D1054927

Rome

timeout.com/rome

Published by Time Out Guides Ltd, a wholly owned subsidiary of Time Out Group Ltd.
Time Out and the Time Out logo are trademarks of Time Out Group Ltd.

© Time Out Group Ltd 2007
Previous editions 1991, 1996, 1998, 1999, 2001, 2003, 2005.

10 9 8 7 6 5 4 3 2 1

This edition first published in Great Britain in 2007 by Ebury Publishing
A Random House Group Company
20 Vauxhall Bridge Road, London SW1V 2SA

Random House Australia Pty Limited 20 Alfred Street, Milsons Point, Sydney, New South Wales 2061, Australia
Random House New Zealand Limited 18 Poland Road, Glenfield, Auckland 10, New Zealand
Random House South Africa (Pty) Limited Isle of Houghton, Corner Boundary
Road & Carse O'Gowrie, Houghton 2198, South Africa

Random House UK Limited Reg. No. 954009

For details of distribution in the Americas, see www.timeout.com

ISBN 10: 1-84670-018-3
ISBN 13: 978184670 0187

A CIP catalogue record for this book is available from the British Library

Printed and bound by Firmengruppe APPL, aprinta druck, Wemding, Germany

The Random House Group Limited makes every effort to ensure that the papers used in our books are made from trees
that have been legally sourced from well-managed and credibly certified forests. Our paper procurement policy can be
found on www.randomhouse.co.uk.

All rights reserved. No part of this publication may be reproduced, stored in a retrieval system, or transmitted in any
form or by any means, electronic, mechanical, photocopying, recording or otherwise, without prior permission from the
copyright owners.

Time Out Guides Limited
Universal House
251 Tottenham Court Road
London W1T 7AB
Tel + 44 (0)20 7813 3000
Fax + 44 (0)20 7813 6001
Email guides@timeout.com
www.timeout.com

Editorial

Editor Anne Hanley
Deputy Editor John Shandy Watson
Listings Editor Federico Lusi
Proofreader Patrick Mulkern
Indexer Lesley McCave

Managing Director Peter Fiennes
Financial Director Gareth Garner
Editorial Director Ruth Jarvis
Deputy Series Editor Dominic Earle
Editorial Manager Holly Pick

Design

Art Director Scott Moore
Art Editor Pinelope Kourmouzoglou
Senior Designer Josephine Spencer
Graphic Designer Henry Elphick
Junior Graphic Designer Kei Ishimaru
Digital Imaging Simon Foster
Ad Make-up Jenni Prichard

Picture Desk

Picture Editor Jael Marschner
Deputy Picture Editor Tracey Kerrigan
Picture Researcher Helen McFarland

Advertising

Sales Director Mark Phillips
International Sales Manager Fred Durman
International Sales Consultant Ross Canadé
Advertising Sales Manager (Rome) Margherita Tedone
Advertising Sales (Rome) Julie Simonsen
Advertising Assistant Kate Staddon

Marketing

Group Marketing Director John Luck
Marketing Manager Yvonne Poon
Sales and Marketing Director North America Lisa Levinson

Production

Group Production Director Mark Lamond
Production Manager Brendan McKeown
Production Coordinator Caroline Bradford

Time Out Group

Chairman Tony Elliott
Financial Director Richard Waterlow
Time Out Magazine Ltd MD David Pepper
Group General Manager/Director Nichola Coulthard
Time Out Communications Ltd MD David Pepper
Time Out International MD Cathy Runciman
Group Art Director John Oakey
Group IT Director Simon Chappell

Contributors

Introduction Anne Hanley. **History** Anne Hanley. **Rome Today** Anne Hanley (*Peace in our time* Agnes Crawford). **Architecture** Anne Hanley (*Lapis tiburtina* Sarah Delaney). **Art in Rome** Frederick Ilchman (*Bernini's babes* Sarah Delaney). **After the Smoke Has Cleared** Phillip Read (*Ratzinger: the facts* Agnes Crawford). **Where to Stay** Natasha Foges. **Sightseeing Introduction** Anne Hanley. **From the Capitoline to the Palatine** Agnes Crawford. **The Trevi Fountain & the Quirinale** Agnes Crawford. **Via Veneto & Villa Borghese** Natasha Foges. **The Tridente** Agnes Crawford. **The Pantheon & Piazza Navona** Julia Crosse. **The Ghetto & Campo de' Fiori** Julia Crosse. **Trastevere & the Gianicolo** Sarah Delaney. **The Aventine, Testaccio & Ostiense** Anne Hanley. **Celio, San Giovanni & San Lorenzo** Sarah Delaney. **Monti & Esquilino** Agnes Crawford. **The Vatican & Prati** Agnes Crawford. **The Appian Way** Agnes Crawford. **The Suburbs** Anne Hanley. **Eating Out** Lee Marshall. **Cafes, Bars & Gelaterie** Julia Crosse. **Shops & Services** Annie Shapero. **Festivals & Events** Natasha Foges. **Children** Philippa Hitchen. **Film** Lee Marshall. **Galleries** Cathryn Drake. **Gay & Lesbian** Peter Douglas. **Music: Classical & Opera** Linda Bordoni. **Nightlife & Live Music** Raffaella Malaguti, Luciano Levrone. **Sport & Fitness** Natasha Foges. **Theatre & Dance** Linda Bordoni. **Trips Out of Town** Nicky Swallow, Anne Hanley. **Directory** Richard McKenna.

Maps LS International Cartography, via Decemviri 8, 20138, Milan. www.geomaker.com

Photography by Gianluca Moggi, except: pages 18, 113 Art Archive; pages 22, 42, 121 AKG Images; page 24 Bettmann/Corbis; page 41 Bridgeman Art Library; page 44 Rex Features; page 261 Kobal; page 276 Pieter van Hattem; page 289 Empics; page 294 Tristram Kenton.
The following image was supplied by the featured artist/establishment: page 263.

The Editor would like to thank Fulvio Marsigliani, Lee and Clara Marshall, and all contributors to previous editions of *Time Out Rome*, whose work forms the basis for parts of this book.

MAD & Co. Advertising & Marketing Director: Margherita Tedone. Tel: +39 06 3550 9145. Fax: +39 06 3550 1775. mad&co@alfanet.it

© **Copyright Time Out Group Ltd**
All rights reserved

Contents

Introduction

Romans are great moaners: they moan if their streets are full of holes and if their route is blocked by road works; they moan if their administration is complacent and if weekends and summer months are log-jammed with crowd-drawing, city-sponsored events; they moan if the glorious *palazzi* that adorn their city fall into disrepair but inevitably find any fresh lick of paint to be the wrong colour.

To listen to them, you'd think that this, your chosen holiday destination, was beyond redemption. But this incorrigible complaining is a foil. For another thing Romans share is an unbounded passion for their city.

History has left them much to be proud of. First of all, there are the vestiges of 500 years as *caput mundi*, hub of the ancient world's greatest empire. Considering the ravages that followed the fall of the Roman Empire – by barbarian marauders, by the passage of time and by Romans themselves, on the look-out for handy building materials in times of hardship – it's a miracle that anything remains, let alone monuments of the magnificence of the Colosseum or Pantheon.

Then there is the heritage of the great popes of the Renaissance and Baroque. We've concentrated on their antics in particular in this eighth edition of the *Rome Guide*. Sybaritic and nepotistic, arrogant and irascible, grasping and corrupt – these towering figures endowed Rome with an artistic and architectural wealth that few cities can match. Their motives were far from pure. And again, much of the papal treasure trove was subsequently carted off, by imperial troops after the devastating Sack of Rome in 1527 (*see p21* **The sack**) and by Napoleonic troops when that emperor swept into this metropolis almost 14 centuries after the fall of the earlier Empire. But despite this, today we're still gasping in awe in front of what remains of the fruits of papal mismanagement.

Romans grow up in the midst of this. Little wonder, then, that they develop an innate sense of their city's superiority. When city luminaries announce year-on-year growth in tourist arrivals of well over ten per cent (2006), they do so not so much in triumph, but rather bemused that anyone would not want to visit. In past decades, this self-satisfaction led to a complacency that meant that visitors were expected to accept the city, warts and all… even without the traditional Roman steam-letting activity of moaning about its drawbacks. These days, however, the Rome of the visitor is a far more streamlined affair, with long-running museums polished up and a swathe of new ones to keep the most demanding of frequent returnees happy.

Not that these latter would find themselves at a loose end anyway. There's something about Rome that gets under the skin of some people, enticing them back again and again, whatever its drawbacks. As they will tell you, there's always something to be discovered, and, above all, always something to sit and observe in this marvellous city where contemporary life weaves itself so effortlessly and beguilingly into the magnificent historical backdrop.

In fact, the only thing that might disturb them is that Rome is now trying a little too hard. It's laudable, certainly, that city hall is striving to iron out some of the Eternal City's eternal chaos. If they manage to make the traffic run smoothly, to provide a public transit system suitable for three million people, to cut red tape and bureaucratic headaches, then our hearty congratulations to them. But what sets Rome apart and gives it its unique charm is its eccentricity, its crankiness… and, of course, its ramshackle loveliness. Is there a danger that in a headlong rush towards modernity, Rome will cancel its own unique identity? We hope not. And we draw comfort from the fact that Rome wasn't built – and nor will it be redeveloped – in a day.

ABOUT TIME OUT CITY GUIDES

This is the eighth edition of *Time Out Rome*, one of an expanding series of Time Out guides produced by the people behind the successful listings magazines in London, New York and Chicago. Our guides are all written by resident experts who have striven to provide you with all the most up-to-date information you'll need to explore the city, whether you're a local or a first-time visitor.

THE LIE OF THE LAND

Rome's *centro storico* is compact, but its warren of medieval streets can make it bewildering. To make the city easier to navigate, we've divided it into areas and assigned each one its own chapter in our Sightseeing section. Most are not official

names you'll see on signposts, but we hope they'll help you to understand the city's layout and to find its most interesting sights. For consistency, the same areas are used in addresses throughout the guide. We've also included phone numbers, website addresses and map references that point to our street maps at the back of the guide. You'll find information on getting around by public transport on page 321.

ESSENTIAL INFORMATION
For all the practical information you might need for visiting the area – including visa and customs information, details of local transport, a listing of emergency numbers, information on local weather and a selection of useful websites – turn to the Directory at the back of this guide. It begins on page 320.

THE LOWDOWN ON THE LISTINGS
We have tried to make this book as easy to use as possible. Addresses, phone numbers, transport information, opening times and admission prices are all included in the listings. However, businesses can change their arrangements at any time. Before you go out of your way, we'd strongly advise you to phone ahead to check opening times and other particulars. While every effort and care has been made to ensure the accuracy of the information contained in this guide, the

publishers cannot accept responsibility for any errors it may contain.

PRICES AND PAYMENT
We have noted where venues accept the following credit cards: American Express (AmEx), Diners Club (DC), MasterCard (MC) and Visa (V). Many also accept travellers' cheques, and/or other cards.

The prices we've listed in this guide should be treated as guidelines, not gospel. If prices vary wildly from those we've quoted, ask whether there's a good reason. If not, go elsewhere. Then please let us know. We aim to give the best and most up-to-date advice, so we want to know if you've been badly treated or overcharged.

TELEPHONE NUMBERS
The area code for Rome is 06. This code must be dialled whether you're phoning from inside or outside the city. For more on telephones and codes, *see p336.*

MAPS
The map section at the back of this book includes street maps of central Rome, a bus map and a plan of metro and local train services. The maps start on page 353, and now pinpoint specific locations of hotels (❶), restaurants (❶), and bars and cafés (❶).

LET US KNOW WHAT YOU THINK
We hope you enjoy the *Time Out Rome Guide*, and we'd like to know what you think of it. We welcome tips for places that you consider we should include in future editions and take note of your criticism of our choices. You can email us at guides@timeout.com.

Advertisers

We would like to stress that no establishment has been included in this guide because it has advertised in any of our publications and no payment of any kind has influenced any review. The opinions given in this book are those of Time Out writers and entirely independent.

There is an online version of this book, along with guides to over 100 international cities, at **www.timeout.com**.

Time Out Travel Guides

Worldwide

All our guides are written by a team of local experts with a unique and stylish insider perspective. We offer essential tips, trusted advice and honest reviews for everything you need to know in the city.

Over 50 destinations available at all good bookshops and at timeout.com/shop

Time Out Guides

Castel Romano Designer Outlet
More than 100 shops of top brands at prices reduced from 30% to 70% all year round.

Book your shopping shuttle from your hotel! For information and booking please contact hotel reception desk within the day before departure and in any case not later than 11.00 AM of the visit date.
Ask your concierge to phone to 06 37350810; 329 4317686.
The cost of the shuttle is 25€
(deposit at the moment of reservation for the service: 5 €)

If you don't feel like driving there is a **shuttle bus** from Central Rome Piazza della Repubblica to the Castel Romano Designer Outlet on Tuesday, Friday Saturday and Sunday.

Vat Refund point: until 30 June 2007, inside Castel Romano Designer Outlet there is a space where you can claim back Vat immediately. If you made purchases using Tax Free Global Refund, also outside of Castel Romano for example in Rome downtown or other cities in Italy, you are eligible to receive vouchers for an additional 10% value that can be used at all of the shops at Castel Romano Designer Outlet.
(These vouchers are valid only on the same day of purchase).

Via Pontina SS 148 Castel Romano (Rome)

Infoline: 0039 06 5050050
tourism@mcarthurglen.com

mcarthurglen.it

In Context

Santo Volto di Gesù. *See p36*.

The **Colosseum**. See p15.

History

Ancient Romans gave the city its form – but Renaissance and Baroque popes provided embellishments.

Each year on 21 April, Romans in their thousands flock to the Campidoglio for fireworks and illuminations marking the Natale di Roma – Rome's birthday. On 21 April 2007 (allowing for some tweaking in calendars over the ages) the Old Girl celebrates the 2,760th anniversary of her birth. How many other cities boast such a precise foundation date? Then again, how many other cities manage to blend myth and history, past and present so seamlessly as Rome?

The tale is categorical: the twins Romulus and Remus were the fruits of a rape by the god of war, Mars, of an Italian princess called Rhea Silvia. Cast adrift as babies and washed into the marshy area below the Palatine hill, the twins were suckled by a she-wolf until found by a shepherd. Romulus became leader of his tribe, quarrelled with and killed his brother, and – on 21 April 753 BC – founded the city of Rome. Then, because his community was short of females, he abducted the women of the neighbouring Sabine tribe, and got to work to raise a nation that would rule the known world.

Digging beneath the legend, you'll find out that ninth-century BC huts have been excavated on the Palatine – proof there was a primitive village there, at least. The first historically documented king of Rome was an Etruscan, Tarquinius Priscus, who reigned from 616 BC. It was probably Etruscans who drained the marshy area between the seven hills to create the Forum, hub of the city's political, economic and religious life.

THE ROMAN REPUBLIC TAKES OVER

According to Roman historians, in 509 BC the son of King Tarquinius Superbus raped Lucretia, the wife of Collatinus, a Roman. The next day, before killing herself, she told her husband and his friend Brutus what had happened, and in revenge they led a rebellion against the Tarquins. The Etruscan dynasty was expelled and the Roman Republic founded, with Brutus and Collatinus as its first consuls.

This account is doubtless as historically (in)accurate as the city's foundation yarn but, in time, Etruscan influence over the region did wane and authority passed to Rome's magistrates. Chief among these were the two annually elected consuls, who guided a council of elders called the Senate. Only the few ancient families or clans who formed the patrician class could participate in the political life of the Republic; only they could vote, be appointed to the Senate or hold important public and religious offices. The lower classes, or plebeians, struggled for a greater say in their own affairs. In 494 BC the office of Tribune of the Plebeians was created to represent their interests, and by 367 BC a plebeian could hold the office of consul. The class system, however, was maintained – rich or successful plebeians were simply designated patricians.

All the Romans of the Republic were united by an unquestioning belief in their right to conquer other tribes. Their superb military organisation, and an agile policy of 'divide and rule' in making alliances, allowed them to pick off the peoples – including the Etruscans – of central and southern Italy, and bring them under Roman control. To ensure the spread of Roman power, new cities were established in conquered territories and an extensive infrastructure was created to support the many conquests. The first great Roman road, the via Appia (*see p171* **The Appian Way**), was begun in 312 BC. Shortly afterwards, work started on the Acqua Appia, the first aqueduct to bring fresh water to the city. The port of Ostia (*see p301* **Ostia Antica**) – founded at the mouth of the Tiber in 380 BC – expanded rapidly. Barges plied the river, bringing corn, wine, oil and building materials into Rome.

Rome's expansion brought the Republic into conflict with two equally powerful peoples: the Carthaginians of North Africa and Spain, and the Greeks, who had colonised southern Italy and Sicily. The latter were expelled from mainland Italy in 272 BC, but the Punic Wars against the Carthaginians lasted for almost 120 years and Rome was more than once in mortal danger. In 218 BC Hannibal made his historic crossing of the Alps, gaining control of much of the Italian peninsula, but was too cautious – and his supply lines were too stretched – to launch an assault on Rome. Carthage was finally destroyed in 146 BC, and the rich land around it sowed with salt, leaving Rome in control of the whole western Mediterranean.

In the early days of the Republic most Romans, whether rich or poor, had been farmers, tending their own land or raising livestock in the surrounding countryside. Wars like those against Carthage, however, required huge standing armies. At the same time, much of the agricultural land in Italy had been laid waste, either by Hannibal or

by the Romans themselves as they attempted to starve the invading Carthaginians into defeat with a scorched-earth policy.

'A parasitic relationship was established, in which all classes in Rome lived off the rest of the empire.'

Wealthy Romans bought huge estates at knock-down prices, while landless peasants flocked to the capital. By the end of the second century BC the Romans were a race of soldiers, engineers, administrators and merchants, supported by tribute in the form of money and goods from defeated enemies and the slave labour of prisoners taken in battle. Keeping the mass of the Roman poor content required the exaction of still more tribute money from the conquered territories. A parasitic relationship was thus established, in which all classes in Rome lived off the rest of the empire.

The political situation in the first century BC became more and more anarchic. Vast armies were required to fight wars on the boundaries of the Republic's empire; soldiers came to owe greater loyalty to their general, who rewarded them with the fruits of conquest, than to the government back in Rome. The result was a succession of civil wars between rival generals.

HAIL CAESAR!

Julius Caesar and Pompey, the two greatest generals of the first century BC, tried to bury their differences in a triumvirate with Crassus, but in 49 BC Caesar, then governor of Gaul, defied the Senate by bringing his army into Italy ('crossing the Rubicon', the muddy stream that marked the border). All opposition was swept aside and for the last six years of his life Julius Caesar ruled Rome as a dictator. The Republican spirit was not quite dead, though: in 44 BC he was assassinated. His death did not lead to the restoration of the Republic: instead, there was a power struggle between Mark Anthony and Caesar's nephew, Octavian, which escalated into a full-blown civil war. Octavian eventually defeated Mark Anthony and Cleopatra at the Battle of Actium in 31 BC. Rome's influence now stretched from Gaul and Spain in the west to Egypt and Asia Minor in the east. To hold it together a single central power was needed. Octavian felt the person to embody such authority was himself and took the name of Augustus (which means 'favoured by the gods').

To give greater authority to his assumption of absolute power, Augustus encouraged the cult of his uncle Julius Caesar as a god, building

The greatest bridge-builder

Romans have never shied away from recycling. Ancient masonry found its way into *palazzi* from the Middle Ages through to the late Baroque, and the bronze cladding from the Pantheon roof made for a superb *baldacchino* over the high altar in St Peter's (*see p164*). Their penchant for recycling also extends to phrases: the acronym SPQR (*senatus populusque romanus* – the senate and people of Rome) still today makes a fitting motto for the Eternal City... even though there is no *Roman* senate (there is, however, an Italian one). And *pontifex maximus* (from where we get the term 'supreme pontiff') is a fine title for the pope.

Literally 'the greatest bridge-builder' (though some experts point to the Etruscan word *pont* – road – as a possible etymology), the office of *pontifex maximus* was probably established under the Etruscan kings of Rome. The commander-in-chief of the *collegium pontificum* (college of priests), he may have been in charge of the bridges over the Tiber or may, less prosaically, have been seen as the bridge between men and their gods. (In fact, as the Tiber was considered to *be* a god, the division is not as clear as it might at first seem.) Originally, the *pontifex maximus* had to be a patrician; from 254 BC anyone could hold this key post. Under the

command of this supreme religious arbiter were the chief priests of the major gods and the Vestal Virgins. The *pontifex maximus* wore part of his toga draped over his head, had magistrate-like status (he was responsible for administering the *jus divinum*, the divine law) but was not allowed to wear the purple-edged toga that marked out the magistrates. He was forbidden from sitting in the Senate or holding any significant political office – until, that is, the Republic gave way to the Empire, and emperors (starting with proto-Emperor Julius Caesar) saw fit to assume this sacred role themselves, as part of their Imperial office.

It wasn't until AD 376 that Emperor Gratian, a fervent Christian, was persuaded by St Ambrose to give up 'unfitting' trappings inherited from his pagan predecessors, including the title of *pontifex maximus*. It's ironic, therefore, that very few years later, Pope Damasus I (reigned 366-383) had already taken over *pontifex maximus* as one of a long list of titles pertaining to the Bishop of Rome (aka the pope). When the current Pope Benedict XVI unveiled a new gate into the Vatican in 2006, it was proudly inscribed 'Benedictus XVI Pont Max Anno Domini MMV Pont 1' – Benedict XVI, *Pontifex maximus*, in the year of our Lord 2005, first year of his pontificate (*pontificatus*).

a temple to him in the Forum (the Temple of Divus Julius; *see p82*). The Ara Pacis (*see p111*), decorated with a frieze showing Augustus and his family, was a reminder that it was he who had brought peace to the Roman world. Later in his reign, statues of Augustus sprang up all over the Empire, and he was more than happy to be worshipped as a god himself.

'The megalomaniac Nero built himself the biggest palace Rome had ever seen.'

Augustus lived on the Palatine hill in a relatively modest house. Later emperors indulged their wealth and power to the full, building a series of extravagant palaces. The last member of Augustus' family to inherit the Empire was the megalomaniac Nero, who built himself the biggest palace Rome had ever seen: the Domus Aurea (Golden House; *see p154*).

When Nero died in AD 68 with no heir, the Empire was up for grabs. Generals converged

from across the Empire to claim the throne, and the eventual winner was a bluff soldier called Vespasian, founder of the Flavian dynasty.

THE GOLDEN AGE OF PAX ROMANA

Over the next 100 years Rome enjoyed an era of unparalleled stability. The Empire reached its greatest extent during the reign of Trajan (98-117). Thereafter it was a matter of protecting the existing boundaries and making sure civil war did not threaten the Empire from within.

Peace throughout the Mediterranean encouraged trade and brought even greater prosperity to Rome. At the same time, however, the power and influence of the capital and its inhabitants declined. Many talented Imperial officials, generals and even emperors were Greeks, North Africans or Spaniards: Trajan and Hadrian were both born in Spain.

To keep an increasingly disparate mass of people content, emperors relied on the policy neatly summed up in the poet Juvenal's scathing phrase *panem et circenses* (bread and circuses). From the first century AD, a regular handout of grain was provided to the poor, ostensibly to maintain a supply of fit young men for the army, but also to ensure that unrest in the city was kept to a minimum. Such generosity to the poor of Rome necessitated still further exploitation of the outlying provinces of the Empire: even in years of famine, Spain and Egypt were required to send grain to Rome.

The other means used to keep more than a million souls loyal to their emperor was the staging of lavish public entertainments. The most famous venue for such spectacles was the Colosseum (*see p85; photo p12*), which was built by emperors Vespasian and Domitian and was completed in AD 80.

Imperial Rome was the most populous metropolis the world had ever seen. In the time of Augustus, it was home to about one million people. By the reign of Trajan a century later it had risen to 1,500,000. No other city would even approach this size until the 19th century. Rome was superbly equipped, too, with eight bridges across the Tiber, magnificent major buildings and 18 large squares.

A SLOW DECLINE
The golden age of Rome ended in AD 180 with the death of Emperor Marcus Aurelius. Defending the eastern provinces and fortifying the borders along the Danube and the Rhine

The **Aurelian Wall**, built to defend Rome.

placed a huge strain on the Imperial purse and the manpower of the legions. Moreover, the exploitative relationship between the Roman state and its distant provinces meant that the latter were unable – and at times unwilling – to defend themselves.

The threat from barbarian invaders and civil wars became so serious that in the third century Emperor Aurelian (270-75) was obliged to fortify the city of Rome with massive defences. The Aurelian Wall, which was later reinforced by medieval popes, still surrounds much of the city. It is a splendid – if misleading – monument to the engineering skills of the ancient Romans. In its heyday, the city needed no defences: its protection lay in the vastness of the Empire and the guaranteed security of the *Pax romana*.

The end of the third century AD was a turning point in the history of Rome. Radical decisions taken by two powerful emperors, Diocletian (284-305) and Constantine (306-37), ensured that the city's days as head of a great empire were numbered. Diocletian established new capital cities at Mediolanum (Milan) and Nicomedia (now in Turkey). He divided the Empire into four sectors, sharing power with a second 'Augustus' – Maximian – and two 'Caesars', Constantius and Galerius. The priorities of the over-extended Empire were now to defend the Rhine and Danube borders against invading Germanic tribes and the eastern provinces from the Persians. Rome was abandoned to itself.

CHRISTIANITY AND CONSTANTINE
The reign of Diocletian is also remembered as one of the periods of most intense persecution of Christians in the Empire. Christian communities had been established in Rome very soon after the death of Jesus, centred in clandestine meeting houses called *tituli*. Christianity, though, was just one of many mystical cults that had spread from the Middle East through the Roman Empire. Its followers were probably fewer than the devotees of Mithraism, a Persian religion open only to men, but Christianity's promise of personal salvation in the afterlife had great appeal among the oppressed – slaves, freedmen, women. Within two decades of Diocletian's persecutions, Emperor Constantine would first tolerate Christianity and then recognise it as the Empire's official religion.

The early part of Constantine's reign was largely taken up with campaigns against rival emperors, the most powerful being Maxentius, who commanded Italy and North Africa. The decisive battle was fought just to the north of Rome at the Milvian Bridge (Ponte Milvio) in 312. Before the battle a flaming cross is said to have appeared in the sky, bearing the words *in hoc signo vinces* (by this sign shall you conquer). As the legend goes, Constantine's cavalry then swept Maxentius' superior forces into the Tiber. The following year, in the Edict of Milan, Constantine decreed that Christianity be tolerated throughout the Empire. Later in his reign, when he had gained control of the Eastern Empire and started to build his new capital city at Byzantium/Constantinople (now Istanbul), it became the state religion.

'To give Rome credibility as a centre of its new religion, fragments of the 'true' cross were brought from the Holy Land.'

Christianity was much stronger in the East than in the West; its effect on Roman life was at first limited, the new faith simply co-existing with other religions. Constantine's reign saw the building of three great basilicas, all on the outskirts of the city. St Peter's and St Paul's Without the Walls (San Paolo fuori le Mura; *see p177*) were built over existing shrines, whereas the Bishop of Rome was given land to build a basilica – San Giovanni in Laterano (*see p150*) – beside the Aurelian Wall. To give Rome credibility as a centre of its new religion, fragments of the 'True' cross were brought from the Holy Land by Constantine's mother, St Helena. Meanwhile, life in fourth-century Rome went on much as before. The departure of part of the Imperial court to Constantinople was a heavy blow to a city accustomed to considering itself *caput mundi*, but the old pagan holidays were still observed, games staged and bread doled out to the poor.

All around, however, the Roman world was falling apart. Constantine learned nothing from the conflicts created by Diocletian's division of power: on his death he left the Empire to be split between his three sons. From this point on, the Western Empire and the Byzantine Empire were two separate entities, united for the last time under Theodosius in the late fourth century. Byzantium would stand for another 1,000 years, while Rome's glorious palaces, temples, aqueducts, statues and fountains were destroyed by waves of Germanic invaders.

THE FALL OF THE WESTERN EMPIRE
The first great shock came in 410, when Alaric's Visigoths marched into Italy and sacked Rome. Even more significant was the conquest of North Africa by the Vandals in 435, which cut Rome off from its main source of grain. In 455 the Vandals, too, sacked Rome,

removing everything they could carry. After this the Western Empire survived in name only. The great aqueducts supplying water to Rome ceased to function, while much of the Italian countryside was laid waste. The emperors in Rome became nothing more than puppets of the assorted Germanic invaders. The last emperor, Romulus, was given the diminutive nickname Augustulus, since he was such a feeble shadow of the Empire's founder. In 476 he was deposed by the German chieftain Odoacer, who styled himself King of Italy. Odoacer was in turn deposed by Theodoric the Ostrogoth, who invaded Italy with the support of Byzantium and established an urbane court in Ravenna, which was to provide stable government for the next 30 years.

In the sixth century much of Italy was reconquered by the Eastern Empire. Then, in around 567, yet another Germanic tribe swept in. The Lombards overran much of the centre of the peninsula, but when they threatened to besiege Rome they met their match in Pope Gregory the Great (590-604), who bought them off with tribute. Gregory was a tireless organiser, overseeing the running of the estates that had been acquired by the Church throughout Western Europe, encouraging the establishment of new monasteries and sending missionaries as far afield as pagan Britain.

He also did a great deal to build up the prestige of the papacy. Rome had been merely one of the centres of the early Church, the others – Byzantium, Jerusalem, Antioch and Alexandria – all being in the East. Disputes were sometimes referred to the Bishop of Rome, but many Christians, particularly in the Eastern churches, did not accord him overall primacy. Then the collapse of all secular government in the West – and above all in Italy – meant that the papacy emerged almost by default as the sole centre of authority, with the pope a political leader as well as head of the Roman Church.

A SHADOW OF ITSELF
The Dark Ages must have been particularly galling for the inhabitants of Rome, living as they did among the magnificent ruins of a vanished golden age. There was no fresh water, as the aqueducts cut during the invasions of the fifth century had never been repaired. Disease was rife. Formerly built-up areas reverted to grazing land, or were planted with vegetables by land-owning religious orders. Fear of attack meant that the countryside around the city was practically deserted. Having reached over a million at the height of the Empire, Rome's population could be counted in no more than hundreds by the sixth century. The ancient ruins became

Popes of the Renaissance

Martin V (1417-31; Oddone Colonna) brought the papacy back to Rome at the end of the Great Schism, ushering in a new age. But Nicholas V (*see below*), philosopher and classicist, is generally considered the first truly Renaissance pope.
Eugenius IV (1431-47; Gabriel Condulmer).
Nicholas V (1447-55; Tommaso Parentucelli).
Callixtus III (1455-58; Alfondo de Borja).
Pius II (1458-64; Enea Silvio Piccolomini).
Paul II (1464-71; Pietro Barbo).
Sixtus IV (1471-84; Francesco della Rovere).
Innocent VIII (1484-92; Giovanni Battista Cibò).
Alexander VI (1492-1503; Rodrigo Borgia; *see p126* and *p129* **Papal mistresses No.1 & No.2**).
Pius III (Oct 1503; Francesco Todeschini Piccolomini).
Julius II (1503-13; Giuliano della Rovere).
Leo X (1513-21; Giovanni de' Medici).
Adrian VI (1522-23; Adrian Florenz) was the last non-Italian pope until the election of Karol Wojtyla – John Paul II – in 1978.

Clement VII (1523-34; Giulio de' Medici; *see p21* **The sack**).
Paul III (1534-49; Alessandro Farnese) summoned the Council of Trent, ushering in the more pious, devotional atmosphere of the Counter-Reformation.
Julius III (1550-55; Giovanni Maria Ciocci del Monte).
Marcellus II (Apr-May 1555; Marcello Cervini).
Paul IV (1555-59; Gian Pietro Carafa).
Pius IV (1559-65; Giovan Angelo de' Medici).
Pius V (1566-72; Antonio Ghislieri).
Gregory XIII (1572-85; Ugo Buoncampagni).
Sixtus V (1585-90; Felice Peretti; *see p155* **Villa Peretti**).
Urban VII (Sept 1590; Giovanni Battista Castagna).
Gregory XIV (1590-91; Niccolò Sfondrati).
Innocent IX (Nov-Dec 1591; Giovan Antonio Facchinetti).
Clement VIII (1592-1605; Ippolito Aldobrandini).
Leo XI (Apr 1605; Alessandro de' Medici).
Paul V (1605-21; Camillo Borghese).
Gregory XV (1621-23; Alessandro Ludovisi).

convenient quarries for builders. Marble and other limestone was burned to make cement, most of which was used to repair fortifications.

For several centuries the city still owed nominal allegiance to the emperor in Byzantium and his representative in Italy, the exarch, whose court was at Ravenna. However, the exarch's troops were normally too busy defending their own cities in north-east Italy to be of much help to Rome. The city did have a military commander – a *dux* – and a *comune* (city council) that met, as the Comune di Roma still does, on the Capitoline hill. But the papacy also had its courts and administration. In the end, the power of the Church prevailed; this would lead to a permanent rift with Byzantium and the Eastern Orthodox churches.

During the Dark Ages, the Roman nobles who controlled the papacy and the city set out to re-establish something akin to the old Empire. When the Lombards seized Ravenna in 751 and threatened to do the same to Rome, Pope Stephen II enlisted Pepin, King of the Franks, as defender of the Church. The papacy's alliance with the Franks grew with the victories of Pepin's son, Charlemagne, over the Lombards and was sealed on Christmas Day 800, when the pope caught Charlemagne unawares in St Peter's and crowned him Holy Roman Emperor.

HOLY ROMAN POLITICS

Rome appeared to have recovered much of its long-lost power and prestige. It had the protection of an emperor (with a power-base comfortably far away in Aachen) and was blessed by the pope, who in return was rewarded by the gift of large areas of land in central Italy. As things turned out, this arrangement caused nothing but trouble for the next 500 years, as popes, emperors and other monarchs vied to determine whose power was greatest. Roman nobles took sides in these disputes, seizing every opportunity to promote members of their own families to the papacy and frequently reducing the city to a state of anarchy. At regular intervals one faction or another would idealistically declare Rome to be a republic once more, to no real effect.

The prestige of the papacy reached a low ebb in the tenth century, when the Frankish Empire collapsed and the papal crown was passed around between a series of dissolute Roman nobles. One of these, John XII (955-64), was obliged to call on the Saxon King Otto for assistance and crowned him Holy Roman Emperor, but then immediately thought better of it. He began to plot against Otto, who rushed to Rome and commanded the clergy and people never again to elect a pope without the consent of himself or his successors.

Paved with good intentions

Nowadays, Romans like to name streets after illustrious (and sometimes not-so-illustrious) personages. In Renaissance Rome, they preferred to name streets after themselves – especially if they were popes and were responsible for having those very streets built.

As the Eternal City emerged from medieval anarchy, it was clear to the popes that any success in imposing order on the city's chaotic topography could be read both literally and figuratively – as a symbol of the Church's ever-firmer grip on its territory and its subjects.

Around the Vatican, **Sixtus IV** created via Sistina (now borgo Sant'Angelo) and **Alexander VI** made via Alessandrina (demolished to make way for via della Conciliazione; see p25 **The longest sulk**). But it was on the opposite side of the Tiber, where the warren in the great bend of the river immediately south of Castel Sant'Angelo was well-nigh impenetrable, that the popes most wished to leave their mark.

In ancient times up to eight bridges spanned the Tiber; in the 15th century there were comfortable crossings only at the Tiber Island and at the Ponte Sant'Angelo (the ancient Pons Aelius), right in front of the papal stronghold at Castel Sant'Angelo.

Little wonder, then, that Sixtus IV, the first of Rome's great town planners, began at the southern end of that bridge, with a three-pronged design (today's *vie* del Panico, del Banco di Santo Spirito and Paola – completed by later popes, including **Paul III** who gave this last his name). Departing from the same spot, Sixtus also tidied up the ancient via Papalis – the route that popes had taken through the centuries to get from the Vatican to the Lateran (see p148 **Ambulatio**).

In 1473, Sixtus decided to expand his area of control, building another bridge – the Ponte Sisto – further downriver. It wasn't until the reign of **Julius II**, however, that Sixtus' plan to connect the two main bridges was fully realised, with the restoration of the via Recta (now via della Lungara) on the right bank, and the creation of via Giulia (named after Julius), hacked through the urban fabric on the left by architect Donato Bramante.

Piazza del Popolo (see p109), the northern gateway into Rome, was another spot where the popes sought to make their presence felt, again to a three-prong plan. From the very rural-looking piazza, **Leo X** kicked off with via Leonina (now via Ripetta). Via Paolina Trifaria (now via del Babuino) was next up, set to

rights by **Clement VII** and Paul III. The central prong leading straight to piazza Venezia – today's via del Corso – was also restored by Paul, who revamped via Trinitatis (today's *vie* Condotti, Fontanella Borghese, del Clementino and di Monte Brianzo, as well as lanes in the area where lungotevere Tor di Nona now lies) to link the two three-prong systems.

Sixtus V (*photo left*) reigned for just five years (1585-90), but they were dramatic years from a town-planning point of view. *His* via Sistina (now *vie* Sistina, Quattro Fontane and Depretis) shoots straight as a die from the top of the Spanish Steps to the basilica of Santa Maria Maggiore (see p160), after which it branches: straight on to Santa Croce in Gerusalemme (see p150) went his via Felice (Sixtus' name was Felice Peretti; now *vie* Carlo Alberto and Santa Croce in Gerusalemme); and dropping south along via Merulana to San Giovanni in Laterano.

Papal independence was reasserted in the second half of the 11th century by Pope Gregory VII (1073-85), who also established many of the distinctive institutions of the Church. It was Gregory who first made celibacy obligatory for priests; he set up the College of Cardinals, giving it sole authority to elect all future popes. He also insisted that no bishop or abbot could be invested by a lay ruler such as a king or emperor, which led to a cataclysmic struggle for power with the Holy Roman Emperor Henry IV.

'The Normans indulged in a three-day orgy of looting, then torched what was still standing.'

When Henry marched on Rome in 1084, bringing with him a new papal candidate, Gregory demanded help from Robert Guiscard, leader of the Normans who had a strong power base in southern Italy. By the time Robert arrived, Rome had already capitulated to Henry's army; in protest, the Normans indulged in a three-day orgy of looting, then torched what was still standing. From the Palatine to San Giovanni in Laterano, little remained but blackened hulks of *palazzi* and smoking ruins of churches. Gregory slunk out of his hiding place in Castel Sant'Angelo and left Rome a broken man; he died the following year.

Despite conflict between rival factions – usually headed by the powerful Colonna and Orsini clans – the 12th and 13th centuries were times of great architectural innovation in Rome. The creative spirit of the Middle Ages is preserved in beautiful cloisters like those of San Giovanni and in Romanesque churches with graceful brick bell towers and floors of finely wrought mosaic.

Rome's prestige, however, suffered a severe blow in 1309, when the French overruled the College of Cardinals and imposed their own candidate as pope, who promptly decamped to Avignon. A pope returned to Rome in 1378, but the situation became farcical, with three pontiffs laying claim to St Peter's throne. Stability was restored only in 1417, when Oddo Colonna was elected as Pope Martin V at the Council of Constance, marking the end of the Great Schism. He returned to Rome in 1420 to find the city and the surrounding Papal States in a ruinous condition.

With the reign of Martin V (1417-31), some semblance of dignity was restored to the office of Christ's Vicar on Earth. It was at this time that the perennial uncertainty as to who would

rule the city was solved: henceforth the city councillors would be nominees of the pope. At this time the popes also made the Vatican their principal residence: it offered greater security than their traditional seat in the Lateran Palace.

Successive popes took advantage of this new sense of authority; Rome became an international city once more. The renewed prestige of the papacy enabled it to draw funds from all over Europe in the form of tithes and taxes. The papacy also developed the money-spinning idea of the Holy Year, first instituted in 1300 and repeated in 1423, 1450 and 1475. Such measures enabled the Church to finance the lavish artistic patronage of Renaissance Rome (*see p17* **Popes of the Renaissance**).

THE RENAISSANCE IS BORN

Nicholas V (1447-55) is remembered as the pope who brought the Renaissance to Rome. A lover of philosophy, science and the arts, he founded the Vatican Library and had many ancient Greek texts translated into Latin. He also made plans to rebuild St Peter's, the structure of which was perilously unstable. The Venetian Pope Paul II (1464-71) built the city's first great Renaissance palazzo, the massive Palazzo Venezia (*see p77*), and his successor Sixtus IV invited leading artists from Tuscany and Umbria – Botticelli, Perugino, Ghirlandaio and Pinturicchio – to fresco the walls of his new Sistine Chapel (*see p166*) in the Vatican.

Since the papacy had become such a fat prize, the great families of Italy redoubled their efforts to secure it, ensuring they always had younger sons groomed and ready as potential popes. The French and Spanish kings usually had their own candidates too. Political clout, rather than spirituality, was the prime concern of Renaissance popes. Sixtus IV and his successors Innocent VIII and Alexander VI (the infamous Rodrigo Borgia) devoted far more of their energies to politics and war than to spiritual matters. Papal armies were continually in the field, carving out an ever-increasing area of central Italy for the Church.

The epitome of the worldly Renaissance pope, Julius II (1503-13), made the idea of a strong papal state a reality, while reviving the dream of restoring Rome to its former greatness as the spiritual capital of the world. He began the magnificent collection of classical sculpture that is the nucleus of today's Vatican Museums (*see p166*) and invited the greatest architects, sculptors and painters of the day to Rome, including Bramante, Michelangelo and Raphael. Julius's rule was not as enlightened as he liked to think, but he did issue a bull forbidding simony (the buying or selling of church offices) in papal elections. In his own financial dealings, he depended on the advice and loans of the fabulously wealthy Sienese banker Agostino Chigi. Julius's successors accomplished far less than he did. Some were simply bon viveurs, like Giovanni de' Medici, who, on being made Pope Leo X in 1513, said to his brother, 'God has given us the papacy. Let us enjoy it.' Enjoy it, he did. A great patron of the arts, his other passions were hunting, music, theatre and throwing spectacular dinner parties. He plunged the papacy into debt, spending huge sums on French hounds, Icelandic falcons and banquets of nightingale pies and peacocks' tongues.

PROTESTANTS AND IMPERIALISM

Later popes had to face two great threats to the status quo of Catholic Europe: the protests of Martin Luther against the Church – and Roman extravagance in particular – and the growing rivalry between Francis I of France and Spanish King/Holy Roman Emperor Charles V, who were establishing themselves as the dominant powers in Europe.

The year 1523 saw the death of Pope Adrian VI, a Flemish protégé of Charles V and the last non-Italian pope until 1978. He was succeeded by Clement VII, formerly Giulio de' Medici, who rather unwisely backed France against the all-powerful emperor. Charles captured the Duchy of Milan in 1525 and threatened to take over the whole of Italy in retaliation for the pope's disloyalty. In 1527 a large and ill-disciplined Imperial army, many of whom were Germans with Lutheran condemnations of Rome ringing in their ears, sacked the city. Chiefly interested in gold and ready money, the looters also destroyed churches and thousands of houses, burned or stole countless relics and works of art, looted tombs, and killed indiscriminately. The dead rotted in the streets for months. (*See also p21* **The sack**.)

Pope Clement held out for seven months in Castel Sant'Angelo, but eventually slunk away in disguise. He returned the following year, crowning Charles as Holy Roman Emperor in Bologna shortly afterwards. In return, Charles grudgingly confirmed Clement VII's sovereignty over the Papal States.

The Sack of Rome put an abrupt end to the Renaissance popes' dream of making Rome a great political power. The primary concerns now were to rebuild the city and push forward the Counter-Reformation, the Catholic Church's response to Protestantism.

THE COUNTER-REFORMATION

The first great Counter-Reformation pope was Alessandro Farnese, Paul III (1534-49), who had produced four illegitimate children during his

riotous youth. He realised that if Catholicism was to hold its own against austere Protestantism, lavish ecclesiastical lifestyles had to be restrained. Paul summoned the Council of Trent to redefine Catholicism and encouraged new religious groups such as the Jesuits – founded by the Spaniard Ignatius of Loyola and approved in 1540 (*see p118* **Ignatius Loyola**) – over older, discredited orders. From their mother church in Rome, the Gesù (*see p123*), the Jesuits led the fight against heresy and set out to convert the world.

Pope Paul IV (1555-59), the next major reformer, was a firm believer in the Inquisition, burning heretics and homosexuals, and strict censorship. He expelled all Jews from the Papal States, except for those in Rome itself, whom he confined to the Ghetto in 1556.

> ## 'The popes continued to spend money as if the Vatican's wealth was inexhaustible.'

By the end of the 16th century the authority of the papacy was on the wane outside Rome, and the papal treasury was increasingly dependent on loans. In the following century popes continued to spend money as if the Vatican's wealth was inexhaustible, commissioning architects of the stature of Bernini and Borromini to design the churches, *palazzi* and fountains that would transform the face of the Eternal City for ever (*see pp31-36* **Architecture**). Inevitably, the economy of the Papal States became chronically depressed.

POOR LOCALS AND RICH TOURISTS

If two centuries of papal opulence had turned monumental Rome into a spectacular sight, squalor and poverty were still the norm for most of its people: the streets of Trastevere and the Suburra – ancient Rome's great slum – in the Monti district were filthy and dangerous, and the Jewish population lived in even less sanitary conditions in the Ghetto. The city was, however, a more peaceful place to live. The rich no longer shut themselves up in fortress-like *palazzi*, but built delightful villas in landscaped parks, such as Villa Borghese. Notwithstanding the waning prestige of the popes, Rome had many attractions. A Europe-wide resurgence of interest in the classical past was under way, and shortly the city would discover the joys – and earning power – of tourism. Rome was about to be invaded again.

By the 18th century a visit to Rome as part of a 'Grand Tour' was near obligatory for any European gentleman, and Romans responded

The sack

On 5 May 1527 an ill-disciplined force gathered beneath Rome's mighty walls. Some 14,000 were German *Landsknechts*, many of them with Martin Luther's fulminations against the new Babylon – Rome – ringing in their ears; 6,000 were Spanish troops under the command of Constable Charles, Duke of Bourbon; the rest were a rabble of mainly Italian deserters and free-booters, mercenaries to a man. All of them were angry: it was months since their nominal commander-in-chief, the Holy Roman Emperor Charles V (aka the Archduke of Austria, King Charles I of Spain…), had paid them. And all of them knew that Rome was a fantastically rich city, bursting with treasure waiting to be looted.

In many ways, Pope Clement VII had brought this situation upon himself. He had gone against papal tradition and turned his back on the Holy Roman Emperor, lining up with France, England and Venice in the League of Cognac after he had angered Charles with a series of diplomatic affronts. But with the Ottomans battering on his eastern borders, Charles's attention was elsewhere as this raggedy 'imperial' army descended on *caput mundi*. Any semblance

of imperial command over these troops disappeared on 6 May when, as the furious assault was launched on the Vatican and the Gianicolo, the emperor's representative, the Duke of Bourbon, was killed. The Sack that followed was pure anarchy.

What the imperial army found as it piled over the walls – making short work of the city's 5,000-odd defenders – must indeed have seemed an El Dorado. This was the city of Michelangelo and Raphael, a city of stupendous villas and sumptuously appointed churches. If St Peter's itself was a building site (construction work on the new basilica wouldn't resume until 1534), not so the great noble *palazzi*.

As Clement high-tailed it along the *passetto* (*see p169; photo below*) into his fortress at Castel Sant'Angelo (*see p170*) protected by his Swiss guard – only 42 of the original 189 survived – the attackers ran amok in an orgy of rape and pillage. Women were dragged into churches to be violated by Lutherans dressed in priestly robes; young children were hurled from high windows; priests suffered unspeakable tortures; corpses piled up in the streets. Cardinal Pompeo Colonna – sworn enemy of the pope and imperial champion – returned to his city, planning to join the free-for-all, but was so sickened at what he found that he turned his family mansion into a refuge.

Clement was forced to capitulate on 6 June, and was fined 400,000 ducats. But it was months before any kind of order returned to the devastated city. In a 1526 census, Rome had 55,000 residents. By the end of 1527 there were no more than 10,000. Many had fled, but as many as 20,000 died – both in the Sack and in the plague that swept through the city towards the end of that *annus horribilis* – some, no doubt, in vicious pogroms.

Not content with the bloodshed that had already occurred, Romans looked for a scapegoat for their misfortunes. They found it in the Jews, who were accused of saving their own skins and profiteering by buying up looted goods from the attackers. The accusations were probably false. But even if they weren't, there's a case to be made that the Jewish community was responsible for salvaging Roman treasures that would otherwise have been lost.

Popes of the Baroque

Urban VIII (1623-44; Maffeo Barberini; see p92 **Barberini trumpeting**). Bernini's *baldacchino* in St Peter's (*see p164*), made in 1625 for the Barberini pope, is considered the first truly Baroque work of art. Determining when the Baroque ends is more difficult: art historians prefer to think of it as a style, rather than a period.
Innocent X (1644-55; Giambattista Pamphili; see p117 **The two-palace pope**; *photo right*).
Alexander VII (1655-67; Fabio Chigi).
Clement IX (1667-69; Giulio Rospigliosi).
Clement X (1670-76; Emilio Altieri).
Innocent XI (1676-89; Benedetto Odescalchi).
Alexander VIII (1689-91; Pietro Ottoboni).
Innocent XII (1691-1700; Antonio Pignatelli).
Clement XI (1700-21; Giovanni Francesco Albani).
Innocent XII (1721-24; Michelangelo de' Conti).
Benedict XIII (1724-30; Pietro Francesco Orsini).
Clement XIV (1730-40; Lorenzo Corsini).

eagerly to this new influx. The city produced little great art or architecture at this time. The two great Roman sights that date from this period, the Spanish Steps and the Trevi Fountain, are a late flowering of Roman Baroque. The few big building projects undertaken were for the benefit of tourists, notably Giuseppe Valadier's splendid park on the Pincio (*see p97*) and the neo-classical facelift he gave to piazza del Popolo.

Although on the surface Rome was a cultured city, there were many customs that reeked of medieval superstition. Smollett, Gibbon and Goethe, forgetting the full brutality of ancient Rome, all remarked on the contrast between the sophistication of vanished civilisation and the barbarism beneath the surface of papal Rome. Some executions were still carried out by means of the *martello*: the condemned man was beaten about the temples with a hammer, before having his throat cut and his stomach ripped open. This method remained in use until the 1820s.

Executions were mostly staged in piazza del Popolo, and often timed to coincide with *carnevale*, a period of frantic merrymaking before Lent. For a few days, via del Corso was one long, masked ball, as bands played and people showered one another with confetti, flour, water and more dangerous missiles. The centrepiece was a race of riderless horses along the Corso. They had heavy balls covered with spikes dangling at their sides, and boiling pitch pumped into their recta to get them moving.

Indeed, Rome was a city of spectacle for much of the year. In summer, piazza Navona was flooded by blocking the outlets of the fountains, and the nobility splashed around in their carriages. The only time the city fell quiet was in late summer, when everyone who could left for their villas in the Alban hills to escape the stifling heat and the threat of malaria.

OCCUPATION, THEN UNIFICATION

In 1798 everything changed. French troops under Napoleon occupied the city and Rome became a republic once more. Pope Pius VI, a feeble old man, was exiled from the city and died in France. Like most attempts to restore the Roman Republic, this one was short-lived. The next pope, Pius VII, elected in Venice, signed a concordat with Napoleon in 1801, which allowed the pontiff to return to Rome. The papacy was expelled for a second time when French troops returned in 1808. Napoleon promised the city a modernising, reforming administration, but Romans were not keen to be conscripted into his armies. When the pope finally reclaimed Rome after the fall of Napoleon in 1814, its noble families and many of the people welcomed his return.

The patchwork of duchies, principalities and kingdoms that had existed in Italy before Napoleon's invasions was restored after 1815. The Papal States were handed back to Pius VII. Nevertheless, the brief taste of liberty under the French had helped inspire a movement for unification, modernisation and independence from the domination of foreign rulers.

The Risorgimento was a movement for the unification of the country, but in itself it was very diverse. Its supporters ranged from liberals who believed in unification for economic reasons, to conservatives who looked to the papacy itself to unify Italy. Initially, the most prominent members were the idealistic republicans of the Giovine Italia (Young Italy) movement, headed by Giuseppe Mazzini. They were flanked by more extreme groups and secret societies, such as the Carbonari.

Two reactionary popes, Leo XII (1823-29) and Gregory XVI (1831-46), used a network of police spies and censorship to put down any opposition. Most of the unrest in the Papal States, though, was in the north; in Rome, life went on much as before. Travellers continued to visit, and Shelley, Dickens and Lord Macaulay all passed through, only to be horrified at the repressive regime.

The election of a new pope in 1846 aroused great optimism. Pius IX (*see also below* **Eviction order**) came to the throne with a liberal reputation and immediately announced an amnesty for over 400 political prisoners. But the spate of revolutions throughout Europe in 1848 radically altered his attitude. In November that year his chief minister was assassinated and Pius fled. In his absence, a popular assembly declared Rome a republic. Seizing the chance to make his dream reality, Mazzini rushed to the city, where he was chosen as one of a triumvirate of rulers. Meanwhile, another idealist arrived in Rome to defend the Republic, at the head of 500 armed followers. He was Giuseppe Garibaldi, a former sailor who had gained military experience fighting in wars of liberation in South America.

Ironically, it was Republican France, with Napoleon I's nephew Louis Napoleon as president, that decided it was duty-bound to restore the pope to Rome. Louis Napoleon's motivation was simple: he wanted to stop Austrian power spreading further within Italy. A French force marched on Rome, but was repelled by the *garibaldini* (followers of Garibaldi) – a ragtag mixture of former papal troops, young volunteers and enthusiastic citizens. The French attacked again in greater numbers, mounting their assault from the gardens of Villa Pamphili. For the whole of June 1849 the defenders fought valiantly from their positions on the Gianicolo, but the end of the Republic was by now inevitable.

Eviction order

Pope Pius IX sat on the throne of St Peter's for 31 years (1846-78), longer than any other pontiff. And for 23 of those, his reign extended over the (increasingly reduced) Vatican States – a huge swathe of land across central Italy.

Initially considered a liberal, Pius began early in his pontificate to make it clear that he was having no dealings with the Church-threatening movement to unify the numerous states that had previously occupied the Italian peninsula. But no amount of conservatism could stop the Risorgimento forces. Already by the end of 1860, King Vittorio Emanuele II of Piedmont, leader of the unification movement, had whittled the Vatican states down to Lazio – the region immediately surrounding Rome. Only the presence of a pro-papal French garrison in Rome held the unification forces beyond Lazio's borders for the ensuing ten years.

In fact, Pius had a foretaste of the inevitable in 1848, that year of Europe-wide upheaval,

when a republic was briefly set up in Rome, and the pope fled south to Gaeta in the Kingdom of the Two Sicilies, not to return until 1850. For 20 more years, Pius held his ground. Then Napoleon III called his French troops from Rome to fight in his war against Prussia, and the way was left open for Vittorio Emanuele to take the city.

Unification troops broke through Rome's Aurelian Walls at Porta Pia (*see p103*) on 20 September 1870. Then – in what had been a pre-arranged face-saving move – they sauntered along what is now via XX Settembre towards the Palazzo del Quirinale (*see p93*), where Pius had been in residence, leaving the pontiff all the time he needed to make good his escape behind the walls of the Vatican. Pius showed no such finesse: when they finally reached the palace, the unifiers found it firmly locked, and had to summon a blacksmith to break in. Victor Emanuel, now king of a fully united Italy, made it his official residence in 1871.

St Peter's square during World War II.

For the next 20 years, while the rest of Italy was being united under King Vittorio Emanuele II of Piedmont, a garrison of French troops protected Pope Pius from invasion. Garibaldi protested vainly to the politicians of the new state – it was, he said, a question of *Roma o morte* ('Rome or death') – but the Kingdom of Italy, established in 1860, was not prepared to take on Napoleon III's France. Meanwhile, the former liberal Pius IX was becoming more and more reactionary. In 1869 he convened the first Vatican Council in order to set down the Catholic Church's response to the upheavals of the industrial age. It did so with intransigence, making the doctrine of papal infallibility an official dogma of the Church for the first time.

A CAPITAL ONCE MORE
Even though it was still under papal rule, Rome had been chosen as the capital of the newly unified kingdom. In 1870, with the defeat of Napoleon III in the Franco-Prussian War, the French withdrew from Rome and unification troops occupied the city. (*See also p23* **Eviction order**.)

There followed the most rapid period of change Rome had experienced since the fall of the Empire. The new capital needed government buildings and housing for the civil servants who worked in them. Church properties were confiscated and for a time government officials worked in converted monasteries and convents. Two aristocratic *palazzi* were adapted to house the Italian parliament: Palazzo di Montecitorio (*see p109*) became the Lower House, and Palazzo Madama (*see p115*) the Senate.

The city's great building boom lasted for over 30 years. New avenues appeared: via Nazionale and via Cavour linked the old city with the new Stazione Termini in the east, and corso Vittorio Emanuele was driven through the historic centre. The new ministries were often massive piles quite out of keeping with their surroundings; still more extravagant was the monstrous Vittoriano (*see p80*), the marble monument to Vittorio Emanuele erected in piazza Venezia.

FASCISM AND THE POST-WAR ERA
Though Rome was little affected by World War I, social unrest broke out following the war, with the fear of Socialism encouraging the rise of Fascism. Benito Mussolini was a radical journalist who, having become alienated from the far left, shifted to the extreme right. He turned to ancient Rome to find an emblem to embody his idea of a totalitarian state: *fasces*, bundles of rods tied round an axe, were carried by the Roman *lictors* (marshals) as they walked in front of the city's consuls. In 1922 Mussolini sent his Blackshirt squads on their 'March on Rome', demanding – and winning – full power in government. He had been prepared to back out at the first sign of real resistance by the constitutional parties, and himself made the 'march' by train.

Mussolini's ambition was to transform the country into a dynamic, aggressive society. Among other things, he wanted to put Italians in uniform and stop them eating pasta, which he thought made them lazy and un-warlike. His ideas for changing the face of Rome were equally far-fetched. He planned to rebuild the city in gleaming marble, with fora, obelisks and heroic statues proclaiming *il Duce* ('the Leader') as a modern Augustus at the head of a new Roman Empire. The most prominent surviving monuments to his megalomania are the suburb of EUR (*see p178*) and the Foro Italico sports complex (*see p175*).

'Italian partisans showed themselves capable of acts of great courage.'

When put to the test in World War II, Fascist Italy rapidly foundered. Mussolini was ousted from power in 1943 and Romans switched their allegiance. During the period of German occupation that followed, Italian partisans showed themselves capable of acts of great courage. Rome was declared an open city – the *Roma, città aperta* of Rossellini's great

film – meaning that the Germans agreed not to defend it, pitching their defence south of the city. While other Italian cities and towns were pounded by bombs, Rome suffered only one serious bombing raid during the whole war.

After the war Italy voted to become a republic and Rome quickly adapted to the new political structures. *Partitocrazia* – government by a group of political parties sharing power and dividing up lucrative government jobs and contracts between them – suited the Roman approach to life. The political unrest that hit Italy in the 1970s and '80s – a spate of right-wing bomb attacks and kidnappings of key figures by the far-left Red Brigades – affected Rome less than it did Milan or Turin. Romans simply swam with the political tide: they voted in their first Communist mayor in 1976.

The city benefited greatly from Italy's post-war economic boom, spreading out along its major arterial roads. The problem for the post-war city authorities has been how to preserve the old city yet still encourage development. Rome's main industry is still being itself, whether as capital of Italy or historical relic, and the city continues to thrive, trading as it has done for the millennium and a half since the Empire fell on its unforgettable past.

The longest sulk

When Pius IX retreated across the Tiber and behind the Vatican walls (*see p23* **Eviction order**), he began one of history's longest sulks – one which was to span 59 years and four papacies. To drive home his displeasure, Pius called a Holy Year in 1875 then failed to sally forth for the traditional opening of the bricked-up Holy Doors in Rome's 'Big Four' basilicas. From 1870 to 1929, in fact, successive pontiffs refused ever to set foot outside the Vatican, proclaiming themselves prisoners of the Italian state – a state that they didn't recognise and that didn't recognise them. And while the rest of the world looked on in embarrassed silence, so the situation remained until Mussolini took the situation in hand and sorted things out with his Lateran Pacts.

When Italy was first unified, the pope was offered the Law of Guarantees, which made him an Italian subject but with regal rights, including sending and receiving ambassadors; it also earmarked a generous sum as compensation for loss of territory. The pope turned his nose up at this, excommunicating Italy's King Vittorio

Emanuele II and threatening Italians who voted – or, even worse, stood – in national elections with fire and brimstone.

It took Pius XI (1922-39) and his diplomatically astute secretary of state Cardinal Pietro Gasparri to find a way out of this impasse. In secret meetings at the Lateran palace, Gasparri and Mussolini's aides hammered out a deal that made the Vatican City a sovereign state and established Catholicism as Italy's state religion (this latter was overturned in changes to the treaty in 1984); in return, the Vatican promised to observe a policy of neutrality, and received compensation – rather less than the Law of Guarantees had offered – for its territorial losses. The Lateran Pacts – also known as *La Conciliazione* – were signed in 1929. Pius celebrated by retaking possession of San Giovanni in Laterano, the official seat of the pope as Bishop of Rome. Mussolini, on the other hand, marked the *rapprochement* by bulldozing picturesque medieval alleyways in the Borgo (*see p169*) to create via della Conciliazione, a 'modern' road that would dignify his own approach to the Holy See.

Sermoneta
gloves ®

The Sermoneta Group has long been a driving force in the Italian economy, thanks to the professionalism of its people and constant market surveys which guarantee the success of the company's expansion policy. The factory was founded in 1965 by Giorgio Sermoneta, although the Sermoneta name goes back some three hundred years thanks to the family's glovemaking and distribution business.

The foundation stone of the SERMONETA Group is the SERMONETA GLOVES store, located at 61, Piazza di Spagna, one of the most evocative locations in the world. SERMONETA GLOVES is world-renowned for its superb quality gloves, its vast selection of styles and its wide range of colours, all readily available in stock. Today SERMONETA GLOVES also has branches in the centre of New York, 609 - 611 Madison Avenue, and Aeroporto Leonardo Da Vinci Fiumicino - Roma Terminal B and terminal C which merely goes to confirm the well-deserved success of the group.

A FAST GROWING COMPANY

PIAZZA DI SPAGNA,61 - 00187 ROMA
TEL.06 6791960 FAX 06 6797167

VIA DELLA SPIGA, 46 - MILANO
TEL.0276318303 FAX 0276318993

SESTRIERE SAN MARCO 2400 /A - CALLE
XXII MARZO - VENEZIA - TEL + FAX 0412777852

AEROPORTO LEONARDO DA VINCI
FIUMICINO - ROMA

TERMINAL B TEL. +39 06 65953933

TERMINAL C TEL. +39 06 65955213

NEW YORK 609-611 MADISON AVENUE
+1 (212)3195946

www.sermonetagloves.com

Rome Today

Can the Eternal City get the balance right?

Between 2 April 2005, when Pope John Paul II died, and 8 April, when his funeral took place, over four million people descended on Rome – mourners, pilgrims, protesters and those *incuriositi* who felt that they simply couldn't miss an event this significant. For a city of 2.8 million people this was, to say the least, a challenge: welcoming, housing, moving, feeding and dealing with the waste of a mass of humanity one and a half times greater than the population of the city itself for six phenomenally intense days.

But Rome – the city of eternal chaos, of 'never do today what can be put off until tomorrow' – coped. In fact, it more than coped: mayors from some of the world's largest metropolises rapidly despatched envoys to witness (and take notes on) the miracle of organisation that successfully dealt with the influx, channelling mourners to St Peter's to pay their last respects with no incidents more serious than some fainting in the warm April weather. Suddenly, Rome was no longer the beautiful, endearing bungler it had always been considered: it was a modern city able to cope with 21st-century numbers even within its burdensome historical framework. It was, in short, a success.

DOWNS AND UPS

Which isn't to say, of course, that Rome in the second half of the first decade of the 21st century is a paragon of streamlined efficiency. Far from it. Ask any taxi driver what state he thinks his city is in today, and chances are that your trip won't be long enough for his litany of woes: the relentless year-on-year increase in cars bumping over the city cobbles (2.1 million – that's 895 vehicles per 1000 inhabitants – in 2006); skyrocketing pollution levels; the disruption caused when the pope or the president or some foreign VIP is whisked through the streets in high-speed, high-security dashes, or when demonstrators process through the city centre; the chaos – occasionally violence – when key football matches are played at the Stadio Olimpico; the transport strikes that bring the city to gridlock; the treacherous potholes; the unending road works; the nose-to-tail tour buses disgorging ever more people into the narrow medieval streets.

All of which is – to some extent – true. But they're all problems that are now being addressed in a way that would have been unthinkable even at the beginning of the 1990s: there's a lot of ground to make up, certainly. And the very nature of Rome throws up problems few other cities have to face. But these days, all but the most jaded complainers will be forced to admit that things in Rome *are* moving.

It all started with the right people being in the right place when large sums of money started to be funneled towards the capital. Some three million pilgrims were expected to visit the Eternal City for the 2000 Holy Year, and the Italian government – a centre-left administration – wanted to put on a good show. Funds were allocated and used effectively for this purpose by then-mayor Francesco Rutelli, of the same political persuasion as central government (in contrast to the fiasco over the 1990 World Cup, from which Rome emerged with endless problems… though it did get a shiny revamped football stadium). Parks were created and historic buildings received a fresh coat of paint. Long-closed museums were spruced up and opened with user-friendly visiting hours. Critics moaned that Rutelli's 'renaissance' was skin-deep, a PR exercise for out-of-towners visiting the *centro storico*. But wheels were put in motion, and Romans – ever ready to moan when roadworks hold them up – began to understand that the inconvenience might, perhaps, be justified by the end result.

BUILDING ON NEW FOUNDATIONS

Since 2001 the mayor's office has been occupied by another centre-left incumbent, cinema- and jazz-loving Walter Veltroni: a quietly-spoken Stakhanovite who has continued the job begun by Rutelli. His task was complicated by hostility from the centre-right national government (2001-06) but, building on the groundwork laid by his predecessor, his efforts to drag his city into the 21st century have certainly borne fruit. His commitment was rewarded when he was swept back to office with 61.4 per cent of the vote in 2006.

In some areas, Rome has leap-frogged other cities to provide services that even the most avant-garde don't have: anyone with wireless-ready equipment, for example, can relax in city-sponsored hotspots in the city's main parks, including Villa Borghese, or switch on in much of the *centro storico* and find themselves directed automatically to the *Viaggio in Roma* site for free tourist information and access to the internet (*see p330* **Internet & email**).

Since its inauguration in 2002, the Renzo Piano-designed Auditorium-Parco della Musica (*see p275*) has revolutionised cultural life in the city. With its intelligent, all-embracing programming philosophy, it sold more tickets in 2005 than London's South Bank complex or Sydney's Opera House. The recently revamped Teatro Palladium (*see p288*) – like the Auditorium, located in a suburb with little or no arts 'tradition' – is equally lively, and the trickle-down effect on the whole cultural and entertainment scene has been dramatic.

'At the bottom of any hole is layer upon layer of history.'

Moreover, while most of Italy has struggled through a rough economic patch, the number of businesses operating in Rome grew by 9.2 per cent and employment leapt by 13.7 per cent (compared to a national figure of 4.6 per cent) from 2001 to 2005, according to research institute CENSIS. Tourism, too, boomed, with overnight stays in the Eternal City rising 22.8 per cent to 19.5 million over the same period, CENSIS reported. In 2005 alone, Rome – traditionally considered (by non-Romans) to be a pen-pushing blood-sucker, draining the resources of the industrially go-ahead north – produced 6.5 per cent of the country's GDP.

That's the upside.

Rome continues to be dogged by problems with transport, due in large part to the fact that the mass-transit system – the *metropolitana* – is woefully inadequate: for decades, the city has limped on with two lines which skirt the city centre and head to outlying residential and business districts. This, in turn, is due to the fact that at the bottom of any hole dug anywhere remotely central is layer upon layer of history. Avid archeologists line up to jump in. In spring 2006, work began on Rome's new metro line C: this will slice north-west to south-east, right through the most visited areas – not, planners hope, ferrying tourists, so much as carrying rushing Romans, thus leaving visitors to enjoy extensive pedestrianised zones above. But this won't happen until 4.3 million cubic metres of earth have been moved (plus an estimated 600,000 for archeological digs), 1.6 million cubic metres of concrete have been poured, 270 million kilograms of steel structures have been erected, €3 billion has been spent and 30 stations have been built along the 25 kilometres (16 miles) of track. All this, authorities say, will have been achieved by 2013. We'll see.

Other headaches stem from the result of the economic boom of the 1960s and '70s. From 1.65 million in 1951, the city's population had risen to 2.78 million by 1971, a 68 per cent leap. To house the new residents, property speculators

In Context

Peace in our time

In 2006, US architect Richard Meier's travertine and glass structure enclosing the **Ara Pacis** (*see p111*) was unveiled in a frenzy of back-slapping on Rome's 2,759th birthday. For the first time since World War II, a modern structure had been built in an historically sensitive part of town, giving the delicate first-century-BC Ara Pacis a luminous, state-of-the-art home.

But not everyone was impressed. From the start, the project had polarised Romans of all ranks and walks of life: the project was compared to a train station, a leisure centre, a shopping mall. Worst of all, critics said, was the colour: like all Meier's designs, the Ara Pacis building is very, very white, and Rome just doesn't do white. Even as the inauguration approached, the chorus of dissent showed no signs of dying down. Before the paint had dried (or, indeed, the loos were completed) the right-wing Alleanza Nazionale party's candidate ran for mayoral elections with the promise to demolish it (he lost, though the pledge may have given him a few extra votes).

Previously, the Ara Pacis had been housed in an elegant pavilion designed by Vittorio Morpurgo, opened with much pomp in 1938. It was a project integral to Mussolini's identification of himself with Augustus, and of his Fascist Era with the 'Golden Age'. As the 'new Augustus', *il Duce* planned to occupy the nearby mausoleum of Augustus himself, and had the surrounding piazza Augusto Imperatore built with characteristic architectural bombast.

In its way, the Meier building was no less of a political statement. Anxious to show that his city was a dynamic, go-ahead kind of place, which had sloughed off its decades-long lethargy then-mayor Francesco Rutelli waived the usual international bidding competition and appointed Meier to create

the museum without any preliminaries; detractors suggested that Rutelli was so dazzled by the star architect that he neglected to stipulate that Meier consider the surroundings when he drew up his plans.

However, the plans were drawn up and – whatever your opinion of the structure itself – the new Museo dell'Ara Pacis is clearly an anomaly in this extraordinary city that has no need of major new architectural statements to attract international attention. Meier's creation would look just as good (perhaps better...) in New York or London, Bilbao or Buenos Aires; Morpurgo's pavilion, on the other hand, would have been out of place anywhere but Rome. Which begs the question: in its current head-long rush towards modernity, is Rome running the risk of losing its identity?

threw up jerry-built high-rises along the major arteries out of town. These developments were unplanned, sometimes unplumbed and largely unconnected with the centre... except for those people who were able to invest in a Fiat 500 and, for their entertainment, pile into a *centro* that was far too small and ill-equipped to accommodate them.

The urban development masterplan – the Piano Regolatore Generale (PRG) – approved in 1962 was a sorry case of shutting the stable

door after the horse had bolted. Its good intentions were tardy and largely ignored thereafter. It wasn't until March 2006 that a replacement – a point of honour for Veltroni and his team – finally went into effect. Already in the period 2000-06, the Rome property sector had seen investments of €19 billion, according to construction industry research institute CRESME. Some of this – inevitably – can be accounted for by sharpsters trying to get their buildings up before the new PRG went into force;

much went, too, into city-sponsored eye-catchers, such as Richard Meier's controversial Ara Pacis Museum (*see p29* **Peace in our time**) and Dio Padre Misericordioso church, Rem Koolhaas' Città dei Giovani and Zaha Hadid's MAXXI.

It has been estimated that the new PRG will entice a further €40 billion to Rome. And that, city hall hopes, will go far towards solving the problems of Rome's run-down *periferie*, providing them with their own centres – shops, theatres and other enticements to give residents a sense of pride, something to do and a reason not to descend en masse on Rome's *centro storico*. Again, we'll see. But in the meantime, the PRG lays down stringent rules on the percentage of territory given over to parks and gardens, and sets out high mandatory targets for energy production – each new building, depending on type and destination, must produce a certain percentage of its energy with solar or photovoltaic panels – and conservation.

WHAT'S IN IT FOR US?

So much for the Rome of the Romans. And the Rome of the visitor? As you hesitate on the kerb, gathering sufficient courage to cross amid life-threatening traffic, or dodge wild-eyed youths screaming down cobbled alleys on silencer-free *motorini*, you might be forgiven for thinking that nothing much has changed in Rome since *Roman Holiday*. But it has.

Anyone who passed through the Eternal City 15 years ago will remember having to get up with the birds in order to see anything: museums – the ones that weren't *in restauro* – generally closed at 1pm. Although we've noted a worrying tendency in the last couple of years to leave less-visited sights (the Galleria Spada or Palazzo Corsini, for example) to their own devices, with severe staff shortages forcing early closures, the major attractions continue to extend opening hours, with online and phone booking becoming increasingly easier.

Besides, there's more to see. The Ara Pacis is now encased in a museum that – love it or hate it – restores its sense of monumentality; the bronze statue of Marcus Aurelius, too, has re-acquired grandeur in its airy new pavilion in the Musei Capitolini. Villa Torlonia is gradually being returned to the city as a green, attraction-packed haven. Digs continue along the via dei Fori Imperiali – the artery hacked through Rome's medieval framework by Mussolini – to reveal more and more of the underlying fora, the history and significance of which will be explained in the new Museo dei Fori Imperiali, scheduled to open sometime in 2007. MACRO's new wing inside the Mattatoio and the exhibition spaces inside the MAXXI building site provide more room for contemporary art.

The events on offer during the long hot Roman summer grow ever more numerous. The free July mega-concert – where Billy Joel, Elton John, Paul McCartney and Simon & Garfunkel have all performed – has now become a fixture: generally held with the Colosseum as its backdrop, in 2007 it was to shift to the Circo Massimo with Genesis on stage (*see p282* **Sounds of summer**). And the menu of offerings during the summertime Estate Romana (*see p253*) was the most extensive yet as that umbrella organisation celebrated its 30th year in 2007. The September Notte Bianca (*see p254*) – during which Rome buzzes, with museums and galleries open, all through one sleepless weekend – draws hundreds of thousands of revellers. On top of that, the new Cinema – Festival Internazionale di Roma (*see p263* **How to launch a film festival**) in October provides a new, glam draw.

'There is always the danger that the Eternal City may fall prey to its own success.'

With Rome on such a roll, and Romans revelling in their increasingly vibrant city, it's difficult to imagine anything but improvements in the offing. Yet there is always the danger that the Eternal City may fall prey to its own success. Already in the *centro storico*, international chains have got wind of the new positive attitude and affluence, and are driving the old one-off shops out of their historical premises… at times to the relief of misguided younger Romans who equate international blandness with worldly sophistication. The near-monopoly of the charming and dependable neighbourhood trattoria has collapsed, undermined by the advent of more sophisticated eating and drinking places. Traditional *vini e olii* – holes in walls where locals quaffed *Castelli* wine as the owner threw together something to eat out back – are more difficult to find. Campo de' Fiori – not so long ago a salt-of-the-earth produce market – is now invaded by hawkers of imitation leather goods by day and becomes a mega-pub by night. Meanwhile, other street markets and corner *alimentari* are being forced out by supermarkets.

The pride of Romans in their unique city – with millennia of uninterrupted history all gloriously still on show – is palpable. But so is their craving for modernity and modern global consumerism. Rome's continued popularity – indeed its very character – will depend on its ability to get the balance right.

Sartogo and Grenon's
Santo Volto di Gesù. *See p36.*

Architecture

A wave of construction is adding to the layers of Rome's glorious built history.

There has never been a time in Rome when architecture wasn't about making a statement – and the statement was, first and foremost, political. From the ancient fora with their marbled temples and towering statues, to the overwhelming churches of the Baroque and the gleaming white EUR district – a Fascist ideal city – the goal was always to awe. Still today, the fact that a swathe of international design superstars have Roman projects on their drawing boards represents city hall's determination to show that *caput mundi* is refusing to rest on its architectural laurels: packed as it is with significant buildings, Rome fully intends to add some more.

THE ANCIENT CITY

The classical ruins we see today are, to an extent, misleading. What's missing (besides roofs and walls) is colour: there was nothing minimalist or pared-back about ancient Rome. Statues, temples and basilicas were multi-hued: buildings and temples were a riot of variegated marbles; statues and bas-reliefs were painted in garish shades. What they still can give is an idea of size: the city's major buildings were designed to express the sophistication and might of Rome. Perhaps for this reason, it was a while before the Romans developed much in the way of architectural style.

The Romans had the Etruscans to thank for insights into hydraulics and town planning. The Greek system of orders was followed for important façades. The main Greek orders – with columns of different proportions based on their width – were Doric (plain and sturdy), Ionic (more slender and ornate) and Corinthian (the most delicate and ornate of all). The **Colosseum** (*see p85*) is a good example of how they were used: hefty Doric at the bottom to support the construction; lighter, more elegant Ionic in the middle; and the decorative Corinthian top layer. It wasn't only columns that were copied from Greece: whole genres of building were based on Greek models: temples were colonnaded and either rectangular or circular; theatres were derived from their Greek counterparts.

Eventually, however, the Romans came up with some ideas of their own: elliptical arenas – known as amphitheatres – designed for blood sports; rectangular meeting houses flanked by columns, known as basilicas; and efficient plumbing and heating systems, complete with hot running water. Perhaps most importantly, the Romans took the arch to unprecedented heights of perfection, giving the world its first large-scale, free-standing masonry.

'The Pantheon was the largest cast-concrete construction made before the 20th century.'

The commonest stone found around Rome was soft, volcanic tufa. This was not an ideal building material, and as early as the third century BC a form of concrete was developed, made of pozzolana (a volcanic ash), lime and tufa rubble. Without concrete, constructing the **Pantheon** (see p119) would have been impossible: the huge hemispherical dome was the largest cast-concrete construction made before the 20th century. Other feats of cast-concrete engineering include the **Terme di Diocleziano** (see p161) and **Terme di Caracalla** (see p141). But concrete was not aesthetically pleasing, so buildings were faced with veneers of coloured marble or travertine (see p33 **Lapis tiburtinus**). Brick, another fundamental Roman building material, was used to face buildings, to lend internal support to concrete walls and as a material in its own right. The most impressive example is the **Mercati di Traiano** (see p80).

EARLY CHRISTIAN ROME
Stylistically speaking, the transition from pagan to paleo-Christian was a smooth one, though this isn't always immediately apparent. You don't need to resort to dank catacombs – a form of burial, what's more, that far pre-dates Christianity. The earliest Christian meeting places – known as *tituli* – were in very ordinary private houses; the first churches happily adopted the basilica form. Churches founded in the fourth and fifth centuries such as **San Paolo fuori le Mura** (see p177), **San Giovanni in Laterano** (see p150), **Santi Quattro Coronati** (see p147), **Santa Maria in Trastevere** (see p135) and **San Pietro in Vincoli** (see p157) are the most tangible connection we have with the interiors of ancient civic Rome: go into any of them and imagine them without the decorations added through the ages. The form is generally simple and stately: most are rectangular, with a flat roof and a

colonnade separating a tall nave from lower aisles. Natural light enters the nave through high windows. Behind the altar, opposite the entrance, is an apse topped by a conch (domed roof). Perhaps the best example of all is **Santa Sabina** (see p139), which was shorn of later additions in a no-holds-barred restoration in the 1930s.

You can trace the fortunes of the Catholic church in Rome's architecture. When it was poor, as in the fifth century, buildings were plain and functional; when it was rich, in the eighth and 12th centuries, churches were adorned with brilliant mosaics. The most magnificent to have survived are in **Santa Maria Maggiore** (see p160), **Santa Prassede** (see p153) and **Santa Maria in Trastevere** (see p135). Many churches were decorated with cosmati-work: choirs, candlesticks and floors inlaid with dazzling patterns in chips of coloured marble and glass. Very occasionally, circular churches were built, perhaps inspired by Roman tombs like Hadrian's mausoleum (now Castel Sant'Angelo, see p170). **Santa Costanza** (see p176) – with its swirling mosaics, which owe little to Christian and much to pagan symbolism – was probably built in the fourth century as a mausoleum for the daughters of Emperor Constantine; its contemporary, **Santo Stefano Rotondo** (see p149), may have been inspired by the church of the Holy Sepulchre in Jerusalem.

During the Middle Ages, Rome's influential families were engaged in an almost constant battle for power – a fact that was reflected in the civic architecture of the city. Construction was unrestricted and unplanned: the tortuous warren of streets in the Monti district is a result. Anyone who could, opted for a fortress-home with lookout towers like **Torre delle Milizie**, behind Trajan's market (see p80).

The quarrels between the families were to have long-lasting effects: with daggers constantly drawn, they failed to impose a Roman candidate on the throne of St Peter's. France stepped in, had Clement V elected, and helped him shift the papacy to Avignon in 1309, where it remained until 1378. The international funds that used to shore up the spendthrift papacy were diverted to the French city and Rome was left bankrupt. The Gothic passed the city by (the one exception being the church of **Santa Maria sopra Minerva**, see p120). The early Renaissance, too, was lost on the shadow of its former self that Rome had become.

THE RENAISSANCE
In the late 14th century a revolution in art, architecture and thought was under way in Tuscany. In crumbling, medieval Rome it was not until the following century that the

Renaissance began to gather momentum (the sole exception being the group of artists around genius Pietro Cavallini). In 1445 the Florentine architect Antonio Filarete created one of Rome's first significant Renaissance works: the magnificent central bronze doors of St Peter's.

'Those with lucrative church connections built fabulous palaces.'

It was Pope Nicholas V (1447-55) who realised that if Rome was to take on fully its role as the focus of Christianity, she had to look the part. As a first step, Nicholas commissioned extensive restoration work on the fourth-century basilica of St Peter, which was in imminent danger of collapse. Meanwhile, those with lucrative church connections built fabulous palaces: in 1508 papal banker Agostino Chigi commissioned a lavish villa, now the **Villa Farnesina** (*see p136*), and in 1515 work started on **Palazzo Farnese** (*see p125*) for Cardinal Alessandro Farnese.

Pope Pius II (1458-64), a cultured Tuscan steeped in classical literature, put a stop to the quarrying of ancient buildings for construction

materials. Sixtus IV (1471-84) had roads paved and widened, churches such as **Santa Maria della Pace** (*see p115*) and **Santa Maria del Popolo** (*see p110*) rebuilt, and the **Sistine Chapel** (*see p166*) built and decorated by some of the foremost artists of the day.

Rome's Renaissance reached its peak with Julius II (1503-13), who made Donato Bramante (1444-1514) his chief architect. Bramante came to Rome from Milan in 1499, and in 1502 built the **Tempietto** (*see p138*) to mark the spot thought to be that of St Peter's execution. With its domed cylinder surrounded by a Tuscan Doric colonnade, the Tempietto came closer than any other building to the spirit of antiquity. Julius also commissioned Michelangelo (1475-1564) to sculpt his tomb and fresco the ceiling of the Sistine Chapel. Raphael (1483-1520) was called in to decorate the *stanze* (private apartments) in the Vatican palace.

Not satisfied with the restoration of **St Peter's** (*see p164*) initiated by his predecessors, the supremely self-assured Julius decided to scrap the basilica that for 12 centuries had been one of the holiest sites in Christendom and start again. The job was given to Bramante, and in 1506 the foundation stone was laid. Work began on Bramante's Greek-

Lapis tiburtinus

You may be forgiven for thinking that Rome is a city of marble. In fact, most of the greyish-cream coloured stone you see in ancient structures and Baroque churches is travertine (*Lapis tiburtinus*). Marble is a metamorphic rock, usually formed from limestone at extremely high temperatures and without fossils and faults. Travertine is a sedimentary rock, formed by percolation of spring water through limestone, and full of imperfections (hence it is pitted with tiny holes and craters). Marble is expensive and had to be brought large distances to Rome. Travertine, on the other hand, is tough, relatively cheap and available in seemingly inexhaustible quantities around Tivoli (*see p311*).

While sculptors of all epochs favoured smoother, polishable marble for their more sophisticated works, Roman architects were happy to make their creations with this, the ultimate local stone: the Colosseum, the façade of St Peter's and the massive columns of Bernini's colonnade in front of that basilica, the Spanish Steps and the Trevi Fountain are all made of travertine. Bernini plumped for travertine in urban

embellishments such as the Fontana dei Quattro Fiumi in piazza Navona and the Fontana del Tritone in piazza Barberini. Add to that the countless churches, bridges, ancient theatres, markets and temples and you begin to appreciate the ubiquity of these great limestone blocks. Not surprisingly, Hadrian made generous use of it in his villa outside Tivoli (*see p312* **Villa Adriana**).

Tivoli's quarries have been in operation since classical times – with the exception of a brief hiccup while barbarians rampaged in the Dark Ages. By the mid-15th century, the building surge in Renaissance Rome saw them working at full tilt again. Would-be emperor Benito Mussolini had travertine used for the construction of his 'Brave New City', EUR (*see p178*) – though he cheated, building in reinforced concrete and merely cladding the structures with travertine. Nowadays, travertine remains a popular material, though as often as not its ends are anything but monumental: as a trawl around the internet will show, you can easily order the stuff in a variety of shades for kitchen tops, garden paths and bathroom floors.

cross design, but was halted after his death in 1514. In 1547 Michelangelo took over, increasing the scale tremendously. During the papacy of Sixtus V (1585-90) – an obsessive planner responsible for the layout of much of modern Rome – Giacomo della Porta (1533-1602) erected the dome to a design by Michelangelo. The second half of the 16th century in Rome was dominated by the austere reforms of the Council of Trent (1545-63), designed to counter the ideas of Martin Luther's Reformation, and by the establishment of heavy-handed new religious orders such as the Jesuits and Oratorians. With the dictates of the Counter-Reformation in mind, Paul V (1605-21) finally scuppered the original Greek-cross design for St Peter's and instead commissioned Carlo Maderno (1556-1629) to lengthen the nave to create a Latin cross.

The earliest churches of the period, such as the **Chiesa Nuova** (*see p113*), were plain and provided with long naves suitable for processions. The **Gesù** (*see p123*), with its wide nave, was deemed ideal for the purposes of the Jesuits, as no architectural obstacles came between the preacher and his flock.

> ### 'The endlessly inventive confections of the Baroque make Rome what it is today.'

As the Counter-Reformation gathered pace, great cycles of decoration teaching the mysteries of the faith (such as the Cappella Sistina of **Santa Maria Maggiore**) or inspiring the onlooker to identify with the sufferings of martyrs (as in the bloodthirsty frescos of **Santo Stefano Rotondo**) began to appear.

THE BAROQUE

Counter-Reformation austerity gave way to an exuberant, theatrical style of architecture: the Baroque. It is to a great extent the endlessly inventive confections of the Baroque that make Rome what it is today. Architects such as Giacomo della Porta and Domenico Fontana (1543-1607) set the scene in which the real shapers of the Baroque grew up: Gian Lorenzo Bernini, Francesco Borromini and Pietro da Cortona.

Bernini (1598-1680) virtually made the Baroque his own, with his imaginative use of marble, bronze and stucco, his combination of sensuality and mysticism. He was jealously guarded by his Barberini family patrons (*see p92* **Barberini trumpeting**), carrying out much of the decoration of the interior of **St Peter's** for the Barberini Pope Urban VIII. He so dominated the arts that Borromini, Rome's other great genius of the era, was relatively neglected.

Bernini said that quarrelsome, neurotic Borromini (1559-1667) 'had been sent to destroy architecture', and for centuries Borromini was vilified as a wild iconoclast. Today he is recognised as one of the great masters of the period, perhaps greatest of all in the inventive use of ground plan and the creation of spatial effects. The most startling examples of his work are **San Carlo alle Quattro Fontane** (*see p92*) and **Sant'Ivo alla Sapienza** (*see p118*), both of which broke all the rules.

Perhaps because of his temperament (he was manic depressive and eventually committed suicide), Borromini never attained Bernini's status, but his lay patrons allowed him a freedom to develop his ideas that he might not have enjoyed had he worked for the popes with their particular agendas.

Meier's **Museo dell'Ara Pacis**. See p36.

Like Bernini, Pietro da Cortona (1597-1669) created some of his greatest works for the Barberini popes. He was principally a painter; his most significant contribution to architecture was his three-dimensional treatment of walls. At **Santa Maria della Pace** (*see p115*) he combined opposing convex forms that, curving sharply at the ends, are nearly flat in the middle. The result is overwhelmingly theatrical.

Throughout the Baroque period the patronage of popes, their families and the religious orders sustained the explosion of architectural and artistic fervour. Popes commissioned the decoration of St Peter's (Urban VIII, 1623-44); the colonnade in front of it (Alexander VII, 1655-67); the layout of **piazza Navona** (*see p116*); and the redecoration of **San Giovanni in Laterano** (Innocent X, 1644-55). Their cardinal nephews inspired many lesser building schemes: the redecoration or restoration of existing churches, and private villas, gardens and palaces.

The religious orders were no less profligate. The Jesuits church of **Il Gesù**, for example, though begun in the 1560s was completed decades later with a façade by Giacomo della Porta. Then, from the 1640s, its interior walls – intended to be bare – started to acquire the alarming profusion of decoration we see today.

NEO-CLASSICISM AND UNIFICATION

During the 18th century the Baroque gained a rococo gloss, as seen in Nicola Salvi's **Fontana di Trevi** (*see p88*), Francesco de Sanctis' **Spanish Steps** (*see p106*) and Fernando Fuga's hallucinatory **Palazzo della Consulta** on piazza del Quirinale. Giovanni Battista Piranesi imposed his neo-classical theories on the city in the later part of the 18th century, creating striking tableaux such as the **piazza dei Cavalieri di Malta** (*see p139*).

The French occupation of the city (1809-14) brought a flurry of Gallic blueprints for changes in town planning. Some plans – such as Giuseppe Valadier's magnificent reorganisation of **piazza del Popolo** (*see p109*) and the **Pincio** (*see p95*) – were carried out under French rule. Still others were adopted after 1815 by the restored papacy and claimed as its own.

In 1870 the city became capital of a united Italy, ruled by the northern Savoy dynasty, which sought to impose order on the chaotic cityscape, providing it with a road system and structures to accommodate the burgeoning bureaucracy… even if this meant razing entire medieval and Renaissance quarters in the process. **Piazza Vittorio** (*see p158*), **Palazzo delle Esposizioni** (*see p93*) and the imperious, jingoistic **Vittoriano** monument (*see p80*) in piazza Venezia are fine examples.

Occasional relief from the pomposity comes in the shape of lovely Liberty (art nouveau) outcrops, such as the **Casina della Civette** (*see p177*), the palazzo housing the Museo Hendrik Christian Andersen (*see p101*), the frescoed **Galleria Sciarra** arcade at via Minghetti 10 and the whole, extraordinary **Coppedè district**, centred on piazza Mincio in the northern suburbs.

20TH CENTURY AND CONTEMPORARY

Italy's inter-war leader Benito Mussolini was obsessed with moving Italians out of cities and back to the countryside. He couldn't, however, stop Rome's urban spread. On the contrary, during the Fascist period (1922-43) the expansion of the city was given a further push by several large-scale projects. One of the most impressive was the **Foro Italico** (*see p175*), a monumental sports complex complete with two stadiums and an army of towering statues of naked athletes. To celebrate the 20th anniversary of the Fascist revolution – and to spearhead Rome's expansion towards the sea – construction also began on a whole new district, initially called E42 but later renamed Esposizione universale romana (**EUR** for short; *see p178*). It is one of the most striking examples of Fascist town planning – or indeed any kind of town planning – anywhere in Europe.

'Thankfully, the outbreak of war stopped Mussolini wreaking too much havoc.'

With construction under way at EUR, Mussolini turned his attention to the *centro storico*: here, according to his Grand Plan, great chunks of the medieval and Renaissance urban fabric would be destroyed, making room for a network of boulevards to improve sight lines between major classical monuments. Thankfully, the outbreak of war stopped *il Duce* wreaking too much havoc. He did, however, manage to bludgeon the **via dei Fori Imperiali** through the ruins of ancient fora from the Colosseum to piazza Venezia.

During his rule, however, young architects built some of Rome's most interesting modern buildings, with a philosophy that was dubbed *razionalismo*, a blend of European functionalism with the rigor and elegance of Mediterranean/classical tradition. They saw Fascism as a modernising force and, participating in the state-sponsored building spree of the 1920s and '30s, contributed some gems: **post office buildings** in via Marmorata, Testaccio, by Adalberto Libera and in piazza Bologna by Mario Ridolfi, and the **Casa della Gioventù** in largo Ascianghi, Trastevere, by Luigi Moretti (all 1933-35), are masterpieces not only of *razionalismo* but of the modern movement. By the '30s, the *razionalisti* realised that they were propaganda pawns. The last great works of the period in which they participated were on the *Città universitaria* campus. Of the group, only Libera stayed on to design the **Palazzo dei Congressi** in EUR.

After the war, with Italians from all over the country drifting to the capital, a number of successful public-housing projects were developed. Economic prosperity in the 1950s – halting at first, then rampant – allowed unfinished projects to be completed: **Termini railway station** was given a magnificent wave-like canopy over its concourse, and building resumed in EUR. Optimism fuelled by this prosperity encouraged the construction of many elegant modernist buildings, including the sports venues built by Pier Luigi Nervi for the 1960 Olympics and, in particular, his glorious reinforced-concrete **Palazzetto dello Sport** next to the Stadio Flaminio (*see p175*).

A growing population with money to spend on real estate was to have dire effects on the capital's outskirts, where property speculators

Hadid's **MAXXI**.

had a field day as a very blind eye was turned to zoning regulations. From the 1960s to the '80s, ugly high-rise blocks galloped across what had been unspoilt countryside. The city centre, luckily, remained largely untouched by unscrupulous development. But though it was spared the worst, the city also suffered from a lack of anything new: work on the first major post-war building project within the Aurelian Walls (the new Ara Pacis pavilion; *see below*), only began in 2000.

Today, thanks mainly to a municipal administration seriously committed to urban regeneration, the decades-long slump in new architecture is over. A string of competitions for new facilities have all been won by highly talented and original architects. Rome's **mosque** (*see p334*), one of the largest in Europe, was completed in 1995 to a visionary design by Italian postmodernist Paolo Portoghesi. In 2002 the last and largest of the three striking concert halls of Renzo Piano's **Auditorium-Parco della Musica** (*see p275*) went into operation and has been a resounding success. American Richard Meier's slick new 'container' for the **Ara Pacis** (*see p29* **Peace in our time**; photo *p34*) was inaugurated in 2006 to much trumpeting and even more criticism, while his **Dio Padre Misericordioso** church (*see p177*) opened in the outskirts of Rome in 2003.

In 2006, the striking travertine and glass **Santo Volto di Gesù** church (**photo** *p31*) by architects Pietro Sartogo and Nathalie Grenon was inaugurated in the southern Magliana district.

Work on Zaha Hadid's **MAXXI** contemporary art museum was struggling ahead as this guide went to press, after a stop-go few years due to budget problems. Work on Odile Decq's new building for **MACRO** (*see p176*) is well underway and the new structure, next to its current site at the converted Peroni Beer factory, is scheduled to open in 2008. The oft-delayed groundbreaking for the **Centro Congressi Italia** at EUR, designed by local talent Massimiliano Fuksas in the shape of a cloud inside a gigantic glass box, finally took place in March 2006, though no one expects the original completion target of 2009 to be met. Rem Koolhaas' startling **Città dei Giovani** (City of Youth) arts and retail development for the old wholesale fruit and vegetable *Mercati generali* on ever-trendier via Ostiense is slowly coming to life. And in the ex-**Mattatoio** (*see p143*), the former slaughterhouse in the Testaccio district, the old holding pens and refrigeration units are being transformed into more exhibition space for MACRO, a branch of the Academy of Fine Arts and an alternative market selling organic foods, eco-friendly holidays and fair-trade products.

Michelangelo's Moses. *See p42.*

Art in Rome

So many Virgins, so little time…

From the Renaissance through the 19th century, an artist's education was not complete without a journey to Rome. From the concentration of artistic treasures young artists distilled the essence of beauty. The sheer number of other artists in the city was also a draw, providing a stimulating – even competitive – creative atmosphere.

As artist Giovanni Battista Armenini wrote in 1587, 'in our times countless youths from almost every part of the world went to Rome moved by the wish to learn good draftsmanship together with painting, which they hoped to do in that city where works and craftsmen of highest excellence flowered in this profession.' The whole city of Rome was seens as an overflowing 'studio' with classical ruins, ancient statues, and the newest works furnishing the models.

Other writers went further, asserting that Rome offered something essential to the education of any civilised being. Rome's

> ▶ For the **Galleria Borghese**, see *p99*;
> for the **Musei Capitolini**, see *p75*;
> for the **Musei Vaticani**, see *p166*;
> for the **Palazzo Altemps**, see *p115*.

monuments provided historical perspective unmatched elsewhere; those who recognised the profundity of Roman art could never be considered ignorant. The entry on Rome in Moroni's *Dizionario di erudizione* of 1852 encapsulates this notion of the Eternal City as the perfect syllabus, and a nurturer of generations to come. Moroni's dictionary cites the Chevalier d'Agincourt, an 18th-century antiquary: 'in Rome, you stroll past fallen grandeurs, you learn the secrets of Europe. Walking over the ruins of the past, you can glimpse the present, you see arise the clamour of factions, which to the eyes of a serene and observant spirit confirms that spectacle of peace and instruction which Rome offers to her sons, and to those who come to entreat her to be a tender mother for them too.'

Although travellers today tend to be less lofty in their goals, and may aim to capture the art of the past with a digital camera rather than a pen and sketchbook, looking closely at the art of Rome still offers a stirring aesthetic experience – and a great education.

Art in Rome is so enjoyable and edifying because it embraces both superlative quality and a stunning chronological range. That the city displays art covering nearly 3,000 years is staggering; that almost all of it was produced right here is even more amazing. No other city can boast as much. Furthermore, many of the greatest paintings and pieces of sculpture are still in their original architectural settings, offering an authentic context that museums can never duplicate.

Yet today, as in the 16th century, visitors can find Rome overwhelming. After all, there is no Louvre to offer one-stop museum shopping, nor an Uffizi to present a comprehensive survey of Italian painting. Moreover, the city's layout can frustrate the most intrepid traveller. With a little planning, good walking shoes and a sense of adventure, however, you can experience Rome's unique continuum of past and present: splendid monuments and intimate spaces, and the layered richness of a hundred generations of artists, patrons and collectors who basked in the absolute certainty that Rome was the centre of the civilised world.

Bernini's babes

One hand clutches her breast, her body writhes and her face looks heavenwards in rapturous agony. Is she in the throes of death or in the midst of an erotic encounter with the Holy Spirit? *La beata Ludovica Albertoni* (1671), whose reclining figure graces the church of **San Francesco a Ripa** (*see p137*), is just one of many sexually and spiritually charged marble women scattered around Rome by Baroque genius Gian Lorenzo Bernini.

An equal in celestial swooning, *L'estasi di Santa Teresa* (1647-52), draws crowds to the church of **Santa Maria della Vittoria** (*see p160, pictured*). Lusty Bernini – father of 11 – was a highly religious individual for whom the distinction between the sensual and the sublime was blurred. Those like him will understand Teresa's tortured transcendence; but cynics viewing this work will likely be musing: 'she ain't thinkin' about heaven.'

Sculptor, architect and darling of a string of popes, Bernini (1598-1680) attended Mass every morning, took communion twice a week, and on the way home from work stopped by regularly at the church of the **Gesù** (*see p123*) where he reportedly underwent the rigorous Spiritual Exercises of the Jesuits. But evidently that didn't preclude a first-hand understanding of intimate female joys and fears. Just look at the terror on the face of Proserpine as Pluto grabs her fleshy thigh in *The Rape of Proserpine* (1621-22); the woeful desperation of Daphne as she turns into a laurel tree to escape Apollo's embrace in *Apollo and Daphne* (1622-25); or the come-hither look of the laid-back *Truth Unveiled by Time* (1646-52), all of which can be admired in the **Galleria Borghese** (*see p99*).

Bernini designed – though his workshop may have carved – the *Four Virtues* group in **Sant'Isidoro** (via degli Artisti 41, 06 488 5359, open 8am-noon Mon-Sat by appointment only), in which *Charity* offers her ample naked bosom with an encouraging smile – an outright solicitation that Bernini's patrons in 1662 didn't seem to find out of place in a church. (It was too much for 19th-century sensibilities though: bronze tunics added to cover her and one of her buxom sisters were not removed until 2002).

Energetic and disciplined, an indefatigable worker who was at home with popes and princes, Bernini lost his head just once, for Costanza Bonarelli, the wife of a fellow artist. So steamy was the affair that Urban VIII had to step in to put out the fire. Bernini subsequently married, had his numerous brood and lived happily until the age of 82. But not before completing, for himself, an exquisite bust of his beloved Costanza (1635, in the Bargello museum in Florence), with an intelligent face and loose blouse. Could she have been the inspiration for his later sensuous ladies?

ART OF THE ANCIENTS

Although the art of Rome has furthered the needs of the Catholic church for nearly two millennia, the single strongest influence has always been the weighty legacy of the ancient world. In few cities are the remains of the past so palpable. Ancient Rome, as *caput mundi*, harvested or created much of the best art of antiquity. Those who successively sacked or occupied the city – from Alaric in 410 to Napoleon in 1808 – pillaged much of this patrimony, but the fraction that survives continues to amaze.

Egyptian obelisks transported across the Mediterranean still mark key squares (*see p107* **Obelisks**) and, while there are not many certain Greek originals in Rome today, the miracle of Greek art can be studied and appreciated in scores of important Roman copies. These marbles – often copies of bronze originals long since destroyed – display the Greek flair for endowing the body with beauty, purpose and a sense of movement. The classical ideal, combining striking naturalism with idealised body types, offered a standard of beauty that was hard to ignore.

Although the most famous Greek sculpture in Rome is the *Ludovisi Throne* – in the Ludovisi family collection housed in Palazzo Altemps – many works are transitional in nature, between Greek and Roman. An outstanding example in this category is the hulking *Belvedere Torso* – a superhuman physique from about 50 BC that inspired Michelangelo – now housed in the Vatican's Pio Clementino Museum.

The Etruscans, the pre-Roman peoples who dominated central Italy from the sixth to the third century BC, produced an exuberant, violent and sensuous art. One of Rome's most pleasant museums is the Villa Giulia (*see p101*), which offers an extraordinary selection of Etruscan art, including life-sized terracotta sculptures from Veio (*see p306*), and a tender terracotta sarcophagus of a married couple. Equally important is the Etruscan work known as the *Lupa Capitolina* (the 'Capitoline She-Wolf'), a bronze treasure that can be found in the Musei Capitolini (*see p75*).

COME THE ROMANS

Beginning in the third century BC the Romans literally built upon this Greek and Etruscan legacy with an unprecedented construction boom. New structural techniques – notably the arch and poured concrete technology – gave birth to daring and spacious buildings (the Pantheon, *see p119*; Domus Aurea, *see p154*). The Romans were also responsible for monumental forms that blur the boundary between architecture and art, such as the triumphal arch ornamented with reliefs (particularly those of Septimus Severus and Titus in the Forum, *see p82*; and that of Constantine, *see p83*) and the independent column ornamented with a spiral band (Colonna di Traiano, *see p81*; Colonna di Marco Aurelio, *see p109*). A further Roman innovation on a smaller scale was the portrait bust, which recorded facial features of the great and the average with arresting honesty.

'*Laocoön* remains perhaps the most dynamic statue in the history of art.'

Much of the best classical art is now concentrated in a few major museums. The Palazzo Altemps, which contains the statue of the *Gaul's Suicide*, is an ideal first stop. The Palazzo Massimo alle Terme (*see p159*) houses important works of Roman painting and sculpture, including two copies of **Myron**'s *Discus Thrower*. The large collections of the Musei Capitolini feature the *Dying Gaul* and beautiful centaurs in dark marble from Hadrian's Villa (*see p312*). Today the sheer size of the classical collection of the Vatican Museums can be demoralising, and the galleries may seem a distraction in one's march toward the frescoes of Raphael and Michelangelo, but it is sobering to be reminded that two centuries ago the Vatican's Pio Clementino Museum was not only the most esteemed part of the Vatican palace, but undoubtedly the most famous museum in the world. Even today one sculpture there gives modern tourists the same frisson that countless other classical works imparted to 18th-century visitors: this is the *Laocoön*, a Hellenistic sculpture showing a powerful man and his sons struggling for their lives against serpents. It remains perhaps the most dynamic statue in the history of art.

A series of accords between the Italian government – in the shape of Cultural Heritage Minister Francesco Rutelli – and a group of major American museums may be the biggest news to hit the ancient art world in recent years. The agreements specify that some pieces of classical art obtained over the past few decades by these American museums without adequate documentation are now the property of the Italian state. This ushers in a new era of openness and cultural collaboration: museums in Europe and Asia are sure to be next.

HOLY INSPIRATION

Christian art flourished in Rome after AD 313, when Emperor Constantine's Edict of Milan legitimised the new religion. Rome was thus

Albergo Cesàri

since 1787

★ ★ ★

Your three stars in the heart of Rome

Established in 1787, the Albergo Cesàri remains an island of peaceful elegance in the heart of Rome, ideally situated between the Fontana di Trevi and the Pantheon.

The hotel was built during the first half of the 18th century, and has accommodated many famous figures, including Stendhal and Gregorovius.

Completely refurbished in 2007, the hotel now features 47 sound-proof guestrooms including new 10 superior rooms. All rooms are equipped with satellite television and pay-per-view, air conditioning, mini-bar, in room safe, hairdryer, direct-dial telephone and complimentary coffee and tea making facilities. Additional amenities include DSL Internet station, Wi-Fi connection free of charge in rooms and throughout the hotel, buffet breakfast and a private garage near the hotel (at extra cost). Non-smoking floors are also available.

The hotel's new Roof Garden has a bar and lounge area with spectacular views of the Eternal City.

A tourist's dream locale, the hotel is close to Rome's most important theatres, trendy restaurants, and fashionable streets such as Via Condotti, Via Veneto, and Piazza di Spagna - home to Armani, Versace, Valentino and many other famous designer boutiques.

LOCATION

Albergo Cesàri is only a few minutes from the Termini Main Railway Station, the Leonardo train to Fiumicino Airport, and is also a convenient walking distance from bus and metro access stations.

00186 Roma - Via di Pietra, 89/a
Tel. + 39 06 6749701 Fax + 39 06 67497030
info@albergocesari.it - booking@albergocesari.it
www.albergocesari.it

Perugino's *Giving of the Keys to St Peter* in the Sistine Chapel.

transformed from a city of temples to one of churches. Little portable early Christian art – the devotional apparatus of the newly recognised religion – survives, but stunning mosaics decorate a number of venerable churches: including Santa Costanza (fourth century, *see p176*), Santa Maria Maggiore (fifth century, *see p160*), Santi Cosma e Damiano (sixth century, *see p84*), and Santa Prassede (ninth century, *see p153*). Two of the most atmospheric early churches are the austere, lovely Santa Sabina (*see p139*), and San Clemente (*see p145*), with its 12th-century mosaics.

Later medieval art can be enjoyed in Santa Cecilia in Trastevere (*see p137*), which contains a ciborium (1283) by **Arnolfo di Cambio** (best known as the architect of the Duomo in Florence) and a pioneering fresco of the *Last Judgment* (1293) by **Pietro Cavallini** above the nun's choir. The little-known Cavallini – who perhaps deserves to rank with Giotto as an early initiator of the Renaissance – also impresses with his narrative mosaics (1291) in nearby Santa Maria in Trastevere (*see p135*).

From 1309 to 1377 the papacy was based in Avignon; Rome withered, and only a fraction of the population remained. Thus the Gothic is largely absent in the Eternal City. The lack of late-medieval art, however, is compensated by the wealth of Renaissance, and particularly High Renaissance, art of the 15th and 16th centuries.

THE RENAISSANCE BEGINS IN ROME

The definitive return of the papacy in 1420 permitted the Renaissance and its doctrine of humanism to take root and eventually flourish in the primary seat of classical glory.

Humanism was preoccupied with reviving the language and art of the ancient Greeks and Romans, and reconciling this pagan heritage with Christianity. Renaissance ideas began to leave their mark on the city with architecture based on ancient examples, and sculpture and painting that assimilated the *contrapposto* grace

and naturalism of the best classical statues. The papacy concluded that patronage of this new art would extend the faith: in 1455, on his deathbed, Pope Nicholas V informed his successors that 'noble edifices combining taste and beauty with imposing proportions would immensely conduce to the exaltation of the chair of St Peter'.

Nicholas' extant contribution to Vatican beautification – the little chapel of Nicholas V, frescoed by **Fra Angelico** and **Benozzo Gozzoli** (1447-79) – may be modest in the light of his ambitions, but it remains an extraordinary jewel of the early Renaissance. Later popes undertook grander campaigns: Sixtus IV (1471-84) engaged the greatest painters of the day – **Perugino, Botticelli, Ghirlandaio** and **Cosimo Rosselli** – to fresco the walls of his Sistine Chapel in 1481-2. And think what you may of the morals of the Borgia pope, Alexander VI, his taste in art was exquisite, as seen in the frescoes (1493-5) by **Pinturicchio** that perpetuate Perugino's sweet style throughout the many rooms of the Borgia Apartments.

Outside the Vatican the grace of 15th-century Florentine art can also be seen in the joyful and energetic frescoes (1489-93) of **Filippino Lippi** in the Caraffa chapel in the church of Santa Maria sopra Minerva (*see p120*). In this and many other Roman churches coins are needed to operate the electric lights.

THE HIGH RENAISSANCE

In the 16th century art and architecture took a monumental turn. In painting, the human figure grew in relation to the pictorial field: the busy backgrounds of 15th-century art were eliminated. Sculptors took their cue from ancient statues, making the human body newly heroic. **Michelangelo** (1475-1564), from Florence, first worked in Rome from 1496 to 1501 for clerics and businessmen. He carved his first *Pietà* (now in St Peter's) for a French cardinal; his 1498 contract challenged the supremacy of classical sculpture in promising to create a piece 'more beautiful

Caravaggio's *David with the Head of Goliath* in the Galleria Borghese. See p43.

than any work in marble to be seen in Rome today'. Michelangelo positioned the dead Christ gracefully in his mother's lap, creating an eternal meditation on death and fulfilling his pledge.

Under Julius II (1503-13) papal patronage called ever greater artists to work on ever larger projects at the Vatican, shifting the centre of the Renaissance from Florence to Rome. Julius summoned Michelangelo back from Florence to begin work on the pope's own monumental tomb, a work destined for the choir of the old St Peter's and crammed with larger-than-life statues. The headstrong Julius soon changed his mind, insisting that the young sculptor paint the ceiling of the Sistine Chapel. Complaining bitterly that he was 'no painter', Michelangelo rapidly frescoed the ceiling (1508-11), retelling the first nine chapters of Genesis with a grandeur and solidity previously associated with sculpture. Although the recent cleaning of the frescoes provoked controversy, the vivid colours we now see are closer to Michelangelo's intentions than the dark, 'sculptural' forms worshipped in the 19th and 20th centuries.

Although a later campaign to fresco the chapel's altar wall produced the triumphant and awe-inspiring *Last Judgment* (1534-41), the tomb for Julius limped to an unsatisfactory conclusion in the early 1540s in San Pietro in Vincoli (*see p157*), employing the powerful *Moses* (c1515; *pictured p37*) as its centrepiece. Following a recent restoration, however, the tomb looks better and brighter than it has for centuries.

Julius initiated his grandest plan of all when he called upon **Donato Bramante** (1444-1514) to design a new basilica of St Peter's. The stateliness of Bramante's style inspired painters as well as other architects. The most influential of the former was **Raphael** (1483-1520).

Julius would occupy the apartments of his dissolute Borgia predecessor; he insisted on a new suite of rooms – the so-called Stanze. These

were decorated by Raphael starting in 1508. The presence of Michelangelo working next door on the Sistine ceiling was a spur to the young painter: the elegant *School of Athens* (1510-11) exemplifies the notion of the High Renaissance, with its re-creation of the philosophers of ancient Greece against a backdrop of imaginary architecture borrowed from Bramante.

If Michelangelo was unsurpassed in depicting the human body in complex poses, the *Stanze* show Raphael's superiority in arranging compositions. The huge demand for this style forced Raphael to run an efficient workshop. His success at delegation is most apparent in the frescoes in the Villa Farnesina (*see p136*), but the astonishingly swift development of the master himself can be seen in a single room of the Vatican Pinacoteca. There, three masterful altarpieces – *The Coronation of the Virgin* (1505), *The Madonna of Foligno* (c1511) and *The Transfiguration* (c1518-20) – chart the amazing shift from a sweetness reminiscent of Perugino to a brooding, dramatic late style. In the same room, note the lavish tapestries, designed by Raphael for the lower walls of the Sistine Chapel.

The Sack of Rome in 1527 (*see p21* **The sack**) halted the artistic boom of the High Renaissance, as frightened artists sought employment elsewhere. The simultaneous spread of the Protestant Reformation directly challenged the legitimacy of the pope and his worldly expenses. This more hardened, pessimistic spirit gave preference to mannerist art, a style of exaggerated proportions and contorted poses that developed out of the mature work of Raphael and Michelangelo. Frescoes (c1545) by Raphael's assistant **Perino del Vaga** (1501-47) in the Castel Sant'Angelo (*see p170*) depict both hyper-elegant humans and statues, playing with the viewer's sense of what is real.

GOING FOR BAROQUE

By the second half of the 16th century the mannerist style had lost its wit and energy. Baroque rescue came through the works of **Annibale Carracci** (1560-1609) of Bologna and the shocking naturalism of Michelangelo Merisi, better known as **Caravaggio** (1571-1610). Carracci, who sought a buoyant version of High Renaissance harmony, has become slightly easier to appreciate here of late. As well as the lovely *Flight into Egypt* in the Galleria Doria Pamphili (*see p119*), Carracci's masterpiece, an ambitious fresco ceiling in the Palazzo Farnese (*see p125*) – home to the French embassy – can now be admired on guided tours of that magnificent structure, after many years under lock and key. Carracci's contemporary Caravaggio left paintings throughout the city during his stormy career.

These works, with their extreme *chiaroscuro*, can be seen in the churches of Sant'Agostino (*see p117*) and Santa Maria del Popolo (*see 110*). His masterpiece may be the *Calling of St Matthew* (c1599-1602) in the church of San Luigi dei Francesi (*see p116*), where the beckoning finger of Christ recalls Michelangelo's *Creation of Adam* in the Sistine Chapel.

'The cruelty often depicted in Caravaggio's paintings mirrored his violent life.'

The Galleria Borghese houses a fine nucleus of Caravaggio paintings, from the coy secular works of his early years to the brooding religious canvases of his maturity, notably the powerful *David with the Head of Goliath* (c1609; *pictured p42*), in which the severed head is Caravaggio's self-portrait. The cruelty often depicted in Caravaggio's paintings mirrored his violent life, and altercations with police and patrons marked his Roman career. After losing a tennis match and killing his opponent, Caravaggio fled south. His bold style persisted for a generation, though, as witnessed in the Vatican Pinacoteca's extraordinary room of Baroque altarpieces by **Domenichino**, **Guido Reni** and **Nicolas Poussin** (taking their cues from altarpieces like Caravaggio's *Deposition* and Raphael's turbulent *Transfiguration*, both also in that museum). Equally weighty Baroque altarpieces can be seen in the Pinacoteca of the Musei Capitolini, with **Guercino**'s *Burial of St Petronilla* (c1623) winning the prize.

The most faithful followers of Caravaggio's style were **Orazio Gentileschi** (1563-1639) and his daughter **Artemisia** (1593-1652), who perpetuated *chiaroscuro*, smooth surfaces and close-up viewpoints. Artemisia had to endure male prejudice (and much worse) to pursue her career, and both artists left Rome, resurfacing together in London in the late 1630s to work for Charles I. Canvases by father and daughter can be seen in the Galleria Spada (*see p123*).

The consummate artist of the Roman Baroque, however, was primarily a sculptor: **Gian Lorenzo Bernini** (1598-1680). Bernini perhaps surpassed Michelangelo in the virtuosity of his marble carving. The confident energy inherent in Baroque art is revealed by comparing Bernini's greatest religious sculpture, *The Ecstasy of St Theresa* (1647-52; *see p38* **Bernini's babes**) in Santa Maria della Vittoria (*see p160*), with Michelangelo's *Pietà*. Michelangelo's mild Virgin shows perpetual, placid bereavement; Bernini's Theresa captures a split second of sensual rapture. The theatricality of sculptures like Bernini's *Apollo*

and Daphne (1622-25) in the Galleria Borghese pushed back the boundaries of sculpture; Bernini tried to capture whole narratives in a frozen instant, and to describe textures more vividly than any previous carver. The Galleria Borghese contains many other Bernini statues.

Similarly, the Galleria Doria Pamphili evokes the epoch with outstanding pictures in a magnificent setting. One small room forces a comparison of two portraits of the Pamphili Pope Innocent X (1644-55): a bust by Bernini and a canvas by the Spaniard Diego Velázquez (the pope found the painting 'too truthful'). Both museums are awash in aristocratic atmosphere.

ART MOVES ON
Subsequent generations insisted further upon the artistic unity of architecture, sculpture and painting pioneered by Bernini. Illusionistic ceiling decoration became more and more elaborate. Ceiling paintings – like those in the Palazzo Barberini (*see p92*) or the church of the Gesù (*see p123*) – depicted heavenly visions: assemblages of flying figures bathed in celestial light, as if the roof of the building had been removed. Perhaps the most inventive practitioner of ceiling painting was **Andrea Pozzo** (1642-1709), a Jesuit painter, architect and stage designer. In the huge church of Sant'Ignazio di Loyola (*see p120*), Pozzo painted both a fresco of the *Glory of St Ignatius Loyola* on the vault of the nave and a false dome on canvas. The latter fools the viewer only from the ideal viewing point, marked by a disc on the floor. The Baroque style and the interest in illusionism limped on well into the 18th century.

The final great artistic movement born in Rome was neo-classicism, a nostalgic – some would say sentimental – celebration of ancient Greek art, expressed in stark white statues and reliefs. **Antonio Canova** (1757-1822) created enormous, muscular statues like *Hercules and Lichas*, which can be seen in the Galleria Nazionale d'Arte Moderna (*see p100*), dignified tombs in St Peter's, and plaster wall panels now on show at the Villa Torlonia (*see p177*).

Later movements of the 19th and 20th centuries can be seen at the Galleria Nazionale d'Arte Moderna and the new MACRO (*see p176*). Contemporary art, also exhibited at MAXXI (*see p175*) and the Palazzo delle Esposizioni (*see p93*), proves that the city isn't (entirely) trapped by its own past.

If this extent of painting, architecture, and sculpture seems dizzying, remember that generations of clerics understood the art of Rome as mere preparation for the greater splendours of paradise. As St Fulgentius marvelled in the sixth century, 'how beautiful must the heavenly city be, if the earthly Rome is so refulgent?'

After the Smoke Has Cleared

Will Benedict XVI, the successor to the jet-setting 'pilgrim pope', be simply 'a humble worker in the Lord's vineyard'?

If it's surreal experiences you're after, nothing beats standing in St Peter's square during the conclave for the election of a new pope.

Just a couple of weeks after the death of Pope John Paul II in April 2005, hundreds of thousands gathered excitedly in the huge piazza surrounded by Bernini's perfect colonnade to fix their gazes on a small chimney poking out of the roof of the Sistine Chapel. Inside, red-robed cardinals from around the globe were sealed off hermetically from the outside world, busy selecting one of their number to be the new pontiff, while outside the crowds waited with bated breath for a steady stream of white smoke to announce a successful vote.

In this first conclave of the high-tech era, mega-screens had been set up at intervals to give a better view of the chimney. In the end they didn't make anything clearer: as often happens, when the smoke did begin to waft up into the mild April evening sky, it was neither white nor black but some indeterminate shade of grey. Confusion ran like an electric current through the crowd but still the square was illuminated by the flashes of millions of mobiles snapping what subsequently proved to be the historic moment. Cheers went up as the huge bells of the basilica began to toll, confirming the cardinals had made their choice – a process that in past centuries could take weeks, months, or even years.

The tension mounted visibly as the crowds awaited the name of their new leader – would it be a cardinal from Africa or South America, where the numbers of Catholics are rapidly overtaking those in the developed northern hemisphere? Would it be the popular but aged former archbishop of Milan, Cardinal Carlo Maria Martini, known for his willingness to discuss many of the thorny issues facing the

Catholic church, or would it be a strongly conservative cardinal determined not to give in to the pressures of an increasingly secular Western society? Underlining the divisions that beset the Christian world today, it's not much of an exaggeration to say that half of the crowd let out wild whoops of joy when the name of Cardinal Joseph Alois Ratzinger was announced, while the other half looked stunned and shocked: their worst fears, it seemed, had just been realised.

But who exactly was this new German pope whom the British press unflatteringly dubbed 'God's Rottweiler' as they searched for stories about his past experiences as a member of the Nazi youth brigades?

For a start, he was, in his way, uniquely qualified for the job. He was one of only two cardinals to have voted in the previous conclave back in 1978. And for the previous two decades he'd been one of John Paul's closest aides, upholding church doctrine and weeding out those who dissented from the faith. While not nearly as photogenic or media-friendly as his predecessor, the almost-80-year-old Pope Benedict XVI was recognised as one of the most brilliant theologians around, with 20 years of experience in dealing with the complex politics and bureaucracy involved in the running of the Vatican city-state. Though he was widely seen as a rather severe and icily intellectual figure, human interest stories soon started emerging – about his simple tastes in food, his enjoyment of Mozart's music, his affectionate fatherly relationship with his flock in his titular parish at Casalbertone in Rome's tough eastern suburbs, his fondness for cats. An unprecedented papal calendar for 2007 contained shots of the pontiff reading, writing, playing the piano and strolling peacefully through the gardens of his summer palace in Castelgandolfo south of Rome.

The press was also swift to pick up on the good looks of his young German secretary, known as 'gorgeous Georg' Gänswein, who soon earned the title of the best bit of clerical eye candy around town.

A NEW PAPAL STYLE
Formerly seen only in plain black suits and berets, once installed on the throne of St Peter's the new pope intrigued observers by developing a keen interest in papal fashion, sporting smart Prada shoes, trendy designer sunglasses and a variety of different hats according to the demands of the seasons. These included the magnificent ermine-fringed *camauro* (*pictured* p44) he donned for a pre-Christmas outing in 2005: no pope had had the courage to wear this kind of headgear since John XXIII in 1963.

If the statistics are to be believed, Benedict continues to draw more visitors to the Vatican than his predecessor, though many of these pilgrims make their way to the Holy See to go into the crypt beneath St Peter's to pay a visit to the simple white tomb of John Paul II as well.

At his inauguration the new pope spoke movingly about the legacy of the man often called 'the pilgrim pope' since John Paul made over a hundred journeys to countries right across the five continents. With a rumoured history of heart problems, the new octogenarian pontiff has no intention of globe-trotting or even trying to set such a hectic agenda, which often had journalists and Vatican officials struggling to keep up with the energetic former footballer Karol Wojtyla.

'Benedict XVI remains every bit the bookish priest he always wanted to be.'

While the Polish pope was a keen sportsman and actor, a master of symbolic gestures, Benedict remains every bit the bookish priest and professor he always wanted to be. During military service as a teenager back in his native Bavaria, Ratzinger was asked by an overbearing colonel what he wanted to become. Unlike his contemporaries, who all had dreams of military or political power, he announced he wanted to enter the Church.

As a teacher and philosopher he has few equals, yet in the first months of his pontificate he discovered that it's one thing to air your views in a small lecture hall surrounded by eager students and quite another to have the world's media monitoring your every move and quoting you out of context. The furious reactions of the Muslim world to his misunderstood speech at Regensburg University provided a steep learning curve for the pope and his newly appointed spokesman about the difficulties of getting a complex message out to the media used to working with 30-second sound bites. Yet just a few months later, on his highly charged visit to Turkey, the sight of the Pope praying in Istanbul's spectacular Blue Mosque alongside the local Muslim leader made it clear that some communication lessons had been learned.

BENEDICT XVI MAKES HIS MARK
Back home, in the first year and a half of his pontificate, Benedict made some sweeping changes among his closest advisers, named over 400 new church leaders to dioceses around the world and wrote his first encyclical on the subject of Christian Love – not quite what the

hardliners had expected from a man they hoped would spearhead a crackdown on anyone with even mildly liberal or enquiring mindsets.

In fact, overall Benedict seems to be a bit of a mystery to those seeking to penetrate the secrets of this papacy – and certainly a disappointment to those hoping for a new crusade against modernity, secularism and relativism. A traditionalist with a rather shy, retiring nature, Ratzinger has little of the authoritarianism and even arrogance he was credited with at the moment of his election. But will he simply be remembered as a transitional pope following in the larger-than-life footsteps of the third-longest papacy since St Peter himself was charged with shepherding the flock

here on earth? Or will he spring a few surprises and find creative ways of healing the divisions, so evident at the moment of his election, between traditionalists and modernists?

Unlike a president, prime minister or company chairman, the job of pope is a job for life and no one – not even those elected with the help of the Holy Spirit in the Sistine Chapel – knows just how long a mandate that's going to be. But if you pick up a copy of that papal calendar, you can't help but note a certain serenity in Benedict's smile that would suggest he's not too bothered about how history will remember him – rather, he's just getting on with the daily business, as he describes it, of being 'a humble worker in the Lord's vineyard'.

Ratzinger: the facts

● Ever the natty dresser, Benedict XVI snubbed Gammarelli – papal tailors since 1792 (near the Pantheon, if you're in the market for some red socks) – by favouring his own personal tailor from his days as a cardinal. He has been spotted wearing Prada loafers.
● He's also been spotted in Gucci sunglasses, although not while wearing the *camauro* (the red cap with 12th-century origins, seen in the portraits of many Renaissance popes, and resurrected by Benedict XVI for chilly winter walkabouts).
● After decades of neglect, the papal residence in the Apostolic Palace has had a makeover. Benedict's elder brother Georg, who has suffered heart problems, is said to now be resident in the palace too.
● Benedict's coat of arms was designed by Archbishop (now Cardinal) Andrea Cordero Lanza di Montezemolo, the diplomatic envoy of the Vatican to Italy (a short commute).
● Said coat of arms shows the Bear of Corbinian, which was on Ratzinger's coat of arms as a cardinal. It refers to the eighth-century Bishop Corbinian who preached in Bavaria and travelled to Rome with a bear carrying his bags. Upon his arrival he released the bear, which made its way back to Bavaria and thus became a symbol of tamed paganism and of the burden of office.
● Also on his coat of arms, and also from Benedict's days as cardinal, is the politically incorrect image of the Moor of Freising, or *caput aethiopum* (Ethiopian head), symbol of the bishops of Munich and Freising. Sometimes said to refer to Balthasar of the Magi or various Moorish martyrs, its origins are vague.

● Upon election, Josef Ratzinger took the name Benedict in memory of the sixth-century founder of western monasticism, St Benedict of Norcia. He also had Benedict XV – pope during World War I – in mind.
● Like his predecessor John Paul II, Ratzinger is a polyglot; he is fluent in six languages (including Latin), and also has good Portuguese and can read ancient Greek and biblical Hebrew.
● His great-uncle Georg Ratzinger was a member of the Reichstag between 1877 and 1878 as a member of the Centre Party.
● His father Josef was a policeman and joined the Ordnugspolizei, the national police force of Nazi Germany, upon its foundation in 1936, but retired the following year.

Where to Stay

Where to Stay   **48**

Features

Hotel Suisse. *See p57.*

Where to Stay

Buona notte.

Il Palazzetto. *See p53.*

Once a city of polar-opposite accommodation options – exorbitantly expensive, often soulless luxury hotels on the one hand; cheap *pensioni* of dubious cleanliness on the other – Rome has only recently started to generate the range of hotels you might expect in one of the most-visited destinations on the planet. The city's ever-increasing popularity has had an inevitable impact on hotel rates; Rome is a more expensive place to stay than most other European capitals. The days of the dirt-cheap hotel bed are well and truly over (though for anyone who doesn't mind a curfew or sleeping under a crucifix, convents remain the ultimate budget option) and you're as unlikely as ever to find a room with a view without making a sizeable dent in your holiday allowance.

It may not come cheap, but the general standard of accommodation has improved dramatically in recent years. The luxury hotel market, in particular, has exploded, due partly to a council scheme to revamp old *palazzi* in

> ❶ Green numbers given in this chapter correspond to the location of each hotel as marked on the street maps. *See pp354-361.*

down-at-heel areas like the Esquilino, and partly to upscale districts such as via Veneto experiencing a resurgence. The recent Italian trend for hotels created by fashion designers had seen haute couturiers sidelining Rome in favour of Florence and Milan; a much-needed injection of glamour came in May 2006 with the opening of Salvatore Ferragamo's swanky **Portrait Suites** (*see p55*).

The mid-range market is also flourishing: fierce competition from boutique hotels popping up all over the *centro storico* means that older-style hotels and *pensioni* are being forced to upgrade both amenities and decor to keep up.

LOCATION

There are now three five-star hotels within a stone's throw of Termini station, but the vast majority of hotels in the area are cheap *pensioni* swarming with budget backpackers. It's not Rome's most picturesque corner, and almost certainly not what you dreamt of for your Roman holiday. It's well worth considering looking further afield, even if it costs you a bit more. Though Termini is only a few minutes' bus ride from the centre, you're likely to end up wishing you were more in the thick of things.

If you're staying for a few days, think about looking for a room in the *centro storico*. A shower between sightseeing and dinner, and a wander (rather than a bus) back to the hotel afterwards can make all the difference. The area around **campo de' Fiori** offers mid-priced hotels with lots of character, and a central piazza that is a lively market by day and a hip Roman hangout by night; the area around the **Pantheon** and **piazza Navona** is generally a bit pricier. Moving distinctly up the price range, Rome's top-end hotels have traditionally clustered around **via Veneto**; though not as lively as it was in its much-hyped *dolce vita* heyday, this famous street is slowly undergoing a makeover; what it lacks in atmosphere, it makes up for in grandeur. The **Tridente** area near the Spanish Steps, hub of designer shopping, is full of elegant hotels at the upper end of the price scale.

If you're looking for some peace, the **Celio**, just beyond the Colosseum, offers a break from the frantic activity of the *centro storico*, as does another of Rome's seven hills: the **Aventine**, an exclusive residential outpost no distance at all from the *centro*.

Heading across the river, the characterful bar- and pizzeria-packed riverside district of **Trastevere** is a pleasant place to stay, with decent bus and tram connections to the major sights; in recent years it has blossomed from hotel-desert to hotel-bonanza, offering an array of price options. Just north of Trastevere, the medieval alleys around the **Vatican** give on to the busy retail thoroughfares of **Prati**: it's lively during the day but hushed at night.

STANDARDS & PRICES

Italian hotels are classified on a star system, from one to five. One star usually indicates *pensioni*, which are cheap but have very few facilities; you may have to share a bathroom. The more stars, the more facilities a hotel will have, but bear in mind the fact that a higher rating is no guarantee of friendliness, cleanliness or decent service.

A double room in a one-star will set you back €50-€100; a two-star, €60-€150; a three-star, €70-€300; a four-star, €120-€450. Five-star prices start at around €300, and don't stop until your bank manager starts to weep. Many hotels charge a lower rate for a double room occupied by one person; we have included these along with the single rates in the listings.

Prices generally rise by a relentless ten per cent a year, but it's worth keeping an eye out for low-season deals on hotel websites. If you're staying in a group or for a longish period, ask about discounts. For our pick of the budget options, *see p67* **Cheap sleeps.**

If you're visiting with children, most hotels will be happy to squeeze a cot or camp bed into a room, but will probably charge 30 to 50 per cent extra for the privilege. Renting an apartment (*see p68*) could prove to be a cheaper and more flexible alternative.

The best Hotels…

For romantic assignations
Eden, *p52*; Inn at the Roman Forum, *p65*; Sant'Anselmo, *p63*.

For cutting-edge design
Aleph, *p52*; Hotel Art, *p55*; Radisson SAS es. Hotel, *p65*.

For glitz & chandeliers
Hassler, *p52*; St Regis Grand, *p64*; Westin Excelsior, *p52*.

For a swim
Cavalieri Hilton, *p53* The suite life; Exedra, *p64*; Radisson SAS es. Hotel, *p65*.

For celeb-spotting
De Russie, *p55*; Hassler, *p52*; Portrait Suites, *p55*.

For honing, toning & buffing
Aleph, *p52*; De Russie, *p55*; Exedra, *p64*.

For conjuring up a bygone era
Hassler, *p52*; Hotel Suisse, *p57*; Hotel Teatro Pace 33, *p59*; La Residenza Napoleone III, *p55*.

For ease of sight-hopping
Abruzzi, *p58*; Capo d'Africa, *p63*; Daphne Trevi, *p51*.

For themed rooms without the cringe factor
Aleph, *p52*; Casa Howard, *p57*; Sant'Anselmo, *p63*.

For archaeological claims to fame
Exedra, *p64*; Inn at the Roman Forum, *p65*; Hotel Teatro di Pompeo, *p59*.

For an *aperitivo*-worthy terrace
Eden, *p52*; Radisson SAS es. Hotel, *p65*; Raphael, *p58*.

F O R T Y 47 S E V E N
A L B E R G O   I N   R O M A

Fortysevenhotel
Via Petroselli 47, 00186 – Rome
Tel +39.06.6787816; Fax +39.06.69190726
contact@fortysevenhotel.com
www.fortysevenhotel.com - www.circusbar.it

SUMMIT
HOTELS & RESORTS

Preferred
BOUTIQUE

47
CIRCUS BAR

BOOKING A ROOM

Always reserve a room well in advance, especially at peak times, which now means most of the year, with lulls during winter (January to March) and in the dog days of August. If you're coming at the same time as a major Christian holiday (Christmas or Easter) it's wise to book weeks, or even months, ahead.

Increasingly, booking is via hotel websites, but you may also be asked to fax confirmation of a booking, with a credit card number as deposit. In high season, smaller hotels may ask for a money order to secure rooms. The **www.venere.com** booking service offers many hotels in all price ranges. If you arrive with nowhere to stay, try the **APT** tourist office (*see p337*), which provides a list of hotels; you have to do the booking yourself. The **Enjoy Rome** tourist information agency (*see p337*) offers a free booking service, as does the **Hotel Reservation** service. Avoid the touts that hang around Termini: you're likely to end up paying more than you should for a very grotty hotel.

Hotel Reservation

Fiumicino airport, Terminals A, B & C arrivals halls (06 699 1000/fax 06 678 1469/www.hotel reservation.it). **Open** 7am-10pm daily. **Credit** AmEx, DC, MC, V.
This agency has details on the availability of numerous hotels at all prices, and runs a shuttle service to the centre from Fiumicino airport. Check out the website for bargain-basement late-booking offers. Staff speak English.
Other locations: Ciampino airport (06 7934 9427); Termini station, at head of platform 24 (06 482 3952).

OUR CHOICE

The hotels listed in this guide have been chosen for their location, because they offer value for money, or simply because they have true Roman character. In the Deluxe category the emphasis is on opulence and luxury. Those in mid- to upper-price ranges are generally smaller, often in old *palazzi*, with pretty, though often small, bedrooms. *Pensioni* are fairly basic, but those listed here are friendly and usually family-run.

A no-smoking law introduced in 2005 applies to hotels' public areas; while a few hotels have extended the ban to include the bedrooms, most are still pretty laissez-faire when it comes to guests lighting up so long as they open a window. Few Roman hotels have access for the disabled (*see p327*); though staff are generally very willing to help guests with mobility difficulties, the real problem is that most places have so many stairs that there's not much they can do. As hotels renovate, they do tend to add a room for the disabled if they can.

Unless stated, the rates listed below are for rooms with private bathrooms. The rates also include breakfast unless indicated otherwise.

Trevi & Quirinale

Moderate

Residenza Cellini

Via Modena 5 (06 4782 5204/fax 06 4788 1806/ www.residenzacellini.it). Metro Repubblica/bus 40Exp, 60Exp, 64, 90Exp, 170, 175, 492, 910. **Rooms** 11. **Rates** €145-€240 double; €165-€280 triple; €165-€260 junior suite. **Credit** AmEx, DC, MC, V. **Map** p357 C5 ❶
This delightfully luminous *residenza* has huge rooms with faux-antique wooden furniture, parquet flooring and comfy beds. The marble bathrooms have jacuzzis or showers with hydro-massage. On the new floor opened in 2007, three of the rooms have balconies and all are decorated in the same classic style; there's an 80sq m (860sq ft) terrace too. The hotel is no-smoking. *Internet (dataport/high-speed/wireless/shared terminal). No-smoking hotel. Parking (nearby, €20-€25). Room service. TV (pay movies).*

Budget

Daphne Trevi

Via degli Avignonesi 20 (06 8745 0087/www. daphne-rome.com). Metro Barberini/bus 52, 62, 63, 95, 116, 119, 492. **Rooms** 7. **Rates** €80-€100 single (shared bath); €110-€150 single; €90-€130 double (shared bath); €120-€200 double; €135-€165 triple (shared bath); €180-€270 triple. **Credit** AmEx, DC, MC, V. **Map** p357 B5 ❷
See p67 **Cheap sleeps.**
Concierge. Internet (dataport/wireless/shared terminal). No-smoking hotel. Parking (nearby, €25-€30).

Veneto & Borghese

Deluxe

155 Via Veneto

Via Veneto 155 (06 322 0404/www.155viaveneto. com). Metro Barberini/bus 52, 62, 95, 116, 119, 492. **Rooms** 120. **Rates** (plus 10% tax) €440-€1,400 double/suite. **Credit** AmEx, DC, MC, V. **Map** p357 B4 ❸
New for spring 2007, this boutique hotel towards the top of via Veneto offers 80 doubles and 40 suites decorated in art deco style, with bathrooms in marble and teak, and luxurious touches such as cashmere blankets and Bang & Olufsen sound systems in some rooms. The ambitious design incorporates a rooftop pool, a lavish lobby with glass dome and, by the end of 2007, a 600sq m (6,500sq ft) spa. *Bar. Concierge. Disabled-adapted rooms. Internet (wireless). Parking (nearby, €25). Pool (outdoor). Restaurant. No-smoking rooms. Spa. TV (widescreen/pay movies).*

The charming **Hotel Suisse** has been family run for more than eight decades. *See p57.*

Aleph

Via di San Basilio 15 (06 422 901/fax 06 4229 0000/www.boscolohotels.com). Metro Barberini/ bus 52, 62, 95, 116, 119, 492. **Rooms** 96. **Rates** €650-€900 double; €1,500-€5,000 suite. **Credit** AmEx, DC, MC, V. **Map** p357 C4

This Adam Tihany-designed flight of fancy has a theme – heaven and hell – with its common areas in various intensities of devil-red, and bright, 'heavenly' bedrooms. Playful touches such as the hologrammed bookcases in the reading room and the outsize backgammon board in the interior courtyard are a world away from the luxe-but-dull decor of many of via Veneto's mega-hotels, and have helped secure its status as a favourite of the fashion set.
Bars (2). Business centre. Concierge. Disabled-adapted rooms. Gym. Internet (dataport/high-speed). Parking (nearby, €35). Restaurants (2). Room service. Spa. TV (pay movies).

Eden

Via Ludovisi 49 (06 478 121/fax 06 482 1584/ www.hotel-eden.it). Metro Barberini/bus 52, 62, 95, 116, 119, 492. **Rooms** 121. **Rates** (plus 10% tax) €480-€650 single; €750-€920 double; €990 studio; €2,100-€5,800 suite. *Breakfast* €49. **Credit** AmEx, DC, MC, V. **Map** p357 B4

Elegant and understated, the historic Eden retains its air of exclusivity thanks in part to its location, a street away from the often aggressive luxury of via Veneto. In addition to its stylish reception rooms and plush but not over-the-top bedrooms, the Eden is also well known for its top-ranked restaurant (La Terrazza) and its roof terrace bar (open to non-residents) with spectacular views.
Bar. Concierge. Disabled-adapted rooms. Gym. Internet (dataport/high-speed/wireless in common areas). Parking (nearby, €18). Restaurant. Room service. TV (pay movies/DVD on request).

Hassler

Piazza Trinità dei Monti 6 (06 699 340/fax 06 678 9991/www.hotelhasslerroma.com). Metro Spagna/ bus 52, 62, 95, 116, 119, 492. **Rooms** 98. **Rates** (plus 10% tax) €430-€460 single; €550-€810 double; €1,600-€3,400 suite. *Breakfast* €33. **Credit** AmEx, DC, MC, V. **Map** p357 A4

Looking down imperiously from the top of the Spanish Steps, the Hassler remains the *grande dame* of the city's deluxe hotels. With acres of polished marble and abundant chandeliers, the relentless luxury may make your head spin, but it's the attentiveness of the staff that really distinguishes this place from the impersonal service often to be found at Rome's top chain hotels. A few steps away, Il Palazzetto (*see p53*) is under the same ownership. *See also p53* **The suite life**.
Bar. Concierge. Internet (dataport/high-speed). Gym. Parking (€30). Restaurants (3). Room service. TV (DVD).

Westin Excelsior

Via Veneto 125 (06 47 081/fax 06 482 6205/www. starwood.com). Metro Barberini/bus 52, 62, 95, 116, 119, 492. **Rooms** 319. **Rates** (plus 10% tax) €520-€970 single; €860-€970 double; €1,600-€8,000 suite; €20,000 Villa La Cupola Suite. *Breakfast* €30-€42. **Credit** AmEx, DC, MC, V. **Map** p357 B/C4

Eclipsing its via Veneto rivals, the vast Excelsior revels in opulence on an undreamt-of scale. A wildly expensive renovation programme was completed in 2002, providing a gym and marble bathrooms throughout the hotel. Rooms are a Hollywood-style fantasy. *See also p53* **The suite life**.
Bars (2). Business centre. Concierge. Disabled-adapted rooms. Gym. Internet (dataport/high-speed/wireless). No-smoking floors. Parking (nearby, €45). Pool (indoor). Restaurant. Room service. Spa. TV (pay movies/DVD on request).

Expensive

Il Palazzetto

Vicolo del Bottino 8 (06 6993 4301/fax 06 6994 1607/www.wineacademyroma.com). Metro Spagna/ bus 52, 62, 95, 116, 119, 492. **Rooms** 4. **Rates** €265-€320 double. **Credit** AmEx, DC, MC, V. **Map** p357 A4 ❽

Some rooms at the International Wine Academy's 19th-century Palazzetto are on the flouncy side; others are more elegant (room 2 is stylishly decked out in cream and black); all have views of the Spanish Steps. The hotel is sister to the impressive Hassler (*see p52*), where breakfast is served. Guests also have free access to the Hassler's gym. **Photo** *p48. Bar. Internet (dataport/high-speed). Restaurant. TV (widescreen).*

The suite life

If you're tempted to blow the budget, do so in style, but be warned: accommodation this luxurious may scupper your sightseeing plans.

There's a suite for all tastes at the **Exedra** (*see p64*). The Executive Suite is all macho glamour, in shades of grey and red, with acres of Carrara marble, leather pouffes and a flame-red mosaic-tiled bathroom. The Adam Tihany-designed Royal Suite has a stylish, pared-down feel, with a vast, circular dining room, cocktail bar, terrace and glass-walled jacuzzi with views of the Terme di Diocleziano and, upstairs, a super-luxe bedroom and office space. The Dalai Lama plumped for the 120sq m (1,300sq ft) Imperial Suite, complete with caramel leather-padded walls, vast bed and hydromassage bath, on a recent trip.

The seventh-floor Penthouse Suite at the **Hassler** (*see p52*) is decked out with paintings from the schools of Tintoretto and Caravaggio, hand-cut crystal chandeliers, antique Venetian mirrors and Louis XV chairs, and opens onto a 160sq m (1,700sq ft) terrace. The rather busy wallpaper and ruched curtains obviously appealed to Tom Cruise and Katie Holmes, who checked in here for some pre-wedding pampering.

The two Executive Suites at the new **Inn at the Roman Forum** (*see p65*) – with their high, beamed ceilings, canopied beds, antique furnishings and designer bathroom, with Bulgari bath products – are splendid enough to satisfy even the most exacting of guests, but the hotel can go one better: when both suites are booked by the same party, they become the Master Garden Suite, an exclusive apartment with private entrance and charming walled garden.

Surely one of the most luxurious B&Bs in the world, **La Residenza Napoleone III** (*see p55*), named after an illustrious former resident, is run by Principessa Letizia Ruspoli in a wing of her own home, the 16th-century Palazzo Ruspoli (*see p109*) near via Condotti.

The three-room suite is magnificent, with hand-stencilled walls, a canopied bed, luxurious drapery and vast oil paintings aplenty (a marble bathroom is hidden behind one, while modern-day amenities that might jar with the imperial ambience – DVD projection screen, hi-fi, kitchenette – are tucked away behind others). The Roof Garden Suite in the attic is more intimate, and has a lovely lavender-planted terrace. A sumptuous breakfast is served on Bulgari silver, and a butler is available on request to attend to guests' every whim.

The **Westin Excelsior** (*see p52*) is home to the priciest pillows in Rome: the mind-boggling Villa La Cupola Suite, which takes its name from the extravagantly frescoed dome (fitted with Bang & Olufsen surround sound, naturally) in the living room. Two floors, 1,100sq m/12,000 sq ft, private cinema, vast terrace, plunge pool, gym: all yours for the princely sum of €20,000 a night. For VIPs who never travel *sans* entourage, a further eight interconnecting rooms along an adjoining corridor can be added, making this the biggest suite in Europe.

You're far from the *centro storico* at the **Cavalieri Hilton** (06 3509 2031, fax 06 3509 2241, www.cavalieri-hilton.it) in the north-western suburbs. But from its Penthouse Suite you get a great view of the whole city while lounging in the jacuzzi on your private 200sq m (2,150sq ft) rooftop terrace, complete with bullet-proof glass screens. Mind you, with another jacuzzi, an extraordinary full-body massage chair and your own wine cellar (pre-ordered from the hotel's 50,000-bottle collection) in your 250sq m (2,700sq ft) room, you may not even make it up on to the roof. Room rates start at €675, and suites run from €1,520 to €7,610 for the penthouse. If you can't afford to splash out on a room, you could always spend a day poolside (*see p293*) or dine at the Michelin-starred La Pergola (*see p212*).

Roma: al centro della città.
Firenze: una villa immersa nel verde.

LA TRADIZIONE
DELL'OSPITALITÀ

www.bettojahotels.it - numero verde: 800.860004

Moderate

Residenza A

Via Veneto 183 (06 486 700/fax 06 4201 2435/ www.hotelviaveneto.com). Metro Barberini/bus 52, 62, 95, 116, 119, 492. **Rooms** 7. **Rates** €150-€215 single; €180-€265 double; €220-€315 triple. **Credit** AmEx, DC, MC, V. **Map** p357 B4 ❾

On the first floor of an imposing palazzo, Residenza A is a 'boutique art hotel' with splashy modern works enlivening its slate-grey and black colour scheme. The rooms have been luxuriously finished, with great extras such as Apple flat-screen computers and free internet, and, in the bathrooms, roomy showers and Bulgari bath products. Specify one of the four rooms overlooking the street for a (soundproofed) view of via Veneto. Reception is open 8am-10pm; guests are given a set of keys to come and go as they like at other times.

Internet (dataport/high-speed). Parking (nearby, €25). TV (DVD).

Budget

Daphne Veneto

Via di San Basilio 55 (06 8745 0087/fax 06 2332 40967/www.daphne-rome.com). Metro Barberini/ bus 52, 62, 63, 95, 116, 119, 492. **Rooms** 8. **Rates** €100-€130 single; €120-€200 double; €180-€270 triple; €280-€570 suite (4-6 people). **Credit** AmEx, DC, MC, V. **Map** p357 B5 ❿

See p67 **Cheap sleeps.**

Concierge. Internet (dataport/wireless/shared terminal). No-smoking hotel. Parking (nearby, €25-€30).

The Tridente

Deluxe

De Russie

Via del Babuino 9 (06 328 881/fax 06 3288 8888/ www.hotelderussie.it). Metro Flaminio/bus 117, 119. **Rooms** 122. **Rates** (plus 10% tax) €440-€480 single; €650-€800 double; €1,320 junior suite; €1,800-€6,500 suite. *Breakfast* (buffet) €28. **Credit** AmEx, DC, MC, V. **Map** p354 E3 ⓫

The De Russie's modern, pared-down elegance – a million miles from the ostentatious glitz of via Veneto – makes it a hit with the international jet set. Film press junkets inevitably take place here: Robert De Niro, Harrison Ford and Richard Gere are recent guests. Rooms are tastefully decorated, and the hotel's fabulous gardens – site of the Stravinskij Bar (*see p220*) – and state-of-the-art spa are major draws, though occasionally abrupt service can fall short of what you might expect from a hotel in this category.

Bar. Business centre. Concierge. Disabled-adapted rooms. Gym. Internet (dataport/wireless/shared terminal). No-smoking rooms. Parking (€44). Restaurant. Room service. Spa. TV (pay movies/ DVD on request).

Hotel Art

Via Margutta 56 (06 328 711/fax 06 3600 3995/ www.hotelart.it). Metro Spagna/bus 117, 119. **Rooms** 46. **Rates** €296-€410 single; €396-€640 double; €650-€1,100 suite. **Credit** AmEx, DC, MC, V. **Map** p354 E3 ⓬

Opened in 2002 on via Margutta, a street famed for its arty, crafty studios, the Hotel Art sticks to its theme throughout. The lobby area – with white pods serving as check-in and concierge desks – sets the modern tone; only the ceiling retains a touch of the classic (it was once a chapel, arched ceilings and all). Hallways are in acidic shades of orange, yellow, green and blue, while the rooms themselves are decorated in a serene palette of neutrals, with parquet floors and chunky wood furniture.

Bar. Concierge. Disabled-adapted rooms. Gym. Internet (dataport/web TV/wireless in common areas/ shared terminal). Room service. TV (pay movies).

La Residenza Napoleone III

Largo Goldoni 56 (06 6880 8083/fax 06 6880 8083/ www.residenzanapoleone.com). Metro Spagna/bus 116, 119. **Rooms** 2. **Rates** €620-€1,650 suite. **Credit** AmEx, DC, MC, V. **Map** p355 E4 ⓭

See p53 **The suite life.**

Internet (dataport/high-speed/wireless). TV (widescreen/DVD).

Expensive

The Inn at the Spanish Steps & The View at the Spanish Steps

Via dei Condotti 85 & 91 (06 6992 5657/fax 06 678 6470/www.atspanishsteps.com or www.theview atthespanishsteps.com). Metro Spagna/bus 116, 119. **Rooms** 24 (Inn); 4 (View). **Rates** (plus 10% tax) *Inn* €200-€820 double. *View* €480-€780 double; €880-€2,200 suite. **Credit** AmEx, DC, MC, V. **Map** p355 E4 & p357 A4 ⓮

The Inn offers luxury boutique accommodation smack in the middle of via Condotti, one of the world's most famous shopping streets, while the View enjoys a slightly more tranquil position on the top floor of a palazzo at the end of the same street. Rooms at the Inn are an extravagant mix of plush fabrics and antiques; some of the deluxe rooms have 17th-century frescoes. The View's decor is more restrained, with sober grey and blue fabrics, dark-wood floors and black and white tiled bathrooms. The junior suite boasts a dead-ahead view of the Spanish Steps. Breakfast is served on the bijou terrace when weather permits.

Bar. Concierge. Internet (dataport/high-speed). Room service. TV (widescreen).

Portrait Suites

Via Bocca di Leone 23 (06 6938 0742/reservations 055 2726 4000/fax 06 6919 0625/www.lungarno hotels.com). Metro Spagna/bus 116, 119. **Rooms** 14. **Rates** (plus 10% tax) €330-€580 double; €580-€730 junior suite; €800-€1,500 suite. **Credit** AmEx, DC, MC, V. **Map** p355 E4 & p357 A4 ⓯

by Latte e Miele

Sleep in Italy
apartments and b&b
in Rome – Florence – Venice

Since 1998 we take care of your needs preserving the perfect relation between price and quality

2oo6 in numbers : 3.825 reservation - 328.500 visitors on the site - more than 830 selected accommodation

web site: www.sleepinitaly.com
tel-fax: +39 063211783
(from 10am to 6pm italian time)
Skype user: sleepinitaly

Opened in 2006, Portrait Suites is the latest in a growing portfolio of luxury boutique hotels owned by fashion designer Salvatore Ferragamo. Though black and white photos and memorabilia from the designer's archives decorate the hallways, the rooms themselves carry little clue of the hotel's fashion pedigree (though eagle-eyed Ferragamo fans might spot the designer's signature *gancino* emblem on the curtains). A somewhat predictable black-and-slate colour scheme is offset with touches of pink and lime, with spacious marble bathrooms, walk-in wardrobes and – ta dah! – a glamorous kitchenette, with all mod cons (though it's hard to imagine the average guest here making use of the dishwasher). Breakfast is served in the rooms or outside on the spectacular terrace; underfloor heating helps keep fashionistas' feet toasty in winter.
Bar. Concierge. Gym (suites only). Internet (wireless). No-smoking rooms. Room service. TV (widescreen/DVD).

Moderate

Casa Howard
Via Capo le Case 18 & via Sistina 149 (06 6992 4555/fax 06 679 4644/www.casahoward.com). Metro Spagna or Barberini/bus 52, 63, 116, 117, 119, 492. **Rooms** 10. **Rates** €130-€210 single; €160-€240 double. *Breakfast* €10. **Credit** AmEx, DC, MC, V. **Map** p357 A5 🄰
Casa Howard (Howard's End) offers beautifully decorated *residenza* accommodation in two locations a stone's throw from the Spanish Steps, with all rooms individually designed. All of the newer (and slightly more expensive) rooms in via Sistina have en suite bathrooms; in via Capo le Case, you may have to go along the hall to your (private) bathroom. Details such as fresh flowers in the rooms, a mini-Turkish bath, kimonos and slippers for every guest, and a sumptuous breakfast served on fine porcelain,

make a stay here into something of a pampering experience. Though the rooms are looked after by a live-in housekeeper, there is no reception and guests are given their own set of keys.
Internet (high-speed/wireless/shared terminal). TV (widescreen in some rooms).

Hotel Suisse
Via Gregoriana 54 (06 678 3649/fax 06 678 1258/ www.hotelsuisserome.com). Metro Spagna/bus 52, 63, 116, 117, 119, 492. **Rooms** 12. **Rates** €85-€100 single; €140-€165 double; €180-€210 triple; €195-€210 quad.* **Credit** AmEx, DC, MC, V. **Map** p357 A/B5 🄱
On the third floor of a tranquil palazzo near piazza di Spagna, Hotel Suisse has been run by the same family since 1921. Rooms are bright and airy, with parquet floors, dark-wood antique furniture and a charming, old-fashioned feel. Breakfast is served in the rooms. Air-conditioning is an extra €10 per night; the two rooms without air-con are cooled by ceiling fans. **Photo** *p52.*
Internet (pay terminal, 1-7.30pm). Room service. TV.

Budget

Pensione Panda
Via della Croce 35 (06 678 0179/fax 06 6994 2151/ www.hotelpanda.it). Metro Spagna/bus 117, 119. **Rooms** 28. **Rates** €65-€68 single (shared bath); €75-€80 single; €98-€108 double; €130-€140 triple. **Credit** AmEx, MC, V. **Map** pp354-355 E3/E4 🄲
Panda's excellent location, just west of piazza di Spagna, is its main selling point. Rooms are very basic but clean; ask for one of the newly renovated rooms, which have terracotta floors and high, wood-beamed ceilings. Air-conditioning is an extra €6 per night. There's no lift and you'll have to go elsewhere for your morning cappuccino, but *centro storico* bargains are hard to come by, and Panda is usually booked solid in high season.
Internet (wireless).

Hotel Teatro Pace 33.
See p59.

Relais Palazzo Taverna. *See p59.*

Pantheon & Navona

Deluxe

Raphael

Largo Febo 2 (06 682 831/fax 06 687 8993/www. raphaelhotelrome.com). Bus 30Exp, 70, 81, 87, 116, 492. **Rooms** 56. **Rates** €260-€290 single; €390-€560 double; €530-€2,000 suite. *Breakfast €22-€26.* **Credit** AmEx, DC, MC, V. **Map** p355 D5 ⑲

This ivy-draped palazzo in a picturesque square is deservedly popular, particularly with politicians (it's close to the Senate). The reception is dotted with an eclectic mix of arty *objets*, including ceramics by Picasso. 'Classic' rooms are decorated with faux-Renaissance columns and flouncy curtains, while 'deluxe' rooms have parquet floors and elegant furnishings. The Richard Meier-designed 'executive' rooms on the third floor have sliding oak panels, black leather sofas, Bose sound systems and Carrara marble bathrooms. Though stylish, the rooms are far from cosy, with furnishings more suited to swish conference facilities than to luxury hotel accommodation. The roof terrace has spectacular views though.
Bar. Concierge. Gym. Internet (dataport/high-speed/ wireless in suites, third-floor rooms & lobby). No-smoking rooms. Parking (nearby, €45). Restaurants (2). Room service. TV (pay movies/ DVD in some rooms).

Expensive

Sole al Pantheon

Piazza della Rotonda 63 (06 678 0441/fax 06 6994 0689/www.hotelsolealpantheon.com). Bus 62, 64, 116, 492, 916/tram 8. **Rooms** 32. **Rates** €200-€290 single; €300-€440 double; €550 suite; €580 apartment. **Credit** AmEx, DC, MC, V. **Map** p355 D5 ⑳

Dating back to the 15th century, this – management will tell you – is the oldest hotel in Europe. Former guests range from Renaissance poet Ariosto to Jean-Paul Sartre. Rooms are fresh and uncluttered, with tiled floors and frescoes. All bathrooms have whirlpool baths. Ask for one of the rooms at the front for superb views over the Pantheon; otherwise console yourself by seeking out the glorious roof terrace where breakfast is served in the warmer months.
Bar. Internet (dataport/high-speed/shared terminal). Parking (nearby, €35-€40). Room service. TV (pay movies).

Moderate

Abruzzi

Piazza della Rotonda 69 (06 9784 1369/fax 06 6978 8076/www.hotelabruzzi.it). Bus 62, 64, 116, 492, 916/tram 8. **Rooms** 25. **Rates** €140-€170 single; €175-€220 double; €210-€280 triple; €280-€380 suite. **Credit** AmEx, DC, MC, V. **Map** p355 E5 ㉑

The splendid location is really this hotel's selling point. Twenty of its 25 rooms have breathtaking views of the Pantheon, and all are outfitted in rich yellow and emerald shades, with wood furnishings. Some rooms are a little cramped. Breakfast is taken nearby, in a café in piazza della Rotonda. TV.

Hotel Teatro Pace 33

Via del Teatro Pace 33 (06 687 9075/fax 06 6819 2364/www.hotelteatropace.com). Bus 40Exp, 64, 81, 492, 916/tram 8. **Rooms** 23. **Rates** €90-€135 single; €140-€235 double; €195-€315 triple; €240-€335 junior suite. **Credit** AmEx, DC, MC, V. **Map** p355 C/D5 & p358 C1 ②

This 17th-century former cardinal's residence lies down a cobbled alley near piazza Navona. An impressive Baroque stone spiral staircase winds up four floors (there's no lift, but chairs are provided every couple of floors). Rooms are spacious and elegantly decorated with wood floors, heavy drapes and marble bathrooms. The original, wood-beamed ceilings are intact in all rooms, but higher on the top two floors. Breakfast is served in the rooms. **Photo** *p57.*
Internet (dataport/high-speed). Room service. TV.

Budget

Pensione Barrett

Largo Argentina 47 (06 686 8481/fax 06 689 2971/ www.pensionebarrett.com). Bus 40Exp, 64, 81, 492, 916/tram 8. **Rooms** 20. **Rates** €100 single; €120 double; €145 triple. *Breakfast* (à la carte) not incl. **No credit cards. Map** p355 D6 & p358 D1 ②

In the same family for 40 years, this *pensione* takes its name from its most famous resident (Elizabeth Barrett Browning stayed here in 1848). A bewildering number of antiques and curios give it a vaguely eccentric feel: the reception is crowded with tapestries and statues; rooms are a mishmash of faux-classical columns, dark wood furniture, original wood-beamed ceilings and pastel walls. Breakfast (costs extra) is served in the rooms, some of which have great views over the square. Air-conditioning is €8 extra per night. *Internet (dataport). TV.*

Relais Palazzo Taverna & Locanda degli Antiquari

Via dei Gabrielli 92 (06 2039 8064/fax 06 2039 8064/www.relaispalazzotaverna.com). Bus 30Exp, 70, 81, 87, 116, 492. **Rooms** 11. **Rates** €80-€150 single; €100-€210 double; €120-€240 triple. **Credit** AmEx, DC, MC, V. **Map** p355 C5 ②
See p67 **Cheap sleeps. Photo** *p58.*
Internet (wireless). TV (widescreen).

Ghetto & Campo de' Fiori

Expensive

Hotel Ponte Sisto

Via dei Pettinari 64 (06 686 310/fax 06 6830 1712/ www.hotelpontesisto.it). Bus 23, 116, 280. **Rooms** 103. **Rates** €190-€315 single; €320-€360 double; €320-€400 junior suite; €400-€500 suite; €80 extra bed. **Credit** AmEx, DC, MC, V. **Map** p358 C2 ②

Once the palazzo of the wealthy Venetian Palottini family, the Hotel Ponte Sisto offers pleasant rooms – some overlooking the gardens of Palazzo Spada, others facing the hotel's palm-lined courtyard – in shades of green and blue, with cherry-wood furnishings and marble bathrooms. The buzzy campo de' Fiori and Trastevere neighbourhoods, equidistant from the hotel, are a short stroll away.
Bar. Concierge. Disabled-adapted rooms. Internet (dataport/wireless in meeting rooms/shared terminal). Parking (€26). Room service. TV (pay movies).

Residenza in Farnese

Via del Mascherone 59 (06 6889 1388/fax 06 6821 0980/www.residenzafarneseroma.it). Bus 23, 116, 280. **Rooms** 31. **Rates** €230-€280 single; €290-€420 double; €450 junior suite; €60 extra bed. **Credit** AmEx, MC, V. **Map** p355 C6 & p358 C2 ②

On a narrow ivy-lined street, this converted convent has been refurbished without losing its charm. An oversized crystal chandelier in the lobby lends a sense of opulence, but details like home-made baked goods and jams for breakfast reflect the homely charm of the place. Rooms run from basic updated cells with small marble bathrooms to more comfortable pastel-hued rooms with hand-painted furnishings to match the frescoes in some parts of the palazzo. Ask for a room overlooking the gardens of Palazzo Spada, or the beautiful Palazzo Farnese. A roof terrace is planned for the near future.
Bar. Disabled-adapted rooms. Internet (dataport/ high-speed). Parking (€20). Room service. TV.

Moderate

Hotel Campo de' Fiori

Piazza del Biscione 6 (06 6880 6865/fax 06 687 6003/www.hotelcampodefiori.com). Bus 23, 116. **Rooms** 22. **Rates** €100-€240 single; €120-€260 double; €190-€300 triple; €260-€340 suite. **Credit** AmEx, DC, MC, V. **Map** p355 D6 & p358 C1 ②

Just off busy campo de' Fiori, this hotel underwent a complete renovation in 2006, and the results are impressive: the rooms, although not particularly spacious, have been elegantly fitted out in rich colours, and the small but elegant bathrooms have bronze-effect tiles with antique mirrors. The pretty roof terrace has great views.
Internet (dataport/high-speed/web TV). TV (widescreen/pay movies).

Hotel Teatro di Pompeo

Largo del Pallaro 8 (06 6830 0170/fax 06 6880 5531/www.hotelteatrodipompeo.it). Bus 23, 116. **Rooms** 13. **Rates** €140-€160 single; €180-€205 double; €195-€240 triple. **Credit** AmEx, DC, MC, V. **Map** p355 D6 & p358 C1 ②

This small, friendly hotel occupies a palazzo built on the site of the ancient Teatro di Pompeo; its *pièce de résistance* is its cave-like breakfast room, dug out of the ancient ruins (patches of the *opus reticulatum* brickwork, circa 55 BC, are still visible). The rooms are simply decorated in neutral

HOTEL FORTE

The Hotel Forte is situated in
the Historic Centre of Rome.
The rooms offer every modern comfort:
bathroom (shower-bath), direct - dial
telephone, air conditioning, mini bar,
satellite colour TV and safe.
This Hotel is covered by
Tin.it spot service. (WiFi Technology).

Via Margutta, 61 - 00187 Roma - Italy
(between Piazza di Spagna e Piazza del Popolo)
Tel. +39 - 06 3207625 - 06 3200408
Fax +39 - 06 3202707 - forte@venere.it

*H*otel *N*avona

A Hotel run by an
Australian Family; rooms with
a bath in a brilliant location;
one minute walk from Piazza
Navona and two minutes from
the Pantheon.
Air Conditioning 1st floor

Tel. (39-06) 6864203
Fax. (39-06) 68803802

Via dei Sediari, 8
00186 Roma

email: info@hotelnavona.com

*R*esidenza *Z*anardelli
roma

A Charming and exclusive residence
with First class rooms. One
minute walk from Piazza Navona
and five minutes from the
Pantheon. Telephone, TV,
Satellite, Air conditioning
First floor with elevator

Tel. (39-06) 68211392
Fax. (39-06) 68803802

Via G. Zanardelli, 7
00187 Roma

www.hotelnavona.com

tones, with terracotta floors and high, wood-beamed ceilings. Opt for one of the attractive rooms in the main hotel building rather than one of the more basic annexe rooms located a few streets away.
Bar. Internet (shared terminal). TV.

Trastevere & Gianicolo

For women-only accommodation, *see p272* **La Foresteria Orsa Maggiore.**

Moderate

Buonanotte Garibaldi

Via Garibaldi 83 (06 5833 0733/fax 06 6830 0793/ www.buonanottegaribaldi.com). Bus 23, 125, 280.
Rooms 3. **Rates** €198-€250 double. **Credit** AmEx, DC, MC, V. **Map** p358 B2
Hidden behind a gated entrance in a peaceful part of the Trastevere neighbourhood, this ex-convent is no ordinary B&B. Fashion designer-turned-artist Luisa Longo's three rooms – arranged around a spectacular courtyard garden – act as a showcase for her distinctive creations: wall panels, bedcovers and curtains in hand-painted silk, organza and velvet. Longo's atelier, in a corner of the courtyard, is open to guests curious to watch the artist at work, and all designs displayed throughout the house are for sale. Guests are greeted after a long day's sightseeing with a restorative glass of wine. **Photo** *p63*.
Internet (wireless). TV (widescreen).

Hotel San Francesco

Via Jacopa de' Settesoli 7 (06 5830 0051/fax 06 5833 3413/www.hotelsanfrancesco.net). Bus 44, 75, 780, H/tram 3, 8. **Rooms** 24. **Rates** €135-€215 double; €180-€235 triple. **Credit** AmEx, DC, MC, V. **Map** p359 C4
On the quieter eastern side of viale Trastevere near San Francesco a Ripa (*see p137*), this ex-seminary opened as a hotel in 2001. It has an attractive marble-floored entrance hall and a lovely roof terrace where breakfast is served when the weather's warm. Rooms are well equipped and reasonably big, though they have a slightly corporate feel. Some look over the internal courtyard of the adjacent convent.
Bars (2). Concierge. Internet (wireless/shared terminal). Parking (€20-€25). Room service. TV.

Hotel Santa Maria

Vicolo del Piede 2 (06 589 4626/06 589 5474/fax 06 589 4815/www.htlsantamaria.com). Bus 780, H/ tram 8. **Rooms** 18. **Rates** €150-€180 single; €165-€220 double; €200-€270 triple; €260-€330 junior suite/quad; €330-€450 suite (up to six beds). **Credit** AmEx, DC, MC, V. **Map** p358 C3
Just off delightful piazza Santa Maria in Trastevere, the Santa Maria opened in 2000 on the site of a 16th-century convent and has since built up a loyal clientele. The bedrooms have tiled floors, slightly bland peach decor and spacious bathrooms. They all open on to a charming, sunny central courtyard planted with orange trees. Bikes are available for

guests to explore Trastevere's winding alleys. As this guide went to press, a sister hotel, the Residenza San Callisto – smaller, but with similar amenities and the same rates – was due to open nearby.
Bar. Disabled-adapted room. Internet (dataport/shared terminal). No-smoking rooms. Parking (€10). TV.

Residenza Arco de' Tolomei

Via dell'Arco de' Tolomei 26C (06 5832 0819/www. inrome.info). Bus 125, H/tram 8. **Rooms** 5. **Rates** €135-€185 single; €150-€210 double; €30 extra bed. **Credit** AmEx, DC, MC, V. **Map** p358 D3
This bijou *residenza*, created by Marco and Gianna Paola Fe' d'Ostiani in their own home, has a cosy, welcoming feel, with beautiful wood flooring and staircase, plentiful antiques and a sunny breakfast room. All bedrooms are individually designed in a whimsical, English country-house style; the three on the upper floor have terraces, while the two below are slightly larger. **Photo** *p64*.
Internet (shared terminal). TV.

Budget

Arco del Lauro

Via dell'Arco de' Tolomei 27 (06 9784 0350/fax 06 9725 6541/www.arcodellauro.it). Bus 125, H/tram 8. **Rooms** 4. **Rates** €85-€110 single; €115-€135 double; €125-€155 triple. **No credit cards.**
Map p358 D3
See p67 **Cheap sleeps**.
Internet (dataport/shared terminal). TV.

Casa di Santa Francesca Romana

Via dei Vascellari 61 (06 5812 1252/fax 06 588 2408/ www.sfromana.com). Bus 780, H/tram 3, 8. **Rooms** 37. **Rates** €77 single; €112 double; €145 triple; €170 quad. **Credit** AmEx, DC, MC, V. **Map** p358 D3

Hotel Teatro di Pompeo. *See p59.*

Hotel Villa del Parco ★ ★ ★

110, Via Nomentana - 00161 Roma
Tel: (39 06) 442 37773
Fax: (39 06) 442 37572

A charming 19th century villa set in
a beautiful garden, situated in a
peaceful residential area very close
to the historic centre. All 30 rooms
are individually furnished and
equipped with modern facilities.
Snack service and parking available.

www.hotelvilladelparco.it

GALLERIA OFFICINA 14
Via G. Giacomo Porro n. 14,
00197 Roma - Tel: 06/8083909
Tuesday-Saturday
from 11:00 a.m. to 13:00 p.m., and from
16:00 p.m to 19:00 p.m.
officinaquattordici@libero.it
www.officina14.it

HOTEL LANCELOT
★★★

*A peaceful haven at a stone's
throw from the Colosseum.*

Friendly English speaking staff.

Via Capo D'Africa, 47- 00184 Roma, Italy
Tel: (39) 0670450615 **Fax:** (39) 0670450640
Email: info@lancelothotel.com
Home page: http://www.lancelothotel.com

On a tranquil side street where Santa Francesca Romana worked many of her miracles and died in 1440, this ex-convent is now a hotel with a predictably churchy feel. It's popular with businessmen on a budget and with families (the quad rooms are spacious and simply but pleasantly decorated). There's a tree-lined central courtyard, which makes a pleasant spot for breakfast in warmer weather. *Restaurant. TV.*

Hotel Antico Borgo Trastevere

Vicolo del Buco 7 (06 588 3774/www.hotelantico borgo.it). Bus 780, H/tram 8. **Rooms** 10. **Rates** €65-€120 single; €95-€140 double; €105-€170 triple. **Credit** AmEx, MC, V. **Map** p358 D3 ⑤
On the quaint eastern side of viale Trastevere, this hotel is hidden down a side street. Rooms are small – but have wood-beamed ceilings and all the basic amenities – and bathrooms minuscule. Breakfast is served in the rooms or at the owners' other hotel, the Domus Tiberina, in a nearby piazza.
Internet (dataport). Room service. TV.

Aventine & Testaccio

Moderate

Sant'Anselmo

Piazza Sant'Anselmo 2 (06 570 057/fax 06 578 3604/www.aventinohotels.com). Metro Circo Massimo/bus 60Exp, 75, 81, 175, 715/tram 3. **Rooms** 34. **Rates** €160-€220 single; €180-€270 double. **Credit** AmEx, DC, MC, V. **Map** p359 E5 ⑥
It may not be in the thick of things – it's in a quiet residential area – but the Sant'Anselmo, lavishly restored in 2005, is dazzling. Themes can be dodgy territory, but the Sant'Anselmo gets it just right: rooms are imaginatively decorated with playful touches. One features famous quotes scribbled over the walls; another, on two levels, boasts its own mosaic-tiled nymphaeum; another is dominated by a vast, sumptuous four-poster bed as well as a free-standing bath. The common areas have also been treated to the full works, with parquet floors and grey walls, enlivened by trendy chandeliers, sleek sofas and floor-sweeping curtains.
Internet (dataport). Parking (free). Room service. TV (pay movies).

Villa San Pio & Aventino

Via di Santa Melania 19 & via di San Domenico 10 (06 570 057/fax 06 574 1112/www.aventinohotels. com). Metro Circo Massimo/bus 60Exp, 75, 81, 175, 715/tram 3. **Rooms** 78 (Villa San Pio); 21 (Aventino). **Rates** €105-€180 single; €120-€240 double; €145-€260 triple; €180-€270 quad (Villa San Pio only). **Credit** AmEx, DC, MC, V. **Map** p359 E5 ⑦
Two of the hotels in the Aventino group are within a stone's throw of each other in a tranquil, leafy neighbourhood (the Sant'Anselmo, *see above*, is the third). Villa San Pio consists of three separate buildings that share the same gardens and an airy breakfast room; recently refurbished, it has a light, pleasant feel. Ask for a room with a terrace for views either of the surrounding greenery or towards Monte Testaccio. Its sister hotel, the Aventino, is less manicured and has yet to be refurbished. Most bedrooms in both places have jacuzzis.
Bar. Disabled-adapted rooms. Internet (dataport/ wireless in lobby). Parking (free). Room service. TV.

Celio & San Giovanni

Expensive

Capo d'Africa

Via Capo d'Africa 54 (06 772 801/fax 06 7728 0801/www.hotelcapodafrica.com). Metro Colosseo/ bus 75, 87, 117, 810/tram 3. **Rooms** 65. **Rates** €320-€340 single; €360-€380 double; €500 suite. **Credit** AmEx, DC, MC, V. **Map** p360 C3 ⑧
Artfully arranged bamboo? Tick. Pastel armchairs? Tick. The Capo d'Africa's hotel-design-by-numbers lobby may set the tone for the rather uninspiring decor throughout, but the hotel's location, on a quiet street near the Colosseum, is a definite mark in its favour. The rooms themselves are spacious and

Buonanotte Garibaldi. *See p61.*

Where to Stay

Residenza Arco de' Tolomei. *See p61.*

comfortable, if bland, and the rooftop breakfast room has knock-out views of the Colosseum and the fourth-century basilica dei Santi Quattro Coronati. *Bar. Disabled-adapted rooms. Gym. No-smoking floors. Internet (dataport/wireless in common areas/ pay terminal). Room service. TV (pay movies).*

Moderate

Domus Sessoriana
Piazza Santa Croce in Gerusalemme 10 (06 706 151/ fax 06 701 8411/www.domussessoriana.it). Bus 571/tram 3, 8. **Rooms** 60. **Rates** €98-€158 single; €147-€198 double; €194-€264 triple; €245-€330 quad; €270-€370 suite. **Credit** AmEx, DC, MC, V. **Map** off p360 E3 ⊕
Built in an Imperial Roman residence, later the church of Santa Croce in Gerusalemme, today this hotel takes up part of the monastery attached to the church (security gates keep the brothers from mingling with hotel guests). Reminders of the building's more devotional past are everywhere, from the huge religious canvases to the narrow ex-refectory where breakfast is served. The tastefully decorated rooms are divided into two wings, 'Conventual' and 'Aurelian'; the rooms in the former, overlooking the monastery's gorgeous vegetable garden, are the most pleasant. The roof terrace has great views. *Disabled-adapted rooms. Internet (dataport/wireless in common areas/pay terminal). Parking (nearby, €18-€20). TV.*

Lancelot
Via Capo d'Africa 47 (06 7045 0615/fax 06 7045 0640/www.lancelothotel.com). Metro Colosseo/bus 75, 87, 117, 810/tram 3. **Rooms** 60. **Rates** €110 single; €170 double; €190 triple; €250-€270 suite. *With half board* €125 single; €200 double; €235 triple; €280-€315 suite. **Credit** AmEx, DC, MC, V. **Map** p360 C3 ⊕
Rooms at this family-run hotel are beautifully kept, and each decorated with elegant mixes of linen, wood and tiles. Some have terraces looking towards the Palatine and Colosseum. The hotel owner moonlights as chef, providing half board for those staying three nights or more; if you're not on half board you can book dinner at an extra cost of €22 (wine and coffee included). Staff are friendly and helpful. *Disabled-adapted rooms. Internet (dataport/wireless/ pay terminal). Parking (€10). Restaurant. TV.*

Monti & Esquilino

Deluxe

Exedra
Piazza della Repubblica 47 (06 489 381/fax 06 480 9800/www.boscolohotels.com). Metro Repubblica/ bus 40Exp, 60Exp, 64, 175, 492, H. **Rooms** 240. **Rates** €600-€800 double; €1,500-€5,500 suite. **Credit** AmEx, DC, MC, V. **Map** p357 D5 ⊕
From its splendid porticoed exterior to its opulent lobby and its stylish rooms, the Exedra is endlessly glamorous. The rooms run from plush and utterly comfortable to outrageous; many overlook the piazza, all have big beds, chic furnishings and marble bathrooms with Etro bath products. From May to September, the rooftop bar/restaurant and pool offer great views. On the lower level, chunks of the Terme di Diocleziano (*see p161*), discovered while the hotel was being done up, are preserved under glass for guests to view. *See also p53* **The suite life.**
Bars (2). Business centre. Concierge. Internet (dataport/web TV/wireless in common areas). No-smoking rooms. Parking (€35). Pool (outdoor). Restaurants (2). Room service. Spa. TV (pay movies/ DVD on request).

St Regis Grand
Via VE Orlando 3 (06 47 091/fax 06 474 737/ www.starwood.com/stregis). Metro Repubblica/ bus 40Exp, 60Exp, 64, 175, 492, H. **Rooms** 161. **Rates** (plus 10% tax) €800-€1,050 double; €1,650 junior suite; €2,800-€13,000 suite. *Breakfast* €31-€43. **Credit** AmEx, DC, MC, V. **Map** p357 C5 ⊕
Founded in 1894 by Caesar Ritz, the father of luxury hotels, the St Regis was treated to a staggering $35-million makeover in 1999, and remains a bastion of old-style luxury to put the recent flood of five-star *arrivistes* in the shade. The original chandeliers hang in massive reception rooms with acres of marble and opulent gold, beige and red furnishings. Rooms have been individually designed and are filled with a mix of Empire, Regency and Louis XV-style furnishings. There are butler (suites and imperial rooms only) and limousine services, and a sauna.

Bar. Business centre. Concierge. Disabled-adapted rooms. Gym. Internet (dataport/high-speed/wireless in common areas). No-smoking rooms. Parking (€55). Restaurant. Room service. TV (DVD on request).

Expensive

The Inn at the Roman Forum

Via degli Ibernesi 30 (06 6919 0970/fax 06 6978 1115/www.theinnattheromanforum.com). Bus 75, 87, 175, 810. **Rooms** 12. **Rates** (plus 10% tax) €210-€610 double; €800-€2,200 suite. **Credit** AmEx, DC, MC, V. **Map** p360 B2 ⓭

Opened in 2006, this boutique hotel's location, near the Forum but on a picturesque street comfortably off the tourist trail, affords it a more exclusive feel than its sister hotels, The Inn and The View at the

Spanish Steps (*see p55*). The rooms are an elegant mix of rich fabrics and antiques; the spacious deluxe double rooms – some with their own fireplace – have canopied beds and marble bathrooms. Breakfast is served on the roof terrace or in a cosy room with open fire in the winter. You can get an ancient-Rome fix on the ground floor, where a crypt is being excavated by archaeologists: curious guests are welcome to have a peek. *See also p53* **The suite life**.
Bar. Concierge. Disabled-adapted room. Internet (dataport/wireless). Parking (nearby, €28). Room service. TV (widescreen/pay movies).

Radisson SAS es. Hotel

Via F Turati 171 (06 444 841/fax 06 4434 1396/ www.rome.radissonsas.com). Metro Termini/bus 70, 71, 105/tram 5, 14. **Rooms** 232. **Rates** (plus 10%

The Inn at the Roman Forum.

Suite

Hotel

Apartments

MOZART
Hotel & Suites
R O M A

Via dei Greci 23\b - 00187 Roma

www.hotelmozart.com - info@hotelmozart.com - tel.+39 06 36001915

Cheap sleeps

For years Rome's budget travellers had to put up with substandard hotel accommodation with next to no amenities and service-with-a-scowl. Now, thanks to a new breed of budget boutique hotels a million times more stylish – though no more costly – than their grim predecessors, it *is* possible to live *la dolce vita* without draining your wallet.

On a picturesque Trastevere backstreet, **Arco del Lauro** (*see p61*) has four rooms, all with private bathroom, decorated in modern, fresh neutrals. Budget *residenze* are few and far between in chi-chi Trastevere, so the Arco del Lauro, with its airy and spotlessly clean rooms, is all the more of a find. Breakfast is taken in a bar in a nearby piazza.

The Beehive (*see p68*) is further proof that going budget needn't entail slumming it. American owners Steve and Linda Brenner mix their penchant for design-icon furnishings (check out the Philippe Starck patio furniture), with reasonable rates and basic amenities, to create a 'youth hostel meets boutique hotel' vibe. There's a sunny garden, a cosy, all-organic restaurant and a yoga studio. The helpful staff provides a free in-house guidebook to the city, and there's free internet access. Breakfast is not included, but can be provided in the Beehive's café for an extra fee on request.

A short walk from St Peter's and the Vatican Museums, **Colors** (*see p68*) offers bright, clean dorm and hotel accommodation that's well above the average for this price bracket. The first two floors, decorated in zingy colours, have self-catering kitchen facilities, with cornflakes and coffee provided for guests to make their own breakfast. More neutral tones have been used in the third-floor superior rooms (all with private bathroom, flat-screen TV, air-conditioning and breakfast). There's a sunny terrace, and the staff is multilingual and very friendly.

Owned by dynamic Italo-American couple Elyssa and Alessandro, **Daphne Inn** (*photo below*) sets the standard for inexpensive but stylish accommodation in Rome. The hotel – in two central locations (the Trevi and Veneto areas; *see p51 and p55*) – is decorated in modern, earthy tones, and the tastefully furnished bedrooms have high ceilings, terracotta or parquet floors and decent-sized bathrooms (some with bathtub). Guests are lent a mobile phone for the duration of their stay, and staff are endlessly helpful. All of the rooms are no-smoking.

There's an interesting contrast between the sleek, modern decor of **Relais Palazzo Taverna** and **Locanda degli Antiquari** (*see p59*) and the 15th-century building (a few steps from the antiques shops that line via dei Coronari) that these twin *residenze* occupy. The spacious, individually styled bedrooms have white-painted wood ceilings, wallpaper with bold graphics, and bedlinen in spicy tones. Breakfast is served in the rooms.

tax) €216-€316 double; €340-€780 suite. *Breakfast* €26. **Credit** AmEx, DC, MC, V. **Map** p360 E1 ❹
Built on the site of an ancient Roman plebeian cemetery (findings are displayed in the excavation area by the entrance), this 'concept' hotel today caters for an altogether different clientele: mainly business clients – who don't baulk at the rather unpromising location, next to a multi-storey car park and opposite the train station – and diehard design fans. The rooftop – more LA than Rome – is a vast decked area with trendy bar and pool. In the all-white

rooms, the bed is set on a low platform, divided from the bathroom by a glass screen; the only splash of colour in sight is the green, turf-effect rugs. Taken over by Radisson a few years ago, there's been no change in the hotel's original image, and its extreme minimalism is starting to feel a little dated.
Bars (2). Business centre. Concierge. Disabled-adapted rooms. Gym. Internet (high-speed/wireless/pay terminal). No-smoking rooms. Parking (nearby, €14). Restaurants (2). Pool (outdoor, open late Apr-late Sept). Room service. Spa. TV (LCD/pay movies/DVD).

Moderate

Nerva

Via Tor de' Conti 3 (06 678 1835/fax 06 6992 2204/ www.hotelnerva.com). Bus 60Exp, 87, 117, 175, 810. **Rooms** 19. **Rates** €100-€160 single; €130-€220 double; €225-€350 suite; €35-€45 extra bed. **Credit** DC, MC, V. **Map** p360 B2 ⓭

The family-run Nerva may be right next door to the famous Forum but there's not a view to be had of it: the hotel faces a wall (though not just any wall: it formed part of the ancient Forum of Nerva; *see p82*). The Nerva is very well located, however, and rooms are pleasant, if a little old-fashioned. The staff and proprietors are a friendly bunch.

Bar. Disabled-adapted rooms. Internet (dataport). Parking. Room service. TV.

Budget

The Beehive

Via Marghera 8 (06 4470 4553/www.the-beehive. com). Metro Termini/bus 40Exp, 64, 492, 910, H. **Rooms** 17. **Rates** €20-26 per bed in dorm; €70-€90 double (shared bath); €30-€35 per person in double, triple or quad room in apartment (shared bath); €180-€240 apartment (6-10 people). *Breakfast* (à la carte) not incl. **Credit** MC, V. **Map** p357 E5 ⓭
See p67 **Cheap sleeps**.
Internet (wireless/shared terminal). Restaurant.

Vatican & Prati

Expensive

Franklin Hotel Rome

Via Rodi 29 (06 3903 0165/fax 06 3975 1652/www. franklinhotelrome.it) Metro Ottaviano/bus 23, 70. **Rooms** 22. **Rates** €100-€320 single; €135-€440 double; €165-€490 triple; €175-€470 quad. **Credit** AmEx, DC, MC, V. **Map** off p354 A2 ⓭
A bit out of the way, beyond the Vatican, the Franklin has a polished modern feel and its rooms are light and airy, if not particularly spacious. Every room has a state-of-the-art CD player – some quarters are outfitted with Bang & Olufsen equipment – and guests can choose from the hotel's extensive CD collection in the reception. Bicycles are available for hire by guests. The entire hotel is no-smoking.
Disabled-adapted room. Internet (dataport/wireless). No-smoking hotel. Parking (nearby, €15-€19). Room service. TV (widescreen/pay movies).

Moderate

Hotel Bramante

Vicolo delle Palline 24 (06 6880 6426/fax 06 6813 3339/www.hotelbramante.com). Bus 23, 40Exp, 62, 280. **Rooms** 16. **Rates** €110-€160 single; €150-€220 double; €170-€235 triple; €175-€245 quad. **Credit** AmEx, DC, MC, V. **Map** p355 A4 ⓭
Hidden down a cobbled street near St Peter's, the

Bramante was once home to 16th-century architect Domenico Fontana, and became an inn in 1873. It has a large, pleasant reception and a little patio. The 16 rooms are simple but elegant; most have high-beamed ceilings, some have wrought-iron beds.
Bar. Internet (dataport/wireless). Room service. TV.

Budget

Colors

Via Boezio 31 (06 687 4030/fax 06 686 7947/ www.colorshotel.com). Metro Ottaviano/bus 23, 492, 990. **Rooms** 21. **Rates** €18-€25 per person in dorm; €40-€60 single (shared bath); €60-€90 single; €60-€90 double (shared bath); €80-€125 double; €75-€110 triple (shared bath); €100-€145 triple. **No credit cards. Map** p354 B3 ⓭
See p67 **Cheap sleeps**.
Internet (dataport/pay terminal). No-smoking rooms.

Pensione Paradise

Viale Giulio Cesare 47 (06 3600 4331/fax 06 3609 2563/www.pensioneparadise.com). Metro Ottaviano/ bus 23, 49, 492. **Rooms** 10. **Rates** €40-€60 single; €60-€95 double; €110-€120 triple; €135-€145 quad. **Credit** AmEx, DC, MC, V. **Map** p354 B2 ⓭
Rooms are on the poky side, as you might expect for this price, but friendly staff and a decent location not far from the Vatican ensure that backpackers keep on coming. There's no breakfast and no air-con (ceiling fans are provided instead), but if you're willing to rough it a little, you could do far worse.
TV.

Self-catering

Consider renting an apartment if you are staying for more than a few days, particularly if there are more than two of you. **Enjoy Rome** (*see p337*) can find a flat for you, as can the **IDEC** agency (www.flatinrome.com), while the London-based **A Place in Rome** (+44 (0)20 8543 2283, www.aplaceinrome.com) offers delightful apartments in the heart of the *centro storico*. **Palazzo Olivia** (06 6821 6986, www. palazzo-olivia.it) has lovely apartments for rent in a newly restored 17th-century palazzo near piazza Navona (minimum stay four nights).

The UK's **Landmark Trust** (+44 (0)1628 825925, www.landmarktrust.org.uk) rents an apartment in the Keats-Shelley House (*see p106*) overlooking the Spanish Steps that sleeps up to four, with a minimum stay of three nights. It costs €2,226 a week in high season, rather less in winter, but is full of lovely details including the original painted wooden ceilings.

The **Bed & Breakfast Italia** agency (06 687 8618, www.bbitalia.it) has hundreds of chic Roman options on their books, including luxury accommodation in *palazzi* – awarded four 'crowns' by the agency's vetters.

Where to Stay

Sightseeing

Features

Maps

St Peter's. *See p164.*

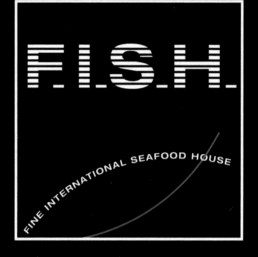

F.I.S.H.

FINE INTERNATIONAL SEAFOOD HOUSE

OYSTERSMAGUR
OTATAKISNAPPE
RCARPACCIOSUS
HISASHIMIMIXYE
LLOWTAILRAVIOL
IMISOSOUPPANA
SIANGRILLSPICY
TUNAROLLNASIG
ORENGTRIPLETA
RTARE.....(*)

viaSerpenti16f-i-s-h.it19.30-00.30Mondayclosed++390647824962

(* and that's just for starters...)

Introduction

There's no place like Rome.

Two things will strike you as you embark on your sightseeing activities in Rome: how history tumbles out of everywhere and is not just confined to museums and galleries; and how compact the city is. Oh, and a third of course: how utterly bewildering and exhausting the Roman experience can be.

It pays to approach this metropolis knowing that you won't see everything; and that if you shut yourself up in the city's extraordinary collections and sites, you'll miss something equally as important and unique – the urban landscape and its inimitable inhabitants. For this you'll need to walk (bring comfy shoes) and lounge: however much seating yourself at a pavement café may crank up the price of your cappuccino, a front-row seat at the magnificent spectacle that is Rome is worth the expense.

To the uninitiated, many *romani* give the impression that looking gorgeous and spending as much time as possible on their *telefonini* is the be-all and end-all of their existence. But they are also feverishly attached to their city, an attachment that recent city councils have done much to enhance. They are rightly proud of their steps forward in preserving their *patrimonio storico*: many historic buildings have been painstakingly restored and are illuminated at night to stunning effect; streets and squares have been repaved with traditional *sampietrini* (square basalt cobbles); and Baroque fountains have been cleaned.

Getting around is easier too: parts of the *centro storico* have been pedestrianised and more central car-free zones are planned for the near future; there are clean green electric buses; and the rather useless metro is being extended to serve the centre. In addition, reliable tourist information is dished out efficiently at a series of kiosks (*see p337* **PIT**).

Despite euro-fuelled inflation, living costs in Rome still compare favourably with other European capitals. Local transport is comparatively cheap, and eating out still an affordable pleasure.

ANCIENT SITES

The heart of the ancient city, and the area with the greatest density of remains, lies between the Capitoline, Palatine, Esquiline and Quirinal hills. Located here are the Colosseum, the Roman Forum and the Palatine, where the sexual excesses of emperors and politicians

St Peter's square. See p162.

were matched only by the passion with which they plotted against and poisoned one another. But ancient Rome doesn't stop there: the Museo Nazionale Romano group (Palazzo Massimo alle Terme, Palazzo Altemps, Crypta Balbi and the Terme di Diocleziano) house an overwhelming collection of ancient statuary, of which there's more in the Vatican and Capitoline museums; and many Renaissance and Baroque churches harbour archeological digs in their cellars.

CHURCHES

Across the centuries, popes, princes and aristocrats commissioned artists and architects to build, rebuild, adorn, fresco and paint their preferred places of worship, with the result that central Rome boasts over 400 churches. Motives were not wholly pious, but the results of all this munificence are some of Rome's most spectacular sights. Churches are places of worship; though only the Vatican imposes its dress code rigidly (both in St Peter's and the Vatican Museums), respect is appreciated. Very short skirts, bare midriffs, over-exposed

Blue Monday

Central Rome has an empty, echoey feel to it on Monday morning, when many shops are closed and so are the majority of museums and galleries. So if you're here for a long-weekend and Monday's your last day, don't make the mistake of leaving the 'best' bits till last.

When you spot that gorgeous pair of shoes, remember that you won't be able to snap them up on Monday morning en route to the airport: only food shops open with the new working week. The rest keep their shutters firmly down until about 3.30pm... though many city-centre shops now open on Sunday.

Most major museums and sights open Tuesday-Sunday only. Notable exceptions to this rule are the **Colosseum**, the **Roman Forum** and the **Palatine**. The **Vatican**, naturally, closes its museums on Sunday (except the last Sunday of every month, when it's free and consequently chaotically packed); on Mondays, they're open – as are **St Peter's** and all of Rome's churches, some of which are as richly endowed, artistically speaking, as museums: this could be your opportunity, for example, to catch the Caravaggios in **San Luigi dei Francesi** (see p116), **Sant'Agostino** (see p117) and **Santa Maria del Popolo** (see p110).

Monday is also a great time for a quiet look at whatever happens to be on display at the **Scuderie Papali al Quirinale** (see p94): few people seem to realise that this exhibition space is open daily during its generally excellent major shows.

Opening hours

Although the winter hours (*orario invernale* – roughly October to May) given in the listings in the following chapters are fairly stable, summer hours (*orario estivo*) can vary greatly, with some sites keeping doors open until as late as 11pm in the warmer months. Check for current times at information kiosks (see p337 **PIT**). Many museums are closed on Mondays (see above **Blue Monday**). *Feriali* on timetables means Monday to Saturday; *festivi* means Sundays and public holidays.

Ticket offices at many museums, galleries and ancient sites stop issuing tickets some time before gates shut; where the gap is an hour or more, this has been indicated in the listings.

Church opening times should be taken as rough guidelines; most open and close an hour later in summer. For many churches, whether doors are open or not depends on anything from priestly whim to finding volunteer staff.

Tickets

Entrance to publicly owned museums and sites is free (*ingresso gratuito*) or reduced (*ingresso ridotto*) for EU citizens (and citizens of other countries with bilateral agreements) aged under 18 or over 65; check tariffs at entrances carefully and remember that you must show photo ID (for children too) at ticket offices to prove that you are eligible. Under-25s in full-time education may also be eligible for discounts, as may journalists, teachers, motoring association members and various others. Make sure you carry a range of ID to take advantage of any savings. Many sights have recently introduced an extra charge for special exhibitions taking place inside; as a general rule, visitors are given no option other than to pay the ticket-plus-exhibition price.

One week each year, usually in the spring, is designated *Settimana dei beni culturali* (Cultural Heritage Week), when all publicly owned museums and sites – plus a few places rarely open to the public – are open long hours and free of charge; check the heritage ministry website (www.beniculturali.it) for details.

shoulders and shorts are all frowned upon. Churches ask tourists to refrain from visiting during services; if you are admitted, you will be expected not to take photos, talk loudly or wander around. A supply of coins for the meters to light up the art works is always handy.

MUSEUMS & GALLERIES

The days of closed doors, wildcat strikes and endless restoration programmes are more or less over. Opening hours are refreshingly longer, though they're still subject to seasonal changes. Much better services at major sights means – unfortunately and unforgivably – that some less-visited museums have suffered: we have indicated where staffing shortages are likely to make opening hours unreliable.

Booking

Booking is mandatory for the **Domus Aurea** (Nero's Golden House; see p154) and **Galleria Borghese** (see p99), where visitors are only admitted at specified times and in small groups, though if you turn up midweek in low season, there's little chance of being turned away.

Booking is possible for many other sites and museums, and recommended for very popular one-off exhibitions.

Bookings for the Ara Pacis, Centrale Montemartini, Colosseum, Crypta Balbi, Palatine, Palazzo Altemps, Palazzo Massimo alle Terme, Terme di Caracalla, Terme di Diocleziano, Tomba di Cecilia Metella, Villa dei Quintili and many other sights are handled on behalf of the city's heritage department by the **Pierreci** agency (06 3996 7700, www.pierreci.it, call centre operates 9am-1.30pm, 2.30-5pm Mon-Sat, credit MC, V), which charges a €1.50 booking fee.

Bookings for Castel Sant'Angelo, Galleria Borghese, Galleria Corsini, Galleria Doria Pamphili, Museo degli Strumenti Musicali, Palazzo Barberini and Villa Giulia are all handled by the **Ticketeria** agency (06 32 810, www.ticketeria.it, call centre operates 9am-6pm Mon-Fri, 9am-1pm Sat, credit MC, V), which charges a €1-€2 booking fee.

In general, tickets must be picked up and, where appropriate, paid for at the museum or site half an hour before your appointment.

Discounts, passes & cards

Rome has finally caught up with Italy's other tourist meccas and now offers a comprehensive multi-entrance-plus-transport card (*see below* **Roma Pass**). However, the city continues to offer a bewildering array of odd discounted tickets in addition to this.

Moreover, the Trambus **110 Open** city-tour bus (*see p323*) offers combination tickets with some of Rome's major museums.

The following tickets can be bought (cash only) at any of the museums and archaeological sites involved or at the APT (*see p337*), where a €1.50 booking fee is charged; booking is also possible online or by phone through the Pierreci and Ticketeria agencies (*see above*); if you pre-book, you're given a code that you quote when picking up tickets at the sites themselves. (For reduced entrance to the museums inside Villa Borghese, *see p97* **Pass?**)

Appia Card
Price €6; €3 concessions. **Valid** 7 days.
Covers Terme di Caracalla, Tomba di Cecilia Metella, Villa dei Quintili.

Archeologia Card
Price €20; €10 concessions. **Valid** 7 days.
Covers the Colosseum, Crypta Balbi, Palatine, Palazzo Altemps, Palazzo Massimo alle Terme, Terme di Caracalla, Terme di Diocleziano, Tomba di Cecilia Metella, Villa dei Quintili. An extra charge of €2 is added when any of the sites involved are staging special exhibitions.

Capitolini Card
Price €8.50; €6.50 concessions. **Valid** 7 days.
Covers Musei Capitolini, Centrale Montemartini. An extra charge of €1.50 is added when either of the museums are staging special exhibitions.

Museo Nazionale Romano Card
Price €6.50; €3.50 concessions. **Valid** 3 days.
Covers Crypta Balbi, Palazzo Altemps, Palazzo Massimo alle Terme, Terme di Diocleziano. An extra charge of up to €2.50 (€3 concessions) is added to the regular price when any of the sites involved are staging special exhibitions.

Locked sites

Some minor – but nonetheless fascinating – archeological sites are kept locked but visits can be arranged through Rome's heritage department. A few days before you want to visit, call 06 6710 3819 to arrange a date and time, when the site will be unlocked for you. You may be asked to send a fax (same number) to confirm. Price for admission is €2.10. Some of these sites can also be visited through the Pierreci agency (*see above*).

Roma Pass

A recent initiative from city hall, the **Roma Pass** is an excellent deal for anyone planning a culture-intensive (or even semi-intensive) short break in the Italian capital. The three-day Pass costs €20 and gives free entrance to any two sights, plus free use of the city's public transport system (though not train services to the airport). Considering that a regular three-day bus pass costs €11, and tickets for most major sights come in at around €6.50-€9, you'll soon recoup your investment.

But there's a raft of other benefits besides: reduced-price tickets for all museums, galleries and archeological sites visited after the first two, discounts for shows and events, plus a bilingual (Italian/English) 'Roma Pass Kit' containing a map and regularly updated news of happenings around the city.

The pass can be purchased at all participating venues, at PITs (*see p337*) and at some *tabacchi* (*see p336*), ATAC transport ticket booths and *edicole* (newsstands). Note that the bus pass lasts not for 72 hours but until midnight of the third day of use. For further information, see www.romapass.it.

Sightseeing

From the Capitoline to the Palatine

The hills are alive with sumptuous museums and extensive ruins.

In the eighth century BC a collection of grass huts was built on a hill overlooking the marshy flood plain of a tributary of the river Tiber. The following century the land was drained, and the settlement expanded down the slopes into what would become the Roman Forum. A thousand years of expansion later, this was the heart of a city of a million people and the hub of the commercial and religious activity of an Empire that stretched from Scotland to Tunisia, from Spain to Iran. The long-forgotten grass huts were replaced with splendid Imperial palaces (the Palatine), great temples were constructed on the neighbouring hill (the Capitoline) and Emperors kept public discontent to a minimum with gory entertainment in the Colosseum. Nowadays the remains of triumphal arches and columns littering the area still speak of these centuries of conquest and Imperial rule.

Piazza Venezia & the Capitoline

Heavily trafficked piazza Venezia is dominated by a brash monument to a disgraced dynasty that produced five kings. **Il Vittoriano** (*see p80*) – aka *l'altare della patria* – is a piece of nationalistic bombast made of unsuitably

dazzling marble brought at vast expense from Brescia; it was constructed between 1885 and 1911 to honour the first king of united Italy, Vittorio Emanuele II of Savoy. Centred on a colossal equestrian statue of the king (before the statue was welded together, metalworkers held a dinner for 20 in the horse's belly), it's also Italy's memorial to the unknown soldier. Favoured by Mussolini for staging rallies, it is totally out of proportion to everything around: it obscures the views of the medieval church of Santa Maria in Aracoeli, the Michelangelo-designed piazza del Campidoglio and the Forum, hub of a millennium of Roman rule.

On the western side of piazza Venezia stands **Palazzo Venezia** (*see p77*). Constructed by the Venetian Pope Paul II in the 15th century, it was to become Mussolini's HQ: *il Duce* addressed the crowds from the central balcony. To the south of the palazzo is **San Marco** (*see p79*), a church founded in the fourth century and remodelled in the 15th century for Pope Paul II.

To the right as you face the Vittoriano are the remains of a Roman *insula* (apartment building), part of which was converted into a church in the Middle Ages; the *insula* itself managed to survive the bulldozers that devastated the area to make way for the Vittoriano (*see p86* **Location, location, location**). Further to the right, steep steps lead up to **Santa Maria in Aracoeli** (*see p79*), built on the spot where, legend says, a sybil prophesied the birth of Christ… and, more recently, venue of AS Roma star Francesco Totti's wedding. Next to that, the more manageable ramped *cordonata* ascends to piazza del Campidoglio.

Il Campidoglio (the Capitoline) was, politically and religiously speaking, the most important of ancient Rome's hills and was the site of the two major temples. Chunks of the

▶ The '**buses to piazza Venezia**' mentioned in this chapter's listings are: bus 30Exp, 40Exp, 44, 46, 60Exp, 62, 63, 64, 70, 81, 85, 87, 95, 117, 170, 175, 492, 571, 628, 630, 780, 810, 850.

one to Jupiter Capitolinus, symbolic father of the city – whose cult chambers also included shrines to Minerva, goddess of wisdom, and Juno, wife of Jupiter – can now be seen inside the Musei Capitolini. The other, to Juno Moneta ('giver of advice'), stood on the site of Santa Maria in Aracoeli. It housed the sacred Capitoline geese, whose honking raised the alarm when Gauls attacked Rome in 390 BC; so failsafe was this alarm system that Rome's first mint was built beside it – from *moneta* comes the word 'money'.

The piazza on the Campidoglio was designed in the 1530s by Michelangelo for Pope Paul III, a symbolic rebuilding of the heart of the city after centuries of degradation. It took about a hundred years to complete, and some of Michelangelo's ideas were modified along the way, but it is still very much as he envisaged it. At the top of Michelangelo's *cordonata* are two giant Roman statues of the mythical twins Castor and Pollux, found near piazza Cenci and placed here in 1583. Looking straight ahead from the top of the steps, you'll see Palazzo Senatorio, Rome's city hall, completed by Giacomo della Porta and Girolamo Rainaldi to Michelangelo's design. To the left is Palazzo Nuovo and to the right Palazzo dei Conservatori, both of which house the **Musei Capitolini** (Capitoline Museums; *see below*). For four centuries the piazza's central pedestal supported a magnificent second-century gilded bronze equestrian statue of Emperor Marcus Aurelius. The statue there now is a copy, with the original inside the Palazzo dei Conservatori. From the top of the *cordonata*, take a right on the road which skirts this palazzo: it leads to a little park with a fantastic view. Beyond a gate, a series of pathways shadowed by oleander hugs the side of the hill (as dusk falls this is Rome's most central gay cruising area). The upper road continues to that part of the hill known as the Tarpeian Rock, where traitors and murderers were flung to their death. There's a great view of the Roman Forum (with the Colosseum in the distance) and, to your left, the back of the Palazzo dei Senatori, which incorporates the great stone blocks of the Tabularium, where the archives of the ancient city were once held.

Musei Capitolini

Piazza del Campidoglio 1 (06 8205 9127/06 6710 2475/www.museicapitolini.org). Buses to piazza Venezia. **Open** 9am-8pm (last entry 7pm) Tue-Sun. **Admission** €6.50; €4.50 concessions. *Special exhibitions* €1.50 extra. *See also p72* **Tickets**. **No credit cards. Map** p358 E2.

Housed in the twin palaces of Palazzo Nuovo and Palazzo dei Conservatori standing on opposite sides of Michelangelo's piazza del Campidoglio, the Capitoline museums constitute the oldest public gallery in the world. Their collection was begun in 1471, when Pope Sixtus IV presented the Roman people with a group of classical sculptures. Sixtus' successors continued to enrich the collection with examples of ancient art (mostly sculptures) and, at a later date, some important Renaissance and post-Renaissance paintings. The entire collection was

Marcus Aurelius in the **Musei Capitolini**.

Roman Forum & the Palatine

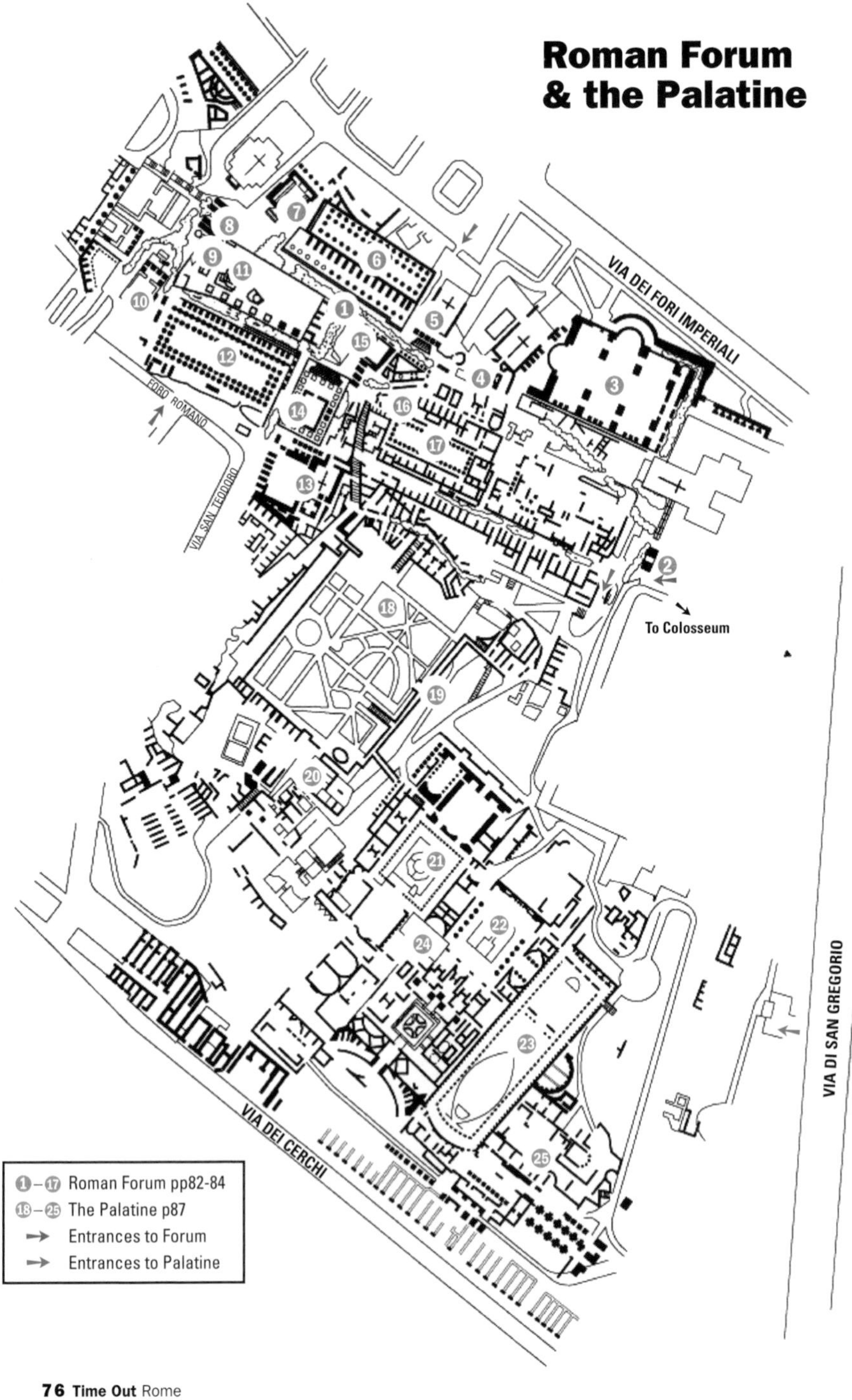

VIA DEI FORI IMPERIALI

FORO ROMANO

VIA DI SAN TEODORO

To Colosseum

VIA DI SAN GREGORIO

VIA DEI CERCHI

①–⑰ Roman Forum pp82-84
⑱–㉕ The Palatine p87
➤ Entrances to Forum
➤ Entrances to Palatine

finally opened to the public in 1734, by Pope Clement XII. Many statues remain frustratingly label-less but there is a decent audioguide.

Entrance to the Musei Capitolini is by the **Palazzo dei Conservatori**, on the right as you come up Michelangelo's stairs. The courtyard contains what's left of the colossal statue of Constantine (the rest was made of wood) that originally stood in the Basilica of Maxentius in the Roman Forum.

Upstairs, the huge Sala degli Orazi e Curiazi (Room 1) is home to a statue (1635-40) by Bernini of his patron Urban VIII in which everything about the pope seems to be in motion. There's also a second-century BC gilded bronze Hercules. Room 2 (Sala dei Capitani) has late 16th-century frescoes of great moments in ancient Roman history. In Room 3 (Sala dei Trionfi), the first-century BC bronze of a boy removing a thorn from his foot, known as the *Spinario*, is probably an original Greek work. There's also a rare bronze portrait bust from the fourth or third century BC, popularly believed to be of Rome's first consul, Brutus.

Room 4 has long been home to the much-reproduced She-Wolf (*lupa*); as this guide went to press, authorities were considering moving the *lupa* – currently being restored – to the new Marcus Aurelius wing (*see below*). This statue is supposedly a fifth-century BC Etruscan bronze, though controversy is raging (*see p85* **Crying wolf**); the suckling twins were added in the Renaissance (attributed to Antonio del Pollaiolo). In Room 5 (Sala delle Oche) is Bernini's pained-looking Medusa and an 18th-century bronze portrait of Michelangelo, believed to have been based on the great master's death mask. Room 6 (Sala delle Aquile) is frescoed with 16th-century Roman scenes amid faux-ancient 'grotesque' decorations. In Room 10 (Sala degli Arazzi) a marvellous marble group shows the Emperor Commodus dressing up as Hercules and being adored by two Tritons. Room 11 (Sala di Annibale) still has original early 16th-century frescoes that show Hannibal riding on an elephant of which Walt Disney would have been proud.

The second-century AD gilded bronze equestrian statue of Marcus Aurelius that for centuries stood in the centre of piazza del Campidoglio has now found a worthy home in an airy new wing of the museums which also contains large sections of a temple to Jupiter (Giove). Though the statue now on the plinth in the piazza outside is a 'perfect' computer-generated copy, it can't compare with the sheer delicacy and majesty of this original.

On the second floor, the **Pinacoteca Capitolina** (Capitoline art gallery) contains a number of significant works. The most striking is Caravaggio's *St John the Baptist* (1596; in the Sala di Santa Petronilla), who has nothing even remotely saintly about him. There's a weepy *Penitent Magdalene* (c1598) by Tintoretto, a *Rape of Europa* by Veronese, and an early *Baptism of Christ* (c1512) by Titian in Room 3. There are also some strangely impressionistic works by Guido Reni in Room 6,

various busy scenes by Pietro da Cortona in the room named after him, and some luscious portraits by Van Dyck in the Galleria Cini, which also contains a self-portrait by Velázquez (1649-51) and some lovely early 18th-century scenes of Rome by Gaspare Vanvitelli. While you're up here, check out the café; the view from the terrace is spectacular.

To get to the other side of the Musei Capitolini, housed in the Palazzo Nuovo, visitors pass through the **Tabularium**, the ancient Roman archive building upon which the Palazzo Senatorio was built. The tufa vaults of the Tabularium date back to 78 BC, and the view from here over the Forum is simply breathtaking, particularly in the evocative light around sunset. Also visible in this area are the ruins of the Temple of Veiovis ('underground Jupiter').

Palazzo Nuovo houses one of Europe's most significant collections of ancient sculpture. The three ground-floor rooms contain portrait busts of Roman citizens, the endearing *Vecchio ubriacone* ('old drunk', part of Bacchus' entourage) and a huge sarcophagus with scenes from the life of Achilles, topped by two reclining second-century AD figures. Dominating the courtyard is the first-century AD river god known as Marforio, reclining above his little fountain.

Upstairs in the long gallery (Room 1), the wounded warrior falling to the ground with his shield is probably a third-century BC discus thrower's top half, turned on its side and given a new pair of legs in the 17th century. Room 2 (Sala delle Colombe) contains a statue of a little girl protecting a dove from a snake, a much-reworked drunken old woman clutching an urn of wine, and a dove mosaic from Hadrian's villa (Villa Adriana; *see p312*) at Tivoli. Room 3 (Gabinetto della Venere) is home to the coy first-century BC *Capitoline Venus*. This was probably based on Praxiteles' *Venus of Cnodis*, considered so erotic by the fourth-century BC inhabitants of Kos that one desperate citizen was caught *in flagrante* with it. In Room 4 (Sala degli Imperatori), portrait busts of emperors, their consorts and children are arranged chronologically, providing a good insight into changing fashions and hairstyles. Next door in Room 5 (Sala dei Filosofi) are ancient portraits of philosophers and poets. Larger statues of mythical figures grace the huge Salone (Room 6). Room 7 (Sala del Fauno) is named after an inebriated faun carved from *rosso antico* marble in the late second century BC; the smirking, pointy-eared statue inspired Nathaniel Hawthorne's *The Marble Faun*. In Room 8 (Sala del Gladiatore) is the moving *Dying Gaul*, probably based on a third-century BC Greek original. Many ancient sculptures long hidden in the storerooms of the Musei Capitolini can now be seen at the Centrale Montemartini (*see p142*).

Museo di Palazzo Venezia

Via del Plebiscito 118 (06 6999 4243). Buses to piazza Venezia. **Open** 8.30am-7.30pm (last entry 6.30pm) Tue-Sun. **Admission** *Museum* €4; €2 concessions. *Special exhibitions* varies. **No credit cards. Map** p358 E1.

Airline flights are one of the biggest producers of the global warming gas CO_2. But with **The CarbonNeutral Company** you can make your travel a little greener.

Go to **www.carbonneutral.com** to calculate your flight emissions then 'neutralise' them through international projects which save exactly the same amount of carbon dioxide.

Contact us at **shop@carbonneutral.com** or call into the office on **0870 199 99 88** for more details.

CarbonNeutral®flights

The collection at Palazzo Venezia contains a hotch-potch of everything from terracotta models by Bernini to medieval decorative art. In Room 1 are Venetian odds and ends, including a double portrait by Giorgione; Room 4 has a glorious zodiac motif on the ceiling. Amid the early Renaissance canvases and triptychs in Room 6 is a breastfeeding *Madonna dell'Umiltà* – a racy show of anatomy for the 14th century, and quite a contrast to the pastel portraits of 18th-century aristos adorning Room 8. Collections of porcelain line the long corridor leading to Rooms 18-26, where you'll find Bernini's terracotta musings for the Fontana del Tritone (*see p91*) and the angels on Ponte Sant'Angelo. Six years in the planning, the *Lapidarium* opened in summer 2006. It occupies the upper level of the cloister of the 'secret garden of Paul II'. As the name suggests, it houses a collection of stone: ancient, medieval and Renaissance sar-cophagi, coats of arms, funerary monuments and assorted fragments. The eastern half of the palazzo often hosts major-sounding exhibitions that don't always live up to expectations, but if you stump up the extra fee you at least get to see Mussolini's old office, the huge Sala del Mappamondo, so-called because of an early map of the world that was kept there in the 16th century.

San Marco

Piazza San Marco (06 679 5205). Buses to piazza Venezia. **Open** 4-7pm Mon; 8.30am-12.30pm, 4-7pm Tue-Sun. **Map** p358 E1.

There's a strong Venetian flavour to this church, which, according to local lore, was founded in 336 on the site of the house where St Mark the Evangelist – the patron saint of Venice – stayed. There are medieval lions, the symbol of St Mark, by the main entrance door; inside are graves of Venetians and paintings of Venetian saints. Rebuilt during the fifth century, the church was further reorganised by Pope Paul II in the 15th century when the neighbouring Palazzo Venezia was built. San Marco was given its Baroque look in the mid 18th century. Remaining from its earlier manifestations are the 11th-century bell tower, a portico attributed to Leon Battista Alberti, the 15th-century ceiling with Paul II's coat of arms, and the ninth-century mosaic of Christ in the apse. Among the figures below Christ is Gregory IV, who was pope when the mosaic was made: his square halo marks him out as bound for sainthood though still alive. In the portico is the gravestone of Vannozza Catanei (*see p126* **Papal mistress No.1**), mistress of Rodrigo Borgia – Pope Alexander VI – and mother of the notorious Cesare and Lucrezia. The chapel to the right at the end of the nave was designed by Pietro da Cortona and contains a funerary monument by neo-classical sculptor Antonio Canova.

Santa Maria in Aracoeli

Piazza del Campidoglio 4 (06 679 8155). Buses to piazza Venezia. **Open** *Apr-Oct* 9am-12.30pm, 3-6.30pm daily. *Nov-Mar* 9.30am-12.30pm, 2.30-5.30pm daily. **Map** p358 E2.

At the head of a daunting flight of 120 marble steps, the Romanesque Aracoeli ('altar of heaven') stands on the site of an ancient temple to Juno Moneta. It was here, legend has it, that a sybil whispered to the Emperor Augustus *haec est ara primogeniti Dei* ('this is the altar of God's first-born'). Though there is an altar purporting to be the one erected by Augustus in the chapel of St Helena (to the left of the high altar), there's no record of a Christian church here until the sixth century. The current basilica-form church was designed (and reoriented to face St Peter's) for the Franciscan order in the late 13th century, perhaps by Arnolfo di Cambio.

Dividing the church into a nave and two aisles are 22 columns purloined from Roman buildings. There's a cosmatesque floor punctuated by marble grave-stones and a richly gilded ceiling commemorating the Christian victory over the Turks at the Battle of Lepanto in 1571. The two stone pulpits in front of the altar have intricate cosmatesque mosaic work – a rare case of work signed by Lorenzo Cosma and his son Jacopo, originators of this much-copied style. Just inside the main door, on a pilaster to the right, is the worn tombstone of a certain Giovanni Crivelli, carved and signed (c1432) by Donatello. The first chapel on the right contains enchanting scenes by Pinturicchio from the life of St Francis of Assisi's helpmate St Bernardino (1486).

In the right aisle, the chapel of San Pasquale Baylon has the recently uncovered remains of a fresco, probably by 13th-century genius Pietro Cavallini, depicting the Madonna and child flanked by saints. The large chapel beside it, with scenes from the life of St Francis, contains a marvellous 13th-century mosaic-encrusted tomb: the upper sec-tion may be by Arnolfo di Cambio; the lower part is a third-century BC Roman sarcophagus.

On the main altar is a tenth-century image of Mary. To the left of the altar, eight *giallo antico* columns mark the round chapel of St Helen, where relics of this redoubtable lady – mother of Emperor Constantine – are kept in a porphyry urn. An ancient stone altar, said to be that erected by Augustus, can be seen behind and beneath the altar. Beyond the chapel, at the back of the transept, is the Chapel of the Holy Child. It contains a much-venerated, disease-healing *bambinello*, which is often whisked to the bedside of moribund Romans. The original – carved, it is said, in the 15th century from the wood of an olive tree from the Garden of Gethsemane – was stolen in 1994 and replaced by a copy; the custodian is keen to impress upon anyone who expresses doubts that this faux-*bambinello* is even holier than the original. The Gothic tomb opposite the Chapel of the Holy Child entrance is that of Matteo d'Acquasparta, who was mentioned by Dante in his *Paradiso*. Over the altar in the third chapel from the main door (along the left aisle) is a fresco of St Anthony of Padua (c1449) by Benozzo Gozzoli. Rome's gypsy community flocks to this church on Christmas eve for a colourful, lively midnight mass.

Il Vittoriano

Piazza Venezia/via di San Pietro in Carcere/piazza Aracoeli (06 699 1718). Buses to piazza Venezia. **Open** *Monument* 9.30am-4pm daily. *Sagrario delle Bandiere* 9am-3pm Tue-Sun. *Museo del Risorgimento* 9.30am-6pm daily. *Complesso del Vittoriano* (06 678 0664; open during exhibitions only; last entry 1hr before closing) 9.30am-7.30pm Mon-Thur; 9.30am-11.30pm Fri, Sat; 9.30am-8.30pm Sun. **Admission** *Monument, Sagrario, Museo del Risorgimento* free. *Complesso del Vittoriano* depends on exhibition. **Credit** AmEx, DC, MC, V. **Map** p358 E1/2.

It's worth climbing to the top of this monument, not only to appreciate the enormity of the thing, but also to see the charmingly kitsch art nouveau propaganda mosaics in the colonnade and – most importantly – to enjoy the view from the only place where you can see the whole city centre without the panorama being disturbed by the bulk of the Vittoriano itself. At the top of the first set of stairs, two soldiers stand guard at the tomb of the *milite ignoto* (unknown soldier), placed here after World War I. Halfway up the terraces on the east side is the very pleasant outdoor Caffè Aracoeli.

In the bowels of the building are various spaces: the **Museo Centrale del Risorgimento** (entrance through unmarked open doors halfway up the steps of the monument or from via San Pietro in Carcere) has all kinds of exhibits on the 19th-century struggle to unify Italy, including the rather fancy boot worn by Giuseppe Garibaldi when he was shot in the foot in 1862, and panels (in English) explaining the key figures and events of the period. Some of the exhibitions held at the Vittoriano give access from the entrance in piazza Aracoeli to a maze of Roman and medieval tunnels extending deep beneath the monument.

The **Sagrario delle Bandiere** (entrance in via dei Fori Imperiali) contains standards from many Italian navy vessels. It also has a couple of torpedo boats, including a manned *Maiale* (Pig) torpedo. On the south-east side of the monument (entrance on via San Pietro in Carcere) is a building whose sign reads 'Museo Centrale del Risorgimento'; it does in fact provide access to the museum, but most of the spaces here are used for special exhibitions of mostly modern art. (Any exhibition advertised as held at the Complesso del Vittoriano will be here.)

The Fora

The oldest of Rome's fora, the **Foro romano** (Roman Forum; *see p82*), started life as a swampy valley used for burials. According to tradition, it was drained in the late seventh century BC by Rome's Etruscan king, Tarquinius Priscus. The Forum was to become the centre of state ceremony, commerce, law and bureaucracy.

As the Empire grew, and the existing fora became too small to cope with the legal, social and economic life of the city, emperors combined philanthropy with propaganda and created new ones of their own: the **Fori imperiali** (Imperial Fora; *see p80*). Clearly visible on either side of via dei Fori Imperiali, there are five separate fora, each built by a different emperor. Mussolini saw fit to slice the road straight through them (propaganda for empire-building of his own) to connect his balcony at Palazzo Venezia (*see p77*) with the Colosseum, demolishing the medieval and early Renaissance buildings that had grown up out of the Roman ruins. Since the 1990s work has been under way to recover tens of thousands of square metres of the ancient remains. Part of Vespasian's forum is incorporated into the church of **Santi Cosma e Damiano** (*see p84*). The recently restored **Torre delle Milizie**, behind the **Mercati di Traiano** (Trajan's Market; *see below*), is a picturesque memento of what the area once looked like.

To reach the Roman and Imperial fora from piazza del Campidoglio, skirt Palazzo dei Senatori to the left. At the bottom of the stairs, on the left, is the entrance to the **Carcere mamertino** (Mamertine Prison; *see below*); beyond, to the right, stretches the Foro romano; further on to the left, the Fori imperiali extend along both sides of via dei Fori Imperiali.

Carcere Mamertino

Clivio Argentario 1 (06 679 2902). Bus 60Exp, 81, 85, 87, 117, 175, 810, 850. **Open** *Apr-Oct* 9am-7pm daily. *Nov-Mar* 9am-5pm daily. **Admission** donation expected. **Map** p360 A2.

Just off the steps leading from the Capitoline hill down to the Roman Forum, the Mamertine Prison was waiting for anyone thought to pose a threat to the security of the ancient Roman state. A dank, dark, tiny underground dungeon, its lower level (built in the fourth century BC) was once only accessible through a hole in the floor. The innumerable prisoners who starved to death here were tossed into the Cloaca Maxima, the city's main sewer. The most famous of the prison's residents, legend has it, were Saints Peter and Paul. Peter caused a miraculous well to bubble up downstairs in order to baptise his prison guards, whom he converted by his shining example.

Fori imperiali & Mercati di Traiano (Imperial Fora & Trajan's Markets)

Visitors' centre *Via dei Fori Imperiali (06 679 7786/06 679 7702). Metro Colosseo/bus 60Exp, 75, 85, 87, 117, 175, 571, 810, 850.* **Open** *Visitors' centre* Apr-Sept 8.30am-6.30pm daily; Oct-Mar 8.30am-4.30pm daily. *Fora* closed for excavations; scheduled to reopen mid 2007. **No credit cards.** **Map** p360 A/B2.

Mercati di Traiano *Via IV Novembre 94 (06 679 0048/06 679 1620). Bus 40Exp, 60Exp, 64, 70, 117, 170.* **Open** (lower site only as this guide went to press; access from piazza della Madonna di Loreto)

9am-2pm (last entry 1pm) Tue-Sun. **Admission** (lower site) €3. **No credit cards. Map** p360 A1. Excavations carried out in the Imperial Fora in the 1990s opened up massive amounts of archaeological space to the public, but the work is far from over. As this guide went to press, the great hemicycle in the upper area of Trajan's markets was still closed for restoration and transformation into the Museo dei Fori Imperiali, a multimedia museum covering the history of urban development in this area. Over the last couple of years the date of completion has been constantly shifting; at the time of writing the expected opening was early to mid 2007. The via dei Fori Imperiali offers a good view over all of the fora, and until the reopening of the Imperial fora you'll have to make do with that. Once the fora reopen, you'll be able to get a closer look by booking a (compulsory) guided tour at the number given above.

The visitors' centre has literature about the fora, a small exhibition area with emperors' busts and bits of pottery, as well as a bookshop, a not very nice café and a public loo.

Foro di Cesare (Caesar's Forum)
The earliest of the Fori imperiali, the Forum of Caesar lies on the south-west side of via dei Fori Imperiali, closest to the Foro romano. Begun by Julius Caesar in 51 BC after the Gallic wars, the forum contained the temple of Venus Genetrix (three columns of which have been reconstructed) and the *basilica argentaria*, hall of the money-changers.

Foro & Mercati di Traiano (Trajan's Forum & Markets)
On the north-east side of via dei Fori Imperiali are the extensive remains of Trajan's forum, the last of the fora, laid out in the early second century AD. At the northern extremity of this forum rises the white marble **colonna traiana** (Trajan's column), an amazingly well-preserved work of Roman sculpture, dedicated in AD 113 to celebrate the triumph over the Dacians. The spiral reliefs, containing over 2,500 figures, depict the campaigns against Dacia (more or less modern-day Romania) in marvellous detail, from the building of forts to the launching of catapults. The higher sections of the column are difficult to discern today, but would have been easily viewed by the ancients from galleries that used to stand nearby. (Plaster casts of the reliefs are now on display at the Museo della Civiltà Romana in EUR; *see p179*). At the top of the column is a bronze statue of St Peter, added in 1587 by Pope Sixtus V to replace the original one of Trajan (now lost). So beloved by the Roman people was Trajan that, when he died in AD 117, his funerary urn was placed in a chamber at the column base (covered with scaffolding as this guide went to press); this made him and his wife, Plotina, the only Romans whose remains were allowed to be placed inside the city's boundary. The height of the column, 38m (125ft), is believed to mark the elevation of that part of the Quirinal hill that stood here before it was cleared away to make room for Trajan's forum.

The Temple of Trajan, mentioned by ancient sources, was also around here, although the exact location is unknown. The rectangular foundation to the south of Trajan's column, where several imposing granite columns still stand, was the basilica Ulpia, an administrative building. Part of the floor of the basilica is now visible at the gallery space

Sightseeing

Temple of Jupiter in the **Musei Capitolini**. *See p75*.

recently acquired and restored by Alda Fendi, of fashion fame (Foro Traiano 1, 06 679 2597, www. fondazionealdafendi-esperimenti.it, open for exhibitions only). To the west, under the walls that support via dei Fori Imperiali, are the remains of one of the libraries that also formed part of Trajan's forum.

The most distinctive feature of the forum complex is the multistorey brick crescent to the south-east of the basilica Ulpia. This great hemicycle, forming part of the **Mercati di Traiano** (Trajan's Markets), was built in AD 107, in part to shore up the slope of the Quirinal hill. Some scholars now argue that it was more of an administrative than a commercial space. When possible, the best way to appreciate its state of preservation is to visit the interior (as this guide went to press, restoration work meant that only the lower site was open, although the markets themselves were due to reopen at some point in 2007). Entering from via IV Novembre, the first room is the Great Hall, a large space possibly used for the corn dole in antiquity. To the south of the Great Hall are the open-air terraces at the top of the great hemicycle, offering spectacular views across to the Capitoline and Foro romano. To the east of the Great Hall, stairs lead down to the so-called via Biberatica, an ancient street flanked by well-preserved shops. The shops here were probably *tabernae* (bars), hence the name 'Biberatica' (*bibere* is Latin for 'to drink'). More stairs lead down through the various layers of the great hemicycle, where most of the 150 shops or offices are still in perfect condition, many with doorjambs still showing the grooves where shutters slid into place when the working day was over. South of the hemicycle, the structure with a loggia with five large arches is the 15th-century **Casa dei Cavalieri di Rodi** (House of the Knights of Rhodes); its somewhat Venetian look is due to having been built by Venetian Pope Paul II. The slightly leaning tower beyond the hemicycle is the 13th-century **Torre delle Milizie**.

Foro di Augusto (Augustus' Forum)

To the south of the House of the Knights of Rhodes is the Forum of Augustus, the second of the Imperial Fora chronologically (inaugurated in 2 BC). The dominant feature here was the Temple of Mars Ultor ('the avenger'), built to commemorate the Battle of Philippi in 42 BC, in which Augustus (then called Octavian) avenged Caesar's death. Three marble columns of the temple are visible on the right side, as is the towering tufa firewall behind it, built to protect the Imperial space from the Suburra slum district just beyond.

Foro di Nerva (Nerva's Forum)

The next forum to the south, which is bisected by via dei Fori Imperiali, is the Forum of Nerva (or *Forum transitorium* because of its connective function from the sprawling Suburra slum to the Foro romano). It was dedicated by Nerva in AD 97. Vestiges of a podium are all that remain of the Temple of Minerva that once stood at the east end of the elongated space, although the frieze around

two marble columns of the portico (visible just before via Cavour) depicts Minerva, goddess of household skills, weaving and spinning.

Foro di Vespasiano (Vespasian's Forum)

The *Templum pacis*, third of the Fori imperiali to be built but the last to be unearthed (recognisable by the potted plants on the west side of via dei Fori Imperiali), was dedicated by Vespasian in AD 75 but devastated by a fire in 192. On display inside this 'Temple of Peace' were the spoils of various wars, including treasures looted from the Temple of Herod during the Sack of Jerusalem in AD 70. The temple's library is now part of the church of Santi Cosma e Damiano. The immense *Forma urbis*, a marble map of the city made in 193 by Septimius Severus, once adorned the brick wall to the left of the church's façade. Taking his cue (as always) from the ancient emperors, Mussolini made some maps of his own: four white-and-black marble maps are still visible against the brick wall on the west side of the road. They show an area that includes Europe, North Africa and the Near East, charting the growth of the Roman Empire through antiquity. There used to be a fifth map too, which showed Mussolini's Fascist 'empire', but it was removed after the war.

Foro romano (Roman Forum)

Entrances from largo Romolo e Remo (via dei Fori Imperiali), via Sacra (piazza del Colosseo), via Foro Romano & via di San Teodoro (06 700 5469/06 3996 7700). Metro Colosseo/bus 60Exp, 75, 85, 87, 117, 175, 571, 810, 850. **Open** (last entry 1hr before closing) *Apr-Sept* 8.30am-6.30pm daily. *Oct-Mar* 8.30am-4.30pm daily. **Admission** free. **Map** p360 A2/3.

Numbers (●) refer to the map on p76.

After its period of glory, the Forum was relentlessly attacked for centuries by barbarians, after which it was gradually dismantled by anyone – from popes to paupers – who needed building materials. There is, clearly, a lot missing; but if you bear in mind that for a thousand-plus years this was treated as little more than a quarry, what's really incredible is how much has survived. With a bit of patience (and a lot of imagination), it's possible to reconstruct what was once the heart of the Western world.

During the early years of the Republic an open space with shops and a few temples sufficed, but from the second century BC, ever spreading, ever conquering Rome needed to give an impression of authority and wealth. Out went the food stalls; in came law courts, offices and immense public buildings with grandiose decorations to proclaim the power of Rome. Space soon ran out, and emperors began to build the new Imperial Fora (*see p80*). But the Foro romano remained the symbolic heart of the Empire, and emperors continued to renovate and embellish it until the fourth century AD. After taking the brunt of barbarian violence, the low-lying land of the Forum was gradually buried by centuries of flood sediment which rose unchecked in a city dramatically depopulated by plague, pestilence and war. The ancient heart of *caput mundi* came to be known as the *campo vaccino* (cow field). Major excavation didn't begin until the 18th century, when digging for antiquities became the hobby of choice for aristocrats from across Europe.

Our tour of the Forum starts at the entrance closest to the Colosseum, where the cobbled **via Sacra** (❶) – the Sacred Way, which ran through the Forum, past its most important buildings – climbs past the towering columns (on the right) of the Temple of Venus and Roma, the two goddesses who protected the city. You can pick up an audioguide (€4) from the office on the left after the Arch of Titus – worth doing as there's very little identification and a total lack of explanation of the Forum's masonry.

At the top of the rise is the **arco di Tito** (arch of Titus; ❷), built in AD 81 to celebrate the sack of Jerusalem by the Emperor Vespasian and his son Titus ten years earlier. One of the bas reliefs shows Roman soldiers with their plundered prize from the Temple of Herod: the menorah and the sacred silver trumpets. The triumphal procession is shown on the east interior wall, with Titus himself accompanied by a winged Victory driving a four-horse chariot. In the centre of the vault there's a square panel that shows Titus riding to the heavens on the back of an eagle, an allusion to his apotheosis.

After the arch bear right, past the church of Santa Francesca Romana (generally closed to the public, but *see p252* Festa di Santa Francesca Romana) and continue on to the towering brick ruins of the **basilica di Massenzio** (❸), begun in 306 by Maxentius but completed in 312 by Constantine. Probably the last really magnificent building constructed before Rome began her decline, its marble-clad walls occupied three times the space now covered. The great vaults are considered to have inspired Bramante when he was designing St Peter's.

Retrace your steps to the via Sacra. Passing the brick remains of a medieval porticus you come to a building with a set of bronze doors: this is the so-called **temple of Romulus** (❹), built in the fourth century and named after the Emperor Maxentius' son, to whom it may or may not have been dedicated. The interior of the temple is under seemingly constant restoration, but is visible from the church of Santi Cosma e Damiano (*see p84*).

Also on the right are the great columns of the **temple of Antoninus and Faustina** (❺) honouring Hadrian's successor, Antoninus Pius, and his wife Faustina, who pre-deceased him. In the seventh or eighth century it became part of the church of San Lorenzo in Miranda, which was heavily remodelled in the 17th century. The distance between the level you're standing on and the bottom of the church's (now-redundant) door is a clear example of the difference between the ancient ground level and that of the 17th century when the new façade was added – a millennium of accumulated mud and filth.

Continuing towards the Capitoline, what's left of the giant **basilica Aemilia** (❻) takes up nearly a whole block. Finished in 34 BC by Lucius Aemilius

Lepidus Paullus with cash he got from Julius Caesar in exchange for his support, it was once a bustling place for administration, courts and business. A large chunk of a dedicatory inscription can be seen on the via Sacra corner. Beyond is the **Curia** (❼). The home of the Senate, it was begun in 45 BC by Julius Caesar and finished in 29 BC by Augustus. (Still under construction on the Ides of March 44 BC, it wasn't here that Julius Caesar was assassinated but at the Curia of Pompey; *see p130* **Extra time**.) It was rebuilt after the fire that heavily damaged the Forum in AD 283; in the seventh century AD it became the church of St Hadrian, almost all trace of which was removed during Mussolini's restoration of 1935-8, although some fresco fragments still cling on inside. The floor is a fabulous example of fourth-century *opus sectile*. The doors aren't the originals, though – they found their way to San Giovanni in Laterano (*see p150*) in 1660. Opposite, directly in front of the arch of Septimius Severus, is a fenced-off, irregular patch of greyish limestone: this is the *lapis niger* (black stone) that was believed to mark the tomb of Romulus.

The **arch of Septimius Severus** (❽) was built in AD 203 to celebrate a victory in Parthia (modern-day Iran). The reliefs of military exploits are now blurred, but some of those at the base of the columns are better preserved, having been buried until the 19th century. These show Roman soldiers (with no head-gear and wearing shoes) leading away their Parthian prisoners (with downcast faces and floppy Smurf hats).

Just to the left after you pass through the arch is a circular brick structure believed to be the *umbilicus urbis* (the navel of the city). Next to it, the curved white steps are all that remains of the **rostra of Julius Caesar** (❾), a platform for the declamation of speeches. Towards the Capitoline hill, the eight massive columns of the **temple of Saturn** (❿) bear an inscription that says it was rebuilt after a fire (probably around AD 360). The cult of Saturn was an ancient one: the first temple to him was built here around 497 BC. The feast dedicated to Saturn, the *Saturnalia*, was celebrated for three days beginning on December 17 and turned the social order on its head, with slaves and servants being served by their masters. With your back to the temple of Saturn, the solitary **column of Phocas** (⓫) is clearly visible. The last monument erected in the Forum before the area became a quarry for Christian structures, it was dedicated to the murderous emperor of Byzantium, Phocas. The inscription on the pedestal records a gold statue erected on top in 608 by Smaragdus, Exarch of Ravenna (although the column itself is recycled, probably dating from the second century).

On the far side of the via Sacra stand the foundations of the **basilica Julia** (⓬), built by Julius Caesar in 55 BC and once a major – and by all accounts very noisy – law court. Following the basilica to the right, you come across an opening to the Cloaca Maxima. At the end of this path is a fenced-off area around the church of **Santa Maria Antiqua** (⓭), where

Sightseeing

beautiful seventh- and eighth-century frescoes were under restoration as this guide went to press. Rising beside the basilica Julia are three elegant columns that formed part of the **temple of Castor** (⑭), one of the twin sons of Jupiter who, according to legend, appeared to Roman troops in 499 BC, helping the Republic to victory over the Latins.

Back towards the centre of the Forum is the **temple of Divus Julius** (⑮). A nondescript mass of concrete masonry beneath a low-pitched green roof is all that remains of the temple dedicated to the memory of the deified Julius by Augustus in 29 BC. It's popularly held to be the place of Caesar's cremation (though in fact this took place at the other end of the Forum, across the via Sacra from the temple of Antoninus and Faustina), and flowers are still left here on March 15 (the Ides) each year.

Between the temples of Castor and Divus Julius are the scant remains of the arch of Augustus, believed to be the arch built in 29 BC to commemorate his victories, including that at Actium over Antony and Cleopatra in 31 BC. Just beyond, three small columns arranged in a curve mark the round **temple of Vesta** (⑯) where the vestal virgins tended the sacred fire. Within its garden, the rectangular **house of the Vestal Virgins** (⑰) was where they lived chastely: if not they could expect to be buried alive in the 'field of wickedness' (*campus scleratus*) by the Quirinale. **Photo** *p76*.

Santi Cosma e Damiano

Via dei Fori Imperiali 1 (06 692 0441). Metro Colosseo/bus 60Exp, 75, 85, 87, 117, 175, 571, 810, 850. **Open** 9am-1pm, 3-7pm daily. **Map** p360 B2.
This small church on the fringe of the Forum incorporates the library of Vespasian's temple of Peace (*see p82*) and the temple of Romulus (visible through the glass panel that forms the front wall; the drop in level is a reminder of the centuries of sediment and muck that swallowed up the Forum). It has a wonderful sixth-century mosaic in the apse: Saints Peter and Paul stand one on each side of the vast figure of Christ descending from the clouds, presenting Saints Cosma and Damian (the patron saints of doctors) to Jesus. On the far left, Pope Felix IV holds a model of the church; on the far right stands St Theodore in memory of Theodoric the Great, who donated the temple of Romulus to the Pope.

The Palatine & the Colosseum

The basket holding infant twins Romulus and Remus was found, legend says, in the swampy area near the Tiber where **San Giorgio in Velabro** (*see p130*) now stands. Later – on 21 April 753 BC, the uncannily precise story continues, the luckier/fratricidal brother Romulus climbed the hill just to the north of the swamp – **the Palatine** (*see p87*) – and founded Rome.

In fact, proto-Romans had already settled on the Palatine hill over a century before that, and maybe much earlier. The presence of Rome's earliest temples on the Palatine hill made the area into illustrious real estate; commerce and bureaucracy were pushed down into the Foro romano as the Palatine became increasingly residential. When Augustus had his house built here he was seeking credibility as the founder of the Empire through a link with the founder of the city. Once he'd set the pattern, many subsequent emperors followed suit.

The valley to the north-east of the Palatine, where the **Colosseum** (*see p85*) and **Arco di Costantino** (*see below*) stand, was hemmed in by the Palatine, Celian and Oppian hills, as well as the Velia, the saddle of land which joined the Oppio to the Palatine. (What was left of the Velia was bulldozed by Mussolini when he drove his via dell'Impero – now via dei Fori Imperiali – through the Imperial Fora; *see p80*.) The dwellings that had accumulated in the valley from the seventh century BC were swept clean by the great fire of AD 64, after which Nero appropriated the land to make a garden for his Domus Aurea (*see p154*). To the south of the Palatine, the **Circo Massimo** (*see below*) is believed to have opened for races in the sixth century BC.

Arco di Costantino (Arch of Constantine)

Piazza del Colosseo. Metro Colosseo/bus 60Exp, 75, 81, 85, 87, 117, 175, 673, 810, 850/tram 3. **Map** p360 B3.
Standing beside the Colosseum, Constantine's triumphal arch was one of the last great Roman monuments, erected in AD 315, shortly before the emperor abandoned the city for Byzantium. Built to commemorate the Battle of the Milvian Bridge (*see p15*), Constantine's is the best preserved of Rome's triumphal arches. Its magnificent relief sculptures and statues were almost all lifted from earlier emperors' monuments around the city; those panels that are Constantinian (the narrow strips above the side arches, for example) give ample evidence of the decline in realism of late antique sculpture, as well as the dearth of skilled artisans and workers.

In front of the arch, the round foundation sunk in the grass is all that remains of an ancient fountain called the *Meta sudans* ('sweating cone'). Much more of this implausibly phallic object – almost all of it, in fact – would have been visible today if it hadn't been for Mussolini's avid bulldozing in the 1930s.

Circo Massimo (Circus Maximus)

Via del Circo Massimo. Metro Circo Massimo/ bus 60Exp, 75, 81, 118, 175, 628, 673/tram 3. **Map** p361 A/B4.
Favoured by 'alternative' youth on summer evenings, the Circus Maximus seen up close is a scrubby dog park littered with broken glass and

Crying wolf

As every student knows, the vestal virgin Rhea Silvia was raped by Mars and gave birth to the twins Romulus and Remus, who were then abandoned in the Tiber. Rescued by a shepherd called Faustulus, they were suckled by a she-wolf (*lupa*) and got into a fratricidal fight, after which Romulus founded Rome.

For centuries, the nature of the she-wolf has been called into question: *lupa* was a Latin word for prostitute. But this has never dampened Romans' devotion to their symbol – a she-wolf suckling the twins – which even today is emblazoned across the chests of Francesco Totti and the AS Roma team. The model for this symbol is a statue in the Capitoline museums (*see p75*). But the authenticity of this statue has recently been called into question.

It has always been known that the figures of Romulus and Remus were added c1471 when the she-wolf was donated to the city by Pope Sixtus IV, but the wolf herself was always believed to date from the fifth century BC. Textbooks have long told Roman kids that the statue was produced by the celebrated Etruscan sculptor Vulca, said to have been called from Veio to decorate the temple of Jupiter on the Capitoline hill. Those books may have to be rewritten. Recent restoration culminated in an announcement in November 2006 that the she-wolf was cast in a single piece. Ancient Etruscan, Greek and Roman bronzes were cast in several pieces and welded together. It was not until the Middle Ages (in part because of the growing market in church bells) that a method for single-jet fusion was developed. If the claims are substantiated it would make Rome's 'ancient' *lupa* at least a millennium more modern than previously believed.

cigarette butts. However, from the Palatine hill (*see p87*) it's still possible to visualise the flat base of the long, grassy basin as the racetrack, and the sloping sides as the stadium stands, and with a lot of imagination the roar of hooves can be heard. Brick remains of the original seating at the southern end are the only visible remains of the structure (the tower there is medieval). Recent excavations have also unearthed a mithraeum from the first century BC. The oldest and largest of Rome's ancient arenas, the Circus Maximus hosted chariot races from at least the fourth century BC. It was rebuilt by Julius Caesar to hold as many as 300,000 people. Races involved up to 12 rigs of four horses each; the first charioteer to complete the seven treacherous, sabotage-ridden laps around the *spina* (ridge in the centre) won a hefty monetary prize and the adoration of the populace. The circus was also used for mock sea battles (with the arena flooded with millions of gallons of water), ever-popular fights with wild animals and the occasional large-scale execution. Perhaps not accidentally, the furious, competitive flow of modern traffic around the circus goes in the same direction that the ancient chariots did.

Il Colosseo (Colosseum)

Piazza del Colosseo (06 700 5469/06 3996 7700). Metro Colosseo/bus 60Exp, 75, 81, 85, 87, 117, 175, 673, 810, 850/tram 3. **Open** 9am-sunset (last entry 1hr before closing) daily. **Admission** (incl Palatine) €9; €4.50 concessions. *Special exhibitions* €2 extra. *See also p72* **Tickets. No credit cards.** **Map** p360 B/C3.
Note: if the queue outside the Colosseum is daunting, you can buy tickets at the Palatine (*see p87*) and make straight for the turnstiles.
Vespasian began building the Colosseum – which has hosted gory battles between combinations of gladiators, slaves, prisoners and wild animals of all descriptions – in AD 72 on the site of a newly drained lake in the grounds of Nero's Domus Aurea (*see p154*). Restoration carried out in 2001 opened up much larger areas of the arena to the public, including a reconstructed section of the sand-covered wood floor that allows visitors to walk across a platform and look down into the elevator shafts through which animals emerged, via trap-doors, into the arena. The top rows of the Colosseum are the best vantage point from which to appreciate the massive scale of the building.

Sightseeing

Location, location, location

In 1927 bulldozers razed the 17th-century church of St Rita (patron saint of hopeless marriages), which was sandwiched between the Vittoriano (*see p80*) and the steep steps leading up to Santa Maria in Aracoeli (*see p79*). Beneath, archeologists found the medieval church of San Biagio (patron saint of sore throats), which had been built into the second and third floors of an *insula* (ancient Roman apartment building).

The apartment block dates from the second century AD and was at least five storeys tall, built against the steep hillside behind – a sort of less grand version of Trajan's Markets (*see p80*). On the ground floor was a row of shops; above was a wooden-floored mezzanine where the shopkeeper and his family would retire after a hard day's wheeling and dealing.

Further up were the type of apartments where the vast majority of Romans lived (or rather slept – washing was done in the public bath complexes and eating in *tabernae*), in rooms illuminated by rectangular windows. The *insula* at piazza Venezia crammed an estimated 380 tenants into less than comfortable surroundings; the higher the floor, the pokier the accommodation.

The poet Martial bemoaned the *ducentas scalas* (two-hundred steps) that he had to clamber up to reach his bed in what we can only imagine was a less than 'des res', while Juvenal lamented the constant dangers of collapse and fire in Rome's teetering residential blocks. All of which is rather surreal to consider as you push your way past thundering traffic and vans selling vastly over-priced soft drinks to peer down nine metres to the ancient street level and picture toga-clad Romans scurrying about their business.

Properly called the Amphitheatrum Flavium (Flavian amphitheatre), the building was later known as the Colosseum not because it was big, but because of a gold-plated colossal statue, now lost, that stood alongside. The arena was about 500 metres (a third of a mile) in circumference, could seat over 50,000 people – some scholars estimate capacity crowds numbered as many as 87,000 – and could be filled or emptied in ten minutes through a network of *vomitoria* (exits) that remains the basic model for stadium design today.

Nowhere in the world was there a larger or more glorious setting for mass slaughter. If costly, highly trained professional gladiators were often spared at the end of their bloody bouts, not so the slaves, criminals and assorted unfortunates roped in to do battle against them. Any combatant who disappointed the crowd by not showing enough grit was whipped until he fought more aggressively. When the combat was over, corpses were prodded with red-hot pokers to make sure no one tried to elude fate

by playing dead. It was not only human life that was sacrificed to Roman blood-lust: wildlife, too, was legitimate fodder. Animals fought animals; people fought animals. In the 100 days of carnage held to inaugurate the amphitheatre in AD 80, some 5,000 beasts perished. By the time wild-animal shows were finally banned in AD 523, the elephant and tiger were all but extinct in North Africa and Arabia. On occasion, however, the tables turned and the animals got to kill the people: a common sentence in the Roman criminal justice system was *damnatio ad bestias*, when thieves and other miscreants were turned loose, unarmed, into the arena, where hungry beasts would be waiting for them.

Entrance to the Colosseum was free for all, although a membership card was necessary, and a rigid seating plan kept the sexes and social classes in their rightful places. The emperor and senators occupied marble seats in the front rows; on benches higher up were the priests and magistrates, then above them the foreign diplomats. Women were confined to the upper reaches – all of them, that is, except the pampered Vestal Virgins, who had privileged seats right near the emperor.

By the sixth century, with the fall of the Roman Empire, bloodsports in the Colosseum were less impressive: chickens pecked each other to death here. The Roman authorities discontinued the games and the Colosseum became little more than a quarry for the stone and marble used to build and decorate Roman *palazzi*. The pockmarks all over the Colosseum's masonry date back to the ninth century, when Lombards pillaged the iron and lead clamps that until then had held the blocks together. This irreverence toward the Colosseum was not halted until the mid 18th century, when Pope Benedict XIV consecrated it as a church. For another century it was left to its own devices, becoming home to hundreds of species of flowers and plants, as well as to a fair number of Roman homeless. After Unification in 1870 the flora was yanked up and the squatters kicked out, in what 19th-century English writer Augustus Hare described as 'aimless excavations'. 'In dragging out the roots of its shrubs,' he moaned in his *Walks in Rome* (1883), 'more of the building was destroyed than would have fallen naturally in five centuries.'

Il Palatino (The Palatine)

Via di San Gregorio 30/piazza di Santa Maria Nova 53 (06 699 0110/06 3996 7700). Metro Colosseo/ bus 60Exp, 75, 85, 87, 117, 175, 271, 571, 673, 810, 850/tram 3. **Open** 9am-sunset (last entry 1hr before closing) daily. **Admission** (incl Colosseum) €9; €4.50 concessions. *Special exhibitions* €2 extra. *See p72* **Tickets**. **No credit cards.**
Map p360 A/B3.
Numbers (●) refer to the map on p76.
While you may not believe the story that Romulus killed his twin brother Remus for crossing the property line he had staked out on the Palatine, archaeological evidence shows that this spot was probably the site of the settlement that would become Rome. Remains have been found of a wall near the Forum area and of primitive huts on the top of the hill dating from the eighth century BC; tradition says one of these latter was Romulus' home.

Later, the Palatine became the home of the movers and shakers of both the Republic and the Empire as sumptuous palaces were built. The choice of location was understandable: the Palatine overlooks the Foro romano, yet is a comfortable distance from the disturbances and riff-raff down in the valley. But the area really came into its own after Augustus built his new home next to the house of Rome's founder; successive emperors constructed massive palaces until the Palatine became virtually one massive Imperial dwelling and government seat. With Rome's decline it became a rural backwater, home to monasteries and their vegetable gardens, its precious marble and statuary toted off by looters. In the 1540s much of the area was bought by Cardinal Alessandro Farnese, who turned it into a pleasure villa and garden.

Entering the Palatine from the Roman Forum, you pass the **Horti farnesiani** (⑱) – originally the Domus Tiberiana – on the right. These gardens – a shady haven full of orange and olive trees but sadly in need of a makeover – were originally laid out in the 16th century, making them one of the oldest botanical gardens in Europe; what you see now is an 'interpretative recreation' from the early 20th century. The 17th-century pavilion at the top of the hill offers a good view over the Forum. Passing beneath the gardens, behind the pavilion, is the **Cryptoporticus** (⑲), a long semi-subterranean tunnel built by Nero either for hot-weather promenades or as a secret route between the Palatine buildings and his palace, the Domus Aurea (*see p154*). Lit only by slits in the walls, the Cryptoporticus is welcomingly cool in summer. At one end there are remnants of a stucco ceiling frieze and floor mosaics.

Head south from the gardens for the site of the 'huts of Romulus', the **Domus Augustus** and the **Domus Livia** (⑳). In the house of Augustus' wife Livia – now beneath a modern brick protective covering – wall paintings dating from the late Republic were found; they include trompe l'oeil marble panels and scenes from mythology.

South-east of here are the remains of the Imperial palaces built by Domitian in the late first century AD, which became the main residence of the emperors for the next three centuries. The nearest section, the **Domus Flavia** (㉑), contained the public rooms. According to Suetonius, Domitian was so terrified of assassination that he had the walls faced with shiny black selenite so he could see anybody creeping up behind him. It didn't work. The strange-looking room with what appears to be a maze in the middle was the courtyard; next to this was the dining room, where part of the marble floor has survived, although it's usually covered for protection. The brick oval in the middle was probably a fountain. Next door is the emperor's private residence, the **Domus Augustana** (㉒), whose name derives from *augustus* ('favoured by the gods' – nothing to do with Emperor Augustus). The oval building next to it (㉓) may have been a garden or a miniature stadium for Domitian's private entertainment. It was surrounded by a portico, visible at the southern end.

Sandwiched between the Domus Flavia and Domus Augustana is a tall grey building that houses the **Museo Palatino** (㉔). Downstairs are human remains and artefacts from the earliest communities of Rome, founded in the Forum and Palatine areas from the ninth century BC. Room 2 has a model of an eighth-century BC wattle-and-daub hut village. Emerging from the floor are the foundations of Domitian's dwelling. Upstairs are busts, gods and some fascinating eave-edgings from the first to the fourth centuries AD.

Walking east, past the stadium, several paths lead to a lower level, from where the remains of the comparatively small **palace and baths of Septimius Severus** (㉕) can be seen. They are some of the best-preserved buildings in the area.

The Trevi Fountain & the Quirinale

The palace of popes, kings and presidents lords over one of Rome's most populist attractions.

The roaring waters of the *acqua vergine* – so called for their purity and low levels of calcium (although legend says their source was indicated to the troops of Agrippa by a virgin) – were fundamental to the development of this area: they supplied the popes' Palazzo del Quirinale and the masses who drew them from the Trevi Fountain in the valley below. On Monday mornings, when workmen turn the water off to clean the fountain, the quarter turns eerily silent.

Water continues to be a key feature of the area: in addition to the fountain, you can hear the rush beneath the ruins of a Roman street at the **Città dell'acqua**, while a miraculous well inside the ancient church of **Santa Maria in Via** (for both, *see p94* **Extra time**) still provides healing cupfuls for sick parishioners.

But this area is also home to art aplenty, notably in the *gallerie* Barberini and Colonna, and at the Accademia di San Luca. And there are two small but superb churches – Sant'Andrea and San Carlino – by the geniuses of Baroque Rome, Bernini and Borromini.

Around the Trevi Fountain

The high walls of the presidential Palazzo del Quirinale (*see p94*) loom over a tangle of

medieval streets, all of which seem in the end to lead to the **Trevi Fountain** (*see below*). The *acqua vergine* that feeds it is said to be the best water in Rome: Grand Tourists used it to brew their tea. Nowadays you'd be hard pressed to get your kettle anywhere near for the coin-tossing hordes elbowing their way through serried ranks of tacky souvenir vendors.

Names like via della Dataria (Ecclesiastical Benefits Office Street) and via della Stamperia (Printing Works Street)recall the era when the whole of the Trevi district acted as a service area for the palace: here were the bureaucratic departments, presses and service industries that oiled the machinery of the Papal States. To keep close to the hub of power, aristocratic families like the Odescalchis, Grimaldis and Barberinis built their palaces close by, as did the Colonna, whose art collection can be seen at the **Galleria Colonna** (*see p89*).

There's more art on display at the **Galleria dell'Accademia di San Luca** (*see p89*), keeper of the flame of artistic orthodoxy. For quite a different kind of art entirely, explore the history of pasta-making at the **Museo Nazionale delle Paste Alimentari** (*see p91*).

Fontana di Trevi (Trevi Fountain)

Piazza di Trevi. Bus 52, 53, 61, 62, 71, 80Exp, 95, 116, 119, 175, 492, 630, 850. **Map** *p357 A5.*
For recent generations, it was Anita Ekberg who made this fountain famous when she plunged in wearing a strapless black evening dress (and a pair of waders… but you don't notice those) in Federico Fellini's classic *La dolce vita.* Don't even think about trying it yourself – wading, washing and splashing in fountains are strictly against local bylaws. And unlike the Grand Tourists, you don't want to drink from it either: the sparkling water is full of chlorine (though there's a chlorine-free spout hidden in a bird-bath-shaped affair at the back of the fountain to the right).

It was an altogether different affair in 19 BC, when spring water was transported here by an aqueduct from the eighth mile of the via Collatina, to the east of Rome. The only aqueduct to pass underground along its whole route into the city, it was the sole survivor of barbarian destruction and other horrors of the early Middle Ages (though after centuries of abandonment the flow has considerably diminished from its heyday, when 100,000 cubic metres gushed into Rome each day). In 1570 Pius V restored the conduit but it wasn't until 1732 that Pope Clement XII called for designs for a new *mostra* – a magnificent fountain to mark the end of the aqueduct. Completed decades later to a design by Nicolò Salvi, the *mostra* – the Trevi Fountain – immediately became a draw for tourists who drank the prized waters to ensure a return to Rome.

Tucked away in a tiny piazza and almost always surrounded by jostling crowds, the fountain's creamy travertine gleams beneath powerful torrents of water and constant camera flashes. It's a magnificent rococo extravaganza of rearing sea horses, conch-blowing tritons, craggy rocks and flimsy trees, erupting in front of the wall of Palazzo Poli. Nobody can quite remember when the custom started of tossing coins in to the waters (as celebrated in *Three Coins in a Fountain*, with its Oscar-winning ditty). The city council made such a poor job of collecting the coins that for 30 years a self-appointed collector waded in every morning and saved them the trouble. Now the money goes to the Red Cross.

Bernini's **Triton Fountain**. *See p91.*

Galleria dell'Accademia di San Luca

Piazza dell'Accademia 77 (06 679 8850/www. accademiasanluca.it). Bus 52, 53, 61, 62, 71, 80Exp, 95, 116, 119, 175, 492, 630, 850. **Map** p357 A5. **Note:** the Galleria was closed for restoration as this guide went to press; it's scheduled to reopen in 2008.

The illustrious Accademia di San Luca (patron saint of artists; St Luke was said to have painted the Virgin and Child from life), housed in Palazzo Carpegno, was founded in 1577 to train artists in the grand Renaissance style (*see p91* **Rebels with a cause**). Although restoration of the gallery shows no sign of coming to an end, the porter is usually willing to let visitors sneak a look at Borromini's staircase; clever and very practical (at least for sedan chairs and mules) the elliptical brickwork ramp to the upper floors of the palace was inspired by the winding ramp inside Hadrian's mausoleum within Castel Sant'Angelo (*see p170*). Access to the ramp is behind a virtuoso piece of stucco work: cornucopiae of overblown buttercups and daisies denote the riches of the earth, while crowns, mitres and chains symbolise what can be achieved by hard work in the course of a long and fortunate career. But without progeny, the allegory continues (the offspring is symbolised by a small child peering out of the herbiage), it is all worthless endeavour; it's not on record whether the few women members of the Academy, such as artistic prodigies Lavinia Fontana (1551-1614) and Angelica Kauffman (1741-1807), agreed with these sentiments.

Galleria Colonna

Via della Pilotta 17 (06 678 4350/www.galleria colonna.it). Bus 40Exp, 60Exp, 64, 70, 117, 170, H. **Open** 9am-1pm Sat. Closed Aug. **Admission** €7; €5.50 concessions. **No credit cards. Map** p357 A6.

Saturday mornings are your only chance to see this splendid six-room gallery, completed in 1703 by Prince Filippo II Colonna, whose descendants still live in the palace. (Among others, the Colonnas produced a pope, a saint, an excommunicated cardinal and Vittoria Colonna, the poetess who befriended Michelangelo.) The entrance leads to the Room of the Column, originally the throne room of Prince Filippo and his successors, who would have sat in state by the ancient column, back-lit by light shining through the window behind, and with a view across to a triumphal arch dedicated to Marcantonio Colonna, the family hero. (Audrey Hepburn behaved regally here too, in *Roman Holiday*.) The cannonball embedded in the stairs down to the Great Hall lies where it landed during the French siege of Rome on 24 June 1849. The mirrored hall may be the work of Gian Lorenzo Bernini, inspired by his visit to Versailles in 1665, while the immense frescoed ceiling pays tribute to Marcantonio, who led the papal fleet to victory against the Turks in the great naval battle of Lepanto in 1571. There are more Turks carved in the legs of the furniture in the next room. The gallery's

Sightseeing

The Legendary Harry's Bar

Legendary Harry's Bar is the unique place that evokes the "Dolce Vita" as if it were a clip from the film, creating a vivid flashback to the golden era of the Via Veneto, when Frank Sinatra sang at the piano and all the stars made their appearance in this bar/restaurant full of glamour and style. As in the roaring sixties, you can still sip an aperitif, enjoy the live piano bar every evening and dive into the magic of the Via Veneto from the exclusive and fascinating Harry's Bar. The refined cuisine recalls the freshness of Mediterranean flavours based on prime ingredients. Tradition and fantasy inspire the elegant dishes, accompanied by the most prestigious labels and a high class service.

Reservations Recommended

Via V. Veneto 150 - 00187 Roma - www.harrysbar.it - info@harrysbar.it
Tel. +39 06 48 46 43 / +39 06 47 42 103 - Fax +39 06 48 83 117
Open from: 11:00 to 2:00 am • Piano Bar 22:00 - 2:00 am (Mon - Sat)

Rebels with a cause

The dues levied by the snobbish **Accademia di San Luca** (*see p89*) – not to mention the conservative styles that this bastion of orthodoxy represented – led early 17th-century artists from northern Europe to set up their own guild called the *Schildersbent* (Dutch for 'painters' clique'), also known as the *Bentvueghels* ('birds of a feather'). Along with the splinter group called the *Bamboccianti* – led by Pieter van Laer, aka *il bamboccio* (the puppet) because of his hunchback – they painted small scenes of warts-and-all peasant life.

These rough-and-ready scenes may have been to the taste of ruddy-cheeked Dutch burghers seeking souvenirs of their Roman holiday but were far removed from the sensibilities of 17th-century Roman aristocrats: the *Bentvueghel* came in for some severe criticism for their lack of decorum. As a result, the vast majority of these paintings have ended up outside Rome, although a couple of examples by Van Laer's follower Johannes Lingelbach can be seen at the **Palazzo Corsini** (*see p135*). They include the splendidly titled *Tooth-puller at piazza Navona*, indicative of the subjects they favoured.

The hard-drinking *Bentvueghels*' refusal to toe the line extended beyond their paintings; as more artists from northern Europe flocked to Rome, the group became increasingly rowdier. Inebriated processions would end up at the lovely church of **Santa Costanza** (*see p176*) on via Nomentana, where the artists would scratch their names on the walls. But it was mock baptisms that tipped them over the edge of acceptability. After this affront to pontifical power, Pope Clement XI outlawed the group in 1720.

most famous and much-reproduced picture is Annibale Caracci's earthy peasant *Bean Eater*. Usually included in the ticket price is a guided tour in English, which starts at noon. Groups of ten or more can arrange tours of the gallery as well as the private apartments at other times during the week.

Museo Nazionale delle Paste Alimentari

Piazza Scanderbeg 117 (06 699 1120/www.museo dellapasta.it). Bus 52, 53, 61, 62, 71, 80Exp, 95, 116, 119, 175, 492, 630, 850. **Open** 9.30am-5.30pm daily. **Admission** €10; €7 children. **No credit cards**. **Map** p357 A5.

All you wanted to know (and much more) about Italy's national staple. Multilingual CD players guide visitors through 11 rooms dedicated to the sophistications of pasta-making: rolling and cutting techniques, the selection and the selection of ingredients. If, after this exhaustive/exhausting introduction to the art of pasta-making, you still have the energy to think of rolling your own, there is a gift shop with all kinds of pasta-related items to take home.

Piazza Barberini & the Quattro Fontane

Art-packed **Palazzo Barberini** (*see p92*) towers above piazza Barberini – once a semi-rural idyll and now a woeful example of the sledgehammer school of city planning. Traffic hurtles north into via Veneto (*see p102*) or south-east towards the Quattro Fontane, while marooned in the midst of the belching fumes is

the last commission Gian Lorenzo Bernini received from the Barberini Pope Urban VIII: the **Fontana del Tritone** (photo p89). The fountain is covered with the bees of the Barberini family emblem, and shows four dolphins supporting a huge open shell on their tails. On the shell sits a Triton blowing into a conch shell to tame the flooding seas, as in a tale recounted by Ovid in his *Metamorphoses*.

North-east of the piazza, charmless *vie* Barberini and Bissolati were redeveloped under Mussolini and now contain airline offices.

Ringing with the noise of life-threatening *motorini*, narrow via Barberini climbs past the Palazzo Barberini gallery to the crossroads, which – for very obvious reasons – are known as the **Quattro Fontane** (four fountains). Four delightful Baroque fountains have stood here since 1593. It's a life-threatening task trying to see them through the traffic, but they clearly represent four river gods: the one accompanied by the she-wolf is the Tiber; the females are probably Juno (with duck) and Diana. But it's anybody's guess who the fourth figure is: some claim it's an allegory of the Nile while others make a case for the Florentine Arno. From here, the staggering view down both sides of the hill takes in three Egyptian obelisks – part of the city's remodeling under obelisk-mad Sixtus V (*see p155* **Villa Peretti**). On one corner stands the little church of **San Carlo alle Quattro Fontane** (*see p92*), one of the great masterpieces of tortured genius Carlo Borromini.

Palazzo Barberini – Galleria Nazionale d'Arte Antica

Via delle Quattro Fontane 13/via Barberini 18 (06 481 4591/bookings 06 32 810/www.galleria borghese.it). Metro Barberini/bus 52, 53, 61, 62, 63, 80Exp, 95, 116, 119, 175, 492, 630. **Open** 8.30am-7.30pm Tue-Sun. **Admission** €5; €2.50 concessions; *see also p72* **Tickets**. **No credit cards.** **Map** p357 B5.

Top architects like Maderno, Bernini and Borromini queued up to work on this vast pile, which was completed in just five years, shortly after Maffeo Barberini became Pope Urban VIII in 1623. Bernini did the main staircase, a grand rectangular affair now marred by an ill-placed lift. Borromini, whose uncle Carlo Maderno drew up the original palace plans, added the graceful oval staircase. Some new rooms were opened in 2006 after a long-running restoration, but more work remains to be done and the paintings will, presumably, continue to shift about the palace. Among masterpieces displayed in the newly opened rooms are Raphael's *Fornarina* (said, probably wrongly, to be a portrait of the baker's daughter he loved and may have been engaged to at the time of his death in 1520), Holbein's pompous *Henry VIII* and Titian's *Venus and Adonis. See also below* **Barberini trumpeting**.

San Carlo alle Quattro Fontane

Via del Quirinale 23 (06 488 3261/www.sancarlino-borromini.it). Metro Barberini/bus 40Exp, 52, 53, 61, 62, 63, 64, 70, 71, 80Exp, 95, 116, 119, 170, 175, 492, 630, H. **Open** 10am-1pm, 3-6pm Mon-Fri; 10am-1pm Sat; noon-1pm Sun. **Map** p357 C5.

Barberini trumpeting

After years swathed in scaffolding and builders' dust, the **Galleria Nazionale d'Arte Antica** at the Palazzo Barberini (*see p92*) reopened in December 2006. A blaze of lights, whirring television cameras, the august presence of the Italian president and jostling crowds of worthy arty types made that inauguration a memorable occasion. But all was not as it seemed. In fact, the trumpeting and publicity served to conceal as much as it unveiled.

Firstly, this was no 'opening' – the gallery had never closed. Throughout its long, drawn-out restoration, large parts had always been open to the public, with important works shunted about the various rooms to keep them on display. Secondly, only nine new rooms were ready for the Big Day, with another 20 or so still to go. Thirdly, and most significantly, the *Circolo Ufficiali delle Forze Armate*, an army officers' club that for many decades has occupied a sumptuous suite here – and for almost as many has been promising to decamp elsewhere – was still firmly in its very comfortable place. (An amicable agreement had been reached, it was said at the inauguration, and the officers were packing their bags; but the furious glare of Culture Minister Francesco Rutelli throughout the ceremony seemed to cast some doubt over this.)

Despite these hiccups, Palazzo Barberini remains a key sight for lovers of the Renaissance. Rome's most magnificent private home, the palace was extended for the family of Pope Urban VIII. Arguably the most extravagant pope of all time, Urban's vast spending on public fountains and fripperies angered hungry Romans who celebrated riotously upon his death in 1644.

To the left of the bookshop by the entrance is the Salone, a public hall where ladies-in-waiting and courtiers would hang about while their superiors entered the inner sanctum. The grandest of its type in any Roman palace, the Salone was a tourist mecca from the moment that Pietro da Cortona completed its ceiling fresco in 1639; the *Triumph of Divine Providence*, an allegory of Urban's rule, is a masterpiece of Baroque propaganda. The Barberini pope claimed divine providence was directly involved in his election in 1623. When votes were counted in the first ballot, one slip was missing. To dispel any doubts about the validity of his election, Urban forced fellow cardinals to stage the vote again, making him the only pope in history to be elected twice – giving him, he reckoned, a right to rule that was to be milked for all it was worth.

Dominating the composition is the central figure of Divine Providence on a cloud above the figure of Time (devouring one of his offspring) and with Virtues floating behind her. At the top, the Barberini crest of bees – supported by Faith, Hope and Charity – buzzes skywards as Immortality reaches to crown it with stars. The goddess Roma holds the papal tiara, and Religion the keys of St Peter.

Also in the Salone are two paintings by Caravaggio (*Narcissus* and the splendidly gory *Judith and Holfernes*); a portrait by Bernini of Urban VIII; and the portrait believed to be of *Beatrice Cenci*, attributed to Guido Reni and the inspiration of writers such as Melville, Shelley and Hawthorne.

Carlo Borromini's first solo composition (1631-41), and the one of which he was most proud, San Carlo (often called Carlino, due to its diminuitive scale) is one of the star pieces of the Roman Baroque. The most remarkable feature is the dizzying oval dome: its geometrical coffers decrease in size towards the lantern to give the illusion of additional height – Borromini is all about illusion – and the subtle illumination, through hidden windows, makes the dome appear to float in mid-air. There is also an austere adjoining courtyard and a simply beautiful library that opens occasionally at the whim of the monastery's residents.

From the Quirinale to via Nazionale

The origins of the name 'Quirinale' are lost in the mists of time; it may refer to a temple of Quirinus which stood here, or perhaps it comes from Cures, a Sabine town north-east of Rome from where, legend relates, the Sabines under King Tatius came to settle on the hill. Throughout the Republican era, the hill was covered in gardens and villas where the great and the good could escape from the malarial heat of the marshy valleys. In the 16th century the pope thought it would be a good idea to do the same thing and the summer **Palazzo del Quirinale** (*see p94*) was begun in 1574 for Gregory XIII (of Gregorian calendar and chant fame). After the collapse of the Papal States in 1870, Pope Pius IX, who was holed up inside the palace, refused to hand over his keys to the troops of King Victor Emanuel; they had to force their way in (*see p23* **Eviction order**). Just 76 years later the reigning Savoia family were forced to quit the palace following a referendum in which the monarchy, disgraced by association with the inter-war Fascist regime, was despatched into exile. Today a constant stream of motorcades swishing across the cobbles serves as a reminder that the Quirinale – now the official residence of the Italian president – is still very much at the decision-making hub of 21st-century Italy.

The space in front of the palace is where the cavalry are put through their paces for visiting heads of state. Officially piazza del Quirinale, it's generally referred to by locals as piazza di Monte Cavallo – Horse Hill Square – on account of the two towering Imperial-era equestrian statues. The giant horses rear up nervously beside the five-metre-high (16 feet) heavenly twins Castor and Pollux. The statues, which had been lying in the nearby ruins of the Baths of Constantine, were artistically arranged by Domenico Fontana, the favourite architect of the city-planner Pope Sixtus V, in the 1580s. Despite Sixtus' predilection for obelisks, it was

Rome's skyline from the **Scuderie**. *See p94.*

Pius VI who dragged the obelisk now standing here from outside Augustus' mausoleum (*see p110*) in 1786; Pius VII added the big granite basin that had been a cattle trough in the Forum. On the far side of the square are the papal stables, now an elegant exhibition space, the **Scuderie del Quirinale** (*see p94*).

Across the road from the palace's long wing stands the splendid church of **Sant'Andrea al Quirinale** (*see p94*), by Bernini. Behind the church, the south-facing slope of the hill, which until Unification was still wooded and wild, is now very much a centre of official Rome, with its state buildings – police stations, court buildings and ministry offshoots – leading down towards the high-street shopping artery of via Nazionale and the **Palazzo delle Esposizioni** (*see below*).

Palazzo delle Esposizioni

Via Nazionale 194 (www.palaexpo.it). Bus 40Exp, 64, 70, 71, 170, H. **Map** p357 C6.
Note: Closed for restoration; due to reopen Sept 2007. This imposing 19th-century purpose-built exhibition space has been *in restauro* for years but is scheduled to reopen for the Notte Bianca (*see p254*).

Sightseeing

Palazzo del Quirinale

Piazza del Quirinale (06 46 991/www.quirinale.it).
Bus 40Exp, 64, 70, 71, 170, H. **Open** 8.30am-noon
Sun. Closed late June-early Sept; occasionally in Apr
& Dec: check website for details. **Admission** €5.
No credit cards. **Map** p357 B6.

The new St Peter's still wasn't finished when Pope
Gregory XIII started building this pontifical summer
palace on the highest of Rome's seven hills; begun
in 1573, the Quirinale was not completed until over
200 years later. The risk that a pontiff (not, on the
whole, renowned for youthful vigour) might keel
over during the holidays was such that it was
decided to build somewhere suitable to hold a
conclave to elect a successor. The Quirinale's
Cappella Paolina (named after Paul V) was designed
by Carlo Maderno and finished in 1617; it is a faithful replica of the Vatican's Sistine Chapel, minus the
Michelangelos. Accommodation for the cardinals
was provided in the *Manica lunga*, the immensely
long wing that runs the length of via del Quirinale
to the rear of the palace. Bernini added the main
entrance door in 1638.

On Sunday mornings, when parts of the palace are
open to the public, you may be lucky enough to catch
one of the noon concerts held in the chapel. The presidential guard changes with a flourish each afternoon outside on the square at any time between 3pm
and 6pm, depending on the season.

Sant'Andrea al Quirinale

Via del Quirinale 29 (06 474 4872). Bus 40Exp, 64,
70, 71, 170, H. **Open** 8.30am-noon, 3-7pm Mon-Fri;
9am-noon, 3.30-7pm Sat, Sun. **Map** p357 B5.

With funding from Cardinal Camillo Pamphili, the
Jesuits commissioned Gian Lorenzo Bernini to build
a church for novices living on the Quirinale. The site
was small and awkward, but Bernini solved the
problem by designing an oval church (1658) with the
entrance and the high altar very unusually on the
short axis. Above the door, a section of the wall
seems to have swung down on to the columns,
creating an entrance porch. Inside, the church is richly decorated with the figure of St Andrew (by Antonio
Raggi, Bernini's star pupil) floating heavenwards
through a broken pediment above the high altar.

Scuderie Papali al Quirinale

Via XXIV Maggio 16 (06 696 270/www.scuderie
quirinale.it). Bus 40Exp, 64, 70, 71, 170, H.
Open during exhibitions only. **Admission** varies.
Credit (phone bookings only) AmEx, DC, MC, V.
Map p357 B6.

The former stables of the Palazzo del Quirinale,
this large space for major exhibitions retains
original features such as the brickwork ramp to the
upper floors, plus acres of chic marble flooring and
space-age lighting. There is a good art bookshop and
a café and – best of all – a breathtaking view
of Rome's skyline (**photo** p93) from the rear staircase as you leave. Exhibitions held here are
generally fascinating, excellent and very over-
subscribed: it pays to book ahead.

Extra time

● First day of the month? Rush over to the
Casino dell'Aurora (via XXIV Maggio 43,
06 482 7224, open 10am-noon, 3-5pm,
first of each month except Jan, free) to
gawp like Grand Tourists *Aurora scattering
flowers before the chariot of the sun*. The
Victorian's darling Guido Reni painted it
in 1614 on the ceiling of the summer
house of the 17th-century Palazzo
Pallavicini Rospigliosi. The rest of the
Pallavicini picture collection is off-limits.
● A stone's throw from the Trevi fountain
are the excavations that came to light
during the remodeling of the ex-Cinema
Trevi (now a Mondadori bookstore, retail
outlet of a publishing house owned by one
S Berlusconi). Called the **Città dell'acqua**
(City of Water; vicolo del Puttarello 25,
339 778 6192, open 4-7.30pm Mon,
11am-3pm Thur-Sun, admission €2, €1
concessions), it incorporates the remains
of an Imperial-age apartment building, part
of a Roman street and a holding tank for
the waters of the *acqua vergine*, which can
be heard rushing by underneath.
● Join well-heeled ladies on a break from
shopping, bronzed youth rendezvous-ing
and snazzily dressed denizens of the
nearby parliament buildings for tea-time
tunes or cocktail-hour blues played on a
concert grand piano in the belle époque
splendour of the air-conditioned, marble-
clad, shop-filled **Galleria Alberto Sordi** (off
piazza Colonna, open 10am-10pm daily).
● Stand in the presence of papal innards
in **Santi Anastasio e Vincenzo** (piazza di
Trevi, open May-Sept 6.45am-12.30pm,
3-8.30pm daily, Oct-Apr 6.45am-12.30pm,
2.30-8pm daily): the liver, spleen and
pancreas of every pope from Sixtus V
(1585-90) to Leo XIII (1878-1903) was
preserved and interred in this church,
before the rest of the body was buried
somewhere grander. The papal offal is not
on view, but there's an an inventory on a
plaque by the altar.
● Perk yourself up with a cupful of
miraculous water in the church of **Santa
Maria in Via** (via Mortaro 24, 06 697 6741,
open 7.15am-1pm, 4-8pm Mon-Fri, 7.15am-
1pm, 4-9pm Sat, 8.30am-1pm, 4-10pm
Sun). In 1286 a stone bearing an image of
the Virgin's face floated to the surface of a
well, over which this church was later built.

Sightseeing

Via Veneto & Villa Borghese

A park full of art.

In the first century BC, Rome's most extensive gardens, the Horti Sallustiani, spread over the valley between the Quirinal hill and the Pincio. During the Renaissance, the area was colonised by aristocratic Roman families such as the Borghese and Boncompagni-Ludovisi, who attempted to out-do one another with the lavishness of their vast suburban estates. In fact, up until the building boom of the late 1800s, only the odd villa or decorative pavilion interrupted the tranquil, leafy parkland from the Pincio to Porta Pia.

When Rome was made capital of Italy in 1871, this green idyll was seen as prime building land, to be dug up and replaced by street after street of grandiose *palazzi*; of the estates, only the Villa Borghese was saved from the property vultures; it is now the city's most central public park.

Villa Borghese & the Pincio

Shortly after Camillo Borghese became Pope Paul V in 1605, his favourite nephew, 26-year-old Scipione Caffarelli Borghese, was made a cardinal. An obsessive love of the arts led Scipione to embark upon the creation of a pleasure park: the **Villa Borghese**. What began as a family vineyard was transformed,

with the acquisition of surrounding lands, into one of the most extensive gardens in Rome since antiquity. A 'Theatre of the Universe', Scipione's vision was a place where sculpture, painting and music could be enjoyed alongside fossil specimens and technological oddities of the day such as orreries, special clocks and lenses. The harmoniously proportioned *Casino nobile* (now the **Galleria Borghese**; *see p99*) was designed to showcase these gems. Begun in 1608, the building was modelled on ancient Roman villas and Renaissance predecessors such as the Villa Farnesina (*see p136*).

An impressive aviary (still visible to the left as you look at the façade of the Galleria Borghese) acted as a backdrop to the land surrounding the *Casino*, which alternated formal gardens dotted with exotic plants,

Pleasure park: **Villa Borghese**.

HOTEL LOCARNO

"Small, intimate, stylish and highly individual, Hotel Locarno has consistently been voted the best 3-star hotel in Rome" (Hip Hotels)

Located in the very heart of Rome, just off the Piazza del Popolo - the city's largest square - and the Via del Corso with its stylish shops and boutiques, the Hotel Locarno opened its Art Deco doors in 1925.

Long a favoured haunt of the film world, actors, directors, scriptwriters and artists have all sampled the hotel's unique atmosphere over the decades. Its 66 rooms and suites, eclectically furnished, all come equipped with private bathroom, air conditioning, telephone, satellite TV, electronic safe and minibar, exude an intimacy and comfort all their own.

The sixth floor roof garden commands a breathtaking view over the Tiber, and in warm weather, breakfast is served in the delightful courtyard garden.

"Understated class" (The Times)

HOTEL LOCARNO Via della Penna 22 - 00186 R
T: +39 06 361 0841 - F: +39 06 321 5249
info@hotellocarno.com - www.hotellocarno.co

fountains and statues with wilder stretches of landscape used for hunting. The villa soon became *the* place to be seen in 17th-century Rome, and the magnificent gardens were further embellished until Scipione's death in 1633. The result was a Baroque amusement park, complete with trick fountains that sprayed unwitting passers-by, automata and erotic paintings, menageries of wild beasts, and an alfresco dining room where the cardinal entertained with due magnificence on summer evenings. Successive generations of the Borghese family altered the park according to changing fashions, though Scipione's descendants proved themselves to be less artistically inclined than their keen-eyed predecessor, selling off a good deal of his priceless collection; one of the worst culprits was Napoleon's notorious sister Pauline, who married into the Borghese family in 1807.

When Rome became capital of a unified Italy, the clan looked set to sell off the estate to property speculators. In a rare example of civic far-sightedness, the state stepped in, in 1901, wresting possession of the villa from the family in a bitter court battle and turning it into a public park.

'The setting, the air, the chord struck, make it a hundred wonderful things,' mused Henry James on strolling around Villa Borghese. Today, the Borghese family's pleasure grounds are a popular spot for jogging, dog-walking, picnicking and cruising. The entire park has been spruced up in recent years, and a spate of arty projects such as the opening in 2006 of the **Museo Carlo Bilotti** (*see p101* and *p102* **Art in the orangery**), cemented its status as a 'park of the arts', of which its founder would have been proud. A wander around Villa Borghese is a great way to recuperate from an overdose of carbon monoxide. Sporty types will find bicycles and in-line skates for hire, and the park can also be a pleasant place to work: there's free internet access at a number of 'wireless hotspots' around the park (see www.romawireless.com for details). Culture vultures head straight to three of Rome's greatest art repositories: the Galleria Borghese itself, the Etruscan museum at **Villa Giulia** (*see p101*) and the **Galleria Nazionale d'Arte Moderna** (*see p100*). The park also houses the **Casa del Cinema** (*see p264*), inaugurated in September 2004, the **Dei Piccoli** children's cinema, the **Bioparco-Zoo** (*see p260*) and the **Museo Civico di Zoologia** (*see p102*). Viale delle Belle Arti and via Omero are crammed with academies and cultural institutes (see www.villaborghese.it for a full list; *see also pp265-267* **Galleries**), which put on occasional exhibitions and concerts. The

British School at Rome (www.bsr.ac.uk), next door to the Galleria Nazionale d'Arte Moderna in an imposing Lutyens-designed pavilion, hosts contemporary art exhibitions, events and lectures.

Other sights worth looking out for include the **piazza di Siena**, an elegantly-shaped grassy hippodrome used for glitzy showjumping events, and, nearby, the pretty **Giardino del Lago**, which has a small lake with rowing boats (for hire from 9.30am to sunset daily) and faux-ancient temples. There is also a good view of the Muro Torto section of the **Aurelian Wall** from the bridge between the Pincio and Villa Borghese. This was the only portion of Rome's ancient walls not repaired and strengthened by Belisarius, on the assurance of the citizens that St Peter himself would protect it; sure enough, the barbarians never attacked here. Once a favourite suicide spot, this is now strung with nets to make sure depressed Romans no longer disturb the traffic below.

Overlooking piazza del Popolo (*see p109*), and now an integral part of the Villa Borghese, is one of the oldest gardens in Rome: the **Pincio**. The Pinci family commissioned the first gardens here in the fourth century. The present layout was designed by Giuseppe Valadier in 1814. The garden is best known for its view of the Vatican at sunset, with the dome

Pass?

In their latest effort to sell the plethora of sights in and around the Villa Borghese park as a single unit, luminaries at Rome's city council have introduced the **Villa Borghese Card**, a 12-month pass costing €10 that gives free entry to one of the venues, and reductions at the rest, plus discounts at the Villa's bars and at book/gift shops in the museums and galleries.

Think carefully before investing: the same sights are covered by the three-day **Roma Pass** (*see p73*), which has free use of the public transport system thrown in. If you do opt for the Villa Borghese Card, you'd do well to blow your one free entrance on the more expensive sights (Galleria Borghese, *see p99*; or Galleria Nazionale d'Arte Moderna, *see p100*). And remember: you'll still need to book to get into the Galleria Borghese (*see also p72* **Tickets**).

The Villa Borghese Card can be purchased at participating venues and at PITs (*see p337*).

The purchase of a mosaic picture is a nice choice and his value increase in time

Il Gruppo Savelli, unica impresa privata a Roma, unisce all'attività di esposizione e vendita di mosaici antichi e moderni anche quella di produzione di opere in mosaico. Gli ambienti in cui risiede, a fianco del colonnato di San Pietro, ospitano un vero e proprio atelier del mosaico nel quale si possono ammirare al lavoro sia mosaicisti esperti che giovani apprendisti.

Savelli Company, unique private enterprise in Rome with exposition and sales of antique and modern mosaics, unites to its activity the production of mosaic works of art. It is situated next to the colonnade of St. Peters, where they host a true mosaic Gallery and you can admire the work of expert and young apprentice of Mosaic.

Savelli, unica empresa privada a Roma en exposicion y ventas de mosaicos antiguos y modernos, une a la actividad la produccion de estas obras de arte. El lugar donde se encuentra, al lado del colonado de San Pedro, hospita una verdadera boutique del mosaico, donde se puede contemplar el trabajo de expertos y jovenes aprendistas del mosaico.

GALLERIA SAVELLI
Religious Articles
Piazza Pio XII, 1-2 - 00193 Roma
Tel. +39.06.68.80.63.83
Fax +39.06.68.80.44.41

SAVELLI Arte e Tradizione
Mosaic Art Gallery
Via Paolo VI, 27-29 - 00193 Roma
Tel. +39.06.68.30.70.17
Fax +39.06.68.80.44.39

TOLL FREE NUMBER from USA and Canada
(011)800.190.22004
From EUROPE (00)

http://www.savellireligious.com
e-mail: vatican@savellireligious.com

of St Peter's silhouetted in gold. The paved area behind the viewpoint is popular with cyclists (bikes can be hired nearby) and skaters.

To the south-east is the **Casino Valadier**. Once a tearoom, it is now a pricey restaurant with a to-die-for view. In the manicured green to the south-east sits the **Villa Medici**, since 1804 the French academy in Rome, where many French artists, from Ingres and David to Balthus, found inspiration. The academy hosts occasional art exhibitions (phone 06 67 611 or consult www.villamedici.it for programme information) and opens its lovely gardens to the public at weekends (10.30am and 11.30am Sat, Sun, tours in Italian and French only, €7, €4.50 concessions).

Between Villa Borghese and the river are two more museums: a striking art nouveau villa houses the **Museo Hendrik Christian Andersen** (*see p101*); the children's museum, **Explora – Museo dei Bambini di Roma** (*see p260*), is in a former bus depot.

Galleria Borghese

Piazzale del Museo Borghese 5 (info & bookings 06 32 810/www.galleriaborghese.it). Bus 52, 53, 95, 116, 910. **Open** (timed entry, every 2hrs) 9am-7pm Tue-Sun. **Admission** (incl booking fee) €8.50; €5.25 concessions; €2 EU citizens under 18 or over 65. *See also p97* **Pass?. Credit** MC, V. **Map** p356 C2. **Note**: numbers are limited and booking at least a day in advance – essential in high season – is always advisable.

Begun in 1608 by Flaminio Ponzio and continued by Jan van Santen (Italianised to Giovanni Vasanzio) upon his death, the Casino Borghese was designed to house Cardinal Scipione Borghese's art collection. One of Bernini's greatest patrons, the cardinal had as good an eye for a bargain as for a masterpiece: he picked up many works – including the odd Caravaggio – at knock-down prices after they were rejected by the disappointed or shocked patrons who had commissioned them. The building's imposing façade was originally adorned with sculptures and ancient reliefs, which, along with many of the gallery's priceless gems, were sold to Napoleon in 1807 and are now conserved in the Louvre. The interior decoration – carried out in 1775-90 by Antonio Asprucci and Christopher Unterberger for Marcantonio IV Borghese – was fully restored in the 1990s.

Visits to the gallery are limited to two hours – sufficient given the building's compactness. With few rooms (but each more magnificent than the one before), the Galleria Borghese is as relaxing and enjoyable as the Vatican Museums can be daunting and agitating. A curved double staircase leads to the imposing entrance salon, with fourth-century AD floor mosaics showing gladiators fighting wild animals; the spectacular *trompe l'oeil* ceiling fresco (Mariano Rossi, 1775-78) shows Romulus received as a god on Olympus by Jupiter and other tales of Roman glory. Also here is the statue of Marcus

Curtius throwing himself into a chasm. (According to legend, when a massive crack appeared in the Roman Forum, threatening to swallow up Rome, the only way to stop it was to sacrifice the city's greatest treasure… so in leaped golden-boy Marcus.) The sculpture is an interesting palimpsest: Marcus' horse dates from the second century, while Marcus himself is the c1618 work of Pietro Bernini (father of the more famous Gian Lorenzo); the whole lot was stuck to the wall in 1776 as part of the villa's 18th-century revamp.

In Room 1 is one of the gallery's highlights: Canova's 1808 waxed marble figure of Pauline, sister of Napoleon and wife of Prince Camillo Borghese, as a topless Venus reclining languidly on a marble and wood sofa, which once contained a mechanism that slowly rotated it. Prince Camillo thought the work so provocative that he forbade even the artist from seeing it after completion. (Asked by a shocked friend how she could bear to pose naked, the irascible Pauline is said to have snapped: 'The studio was heated'.)

Rooms 2 to 4 contain some spectacular sculptures by Gian Lorenzo Bernini, made early in his career and already showing his genius. His *David* (1624) merits observation from different points of view in Room 2; the tense, concentrated face on the biblical hero as he is about to launch his shot is a self-portrait of the artist. Room 3 houses perhaps Bernini's most famous piece: *Apollo and Daphne* (1625), a seminal work of Baroque sculpture. As the nymph flees the amorous sun god, her desperate plea for help is answered by her river-god father; as Apollo reaches her she morphs – fingertips first – into a laurel tree. Ovid's tale was given a moral twist by Maffeo Barberini – later Pope Urban VIII – who composed the Latin inscription on the base: 'When we pursue fleeting pleasures, we reap only bitter fruits'). Bernini's virtuosity is especially evident in the cluster of paper-thin marble leaves separating the god and the girl. In Room 4, Pluto's hand presses into Proserpine's marble thigh in *The Rape of Proserpine* (1622), as she flexes her toes in tearful struggle.

Room 5 contains important pieces of classical sculpture, many of them Roman copies of Greek originals. Among the most renowned are a Roman copy of a Greek dancing faun and a copy of sleeping Hermaphroditus, offspring of Hermes and Aphrodite, displayed with his/her back to the onlooker so that the breasts and genitals are invisible. Bernini's *Aeneas and Anchises* (1620) dominates Room 6, showing the family fleeing as Troy burns, a theme reflected in the ceiling with Pecheux's painting of the gods deciding the fate of the city. Room 7 is Egyptian-themed: the ceiling paintings by Tommaso Maria Conca (1780) include an allegory of the richness of Egypt, while among the classical statues is a second-century Isis with black marble clothing.

The six Caravaggios in Room 8 include the *Boy with a Basket of Fruit* (c1594) and the *Sick Bacchus* (c1593), believed to be a self-portrait. His *David with the Head of Goliath*, also thought to be a self-portrait, was sent to Scipione Borghese as a desperate plea for pardon:

Sightseeing

Marks men

Noble, pope-producing families liked to make their presence felt by stamping their family crests on monuments around the city. Papal hallmarks are very much in evidence around Villa Borghese and via Veneto.

● Eagles and dragons, emblems of the Borghese family (Paul V, 1605-21), are the silent sentinels of Villa Borghese.
● The dragon of the Boncompagni family (Gregory XIII, 1572-85) can be spied on the façade of Palazzo Margherita, now the US embassy. The family later sold the building to Italy's royal Savoia family, whose crest can also be seen on the building's exterior, along with that of the US armouries.
● The bees of Bernini's patron Maffeo Barberini (Urban VIII, 1623-44) decorate the sculptor's Fontana delle Api (*pictured left*) at the lower end of via Veneto. The original inscription read that the pope built it 'in the XXII year of his papacy', though it was in fact completed two months before the date inscribed. A stone-cutter was hastily dispatched to remove an 'I', an action which was judged a curse on the pope... who duly popped his clogs eight days before reaching his 22nd year.
● Michelangelo was duty-bound to place the emblem of the Medici family (Pius IV, 1499-1565) – balls on a shield – on the façade of the Porta Pia. The emblem is variously thought to represent pawnbrokers' coins, a dented (but unyielding) shield or, most likely considering the family's origins, as apothecaries, medicinal pills.

since his exile for the murder of his opponent in a tennis match in 1606, the artist had been dogged by a terror of execution. The painting uses the same young model as *St John the Baptist* (1610), possibly Caravaggio's last painting. (Finally given a papal pardon in 1610, Caravaggio set sail for Rome but never made it; he was mistakenly arrested at Porto Ercole, where he became ill and died.)

Upstairs, the picture gallery is packed with one masterpiece after another. Look out in particular for: Raphael's *Deposition*, Pinturicchio's *Crucifixion with Saints Jerome and Christopher* and Perugino's *Madonna and Child* (Room 9); Correggio's *Danaë*, commissioned as 16th-century soft porn for Charles V of Spain (as told in Ovid's *Metamorphoses*, Jupiter – disguised as a 'golden shower' – attempted to seduce the reclining, half-naked maiden) and Lucas Cranach's *Venus and Cupid with Honeycomb* (Room 10); a dark, brooding *Pietà* by Raphael's follower Sodoma (Room 12); two self-portraits and two sculpted busts of Cardinal Scipione Borghese by Bernini (Room 14); Jacopo Bassano's *Last Supper* (Room 15); and Rubens' spectacular *Pietà* and *Susanna and the Elders* (Room 18). Titian's *Venus Blindfolding Cupid* and *Sacred and Profane Love*,

the work that originally put the gallery on the map, are the centrepieces of Room 20. In 1899 the Rothschilds offered to buy the latter work at a price that exceeded the estimated value of the entire gallery and all of its works put together; the offer was turned down. Other highlights of Room 20 include works by Veronese, Giorgione and Carpaccio, and *Portrait of a Man* by Antonello da Messina.

Galleria Nazionale d'Arte Moderna e Contemporanea

Viale delle Belle Arti 131 (06 3229 8301/www.gnam. arti.beniculturali.it). Bus 52, 95/tram 3, 19. **Open** 8.30am-7.30pm Tue-Sun. *Ticket office* 9am-2pm Mon-Fri. **Admission** *Gallery* €6.50; €3.25 concessions. *Gallery & exhibitions* €9; €7 concessions. *See also p97* **Pass?**. **No credit cards**. **Map** p356 A2.

Several of the villas dotted around the park are the remains of a world exposition held here in 1911, and this neo-classical palace, dedicated to 19th- and 20th-century art, is one of the most eye-pleasing. The permanent collection begins with the 19th century, when big was beautiful: an enormous statue of *Hercules* by Canova (with artfully positioned fig-leaf) dominates Room 4 of the left wing; Ettore

Ferrari's plaster model for the bronze of Giordano Bruno in Campo de' Fiori stands opposite, in Room 4 of the right wing.

In the Palizzi Room (Room 5, left wing) are smaller pieces, including romantic views of the Neapolitan hinterland and views of Rome before the dramatic changes wreaked upon the urban landscape in the late 19th century. The 20th-century component (upper right and left wings) includes works by De Chirico, Modigliani, Morandi and Marini, and a powerful altarpiece to Fascism by Gerardo Dottori. International stars include *The Three Ages* by Klimt and *The Gardener* and *Madame Ginoux* by Van Gogh. Cézanne, Braque, Rodin and Henry Moore are also represented here.

Museo Carlo Bilotti

Viale Fiorello La Guardia (06 8205 9127/www .museocarlobilotti.it). Bus 52, 53, 95, 910. **Open** 9am-7pm Tue-Sun. **Admission** €4.50; €2.50 concessions. *See also p97* **Pass?**. **No credit cards**. **Map** p356 A3.

This contemporary art museum (*see also p102* **Art in the orangery**) is housed in a palazzo that was bought by Scipione Borghese in 1616 and used as a resting place during hunts. Damaged by French cannon fire in 1849, it was then variously used as a storehouse for oranges, a religious institute and city offices. Billionaire tycoon Carlo Bilotti opened it as a museum in 2006 to house his superlative collection of modern art. The De Chirico paintings and sculptures that form the nucleus of the 22 works in the permanent collection (on the first floor) perhaps influenced Bilotti to choose Rome as the city in which to display them (De Chirico spent much of his life in Rome, and died here in 1978). Also on the first floor, an entire room is devoted to the Bilotti family: the highlights are a Larry Rivers portrait of Mr Bilotti posing before a Dubuffet canvas and a poignant 1981 Warhol portrait of Bilotti's wife and daughter, who died aged 20. A wall of photos capture the family schmoozing with various high-profile figures on the contemporary art scene. The ground floor hosts temporary exhibitions by world-renowned artists.

Museo Hendrik Christian Andersen

Via PS Mancini 20 (06 321 9089/www.gnam. arti.beniculturali.it). Metro Flaminio/bus 95, 490, 495, 628/tram 2, 19. **Open** 9am-7pm Tue-Sun. **Admission** free. **Map** p354 D2.

This offshoot of the Galleria Nazionale d'Arte Moderna (*see p101*) occupies an art nouveau villa between the river and viale Flaminia. This was the studio-home of Hendrik Christian Andersen, a Norwegian-American whose artistic ambitions were monumental but whose fans were few (with the notable exception of Henry James, who, reportedly, had his eye on the man rather than his works). Andersen favoured the bombastic homoerotic style of which Mussolini was so fond. His massive bronze and plaster figures stride manfully across the studio; more interesting, perhaps, is his megaloma-

niacal plan for a 'world city' (1913). Temporary exhibitions in the upper rooms are rather hit-and-miss, though the top-floor café's terrace (9am-4pm Mon-Fri) is a pleasant spot on a sunny day.

Museo Nazionale Etrusco di Villa Giulia

Piazzale di Villa Giulia 9 (06 322 6571). Tram 2, 3, 19. **Open** 8.30am-7.30pm (last entry 6.30pm) Tue-Sun. **Admission** €4; €2 concessions. *See also p97* **Pass?**. **No credit cards**. **Map** p354 E1.

Founded in 1889 in the splendid Villa Giulia, this collection charts the development of the sophisticated, mysterious Etruscans. The villa was originally constructed in the mid-16th century as a sumptuous summer residence for Pope Julius III; Michelangelo gave his friend Vignola a hand with the design. The rustic façade leads into an elegantly frescoed loggia. Across the courtyard, stairs go down to the nymphaeum. Restored in 2004, the sixth-century BC *Apollo of Veio*, in coloured terracotta, is in a separate room by the nymphaeum.

In the main body of the museum, a number of rooms are dedicated to objects unearthed at the

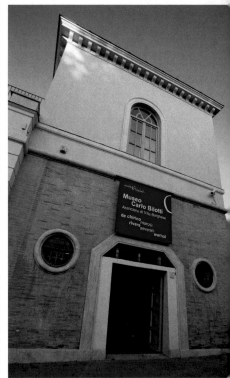

Modern masterpieces: **Museo Carlo Bilotti**.

Art in the orangery

The Museo Carlo Bilotti (*see p101*) opened in 2006, with an ebullient Italian-American perfume executive from Palm Springs as its benefactor. Something of a latter-day Scipione Borghese, Bilotti bought his first important work, a De Chirico, at age 20. He soon amassed an array of masterpieces – befriending the likes of Warhol, De Chirico and Dali in the process – and became the patron of many an up-and-coming artist.

Armed with his superlative collection, a big dream and an ego to match, in 2003 Bilotti approached Rome's mayor Walter Veltroni with the idea of creating an eponymous museum to house some of his accumulated masterpieces. Veltroni agreed, offering the 16th-century *aranciera* (orangery), smack in the middle of Villa Borghese.

The museum's opening in May 2006 was something of a coup for all concerned: it was the first time the city had been involved with a private donor on such a scale. Asked why Rome had been chosen as the object of his largesse, Bilotti was frank: in Florida, he reasoned, he would get a wall or a room; 'in Italy, I get a museum with my name on it' (and besides, Boca Raton just ain't Rome).

Just a few months after making his dream museum a reality, Carlo Bilotti died, but not before he had set in motion an ambitious new project: he enlisted Veltroni's help in finding a 'deconsecrated temple' – the long-abandoned Chapel of Divine Love on the edge of the Villa Ada park (*see p176*) – to be made over by an undisclosed contemporary artist.

Etruscan necropolis at Cerveteri (*see p305*); the centerpiece is the almost life-size sixth-century BC sarcophagus of a married couple, reclining as though at a dinner party. The Etruscan fondness for eating and drinking is apparent from the vast number of bronze cooking utensils, as well as ceramic cups and *amphorae* (often decorated with scenes from imported Greek myths). The Room of the Seven Hills (a frescoed frieze names them) contains the Castellani collection of extraordinarily delicate jewellery from the eighth century BC right up to the 19th century. Next door is the Room of Venus, with pieces unearthed at the fifth-century BC temples of Pyrgi (*see p305*). The Etruscans went well prepared to their graves, and the majority of the collection comes from excavations of tombs: hundreds of vases, pieces of furniture and models of buildings made to accompany the dead. Detailed notes in English detail the excavation sites and provide information on how gold, bronze and clay were worked. In the gardens there is a reconstruction of an Etruscan temple and a pleasant café. As this guide went to press, part of the collection (not including pieces mentioned here) was closed for restoration.

Museo Civico di Zoologia

Via U Aldrovandi 18 (06 6710 9270/www.museo dizoologia.it). Bus 217, 910/tram 3, 19. **Open** 9am-5pm Tue-Sun. **Admission** €4.50; €2.50 concessions. *See also p97* **Pass?. No credit cards**. **Map** p356 B1.
On the north-east side of the Bioparco-Zoo (*see p260*) is the Museo di Zoologia, with a room dedicated to the wetlands of Lazio and sections on animal reproduction, biodiversity and extreme habitats. A vast collection of dusty and moth-eaten stuffed animals lingers in its old wing. Access is from via Aldrovandi, or through the zoo for ticket-holders.

Via Veneto & the Quartiere Ludovisi

Despite an extensive revamp in 2006, **via Vittorio Veneto** (VEH-neto) is still struggling to live up to its *dolce vita* glory days, when Fellini made it Rome's most glamorous hangout. The street's 'restoration project' – largely financed by restaurant owners nostalgic for the days when Burton, Taylor and pals used to run up astronomical bills in their establishments – involved widening pavements, improving street lighting and giving some of the older *palazzi* a facelift… but sadly did nothing for the lack of atmosphere. The modern-day Taylors and Burtons, when they're in town, do their hell-raising elsewhere. This tree-lined slalom curve still manages to rake in the euros, however, mainly thanks to its vast luxury hotels groaning under the weight of their own chandeliers, and its cripplingly expensive, glass-enclosed pavement cafes. Aimed entirely at expense-account travellers and unwitting tourists, restaurants in the area came under scrutiny in 2006 when a spate of scams culminated in a Japanese tourist being charged €990… for a bottle of beer.

This area is known as the **Quartiere Ludovisi**, after the 17th-century Villa Ludovisi, the palace and gardens of which stood here until the 1870s. Following the Unification of Italy, the Ludovisi family, like other aristocratic landowners of the day, sold their property off to building speculators; what had once been a slope of verdant tranquillity

Sightseeing

was swiftly gobbled up by pompous Piedmontese *palazzi* (nearby Villa Borghese only narrowly escaped the same fate).

Prince Boncompagni-Ludovisi (whose surnames have been given to two local in the area) put the proceeds of the sale of his glorious estate towards building a huge palace on part of his former grounds. Crippled by running costs and the capital gains bill on the sale of his land, he was forced to sell his new abode to Margherita, widow of King Umberto I, who was to give her name to the classic pizza, as well as to this monument to the prince's lack of financial acumen. Halfway along via Veneto, Villa Margherita is now part of the massively barricaded US embassy.

As the new *palazzi* sprang up, the area began to acquire the reputation for luxury that it retained throughout the mid-20th century. Its fame in the 1950s was due mostly to the enormous American presence at Cinecittà (*see pp261-264* **Film**). Fellini's 1960 film *La dolce vita*, starring the late and much-lamented Marcello Mastroianni, consecrated the scene and coined the term 'paparazzo', the surname of a character in the film modelled on legendary photographer Tazio Secchiaroli who made his name snapping away in this glam neighbourhood.

The lower reaches of via Veneto are home to the eerie **Santa Maria della Concezione** and to Bernini's Fontana delle Api (Bee Fountain; *see also p100* **Marks men**).

Santa Maria della Concezione

Via Veneto 27 (06 487 1185). Metro Barberini/ bus 52, 62, 95, 116, 119. **Open** *Church* 7am-noon, 3-7pm daily. *Crypt* 9am-noon, 3-6pm Mon-Sat; 9am-noon, 3-7pm Sun. **Admission** *Crypt* donation expected. **Map** p357 B5.

Commonly known as *i Cappuccini* (the Capuchins) after the long-bearded, brown-clad Franciscan sub-order to which it belongs, this Baroque church has a *St Michael* (1635) by Guido Reni (first chapel on the right), which was a major hit with English Grand Tourists, and a fine *St Paul's Sight Being Restored* (1631) by Pietro da Cortona (first chapel on the left). The real draw, though, is the crypt, which holds Rome's most macabre sight: the skeletons of over 4,000 monks, meticulously dismantled and arranged in swirls, sunbursts and curlicues through four subterranean chapels. Delicate ribs hang from the ceiling in the form of chandeliers, and inverted pelvic bones make the shape of hourglasses – a reminder (as a notice states) that 'you will be what we now are'.

Piazza Sallustio & Porta Pia

East of Villa Borghese, street after street of imposing, late 19th-century *palazzi* cover what was ancient Rome's greatest garden: the Horti Sallustiani, on land that passed from Julius Caesar to the historian and politician Gaius Crispus Sallustius around 40 BC. Ruins are still visible in the hexagonal **piazza Sallustio**: you'll need a good imagination to get an idea of the lost grandeur by peering at the masonry in the hole in the middle of the piazza.

A couple of streets north-east is **Porta Pia**, its city-facing façade designed by Michelangelo for the Medici pope Pius IV in 1561. It was by this monumental entrance gate that a hole was blown on 20 September 1871, allowing Unification troops to march along what is now via XX Settembre and evict the pope from his last stronghold in the Quirinal palace (*see p23* **Eviction order**). Next to the gate is the heavily guarded British embassy. Completed in 1971, the travertine-clad structure designed by architect Sir Basil Spence (of Coventry Cathedral fame) replaced a 19th-century villa demolished after a bomb explosion in 1946. Though often bemoaned for being out of place next to the Porta Pia, it does have a towering Henry Moore sculpture in its decorative pool by way of compensation.

Extra time

● If you manage not to flinch at the prices, go for a cocktail in the spectacularly flouncy **Harry's Bar** (via Veneto 150, 06 484 643); its *dolce vita* photo gallery is a poignant reminder of via Veneto's better days.

● Ogle the cavalry (in their Armani-designed uniforms) at their **Villa Umberto** HQ, on the corner of via Raimondi and via Pinciana.

● The home of sculptor **Pietro Canonica** (viale Pietro Canonica 2, open 9am-7pm Tue-Sun, €4.50, €2.50 concessions; *see also p97* **Pass?**), tucked away in Villa Borghese, is spookily unaltered since his death in 1959. It contains 19th-century paintings and furniture, Flemish tapestries and the artist's own work.

● Shakespeare buffs should catch a play at the open-air **Silvano Toti Globe Theatre**, in Villa Borghese (largo Acqua Felix, near piazza di Siena, 06 8205 9127,www.globe theatreroma.com, open June-Sept, tickets €5.50-€18; *see also p97* **Pass?**), for the novelty value of seeing the bard performed in Italian. Opened in 2005, it's a replica of London's Globe theatre. Tickets are free on Sunday mornings.

Sightseeing

Clean water. It's the most basic human necessity. Yet one third of all poverty related deaths are caused by drinking dirty water. Saying *I'm in* means you're part of a growing movement that's fighting the injustice of poverty. Your £8 a month can help bring safe water to some of the world's poorest people. We can do this. We *can* end poverty. Are you in?

shouldn't everyone get clean water? I don't think that's too much to ask for

Let's end poverty together.
Text 'WATER' and your name to 87099 to give £8 a month.

Standard text rates apply. Registered charity No.202918

oxfam.org.uk

i'm in

Oxfam

Sarite Morales, Greenwich

The Tridente

Rome's fashionable triangle.

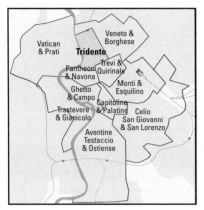

Presumably hoping to keep his favoured haunts to himself, Federico Fellini set his film *La dolce vita* on via Veneto (*see p102*), where gawpers from the provinces then flocked in droves, hoping for a glimpse of the glam and famous. The A-class hipsters, however, favoured the Tridente, the triangle enclosed by the three prongs – *vie* Ripetta (where Fellini lived), del Corso and Babuino – emanating from piazza del Popolo.

The super-smart grid of streets at the foot of the Spanish Steps was no stranger to jet-set attention: as long ago as the 18th century it had a *dolce vita* all of its own when this was the little St James's of the Grand Tourists. Thousands of English 'milords' took lodgings in piazza di Spagna, kitted themselves out in the latest local fashions and sat for portraits to show the folks back home. They used the services of a banker or agent here, availed themselves of a plausible *cicerone* to guide them through impenetrable ruins and relaxed with fellow Tourists over coffee at the (sadly long gone) fashionable Caffè degli Inglesi (with its daring interior decor by Piranesi, all pyramids, obelisks and sphinxes) on the corner where via delle Carozze meets the piazza.

Even today there are still people who visit Rome without ever straying out of the Tridente area: between one glorious fashion outlet and another, cosmopolitan shopaholics might just do a spot of sightseeing, but they are more likely to admire the vistas from a handy café or restaurant table.

Via del Babuino & piazza di Spagna

Piazza di Spagna is where everybody meets, congregating in the summer on whichever side of the grand staircase is in the shade. In spring the loafers, courting couples, exhausted tourists and those whose dates are seriously late are temporarily turfed off the steps while an army of gardeners arranges a display of azaleas.

While here, spare a thought for the coughing, consumptive 25-year-old Keats, who spent a few wretched months in the winter of 1820-1 in the Casina Rossa, now the **Keats-Shelley Memorial House** (*see p106*), at the foot of the Spanish Steps.

Though the Spanish have a magnificent embassy in the square, it's hardly fair that the area was named after them: it is the French who should be thanked for creating this sophisticated urban landscape with its grand **Spanish Steps** (*see p106*), which lead down from the French preserve of Villa Medici – the glorious Renaissance villa that gives hospitality to artistic and musical winners of the coveted annual *Prix de Rome* – and the **Trinità dei Monti** church and convent at the top. Don't be daunted by the steep climb – though one of the best-kept secrets of the area is the passenger lift, concealed on the left just inside the main entrance to the Spagna metro station. (This is also the easiest way up to the Villa Borghese.)

From the top of the steps you can get the lie of the land: just beyond the *barcaccia,* a charming fountain in the shape of a half-sunken boat, is via Condotti with its high-fashion boutiques, the Gucci and Prada emporia immediately recognisable even at this distance by the neat lines of Japanese tourists clutching lengthy shopping lists for cult-status luxury leather goods. Here too is the legendary **Café Greco** (*see p218*), where clientele included Casanova and mad King Ludwig of Bavaria. If it's tea you crave, try **Babington's** tea rooms – that other august institution, located on piazza di Spagna – which has been serving reviving beverages and English-style snacks for 110 years.

To the north-west the incongruously neo-Gothic spire of All Saints' English church (*see p333*) pokes up above the rooftops along **via del Babuino**. The origin of this oddly (and, to Roman ears, rudely) named street lies in the

Everybody meets on the **Spanish Steps**.

Spanish Steps

Metro Spagna/bus 52, 53, 61, 71, 80Exp, 85, 95, 116, 160, 850. **Map** p357 A4.
Piazza di Spagna takes its name from the Spanish Embassy to the Vatican, but is famous for the Spanish Steps (Scalinata di Trinità dei Monti), an elegant cascade down from the church of Trinità dei Monti. The steps (completed in 1725) could more accurately be called French: they were funded by French diplomat Etienne Gueffier, who felt the muddy slope leading up to the church – itself built with money from a French king – needed a revamp. At Christmas a crib is erected halfway up; in spring the steps are adorned with huge tubs of azaleas; sometimes fashion shows are held here. At the foot of the stairs is a delightful boat-shaped fountain, the *barcaccia*, designed in 1627 by Gian Lorenzo Bernini and/or his less famous father Pietro; it's ingeniously sunk below ground level to compensate for the low pressure of the delicious *acqua vergine* that feeds it.

Via del Corso & piazza del Popolo

Via del Corso is the last urban stretch of the ancient via Flaminia, which linked Rome with the north Adriatic coast. Over the past 2,000 years it has been successively a processional route for Roman legions, a country lane, a track for *carnevale* races and, from the late 1800s, a principal showcase street for the capital.

The street's liveliest period began in the mid 15th century, when Pope Paul II began to fret over the debauched goings-on at the pre-Lenten *carnevale* celebrations in Testaccio (*see p141*). He decided to move the races and processions somewhere more central, where he and his troops could keep an eye on things. The obvious spot was via Flaminia – then known simply as via Lata ('wide street') – at the end of which he built his Palazzo Venezia (*see p77*). The pope had the stretch of the street within the city walls paved (using funds from a tax on prostitutes) and renamed il Corso. For over four centuries Romans flocked there at *carnevale* time to be entertained by such edifying spectacles as races between press-ganged Jews, hunchbacks, prostitutes and horses with hot pitch squirted up their recta to make them run faster.

These grotesqueries only stopped after Italian Unification in the 1870s, when the new national government set up shop halfway along via del Corso. The cheap shops and eateries that lined the street were shut down, to be replaced by pompous neo-classical offices for banks and insurance companies. This set the tone for what remains the country's political heart: the Lower House (Camera dei deputati) is in **Palazzo di Montecitorio** (*see p109*), in the piazza of the same name, and **Palazzo Chigi**, the prime

ugly statue draped over an old drinking trough, which reminded inhabitants of a member of the monkey family – another incongruity in the street to which all Rome's most beautiful people flock for their shopping.

Parallel to via del Babuino is **via Margutta**, focus of the 1960s art scene. Federico Fellini lived here until his death in 1993. This was always an artists' quarter: models would ply for trade on the Spanish Steps. Once a year artists who still live here open their studios to the public. A collection of somewhat higher-standard modern works can be seen at the **Galleria Comunale d'Arte Moderna e Contemporanea** (*see p111* **Extra time**).

Keats-Shelley Memorial House

Piazza di Spagna 26 (06 678 4235/www.keats-shelley-house.org). Metro Spagna/bus 52, 53, 61, 71, 80Exp, 85, 95, 116, 160, 850. **Open** 9am-1pm, 3-6pm Mon-Fri; 11am-2pm, 3-6pm Sat. Closed 1wk Dec. **Admission** €3.50. **No credit cards**. **Map** p357 A4.
The house at the bottom of the Spanish Steps where the 25-year-old John Keats died of tuberculosis in 1821 is crammed with mementos. A lock of Keats' hair and his death mask, a minuscule urn holding tiny pieces of Shelley's charred skeleton, copies of documents and letters, and a massive library make this a Romantics enthusiast's paradise. Bring a box of tissues: even the hardest-hearted can be moved to tears by the sight of manuscripts written by con-sumptive poets with shaky hands. Devotees should also make the pilgrimage to the Cimitero acattolico (Protestant Cemetery; *see p142*) where both Keats and Shelley are buried. The apartment above the Keats-Shelley House can be rented for holidays (+44 (0)1628 825 925/bookings@landmarktrust.org.uk).

Obelisks

For the Egyptians, obelisks were needles that channelled the energy of the sun. For the Romans, they became both a symbol of conquest and of the Egyptian culture that was so readily embraced in *caput mundi*. After the fall of the Empire, Rome's obelisks spent centuries lying about in the mud, only to be resurrected first by urban-planner Pope Sixtus V (1585-90) to indicate key points of pilgrimage, and later by his successors. Today 13 obelisks still grace the cityscape.

Palazzo Massimo alle Terme (*see p159*): like its twin in Florence's Boboli Gardens, the obelisk in the small park in front of this palazzo dates from the reign of Rameses II and was originally poached from Heliopolis. Discovered in 1883 near Santa Maria sopra Minerva, it probably once stood in Domitian's Isaeum Campense – the temple to Isis built by the emperor – which occupied the area that today lies between the Pantheon and piazza del Collegio Romano.

Piazza della Minerva: also from the Isaeum, and now in front of the church of **Santa Maria sopra Minerva** (*see p120*), this obelisk was originally erected at Sais by the Pharaoh Apries. In 1667 Bernini mounted it atop an elephant for his patron Alexander VII.

Piazza di Montecitorio: made for King Psammetichus II, this sixth-century BC obelisk was brought back from Heliopolis by Augustus in 10 BC and set up in the *Campus martius*, where it was the gnomon for the horologium (a giant sundial). It was placed in front of **Palazzo di Montecitorio** (*see p109*) in 1792.

Piazza Navona (*see p116*): although this obelisk was custom-made in Egypt by order of Domitian, its hieroglyphs – describing the Emperor as eternal pharaoh – were cut in Rome. It stood at the Isaeum Campense and was later erected at the Circus of Maxentius, where it remained until being relocated to piazza Navona in 1651 by Innocent X.

Piazza del Popolo (*see p109*): brought to Rome in 10 BC by Augustus, who placed it in the centre of the Circus Maximus, this obelisk was first erected by Rameses II at Heliopolis. It was later found in three pieces, which were reassembled as the focal point of Rome's northern gateway in 1589 by Sixtus V.

Piazza del Quirinale (*see p93*) and **Piazza dell'Esquilino** (map p357 D6): after visiting Alexandria, Augustus decided to emulate Alexander the Great by erecting two obelisks at

the entrance to his mausoleum. One of them is now in piazza del Quirinale, where it was erected by Pius VI in 1786, two centuries after obelisk-mad Sixtus V placed its twin in piazza dell'Esquilino (behind Santa Maria Maggiore).

Piazza della Rotonda: the obelisk in front of the Pantheon (*see p119*) is dedicated to Rameses the Great and dates from the 14th century BC. It originally stood before the temple of Ra at Heliopolis; Domitian moved it to the Isaeum in around AD 80. It was placed atop the fountain here in 1711.

Piazza San Pietro (*see p164*): this obelisk was erected in Alexandria by the Romans in the first century BC and dedicated to Augustus. A vast ship was required to move it to Rome; having completed its mission, the ship was then sunk to form a new jetty at Ostia (*see p300*). Caligula placed the obelisk in the Circus he had built in the Vatican field, where it stayed until Sixtus V ordered Domenico Fontana to shift it (with the help of 8,000 men) to its current spot in 1586.

Piazza Trinità dei Monti (*see p105*): the hieroglyphs on this obelisk are Roman copies of those inscribed on the one in piazza del Popolo. Erected at its current site in 1789 by Pius VI, it originally stood in the splendid Horti Sallustiani (Gardens of Sallust; *see p103*).

San Giovanni in Laterano (*see p150*): the largest obelisk in the world was erected by Thutmose III in the 15th century BC in front of the Temple of Ammon at Thebes. Constantine brought it down the Nile to Alexandria; later (in AD 357), Constantius transported it to Rome. The last of the obelisks to be brought to the city, it was set up on the *spina* of Circus Maximus. In 1587 it was shifted to San Giovanni in Laterano by Sixtus V.

Viale dell'Obelisco: inside the Villa Borghese (*see p95*) is a monolith brought to Rome by Egypto-maniac Hadrian. Dedicated to the Emperor's dead lover Antinous, it identifies him with Osiris and may have been erected on the site of Antinous' burial. Discovered near Santa Croce in Gerusalemme (*see p150*) in the 16th century, it was eventually erected here for Pius VII in 1822.

Villa Celimontana (*see p149*): this obelisk was presented in 1582 by the Senate to Ciriaco Mattei, who placed it in his villa. Previously it had been at the foot of the steps leading to Santa Maria in Aracoeli (*see p79*), but probably had been moved there from the Isaeum.

Sightseeing

YOU KNOW
WHERE TO GO.

ROME
VIA VITTORIO VENETO 62A • +39-06-4203051

FREE COLLECTIBLE SOUVENIR FOR
ALL TIME OUT ROME GUIDE FRIENDS,
PARTNERS AND READERS WITH
A MINIMUM BILL OF 25 EUROS AT HRC ROME.

minister's office, is next door in piazza Colonna, so named for the magnificent second-century AD **colonna di Marco Aurelio** (column of Marcus Aurelius; *see below*) that graces it. Legends of Machiavellian wheeling and dealing cling to every restaurant and bar around the parliament building.

North from Palazzo Chigi, imposing edifices such as **Palazzo Ruspoli** (*see below*) give way to lower-end clothing outlets, which attract a seething mass of suburban teenagers at the weekend.

The pedestrianised **piazza San Lorenzo in Lucina**, with the church of the same name (*see p109*), is a welcome retreat from the fumes and crowds in search of a bargain.

Well hidden among the retail crush is the **Casa di Goethe** (*see p111* **Extra time**), the house where the German poet stayed during a visit to the Eternal City in 1786. Beyond, the symmetrically elegant **piazza del Popolo** (*see below*) – once the papacy's favourite place for executions – is graced by the Caravaggio-packed church of **Santa Maria del Popolo** (*see p110*). The piazza has been gloriously restored and is virtually traffic-free.

Colonna di Marco Aurelio (Column of Marcus Aurelius)

Piazza Colonna. Bus 52, 53, 61, 63, 71, 80Exp, 85, 95, 116, 119, 160, 850. **Map** p355 E5.

The 30m (100ft) column of Marcus Aurelius was built between AD 180 and 196 to commemorate the victories on the battlefield of that most intellectual of Roman emperors. Author of the *Meditations*, he died while campaigning in 180. The reliefs on the column, modelled on the earlier ones on Trajan's column (*see p81*) in the Imperial Fora, are vivid illustrations of Roman army life. In 1589 a statue of St Paul replaced that of Marcus Aurelius on top of the column.

Palazzo di Montecitorio

Piazza di Montecitorio (06 67 601/http://english.camera.it). Bus 52, 53, 61, 63, 71, 80Exp, 85, 95, 116, 119, 160, 850. **Open** 10am-5pm 1st Sun of mth. **Admission** free. **Map** p355 E5.

Since 1871 this has been the Lower House of Italy's parliament, which is why police and barricades sometimes prevent you from getting near its elegantly curving façade. (It's best to check the website: open days can be cancelled for important parliamentary events.) Designed by Bernini in 1650 for Pope Innocent X, much of the building has been greatly altered, but the clock tower, columns and window sills of rough-hewn stone are his originals. In piazza di Montecitorio stands the tenth-century BC obelisk of Psammeticus. It was brought from Heliopolis by Augustus to act as the gnomon (projecting piece) for the emperor's great sundial. As part of a recent refurbishment of the square, a new sundial of sorts was set into the cobblestones.

Palazzo Ruspoli-Fondazione Memmo

Via del Corso 418 (06 6830 7344/www.fondazione memmo.it). Bus 52, 53, 61, 63, 71, 80Exp, 85, 95, 116, 119, 160, 850. **Open** times vary. **Admission** varies with exhibition. **No credit cards. Map** p355 E4.

This palace of one of Rome's old noble families is today used for touring exhibitions of photography, art, archaeology and history. It opens late at least one night a week. The basement rooms often host photo exhibitions, and admission is sometimes free.

Piazza del Popolo

Metro Flaminio/bus 88, 95, 117, 119, 490, 491, 495/tram 2. **Map** p354 D2.

For centuries, piazza del Popolo was the first glimpse most travellers got of Rome, for it lies at the end of the ancient via Flaminia and directly inside the city's northern gate, the Porta del Popolo. If Grand Tourists arrived during *carnevale* time, they were likely to witness condemned criminals being tortured here for the edification and/or entertainment of the populace. The piazza was given its present oval form by Rome's leading neo-classical architect, Giuseppe Valadier, in the early 19th century; the obelisk in the centre was brought from Egypt by Augustus and stood in the Circo Massimo until 1589, when it was moved to its present site by Pope Sixtus V. It appears to stand at the apex of a perfect triangle formed by via Ripetta, via del Corso and via del Babuino, although this is an illusion. The churches on either side of via del Corso – Santa Maria dei Miracoli and Santa Maria di Monte Santo – look like twins, but are actually different sizes. Carlo Rainaldi, who designed them in the 1660s, made them and the angles of the adjacent streets appear symmetrical by giving one an oval dome and the other a round one. The immense Porta del Popolo gate was given a facelift by Bernini in 1655 to welcome Sweden's Queen Christina, who had shocked her subjects by abdicating her throne to convert to Catholicism. The plaque wishing *felice fausto ingressui* ('a happy and blessed arrival') was addressed to the Church's illustrious new signing. The piazza's greatest monument is the church of Santa Maria del Popolo (*see p110*), and the piazza contains those eternally fashionable meeting points: cafés Rosati and Canova (for both, *see p218*).

San Lorenzo in Lucina

Piazza San Lorenzo in Lucina 16A (06 687 1494). Bus 52, 53, 61, 63, 71, 80Exp, 85, 95, 116, 119, 160, 850. **Open** *Church* 8am-8pm daily. *Roman remains* guided tour 4.30pm 1st Sat of mth. **Admission** *Roman remains* €2. **No credit cards. Map** p355 E4.

This 12th-century church was built on the site of a titulus, which in turn is believed to stand on the site of an ancient well sacred to Juno. The church's exterior incorporates Roman columns, while the 17th-century interior contains Bernini portrait busts in the Fonseca Chapel, a kitsch 17th-century *Crucifixion* by Guido Reni and a monument to

Via Margutta. See p106.

a pair of scales. The chapel was completed by Bernini, who, on the orders of Agostino's descendant Pope Alexander VII, added the statues of Daniel and Habakkuk. The church's most-gawped-at possessions, however, are the two masterpieces by Caravaggio to the left of the main altar, in the Cerasi Chapel. On a vast scale, and suffused with lashings of the master's particular light, they show the martyrdom of St Peter and the conversion of St Paul. To the left of the main door is a memorial to 17th-century notable GB Gisleni: grisly skeletons, chrysalids and butterflies remind us of our brief passage through this life before we exit the other end.

Via Ripetta

Halfway down the third arm of the Tridente, **via Ripetta**, is stark piazza Augusto Imperatore, built by Mussolini around the rather neglected **Mausoleo di Augusto** (*see below*) – the funeral mound of the Emperor Augustus – with the intention of having himself buried there with the Caesars. Above is the Ara Pacis Augustae, erected by Augustus to celebrate peace after his conquest of Gaul and Spain, and recently provided with a new showcase – the **Museo dell'Ara Pacis** (*see p111*), designed by American architect Richard Meier. The piazza where these two monuments stand will be made over and pedestrianised in the next few years, while the riverside road beyond the Ara Pacis is destined to be rerouted underground, to make an esplanade from the Ara Pacis across to the river bank.

French artist Nicolas Poussin, who died in Rome in 1665. In the first chapel on the right is a grill, reputed to be the one on which the martyr St Lawrence was roasted to death.

Santa Maria del Popolo

Piazza del Popolo 12 (06 361 0836). Metro Flaminio/bus 88, 95, 117, 119, 490, 491, 495/ tram 2. **Open** 7am-noon, 4-7pm Mon-Sat; 7.30am-1.45pm, 4.30-7.30pm Sun. **Map** p354 D2.
According to legend, Santa Maria del Popolo occupies the site of a garden in which hated Emperor Nero was buried. The site was still believed to be haunted by demons 1,000 years later; in 1099 Pope Paschal II built a chapel there to dispel them. Nearly four centuries later, beginning in 1472, Pope Sixtus IV rebuilt the chapel as a church, financing it by taxing foreign churches and selling ecclesiastical jobs.

In the apse are, unusually for Rome, stained-glass windows, a northern touch created by French artist Guillaume de Marcillat in 1509. The apse itself was designed by Bramante, while the choir ceiling and first and third chapels in the right aisle were frescoed by Pinturicchio, the favourite artist of the Borgias. In Pinturicchio's exquisite works (1508-10), the Virgin and a host of saints keep company with some very pre-Christian sibyls. Most intriguing is the Chigi Chapel, designed by Raphael for wealthy banker Agostino Chigi. The mosaics in the dome depict God creating the sun and the seven planets, and Agostino's personal horoscope: with binoculars you can just about make out a crab, a bull, a lion and

South of the square stand two fine churches: **San Girolamo degli Illirici**, serving Rome's Croatian community, and **San Rocco**, built for local innkeepers and Tiber boatmen by Alexander VI (1492-1503). Heading back towards via del Corso, the giant, curving walls of the **Palazzo Borghese** come into view; acquired in 1506 by Camillo Borghese, the future Pope Paul V, it was later the home of Napoleon's sister Pauline.

Mausoleo di Augusto (Mausoleum of Augustus)

Piazza Augusto Imperatore/via Ripetta. Bus 30Exp, 70, 81, 87, 186, 492, 628, 913. Not open to the public. **Map** p355 D3.
It's hard to believe that this forlorn-looking brick cylinder was one of the most important monuments of ancient Rome. It was originally covered with marble pillars and statues, all of which have long since been looted. Two obelisks that stood either side of the main entrance are now in the piazza del Quirinale and piazza dell'Esquilino. The mausoleum was built in honour of Augustus, who had brought peace to the city and its Empire, and was begun in 28 BC. The first person buried here was Augustus' nephew, favourite son-in-law and heir apparent, Marcellus.

Augustus himself was laid to rest in the central chamber in AD 14, and many more emperors went on to join him. In the Middle Ages the mausoleum was used as a fortress; in the Renaissance it housed gardens. Mussolini had it restored, reportedly because he thought it a fitting place for his own illustrious corpse. He also planted the cedars and built the square that now surrounds the tomb.

Museo dell'Ara Pacis

Via Ripetta/lungotevere in Augusta (06 6710 6756/ 06 3600 4399/fax 06 3600 3471/www.arapacis.it). Bus 30Exp, 70, 81, 87, 186, 492, 628, 913. **Open** 9am-7pm (last entry 6pm) Tue-Sun. **Admission** €6.50, €3 concessions. **Map** p355 D3.

Whatever you make of its new container (*see p29* **Peace in our time**), it's a relief that Augustus' great monument has finally been liberated after years hidden beneath scaffolding: its Luna marble glows in architect Richard Meier's luminous space.

Outside, the flank of the building towards piazza Augusto Imperatore has been carved with the *Res Gestae*, Augustus' testament to his 'things done'.

Inaugurated in 9 BC, the altar of Augustan peace celebrated the end of the civil war and strife that had characterised the last years of the Republic, and the wealth and security brought by Augustus' victories. Originally located a few hundred metres away (off via in Lucina, behind the church of San Lorenzo in Lucina; *see p109*), the *ara* was designed to overlook the urban stretch of via Flaminia (now via del Corso) by which Augustus had re-entered the city after three years' absence in Spain and Gaul. The altar as we see it now was reconstructed by the Fascists in the 1930s, after major excavations under the palazzo that had been built over the altar – its position known from fragments discovered during building work in the 16th century – and an equally major trawl through the world's museums looking for missing bits.

Extra time

● A whole dynasty of sculptors worked in the **Museo-Atelier Canova-Tadolini** at via del Babuino 150. The studio, now an extraordinary café (*see p218*), originally belonged to 18th-century sculptor Antonio Canova; he bequeathed it (together with his sketches, models and tools) to his student and assistant Adamo Tadolini, from whom it passed to two more generations of Tadolini sculptors. You can take tea or coffee here, and sample the chocolate gateau, comforted by the sight of those perfect forms preferred by the genius who created the *Three Graces*.
● After visiting his studio museum (*see above*), pay further respects to neo-classical sculptor Antonio Canova by walking past the exterior of his fragment-encrusted house in the nearby street that bears his name. The great man's works are sadly out of fashion, but surely he's overdue for reappraisal?
● Famed for his bleakly metaphysical paintings, De Chirico is celebrated at the **Casa-Museo Giorgio De Chirico** (piazza di Spagna 31, www.fondazionedechirico.it). Here you can nose around his attic-studio – complete with the artist's last colours dried on to palettes and brushes, favourite reading material open on his bedside table and crowded on to library shelves, and well-worn props (including some frightful plastic fruit).
● After the seven veils business, Salome convinced King Herod to cut off John the Baptist's head and present it to her on a silver tray. By tortuous routes the relic ended up in a side chapel of **San Silvestro** in piazza

San Silvestro, where the blackened skull is still on display to this day.
● The Lombard community in Rome built the vast church of **San Carlo** (via del Corso 437) to celebrate the canonisation of Milanese archbishop Carlo Borromeo in 1610. Newly and magnificently restored, the church offers Romans a reminder of the wealth and power of Italy's rival capital.
● Gian Lorenzo Bernini lived in a fine house (now Palazzo Bernini, with commemorative plaque) in via della Mercede. From out of his window he saw – and had a hand in rebuilding – **Sant'Andrea delle Fratte** (via Sant'Andrea delle Fratte 1), the church of the Scots in Rome until 1585. Inside, in front of the main altar, are two stunning marble angels carved by the great man.
● The German poet Johann Wolfgang von Goethe, who breezed into town from Weimar in 1786, had a jolly time in the house on via del Corso that he shared with the painter Hans Tischbein. The **Casa di Goethe** (via del Corso 18, www.casadigoethe.it) preserves many of his diaries and letters, and hosts concerts, films and cultural events.
● The **Galleria Comunale d'Arte Moderna e Contemporanea** (via F Crispi 24, 06 474 2848) was always a stop-gap, where some of the city's modern art collection was shown in cramped quarters before the restoration and opening of MACRO (*see p176*). A fairly minor collection of early 20th-century works was left here when the more exciting stuff found its way to MACRO.

The Pantheon & Piazza Navona

Rome's historic centre is packed with architectural gems, handsomely displayed in obelisk-punctuated *piazze* or tucked away down narrow alleys.

Much of what is now Rome's *centro storico* flooded regularly and therefore was not properly settled in antiquity; instead it was used as a vast training ground – the *Campus martius* or Field of Mars (Mars was the god of war) – for the Roman military machine. It was not until the third century AD that the Aurelian Wall encompassed the area, which by then was fitted out with military R&R facilities such as marbled bathhouses, theatres, grand temples like the Pantheon (*see p119*) and a 30,000-seat athletics stadium where track-shaped piazza Navona (*see p116*) stands today.

Water, and the lack of it, was a key factor in the fifth-century decline and fall of the city. Barbarians cut Rome's aqueducts, driving the remaining population of a fatally wounded city down towards its alternate water supply, the filthy Tiber. The *Campo marzio* beside the river became prime construction territory. Every medieval wall here tells a tale of primitive recycling: grander *palazzi* were built using dressed stone pinched from disused military facilities; humbler souls blithely constructed their own little houses among the ruins.

After Unification in the 1870s, the flooding problem was dealt with once and for all by the construction of the massive *banchine* along the

river banks. Practical as they were, these embankments cut the Romans off from their river and utterly changed the topography. To see to what extent, take a look at the Roman views churned out for Grand Tourists (the Museo di Roma, *see p113*, displays some charming examples): cows graze in water meadows and rowing boats are pulled up in front of houses.

Even now the river ebbs away to a trickle over the long, hot summer, leaving reed banks and old bits of masonry sticking out of the mud; but after a few days of Rome's often monsoon-like rain, or when winter snow melts high in the mountains of Tuscany where the Tiber begins – then the brown swirl races under bridges, rises high over tow paths, and creeps up, and up, the immense walls.

Today, this section of the *centro storico* retains its historical mix of the very grand and the very humble: mink-coated *contessas* mingle with wrinkled pensioners, craftsmen and tradesmen. There's a good chance that they may all live, or make a living, in parts of the same palazzo. It's a chic area after dark, with smart restaurants and hip bars. Next morning, however, it's back to business, with wheeling and dealing taking place against a stunning backdrop.

West of piazza Navona

After arriving at the northern entrance to the city at piazza del Popolo (*see p109*), pilgrims were funnelled past a succession of rosary-makers (*coronari*) – the hard-selling souvenir touts along **via de' Coronari** – who vied to empty the travellers' pockets before they reached St Peter's. The faithful also paid a swingeing toll to cross the Castel Sant'Angelo bridge to reach their final destination.

Nowadays, in the golden triangle that extends south from via de' Coronari's southern tip as far as via del Governo Vecchio, taking in via della Pace and piazza del Fico, humanity flows along in a continuously moving wave. Here, VIPs and movie stars parade their assets (but never before midnight) in *dolce vita*-style bars before a backdrop of dazzling Renaissance beauty, including the stunning façade of **Santa Maria della Pace** (*see p115*).

At the south-western tip of piazza Navona, in piazza Pasquino, a severely truncated classical statue nestling against the back wall of Palazzo Braschi – now home to the **Museo di Roma** (*see p113*) – is the most famous of Rome's 'talking' statues; in the days when Vatican walls had ears and you could lose your head for an offhand irreverent remark, Romans let off steam by pinning scurrilous verse to sculptures. Rumour had it that Pasquino (after whom the piece was named in 1501) was a tailor to the Vatican and that much of papal Rome's gossip emanated from his nearby shop. The cutting witticisms came to be known as *pasquinate* (pasquinades). The statue is still in use: a certain media magnate and ex-prime minister features in much of the doggerel.

Nearby, **corso Vittorio Emanuele II** (known simply as corso Vittorio) shoots north-west towards the river. When it was hacked through the medieval area after Unification in the 1870s, only the most grandiose of homes – like **Palazzo Massimo alle Colonne** (*see p115*) and Palazzo Braschi – were spared. Traffic can be heavier at three in the morning than three in the afternoon; but get here too late and you'll miss the Rubens altarpieces in the magnificent **Chiesa Nuova** (*see below*).

The Ludovisi throne in **Palazzo Altemps**. See p115.

Chiesa Nuova (Santa Maria in Vallicella)

Piazza della Chiesa Nuova (06 687 5289/www.chiesa nuova.net). Bus 30Exp, 40Exp, 46, 62, 63, 64, 70, 81, 116, 492, 628, 630, 780, 916. **Open** *Apr-Oct* 8am-1pm, 4.30-7.30pm daily. *Nov-Mar* 8am-1pm, 4-7.30pm daily. **Map** p355 C5.

Filippo Neri (1515-95) was a wealthy Florentine who abandoned the cut and thrust of the business world to live and work among the poor in Rome. He experienced an 'ecstasy' of divine love at the Catacombs of San Sebastiano (*see p173*) in 1544, after which he founded the Oratorian order. In 1575 work began on the order's headquarters, the Chiesa Nuova, on the site of Santa Maria in Vallicella (donated by Gregory XIII). Neri wanted a large, simple building; the plain walls were covered with exuberant frescoes and multicoloured marbles only after his death. Pietro da Cortona painted *Neri's Vision of the Virgin* (1665) in the vault, the *Trinity in Glory* (1647) in the cupola and the *Assumption of the Virgin* (1650) in the apse. The *Virgin and Child*, over the altar, and saints Gregory and Domitilla, to the left and right, are by Rubens (1607-08). Neri was canonised in 1622, and his body lies in an ornately decorated chapel to the left of the main altar. His rooms are open to all on 26 May (his feast day) – though you can also get in on Tuesday, Thursday and Saturday between 10am and noon by booking a 30-minute guided tour (06 6880 4695). Singing was an important part of Oratorian worship, and oratory as a musical form developed out of the order's services. Next to the church, Borromini designed the brick Oratorio dei Filippini (1637-52).

Museo di Roma

Palazzo Braschi, piazza San Pantaleo 10 (06 6710 8346/www.museodiroma.comune.roma.it). Bus 30Exp, 40Exp, 46, 62, 63, 64, 70, 81, 116, 492, 628, 630, 780, 916. **Open** 9am-7pm (last entry 6pm) Tue-Sun. **Admission** €6.50; €3 concessions. *Special exhibitions* €2.50 extra. S*ee also p72* **Tickets. No credit cards. Map** p355 D6.

A rotating collection displayed over two floors recounts the evolution of the Eternal City from the Middle Ages to the early 20th century. Paintings and drawings include portraits of Roman movers and shakers, and views of what the city looked like before 17th- and 19th-century building projects, such as the *banchine* flood walls along the Tiber, dramatically changed it. Sculpture, clothing, furniture and photographs help to put the city's monuments in a human context, and oddities like the Braschi family sedan chair (used by Pius VI) and the papal railway carriage (used by more recent pontiffs) round out the collection. The palazzo was built by Luigi Braschi (nephew of 18th-century Pope Pius VI) in one of the last great flurries of papal nepotism. Sold to the Italian state in 1871 and intended to house the Interior Ministry, the palazzo later became the Fascist party HQ. The bookshop is well stocked, and the reading room has a selection of Rome-oriented reference books (in Italian).

Sightseeing

Time Out
Travel Guides

Italy

Available at all good bookshops
and at timeout.com/shop

PHOTO CREDIT: JONATHAN PERUGIA

Time Out
Guides

Palazzo Massimo alle Colonne

Corso Vittorio Emanuele 141 (06 6880 1545).
Bus 30Exp, 40Exp, 46, 62, 63, 64, 70, 81, 116,
492, 628, 630, 780, 916. **Open** (16 Mar only)
8am-1pm. **Map** p355 C6.

The aristocratic Massimo family claims to trace
their line back to ancient times. After their palace
was destroyed during the Sack of Rome in 1527 (*see*
p21 **The sack**), this replacement was designed by
Baldassare Peruzzi (1532-36). The curved façade
incorporates a portico and follows the plan of the
stands in Domitian's Odeon, which was closely
linked to the same emperor's stadium – where
piazza Navona now stands. The private church
(church, mind you, not chapel: this is the only family
church in Rome) has been open to the public on 16
March ever since 1583, when a young Massimo was
supposedly raised from the dead by San Filippo Neri
(*see p113* Chiesa Nuova). Behind the palace, the
piazza de' Massimi is dominated by an ancient
column from the Odeon, a small theatre for poetry,
music and oratory used at the time of Emperor
Domitian's games.

Santa Maria della Pace

Vicolo del Arco della Pace 5 (06 686 1156). Bus
30Exp, 40Exp, 46, 62, 63, 64, 70, 81, 116, 492,
628, 630, 780, 916. **Open** 10am-noon, 4-6pm
Mon-Sat; 10am-noon Sun. **Map** p355 C5.
Note: opening hours depend on the presence of the
custodian, but the church is always open for mass
on Saturday from 4.30pm to 6pm.

Built in 1482 for Pope Sixtus IV, Santa Maria della
Pace was given its theatrical Baroque façade by
Pietro da Cortona in 1656. The church's most famous
artwork is just inside the door: Raphael's *Sibyls*,
painted in 1514 for Agostino Chigi, the playboy
banker and first owner of the Villa Farnesina (*see*
p136). Even if the church is closed, you can visit the
beautifully harmonious cloister by Bramante, his
first work after arriving in Rome in the early 16th
century. Paying exhibitions are often held here (*see*
p120 **Extra time**), but no ticket is required to see
the cloister itself. Walk in and climb to the upper
level (where there's a pleasant bar, and a bookshop
offering a tantalising glimpse of Raphael's *Sibyls*).

Piazza Navona & east

Piazza Navona (*see p116*) was the great
theatre of Baroque Rome: at times it would be
flooded in order to amuse the aristocracy with
mock naval battles. Its graceful sweep – with
Bernini's fountains, Borromini's church of
Sant'Agnese in Agone (*see p116*) and
picturesque pavement cafés – is now frequented
by more prosaic denizens, from tarot-readers,
caricaturists, buskers and suburban smoothies
to tourists, nuns and businessmen.

Just north of piazza Navona are **Palazzo
Altemps** (*see below*), with its spectacular
collection of antique statuary; **Sant'Agostino**

(*see p117*), with its Caravaggio masterpiece;
and the **Museo Napoleonico** (*see p120*
Extra time). Due east from the piazza are
the Italian Senate, **Palazzo Madama** (*see*
below); the church of **San Luigi dei Francesi**
(*see p116*), with yet more Caravaggios; and
Borromini's breath-taking **Sant'Ivo alla
Sapienza** (*see p118*).

Palazzo Altemps

Piazza Sant'Apollinare 46 (06 683 3759). Bus
30Exp, 40Exp, 46, 70, 81, 87, 116, 492, 628.
Open 9am-7.45pm (last entry 6pm) Tue-Sun.
Admission €7; €3 concessions; *see also p72*
Tickets. **No credit cards**. **Map** p355 D5.
The 15th- to 16th-century Palazzo Altemps has been
beautifully restored to house part of the state-owned
Museo Nazionale Romano stock of Roman treasures
(the rest is spread between the Palazzo Massimo alle
Terme and the Terme di Diocleziano; *see p159* and
p161). Here, in perfectly lit salons, loggias and court-
yards, you can admire gems of classical statuary
from the formerly private Boncompagni-Ludovisi,
Altemps and Mattei collections.

The Ludovisis were big on 'fixing' statues broken
over the ages or which simply didn't appeal to the
tastes of the day. In Room 9, for example, a stately
Athena with Serpent was revamped in the 17th
century by Alessandro Algardi, who also 'improved'
the *Hermes Loghios* in Room 19 upstairs. In Room
20, the former dining room with pretty 15th-
century frescoes on foody themes, is an *Ares*
touched up by Bernini. Room 21 has the *Ludovisi
Throne*, the museum's greatest treasure… or its
greatest hoax, if you subscribe to the theory of the
late, great art historian and polemicist Federico Zeri.
(On what may – or, then again, may not – be a fifth-
century BC work from Magna Grecia, Aphrodite is
being delicately and modestly lifted out of the sea
spray from which she was born; on one side of her
is a serious lady burning incense, and on the other
is a naked one playing the flute.) In Room 26, a
Roman copy of a Greek *Gaul's Suicide* was
commissioned, recent research suggests, by Julius
Caesar. Also here is the Ludovisi sarcophagus,
which bears some action-packed high reliefs of
Roman soldiers trouncing barbarians. **Photo** p113.

Palazzo Madama

Corso Rinascimento (06 67 061/www.senato.it).
Bus 30Exp, 70, 81, 87, 116, 204, 280, 492, 628.
Open *Guided tours only* (in Italian) 10am-6pm 1st
Sat of mth. **Admission** free. **Map** p355 D5.
Home to the Italian Senate since 1871, this palazzo
was built by the Medici family in the 16th century
as their Rome residence. Its rather twee façade, with
a frieze of cherubs and bunches of fruit, was added
a hundred years later. The 'Madama' of its name
refers to Margaret of Parma (1522-86), the illegitimate daughter of Emperor Charles V, who lived here
in the 1560s before moving to the Netherlands,
where she instigated some of the bloodiest excesses
of the religious wars.

Bernini's abstinent elephant. *See p119.*

Piazza Navona

Bus 30Exp, 40Exp, 46, 62, 63, 64, 70, 81, 87, 116, 492, 628, 630, 780, 916. **Map** p355 D5.

This tremendous theatrical space, centred on the gleaming marble composition of Bernini's Fontana dei Quattro Fiumi (Fountain of the Four Rivers), is the hub of the *centro storico*. The piazza owes its shape to an ancient athletics stadium, built in AD 86 by Emperor Domitian, which was the scene of sporting events, and at least one martyrdom. Just north of the piazza, at piazza di Tor Sanguigna 16, you can still see remains of the original arena, sunk below street level. These remains are partially visible from the street; they can also be visited on guided tours on Saturdays and Sundays (10am-1pm; phone 06 6710 3819 for bookings and information).

The piazza acquired its current form in the mid-17th century under Pope Innocent X of the Pamphili family (*see p117* **The two-palace pope**). Its western side is dominated by Borromini's façade for the church of Sant'Agnese in Agone (*see below*) and the adjacent Palazzo Pamphili (now the Brazilian embassy), built in 1644-50. The central fountain, finished in 1651, is one of the most extravagant masterpieces designed – though only partly sculpted – by Bernini. Its main figures represent the longest rivers of the four continents known at the time; the Ganges of Asia, Nile of Africa, Danube of Europe and Plata of the Americas, surrounded by geographically appropriate flora and fauna. The

figure of the Nile is veiled, because its source was unknown. For centuries, the story went that Bernini designed it that way to show the river god recoiling in horror from the façade of Sant'Agnese, designed by his arch-rival Borromini; in fact, the church was built after the fountain was finished. The obelisk at the fountain's centre, moved here from the Circus of Maxentius on the Appian Way, was carved in Egypt under the orders of Domitian (the hieroglyphics are a Roman addition describing him as 'eternal pharaoh'). The less spectacular Fontana del Moro is at the southern end of the piazza. The central figure of the Moor was designed by Bernini in 1653, and executed by Antonio Mari.

San Luigi dei Francesi

Piazza San Luigi dei Francesi (06 688 271/www. saintlouis-rome.org). Bus 30Exp, 70, 81, 87, 116, 204, 280, 492, 628. **Open** 8.30am-12.30pm, 3.30-7pm Mon-Wed, Fri-Sun; 8.30am-12.30pm Thur. **Map** p355 D6.

Completed in 1589, San Luigi (St Louis) is the church of Rome's French community. Most visitors ignore the gaudily lavish interior, and make a beeline for Caravaggio's spectacular scenes from the life of St Matthew in the fifth chapel on the left. Painted in 1600-02, they depict Christ singling out a very reluctant Matthew (left), Matthew being dragged to his execution (right) and an angel briefing the evangelist about what he should write in his gospel (over the altar). Don't let Caravaggio's brooding brilliance and dramatic effects of light and shade blind you to the lovely frescoes of scenes from the life of St Cecilia by Domenichino (1615-17), which are in the second chapel on the right. Take a few coins for instant meter-operated illumination.

Sant'Agnese in Agone

Piazza Navona/via Santa Maria dell'Anima 30A (06 6819 2134/www.santagneseinagone.org). Bus 30Exp, 40Exp, 46, 62, 63, 64, 70, 81, 87, 116, 492, 628, 630, 780, 916. **Open** 9am-noon, 4-7pm Tue-Sat; 10am-1.30pm, 4-8pm Sun. **Map** p355 D5.

Legend says that pubescent Agnes was cast naked into the stadium of Domitian around AD 304 when she refused to renounce Christ and marry some powerful local buck (possibly Romulus, the son of Emperor Maxentius), but her hair grew miraculously to save her from embarrassment. She was condemned to burn but when the fire refused to catch light, her pagan persecutors chopped her head off, supposedly on the exact spot where this church now stands. Carlo and Girolamo Rainaldi began the church for Pope Innocent X in 1652; after they quarrelled with the pope, Borromini was appointed in their place. He revised the design considerably, adding the splendidly fluid concave façade. The trompe l'oeil side chapels contain statues of St Agnes and another victim of a botched martyrdom, St Sebastian. The doorway in the chapel to the left of the high altar contains a reliquary with Agnes's implausibly small skull. Around the church are reliefs with cherubs holding symbols associated with the martyrdom, including the lamb most commonly used to represent her. Admire Borromini's sacristy during a Sunday early-evening concert.

Sant'Agostino

Piazza Sant'Agostino (06 6880 1962). Bus 30Exp, 70, 81, 87, 116, 204, 280, 492, 628. **Open** 7.45am-noon, 4-7.30pm daily. **Map** p355 D5.

Built over a ninth-century church that marked the burial place of St Monica, St Augustine's mother, the 15th-century church of Sant'Agostino has one of the earliest Renaissance façades in Rome, fashioned out of travertine filched from the Colosseum. Inside, the third column on the left bears a fresco of Isaiah by Raphael from 1512 (when its commissioner complained that the artist had charged him too much for the work, Michelangelo is said to have snapped: 'the knee alone is worth that'). Immediately below is a beautiful sculpture of Mary, her mother Anne and the Christ-child by Andrea Sansovino (also 1512). In the first chapel on the left is Caravaggio's depiction of the grubbiest, most threadbare pilgrims ever to present themselves at the feet of the startlingly beautiful *Madonna of the Pilgrims* (1604). So dirty were

The two-palace pope

If you look up and see a heraldic crest featuring a dove with an olive branch in its beak, the chances are you are standing in front of one of the many palaces and churches built by the powerful Pamphili family. The Pamphili fiefdom centred on piazza Navona, where the aristocratic family transformed a row of modest houses beside the ancient Roman racetrack into increasingly noble premises.

What is now the magnificent quarters of the Brazilian embassy was the result of a massive rebuild after the family finally got its pope – Giambattista Pamphili became Innocent X in 1644. The **Palazzo Pamphili** (*pictured right*) has three courtyards, dozens of chandelier-lit, frescoed rooms that twinkle at night when the Brazilians are holding grand receptions, and a liberal spattering of family doves and twigs.

To tidy things up, Pope Innocent asked Bernini, virtuoso sculptor and an architect of St Peter's, to landscape the piazza for him (and stick up a spare obelisk that were lying around Rome); the result was the staggeringly theatrical Fountain of the Four Rivers.

With the pope busy at the Vatican or in the Quirinal palace (*see p93*), Donna Olimpia Maidalchini – Innocent's widowed, and extremely wealthy, sister-in-law – became chatelaine of the vast palace. The Romans couldn't stand her, and it wasn't long before the city seethed with rumours about impropriety, and worse; they particularly despised her meanness. Unquestionably Donna Olimpia was an interfering, overbearing old busybody, with disproportionate influence on both *urbi et orbi*. Sculptor Francesco Algardi captured the domineering nature of the old bat in his masterly marble bust, complete with billowing marble veil, in the family's spectacular art collection across at the other main Pamphili gaff, now home to the **Galleria Doria Pamphili** (*see p119*).

The 75-year-old Pope Innocent, who was 'tall in stature, thin, choleric, splenetic, with a red face, bald in front with thick eyebrows bent above the nose,' was luckier with the image he presented to posterity. He chose Spanish court painter Diego Velázquez to paint his best side. Velázquez's image of the beady-eyed pontiff is arguably one of the finest portraits ever painted, and the star exhibit of the Galleria's collection.

This second palace came to the family when Donna Olimpia's son Camillo, the papal nephew and sometime cardinal, decided to marry. He hitched himself to a fabulously wealthy widow whose property portfolio included this magnificent mini-Versailles on via del Corso, as well as one of the finest collections of old masters in Italy.

they, in fact, that the church that originally commissioned the picture refused point-blank to have it. The two highest angels of the main altar are the work of Bernini (1628); below is a Byzantine Madonna.

Sant'Ivo alla Sapienza

Corso Rinascimento 40 (06 686 4987). Bus 30Exp, 70, 81, 87, 116, 204, 280, 492, 628. **Open** 10am-noon Sun. **Map** p355 D5.

You can peer, and wander, into the magnificent Renaissance courtyard of the state archives, but pick a Sunday morning to do real justice to this crowning glory of Borromini's tortured imagination. The concave façade of Sant'Ivo is countered by the convex bulk of the dome, which terminates in a bizarre corkscrew spire. The floor plan is based on a six-pointed star, but the forms of classical architecture (solid pediments, columns and logical arches, squares and circles) melt into an altogether more fluid play of convex and concave surfaces on the walls and up into the dome, in a dizzying whirl that soars up to the unknowable, intangible realm of the heavens… leaves you feeling like someone spiked your cappuccino.

From the Pantheon to via del Corso

With the **Pantheon** (*see p119*) as backdrop, all human life plays out its part in **piazza della Rotonda**. A 16th-century fountain is topped by an Egyptian obelisk dedicated to Rameses II. On the steps of the fountain, pierced punks with dogs on limp string hang out with hippies who forgot to go home. All seem oblivious to the bemused tour groups taking photographs and

Ignatius Loyola

message. In fact, it took Rome a while to see the positive side of Ignatius' teachings, which initially brought him and his band of disciples up against the Inquisition: they were imprisoned and beaten up, as well as being generally laid low with every kind of suffering, pestilence, illness and insult.

But the dour self-flagellatory stance of Ignatius – who preached utter submission, *perinde ac cadaver* ('well-disciplined as a corpse'), to the Church and the pope – attracted a large following in troubled Counter-Reformation Catholic Europe, and his Society of Jesus (from whence 'Jesuits') was given the papal seal of approval in 1540. Donations from powerful supporters who followed Loyola's 'Spiritual Exercises' quickly mounted up. Ignatius' beatification in 1609, and canonisation in 1622, gave impetus to an extraordinary flurry of church-building; by then the Jesuits were out in missionary force, pushing to the ends of the known world in search of souls to save. The iconography of Bernini's Fountain of the Four Rivers (*see p16*) in piazza Navona expresses the movement's global reach.

Ignatius' canonisation coincided with the zenith of Roman Baroque architecture: the order's mother-church, the **Gesù** (*see p123, pictured left*), is a jaw-dropping example of theatricality and opulence. Free evening choral concerts at **Sant' Ignazio** (9pm, days vary; *see p120*), the other barn-like Jesuit church, will give you time to stare at the trompe l'oeil ceiling, which records the ecstasies and agonies of the Spanish saint.

Born in the Spanish Basque Country, Ignatius (Iñigo) Lopez de Loyola (1491-1556) was the aristocratic founder of what was to become arguably the most powerful and influential (and, in many circles, least-liked) religious movement of the Catholic church: the Jesuits. After a dissolute youth and wartime leg injury, the reformed and fervently pious Ignatius experienced a vision at La Storta outside Rome that laid the foundation for the success of his mission: *ego vobis Romae propitius ero* (basically: 'Rome's the place') was God's the well-heeled tourists paying through the nose for a cappuccino-with-a-view at the cafés.

South of the Pantheon, central Rome's only Gothic church, **Santa Maria sopra Minerva** (*see p120*), stands in piazza della Minerva. In front is *il Pulcino della Minerva*, aka 'Bernini's elephant'. This cuddly marble animal, with wrinkled bottom and benign expression, has stood here since 1667. It was designed by Bernini as a tribute to Pope Alexander VII: elephants were both a symbol of wisdom and a model of abstinence. They were believed to be monogamous and to mate only once every five years, which, the Church felt, was the way things should be. Bernini perched a 12th-century BC Egyptian obelisk on its back; like its neighbour in piazza della Rotonda, this obelisk came from a temple to the Egyptian goddess Isis that stood nearby (*see also p107* **Obelisks**).

Further east, piazza del Collegio Romano contains one of Rome's finest art collections in the **Galleria Doria Pamphilj** (*see below*). The charmingly rococo piazza Sant'Ignazio looks just like a stage set despite its severe Jesuit church, **Sant'Ignazio di Loyola**. In neighbouring piazza di Pietra, the columns of the Temple of Hadrian can be seen embedded in the walls of Rome's ex-stock exchange, where the occasional exhibition is now held. The quieter lanes close to via del Corso contain outposts of the parliament; journalists, MPs and assorted hangers-on haunt the area's bars. On the lower reaches of via del Corso is the privately owned **Museo del Corso** (*see below*).

Galleria Doria Pamphilj

Piazza del Collegio Romano 2 (06 679 7323/www. doriapamphilj.it). Bus 62, 63, 81, 85, 95, 117, 119, 160, 175, 492, 628, 630, 850. **Open** 10am-5pm (last entry 4pm) Mon-Wed, Fri-Sun. **Admission** (incl audio guide) €8; €5.70 concessions; *see also p72* **Tickets**. **No credit cards**. **Map** p355 E5.

The collection of one of the great families of Rome's aristocracy (spelled either Pamphili or Pamphilj) now headed by two half-British siblings, is a very personal one: hung according to an inventory of 1760, some extraordinarily good paintings are packed in with the occasional bad copy to give a unique view of the tastes of late 18th-century Rome. The entrance is through the state apartments planned by Camillo Pamphili in the mid-16th century (*see also p117* **The two-palace pope**). The nephew of Pope Innocent X, Camillo escaped the College of Cardinals to marry fabulously wealthy Olimpia Aldobrandini, to whom the oldest part of the palace belonged, and who had already been left a widow by a member of the Borghese family. The family chapel was designed in 1689 by Carlo Fontana but heavily altered in the 18th and 19th centuries when the trompe l'oeil ceiling was added. The star turns are the corpses of two martyrs: St

Justin, under the altar, and St Theodora, visible to the right of the door. The main galleries are on all four sides of the central courtyard. Hard-nosed Olimpia is shown in Algardi's stylised portrait bust by the windows in the first gallery. Velázquez's portrait of a no-nonsense Pope Innocent X is the highlight of the collection. With Bernini's splendid bust next to it, it's difficult to see how the vital presence of Innocent X could be bettered. At the end of the Galleria degli Specchi (Gallery of Mirrors) are four small rooms ordered by century. In the 17th-century room, Caravaggio is represented by *Rest on the Flight into Egypt* and *Penitent Magdalene*. The 16th-century room includes Titian's shameless *Salome*, and a *Portrait of Two Men* by Raphael. In the 15th-century room is a beautifully tragic *Deposition* by Hans Memling. At the end of the third gallery, steps lead to the Salone Aldobrandini, where ancient sculpture is on display (much of it damaged when snow brought down the ceiling in the 1950s). On the way, keep an eye out for Guercino's *St Agnes* failing to catch fire and Pieter Breugel the Elder's northern view of an imaginary sea battle in the bay of Naples. Sadly, the private apartments are closed indefinitely.

Museo del Corso

Via del Corso 320 (06 678 6209/www.museo delcorso.it). Bus 62, 63, 81, 85, 95, 117, 119, 160, 175, 492, 628, 630, 850. **Open** 10am-8pm Tue-Sun. **Admission** varies with exhibition. **No credit cards.** **Map** p355 D5.

This privately owned space stages exhibitions on artistic, historical and literary themes; the presentation is often more impressive than the content.

Pantheon

Piazza della Rotonda (06 6830 0230). Bus 30Exp, 40Exp, 46, 62, 63, 64, 70, 81, 85, 87, 95, 117, 119, 160, 175, 492, 628, 630, 780, 850, 916/tram 8. **Open** 8.30am-7.30pm Mon-Sat; 9am-6pm Sun; 9am-1pm public hols. **Admission** free. **Map** p355 D5.

The Pantheon is the best-preserved ancient building in Rome. It was built (and possibly designed) by Hadrian in AD 119-128 as a temple to the 12 most important classical deities; the inscription on the pediment records an earlier Pantheon built a hundred years earlier by Augustus' general Marcus Agrippa (which confused historians for centuries). Its fine state of preservation is due to the building's conversion to a Christian church in 608, when it was presented to the pope by the Byzantine Emperor Phocas. The Pantheon has nevertheless suffered over the years – notably when bronze cladding was stripped from the roof in 667, and when Pope Urban VIII allowed Bernini to remove the remaining bronze from the beams in the portico to melt down for his *baldacchino* in St Peter's in 1628. The simplicity of the building's exterior remains largely unchanged, and it retains its original Roman bronze doors. Inside, the Pantheon's real glory lies in the dimensions, which follow the rules set down by top Roman architect Vitruvius. The diameter of the hemispherical dome is exactly equal to the height of the whole

Extra time

● Joseph Ratzinger's election as pope was hugely popular at **Santa Maria dell'Anima** (06 6880 1394, www.santa-maria-anima.com), Rome's German church. It contains the fine Renaissance tomb of Dutch Pope Adrian VI, with an inscription that reads: 'How important, even for the best of men, are the times in which he finds himself.' Adrian ruled over particularly difficult times and lasted barely two years; he was the last non-Italian pontiff until John Paul II in 1978.

● Blink and you could miss any mention of Napoleon's reign in Rome – from 1798 to 1814 – in standard accounts of the city. But dreams of empire were the Corsican's fatal fantasy; he even shipped in Pope Pius VII for his imperial coronation in Paris in 1804. Rome was mostly an opportunity for grabbing as much loot as his army could carry, hauling back cartloads of marbles and old masters. But the emperor's mother Letizia lived happily in the Palazzo Bonaparte on piazza Venezia for many years, spying on the locals from behind the dark green shutters of her *kiosk*. Meanwhile, his sister Pauline posed in the nude for sculptor Canova (*see p99* Galleria Borghese) and ran up huge bills for her millionaire Roman husband, Prince Camillo Borghese. The **Museo Napoleonico** (piazza di Ponte Umberto I, 06 6880 6286, www.comune.roma.it/museonapoleonico, closed Mon) contains pieces relating to the imperious Frenchman's family.

● Urbino-born architect Donato Bramante is credited with kick-starting the Roman High Renaissance. He began with the beautiful **Chiostro del Bramante** (Arco della Pace 5, 06 6880 9036, www.chiostrodelbramante.it) in 1500-4.

● Saint Eustace is supposed to have been martyred while hunting on the very spot where the church of **Sant'Eustachio** – in the eponymous square – was (according to legend) founded by Emperor Constantine. Antlers figure on the church's 18th-century façade because, while out hunting one day, the soldier who would become the patron saint of hunters had a vision of a stag with a cross between its antlers. Most people come here for the legendary *gran caffè* across the piazza at the superb **Caffè Sant'Eustachio** (*see p221*).

building; it could potentially accommodate a perfect sphere. At the exact centre of the dome is the oculus, a circular hole 9m (30ft) in diameter, the only source of light and a symbolic link between the temple and the heavens. The building is still officially a church, and contains the tombs of eminent Italians, including the artist Raphael and united Italy's first king, Vittorio Emanuele II. Until the 18th century the portico was used as a market: supports for the stalls were inserted into the notches still visible in the columns.

Santa Maria sopra Minerva

Piazza della Minerva 42 (06 679 3926/www.basilica minerva.it). Bus 30Exp, 40Exp, 46, 62, 63, 64, 70, 81, 87, 492, 628, 630, 780, 916/tram 8. **Open** 8am-7pm daily. **Map** p355 E5.

Central Rome's only Gothic church was built on the site of an ancient temple of Minerva in 1280 and modelled on Santa Maria Novella in Florence. It was heavily (over-) restored in the 'Gothick' style in the mid-19th century. The best of its works of art are Renaissance: on the right of the transept is the superb Carafa chapel, with late 15th-century frescoes by Filippino Lippi (1457-1504), commissioned by Cardinal Oliviero Carafa in honour of St Thomas Aquinas. Carafa took Renaissance self-assurance to extremes: the altar painting shows him being presented to a patient Virgin, right at the moment when Gabriel informs her she has conceived. The tomb of the Carafa Pope Paul IV (reigned 1555-59) is also in the chapel. He was one of the prime movers of the Counter-Reformation, chiefly remembered for the institution of the Jewish Ghetto and ordering Daniele da Volterra to paint loincloths on the nudes of Michelangelo's *Last Judgment*. A bronze loincloth was also ordered to cover Christ's genitals on a work by Michelangelo here: the statue was finished by Pietro Urbano (1514-21) and depicts a heroic Christ holding up a cross. An early Renaissance work is the *Madonna and Child*, believed by some to be by Fra Angelico, in the chapel to the left of the altar, close to the artistic monk's own tomb. On either side of the altar are the tombs of Medici popes: corpulent Leo X and Clement VII. The father of modern astronomy Galileo Galilei was tried for heresy in the adjoining monastery in 1633.

Sant'Ignazio di Loyola

Piazza Sant'Ignazio (06 679 4406/www.chiesa santignazio.org). Bus 62, 63, 81, 85, 95, 117, 119, 160, 175, 492, 628, 630, 850. **Open** 8am-12.15pm, 3-7.15pm daily. **Map** p355 E5.

Sant'Ignazio was begun in 1626 to commemorate the canonisation of St Ignatius, founder of the Jesuit order (*see p118* **Ignatius Loyola**). Trompe l'oeil columns soar above the nave, and architraves by Andrea Pozzo open to a cloudy heaven. Trickery was also involved in creating the dome: the monks next door claimed that a real dome would rob them of light, so Pozzo simply painted a dome on the inside of the roof. The illusion is fairly convincing if you stand on the disc set in the floor of the nave. Walk away, however, and it dissolves.

The Ghetto & Campo de' Fiori

Rome's medieval heart still beats strong.

Campo de' Fiori is the heart of medieval Rome. This is the one area of the city where you are not overawed by towering classical remains or Mussolini-era boulevards, but rather drawn into a web of tightly wedged, gaily coloured buildings, and cobbled alleys where life with its daily markets and washing-line draped courtyards goes on much as it did (bar the odd satellite dish and rusting scooter) at the time of Lucrezia Borgia (*pictured right*) and her mother, Vannozza Catanei (*see p126* **Papal mistress No.1**).

In ancient times, the *Campus martius* (field of war) occupied much of this low-lying area along the river Tiber: it was here that Roman males did physical jerks to stay fighting fit. But with theatrical entertaintainment banned in the serious city centre, this was also where ancient locals headed for low-brow fun: the Teatro di Pompeo occupied much of the area between largo Argentina and campo de' Fiori; and there were the theatres of Marcellus and Balbus as well.

After barbarian hordes rampaged through Rome in the fifth and sixth centuries, the area fell into ruin. The ancient structures proved handy quarries for building materials; what then remained of the glory that had been Rome was built into and over during the Dark Ages with no planning and even less respect. By the late Middle Ages, this had become a densely populated, highly

insalubrious part of town. It was not until the pope made the Vatican – just across the river – his main residence in the mid 15th century that the area's fortunes began to look up. With a papal court and its visitors to cater to, business flourished.

East of via Arenula, a warren of narrow winding streets and colossal ancient ruins make the Ghetto (*see p126*) a picturesque haven. But the picturesque appearance masks a sorry history of prejudice, isolation and deportation.

From largo Argentina to campo de' Fiori

Largo Argentina today is a polluted transport hub and rendezvous point for milling teenagers, who, like the bus drivers, rarely give a second

Papal daughter: Lucrezia Borgia. *See p126.*

Sightseeing

thought to the expanse of ancient ruins that fill the hole in the centre of the square. It's officially called **largo di Torre Argentina**. The name has nothing to do with the Latin American country though; it refers to a tower – *torre* – in a nearby street, which was the home of Johannes Burckhardt, the powerful master of ceremonies – and entertaining diarist – of the Borgia papacy; Burckhardt's home town was Strasbourg, the diocesan name of which was Argentinensis. His house and tower are now occupied by a theatre museum, the **Biblioteca e Raccolta Teatrale del Burcardo** (via del Sudario 44, 06 681 9471, www.burcardo. org, 9am-1.30pm Mon-Fri, closed Aug).

Visible when you peer over the railings in largo Argentina are columns, altars and foundations from one round and three rectangular temples dating from the mid third century BC to c100 BC. The frescoes on the taller brickwork are from the 12th-century church of San Nicola de' Cesarini, which was built into one of the temples. If you want to take a closer look, you'll have to cosy up to the ladies of the **Rifugio Felino di Torre Argentina** cat sanctuary (06 687 2133, www.romancats.de, open noon-6pm daily). They lavish care and nourishment on some 250 abandoned and wild cats each year among the ruins, and offer guided tours of the site and its feline residents (3pm Mon-Wed & Sat, 4pm Thur & Fri, donation appreciated).

To the east of the square, in via delle Botteghe Oscure, is the **Crypta Balbi** (*see below*), a tribute to Rome's architectural accretions through the ages; in via del Plebiscito, on the other hand, is **Il Gesù** (*see p123*), chief church of the Jesuit order.

West along corso Vittorio Emanuele II (universally known as corso Vittorio) is the church of **Sant'Andrea della Valle** (*see p125*), topped by Rome's second-tallest dome; the first act of *Tosca* is set here. Further on are the **Museo Barracco** (*see p125*), with its collection of ancient sculpture, and the Vatican-owned Renaissance gem, the **Palazzo della Cancelleria** (*see p125*).

To escape the unbreathable air and decibels, take any left off corso Vittorio. Narrow alleys and cramped buildings are home to countless little shops. Façades are dotted with Latin lapidaries and shrines to the Madonna. Café tables occupy cobbled pavements.

The streets converge on lively **campo de' Fiori** (*below*). The campo and its surrounding streets have for centuries been a fascinating mix of the very smart and the very rough. A stone's throw from the riotous campo, Pope Alexander VI – aka Rodrigo Borgia – sired four of his children, including the sadly

misrepresented Lucrezia: the building on the corner of via del Gallo, above the busy *forno* (bakery), bears the coat of arms of Vannozza Catanei, their mother (*see p126* **Papal Mistress No.1**). The powerful Farnese clan – which spawned Pope Paul III (*see p129* **Papal Mistress No.2**) – staked its claim in **piazza Farnese**, a stately square with a pair of fountains made with giant Roman tubs from the baths of Caracalla (*see p141*). The Renaissance **Palazzo Farnese** (*see p125*) – now the French embassy – sits solidly as the undisputed elder statesman of the square. To the north and west are streets packed with antique stores and eateries. Gold and jewellery shops cluster to the south, near the old Monte di Pietà, the state-run pawn shop. Via dei Giubbonari (jacket-makers' street) seethes with clothing stores, while the **Galleria Spada** (*see p123*) is in a pretty palazzo in parallel via Capo di Ferro.

Campo de' Fiori

Bus 30Exp, 40Exp, 62, 63, 64, 70, 81, 87, 116, 492, 571, 628, 630, 780, 916/tram 8. **Map** p358 C1.
Campo de' Fiori has been a hub of Roman life since the 15th century, when the pope moved his chief residence to the Vatican; noble families flocked to this area and built palaces, just across the river from the centre of power. Tradesmen and craftsmen set up shop in via del Pellegrino and via Giulia. And inn-keepers and food-purveyors clustered in the campo.

Despite galloping gentrification and a substantial population of foreign students and professionals seeking to soak up *romanitas*, the campo has retained some neighbourhood spirit; its friendly, chaotic energy remains magnetic. By day the picturesque but costly food and flower market bustles from about 6am to 2pm (Mon-Sat). Restaurant tables ringing the square fill up for lunch. Afternoons are slow and quiet, except for a perpetual group of alternative types with flea-bitten dogs, bongo drums and – bitter, sleep-deprived locals allege – a flourishing sideline in drug dealing. At sunset the square fills up again for *aperitivo* hour and dinner. Wine-quaffers and beer-chuggers take over the square in a noisy, drunken open party that lasts through the wee hours.

When emptied of its market stalls, the campo is dominated by the dark statue of a brooding, book-clutching Giordano Bruno, burned at the stake here in 1600 after a run-in with the Inquisition. Many an Anglo-Saxon rendezvous in the campo is invariably arranged beneath the dour figure of 'Gordon Brown', as Giordano Bruno translates so neatly. **Photo** *p127*.

Crypta Balbi

Via delle Botteghe Oscure 31 (06 678 0167). Bus 46, 62, 70, 87, 186, 492, 571, 810, 916/tram 8. **Open** 9am-5pm Tue-Sun. **Admission** €7; €3 concessions; *see also p72* **Tickets**. **No credit cards. Map** p358 D2.

Part of the Museo Nazionale Romana, the Crypta Balbi is often overlooked on travellers' itineraries. It's a pity: not only does it display one of Rome's more interesting recent archaeological finds, it also combines the best of the ancient with state-of-the-art technology, and is packed with displays, maps and models that explain (in English) Rome's evolution from its bellicose pre-Imperial era, to early Christian times and on through the dim Middle Ages. The underground ruins themselves, which are open for about 15 minutes every hour, on the hour (no guide), show the foundations of the gigantic *crypta*, or theatre lobby, built by Cornelius Balbus, a Spaniard much in favour at the court of Augustus. The lavish theatre that Balbus built next to the *crypta* remains hidden under buildings but new excavations have brought to light parts of the adjacent Porticus Minucia, where grain was doled out to the have-nots in Republican Rome. New digs have also unearthed a mithraeum. Upstairs is a display of the minutiae of everyday life in ancient Rome: plates, bowls, glasses, amphorae, oil lamps and artisans' tools. The upper levels provide a fantastic view of Roman rooftops.

Bridge at **Palazzo Farnese**. See p125.

Galleria Spada

Piazza Capo di Ferro 3 (06 687 4896/www.galleria borghese.it/spada/it). Bus 23, 30Exp, 40Exp, 46, 62, 63, 64, 70, 81, 116, 280, 492, 630, 780, 916, H/tram 8. **Open** 8.30am-7.30pm Tue-Sun. **Admission** €5; €2.50 concessions; *see also p72* **Tickets**. **No credit cards. Map** p358 C2.

Note: staff shortages sometimes force this gallery to adopt irregular opening hours in the afternoons. You can admire the Borromini perspective while the warders take breaks.

Time was when this ornate gem of a palace contained one of Rome's most charming little museums; but staffing cuts and general neglect by authorities (the long-suffering staff-survivors couldn't be nicer) have reduced it to four dusty hard-to-find rooms – no longer bewitching enough to make you forget that most of the contents are second-rate 17th-century leftovers. The Italian Consiglio di Stato – a kind of appeals court – now sprawls through the palace, which was built in 1540, and acquired by Cardinal Bernardino Spada in 1632.

Spada was an avid art collector, and very fond of having his portrait painted, as demonstrated in Room 1 of the gallery. The walls of the four small upstairs *saloni*, entered by the back stairs, are crammed and old-style, but notes (in English) in each room help you to make sense of them all. There are some big names here: Domenichino, Guercino and Guido Reni – see his *San Girolamo* and *Slave of Ripa Grande* – plus the father-daughter Gentileschi duo, Orazio and Artemisia. Her *Madonna Nursing the Infant Jesus* gives a rare female view of the subject. Cleopatra gets odd treatment: in Room 2, she is adorned with a wacky hat by Lavinia Fontana, while in Room 3, Francesco Trevisani pictures the Egyptian queen as a blonde at an intimate dinner with Mark Anthony. The main attraction, however, is the Borromini perspective, which shows that the manic-depressive architect had a sense, if not of humour, at least of irony. If you're lucky to get there at the right moment (there appears to be no timetable) you'll be taken to a courtyard and misled into believing a 9m-long (30ft) colonnade is much longer by perspective trickery. In theory, an art historian conducts guided tours around the impressive art works in the Consiglio di Stato spaces on the first Sunday of each month; phone for details and to book.

Il Gesù

Piazza del Gesù (06 697 001/Loyola's rooms 06 6920 5800/www.chiesadelgesu.org). Bus 30Exp, 40Exp, 46, 62, 63, 64, 70, 81, 87, 492, 630, 780, 916, H. **Open** *Church* 6am-12.30pm, 4-8pm daily. *Loyola's rooms* 4-6pm Mon-Sat; 10am-noon Sun. **Admission** free. **Map** p358 D1.

The huge Gesù is the flagship church of the Jesuits, the order founded by Basque soldier Ignatius Loyola in the 1530s (*see also p118*). Realising the power of a direct appeal to the emotions, Loyola devised a series of 'spiritual exercises' aimed at training devotees to experience the agony and ecstasy of the saints. The Gesù itself (built 1568-84) was designed

Sightseeing

Hotel Bernini Bristol
and Roof Garden L'Olimpo

In the city centre, at the beginning of Via Veneto
and the most fashionable shopping area.
127 rooms and suites recently renovated both
in traditional and contemporary style.
New Wellness Club with treatments.
Entirely WI-FI.
Rooftop restaurant "L'Olimpo" for a breathtaking
360° panoramic view over Rome offering
a delicious traditional Mediterranean cuisine.

SINA
FINE ITALIAN HOTELS

HOTEL BERNINI BRISTOL AND ROOF GARDEN L'OLIMPO
PIAZZA BARBERINI 23 • 00187 ROME • TEL. +39 06488931 • FAX +39 064824266
www.berninibristol.com

to involve the congregation as closely as possible in the proceedings, with a nave unobstructed by aisles, offering a clear view of the main altar. Giacomo della Porta added a façade that would be repeated *ad nauseam* on Jesuit churches across Italy (and the world) for decades afterwards. As befitted a construction of the immediate post-Reformation era – with Martin Luther's fulminations against material manifestations of God's glory still echoing – the Gesù started out life as a very austere affair. Over the next century, however, there was much embellishment. A large, bright fresco, *Triumph in the Name of Jesus*, by Il Baciccia (1676-79) – one of Rome's great Baroque masterpieces – decorates the gilded ceiling of the nave, which seems to dissolve on either side as stucco figures (by Antonio Raggi) and other painted images are sucked up into the dazzling light of the heavens. (The figures falling back to earth are presumably Protestants.) On the left is another spectacular Baroque achievement: the chapel of Sant'Ignazio (1696-1700) by Andrea Pozzo, which is adorned with gold, silver and coloured marble; the statue of St Ignatius is by Antonio Canova. Towering above the altar is what was long believed to be the biggest lump of lapis lazuli in the world… in fact, it's covered concrete. Check out the sculpture group to the left and prepare to wince: an ugly hag (Idolatry) has her breast tugged by a vicious serpent as a virtuous Faith triumphs over them and a pagan Roman soldier. Outside the church, at piazza del Gesù 45, you can visit the rooms of St Ignatius, which contain a wonderful painted corridor with trompe l'oeil special effects by Pozzo, and mementoes of the saint, including his death mask.

Museo Barracco di Scultura Antica

Corso Vittorio 166 (06 687 5657). Bus 40Exp, 46, 62, 64, 116, 571, 916. **Open** 9am-7pm Tue-Sun. **Admission** €3; €1.50 concessions. **No credit cards. Map** p358 C1.

This small collection of mainly pre-Roman art was amassed in the first half of the 20th century by Giovanni Barracco. His interests covered the whole gamut of ancient art: there are Assyrian reliefs, Attic vases, Egyptian sphinxes and Babylonian stone lions, as well as Roman and Etruscan exhibits and Greek sculptures. Don't miss the copy of the *Wounded Bitch* by the fourth-century BC sculptor Lysippus, on the second floor.

Palazzo della Cancelleria

Piazza della Cancelleria. Bus 40Exp, 46, 62, 64, 116, 571, 916. **Closed to the public. Map** p358 C1.

One of Rome's most refined examples of Renaissance architecture, the Palazzo della Cancelleria was built, possibly by Bramante, between 1483 and 1513 for Raffaele Riario. Although his great-uncle, Pope Sixtus IV, made him a cardinal at the age of 17, Raffaele didn't allow his ecclesiastic duties to cramp his style. He is said to have raised a third of the cost of this palace with his winnings from a single night's gambling. He was involved in plotting against the powerful Florentine

Medici family; in retaliation, the palace was confiscated for the church when Giovanni de' Medici became Pope Leo X in 1513. It later became the papal Chancellery and is still Vatican property (one of the offices housed here is the Rota romana, which grants or denies marriage annulments). There is a lovely courtyard. The palazzo incorporates the fourth-century church of San Lorenzo in Damaso and, as archaeologists discovered in the 1940s, sits atop a mithraeum and part of a canal connecting the Baths of Agrippa – located just north of largo Argentina – to the Tiber. These ruins are usually visible with permission (06 6988 5318, fax 06 6988 5518), but at the time of writing were closed for further digs.

From time to time chances arise to enter the palazzo. You might be lucky enough to find tickets for the occasional chamber-music concerts held here; alternatively look out for exhibitions on religious themes mounted in the magnificently frescoed rooms.

Palazzo Farnese

Piazza Farnese (06 6889 2818/www.france-italia.it). Bus 30Exp, 40Exp, 46, 62, 63, 64, 70, 81, 87, 116, 492, 571, 628, 630, 780, 916. **Open** (guided tours only; in Italian or French) 3pm, 4pm, 5pm Mon, Thur. Closed 6wks July-Sept. **Admission** free. **Map** p358 C2.
Note: tours *must* be pre-booked, the earlier the better; organisers suggest two months in advance.

This palazzo has housed the French embassy since the 1870s. Considered by many to be the finest Renaissance palace in Rome, the huge building – recently and dramatically restored – was begun for Cardinal Alessandro Farnese (later Pope Paul III) in 1514 by Antonio da Sangallo the Younger. Sangallo died before it was completed, and in 1546 Michelangelo took over. He was responsible for most of the upper storeys, the grand cornice along the roof, and the inner courtyard. Vignola and Giacomo della Porta completed the rear façade, which gives out to a large garden. Several generations of Farneses passed through the palazzo; it was Cardinal Odoardo who called in Annibale Carracci to paint the magnificent frescoes in the gallery. Odoardo also was responsible for the picturesque bridge across via Giulia (*pictured p123*), which connected the garden to what was then known as the *Camerini farnesiani*, where the family kept its sculpture collection.

Sant'Andrea della Valle

Corso Vittorio 6 (06 686 1339). Bus 30Exp, 40Exp, 46, 62, 63, 64, 70, 81, 87, 116, 492, 571, 628, 630, 780, 916. **Open** 7.30am-12.30pm, 4.30-7.30pm daily. **Map** p358 D1.

Many architects got their hands on this church. Originally designed in 1524 by Giacomo della Porta, it was handed over to Carlo Maderno, who stretched the design upward and added the dome, which is the highest in Rome after St Peter's. He left much of the façade design to Carlo Rainaldi, who in turn commissioned artist Giacomo Antonio Fancelli to sculpt two angels to adorn it. When the first one (on the

Sightseeing

left) was complete, the story goes, it was criticised by Pope Alexander VII. Fancelli quit the job in a huff saying the pope could do the other one himself; it was never done. Giovanni Lanfranco nearly died while painting the dome fresco, allegedly because his rival Domenichino had sabotaged the scaffolding on which he was working. Puccini set the opening act of *Tosca* in the chapel on the left.

The Ghetto

Rome's Jews occupy a unique place in the history of the diaspora, having maintained a presence in the city uninterrupted for over 2,000 years. This makes them Europe's oldest Jewish community; they have enjoyed a surprising degree of security, even at times (such as the years following the Black Death, or after the Sack of Rome, *see p21* **The Sack**) when waves of anti-Semitism were sweeping the rest of the Continent.

It may seem odd that the city that was the great centre of power for the Catholic church represented such a safe haven for Jews, but their security came at a price. The popes took on the double role of protectors (curbing popular violence against Jews) and oppressors, bringing Jews under their direct jurisdiction and making sure they paid for the privilege. The first documented tax on Roman Jews, dating back to 1310, set the pattern for the tradition of blackmail that was to characterise the Church's relations with the Jewish community until the 19th century. Payment of this tax exempted Jews from the humiliating *carnevale* games, during which they were liable to be packed into barrels and rolled from the top of Monte Testaccio (*see p143*).

In September 1943 the German occupiers demanded 50 kilograms (110 pounds) of gold from the Jewish community, to be produced in 36 hours. After an appeal – to which both Jews

Papal mistress No.1

Before he became Pope Alexander VI in 1492, Spanish Cardinal Rodrigo Borgia – whose family name became a byword for incest, poisoning and murder – lived openly with his mistress Vannozza (or Giovanna) Catanei and their children at various addresses around campo de' Fiori.

Alexandre Dumas, who penned a splendid potboiler on the dynasty's darker deeds, says Vannozza was the dazzlingly pretty 15-year-old daughter of one of Rodrigo's earlier Spanish mistresses. Wherever she originated, Vannozza was married off by Rodrigo to a series of elderly, frail and presumably compliant Italian husbands.

Vannozza bore Rodrigo four children, acknowledged as papal 'nephews' on his election in 1492. The eldest, Cesare – born at 56 via del Pellegrino – was a handsome psychopath and barely 17 when his father's flagrant vote-rigging ensured victory in the papal conclave; Cesare was promptly ushered in as an unlikely teenage cardinal, but later made a ruthless leader of the powerful army of the papal states. Vannozza's daughter Lucrezia (*pictured p121*), rumoured to be a victim of incest at the hands of both her father and brother, was used as a dynastic pawn in a series of unhappy marriages. The pope's favourite son, Juan, was murdered, probably by Cesare's henchmen, and buried (like Vannozza) in the church of Santa Maria del Popolo (*see p110*), though their graves there

were later moved and Vannozza's tombstone can now be found at San Marco (*see p79*). Frescoes in the Vatican's Borgia apartments show them all: Cesare, Juan and Jofré as Roman soldiers in the Resurrection scene; and Lucrezia as St Catherine of Alexandria.

The Borgia palace still stands at the top of via dei Banchi Vecchi (**map** p355 C5), the wide (for those times), paved, pilgrim road Rodrigo drove through to reach the papal apartments at Castel Sant'Angelo and St Peter's beyond: it was given a new façade when corso Vittorio Emanuele II was built in the 19th century, but you can glimpse its original Renaissance arches though the courtyard of Palazzo Sforza Cesarini, and, if the lights are on upstairs, tantalising glimpses of magnificent painted ceilings.

Just before he became pope (and found another mistress; *see p129* **Papal mistress No.2**), Rodrigo provided sufficient funds and real estate around campo de' Fiori for Vannozza to set herself up as proprietor of a chain of successful inns such as the Biscione (the Snake), in via del Biscione, and La Vacca (the Cow), on the corner of the campo and via del Gallo; Vannozza's coat of arms, incorporating the Borgia bull, can still be seen there. Amazingly, given her family's reputation, Vannozza died of natural causes in 1518 at the ripe old age of 76, long outliving Rodrigo, who died in 1503 – probably poisoned, according to his diarist Johannes Burkhardt.

Morning market, evening excess: **campo de' Fiori.** *See p122.*

and non-Jews responded – the target was reached, but this time accepting blackmail did not bring security. On 16 October more than 1,000 Jews – mostly women and children – were rounded up and deported in cattle trucks to Auschwitz. A quarter of Rome's Jews died in concentration camps, a proportion that would have been higher had it not been for the help given by wide sections of Roman society, including the Catholic priesthood (though not, many would argue, the Vatican).

Rome's Jews had originally settled in Trastevere but by the 13th century they had started to cross the river into the area that would become the Jewish Ghetto, a cramped quarter in one corner of the *centro storico*, immediately north of the Tiber Island. The Ghetto (the word is Venetian in origin) was walled off from the rest of the city in 1556 after the bull *Cum nimis absurdum*, issued by the anti-Semitic Pope Paul IV, ordered a physical separation between Jewish and Christian parts of the cities. Many Jews actually welcomed the protection the walls and curfews afforded, despite the fact that they were also obliged periodically to attend mass to be lectured on their sinfulness.

However, over-crowding, the loss of property rights, and trade restrictions imposed on the community all took their toll, and the Ghetto experienced a long decline from the 16th to the 18th centuries. When Pius IX became pope in 1848, he opened up the Ghetto gates with a promise of more tolerance and integration. But winds of revolution and secularisation were sweeping Italy, and he closed them again two years later, issuing a series of race laws that prohibited Jews not only from owning property but from attending secondary school or

university, undertaking scientific or artistic careers and receiving treatment in public hospitals. By the time of Italian Unification in 1870, conditions for the more than 5,000 people who lived in the Ghetto had become desperately squalid. The new government ordered that the walls be destroyed.

Some 15,000 Jews live in Rome now, but few of them choose to live in the old Ghetto area. They flock there for weekends and holidays, however, and to visit its chief landmark – the imposing synagogue, begun in 1874. This incorporates the **Museo d'Arte Ebraica** (*see p128*), a fascinating museum tracing the history and ritual of Roman Jewish life.

Via Portico d'Ottavia, an anarchic hotchpotch of ancient, medieval and Renaissance architecture leading to the **Portico d'Ottavia** itself (*see p128*), used to mark the boundary of the Ghetto. This street is still the centre of Rome's Jewish life, though many of the people you'll see sitting around chatting in the evening or at weekends have come in from the suburbs. It's also a good place to sample a unique hybrid: Roman-Jewish cuisine. Restaurants like Sora Margherita (*see p197*) specialise in delicacies such as artichokes deep-fried Jewish-style; in a tiny unmarked cornershop (the Forno del Ghetto, *see p241*) you'll find the bakery that turns out a *torta di ricotta e visciole* – ricotta and damson tart – that has achieved legendary status among Roman gourmets. The Ghetto's winding alleys also hide non-comestible gems that include the beautiful, delicate **Fontana delle Tartarughe** (*see below*).

Fontana delle Tartarughe

Piazza Mattei. Bus 30Exp, 40Exp, 46, 62, 63, 64, 70, 81, 87, 492, 628, 630, 780, 916/tram 8. **Map** p358 D2.

Four *ephebes* (adolescent boys) cavort around the base of one of Rome's loveliest fountains, gently hoisting tortoises up to the waters above them. According to legend, Giacomo della Porta and Taddeo Landini built the fountain for the Duke of Mattei at some point in the 1580s. The duke, so the story goes, had lost all his money and hence his fiancée, and wanted to prove to her father that he could still achieve great things. He had the fountain built overnight in the square outside his family palazzo (you can wander freely into the classical, carving-clad courtyard of the palazzo, now home to an American studies centre); the next morning he triumphantly displayed his accomplishment from a palace window. The wedding was on again, but he had the window walled up, and so it remains. The turtles were probably an afterthought, added by Bernini during a restoration. The ones there today are copies: three of the originals are now in the Capitoline museums; the fourth was stolen and presumably graces some private fountain.

Museo d'Arte Ebraica

Lungotevere Cenci (06 6840 0661/www.museo ebraico.roma.it). Bus 23, 63, 280, 630, 780/tram 8. **Open** *June-Sept* 10am-7pm Mon-Thur, Sun; 9am-4pm Fri. *Oct-May* 10am-5pm Mon-Thur, Sun; 9am-2pm Fri. Closed on Jewish holidays. **Admission** €7.50; €3 concessions. **No credit cards. Map** p358 D2.
Inscriptions and carvings from the old Cinque Scole – where Catalonian, Aragonese and Sicilian Jews traditionally worshipped with Roman Jews in the Ghetto – line the entrance passage to this fascinating museum, which details the history of the city's Jewish community. The recently extended and refurbished display is housed beneath the magnificent neo-Assyrian, neo-Greek Great Synagogue inaugurated in 1904. As well as luxurious crowns, Torah mantles and silverware, this museum presents vivid reminders of the persecution suffered by Rome's Jews at various times through history. Copies of the 16th-century papal edicts that banned Jews from a progressively longer list of activities are a disturbing foretaste of the horrors forced on them by the Fascists and Nazis; the Nazi atrocities are in turn represented by stark photographs and heart-rending relics from the concentration camps, as well as film footage from the post-war period. There are also displays on the ancient Roman synagogue excavated at Ostia in 1964, as well as Jewish items from the city's catacombs. Admission to the museum includes guided tours of the synagogue in English and Italian. Services are held daily; *see also p333.*

Portico d'Ottavia

Via Portico d'Ottavia. Bus 23, 30Exp, 44, 63, 81, 95, 160, 170, 280, 628, 715, 716, 781. **Open** always visible from street level. *Lower area walkway* 9am-6pm daily. **Admission** free. **Map** p358 D2.
Great ancient columns and a marble frontispiece, held together with rusting iron braces, now form part of the church of Sant'Angelo in Pescheria. They were originally the entrance of a massive colonnaded square (*portico*) containing temples and libraries, built in the first century AD by Emperor Augustus and dedicated to his sister Octavia (this, in turn, had been built over a first-century BC square). The mighty structure was decorated with 34 bronzes by Lysippus depicting bellicose events from the life of Alexander the Great; these are long lost. The isolated columns outside, and the inscription above, date from a later restoration, undertaken by Septimius Severus in AD 213. After lengthy digs and restoration work in the 1990s, a walkway has been opened allowing you to stroll through the *forum piscarium* – the ancient fish market, which remained in operation hereabouts until medieval times, hence the name of the church – and get a closer look at the massive remains. Atmospheric (if slightly rubbish-strewn) as the place is, there are no explanations of what you're looking at. The walkway continues past a graveyard of broken columns and dumped Corinthian capitals to the Teatro di Marcello (*see p131*), passing by three towering columns that were part of the Temple of Apollo, dating from 433 BC.

Tiber Island & the Bocca della Verità

When the last Etruscan king was driven from Rome, the Romans uprooted the wheat from his fields and threw it in baskets into the river. There the baskets lay, with silt accumulating around them until that silt formed an island. When the Roman god of medicine, Aesculapius, came to Rome on a boat to deal with a plague epidemic in the third century BC, his snake jumped out at that spot, indicating that this was the spot for a sanctuary. That's what the legend says, anyway, and from that moment on the island has had a vocation for public health. Today the busy Fatebenefratelli hospital occupies the north end of the island that *romani* simply call *l'Isola tiberina* – the **Tiber Island**. The church of San Bartolomeo – an apostle flayed alive by Armenians – is built over the original sanctuary. Remains of the ancient building can be seen from the wide footpath around the island, down by the muddy, rushing Tiber: a sculpted boat-shaped outcrop of travertine is decorated with a rod and snakes, the symbol of the god of healing. Ignore the tattered bits of plastic bags decorating the trees hugging the island's banks and head for the southern tip for a glimpse of the **Ponte Rotto** (broken bridge), Rome's oldest, and of the mouth of the **Cloaca Maxima**, ancient Rome's great sewer (for both, *see p129*).

Across on the left (east) bank of the river stood ancient Rome's cattle market (*forum boarium*) and vegetable market (*forum*

Papal mistress No.2

Rodrigo Borgia marked his election to the papacy by adopting the name Alexander VI and by ditching his then mistress Vannozza Catanei (*see p126* **Papal mistress No.1**) for a more fittingly high-born one. And to show just how serious he was about this relationship, he ordered Vatican painter Pinturicchio to portray his new conquest – the lovely Giulia from the powerful Farnese family – as the Madonna (though it's not recorded whether the Christ child that his Holiness kneels to adore in the same painting is the couple's Laura, born around 1492).

Rodrigo was 62 and Giulia 15 when the liaison began. Heart-melting good looks and a top-notch pedigree made her a perfect companion for both the pope, and for the pope's own spirited and beautiful daughter Lucrezia, who became her best friend. To keep up appearances, Rodrigo married Giulia off to the son of a distant cousin; the hapless husband's chief virtue (for Rodrigo) was that he had a terrible squint.

The Farneses were rewarded for Giulia's papal 'duties' with the appointment in 1493 of the papal mistress's younger brother Alessandro as cardinal. (Alessandro eventually took the papal tiara himself, in 1534, becoming Paul III). Cynics in the Eternal City made no secret of their suspicions that Alessandro's 'pimping', as they put it, had gone a long way towards securing his ecclesiastical advancement.

But headstrong Giulia – *la bella*, as Romans called her – was certainly no mere pawn. She proved more than a match for the pope, who coughed up a huge ransom for her when she was kidnapped by the French on a return trip from Naples – despite the fact that the pope had expressly forbidden her to travel to Naples where another of her brothers was dying.

The moment both husband and lover were safely dead, Giulia embarked on a series of relationships before marrying again, then retired from Rome to become the autocratic governor of the small town of Carbognano, near Viterbo. Her daughter Laura made an excellent marriage to the nephew of Giuliano della Rovere, who succeeded Alexander VI as Pope Julius II.

---

holitorium) – a bustling place from the time of the Etruscan kings, chunks of which can be seen beneath the church of **San Nicola in Carcere** (*see p130*). Further south are two delightful Republican-era **temples** (*see p131*) and **Santa Maria in Cosmedin** (*see p131*), with its *'bocca della verità'* (mouth of truth). Skirt left around Santa Maria in Cosmedin for the touchingly unadorned arch of Janus and the church of **San Giorgio in Velabro** (*see below*). Both these churches have strong British associations: Santa Maria in Cosmedin was from 1532 the titular church of the last Catholic Archbishop of Canterbury, Reginald Pole, while, from 1879-90, San Giorgio in Velabro was the titular church of Cardinal John Henry Newman (on track to be England's first saint since the Reformation).

Ponte Rotto & Cloaca Maxima
Views from Ponte Palatino, Isola Tiberina & lungotevere Pierleoni. Bus 23, 63, 280, 630, 780, H/tram 8. **Map** p358 D/E3.
The Ponte Rotto – literally, 'Broken Bridge' – stands on the site of the Pons aemilius, Rome's first stone bridge, built in 142 BC. It was rebuilt many times – even Michelangelo had a go – before 1598, when great chunks collapsed (yet again) into the river and it was decided to give up trying to keep it up. To the east of the bridge is a tunnel in the embankment: the gaping mouth of the Cloaca Maxima, the city's great sewer. Built under Rome's Etruscan kings in the sixth century BC to drain the area around the Forum, it was given its final form in the first century BC.

San Giorgio in Velabro
Via del Velabro 19 (06 6920 4534/www.oscgeneral. org/sgiorgio.html). Bus 30Exp, 44, 63, 81, 95, 160, 170, 628, 715, 716, 781. **Open** 10am-12.30pm, 4-6.30pm daily. **Map** p358 E3.
The soft light from the windows in the clerestory give a wonderfully peaceful aura to this austere little church of the fifth century. A swingeing restoration in 1925 did away with centuries of decoration and restored its original Romanesque simplicity. The 16 columns, pilfered from the Palatine and the Aventine hills, are all different. Pieces of an eighth- or ninth-century choir, including two slender columns, are incorporated into the walls. In the apse is a much-restored fresco by the school of Pietro Cavallini showing St George with a white horse and the Virgin on one side of the central Christ figure, and St Peter and St Sebastian opposite. The 12th-century altar is a rare example of the Byzantine-inspired 'caged and architraved' ciborium, a canopy on columns. A church was first built here by Greeks and was dedicated to St Sebastian, who was believed to have been martyred in the swampy area hereabouts. It was later rededicated to St George of Capadoccia (of dragon-slaying fame); a piece of the

Extra time

● You don't need much imagination to picture the ancient temple to Aesculapius (the god of medicine) that lies beneath the church of **San Bartolomeo** on the Tiber Island: the precious marble columns in the nave are the very ones that adorned the original temple, which was inaugurated in 293 BC. But if you need help to imagine how things were when Otto III built this church in 998, then check out the massive bronze vessel (protected by an iron grille on the right-hand wall of the nave, by the altar) in which the 18-year-old German-born Holy Roman Emperor brought relics of the apostle Bartholomew from Benevento.

● It was in the once-marshy area now known as the **Velabro** (from *velum*, Etruscan for marsh) that the twins Romulus and Remus were reportedly found in their basket. Close to Rome's main river port, the marsh was too tempting a real-estate opportunity and was soon drained by means of the **Cloaca Maxima** sewer system. Chunks of this ingenious Etruscan-built infrastructure can be seen (with special permission; *see p73* **Locked sites**) beneath what is popularly (but wrongly) known as the **Arco di Giano** (Arch of Janus), the touchingly depleted gateway that marked the eastern entrance to the *forum boarium* (cattle market) in what is now via del Velabro. The niches lost their statues long ago but reliefs of four goddesses – probably Juno, Minerva, Ceres and Roma – can still be seen.

● Exuberant *latinisti* like to hold toga parties on the Ides (15th) of March, when Julius Caesar was knifed by Brutus & Co in the **Teatro di Pompeo** – Rome's first permanent theatre structure, built in the mid first century BC – where the Senate was meeting after its building in the Forum was destroyed by fire. Several establishments around the campo de' Fiori area – restaurants Da Costanzo (in piazza del Paradiso) and Da Pancrazio (in piazza del Biscione), and the Hotel Teatro di Pompeo (in largo del Pallaro) –

all conceal chunks of the ancient walls, or at least keep their wine in hugely deep cellars, which were the ground floor of the theatre. Nearby, via di Grottapinta clearly follows the curve of the *cavea* (semicircular seating area), while via dei Chiavari and piazza dei Satiri mark where the stage stood.

● The ghastly story of Beatrice Cenci has inspired generations of artists and writers, from Guido Reni to Shelley, Stendhal and Moravia. It's a 16th-century tale of child abuse, incest, violence and murder, which ended with a sensational mass public execution of the entire family – including beautiful, aristocratic 22-year-old Beatrice – in front of Castel Sant'Angelo. Hidden deep in the Ghetto, the unassuming **Palazzo Cenci**, in vicolo dei Cenci, was the family house of horrors.

● Since 1361, a pilgrim hostel has stood on the site where the **Venerable English College** (via Monserrato 45, 06 686 5808, www.englishcollegerome.org) has been training Catholic priests since 1579. During persecutions in turbulent 16th-century England, 41 priests who had trained at the college were martyred for their faith the moment they set foot in that popery-hating country. Visit the college and its church – dedicated to the Holy Trinity and St Thomas of Canterbury – by appointment, or catch mass at 10am daily from late September to late May.

● To serve the spiritual needs of the Florentine merchants who lived close to the river, near where their ships came in, Michelangelo made detailed plans for a huge church dedicated to **San Giovanni dei Fiorentini** in via Giulia/piazza dell'Oro. However, he lost the commission; it was instead entrusted to architect Antonio Sangallo, whose style better reflected the new austerity imposed by the Council of Trent. It's the perfect antidote to all that Baroque excess.

skull of the valorous third-century saint is kept under the altar. The portico and bell tower are 12th-century additions. Outside, to the left, is the *arco degli Argentari*, built in AD 204; it was a gate on the road between the main Forum and the *forum boarium* (cattle market), along which moneychangers (*argentari*) plied their trade. The church and other monuments were damaged by a Mafia bomb in 1993 but have since been repaired.

San Nicola in Carcere

Via del Teatro di Marcello 46 (06 6830 7198). Bus 23, 30Exp, 44, 63, 81, 95, 160, 170, 628, 715, 716, 781. **Open** 7am-7pm daily. **Map** p358 E2.

The 12th-century San Nicola was built over three Roman temples: dating from the second and third centuries BC, these were dedicated to two-faced Janus, protector of the gates; to the goddess Juno Sospita, who may have been a protectress of commerce; and to Spes (Hope). An informal guided tour (small donations appreciated) takes you down to these, and even deeper to see a slab from the Etruscan *forum holitorium* (vegetable market), a busy commercial exchange near the main river. On the outside of the church, six columns from the Temple of Janus can be seen on the left; the ones on the right are from the Temple of Spes. The church's façade was added by Giacomo della Porta in 1599. The name, *in carcere* (prison), probably comes from a seventh-century jail that stood nearby.

Santa Maria in Cosmedin
Piazza della Bocca della Verità 18 (06 678 1419).
Bus 44, 63, 81, 95, 160, 170, 628, 715, 716, 781.
Open *Apr-Sept* 9am-6pm daily. *Oct-Mar* 9am-5pm daily. **Map** p358 E3.
Despite an over-enthusiastic recent restoration, this remains a lovely jumble of early Christian, medieval and Romanesque church design – with a touch of kitsch to boot. Santa Maria in Cosmedin was first built in the sixth century and then enlarged in the eighth. The beautiful campanile was a 12th-century addition. Between the 11th and 13th centuries much of the original decoration was replaced with Cosmati work, including the spiralling floor, the throne, the choir and the 13th-century *baldacchino*. This last is located above the ultimate example of recycling – a Roman bathtub used as an altar. In the sacristy/ souvenir shop is a fragment of an eighth-century mosaic of the Holy Family, brought here from the original St Peter's. In the crypt are ruins of the Ara maximus, a monument to Hercules over which the church was built; scholars believe it may have been erected here even before the founding of the city. The name Cosmedin comes from the Greek, meaning splendid decoration; this has always been the church of the Greek community, many of whom were expelled from Constantinople in the eighth century; Byzantine rite services are still held here at 10.30am on Sundays.

The church is better known as the *bocca della verità* (the mouth of truth), after the great stone mask of a horned, bearded man with a gaping mouth on the portico wall – probably, in fact, an ancient drain cover. Anyone who lies while their hand is in the mouth will have that hand bitten off, according to legend. It was reportedly used by Roman husbands to determine the fidelity of their wives. A scene in *Roman Holiday* where Gregory Peck ad-libs having his hand munched, eliciting a (reportedly) unscripted shriek of genuine alarm from Audrey Hepburn, is one of the most delightful moments in cinema. Nowadays, busloads of tourists are the main takers of this opportunity to see if one's essential integrity passes muster – in high season, queues snake down the road outside.

Teatro di Marcello
Via Teatro di Marcello. Bus 30Exp, 44, 63, 81, 95, 160, 170, 628, 715, 716, 781. **Open** by appointment only; *see p72* **Locked sites**. **Map** p358 D/E2.

This is one of the strangest and most impressive sights in Rome: a Renaissance palace – still inhabited, though now divided up into apartments – grafted on to an ancient, time-worn theatre. Julius Caesar began building a massive theatre here to rival Pompey's in the *Campus martius*, but it was finished in 11 BC by Augustus, who named it after his favourite nephew. At one time it was connected to the Portico d'Ottavia, and originally had three tiers in different classical styles (Ionic, Doric and Corinthian): the top one has collapsed. Its 41 arches were topped with great marble theatrical masks. It seated up to 20,000 people.

After the theatre was abandoned in the fourth century AD it had various uses: at the end of the 12th century the powerful Savelli clan turned it into the family fortress; in the 16th century they commissioned Baldassare Peruzzi to convert it into a less defensive-looking family pile.

Now known as the Palazzo Orsini (little bear… stone interpretations of which can be seen on the gateposts and elsewhere) after another owner, it has been split up into luxury apartments. The shops that filled the ground-level archways were thrown out in the 1930s, leaving the structure in splendid if rather sad isolation, its travertine blocks looking rather like they're suffering from some wasting disease. Get a close-up look from the walkway below the Portico d'Ottavia (*see p128*).

Tempii di Ercole & Portuno (Temples of Hercules & Portunus)
Piazza della Bocca della Verità. Bus 44, 63, 81, 95, 170, 628, 715, 716, 781. **Open** by appointment only; *see p72* **Locked sites**. **Map** p358 E3.
Like the Pantheon, these diminutive Republican-era temples owe their good state of preservation to their conversion into churches in the Middle Ages. The round one, which looks for all the world like a delightful English folly, was built in the first century BC and dedicated to Hercules. Early archaeologists were confused by its shape, which is similar to the Temple of Vesta in the Roman Forum, and dubbed it the Temple of Vesta. Recently restored, it's the oldest marble building still standing in Rome (the marble blocks on the temple's bottom half are what remain of the original). The original upper section, perhaps domed, has been lost, although 19 of its 20 marble columns have survived; the roof is modern.

To its right stands the square temple dedicated to Portunus (god of harbours), as ancient Rome's river port was near by. (Inexplicably, early archaeologists attributed this one to *Fortuna Virilis* – manly fortune.) The two temples were deconsecrated and designated ancient monuments in the 1920s on Mussolini's orders. Once picturesquely placed amid glorious clumps of oleander, the temples now tower over struggling rose bushes and sparse lawns. The Triton fountain in front, by Francesco Bizzaccheri (1715), was inspired by, but definitely doesn't equal, Bernini's in piazza Barberini (*see p91*).

Trastevere & the Gianicolo

The other side of Rome.

Trastevere is a great treat if you've spent your time diligently observing ancient ruins, and admiring statuary on the other, serious side of the river. Across the Tiber *(trans tiberim)*, your main tasks include rambling in leisurely fashion through narrow, cobbled streets, keeping your ear out for some of the thickest *romanaccio* accents in town and selecting the bar you like best for *aperitivi* and people-watching.

Trastevere (pronounced Tras-TEV-ver-ray) still lives up to your oh-so *pittoresco* Roman fantasy – at least partially. It's true that much of the boisterous and very communal street life and artisan trade that gave Trastevere its flavour has given way to wine bars and trendy restaurants. An inevitable transformation, you might say, for a neighbourhood that for centuries has attracted artists and writers, brawlers and hookers, all drawn by its particular lively yet langorous quality.

Notoriously proud of their identity, *trasteverini* claim descent from indigenous Etruscans as well as slave stock, including first-century AD sailors lured upriver from the port at Ostia. Through the Imperial period, much of the *trans tiberim* area was agricultural, with farms, vineyards, country villas and gardens laid out for the pleasure of the Caesars. Later, Syrian and Jewish trading communities set up

here before moving in the Middle Ages to the Ghetto across the river. Trastevere was a working-class district in papal Rome and remained so until well after the Unification in 1870. Today, *trasteverini* boast they are the only true Romans, and celebrate their exclusive heritage in a two-week-long street festival each July called the *festa di noiantri* ('we others').

Hugging the river from Ponte Sublicio in the south almost to the Vatican in the north, the district has at least three distinct personalities.

The streets and *piazzette* to the east of thundering viale Trastevere, with vines and creepers decking charming houses, almost seem painted to please a foreigner's aesthetics. This is a quiet part of the neighbourhood – contemplative, rather than party-going.

A wholly different demographic gathers to the west of viale Trastevere: by day, action centres around the food market in piazza San Cosimato; come late afternoon, a buzz begins on the small streets that fan out from piazza Santa Maria in Trastevere, growing in volume and intensity as the evening progresses. Night brings an international crowd to the scores of cafés, pubs and restaurants; there to meet them is a rather louche bunch, some selling trinkets in (rather more upmarket) piazza Sant'Egidio (**photo** p133) and (decidedly squalid) piazza Trilussa. By the wee hours, the result can be charmingly picturesque – or can degenerate unpleasantly: sales of glass bottles have been banned in the area as overly enthusiastic revellers have been known to spoil the party.

Moving towards the Vatican, via della Lungara is flanked by stately villas once owned by some of papal Rome's most illustrious families. Here also is Rome's arguably most infamous prison, the *Regina Coeli.*

The traffic in the warren of alleys is chaotic, despite severe restrictions introduced recently on cars in the evening. Fur-coated Roman matrons venturing over from the other side of the Tiber instinctively transfer their designer bags on to the curbside shoulder, beyond the reach of Vespa-borne opportunists.

Up above Trastevere, the **Gianicolo** (*see p138*) is Rome's highest hill – though not one of the official seven. A park with spectacular views over the *centro storico* runs most of its length; elsewhere, comfortable apartment blocks stand in leafy tranquillity.

West of viale Trastevere

Ponte Sisto, an elegant footbridge that was constructed by Pope Sixtus IV, links Trastevere to Rome 'proper'. Alternatively, you can cross the heavily trafficked Ponte Garibaldi and take via della Lungaretta to the heart of Trastevere and **Santa Maria in Trastevere** (*see p135*). Nearby, the market square of **piazza San Cosimato** (photo p136) has recently undergone a major makeover, becoming a meeting place for locals after years as a construction site. Despite the preponderance of cement, it attracts children, elderly residents and football-playing youngsters at all times of the day.

On the other (northern) side of piazza Santa Maria in Trastevere, piazza Sant'Egidio is the site of the unassuming **Museo di Roma in Trastevere** (*see below*) and home to lively open-air stalls where geegaws of varying quality from faraway places are peddled.

Further north still, the backstreets nestled against the Gianicolo (Janiculum hill, *see p138*) allow you a glimpse of the less commercial side of Trastevere. Smoggy via della Lungara (*see p18* **Paved with good intentions**) leads to the lovely **Orto Botanico** (botanical gardens; *see below*), the **Villa Farnesina**, with its frescoes by Raffaele, and **Palazzo Corsini** (*see p135*), which now houses part of the national art collection. Near the start of via della Lungara, by the imposing Porta Settimiana – a third-century gate rebuilt in the 15th century – the humble **Casa della Fornarina** (*see below*) is where the artist Raphael's mistress is said to have lived.

Casa della Fornarina

Via di Santa Dorotea 20 (no phone). Bus 23, 280, 780, H/tram 8. Closed to the public. **Map** p358 B2.

Just inside the Porta Settimiana is an unassuming house, now a restaurant, with a pretty window high on the façade and a granite column embedded in its wall. It is believed to have been the home of Margherita, known as *la fornarina,* the baker's daughter who reputedly stole the heart of Renaissance genius Raphael and whose seductive portrait hangs in the Palazzo Barberini (*see p91*); the artist couldn't resist staking his claim – his name is inscribed on a bangle on her naked arm.

Museo di Roma in Trastevere

Piazza Sant'Egidio 1B (06 581 6563/www2.comune. roma.it/museodiroma.trastevere). Bus 23, 44, 75, 280, 780/tram 3, 8. **Open** 10am-8pm (last entry 7pm) Tue-Sun. **Admission** €3; €1.50 concessions. *Special exhibitions* varies. **No credit cards. Map** p358 C3.

If you happen to be in Trastevere with nothing much to do, you could take in this modest museum and be pleasantly surprised, especially if you have children along. A small collection of watercolours by Ettore Roesler Franz illustrates scenes of everyday 19th-century Roman life; a series of rooms with waxwork tableaux shows humble folks drinking in the osteria, dancing the *saltarello* or playing the *zampogne* (bagpipes). There are also occasional photographic exhibitions.

Orto Botanico

Largo Cristina di Svezia 24 (06 4991 7135). Bus 23, 280, 780, H/tram 3, 8. **Open** Apr-Oct 9.30am-6pm Mon-Sat. Nov-Mar 9.30am-5.30pm Mon-Sat. **Admission** €4; €2 concessions. **No credit cards. Map** p358 B2.

Rome's Botanical Gardens were established in 1833, within the gardens of the Palazzo Corsini (*see p135*), which had been the home of Queen Christina of Sweden (*see also p135* **Queen Christina**). But this verdant area at the foot of the Gianicolo had first been planted in the 13th century, by order of Pope Nicholas III, and was devoted to simples (medicinal

Sightseeing

Evening action in **piazza Sant'Egidio**. *See p132.*

DISCOVER MORE CITIES

Tell us what you think and you could win £100-worth of City Guides

Your opinions are important to us and we'd like to know what you like and what you don't like about the Time Out City Guides

For your chance to win, simply fill in our short survey at
timeout.com/guidesfeedback

Every month a reader will win £100 to spend on the Time Out City Guides of their choice – a great start to discovering new cities and you'll have extra cash to enjoy your trip!

Time Out
Guides

Queen Christina

In 1655, Queen Christina abdicated the Swedish throne and came to Rome, entering triumphantly through a gate in piazza del Popolo (*see p109*), designed for the event by Gian Lorenzo Bernini. She was to spend the next 34 years in the Eternal City, her intellect, culture, audacity and ambiguous sexuality making her an object of admiration and gossip – and an embarrassment to the Church.

Christina became queen at age six, but soon managed to alienate her people not only by her conversion to Catholicism in that rigidly Protestant country, but because she dressed and behaved like a man, demanded to be king rather than queen and ruled in an erratic fashion that plunged her exchequer into debt.

Despite these signs, such a high-class conversion to a Church in the throes of an ideological battle with the followers of Martin Luther made her a darling of the Catholic hierarchy. Once in Rome, though, Christina gave Pope Alexander VII nothing but grief.

Her devotion to Catholicism was questioned, but not her attachment to a Catholic priest, Decio Azzolino, to whom she left her entire patrimony. Her tastes (sexual and otherwise) were unshackled, her mentality was decidedly 'out of the box', offending and confounding the conventions of the day. During her three decades in Rome – mostly in the Palazzo Riario (now Corsini; *see below*) – she surrounded herself with the greatest philosophers and artists of the time; she patronised them all, amassing a connoisseur's collection of art, despite often-shaky finances. Her parties were legendary. She studied alchemy and astrology. Her attachment to a series of women fuelled speculation about Sapphic leanings. (After her death, her body was examined for possible hermaphroditic characteristics: reports say that no conclusions were reached.)

Short, stout, pockmarked and with a hump on her shoulder, Christina – contemporary sources said – exerted an extraordinary degree of fascination, right up until her death in 1689 when she was buried, against her explicit wishes, in St Peter's.

plants) and citrus groves. Today the Orto Botanico is a delicious haven from the rigours of a hot, dusty day, with its Baroque stairs flanked by cascading waterfalls, formal tableaux around fountains and statues, its bamboo grove, and varieties of exotic plants and flowers. Check out the cactus garden, the orchids and the touching and smelling collection for the vision-impaired. One of Rome's most under-appreciated gems.

Palazzo Corsini – Galleria Nazionale d'Arte Antica

Via della Lungara 10 (06 6880 2323/www.galleria borghese.it). Bus 23, 280, 780, H/tram 3, 8. **Open** 9.30am, 11am, 12.30pm Tue-Sat. **Admission** €4; €2 concessions. **No credit cards. Map** p358 B2.
Note: severe staff shortages mean that the gallery theoretically only opens its doors for three 15-minute periods (at the times above); once inside, you can remain until 1.50pm. But even these openings aren't guaranteed – it pays to call ahead.
In the 1933 film *Queen Christina*, Greta Garbo played the former owner of this palace as a graceful tussler with existential angst; in real life, the stout 17th-century Swedish monarch smoked a pipe, wore trousers and entertained female – and a fair number of (ordained) male – lovers. 'Queen without a Realm, Christian without a faith, and woman without shame' ran one of the contemporary epithets on Christina. But Christina was also one of the most cultured and influential women of her age. The century's highest-profile convert to Catholicism, she

abdicated her throne and established her glittering court here in 1662, filling what was then Palazzo Riario with her fabled library and an ever-expanding collection of fabulous old masters. She threw the best parties in Rome and commissioned many of Scarlatti and Corelli's hit tunes before dying here in 1689. (*See also above* **Queen Christina**.)

Today the palace – later redesigned by Ferdinand Fuga for the Corsini family – houses part of the national art collection. The galleries have beautiful frescoes and trompe l'oeil effects, and contain paintings of the Madonna by Van Dyck, Filippo Lippi and Orazio Gentileschi, two St Sebastians (one by Rubens and one by Annibale Carracci) and a pair of Annunciations by Guercino. Among the works by Caravaggio is an unadorned *Narcissus*. There's also a triptych by Fra Angelico and a melancholy *Salome* by Guido Reni.

Palazzo Corsini is also the HQ of the prestigious Accademia dei Lincei, a scientific society that has been going since 1603.

Santa Maria in Trastevere

Piazza Santa Maria in Trastevere (06 581 4802). Bus 23, 280, 780, H/tram 3, 8. **Open** 7.30am-9pm daily. **Map** p358 C3.
This stunning church, with its welcoming portico and façade with shimmering 13th-century mosaics, overlooks the traffic-free piazza of the same name and is the heart and soul of Trastevere. According to legend, a well of oil sprang miraculously from the

Sightseeing

Piazza San Cosimato. *See p132.*

ground where the church now stands the moment Christ was born, and flowed to the Tiber all day. A small street leading out of the piazza, via della Fonte dell'Olio, commemorates this.

The façade we see today was designed by Carlo Fontana in 1692, but the mosaics pre-date it by four centuries: they show Mary breastfeeding Christ, flanked by ten women with crowns and lanterns, on a solid gold background.

The present 12th-century Romanesque church, built for Pope Innocent II, replaced a basilica from the late third or early fourth century (though legend has it that it was founded by Pope Callistus I, who died in 222) – one of the city's oldest and the first dedicated to the Virgin. That in turn probably topped the site of a *titulus* – a place of worship in the house of an early Christian. The 22 granite columns with Ionic and Corinthian capitals that line the nave are thought to be from the Baths of Caracalla (*see p141*). The apse is made magnificent by a 12th-century mosaic of Jesus and the Virgin Mary; the figure on the far left is Pope Innocent. Further down, between the windows, are mosaics of the Virgin from the 13th century, attributed to Pietro Cavallini, whose relaxed, realistic figures represent the re-emergence of a Roman style after long years of the hegemony of stiff Byzantine models. The Madonna and Child with rainbow overhead is also by Cavallini. Through the wooden door on the left, just before entering the transept, there are two tiny, exquisite fragments of first-century AD mosaics from Palestrina (*see p314*), and in the Altemps chapel to the left of the high altar is a very rare seventh-century painting on wood of the Virgin, known as the Madonna of Clemency. Still on the left side is the 17th-century Avila chapel with its elaborate cupola by Antonio Gherardi. The wood-carved ceiling and centrepiece painting of the *Assumption* is by Domenichino. Throughout the nave, fine marble mosaic in the cosmatesque style graces the floor, but the original 12th-century work was almost completely replaced in the late 18th century.

Villa Farnesina

Via della Lungara 230 (06 6802 7268/www.lincei.it). Bus 23, 280, 780, H/tram 3, 8. **Open** 9am-1pm Mon-Sat. **Admission** €5; €4 concessions. **No credit cards**. **Map** p358 B2.

Villa Farnesina was built between 1508 and 1511 to a design by Baldassare Peruzzi as a pleasure palace and holiday home for the fabulously rich papal banker Agostino Chigi. Treasurer to Pope Julius II, Chigi was one of Raphael's principal patrons. In its day the villa was stuffed to the rafters with great works of art, although many were later sold to pay off debts. Chigi was known for his extravagant parties, where guests had the run of the palace and the magnificent gardens. Just to make sure his guests knew that money was no object, he would have his servants toss the silver and gold plates on which they dined into the Tiber – into underwater nets, to be fished out later and used again. The powerful Farnese family bought the villa and renamed it in 1577 after the Chigis went bankrupt.

The stunning frescoes are homages to the pagan and classical world; the works on the ground-floor Loggia of Psyche were designed by Raphael but executed by his friends and followers, including Giulio Romano; according to local lore, the master himself was too busy dallying with his mistress, *la fornarina* (baker's girl) to apply any more paint than was strictly necessary himself. The Grace with her back turned, to the right of the door, is attributed to him though. Around the corner in the Loggia of Galatea, Raphael took brush in hand to create the victorious goddess in her seashell chariot. Upstairs, the Salone delle Prospettive was decorated by Peruzzi with views of 16th-century Rome. Next to it is Agostino Chigi's bedroom, with a fresco of the *Marriage of Alexander the Great and Roxanne* by Raphael's follower Sodoma. Like most of his paintings, this is a rather sordid number showing the couple being undressed by vicious cherubs.

The villa stays open until 4pm on Mondays and Saturdays from mid March to July, from mid September to December. It also opens 9am-1pm on the first Sunday of every month.

East of viale Trastevere

In this achingly charming part of Trastevere, you won't have to battle crowds or hawkers as you wander between pretty *piazze* and washing-festooned streets. It's easy, here, to imagine Roman life as it was two or three centuries ago. The area is dominated by the basilica of **Santa Cecilia** (*see p137*) with its underground treasures and Cavallini frescoes, but unexpected gems can be found in the **Chiostro dei Genovesi** (*see p137*) and in the church of **San Francesco a Ripa** (*see p137*).

This was a busy commercial area from the 15th century through to Unification in the late 19th century, due to its proximity to the busy

Ripa Grande port. The port is commemorated in a statue on the riverside façade of the huge structure of San Michele, a former hospice, orphanage and reform school, now housing offices of the cultural heritage ministry.

Chiostro dei Genovesi

Via Anicia 12 (no phone) Bus 3, 23, 75, 115, 280, 630, 753, 780, H/tram 8. **Open** *Apr-Sept* 3-6pm Tue, Fri. *Oct-Mar* 2-4pm Tue, Fri. **Admission** free. **Map** p359 C4.

To the left of the 15th-century church of San Giovanni dei Genovesi is a wooden door (ring the bell marked 'Sposito' to get in) that opens into a glorious flower-filled cloister with a well, part of a 15th-century hospice for Genoese sailors designed by Baccio Pontelli. Concealed among the octagonal columns supporting the double loggia is a plaque commemorating Rome's first palm tree, planted here in 1588.

San Francesco a Ripa

Piazza San Francesco d'Assisi 88 (06 581 9020). Bus 23, 44, 75, 115, 280, 630, 753, 780, H/tram 8. **Open** 7am-noon, 4-7pm Mon-Sat; 7am-1pm, 4-7.30pm Sun. **Map** p359 C4.

Rebuilt in the 1680s, this church took the place of a 13th-century one that held now-lost frescoes by Pietro Cavallino chronicling the life of St Francis of Assisi. The saint stayed in the adjoining convent when he visited Rome in 1229: if you ask the sacristan, he may show you the cell where St Francis lived and the rock on which he placed his head to sleep. An orange tree in the garden was supposedly planted by the saint, ever in harmony with nature. Nowadays, though, most visitors stop here to see a 1674 sculpture by Gian Lorenzo Bernini of the Beata Ludovica Albertoni, a Franciscan nun of noble origins who is shown in a dramatic, sexually ambiguous Baroque ecstasy with a few plaster *putti* heads thrown in years later for effect (*see p38* **Bernini's babes**).

Santa Cecilia in Trastevere

Piazza Santa Cecilia (06 581 2140). Bus 2, 23, 75, 115, 280, 780, H/tram 8. **Open** *Church* 9.30am-1.15pm, 4-8pm daily. *Cavallini frescoes* 10.15am-12.30pm Mon-Sat; 11.30am-12.30pm daily. *Archeological site* 7am-12.30pm, 4-6.30pm daily. **Admission** *Frescoes* €2.50. *Archeological site* €2.50. **No credit cards**. **Map** p358 D3.

The current 16th-century church of this magnificent religious complex was built above a fifth-century basilica, which in turn incorporated a titulus, or house where early Christians met. In this case,

Sightseeing

Extra time

● The new **Casa della Memoria e della Storia** (via San Francesco di Sales 5, 06 687 6543, open 10am-6pm Mon-Sat, library 10am-2pm Mon-Sat) is a documentation centre and exhibition space focusing on those who suffered under – and fought against – Nazi-Fascism: Italian partisans, Jewish groups and historians contribute to the centre's events.
● The **Vecchia Farmacia della Scala** (piazza della Scala 23, 06 580 6217) has been whipping up cures – including one, reportedly, for the plague – since the 16th century. Check out the collection of beautiful ceramic medicinal-herb containers.
● Water splashes merrily from wine cask to barrel in the charming **Fontana delle Botte** on via Cisterna. It may look venerable but it's a 20th-century tribute to the wine-loving spirit of the locals. In 1927, Rome authorities got architect Pietro Lombardi to design a series of fountains to define various neighbourhoods: these also include the Fontana delle Anfore (amphorae; *see p140* **Ambulatio**) in Testaccio, Fontana dei Libri (books) near Palazzo Madama (*see p115*) and many others.
● A recent revamp of piazza San Cosimato has given new prominence to the 12th-century entrance to the convent of **Santi**

Cosma e Damiano. Originally it was a Camaldolese monastery but it was taken away from this order after just four years due to reports of improper behaviour. Poor Clare nuns took it over, and their successors still run it as a hospice for the elderly.
● Rome's architectural riches are so immense that locals can get blasé. But even laid-back *trasteverini* are horrified at the conversion of the complex around Borromini's church of **Santa Maria dei Sette Dolori** (via Garibaldi 27, *pictured*) into a luxury hotel. As this guide went to press, the17th-century façade was hidden behind scaffolding.

gruesome legend relates, that house belonged to Roman patrician Valerio, who lived at the time of Emperor Marcus Aurelius. So impressed was Valerio by his wife Cecilia's vow of chastity that he too converted to Christianity. Valerio was murdered for his pains, and Cecilia was arrested while she tried to bury him. Doing away with the saintly Cecilia proved a difficult job for the Romans. After a failed attempt to suffocate her in the hot baths of her house (on the site) her persecutors tried to behead her. But only three strokes of the axe were permitted by law, and even the third failed to do the job immediately. As she was slowing dying she sang, thereby securing her place as the patron saint of music. When her tomb was reopened in 1599, her body was uncorrupted. Sculptor Stefano Maderno portrays her prone with her head delicately turned away in an exquisite marble rendering beneath the altar. Her sarcophagus is in the crypt.

The excavations below the church provide extensive evidence of early Roman and palaeo-Christian buildings; here too is the pretty decorated crypt where Cecilia's body lies.

On the first floor, on the other hand, is a choir from where nuns from the adjoining convent could look down over the interior of the basilica from behind a grill. On one wall is what remains of what was possibly Rome's greatest 13th-century fresco – a *Last Judgment* by little-known genius Pietro Cavallini. With its rainbow-winged angels of all ranks and desperate sinners writhing hellwards, the once-monumental fresco shows Cavallini breaking away from the Byzantine style and giving new light and humanity to the figures.

The Gianicolo

This luxuriously verdant hilltop neighbourhood is one of Rome's most beautiful. A couple of winding roads lead up from Trastevere past decidedly patrician villas, many of which are now embassies and cultural institutions. Up via Garibaldi is Bramante's lovely **Tempietto** (*see below*), in the courtyard of the church of San Pietro in Montorio (which is part of a complex that also includes the Spanish cultural centre). It contrasts oddly with the squat Fascist-era monument across the road: the **Ossario Garibaldino** (open 9am-1pm Tue-Sun). Inscribed with the words *Roma o morte* (Rome or death) – the rallying cry of Unification hero Giuseppe Garibaldi – the monument contains the remains of Risorgimento heroes, including Goffredo Mameli, composer of Italy's stirring national anthem.

A grand belvedere at the **Fontana Paola** (*see below*) is one of the best places to gaze down over the Eternal City.

At the top of the hill, the imposing bronze **statue of Giuseppe Garibaldi** on his dashing steed is a reminder of his role in the creation of Italy as a nation – in 1849 this breathtaking lookout spot was the scene of one of the fiercest battles in the struggle for Italian unity (the Risorgimento; *see p23*). Freedom fighter Garibaldi and his makeshift army of red-shirted *garibaldini* – a hotchpotch of former papal troops and starry-eyed young enthusiasts – tried valiantly (but ultimately failed) to defend the short-lived Roman Republic against French troops sent to restore papal rule. From beneath this balcony a cannon fires one shot each day at noon. To the north, Garibaldi's South American wife Anita sits astride her own bronze horse, baby in one arm and pistol in the other. The busts that line the road depict Risorgimento martyrs. A lighthouse donated by Italian emigrants to Argentina flashes its light from this promontory.

Fontana Paola
Via Garibaldi. Bus 44, 75, 115, 710, 870.
Map p358 B3.
This grandiose fountain, which sends lavishly splashy cascades into an equally grand pool, is fed by water that has travelled 35km (22 miles) through a Trajan-era aqueduct from Lake Bracciano, to the north of Rome. Pope Paul V had Flamino Ponzio and Giovanni Fontana design the fountain for him in 1621, in a bid to out-do his predecessor Sixtus V, who had harnessed a third-century AD aqueduct to supply his Fontana dell'Acqua Felice (*see p158*) 20 years earlier. A theatre is housed in the massive chamber above the fountain, offering outdoor performances in summer and an attractive café besides.

Tempietto di Bramante & San Pietro in Montorio
Piazza San Pietro in Montorio 2 (06 581 3940).
Bus 44, 75, 115, 710, 870. **Open** *Tempietto* Apr-Sept 9.30am-12.30pm, 4-6pm Tue-Sun; Oct-Mar 9.30am-12.30pm, 2-4pm Tue-Sun. *Church* 8am-noon, 4-6pm daily. **Map** p358 B3.
High up on the Gianicolo, on one of the spots where St Peter is believed to have been crucified (St Peter's is another), San Pietro in Montorio conceals one of Rome's greatest architectural jewels in its courtyard: the Tempietto, designed by Donato Bramante in 1508 for Cardinal Giuliano della Rovere, who was to become Pope Julius II (and who also got him working on St Peter's basilica). The small circular structure, with its Doric columns, has classical symmetry that was subsequently imitated by many architects. Bernini got his hands on it in 1628, adding the staircase that leads down to the crypt. The church next door, founded in the late ninth century and rebuilt in the late 15th, contains a chapel by Bernini (second on the left) and one by Vasari (fifth on the right). Paintings include Sebastiano del Piombo's *Flagellation*, and *Crucifixion of St Peter* by Guido Reni. The name Montorio, or golden hill, refers to the way the sun hit sand on the Gianicolo, turning it gold.

The Aventine, Testaccio & Ostiense

Workaday (and party-night) neighbourhoods overlooked by a high-class hill.

The leafy, upmarket Aventine hill couldn't be more different from the busy, workaday districts of Testaccio and Ostiense that lie at its southern feet. Yet there's a grudging respect between them that runs both ways. Without the proximity of Testaccio's bars and markets, and Ostiense's burgeoning cultural and nightlife scene, the Aventine would be a lifeless enclave of privilege; whereas inhabitants of the lower areas are wont to seek respite from the bustle and din that surrounds them with a wander up to the peaceful hill that overlooks them.

The Aventine

First settled by King Ancius Marcius in the seventh century BC, the Aventine was later colonised by sailors, merchants and other undesirables who crept inexorably up the hill from the rough-and-tumble port below.

In 456 BC the whole of the Aventine hill was earmarked for plebeians to construct homes. And there the plebs remained, organising their guilds and building their temples. As they became more successful, so their villas became gentrified. By the time the Republic gave way to the Empire, this had become an exclusive neighbourhood. By the fifth century AD there were two bath complexes here and many luxurious *palazzi*.

What the Aventine is best for nowadays is a walk: the delightful **Parco Savello**, still surrounded by the crenellated walls of a 12th-century fortress of the Savello family, has dozens of orange trees and a spectacular view. Contemplate the beauty of the basilica of **Santa Sabina** (*see below*) or peek through the keyhole of the **priory of the Knights of Malta** at nearby piazza Cavalieri di Malta 3 to enjoy the surrealistic surprise designed by Gian Battista Piranesi – a telescopic view of St Peter's dome.

Across thundering viale Aventino is the *piccolo Aventino*, aka the San Saba district (*see p142* **Extra time**). Beyond the white cuboids of the UN's Food and Agriculture Organisation – once Mussolini's Colonies Ministry – stand the towering remains of the **Terme di Caracalla** (Baths of Caracalla; *see p141*).

Santa Sabina
Piazza Pietro d'Illiria 1 (06 574 3573). Bus 81, 160, 175, 628, 715. **Open** 6.30am-12.45pm, 3-7pm daily. **Map** p359 E4.
Try to visit Santa Sabina on a sunny day, when the light shines softly into this magnificent, solemn basilica. It was built in the fifth century over an early Christian titulus believed to have belonged to a

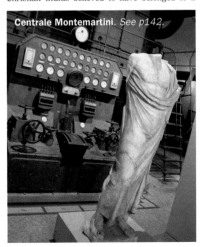

Centrale Montemartini. *See p142.*

Ambulatio Emporium

Much of early Rome's might rested on commerce. The *Portus tiberinus*, on the river's left bank across from the Tiber Island, was active from the eighth century BC. The commodities and luxuries that the expanding metropolis demanded arrived by ship from all over the known world at the sea port of Ostia (*see p300*), then were transferred to *caudicariae* (barges) and pulled upriver by oxen.

By the early second century BC, Rome had outgrown its old port. In 193 BC, construction began on a new structure, the **Emporio** (*see p143*), in what is now Testaccio. Steps led up from this wharf area to the Porticus Aemilia, a huge covered warehouse 60 metres (200 feet) wide and almost 500 metres (1,600 feet) long. Behind the *porticus* were the *horreae* (grain warehouses), built under Tiberius (AD 14-37) to implement the Imperial grain monopoly.

Buses 23, 75, 95, 280 and 716, and tram 3, will deposit you in **piazza dell'Emporio**, where the **Fontana delle Anfore** by Pietro Lombardi (1927) is a reminder of the area's vocation. From the riverbank here you can peer down into the *emporium*. The object of frantic digging in the 1980s and '90s, it is now largely abandoned, its few remaining arches providing shelter for any homeless people able to scale fences. Continue south along the riverbank to the traffic lights, and turn into via Rubattino. Chunks of the *porticus* emerge from behind a motley stone wall. Turn right here into via Vespucci.

For an idea of the vast size of this structure, turn around. One end nestled beneath the Aventine hill, way off in the distance. To get to the other end, walk down via Vespucci and turn left into via Florio, where more *porticus* fragments are visible. Take a right into via Branca and continue to the technical school's gates (where this road meets via Beniamino Franklin); look through and you'll be able to

see the end wall of the *porticus*. Take a left into via Franklin, where, as this guide went to press, excavations were under way of one of the *horreae*. At the end of via Franklin are (right) the **Mattatoio** (*see p143*) and (left) **Monte Testaccio**.

This 36-metre-high (120-foot-high) 'mountain' covered by scruffy plants is a quirky sidebar to the commercial might of the Roman Empire in the second and third centuries. What appears to be a substantial hill is in fact a collection of pieces of broken amphorae dumped here during the port's heyday. The jars held olive oil from Betica (Andalucía) and North Africa. In the Middle Ages, Monte Testaccio and the area below it were the venue for pre-Lenten *carnevale* celebrations, with the horse races and religious pageants of the nobility vying with the less-refined sport of the people. Pigs, bulls and wild boar were packed into carts at the top of the hill and sent careering down: survivors of the impact were finished off with spears. Jews, too, were subjected to indignities of all kinds. *Osterie* were bored into the flanks of the hill in the 17th century. Today, clubs and restaurants are still tucked away there, many of them with glass rear walls that show the clay-pot innards of the hill.

Skirt the hill by first heading left along via Galvani and then right on via Zabaglia. This latter passes between the **British military cemetery** on the right and the **Cimitero Acattolico** (Protestant Cemetery; *see p142*) on the left. Just before the graveyards, turn left into via Caio Cestio and follow the high wall of the Protestant Cemetery to the end of the road. Turn right, and a few moments' walk takes you to the unlikely **pyramid** (*see p142* **Extra time**) and piazzale Ostiense, the hell-for-leather roundabout surrounding the third-century **Porta San Paolo** gate. Formerly the Porta Ostiense, it is from here that via

martyred Roman matron named Sabina; the only trace of this ancient place of worship is a bit of mosaic floor visible through a grate at the entrance. The church was subjected to a merciless restoration in the 1930s: what you see today is arguably the closest thing – give or take a 16th-century fresco or two – in Rome to an unadulterated ancient basilica. The late fifth-century cypress-wood doors are carved with biblical scenes, including one of the earliest renderings of the Crucifixion; ten of the original 28 panels have been lost. The high nave's elegant Corinthian

columns support an arcade decorated with ninth-century marble inlay work; the *schola cantorum* (choir) dates from the same period. Selenite has been placed in the high, stone-grated arched windows, as it would have been in the ninth century. Above the entrance, the fifth-century mosaic recalls that the priest Peter of Illyria built the church while Celestine was pope; two figures on either side of the inscription represent the church members converted from paganism and Judaism. Later additions in the church include Taddeo Zuccari's 16th-century fresco in the apse.

Ostiense begins its 30-kilometre (19 miles) route to the ancient seaport at Ostia Antica (*see p302*). Inside the gate – be prepared to take your life into your hands and plunge into the traffic bedlam – is the **Museo della Via Ostiense** (*see p143*).

It's a humble but oddly charming little museum, containing artefacts and prints pertaining to via Ostiense and the port at its far end. There are large-scale models of old Ostia and the port of Trajan (*see p301*) and, on the upper level, a 13th-century fresco of the Madonna and Child and a fine view over Roman driving skills.

To round off your itinerary, cross piazzale Ostiense to the Roma–Ostia station and hop on a train to Ostia Antica. It was the exponential growth of this port – and its grain-stocking facilities in particular – along with improvements in road transport that sounded the death knell for Testaccio's *emporium* in the third century AD.

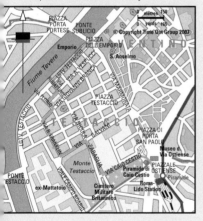

A tiny window in the entrance porch looks on to the place where St Dominic is said to have planted an orange tree brought from Spain in 1220. The adjoining monastery contains a cell (usually closed) where the saint stayed. A peaceful 13th-century cloister is reached by a sloping corridor near the main door. Excavations here in the 19th century unearthed parts of the fourth-century BC Servian Wall; a house from the second century BC; a third-century AD bath complex; and a third-century BC temple (can be seen by appointment only).

Terme di Caracalla (Baths of Caracalla)

Viale delle Terme di Caracalla 52 (06 3996 7700). Bus 118, 160, 628. **Open** (last entry 1hr before closing) 9am-2pm Mon; 9am-sunset Tue-Sun. **Admission** €6; €3 concessions. *See also p72* **Tickets. No credit cards. Map** p361 B/C5.

The high-vaulted ruins of the Baths of Caracalla, surrounded by trees and grass, are pleasantly peaceful today, but were anything but tranquil in their heyday, when up to 1,600 Romans could sweat it out in the baths and gyms. You can get some idea of the original splendour of the baths – built between AD 213 and 216 – from the fragments of mosaic and statuary littering the grounds, although the more impressive finds are in the Vatican Museums (*see p166*) and the Museo Archeologico in Naples.

The two cavernous rooms down the sides were the *gymnasia*, where Romans engaged in strenuous sports like toss-the-beanbag. There was also a large open-air *natatio* (pool) for lap-swimming. After exercising, they cleansed themselves in saunas and a series of baths of varying temperatures. The baths were usually open from noon until sunset and were social centres where people came to relax after work. The complex also contained a library, a garden, shops and stalls. Underneath it all were 9.5km (six miles) of tunnels, where slaves scurried about, treading the giant wheels that pumped clean water up to bathers and tending to huge braziers that heated the chambers from below the tiles and through pipes in the walls. Caracalla's baths were in use for more than 300 years: the fun dried up in 537 when the Visigoths sacked Rome and severed the city's aqueducts.

After years without a home, the Teatro dell'Opera's summer season (*see p277*) has now moved back here, they are sensitive about what they perform: gone, alas, are the days of full-scale productions of *Aida* with foundation-shaking elephants.

Testaccio & Ostiense

Tucked below the quiet heights of the Aventine is bustling **Testaccio**, where longtime residents are stridently – even brusquely – Roman (though a more recent influx tends to be urban and professional). The produce market in piazza Testaccio is arguably Rome's best.

Today's Testaccio is strictly residential-commercial. Historically, though, Testaccio was a place of industry and trade (*see p140* **Ambulatio**). This was the site of ancient Rome's great inner-city port. With the decline of Rome as a trading power, so Testaccio became a tranquil place of vegetable gardens and vineyards belonging to the great religious orders up on the Aventine, only to be built over after Italian Unification in the 1870s: dwellings went up for the under-class who manned the municipal slaughterhouse – **il Mattatoio** (*see p143*) – and the other noisy industries shifted

Sightseeing

Extra time

● Check out the white **pyramid** that sticks out like a sore thumb in piazzale Ostiense. An obscure first-century BC magistrate and tribune named Caius Cestius took the prevailing *aegyptomania* to extremes when he decided to build himself a tomb that was fit for a pharaoh. Faint traces of fresco in the pyramid's small inner chamber can be seen by prior appointment (*see p73* **Locked sites**).
● The Aventine's minor churches deserve a visit: in **Sant'Alessio** (via Sant'Alessio 23), Alexis lies in marble agony, with a bizarre wooden staircase hanging over his head, presumably for a speedy getaway to heaven; beneath **Santa Prisca** (via Santa Prisca 11) is Rome's best-preserved mithraeum (to get in, *see p73* **Locked sites**); at **Sant'Anselmo**, the Rome HQ of the Benedictine order, Gregorian chant evensong is sung every day at 7.15pm.
● Cross viale Aventino for a look around the '*piccolo Aventino*' – the San Saba district – a leafy neighbourhood with a morning market in its main square, piazza Bernini, not far from the eighth-century church of **San Saba** and a series of charming detached villas with gardens, built in the early 20th century (to a design by Quadrio Pirani) as a public-housing project.

here from the *centro storico*. Testaccio has no wondrous monuments, just sites that tell of its industrious past, such as the ancient port – **Emporio** – and a rubbish tip of discarded potsherds – **Monte Testaccio** (for both, *see p140* **Ambulatio**). The ex-Mattatoio is now destined to become a cultural centre.

Other noteworthy stops include the charming **Museo della Via Ostiense** (*see p143*); the **Cimitero Acattolico** (non-Catholic cemetery; *see below*), with its illustrious company of defunct foreign artists and writers; and the totally out-of-place **pyramid**, the mausoleum of a Roman with an inflated sense of self.

Testaccio also boasts the city's best nightlife, with clubs, eateries and bars dug into the base of Monte Testaccio: you can see the broken clay pieces piled up in some of the establishments on via Galvani. If you have a strong stomach, try a typical *testaccino* meal in the vicinity of the old slaughterhouse: bits of the beast that no one else wanted go into specialities such as *rigatoni alla pajata*, *trippa alla romana* and *coratelli ai carciofi* (*see p341* **The menu**).

Due south from Testaccio, **via Ostiense** slices through the once-run-down area of the same name, which is now destined for greater things. To the east of this ancient road is a dense concentration of nightspots, especially around **via Libetta**; the shiny, bustling new campus of the **Università Roma Tre**; and the old wholesale fruit and veg market, currently being transformed into the **Città dei Giovani** (City of Youth) – a youth-orientated arts and entertainment hub designed by Dutch architect Rem Koolhaas. To the west of via Ostiense, things are moving more slowly: though the low-rise workers' housing now sells for eye-watering prices, and some nightspots have opened up, the long-awaited Città delle Scienze science park (www2.comune.roma.it/citta scienza) in the decommissioned gasworks is still firmly on the drawing board. The glorious display of classical statuary in a former power station, the **Centrale Montemartini** (*see below*), is, however, a taste of what's to come.

Centrale Montemartini

Via Ostiense 106 (06 574 8030/www.musei capitolini.org). Bus 23, 271, 769. **Open** 9am-7pm Tue-Sun. **Admission** €4.50; €2.50 concessions. *See also p72* **Tickets**. **No credit cards**. **Map** p143 B3.
It may be true that the Centrale Montemartini contains merely the leftover ancient statuary from the Musei Capitolini (*see p75*) but, this being Rome, the dregs are pretty impressive; moreover, the setting itself makes this spot worth a visit. You enter through the headquarters of Rome's electricity company, beneath the skeleton of its old gasworks. Inside are fauns and Minervas, bacchic revellers and Apollos, all starkly white but oddly at home against the gleaming machinery of the decommissioned generating station. There's a (variable) extra charge when special exhibitions are being staged here. **Photo** *p139*.

Cimitero Acattolico

Via Caio Cestio 6 (06 574 1900/www.protestant cemetery.it). Metro Piramide/bus 23, 30Exp, 75, 95, 118, 271, 280, 716, 769/tram 3. **Open** 9am-5pm Mon-Sat. **Admission** free (donation of €2 expected). **Map** p359 D/E6.
This heavenly oasis of calm in the midst of a ruckus of traffic has been the resting place for foreigners who have passed on to a better world since 1784. Verdant and atmospheric, it's a dependable mecca for modern-day travellers keen to recapture the Grand Tour ethos. Unofficially known as the Protestant Cemetery, this charmingly old-world corner of the city also provides a final resting place for Buddhists, Russian Orthodox Christians and atheists; a sign points to the grave of Antonio Gramsci, founder of the Italian Communist Party. In the older sector is the grave of John Keats, who coughed his last at the age of 26, after only four months in Rome; in fine Romantic fashion his anonymous epitaph concludes: 'here lies one whose name

Sightseeing

was writ on water' (which was all the poet wanted: his executors added the rest). Next to him lies his companion, Joseph Severn. Close by is the tomb of Shelley, who died a year after Keats in a boating accident.

Emporio-Porto Fluviale

Lungotevere Testaccio. Bus 23, 30Exp, 75, 95, 170, 280, 716, 781/tram 3. **Open** *by appointment only, see p73* **Locked sites**; *visible from lungotevere Testaccio & Ponte Sublicio.* **Map** *p359 D4. See p140* **Ambulatio**.

Il Mattatoio

Piazza Giustiniani/via di Monte Testaccio. Bus 23, 30Exp, 75, 95, 170, 280, 673, 716, 719, 781/ tram 3. **Map** *p359 C6.*
The bizarre statue of a winged hero slaughtering an ox atop the Mattatoio (slaughterhouse) leaves little doubt about its mission. Hailed as Europe's most advanced abattoir when it opened in 1891, the 24-acre complex extending from the Tiber to Monte Testaccio and the Aurelian Walls coped with an eightfold increase in the city's population, was the source of meat for the whole of central Italy and provided Testaccio's residents with work until 1975.

For decades, bickering between politicians, architects and planners left the structure in picturesque abandon: now, the whole area – including the *campo boario* (cattleyards), home to the Villaggio Globale *centro sociale* (*see p279*) – is being reclaimed and transformed into a university architecture department, a centre for fair-trade sales, spaces for multi-media projects and exhibitions, as well as an outpost of the MACRO gallery (*see p176*). In the meantime, you can wander in for a look: the Mattatoio is still home to the horses that draw tourist carriages (and the homeless, who rent mattresses in the stables).

Monte Testaccio

Via Zabaglia 24. Bus 23, 30Exp, 75, 95, 280, 673, 716/tram 3. **Open** *by appointment only, see p73* **Locked sites**. **Map** *p359 D6. See p140* **Ambulatio**.

Museo della Via Ostiense

Via R Persichetti 3 (06 574 3193). Metro Piramide/ 23, 30Exp, 75, 95, 118, 271, 280, 716, 769/tram 3. **Open** *9.30am-1.30pm, 2.30-4.30pm Tue, Thur; 9.30am-1.30pm Wed, Fri, 1st & 3rd Sun of mth.* **Admission** *free.* **Map** *p359 E6. See p140* **Ambulatio**.

Sightseeing

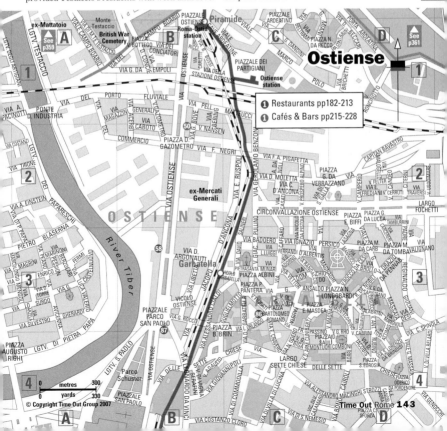

Celio, San Giovanni & San Lorenzo

Parks and churches mark where Christianity suffered its growing pains.

There are few finer places than the **Celio** to get a feel for the clash between powerful pagan Rome and early Christianity – from the new religion's struggle to get a foothold to its eventual triumph. The area is rife with testimony to martyrdom and conversion, gruesome violence and miracles, Imperial grandeur and pious humility. The monuments themselves are evidence of this rich palimpsest of Roman history, with each era literally building on the foundations of the previous one, discarding the old and adding its own innovations. The painful progression of Christianity from obscure cult to state religion provided the inspiration for much of the art and architecture in this district: from the scenes of the watery martyrdom of San Clemente under the church bearing his name, to the shrine to the self-sacrificing Roman soldier in Santi Giovanni e Paolo, to the frescoes depicting the conversion of Constantine in the church of the Quattro Coronati. The great basilica of **San Giovanni in Laterano** is testimony to the ultimate victory of the Christians.

A 20-minute walk past the basilica and nearby Santa Croce in Gerusalemme, where relics of the True Cross brought to Rome by Constantine's mother are revered, is the working class neighbourhood of **San Lorenzo**.

Known as a left-wing bastion, it was the only Roman quarter to be pounded by Allied bombs during the Nazi occupation. The beautiful basilica dedicated to San Lorenzo took a direct hit and was almost totally rebuilt after the war.

Celio

Once the residential area of choice for Roman senators, nobility and wealthy entrepreneurs, the Caelian hill (one of the famous seven) was – like the rest of Rome – overrun in AD 410 by Alaric the Goth. Its patrician villas and shops remained largely deserted for centuries thereafter, crumbling back to nature. Today the hill itself retains a bucolic character, with much of it occupied by monasteries and convents, churches and nursery schools.

The greater Celio neighbourhood stretches roughly from the via delle Terme di Caracalla on the south, to the Palatine on the west, the Colosseum to the north and San Giovanni in Laterano (*see p150*) to the east. An arduous but rewarding (and crowd-free) walking tour of the area could begin at the church of **San Gregorio Magno** (*see p145*), pass under the medieval arcade to the church of **Santi Giovanni e Paolo** (*see p146*), with its fabulous Roman house underneath, and skirt the out-of-place flagship television studio belonging to former prime minister and media magnate Silvio Berlusconi. The lovely, leafy **Villa Celimontana** (*see p149*) park is a good place to rest your feet.

The high-walled road along the park's northern edge leads to a chunk of the once-glorious **Acqua Claudia** aqueduct (*see also p172* **Parco degli acquedotti**). At the top of the supporting arch is a blue and red Greek cross, the symbol of the Trinitarian order whose 12th-century mission was to raise money to pay the ransom of crusaders captured by the infidels.

Past that arch, and right into via della Navicella, two churches face off across the street. On the right, **Santa Maria in Domnica** (*see p149*) has pretty ninth-century mosaics and a delicate sculpture of a little Roman boat (*navicella*) in front of it. Across the road, assorted martyrdoms are depicted in the odd and gruesome frescoes in **Santo Stefano Rotondo** (*see p149*). Further on to the left, the monolithic **Santi Quattro Coronati** (*see p147*) complex comes into view, with its charming cloister and secret chapel. Below it is the multi-layered **San Clemente** (*see below*).

San Clemente

Via San Giovanni in Laterano (06 774 002/www. basilicasanclemente.com). Metro Colosseo/bus 60Exp, 75, 85, 87, 117, 571, 810, 850/tram 3. **Open** 9am-12.30pm, 3-6pm Mon-Sat; noon-6pm Sun. **Admission** *Church* free. *Excavations* €5. **No credit cards. Map** p360 D3.

A favourite with kids for its dungeon-like underground level, this 12th-century basilica is a three-dimensional Roman time-line, a church above a church above an even older Imperial building – a full 18m (60ft) of Roman life separates the earliest structure from the one we see today.

In 1857 the Irish Dominicans – who have run the church since the 17th century – began digs that unearthed the church's fourth-century predecessor, and, beneath, an early Christian *titulus* (meeting place). The fourth-century structure was razed in the Norman sack of 1084, but the *schola cantorum* (choir), with its exquisite carving and mosaic decorations, survived and was moved upstairs to the new church, where it still stands.

Also in the upper church is the 12th-century mosaic in the apse, still in Byzantine style but with a theological complexity unusual for its period. Against a gold backdrop, cobalt blues, deep reds and multi-hued greens make up the crucified Christ. From the drops of Christ's blood springs the vine representing the Church, which swirls around peasants at their daily tasks, Doctors of the Church spreading the divine word and a host of animals. Above the cross, the hand of God links heaven and earth, while below, sheep represent Christ and the 12 apostles. The Latin inscription above the sheep says 'I am the vine, you are the branches'. Towards the back of the church, in the chapel of St Catherine of Alexandria, a series of frescoes by Masolino (c1430), possibly with help from Masaccio, depict the life of the saint – she is shown calmly praying as her torturers prepare the wheel to which she was strapped and stretched to death (and for which the firework was later named) – as well as Christ on the cross in between the two thieves.

From the sacristy, steps lead down to the fourth-century basilica, the space broken up by walls supporting the structure above. Fading frescoes show scenes from the life of St Clement, the fourth pope, exiled to the Crimea by Emperor Trajan. Even in exile, he didn't give up proselytising and so was hurled into the Black Sea, tied to an anchor. A year later, the sea receded, revealing a tomb containing Clement's body. After that, the sea would recede once a year and another miracle would occur.

Near the far end of the underground basilica is a modern shrine to St Cyril, the inventor of Cyrillic script was a great figure of the Orthodox churches and credited with bringing Clement's body to Rome.

A stairway leads down to an ancient Roman alley. On one side are the remains of a second-century Roman *insula*, or apartment building, containing a site where the Persian god Mithras was worshipped. There are three rooms devoted to the cult, which was as popular as Christianity in the late Imperial age. Persian mythology said that Mithras was born of a virgin who was called 'mother of God'… Sound familiar? In the sanctuary, a fresco depicts the god killing a bull. On the other side of the lane are the ground-floor rooms of a Roman house used by early Christians as a *titulus*. At one of the turns in this warren of antiquity, you can hear water rushing through an ancient sewer on its way down to the Tiber.

San Gregorio Magno

Piazza di San Gregorio Magno 1 (church 06 700 8227/oratories 06 7049 4966). Bus 60Exp, 75, 81, 175, 271, 673/tram 3. **Open** 8.30am-1pm, 3.30-7pm daily. **Map** p361 B4.

This impressive Baroque church with a grandiose staircase, finished by Giovanni Battista Soria in 1633, stands on the site of the home of one of the most

Medieval arcade: Clivio Scauro. *See p144.*

Sightseeing

remarkable popes, Gregory I (the Great; 590-604). Gregory was steered by his affluent family towards a career in public administration, but instead he embraced the monastic life and converted his house into a monastery. He became Pope Pelagius II's right-hand man and was tapped for the papacy when Pelagius died. Popular lore says he fled Rome when he heard the news; dragged back, he spent his 14-year pontificate vigorously reorganising the Church.

Inside the church, in a chapel on the right, is a marble chair dating from the first century BC, said to have been used by Gregory as his papal throne. Also here is the tomb of diplomat Sir Edward Carne, who visited Rome several times to persuade the pope to annul the marriage of Henry VIII and Catherine of Aragon, so that the king could marry Anne Boleyn.

Outside, across a pine-scented garden maintained by the nuns of Mother Teresa's order, stand three chapels, or *oratori* (closed Aug). The chapels of Santa Barbara and Sant'Andrea are medieval structures, heavily restored in the early 17th century and popularly believed to have been part of the house of Gregory the Great and his mother St Sylvia; Sant'Andrea has frescoes by Guido Reni and Domenichino. The chapel of St Sylvia itself dates from the 17th century. Behind the chapels are remains of shops that lined this ancient road, the Clivus Scauri.

Santa Maria in Domnica
Via della Navicella 10 (06 7720 2685). Bus 81, 117, 673. **Open** 8.30am-12.30pm, 4.30-7pm daily. **Map** p361 C4.

Santa Maria in Domnica.

Santa Maria in Domnica is known to the locals as the *navicella* (little ship), after the Roman statue that stands outside (which was the inspiration for the 16th-century *barcaccia* fountain at the Spanish Steps). A church was built here in the seventh century, over the barracks of a corps of Roman *vigiles* (firefighters). It was reconstructed in the ninth century by Pope Paschal I, who commissioned the apse mosaic – one of the most charming in Rome. The pope is portrayed sitting at the feet of the Virgin and Child with a square halo that indicates he was living when the mosaic was made. What sets this lovely design in gold and rich blues, reds and aquamarines apart is that Mary and Jesus don't show the melancholy prescience of what was to befall them as did most such depictions until then: the cherry-red daubs of blush on their cheeks give them a healthy and cheerful glow. They are surrounded by a host of angels; above, the apostles appear to be skipping through a meadow. The interior of the church is austere and peaceful, with 18 ancient marble columns supporting the graceful arches of the nave. The carved wood ceiling and porticoed façade are the result of a 16th-century restoration.

Santi Giovanni e Paolo
Piazza Santi Giovanni e Paolo 13 (church 06 700 5745/excavations 06 7045 4544/www.case romane.it). Bus 60Exp, 75, 81, 175, 673/tram 3. **Open** *Church* 8.30am-noon, 3.30-6pm daily. *Excavations* 10am-1pm, 3-6pm Mon, Thur-Sun. **Admission** *Church* free. *Excavations* €6; €4 concessions. **No credit cards. Map** p360 C3.

In the fourth century, a church was built over the house (and probably the bones) of John and Paul, two officers at the Imperial court who were martyred in 362. The original church was hacked away, first by Goths and later by Normans, but traces of it can still be seen in the 12th-century façade on lovely piazza Santi Giovanni e Paolo, which is overlooked by a 12th-century bell tower attached to the nearby convent. Two time-worn lions flank the entrance; one seems to be gnawing on a helpless babe.

An 18th-century restoration left the church with its present lugubrious ambience inside. Better to head around the corner, beneath the medieval buttresses of Clivus (clivio) Scauro to locate the door leading to the labyrinthine excavations of the martyrs' house. Digs in the 19th century and others in the final years of the 20th led to the discovery of more than 20 rooms on several levels. From four different buildings, and dating from the first century AD, these rooms include some evidently used for secret Christian worship. Among these are spaces bought in the fourth century by wealthy senator Pammachius, who, after embracing Christianity, donated generously to the poor and made his home into a church. Three other Christian martyrs are said to be buried there; a well-preserved fresco from the late fourth century in the *confessio* honours them. In the nymphaeum, *putti* in brightly coloured boats flank a naked female divinity, perhaps Proserpine. There are several other frescoes in good condition

Sticky ends

You needed broad shoulders indeed to embrace Christianity in its early years. Nero was the first emperor to make Christian-harrassing official policy: blamed for setting the infamous fire of AD 64, he sought to take the heat off himself by blaming, and punishing, members of this pesky new sect. Emperors Domitian, Decius and Diocletian carried out some of the worst Christian-cleansing, though most of Rome's rulers (even after Constantine) indulged in at least a bit of persecution.

Martyrdom guaranteed a fast track to heaven, and there was no shortage of victims, whether willing or incidental. Accurate numbers of those who died for their faith don't exist. German historian Ludwig Hertling reckoned that around 100,000 met sticky ends between AD 30 and 313, when Christianity was legalised by Constantine. Perhaps more realistically, Edward Gibbon (in his *Decline and Fall*) estimated anything between 1,500 and 2,000 in that period. In *Ecclesiastical History*, Eusebius gives a host of graphic descriptions of some of the torments suffered by the faithful. The Celio harbours some stirring examples...

● John and Paul were brothers employed in the imperial household in the fourth century; John was a butler and Paul served Costanza, Constantine's daughter. When the Emperor Julian, later known as the Apostate, tried to reverse Constantine's swing towards Christianity, he gave the brothers a chance to recant. They refused and were beheaded in their home, now visibile under the church of **San Giovanni e Paolo** (*see p146*). Three hapless worshipers – Crispin, Crispiniano and Benedetta – who happened to be there at the time, also met their maker.

● No one knows who is commemorated in the church of **Santi Quattro Coronati** (*see p147*; literally, 'four crowned saints' – a crowned saint is a martyr). Popular lore says that the 'four' were either soldiers who refused to bow to the god Esculapius or stonemasons who refused to sculpt the deity during the reign of Diocletian. Both versions of the story of the men – who were scourged to death – are depicted here.

● St Clement – the fourth pope, commemorated in the church of **San Clemente** (*see p145*) – is always depicted with an anchor, the instrument of his martyrdom. Condemned to hard labour in the mines of the Crimea, Clement continued proselytising and so Romans threw him into the Black Sea. A year later the waters receded to reveal his tomb, a 'miracle' that was then repeated annually. On one such occasion, a boy touched the tomb, only to be sucked into the sea. The next year, there he was, safe and sound inside the tomb.

● With its ethereal lighting and round shape, **Santo Stefano Rotondo** (*see p149*) is the *martyrium* par excellence. In the late 16th century, German monks were trained here to be despatched back to their country to re-convert those who had left the mother church to follow Martin Luther. In 1585, artists Pomarancio, Tempesta and Bril were called upon to paint 34 frescoes showing the grisly fates that might await them there: among the precedents on display are Christians being torn apart by dogs under Nero; baked in furnaces under Marcus Aurelius; split lengthwise by being tied to two bound trees then released; boiled in hot lead... and so on *ad nauseum*.

throughout the site. Guided tours in English for large groups can be booked; smaller groups can book private visits on Tuesday and Wednesday. This is an especially good and little-visited place to time-travel through Roman history.

The sacristan may let you in through the gates at the foot of the bell tower: from there you'll get a glimpse of the massive foundations of the Temple of Claudius. **Photo** p150.

Santi Quattro Coronati

Via dei Santi Quattro 20 (06 7047 5427). Bus 85, 87, 117, 571, 810, 850/tram 3. **Open** *Church & cloister* 9.30-11.50am, 4-5.30pm Mon-Sat; 9.30-10.30am, 4-5.50pm Sun. *Oratory* 9.30am-noon, 3.30-6pm daily. **Map** p360 D3.

The secret places in the basilica of the Four Crowned Saints make it a good candidate for dragging listless kids to. The church dates from the fourth century and was probably named for four Roman soldiers who refused to pray before the statue of Esculapius, the Roman god of healing. Another version has it dedicated to early stonemasons who refused to sculpt the aforementioned deity, making the church especially dear to present-day masons. Like San Clemente and Santi Giovanni e Paolo, it was burnt down by rampaging Normans in 1084. It was rebuilt as a fortified monastery, with the church itself reduced to half its original dimensions; the outsize apse, visible as you look uphill along via dei Santi Quattro, remains from the original church. The early basilica form is still discernible, and the columns that once ran along the aisles are embedded in the walls of the innermost courtyard. The church has a fine cosmatesque floor and an upper-level *matronium*, to which women were relegated during religious functions. There is also one of Rome's most beautiful cloisters, from about 1220, with lovely, slender columns supporting delicate arches and a double-cupped fountain gurgling amid its flowerbeds. The musty chapel of Santa Barbara conceals a pair of frescoes: a 12th-century *Madonna and Child* and a ninth-century unidentified saint. Just ring the bell at the door on the left side of the nave and a kind-hearted nun will proabably let you have a peek.

In the oratory outside the church (ring the bell and ask for the key) is a fresco cycle depicting the *Donation of Constantine* – a false story put forward for centuries by the papacy as justification for its authority. According to the legend, an early pope, Sylvester, cured Emperor Constantine of leprosy, after which the august personage was so grateful that he granted the Bishops of Rome spiritual and worldly authority over the whole of the Western Empire (Constantine, from his capital at Constantinople, lorded it over the Eastern Empire). The frescoes, a first-class example of political propaganda, were painted in the 13th century. They show a pox-ridden Constantine being healed by Sylvester, crowning him with a tiara and giving him a cap to symbolise the pope's spiritual and – more importantly – earthly power. In one scene, Constantine's mother, Helen, indicates Christ's cross on the hill of Golgotha. Visitors should be as silent as possible: the monastery is still home to an enclosed order of Augustine nuns.

Ambulatio Il Possesso

Since the beginning of the Christian era, 'pope' has equalled 'pomp', and one of the most pomp-filled events is the papal procession from the Vatican to the basilica of San Giovanni in Laterano. Each newly elected pope, ten days after his coronation in St Peter's, takes possession of the Lateran, his official seat in his role of Bishop of Rome.

For centuries, pontiffs processed – with thousands of adulating Romans flanking the way – on horseback, in carriages and finally in motorcades in the ceremony known as *il possesso*. They did so along the ancient route called the via Papalis.

Over the years, changes were introduced. In the Middle Ages, a detour was made, legend recounts, after the newly elected pope – subsequently known as Joan – had to stop and give birth (*see p152* **Extra time**) on a street corner below Santi Quattro Coronati. In the 16th century, Sixtus V tidied up the via Papalis as part of his massive urban renewal plan (*see also p18* **Paved with good intentions**). Since losing temporal power, the pope has been greeted at the bottom of Michelangelo's great *cordonata* – the steps leading up to the Campidoglio – by Rome's mayor, after which he takes the via dei Fori Imperiali rather than trying to cruise through the Forum.

The route's a satisfying one to follow, passing by many of the Eternal City's major monuments. It's a long walk for a single day, but you could divide it over two, or speed things up by hopping on a bus from time to time.

From **St Peter's** (*see p164*), head straight along via della Conciliazione to **Castel Sant'Angelo** (*see p170*) and cross the river at the Ponte Sant'Angelo, into the heart of medieval Rome along via del Banco di Santo Spirito. Lined with chic boutiques, *vie* dei Banchi Nuovi and then del Governo Vecchio lead to *piazze* Pasquino and San Pantaleo. Urban redevelopment over the centuries means that the old path from here to the Campidoglio is not easy to track, so pick up one of the huge numbers of buses that travel along corso Vittorio and via delle Botteghe Oscure to piazza Venezia (some stop at nearby piazza d'Aracoeli).

To the right of the Vittoriano monument, Michelangelo's *cordonata* leads up to the **Campidoglio** (*see p74*). Climb the steps, cut across piazza del Campidoglio and descend again by the stairs on the left of the Palazzo Senatorio (in front of you on the square). From here, you can cut a straight line through the **Roman Forum** (*see p82*). Skirt to either side of the **Colosseum** (*see p85*) and head up the hill along via di San Giovanni (the 85 and 117 buses travel along this street; the 3 tram runs on parallel via Labicana) to the basilica of **San Giovanni in Laterano** (*see p149*).

When his turn came, Benedict XVI ruined the party. For 'security reasons', he snuck out of a Vatican side gate at 5.15pm on 7 May 2005 and drove a top-secret route to the Lateran, where he was led to his episcopal throne, sorely disappointing Romans hoping to take part in the festivities along the ancient route. After all, what's a pope without pomp?

Santo Stefano Rotondo

Via di Santo Stefano Rotondo 7 (06 421 191).
Bus 81, 117, 673. **Open** *April-Sept* 9am-noon,
4-6pm Tue-Sun. *Oct-Mar* 9.30am-12.30pm, 3.30-
5.30pm Tue-Sun. **Map** p361 C4.

Perhaps inspired by the Church of the Holy
Sepulchre in Jerusalem, this unusual round church
dates from the fifth century; in its measurements,
some say, lies the secret of the Holy Number of God.
It rests on parts of a patrician Roman villa and a
mithraeum, one of many in this area of Rome. In its
original form, the church must have been exceptionally beautiful, with its Byzantine-inspired
simplicity – three concentric naves separated by
rings of antique columns set within a Greek cross –
and play of natural light. This effect was disturbed
when arches were built to shore it up in the 12th century, and the portico was added. The outer ring was
walled in 1450, and the atmosphere changed defini-
tively with a 16th-century attempt at mind control:
34 horrifically graphic frescoes of martyrs being
boiled, stretched and slashed (*see p147* **Sticky
ends**) were added to the interior walls for the edification of the faithful. Visit when the sun is stream-
ing in from the upper windows and you'll catch
something of the original contemplative aura. An
underground shrine to the Persian god Mithras can be
visited by appointment. At the time of writing, the
church and its lovely grounds – where composer
Palestrina penned some of his polyphonic masterpieces
in the 16th century – were undergoing restoration, but
should be open by the time this guide is published.

Villa Celimontana

*Via della Navicella/via San Paolo della Croce
(no phone). Bus 60Exp, 75, 81, 117, 175, 271,
628, 673/tram 3.* **Open** dawn to dusk daily.
Admission free. **Map** p361 C4.

This is a pretty, leafy walled garden, with a rather
pokey playground; which doesn't stop swarms of
local kids from climbing, running and holding birthday picnics here. The pleasant lawns are dotted with
bits of marble from the collection of the Mattei
family, which owned the property from 1553 until
1928, when it became a public park. The graceful
family villa, now housing the Italian Geographic
Society, was built in the 16th century. Forlorn and
forgotten at the southern end is one of Rome's
Egyptian obelisks (*see p107* **Obelisks**). In summer
the villa becomes the gorgeous venue for big-name
evening jazz concerts (*see p283*).

From San Giovanni to Santa Croce in Gerusalemme

Seat of the Bishop of Rome (ie the pope in his
local role), and first and foremost of the four
great Roman basilicas, **San Giovanni in
Laterano** (*see p150*) is high on any pilgrim's
must-do list. Many non-religious visitors write
it (and the area around it) off as too far from the

centro storico, with first-class sights thin on
the ground. This is a pity because a stop at this
grandiose – if rather impersonal – cathedral
and nearby monuments provides a good picture
of Christianity as a fledgling state religion.

San Giovanni stands on the spot donated
in the third century by Emperor Constantine
for the construction of the first Christian
basilica: note its location inside the city walls
but in a then-quiet corner far away from the
centre of political power. For centuries it was
to be the papal seat and residence, its
importance underscored by the presence of
many holy souvenirs carted here from the Holy
Land by Constantine's mother Helena, an early
convert to the new faith. The 28 steps of the
Scala Santa, for example, across the road to
the north of the basilica, were said to be the
very ones that Christ climbed to hear Pontius
Pilate's non-verdict that essentially condemned
him to death. At the top is the recently restored
Sancta Sanctorum (*see p151*), containing
super-sacred relics. (A few blocks north of here
is the **Museo Storico della Liberazione
di Roma**, a grim testament to the notorious
prison where Nazi SS officers tortured and
killed suspected partisans.)

On the west side of the basilica complex
are the Lateran palace, now used for the
administration of the Church in Italy, the
Pontifical University and the octagonal
baptistry. Stranded in the middle of thundering
traffic in the unappealing piazza is another
of Rome's Egyptian obelisks (*see p107*
Obelisks). South of the church, on the other
hand, are the sunken ruins of **Porta Asinaria**,
an ancient gate belonging to the third-century
Aurelian Wall. The **Porta San Giovanni** is
the starting point of the modern via Appia
Nuova, a retail-intensive main drag that leads
south out of town to the Alban Hills.

A park has been created beneath the
impressive stretch of Aurelian Wall that runs
from San Giovanni east towards **Santa Croce
in Gerusalemme** (*see p150*), a basilica
that bristles with relics brought back by the
redoubtable St Helena after her pilgrimage
to the Holy Land at the age of 80: pieces of the
cross, a nail and thorns from Christ's crown
among them. A lovely vegetable garden,
recently restored and lovingly tended by monks
of the adjoining monastery, can be visited by
appointment. The church was built over a part
of Helena's own house, known as the Sessorium,
a palace that originally belonged to the
Emperor Septimius Severus (193-211).

Dotted around is a panoply of minor **Roman
ruins**: through the opening in the Aurelian
Wall to the right of the church is the
Amphitheatrum Castrum, and part of the Circus

Sightseeing

Santi Giovanni e Paolo. *See p146.*

Varianus, both dating from the reign of Elagabulus; the Baths of Helena, of which only the cistern is visible; and the monumental travertine archway built by Emperor Claudius in the first century AD to mark the triumphal entrance of the aqueducts in to the city (and later incorporated into the Aurelian Wall).

To the left of the basilica is the delightful **Museo Nazionale degli Strumenti Musicali** (museum of musical instruments).

The oven-shaped Tomb of Eurysaces (an ancient Roman baker) stands just outside the well-preserved third-century Porta Maggiore. North from here, beyond the railway tracks, is the district of San Lorenzo (*see p152*).

Museo Nazionale degli Strumenti Musicali

Piazza Santa Croce in Gerusalemme 9A (06 701 4796/mnsm@virgilio.it). Metro San Giovanni/bus 105, 571, 649/tram 3. **Open** 8.30am-7.30pm Tue-Sun **Admission** €4; €2 concessions. **No credit cards. Map** off p361 E4.

This small museum is a treat for musicians and music-lovers. A recent wash-and-brush-up means that this formerly musty collection now has video loops and good explanations in English. From prehistoric to Baroque, an astonishing variety of drums, lutes, flutes and spinets showcases the evolution of instrument-making in Italy, the rest of Europe, Africa and Japan.

San Giovanni in Laterano

Piazza San Giovanni in Laterano 4 (06 6988 6433). Metro San Giovanni/bus 16, 85, 87, 117, 186, 218, 571, 650, 665, 714, 850/tram 3. **Open** *Church* 7am-6.30pm daily. *Baptistry* (06 6988 6452) 7.30am-12.30pm, 4-6.30pm Tue-Sat; 9am-12.30pm, 4-6.30pm Sun. *Cloister* 9am-6pm daily. *Museum* 9am-1pm Mon-Sat. **Admission** *Church* free. *Cloister* €2 (free with Vatican museum ticket). *Museum* €4. **No credit cards. Map** p361 E4.

The Catholic faithful earn indulgences for visits to this major basilica. Along with the Lateran palace, it was the site of the original papal headquarters until the move across the river to St Peter's and the Vatican in the 14th century. Constantine's second wife, Fausta, gave the plot of land to Pope Melchiades to build the papal residence and church in 313. There are few traces of the of the original basilica, which was done in by fire, earthquake and barbarians. It has been heavily restored and rebuilt: the end result is a vast, impersonal, over-decorated hangar.

The façade with its 15 huge statues of Christ, the two Johns (Baptist and Evangelist) and 12 Doctors of the Church, is part of the 1735 rebuilding by Alessandro Galilei. The interior bears the stamp of Borromini, who transformed it in 1646; for centuries he was derided for encasing the original columns in stucco, though experts now believe that the ancient supports had been replaced by nondescript ones in the 15th century. A few treasures from earlier times survive: a much restored 13th-century mosaic in the apse, a fragment of a fresco attributed to Giotto (hidden behind the first column on the right) showing Pope Boniface VIII announcing the first Holy Year in 1300, and the Gothic *baldacchino* over the main altar.

Off the left aisle is the 13th-century cloister, with delicate twisted columns and fine cosmatesque work by the Vassalletto family. A small museum off the cloister contains papal vestments and some original manuscripts of music by Palestrina.

The north façade was designed in 1586 by Domenico Fontana, who also placed Rome's tallest Egyptian obelisk out front. This was part of Pope Sixtus V's 16th-century urban renewal scheme (*see p18* **Paved with good intentions**). Also on this side is the octagonal baptistry that Constantine had built. The four chapels surrounding the font have mosaics from the fifth and seventh centuries, and bronze doors said to come from the Baths of Caracalla.

Santa Croce in Gerusalemme

Piazza Santa Croce in Gerusalemme 12 (06 701 4769/www.basilicasantacroce.it). Bus 81, 85, 87, 105, 571, 649/tram 3, 5, 14. **Open** *Church* 7am-12.45pm, 2.30-7pm Mon-Sat; 8am-12.45pm, 2.30-7pm Sun. *Chapel of the Relics* 8am-12.30pm, 2.30-6.30pm daily. **Map** off p361 E4.

Founded in 320 by St Helena, mother of Emperor Constantine (who legalised Christianity in 313), this church began as a hall in her home, the Palatium Sessorium. The church was rebuilt and extended in the 12th century, and again in 1743-44. Helena had her church constructed to house relics brought back from the Holy Land by the redoubtable lady herself. The emperor's *mamma* came back with an enviable shopping-bagful: three chunks of Christ's cross, a nail, two thorns from his crown and the finger of St Thomas – allegedly the very one that the doubting saint stuck into Christ's wound. All of these are displayed in a chapel at the end of a Fascist-era hall at the left side of the nave. Apart from the wood, those venerable objects are rather hard to identify, inside their gold reliquaries. In the mosaic-ceilinged lower chapel (under the altar) is Helena's stash of soil from Jerusalem. Helena's Holy Land souvenir-collecting sparked a relic-craze that was exploited to the full for centuries by the wily merchants of the Holy Land; when Jesus-related bits were in short supply, scraps of saints and martyrs were fair game too.

Scala Santa (Holy Stairs) & Sancta Sanctorum

Piazza di San Giovanni in Laterano (06 772 6641). Metro San Giovanni/bus 16, 85, 87, 186, 218, 571, 650, 665, 714/tram 3. **Open** *Scala Santa* Apr-Sept 6.15am-noon, 3.30-6.30pm daily; Oct-Mar 6.15am-noon, 3-6pm daily. *Sancta Sanctorum* (booking obligatory) Apr-Sept 10.30-11.30am, 3.30-4.30pm daily; Oct-Mar 10.30-11.30am, 3-6pm daily. **Admission** *Scala Santa* free. *Sancta Sanctorum* €3.50. **No credit cards. Map** p360 E3.

According to tradition, these steps (now covered with wooden plants) are the very ones Jesus climbed in the house of Pontius Pilate only to see the Roman governor wash his hands of the self-styled messiah. Emperor Constantine's mother St Helena brought these back in the fourth century. A crawl up the

Scala Santa has been a fixture on every serious pilgrim's list ever since. In 1510 Martin Luther gave it a go, but halfway up he decided that relics were a theological irrelevance and walked back down again. Don't climb them unless you know 28 different prayers (one for each step); walking up is not allowed. Prepare for a queue on Good Friday.

At the top of the Holy Stairs (but also accessible by non-holy stairs to the left) is the Sancta Sanctorum ('Holy of Holies'), the *privatissima* chapel of the popes and one of the only monuments around here that escaped Sixtus V's revamping. Some of the best early Christian relics were kept in the crypt under the altar at one time – including the heads of saints Peter, Paul and young Agnes. Most of them have now been distributed to other churches around the city, but displayed in a glass case on the left wall is a fragment of the table on which the Last Supper was supposedly served. The real treasures here, however, are the exquisite 13th-century frescoes in the lunettes and on the ceiling, attributed to Cimabue. Once, no one but the *pontifex maximus* himself was allowed to set foot in the Sancta Sanctorum, but the exclusive entry policy has since been relaxed: anyone with €3.50 is welcome.

Sightseeing

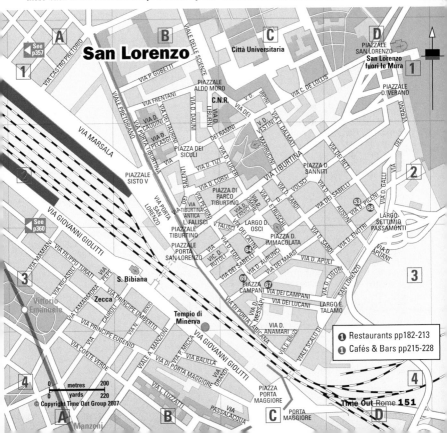

San Lorenzo

Map p151.

Colourful and hopping, the San Lorenzo neighbourhood still retains some of its original threadbare working-class character. Its proximity to Rome's **La Sapienza** university keeps it youthful and lively. A constant influx of students and artists mingles with a (diminishing) local population proud of its unswerving anti-Fascist and partisan history.

Constructed in the 1890s as a ramshackle ghetto for the poor, San Lorenzo became a hotbed of anarchist and left-wing activity. Hemmed in by urban infrastructure, such as the freight train depot and the sprawling cemetery of Il Verano, *sanlorenzini* were isolated in poverty from the rest of the city. Maria Montessori, who opened her first school here in 1907, said, 'when I first came to this quarter where respectable people only come when they're dead, I had the impression that some huge disaster had struck.'

Unbowed by their circumstances, the locals were ready with rocks and bricks to hurl from buildings when Fascists first came calling some years later. Alas, their anti-Fascism didn't help them in World War II: on 19 July 1943, Allied planes launched a strike on the Nazi-occupied train station – in the process knocking out several buildings, including the lovely (now restored) **San Lorenzo fuori le Mura** (*see below*), and killing 3,000 civilians. The scars still show, as do other vestiges of the district's history and vocation. But besides the many emporia selling tombstones, coffins and memorial lanterns, there's a happy mix of artisans, second-hand clothing shops, clubs and restaurants, plus purveyors of regular items like food and hardware to show that real people still live here. It's also home to Rome's only converted-loft artists' community.

To the north east, some 120,000 students study at La Sapienza university, a sprawling complex of Fascist-era buildings by the likes of Marcello Piacentini and Arnaldo Foschini.

San Lorenzo fuori le Mura

Piazzale del Verano 3 (06 491 511). Bus 71, 492/ tram 3, 19. **Open** *Apr-Sept 7.30am-12.30pm, 3-8pm daily. Oct-Mar 7.30am-12.30pm, 3-7pm daily.* **Map** p151 D1.

This spacious church, with its unusual chancel and ethereal light, gives a sense of calm, a feature of the Romanesque tradition to which it belongs. Like most Roman places of worship, it's a patchwork of 'improvements' over the centuries. St Lawrence, whose remains lie in a crypt beneath the church, was martyred in the mid-third century; convert-Emperor Constantine had a basilica built over his tomb in the fourth century. Several popes were subsequently laid to rest in the same underground catacombs.

In the late sixth century, Pope Pelagius II rebuilt the basilica; from this incarnation comes the broad chancel with its Corinthian columns, marble ciborium and stylised Byzantine mosaic of Pelagius and St Lawrence, with Christ seated on an orb. The nave is a 13th-century addition by Pope Honorius, though much of it is a faithful restoration undertaken after it was demolished by American bombs in 1943. In the portico are 13th-century frescoes depicting the life of the saint. A lovely courtyard, to the right of the nave, encloses orderly gardens as well as a piece of the errant bomb that wreaked havoc on the church. A ramp on the right leads behind the chancel, to the crypt of Blessed Pope Pius IX, the last pope to rule over the Vatican States; his reportedly uncorrupted body lies with a creepy silver mask over his face. *See also p25* **The longest sulk**.

Extra time

● On her way to be crowned in San Giovanni Laterano, legend says, **Pope Joan** gave her dark secret away when she had to pull over to have a baby. After which she was either stoned on the spot or sent into exile, depending on who you ask. A forlorn shrine at the corner of *vie* dei Querceti and dei Santi Quattro marks the spot.

● One of Rome's best-kept small parks is in front of the Celio military hospital, on via Celimontana. A decent playground for kids, and a great place for hanging out with infants, old folks and dogs.

● Sandwiched between via San Giovanni in Laterano and via Labicana is the partially excavated first-century AD **Ludus Magnus**, home and training ground for gladiators, just a short walk from the Colosseum where they would meet death or glory. It's particularly lovely in the spring when overrun with brilliant red poppies.

● At the eastern end of via San Paolo della Croce stands the **arco di Dolabella**, a pre-existing Roman arch incorporated by Nero into an aqueduct that carried water from the Acqua Claudia (*see p172*) to his artificial lake on the spot where the Colosseum was subsequently built. The buildings by the arch – the church of **San Tommaso in Formis** and the Istituto Sperimentale per la Nutrizione delle Piante – were once part of a hospital for clergy and for Christian slaves freed by the Trinitarian order in medieval times. A 12th-century mosaic of Christ freeing two slaves adorns the door of the botanical institute.

Monti & Esquilino

Glittering mosaics and the Domus Aurea contrast with gritty urbanity.

The area now covered by the *rioni* (city districts) of Monti and Esquilino has always been one of contrasts: in ancient times the notorious Suburra – a giant slum where streets ran with effluent – was cheek by jowl with the Imperial fora (*see p80*) and Nero's Domus Aurea (*see p154*). The more salubrious Esquiline hill above was home to first-century BC magnate-impressario Maecenas and, later, to Felice Peretti (Pope Sixtus V), whose exquisite Villa Peretti sprawled across the hill (*see p155* **Villa Peretti**).

Nowadays the twisting alleyways of Monti – roughly the Suburra area – are bustling, noisy and very hip. The Esquiline hill, by contrast, was swallowed up in the 1870s by solid, soulless *palazzi*, built after Italy was unified to house the official buildings (and the officials) of the new state; these have seen better days, and despite claims that the whole area is undergoing a rebirth, it remains predominantly grubby and gloomy. If you arrive in Rome by bus or train, your first stop will be right here, at Termini station, and first impressions may be less than favourable. But both Monti and Esquilino have their sights and charms: a little patience, and looking in the right places, will reveal them.

Monti

The marshy ground between the Quirinal, Viminal and Esquiline hills was home to the steamy, squelchy, overcrowded Suburra, which was described by Roman writers fond

of excursions into the *demi-monde*. Propertius spent time here waiting for his mistress Cynthia to climb out of a first-floor window, down a rope and into his arms. Juvenal, who lived in the heart of this hottest, noisiest and most chaotic quarter of the city, reported in his *Satires* that the most common cause of death was insomnia.

The area of Monti that was the Suburra – the enclave stretching east from the Forum between *vie* Nazionale and Cavour – is just as noisy, cosmopolitan and full of life today as it was then. Streets are cleaner, and property prices higher, but the narrow, chaotic streets full of funky clothes shops, wild bars and ethnic restaurants pulsate with the same kind of frenetic activity.

The post-Unification developers who did their worst to the Esquiline also left their mark on parts of Monti: **via Nazionale** has roaring traffic, drab carbon-copy high-street fashion emporia and rip-off tourist restaurants; via Cavour is singularly bland. The lumpen Bank of Italy HQ in Palazzo Koch on via Nazionale and the lab on undulating via Panisperna where Enrico Fermi and Ettore Majorana first split the atom in 1934 are oppressive. There's relief, however, in the streets south of Santa Maria Maggiore (*see p160*), where two stunning early churches dedicated to two sister saints, **Santa Prassede** (*see p153*) and **Santa Pudenziana** (*see p154*), glow with extraordinary mosaics.

For a verdant break and splendid views, head for the **Villa Aldobrandini** gardens high up above the south-western end of via Nazionale (access from nearby via Mazzarino). Built in the 16th century, the garden's formal lawns and gravel paths are disturbed only by tramps sleeping on benches (and the traffic noise below).

Santa Prassede

Via Santa Prassede 9A (06 488 2456). Bus 16, 70, 71, 75, 84, 360, 649, 714. **Open** 7.30am-noon, 4-6.30pm Mon-Sat; 8am-noon, 4-6.30pm Sun. **Map** p360 D1.
This church was built in the ninth century on the spot where St Praxedes is said to have harboured Christians. The saint, the story says, sponged up the blood of 23 martyrs who were discovered and killed before her, throwing the sponge into a well; its location is now marked by a porphyry disc on the floor of the nave. This tale is depicted in the 1735 altarpiece by Domenico Muratori. This church is a scale copy of the old St Peter's, a ninth-century attempt to recreate an early Christian basilica, although uneven brickwork shows that the Romans had lost the knack.

Sightseeing

Ex-Piazza Vittorio market. *See p158.*

Roman mosaicists were no better, so Pope Paschal I imported artists from Byzantium (*see p159* **All that glitters**). In a room to the right of the chapel of St Zeno is a portion of column said to be part of the very one that Jesus was tied to for the flagellation.

Santa Pudenziana

Via Urbana 160 (06 481 4622). Metro Cavour/bus 16, 70, 71, 75, 84, 360, 649, 714. **Open** 8am-noon, 3-6pm Mon-Sat; 9am-noon, 3-6pm Sun. **Map** p360 C1.
Tradition says St Pudenziana was the sister of St Praxedes; their father Pudens was a senator who harboured St Peter in a house on the spot where this church now stands. A purpose-built church was constructed in the fourth century, restored in the eighth and 11th centuries and brutally remodelled in the 16th century. Still very active, the church is now used by Rome's Filipino community. Among the glowing sacred hearts, the undoubted star is the apse mosaic. (*See also p159* **All that glitters**).

Colle Oppio

The serene, green Colle Oppio was the site of Nero's **Domus Aurea** (*see below*), an all-too-vivid reminder of the hated emperor that was torn down, filled in and replaced with bath complexes, first by Titus (on the south-west side of today's park) and later Trajan (on the northern side). On via Terme di Traiano is a structure – closed to the public – called the *Sette sale* (seven rooms), which was in fact a nine-chamber water tank estimated to have

held eight million litres of water. Nowadays the lower reaches of the Colle Oppio park, towards via Labicana, are peopled by swarms of Roman mums and their toddlers during the day. A string of unpleasant incidents involving far-right local youths, homeless immigrants and a sprinkling of the city's more foolhardy gays has resulted in the park being firmly locked after darkness falls.

On the western slope, **San Pietro in Vincoli** (*see p157*) contains important relics and a mighty Michelangelo. Further north, on the border with Monti, the church of **Santi Silvestro e Martino ai Monti** (*see p157*) stands above a Roman house. Nearby, on via Merulana, the **Museo Nazionale d'Arte Orientale** (*see p155*) provides an exotic break from ancient Rome.

Domus Aurea (Golden House)

Via della Domus Aurea (06 3996 7700). Metro Colosseo/bus 60Exp, 75, 81, 85, 87, 117, 175, 186, 204, 673, 810, 850/tram 3. **Open** (for guided tours; by appointment only) 10am-4pm Tue-Fri.
Admission €4.50. **Map** p360 C2.
In the summer of AD 64 fire devastated a large part of central Rome. (Some blame Nero for setting the blaze intentionally, but fire was a real risk and a common occurrence.) The ashes of patrician palaces mingled with those of slums. Afterwards, anything in the area east of the Forum left unsinged was knocked down to make way for a home fit for the sun-god that Nero liked to think he was.

Work began on the emperor's Domus Aurea (Golden House) immediately after the fire had died down. A three-storey structure, its main façade faced south and was entirely clad in gold; inside, every inch not faced with mother-of-pearl or inlaid with gems was frescoed by Nero's pet aesthete Fabullus. Fountains squirted perfumes, and baths could be filled with sea or mineral water. In one room, Suetonius claimed, an immense ceiling painted with the sun, stars and signs of the zodiac revolved constantly, keeping time with the heavens. Lakes were dug, forests planted and a 35m-high (116ft) gilded bronze statue of Nero erected.

After Nero's death in AD 68, a *damnatio memoriae* was issued and work was begun to eradicate every vestige of the hated tyrant. Vespasian drained the lake to build his amphitheatre (the tight-fisted emperor kept Nero's colossus, simply putting a new head on it, and so the stadium became known as the Colosseum), and Trajan used the brickwork as a foundation for his baths. So thorough was the cover-up job that for decades after the house's frescoes were rediscovered in 1480, no one realised it was the Domus Aurea that they had stumbled across. The frescoed 'grottoes' became an obligatory stopover for Renaissance artists, inspiring – among other things – Raphael's weird and wonderful frescoes in the Vatican (and also giving us the word 'grotesque'). The artists' signatures can still be seen scratched into the ancient stucco. After decades of restoration, some 30 rooms of the Domus Aurea reopened in June 1999 only to suffer a partial collapse after heavy rains in the winter of 2005. In February 2007 the Domus partially reopened for guided tours, which allow visitors a close-up look at the frescoes and plaster mouldings from high up on the restorers' scaffolding.

Museo Nazionale d'Arte Orientale

Via Merulana 248 (06 469 748). Bus 16, 85, 87, 714, 810, 850/tram 3. **Open** 8.30am-2pm Mon, Wed, Fri, Sat; 9am-7pm Tue, Thur, Sun. Closed 1st & 3rd Mon of mth. **Admission** €4; €2 concessions. **No credit cards. Map** p360 D2.

If you've had enough of ancient and papal Rome, try this impressive collection of Oriental art, in a dusty palazzo near Santa Maria Maggiore. It's arranged geographically and roughly chronologically. First are ancient artefacts from the Near East – pottery, gold, votive offerings – some from the third millennium BC. Then come 11th- to 18th-century painted fans from Tibet, sacred sculptures, and some Chinese pottery from the 15th century. Perhaps most unusual are artefacts from the Swat culture, from Italian-funded excavations in Pakistan.

Villa Peretti

The last thing that comes to mind as you elbow through crowds in Termini railway station or gasp for breath in fume-filled piazza dei Cinquecento is bucolic idylls and magnificent estates. Yet that was what this area was known for until the late 19th-century developers got their hands on the glorious Villa Peretti. All that remains of this villa today is the name of the street in front of Palazzo Massimo alle Terme. Once punctuated by avenues of cypresses, ancient sculpture and delightful fountains, the villa was the residence of Cardinal Felice Peretti, who was to become Pope Sixtus V in 1585.

The Iron Pope was an avid town-planner, and his own verdant part of the city benefited as much as any from his redevelopments. He was responsible for building the Acqua Felice aqueduct, which followed the route of the Acqua Alessandrina, constructed by Alexander Severus in the third century AD and destroyed by pillaging barbarians in the fifth. This aqueduct provided his estate (and some lucky neighbours) with water; it still gushes into the grubby Fontana dell'Acqua Felice in largo Santa Susanna. Across Rome in via Garibaldi, below the church of San Pietro in Montorio (*see p138*), stands another fountain

shifted there from its original home in Villa Peretti: the lions and pears that decorate it are the symbols of Sixtus.

As well as beautifying his villa, Peretti sought to impose order on the higgledy-piggledy chaos of medieval Roman streets when he rose to the throne of St Peter. To make life easier for visiting pilgrims, he began re-erecting the Egyptian obelisks that had been lying around in mud since the collapse of the Empire, putting them to use as signposts for points of pilgrimage. Between the obelisks, Sixtus had straight-as-a-die roads constructed: today, via Sistina is the name of a stretch running from the top of the Spanish Steps to piazza Barberini, but study the map and you'll see that the same road continues on to the major basilicas of Santa Maria Maggiore (*see p160*) and San Giovanni in Laterano (*see p149*). (*See also p18* **Paved with good intentions** and *p107* **Obelisks.**)

Before expiring of malaria in 1590, Sixtus also rebuilt much of the complex around San Giovanni in Laterano, and completed the dome of St Peter's. All of which served to ingratiate him not at all with his people: upon his death a mob tore down his statue on the Capitoline.

Sightseeing

OUR CLIMATE NEEDS
A HELPING HAND TODAY

Be a smart traveller. Help to offset your carbon emissions
from your trip by pledging Carbon Trees with Trees for Cities.

All the Carbon Trees that you donate through Trees for Cities
are genuinely planted as additional trees in our projects.

Trees for Cities is an independent charity working with local
communities on tree planting projects.

www.treesforcities.org   Tel 020 7587 1320

Trees for Cities
Charity registration number 1032154

San Pietro in Vincoli

Piazza di San Pietro in Vincoli 4A (06 9784 4952).
Metro Cavour/bus 16, 70, 71, 75, 84, 360, 649,
714. **Open** 8am-noon, 3-6pm daily. **Map** p360 C2.

First mentioned in 431, the church was rebuilt in 439 by Sixtus III with backing from Emperor Valentian III's wife Eudoxia, and dedicated to Saints Peter and Paul. In 442 Eudoxia gave Pope Leo I the chains that had held Peter in prison in Jerusalem; he put them together with the chains that had bound the saint at the Carcere Mamertino (Mamertine Prison; *see p80*), whereupon they miraculously fused. It was only in the 11th century, however, that Gregory VII changed the dedication to St Peter *ad vinculum* – in chains. The church was repaired in the 15th century, and then modified and restored in the 19th.

The chains are in a reliquary beneath the high altar and are the objective of the pilgrims who flock to the church. Secular tourists head for the funerary monument of Pope Julius II with Michelangelo's imposing *Moses* (c1513) as its central figure. Julius had wanted an enormous sepulchre with 40 life-size statues in a vast free-standing architectural framework. The proposed scale of the tomb was one of the reasons for the rebuilding of St Peter's, but it quickly became clear that neither the tomb nor the basilica would be finished before the sickly pope expired. So Julius shifted Michelangelo to work on another pet project: redecorating the cracked ceiling in the Sistine Chapel. After the completion of the ceiling Michelangelo went back to work on the tomb, but seven months later syphilis got the better of Julius and the tomb was put on a back-burner. This considerably abbreviated version was cobbled together by Michelangelo's pupils. The magnificent *Moses* (horned, from an archaic mistranslation of an Old Testament phrase really meaning 'with light emanating from his head') dominates the composition. The master's hand can be seen in the statues of Leah and Rachel to either side of the patriarch. After a recent restoration, experts came to the conclusion that he may have carved the pope's head too, although he clearly had nothing to do with the rest of poor Julius, which is by Maso del Bosco. When completed, the monument was placed here where Julius had been titular cardinal. His body ended up in an unmarked grave across the river in the Vatican.

Santi Silvestro e Martino ai Monti

Viale del Monte Oppio 28 (06 478 4701). Metro
Cavour or Vittorio/bus 16, 70, 71, 75, 84, 360, 649,
714. **Open** *Church* 7.30-11.30am, 4-6.30pm Mon-Sat;
7.30am-noon, 3.30-7pm Sun. *Titulus* 9.30-11.30am
Thur. **Admission** *Church* free. *Titulus* donation
expected. **Map** p360 D2.

The first church on this site was founded by St Sylvester in the fourth century. It was in that earlier church in 325 that the findings of the Council of Nicea (which established God the Father and Christ as one and the same) were presented to Constantine: the event is commemorated in the fresco on the left as you enter. The church was rebuilt in the ninth

century and remodeled c1650. On the far left and right of the left-hand aisle, two frescoes show respectively San Giovanni in Laterano (*see p149*) as it was before Borromini's changes and the interior of the original St Peter's. On the wall of the right-hand aisle, the mid 17th-century frescoes by pioneering landscape artist Gaspard Dughet caught the eye of many a Roman aristocrat, sparking the fashion for landscaped rooms in grand residences such as *palazzi* Colonna (*see p89*) and Doria-Pamphili (*see p119*). Beneath the ninth-century church is a third-century *titulus* (Roman house used as a place of worship); if you're here on a Thursday morning, ask the sacristan to unlock the gate for you. It's a spooky place, littered with bits of sculpture, decaying mosaics and frescoes. But it doesn't have the usual jungle of newer foundations sunk through Roman brickwork, so it's not difficult to picture this as an ancient dwelling and/or place of worship.

Esquilino

If you've come to Rome on a budget package or picked up a last-minute deal, chances are you'll end up in a hotel on the Esquilino, around Termini railway station. It may come as a shock. Despite heroic efforts by the municipal authorities to convince us that a renaissance is under way here, the Esquilino's grimy *palazzi* and questionable after-dark denizens may not

Fontana dell'Acqua Felice. *See p158.*

Sightseeing

be what you expected of the Eternal City. Don't despair. They're well hidden, but the Esquilino's charms and attractions are many.

The ancient ruins and Renaissance villas that dotted the area were swept away, and a whole new city-within-a-city built in the grid mode favoured by the Torinese planners who followed Italy's new royal family from the north after Italian Unification in the 1870s. **Piazza Vittorio Emanuele II** – the city's biggest square and always known simply as piazza Vittorio – was the new capital's showcase residential area. From optimistic beginnings the once-proud *palazzi* saw a steady decline into characterless slumhood. In the 1980s the first arrivals of a multi-ethnic community settled in the area, injecting life and colour, but no prosperity, into the run-down streets around the square. The noisy, smelly and characterful market that once occupied the pavements around the garden at the centre of the square was moved in 2002 into more salubrious covered quarters in a former army barracks in via Lamarmora (*see p247; photo p154*). The pavement where the market stood has been refurbished and the shady central gardens have been valiantly brought back into play. In the gardens, have a go at breaking the still-encoded recipe for changing base metal into gold on the **Porta Magica** in the northern corner; this curious door, with hermetic inscriptions dating from 1688, is all that remains of the Villa Palombara, an estate that once occupied this site. The gardens' benches are taken over by assorted down-at-heel immigrants who clearly haven't cracked the code; the flat travertine paving is perfect for the early-morning t'ai chi sessions attended by droves of Chinese.

North-west of the piazza, **Santa Maria Maggiore** (*see p160*) – its ceiling gilded with the first gold brought back from the New World – is one of the four patriarchal basilicas, and has splendid mosaics.

Due north of piazza Vittorio is **Termini railway station**. The railway reached Termini (the name comes from the nearby Terme di Diocleziano, and has nothing to do with its being a terminus) in the 1860s. The first station building (1864-71) was demolished to make way for what is one of Italy's most remarkable modern buildings, a triumph of undulating horizontal geometry. Architect Angiolo Mazzoni designed the lateral wings, complete with tubular towers of metaphysical grace straight out of a De Chirico painting; building began in 1937 as a key part of feverish preparations for the Fascist Universal Expo planned for 1942 (World War II stymied the Expo). In 1947 a judging commission hedged its bets by selecting two projects in a competition for the design for a new main station building. Despite the compromise, the result is staggering. The great reinforced concrete 'wave' was completed in time for the 1950 Holy Year. In the late '90s the station – and piazza del Cinquecento with its bus terminus – underwent a major facelift but the whole area remains less than charming. Pass through piazza del Cinquecento as dusk approaches and you'll see swirling clouds of starlings driven to insanity by the constant light and diesel fumes: the nitrogen-rich stench whenever it rains is a clue to watch your head.

Proximity to the railway terminus made the surrounding area particularly interesting to developers. Architect Gaetano Koch designed a ministerial and administrative district, focusing on the semicircular arcaded **piazza della Repubblica** (1888), once the exedra (anteroom) of the massive **Terme di Diocleziano** bath complex (*see p161*) and still frequently referred to as piazza Esedra by locals. After a recent renovation, Koch's *palazzi* are stunningly white.

This heavily trafficked roundabout is the traditional starting point for many major demonstrations, and a favourite hangout for the motley overflow from Stazione Termini. The **Fontana delle naiadi** at its centre was due for unveiling in 1901, but the nudity of the art nouveau nymphs cavorting seductively with sea monsters so shocked the authorities that it was boarded up again for years. Locals, fed up with the eyesore, eventually tore the planks down – a rather undignified inauguration. Sculptor Mario Rutelli is said to have returned to Rome once a year for the rest of his life to take his buxom models out to dinner.

The extraordinary Museo Nazionale Romano collection of ancient artefacts, which used to be confined to the Terme di Diocleziano, has spilled over into the **Palazzo Massimo alle Terme** (*see p159*) on the south-east fringe of the square. To the north-west is the church of **Santa Maria della Vittoria** (*see p160*), containing one of Bernini's most extraordinary sculptures, and the **Fontana dell'Acqua Felice** (*photo p157*). Designed by Domenico Fontana in the form of a triumphal arch, this fountain was completed in 1589. It was one of many urban improvements that were commissioned in Rome by Pope Sixtus V, and provided this district with clean water from an ancient aqueduct. The statue of Moses in the central niche of the fountain, by Leonardo Sormani, has been condemned as an atrocity against taste ever since it was unveiled in 1586.

To the south-west of piazza della Repubblica, via Nazionale descends to the old centre, passing the American church of **San Paolo entro le Mura** (via Napoli 58, 06 488 3339, www.stpaulsrome.it, open 9am-4.30pm Mon-Fri), with its Arts and Crafts movement

All that glitters

A few streets away is the church of **Santa Prassede** (*see p153*), dedicated to Pudenziana's sister. In the early ninth century, Pope Paschal I was looking for artists to decorate the chapel of San Zeno here as a mausoleum dedicated to his mother, St Theodora. With the Roman Empire long dead, the pick of mosaic artists was thriving across in Byzantium, where the traditionally Roman art of mosaic took on a flashier and more colourful style, with coloured glass tesserae often backed with gold or silver. Undoubtedly the finest expression of Byzantine art in Rome, the chapel is topped with a vault showing a fearsome Christ supported by four angels, while around the walls are various saints, including St Theodora herself with the blue square halo that tells us she was still alive when she posed for her mausoleum mosaic. On the right the Anastasis shows Christ reaching into hell to rescue Adam, Eve and assorted Old Testament characters.

Until the late 13th century, church decoration was dominated by mosaic. With the dawn of the Renaissance, heightened naturalism was the order of the day and advances in fresco techniques meant that mosaic was all but abandoned as an outmoded method, staying out of favour until a resurgence in interest in the 19th century. On the Esquiline hill, the basilica of **Santa Maria Maggiore** (*see p160*) undoubtedly has the most trumpeted mosaics of the area, but in two less-visited churches are oft-overlooked masterpieces.

Santa Pudenziana (*see p154*) has one of the earliest examples of Christian mosaics in Monti, from the early fifth century (although damaged in the 16th century). A marvellous example of the continuity between pagan and Christian art, Christ is enthroned in majesty and the apostles on either side are depicted as wealthy Roman citizens in a Roman cityscape (albeit with the symbols of the Evangelists flying over their heads). Santa Pudenziana herself is very naturalistically depicted on the right wearing a gold cloak.

In the apse, Christ riding on a cloud is being introduced to the martyr St Praxedes by St Paul on the right, while St Peter is doing the honours on the left for her sister St Pudenziana. Pope Paschal is there too, holding a model of the church.

While today we can appreciate the mosaics with a few coins in the light meter outside the chapel, in Paschal's day light bulbs weren't up to much – hence the vast numbers of gloom-lightening gold tiles.

Sightseeing

mosaics, along the way. If you've had your fill of the picturesque and need a shot of the Kafkaesque, take a look at such monolithic examples of Italian public architecture as the Interior Ministry in piazza del Viminale or the Teatro dell'Opera (*see p276*) along via Firenze.

Palazzo Massimo alle Terme

Largo di Villa Peretti 1 (06 480 201/bookings 06 3996 7700). Metro Repubblica/bus 16, 36, 38, 40Exp, 64, 86, 90Exp, 92, 105, 157, 170, 175, 204, 217, 310, 360, 492, 590, 649, 714, 910, C, H. **Open** *9am-7pm Tue-Sun.* **Admission** *€7; €3.50 concessions. Special exhibitions €2 extra. See also p72* **Tickets. No credit cards. Map** *p357 D5.*

The Italian state's spectacular collection of ancient art underwent a radical reorganisation in the run-up to 2000. It is now divided between the Terme di Diocleziano (*see p161*), Palazzo Altemps (*see p115*) and here at the Palazzo Massimo alle Terme.

In the basement of the Palazzo Massimo is an extensive collection of numismatics showing coins from Roman times to the euro. On the ground and first floors are busts of emperors, their families and lesser mortals, in chronological order (allowing you to track changing fashions in Roman hairstyles). The ground floor covers the period up to the end of the Julio-Claudian line. In Room 5 is a magnificent statue of Augustus as *pontifex maximus*. Room 7 houses the undoubted stars of the ground floor, two bronzes found on the Quirinale showing a Hellenistic hero in the triumphant pose of Hercules and an exhausted boxer.

The first floor begins with the age of Emperor Vespasian (AD 69-79); portrait busts in Room 1 show the gritty no-nonsense soldier. Room 5 has decorations from Imperial villas – statues of *Apollo* and of a young girl holding a tray of religious objects are both from Nero's coastal villa at Anzio, and a gracefully crouching *Aphrodite* taking her bath is from Hadrian's Villa at Tivoli (*see p312*). Room 6 has two discus throwers, second-century marble copies of a Greek bronze original from the fifth century BC. In Room 7 is a peacefully sleeping hermaphrodite, another second-century AD copy of a Greek original.

The real highlight of the Palazzo Massimo, though, lies on the second floor, where rare wall paintings from assorted villas have been reassembled. The spectacular fresco from the *triclinium* (dining room) of the villa of Livia shows a fruit-filled garden bustling with animal life and displays a use of perspective that was rarely seen again until the Renaissance. Another, from the *triclinium* of the Roman Villa Farnesina (in Room 3), has delicate white sketches on a black background, surmounted by scenes of courts handing down sentences that have baffled experts for centuries. Also in Room 3 is a lively naval battle, from a frescoed corridor in the same villa. The three *cubicoli* (bedrooms) in Room 5 all have decorative stuccoed ceilings.

Santa Maria della Vittoria

Via XX Settembre 17 (06 4274 0571). Metro Repubblica/bus 16, 36, 38, 60Exp, 61, 62, 84, 86, 90Exp, 92, 217, 360, 910. **Open** 8.30am-noon, 3.30-6pm Mon-Sat; 3.30-6pm Sun. **Map** p357 C5.

This modest-looking Baroque church, its interior cosily candlelit and adorned with marble and gilt, holds one of Bernini's most famous works. The *Ecstasy of St Teresa*, in the Cornaro chapel (the fourth on the left), shows the Spanish mystic floating on a cloud in a supposedly spiritual trance after a teasing, androgynous angel has pierced her with a burning arrow; the result is more than a little ambiguous (*see also p38* **Bernini's babes**). A French president in the 19th century remarked 'if that's heavenly love I know all about it.' (Writing of the angel incident in her *Life*, Teresa recalled: 'so intense was the pain I uttered several moans; so great was the sweetness caused by the pain that I never wanted to lose it.') When the chapel is seen as a whole, with the heavens painted in the dome, the light filters through a hidden window reflecting gilded rays and bathing Teresa in a heavenly glow. She is surrounded by a row of witnesses – members of the Cornaro family.

Santa Maria Maggiore

Piazza Santa Maria Maggiore (06 483 195/museum 06 483 058). Bus 16, 70, 71, 75, 84, 105, 204, 360, 590, 649, 714/tram 5, 14. **Open** *Church* 7am-7pm daily. *Museum* 9am-6pm daily. *Loggia* (guided tours only) usually 9am & 1pm daily; book by phone or at the ticket office. **Admission** *Church* free. *Museum* €4; €2 concessions. *Loggia* €3. **No credit cards. Map** p357 D6.

Behind this blowsy Baroque façade is one of the most striking basilica-form churches in Rome. Local tradition says a church was built on this spot in c366; documents place it almost 100 years later. The fifth-century church was first extended in the 13th century, then again prior to the 1750 Holy Year, when Ferdinando Fuga redid the interior and attached the façade that we see today. Inside, a flat-roofed nave shoots between two aisles to a triumphal arch and apse. Above the columns of the nave, heavily restored fifth-century mosaics show scenes from the Old Testament. Thirteenth-century mosaics in the apse by Jacopo Torriti show Mary, dressed as a Byzantine empress, being crowned Queen of Heaven by Christ.

Terme di Diocleziano. *See p161.*

The Virgin theme continues in fifth-century mosaics on the triumphal arch. The ceiling in the main nave is said to have been made from the first shipment of gold extracted from the Americas by Ferdinand and Isabella of Spain, and was presented to the church by the Borgia Pope Alexander VI. The Borgias' heraldic device of a bull is very much in evidence. In the 16th and 17th centuries two incredibly flamboyant chapels were added. The first was the Cappella Sistina (last chapel on the right of the nave), designed by Domenico Fontana for Sixtus V (1585-90), and decorated with multicoloured marble, gilt and precious stones. Directly opposite is the Cappella Paolina, an even gaudier Greek-cross chapel, designed in 1611 by Flaminio Ponzio for Paul V to house an icon of the Madonna (dating from the ninth, or possibly the 12th, century) on its altar.

To the right of the main altar a plaque marks the burial place of Rome's great Baroque genius, Gian Lorenzo Bernini. In the loggia, high up on the front of the church (book tours in advance; notes are provided in English), are glorious 13th-century mosaics that decorated the façade of the old basilica, showing the legend of the foundation of the church. The lower row shows Mary appearing to Giovanni the Patrician, who, with Pope Liberius, then sketches the plan for the basilica. The legend goes that the Virgin told Giovanni to build a church on the spot where snow would fall the next morning. The snow fell on 5 August 352, a miracle that is commemorated on that day every year, when thousands of flower petals are released from the roof of the church in the Festa della Madonna delle Neve (see p254). The Cappella Paolina also contains a relief (1612) by Stefano Maderno showing Liberius tracing the plan of the basilica in the snow.

Terme di Diocleziano

Via Enrico De Nicola 79 (06 3996 7700/www.archeorm.arti.beniculturali.it/sar2000/diocleziano). Metro Repubblica/bus 36, 38, 40Exp, 64, 86, 90Exp, 92, 105, 157, 170, 175, 217, 310, 714, 910. **Open** 9am-7.45pm Tue-Sun. **Admission** €7; €3.50 concessions. *See also p72* **Tickets**. **No credit cards**. **Map** p357 D5.

Part of the Museo Nazionale Romano, Diocletian's baths were the largest in Rome when they were built in AD 298-306, able to accommodate 3,000 people at a time. For an idea of the immense size of the structure, tour the remaining fragments: the tepidarium and part of the central hall are in Santa Maria degli Angeli (*see right* **Extra time**); a circular hall can be seen in San Bernardo alle Terme (piazza San Bernardo); and the Aula Ottagona (octagonal hall) – which used to house Rome's planetarium and now is occasionally used for exhibitions – is in via Romita.

A convent complex was built around the largest surviving chunk of the baths by Michelangelo in the 1560s: it now contains inscriptions and other items from the Museo Nazionale Romano ancient artefacts collection, including some of the hut-shaped funerary urns found in Lazio, which give an idea of what eighth-century BC houses looked like. **Photo** *p160*.

Extra time

● The basilica of **Santa Maria degli Angeli** (piazza della Repubblica), which Michelangelo ingeniously 'dropped' into the massive ruins of the Baths of Diocletian (*see left*), is one of the city's grandest churches. It is also famous for Clement XI's magnificent 45-metre-long (148 feet) bronze meridian (1702), which runs across the marble floor, marking the zodiac signs of the constellations and, importantly, the exact point of the spring equinox, from which the date of Easter (first Sunday after the first full moon following the spring equinox) was calculated. Until 1870, all clocks in Rome took their cue from this sophisticated time-piece.

● The **Tempio di Minerva Medica** (via Giolitti) is one of the landmarks you see from the train as you approach Termini railway station. The much-engraved ruin owes its name to the statue of a goddess that was found here, although it has long been established that the building was never a temple at all but a third-century dining pavilion of an extensive garden complex belonging to the Licinii family, which had produced Emperor Gallienus. As the trains hurtle by it's difficult to imagine the emperor holding summer court here.

● Just by the Tempio di Minerva Medica, and equally unexpected in this scene of urban desolation, is the little church of **Santa Bibiana** (St Vivian; via Giolitti 154), who was martyred on this spot. The fifth-century church was rebuilt in 1625 by Gian Lorenzo Bernini, who also carved the statue of the saint in the niche over the altar. Frescoes are by Agostino Ciampelli (on the right) and Pietro da Cortona (left).

● When things were at their most violent in medieval Rome, rival clans took to their towers and pulled up the ladders. By the 13th century, when anarchy had reached its peak, the city bristled with over 200 towers. Of these, about a dozen remain; half are in Monti. The **Torre dei Conti**, erected in 1203, stands skyscraper-close to the famous **Torre delle Milizie** (*see p80*). Another pair of towers – built by the Graziani and Capocci families – stands in piazza San Martino ai Monti. **The Torre dei Margani** was transformed into the belfry of the church of San Francesco di Paola (piazza San Francesco di Paola 10).

Sightseeing

The Vatican & Prati

The pope's home and 'hood.

Once the *Ager* or *Campus vaticanus* was marshland lying between the Monti Vaticani (stretching from the Gianicolo to modern-day Monte Mario) and the Tiber, across the river from the city centre and known mainly for its poor-quality wine. Then, in the first century, the mad, bad Emperor Caligula decided it would be a good spot for a circus and a practice-ground for the most glamorous of sports, chariot-racing.

Nero completed Caligula's circus in AD 54 and built a bridge, the Pons Neronianus, to connect it with the centre. In the summer of AD 64, a fire destroyed half of the city. When people starting muttering that Nero was the fire-setter, he in turn blamed the Christians – and the persecution of this pesky new cult began in earnest. Nero's circus was the main venue for Christian-baiting: legend says they were covered in tar and burned alive here. Top apostle Peter is traditionally believed to have been crucified in the circus then buried close by on the spot where, 250 years later, in AD 326, Constantine built the first church of St Peter.

Not all of the following 264 popes resided here – they began in the Lateran (*see p150* San Giovanni in Laterano), in fact, before history drove them to many other places, including Viterbo (*see chapter* **Trips Out of Town**), Anagni (south of Rome) and Avignon, France – but throughout the Christian era, pilgrims have continued to flock to the tomb of the founder of the Roman Church.

All around, the **Borgo** grew up to service the burgeoning Dark Age tourist industry. Pope Leo IV (847-55) enclosed the Borgo with the 12-metre-high (40 feet) Leonine Wall, following a series of Saracen and Lombard raids. Pope Nicholas III (1277-80) extended the walls and provided a papal escape route, linking the Vatican to the impregnable Castel Sant'Angelo by way of a long *passetto* (covered walkway). He never used his getaway, but Clement VII did, in 1527, during fierce fighting with the troops of Emperor Charles V (*see p21* **The sack**). The nine-month siege and subsequent Sack of Rome was a watershed: things in the papal stronghold were never the same again. Almost the whole papal army was slaughtered, the city was burned and looted, and the Sistine Chapel was used as a stables by the Protestant mercenaries – their graffiti in the Papal Suite (*see p168* Stanze di Raffaello) is still visible. After Paul III got Michelangelo in to build bigger, better walls, the popes withdrew back across town to the old Lateran palace, and then to the grand new Quirinal palace (*see p93*), where they stayed until the troubles of 1870 forced them back across the Tiber once more.

The Vatican

In 1870, when Italian troops breached Rome's walls at Porta Pia (*see p23* **Eviction order**), centuries of rule by the occupant of the throne of St Peter were put to an end. Over the years, foreign despots had been either seen off or paid off but in 1870 it all went wrong: the pope lost control of a vast, rich swath of central Italy and was ignominiously forced back into the Vatican palace behind the hefty walls. Between 1870 and 1929 the pope pronounced the Italian state to be sacrilegious and national elections to be illegal. Something had to be done, and on 11 February 1929 Pius XII and Mussolini signed the Lateran Pacts, a treaty designed to sort out the status of the Vatican once and for all. The terms of the reconciliation treaty (*La Conciliazione*) awarded the Church a huge cash payment, tax-free status and a constitutional role that led to an important continuing moral influence over future legislation on social issues such as education and divorce. To commemorate the historic agreement, Mussolini demolished a particularly picturesque part of the medieval Borgo, replacing it with a short but 'modern' approach road to St Peter's: via della Conciliazione.

The Vatican City occupies an area of less than half a square kilometre, making it the smallest state in the world. Despite having fewer than 800 residents, it has its own diplomatic service, postal service, army (the Swiss Guard), heliport, railway station, supermarket, and radio and TV stations. It has observer status at the UN, and issues its own stamps and currency (Vatican euros have a tiny circulation; the Holy See keeps a few knowledgeable collectors happy with occasional issues of coins that increase exponentially in value). It also contains one of the world's finest collections of art and antiquities, including the largest array of pagan and non-Christian works.

PAPAL AUDIENCES

When the Pope is in Rome, crowds gather in St Peter's square at noon on Sunday to hear him address pilgrims from the window of his study in the Apostolic Palace. On Wednesday mornings he holds a general audience in St Peter's square, if the weather is fine, otherwise in the modern Sala Nervi audience hall.

Apply well in advance to the Prefettura della Casa Pontificia for tickets (06 6988 3114, 6988 3273, fax 06 6988 5863, open 9am-1.30pm Mon-Sat), which are free and can be picked up on the morning of the audience. Entry is through the bronze door, just to the left of the basilica. For a private audience, your local bishop has to make a written request, which can take between three months and a year to be granted.

VATICAN GARDENS

The Vatican walls surround splendid formal gardens, which can be glimpsed from some windows in the Vatican Museums or visited on guided tours aboard a minibus that wends its way through the Pope's backyard. Tours (€12, €8 concessions) take place daily, weather permitting; times vary. Booking is essential and must be done at least one week in advance by fax (06 6988 4676) or email (vistireguideate.musei@scv.va).

TOURIST INFORMATION

The Vatican's own tourist information office (06 6988 1662, open 8.30am-6.30pm Mon-Sat), situated on the left of St Peter's square as you face the basilica, dispenses information, organises guided tours, has a bureau de change, offers postal and philatelic services, and sells souvenirs and publications. The number of the Vatican switchboard is 06 6982; the general Vatican website is www.vatican.va.

DRESS CODE

The Vatican enforces its dress code strictly, both in St Peter's and in the Vatican Museums. Anyone wearing shorts or a short skirt, or with bare shoulders or midriff, will be turned away.

Sightseeing

St Peter's basilica: centre of the Catholic world. *See p164.*

St Peter's

*Piazza San Pietro (06 6988 1662). Metro Ottaviano/
bus 23, 40Exp, 62, 64.* **No credit cards.** **Map** p165
& off p355 A4/5.
Basilica: **Open** *Apr-Sept* 7am-7pm daily. *Oct-Mar*
7am-6pm daily. **Admission** free. Audio guide (€5)
available at cloakroom after the security check.
Dome: **Open** *May-Sept* 8am-6pm daily. *Oct-April*
8am-5pm daily. **Admission** €4. *With lift* €7.
Note: there are 320 steps to climb after the lift has
taken you to the first level.
Grottoes: **Open** *Apr-Sept* 7am-6pm daily. *Oct-Mar*
7am-5pm daily. **Admission** free.
Necropolis: Apply at the *Uffizio degli Scavi (06
6988 5318/fax 06 6988 5518 or 6987 3017/
scavi@fsp.va).* **Open** *Guided tours* 9am-5pm
Mon-Sat. **Admission** €10. English-language tours
must be booked at least 25 days in advance, though
if you're in Rome without a reservation it's always
worth asking at the *Ufficio degli Scavi* (beyond the
Swiss Guard post on the left of St Peter's as you
face the basilica) for any spaces. Under-12s are
not admitted; 12- to 15-year-olds must be
accompanied by an adult.
Treasury Museum: **Open** *Apr-Sept* 9am-6.15pm
daily. *Oct-Mar* 9am-5.15pm daily. **Admission** €6;
€4 children.

After 120 years as a building site, the current
St Peter's was consecrated on 18 November 1626
by Urban VIII – exactly 1,300 years after the conse-
cration of the first basilica on the site.

The earlier building was a five-aisled classical
basilica, fronted by a large courtyard and four
porticoes. Enlarged and enriched, it became the
finest church in Christendom. By the mid 15th
century, however, its south wall was collapsing.
Pope Nicholas V had 2,500 wagonloads of masonry
from the Colosseum carted across the Tiber, just for
running repairs. No one wanted to take responsibility for demolishing Christianity's most sacred

church. It took the arrogance of Pope Julius II and
his pet architect Donato Bramante to get things
moving. In 1506 some 2,500 workers tore down the
1,000-year-old basilica, and Julius laid the foundation stone for its replacement.

Following Bramante's death in 1514, Raphael took
over the work and scrapped his predecessor's design
for a basilica with a Greek-cross plan, opting for an
elongated Latin cross. In 1547 Michelangelo took
command and reverted to a Greek cross. He died in
1564, aged 87, but not before coming up with a plan
for a massive dome and supporting drum. This was
completed in 1590, the largest brick dome ever constructed, and still the tallest point of any building in
Rome. In 1607 Carlo Maderno won the consent of
Pope Paul V to demolish the remaining fragments
of the old basilica and put up a new façade, crowned
by enormous statues of Christ and the apostles.

After Maderno's death Bernini took over and,
despite nearly destroying both the façade and his
reputation by erecting towers on either end (one of
which fell down), he became the hero of the hour
with his sumptuous *baldacchino* and elliptical
piazza. This latter was built between 1656 and 1667,
its colonnaded arms reaching out towards the
Catholic world in a symbolic embrace. The oval measures 340 by 240 metres (1,115 by 787 feet), and is
punctuated by the central Egyptian obelisk (erected
by a workforce of 800 in 1586) and two symmetrical
fountains by Maderno and Bernini. The 284-column,
88-pillar colonnade is topped by 140 statues of saints.

In the portico (1612), opposite the main portal, is a
mosaic by Giotto (c1298) from the original basilica.
Five doors lead into the basilica: the central ones
come from the earlier church, while the others are
all 20th-century. The last door on the right is opened
only in Holy Years by the pope himself (and, as seen
from the inside, is firmly cemented shut).

Inside, the basilica's size is emphasised on the
marble floor, where a boastful series of brass lines
measure the lengths of other churches around the
world that haven't made the grade (second longest
is St Paul's, London). But it is Bernini's vast *baldacchino* (1633), hovering over the high altar, which
is the real focal point. Cast from bronze purloined
from the Pantheon by Bernini's patron, Pope Urban
VIII, of the Barberini family, it prompted local wits
to quip '*quod non fecerunt barbari, fecerunt
Barberini*' ('what the barbarians didn't do, the
Barberini did'). An extraordinary piece of Baroque
design, it takes its form from a Mesopotamian
tradition in which woven silken cloth was draped
over a framework to mark a sacred spot. In Bernini's
hands it became a hundred feet of gilded bronze. The
canopy stands over the high altar officially reserved
for the Pope; below, two flights of stairs lead beneath
the altar to the *confessio*, where a niche contains a
ninth-century mosaic of Christ, the only thing from
old St Peter's that stayed in the same place when the
new church was built. Far below lies the site of what
is believed to be St Peter's tomb, discovered during
excavations in 1951.

Bernini's **Tomb of Alexander VII.**
See p165.

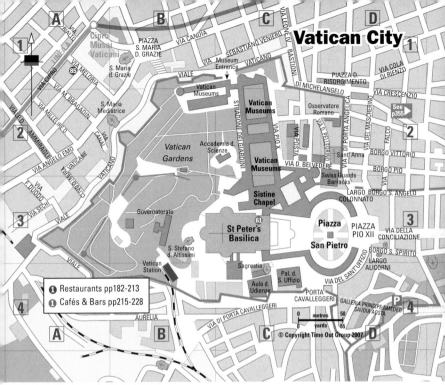

Vatican City

- A1 Cipro Musei Vaticani
- A1 PIAZZA S. MARIA D. GRAZIE
- A1 S. Maria d. Grazie
- A2 S. Maria Mediatrice
- B2 Vatican Gardens
- B2 Accademia d. Scienze
- C1 Vatican Museums
- C1 Osservatore Romano
- C2 Vatican Museums
- C3 Sistine Chapel
- C3 St Peter's Basilica
- D3 Piazza San Pietro
- A3 Governatorato
- A3 S. Stefano d. Altissimi
- A3 Vatican Station
- C3 Sagrestia
- C4 Pal. d. S. Uffizio
- C4 Aula d. Udienze
- C4 PORTA CAVALLEGGERI
- C2 Sant'Anna
- C2 Swiss Guards Barracks

❶ Restaurants pp182-213
❶ Cafés & Bars pp215-228

© Copyright Time Out Group 2007

Pilgrims head straight for the last pilaster on the right before the main altar, to kiss the big toe of Arnolfo da Cambio's brass statue of St Peter (c1296), worn down by centuries of pious lips, or to say a prayer before the crystal casket containing the mummified remains of much-loved Pope John XXIII, who was beatified in 2002. Tourists, on the other hand, make a beeline for the first chapel on the right, where Michelangelo's first major work, the *Pietà* (1499), is found. He signed his name on the thin sash across the Virgin's chest in response to cynics who claimed that he was too young at 25 to have produced the piece himself. The statue's position behind bullet-proof glass means the signature is only visible with strong binoculars or on postcards. Proceeding around the basilica in an anti-clockwise direction, notice Carlo Fontana's highly flattering monument to the unprepossessing Queen Christina of Sweden, a convert to Catholicism in 1655 (*see p135* **Queen Christina**), to the left of the *Pietà* chapel. The third chapel has a tabernacle and two angels by Bernini, plus St Peter's only remaining painting: a *Trinity* by Pietro da Cortona (the others have been replaced by mosaic copies). In the first chapel beyond the right transept is a tear-jerker of a neo-classical tomb (1792), the last resting place of Pope Clement XIII, by Antonio Canova.

Bernini's Throne of St Peter (1665), flanked by papal tombs, stands at the far end of the nave beyond the high altar, under a stained-glass window.

Encased within Bernini's creation is a wood and ivory chair, probably dating from the ninth century but for many years believed to have belonged to Peter himself. To the right of the throne is Bernini's 1644 monument to his patron Urban VIII, who commissioned the bronze portrait (between statues of *Charity* and *Justice*) before his death. On the pillars supporting the main dome are much-venerated relics, including a chip off the True Cross above the statue of St Helena bearing the cross she is said to have brought back from the Holy Land.

In the left aisle, beyond the pilaster with St Veronica holding the cloth with which she wiped Christ's face, Bernini's tomb for Pope Alexander VII (another of his patrons) shows the pope seated above a doorway shrouded with a cloth of reddish marble, from beneath which struggles a skeleton clutching an hourglass: a grim reminder of the fleeting nature of life.

Near the portico end of the left aisle is a group of monuments to the Old Pretender James Edward Stuart (the 18th-century claimant to the throne of England and Scotland, and here recorded as King James III), his wife Maria Clementina Sobieski and their sons Charles Edward (Bonnie Prince Charlie) and Henry Benedict. They are buried in the grottoes below.

Beneath the basilica are the Vatican Grottoes – Renaissance crypts containing papal tombs. The Necropolis, where St Peter is said to be buried, lies under the grottoes. The small treasury museum off the left nave of the basilica contains some stunning liturgical relics. The dome, reached via hundreds of stairs (there's a cramped lift as far as the basilica roof), offers fabulous views of the Vatican gardens.

Vatican Museums (Musei vaticani)

Viale del Vaticano (06 6988 3333/mv.vatican.va). Metro Ottaviano or Cipro–Musei Vaticani/bus 23, 32, 34, 49, 81, 492/tram 19. **Open** (last entry 1hr 15mins before closing) *Mar-Oct* 10am-4.45pm Mon-Fri; 10am-2.45pm Sat. *Nov-Feb* 10am-1.45pm Mon-Sat. *Year-round* last Sun of each month 9am-1.45pm. Closed Catholic holidays. (*See also p168* **Blame Dan Brown**.) **Admission** €13; €8 students under 26 years. Free to all last Sun of month. **No credit cards. Map** p165.

It's a brisk ten-minute walk around the Vatican walls from St Peter's to the Vatican Museums.

Begun by Pope Julius II in 1503, this immense collection represents the accumulated fancies and obsessions of a long line of strong, often contradictory personalities. The popes' unique position allowed them to obtain treasures on favourable terms from other collectors, and artists often had little choice as to whether they accepted papal commissions.

One-way routes cater for anything from a dash to the Sistine Chapel to a five-hour plod around the lot (if opening hours permit). There are also a number of itineraries for wheelchair users, with facilities en route. Wheelchairs can be borrowed at the museum: you can't book them, but call ahead (06 6988 3860) to check there's one free. The following are selected highlights from the collections (in alphabetical order).

Museo dell'Arte Sanitaria. *See p170.*

Appartamento Borgia

This six-room suite, known as the Borgia Rooms, was adapted for the Borgia Pope Alexander VI (1492-1503) and decorated by Pinturicchio with a series of frescoes on biblical and classical themes. In 1973 some 50 rooms adjoining the Borgia Apartments were renovated to house the Collezione d'Arte Religiosa Moderna.

Cappella Sistina (Sistine Chapel)

The world's most famous frescoes cover the ceiling and one immense wall of the Cappella Sistina, built for Sixtus IV in 1473-84. For centuries it has been used for papal elections. In the 1980s and '90s, the 930 sq m (10,000 sq ft) of *Creation* – on the ceiling – and the *Last Judgement* – on the wall behind the altar – were subjected to the most controversial restoration job of all time. The result is very blue.

In 1508 Michelangelo was commissioned to paint a simple decoration on the ceiling of the Sistine Chapel. Julius II may have been egged on to employ a sculptor with no experience in fresco by his architect Bramante, who was jealous of the pope's admiration for Michelangelo and desperately wanted to see him fail. Michelangelo responded by offering to do far more than mere decoration, and embarked upon his massive venture alone. He spent the next four and a half years standing (only Charlton Heston lay down) on 18m-high (60ft) scaffolding with paint and plaster dripping into his eyes. Despite a fairly handsome payment (in four years he earned as much as a regular artist could expect to earn in 15), he complained to his brother in 1511, 'I could well say that I go naked and barefoot.' Under pressure from the dying Julius II (syphilis got him in the end) to finish as quickly as possible, Michelangelo complained in another letter: 'I have no friends and no need of them; I wish simply to eat a hot meal in peace.'

The ceiling work was completed in 1512, just seven months before the death of Julius, and is exemplary of the confident pursuit of beauty of the High Renaissance. Beginning at the *Last Judgment* end, scenes depict the *Separation of Light from Darkness*, the *Creation of Sun, Moon and Planets*, the *Separation of Land and Sea* and the *Creation of Fishes and Birds*; the *Creation of Adam*, the *Creation of Eve*, the *Temptation* and *Expulsion from Paradise*; the *Sacrifice of Noah* (which should have appeared after the *Flood*, but for lack of space), the *Flood* and the *Drunkenness of Noah*. Michelangelo painted these scenes in reverse order, beginning with Noah's drunkenness. They are framed by monumental figures of Old Testament prophets and classical sibyls foretelling the birth of Christ.

Twenty-three years later, aged 60, Michelangelo was dragged back by Paul III in 1535. Between the completion of the ceiling and the beginning of the wall, Rome had suffered. From 1517, the Protestant Reformation threatened the power of the popes, and the sack of the city in 1527 was seen by Michelangelo as the wrath of God descending on the corrupt city. The *Last Judgment* dramatically

Vatican essentials

Remember

● Entrances to St Peter's basilica and to the Vatican Museums are in separate places and involve two lengthy queues (*see also* p168 **Blame Dan Brown**), as well as a ten-minute hike around the outside of the Vatican walls to get from one to the other. There is one way of avoiding this: from the Sistine Chapel (if you don't have an audioguide to return), try diving out through the exit to the right of the papal entrance marked 'authorised tour groups only', which leads straight to St Peter's... though there is a small chance you may be turned back.

● Since the post-9/11 introduction of security checks at St Peter's, the queue (*pictured right*) to enter the basilica is almost always daunting, sometimes wrapping itself most of the way around Bernini's colonnade. Take comfort in the fact that the queue moves reasonably swiftly. But before you join it, (1) make sure you're not going to be turned away once you get there because you're unsuitably dressed (no shorts, very short skirts, or bare midriffs or shoulders) and (2) bear in mind that the doors close at the advertised times, no matter how many people are waiting outside.

Must-haves

● Sensible shoes: absolutely essential if you are to attempt the ascent of the dome, as the 320 marble stairs after you emerge from the lift are very slippery.
● Water: only the Galleria degli Arazzi and the Sistine Chapel are air-conditioned and people have been known to keel over in the

summer. There's no water, holy or otherwise, to be had between the entrance to the museums and the Sistine Chapel. There's a similar shortage of toilets.
● Binoculars: a good idea for looking at the details of frescoes in the Sistine Chapel, as well as for appreciating the view if you're planning an ascent of the dome.
● A museum guide book or audio guide (from the desk after the ticket barrier): these are possibly the worst-labelled museums anywhere.

reflects this gloomy and pessimistic atmosphere. Hidden among the larger-than-life figures that stare, leer and cry out from their brilliant ultramarine background, Michelangelo painted his own frowning, miserable face on the wrinkled human skin held by St Bartholomew, below and to the right of the powerful figure of Christ the Judge. In 1555 Paul IV objected to the nudity and added modest loincloths, removed in the recent restoration.

Before Michelangelo set foot in the chapel, the stars of the 1480s had created the paintings along the walls. On the left-hand wall (as you look at the *Last Judgment*) are: the *Journey of Moses* by Perugino; *Events from the Life of Moses* by Botticelli; *Crossing the Red Sea* and *Moses Receives the Tablets of the Law* by Cosimo Rosselli; *The Testament of Moses* by Luca Signorelli; and *The*

Dispute over Moses' Body by Matteo da Lecce. On the right-hand wall are *The Baptism of Christ* by Perugino; *The Temptations of Christ* by Botticelli; *The Calling of the Apostles* by Ghirlandaio; *Handing over the Keys* by Perugino; *The Sermon on the Mount* and *The Last Supper* by Cosimo Rosselli; and *The Resurrection* by Hendrik van den Broeck (van den Broeck and Lecce replaced the paintings lost after the collapse of the Popes' entrance in 1565). The portraits are by the same masters.

Galleria Chiaramonte

Founded by Pius VII in the early 19th century and laid out by the sculptor Canova, this is an eclectic collection of Roman statues, reliefs and busts. Don't miss the replica of a Greek statue by Polyeuctos of stuttering orator Demosthenes or the copy of a *Resting Satyr* by the Greek sculptor Praxiteles.

Blame Dan Brown

Visiting the Vatican Museums – always a purgatory of endless queues – got even more tricky from January 2007. In what cynics describe as a deal with the tour-bus 'mafia', the museums will admit only authorised, pre-paid groups before 10am, leaving individual visitors from 10am until the ridiculously early closing time (for exact hours, *see p166*) to run for the Sistine Chapel.

Behind the short openings is a series of intrigues, from the museum guards' point-blank refusal to have their cushy contracts altered, to the enormous earnings from exclusive 'after hours' visits: from January 2007, charges for these latter were to rise to a whopping €2,500 plus €15 per person for groups of up to 30, and €20,000 plus €15 per person for groups of up to 400.

Despite the changes, the Vatican Museums remain a 'must-see' destination. To ease the pain, avoid Saturdays, Mondays and days after public and religious holidays. Wednesdays around 10.30am – when many punters have piled into St Peter's square for the papal audience – is a good time. Long summer opening hours mean that if you roll up at 12.30pm the queues should be shorter. But for some years now there's been no real low season at the Vatican, and 'shorter' here is a relative concept. We blame Dan Brown...

Gallerie dei Candelabri & degli Arazzi
The long gallery studded with candelabra contains Roman marble statues, while the next gallery has ten huge tapestries (*arazzi*), woven by Flemish master Pieter van Aelst from the cartoons by Raphael that are now in London's Victoria & Albert Museum.

Galleria delle Carte Geografiche
Pope Gregory XIII (who was responsible for introducing the Gregorian calendar) had a craze for astronomy, and was responsible for this 120m-long (394ft) gallery, with its Tower of the Winds observation point at the north end. Ignazio Danti of Perugia drew the maps, which were then frescoed (1580-83), and show each Italian region, city and island with extraordinary precision.

Museo Egiziano
Founded by Gregory XVI in 1839, in rooms which are partly decorated in Egyptian style, this is a representative selection of ancient Egyptian art from 3000 BC to 600 BC. It includes statues of a baboon god, painted mummy cases and a marble statue of Antinous, Emperor Hadrian's lover, who drowned in Egypt and was declared divine by the emperor. A couple of real mummies help make this the most exciting bit of the whole Vatican if you have grisly-minded kids in tow.

Museo Etrusco
Founded in 1837 by Gregory XVI, and enlarged in the 20th century, this collection contains Greek and Roman art as well as Etruscan masterpieces, including the contents of the Regolini-Galassi Tomb (c650 BC), the Greek-inspired fourth-century BC *Mars*, and the fifth-century BC *Young Man and Small Slave*.

Museo Paolino
This collection of Roman and neo-Attic sculpture has been housed here since 1970. Highlights include the beautifully draped statue of Sophocles from Terracina, a trompe l'oeil mosaic of an unswept floor and the wonderfully elaborate Altar of Vicomagistri.

Museo Pio-Clementino
In the late 18th century Pope Clement XIV and his successor Pius VI began the world's largest collection of classical statues; it now fills 16 rooms. Don't miss the first-century BC *Belvedere Torso* by Apollonius of Athens; the *Apollo Sauroctonos*, a Roman copy of the bronze *Lizard Killer* by Praxiteles; and, in the octagonal Belvedere Courtyard, the exquisite *Belvedere Apollo* and *Laocoön*, the latter being throttled by the sea serpents Athena had sent as punishment for warning the Trojans to beware of the wooden horse.

Pinacoteca
Founded by Pius VI in the late 18th century, the Pinacoteca (picture gallery) includes many of the pictures that the Vatican hierarchy managed to recover from Napoleon after their forced sojourn in France in the early 19th century. The collection ranges from early paintings of the Byzantine School and Italian primitives to 18th-century Dutch and French old masters, and includes Giotto's *Stefaneschi Triptych*; a *Pietà* by Lucas Cranach the Elder; several delicate Madonnas by Fra Filippo Lippi, Fra Angelico, Raphael and Titian; Raphael's very last work, *The Transfiguration*; Caravaggio's *Entombment*; and a chiaroscuro *St Jerome* by Leonardo da Vinci.

Pio Cristiano Museum
The upper floor of the Museo Paolino is devoted to a collection of early Christian antiquities, mostly sarcophagi carved with reliefs of biblical scenes.

Stanze di Raffaello, Loggia di Raffaello & Cappella di Niccolò V
The Raphael Rooms were part of Nicholas V's palace, and were originally decorated by Piero della Francesca. Julius II then let Perugino and other Renaissance masters loose on them. He later discovered Raphael, and gave the 26-year-old *carte blanche* to redesign four rooms of the Papal Suite. The order of the visit changes from time to time; if

possible, try to see the rooms in the order in which they were painted. The Study (Stanza della Segnatura) was the first one Raphael tackled (1508-11), and features philosophical and spiritual themes – the triumph of Truth, Good and Beauty. Best known is the star-packed *School of Athens* fresco, with contemporary artists as classical figures: Plato is Leonardo; the glum thinker with the big knees on the steps at the front – Heraclitus – is Michelangelo; Euclid is Bramante (note the letters RUSM, Raphael's signature, on his gold collar); and Raphael himself is on the far right-hand side just behind a man in white, believed to be his pupil Sodoma. Raphael next turned his hand to the Stanza di Eliodoro (1512-14), frescoed with *The Expulsion of Heliodorus*. The portrayal of God saving the temple in Jerusalem from the thieving Heliodorus was intended to highlight the divine protection enjoyed by Julius himself (the pope's portrait is shown twice: both as the priest of the temple in the centre wearing blue and gold, and as the red-capped figure carried on a bier on the left).

The Dining Room (Stanza dell'Incendio, 1514-17), painted after Julius' death, is dedicated to his successor, Leo X (the most obese of the Popes, he died from gout aged 38), and shows other (more virtuous) Pope Leos with the face of Leo X. The room is named for the Fire in the Borgo, which Leo IV apparently stopped with the sign of the cross. (Note the first church of St Peter's in the background).

The Reception Room (Sala di Constantino, 1517-24) was completed by Giulio Romano after Raphael's death in 1520, but was based on Raphael's sketches of the Church's triumph over paganism, and tells the legend of Constantine's miraculous conversion.

The long Loggia di Raffaello (almost never open to the public) has a beautiful view over Rome. Started by Bramante in 1513, and finished by Raphael and his assistants, it features 52 small paintings on biblical themes, and leads into the Sala dei Chiaroscuri (Gregory XIII obliterated Raphael's frescoes here, but the magnificent ceiling remains). The adjacent Cappella di Niccolò V (Chapel of Nicholas V, usually open), has outstanding frescoes of scenes from the lives of saints Lawrence and Stephen by Fra Angelico (1448-50).

The Vatican Library

Founded by Pope Nicholas V in 1450, this is one of the world's most extraordinary libraries, containing 100,000 medieval manuscripts and books, and over a million other volumes. It is open to students and specialists on application to the Admissions office (06 6987 9403, bavsegre@vatlib.it). *See also p330.*

Borgo & Prati

In the 1930s Mussolini's broad avenue, via della Conciliazione, was bulldozed through much of the Borgo and its fascinating warren of medieval streets. A few of the streets remain, however, and salt-of-the-earth Romans mingle here with off-duty Swiss Guards and immaculately robed priests from the Vatican *Curia* (administration). Before his elevation, Josef Ratzinger lived above souvenir tat in a gloomy Fascist-era building just outside Bernini's colonnade and near the raised, covered *passetto*, the 13th-century escape route to **Castel Sant'Angelo** (*see p170*). In Medieval Rome's Anglo-Saxon enclave, to the south of via della Conciliazione, you'll find the **Museo Storico Nazionale dell'Arte Sanitaria** (*see p170*).

After Rome became capital of the unified Italian state in 1871, the meadows (*prati*) around the Renaissance ramparts north of the Borgo were suddenly required for housing for

Sightseeing

Fiery message at the **Museo delle Anime dei Defunti**. *See p170.*

the staff of the new ministries and parliament across the Tiber. The largest of the *piazze* by the Vatican walls was provocatively named after the Risorgimento, the movement that had destroyed the papacy's hold over the whole of central Italy. Broad avenues were laid out and named after anti-papal figures such as 14th-century 'freedom fighter' Cola di Rienzo, and decidedly pre-Christian (ie pagan) leaders such as Octavian and Julius Caesar.

Still a solidly bourgeois district, Prati's main drag, via Cola di Rienzo, provides ample opportunities for retail therapy – a good antidote to a surfeit of culture. Endless imposing military barracks line viale delle Milizie; quiet, tree-lined streets lead towards the river; and the massive, bombastic Palazzo di Giustizia (popularly known as *il palazzaccio*, 'the big ugly building') is between piazza Cavour and the Tiber. On the riverbank is one of Catholic Rome's truly weird experiences: the **Museo delle Anime dei Defunti** (*see below*).

Castel Sant'Angelo

Lungotevere Castello 50 (06 681 9111). Bus 23, 40Exp, 49, 87, 280, 926. **Open** 9am-7pm (last entry 6pm) Tue-Sun. **Admission** €5; €2.50 concessions. *With exhibition* €8; €4 concessions. **No credit cards.** Map p355 B4.

Extra time

● Classicists may get a kick out of translating the long plaque at the massive and highly controversial multi-storey car park built beneath the Gianicolo hill for the 2000 Holy Year. All official Vatican documents are still written in the language of the Caesars, though words like 'car park' can pose something of a challenge.
● Learn the secrets of the world's most nattily dressed police force in the **Museo Storico dell'Arma dei Carabinieri** at piazza del Risorgimento 46 (06 689 6696, open 8.30am-12.30pm Tue-Sun, admission free).
● Over the last couple of summers, attempts have been made to create a 'beach' on the banks of the Tiber by the **Castel Sant'Angelo**, and summer evening events are staged on the terraces of the castle (www.castelsantangelo.com).
● If your strength ebbs at the very sight of the 320 steps ascending from the top of the lift to the top of St Peter's dome, grant yourself some Dutch courage (in strictly non-alcoholic form) at **Il Ristoro** (*see p228*), the basilica's own cafe.

Begun by Emperor Hadrian in AD 135 as his own mausoleum, Castel Sant'Angelo has variously been a fortress, prison and papal residence. It now plays host to temporary art shows, although the real pleasure of a visit to Castel Sant'Angelo lies in wandering from Hadrian's original spiralling ramp entrance to the upper terraces, with their superb views of the city and beyond. Be careful, though – Puccini had Tosca hurl herself to her death from here. In between there is much to see: lavish Renaissance salons, decorated with spectacular frescoes and trompe l'oeil; the glorious chapel in the Cortile d'Onore, designed by Michelangelo for Leo X; and, halfway up an easily missed staircase, Clement VII's surprisingly tiny personal bathroom, painted by Giulio Romano. In the summer the *passetto* – linking the castle to the Vatican – is occasionally open (to the halfway point; you won't find yourself in Benedict's bedroom) and well worth a visit.

Museo delle Anime dei Defunti

Lungotevere Prati 12 (06 6880 6517). Bus 23, 30Exp, 34, 40Exp, 49, 70, 80Exp, 81, 87, 280, 492, 913, 926. **Open** *July-mid Sept* 7-10am, 5.30-7.30pm daily. *Mid Sept-June* 7-11am, 4.30-7.30pm daily. **Admission** free. **Map** p355 D4.
This macabre collection, attached to the neo-Gothic church of Sacro Cuore di Gesù in Prati, contains hand- and fingerprints left on the prayer books and clothes of the living by dead loved ones, to request masses to release their souls from purgatory. Begun just over a century ago, the collection includes an incandescent handprint supposedly left by Sister Clara Scholers on the habit of a fellow-nun in Westphalia in 1696, and second bank notes left by a dead soul outside a church where he wanted a mass said. **Photo** *p169*.

Museo Storico Nazionale dell'Arte Sanitaria

Lungotevere in Sassia 3 (06 689 3051). Bus 23, 40Exp, 62, 280. **Open** 10am-noon Mon, Wed, Fri. Closed Aug. **Admission** €3. **No credit cards.** Map p355 B4.
A hostel and church was established around 726 by King Ine of Wessex to cater for weary and sick pilgrims who descended from the north. Known as the *burgus saxonum* or *in Sassia*, this district became the nucleus of the world's first purpose-built hospital. The name *in Sassia* persists although British funds for the hostel were cut off with the Norman invasion of England in 1066, after which it passed into papal hands and thence to the Templar knight Guy de Montpellier, who founded the Order of the Holy Spirit (Santo Spirito). A few rooms of the modern hospital of Santo Spirito house a gruesome collection of medical artefacts, dating from ancient times to the 19th century. The two massive 15th-century frescoed wards, the gloriously elegant fruit of a rebuilding programme in Renaissance times, were only recently emptied of their beds to provide space for itinerant exhibitions. Any rare opportunity to visit them should be seized. **Photo** *p166*.

The Appian Way

Roam the old way.

Appius Claudius Caecus, censor of 312 BC, had a couple of inspired ideas. One was to build a straight road to move troops and materials as efficiently as possible from Rome to the second city of the Republic, Capua. Appius Claudius and his engineers took advantage of a lava stream from a volcanic eruption some 270,000 years earlier in the Alban Hills to the south; it provided a solid base out from the spot where the tomb of Cecilia Metella (*see p174*) stands. Soon after, the road was extended to Brindisi, opening up *caput mundi* towards the East. Officially named after its creator, the Appia became known as the *regina viarum*, 'queen of roads'.

Today this is undoubtedly the most picturesque of the ancient Roman *vie consolari*. In ancient times it was a prime spot for the real estate of the after-life; the remains of the dead – whether cremated or buried – had to be kept outside the *pomerium* (a sacred city boundary), and well-to-do Roman families began setting up their family mausoleums alongside the major road into the city. It was once lined with tombs, vaults, sarcophagi and every kind of magnificent mortuary decoration imaginable – an exquisitely picturesque gallery of the pagan departed, of which fragments remain.

Christians, too, began burying their dead here, initially in common necropoli. Later, as land became too expensive, they laid their dead to rest underground, creating the estimated 300-kilometre (200-mile) network of underground cemeteries known as the **catacombs**. This system wasn't used for secret worship in times of persecution as once thought: Roman authorities were perfectly aware of its existence. But for pagans, death and its rituals were sacred whatever the religion. Besides, having the cemetery close by meant that they could keep an eye on those pesky cultists. Jews also used the catacomb method for their burials; a Jewish catacomb can still be visited at Vigna Rondanini, via Appia Antica 119 (by appointment only, *see p73* **Locked sites**).

Via Appia Antica suffered at the hands of marauding Goths and Normans, although pilgrims continued to use it as the first leg of their long trip to the Holy Land. Successive popes did as much damage as barbarians had, grabbing any good pieces of statuary or marble that remained and reducing the ancient monuments to unrecognisable stumps of brick.

Miraculously, there are still things to see: the mausoleum of Priscilla, where via Appia Antica meets via Ardeatina, the tomb of Cecilia Metella and, further down the road, the Casal Rotondo and the mausoleums of the Orazi and Curiazi, maintain more or less their original shape.

With all these reminders of antiquity, this is a wonderful area to spend a day, preferably a Sunday or holiday when all but local traffic is banned. Explore more extensively by renting a bike at the Centro Visite Parco Appia Antica (*see p172*), past the Porta San Sebastiano gate.

Appius Claudius' other good idea was to bring water to Rome from the springs of the verdant limestone hills around the city. The first aqueduct ran 12 kilometres (7.5 miles) from

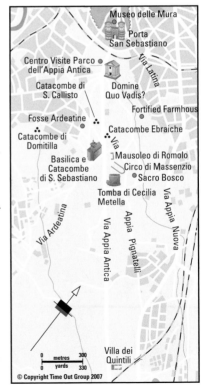

© Copyright Time Out Group 2007

Sightseeing

the Alban Hills and was called the Acqua Appia. Nothing remains of this, but the majestic ruins of other, more copious aqueducts can be seen in the **Parco degli Acquedotti** (*see below*).

BUSES ON THE WAY

You can take the **Archeobus** (*see p323*) from Termini station, which stops by most major sights. The following regular bus services each cover some portion of the Appian Way as well.

118 Viale Aventino (outside Circo Massimo metro station) – Terme di Caracalla – Porta San Sebastiano – along via Appia Antica to Domine Quo Vadis? and the catacombs of San Callisto and San Sebastiano – Via Appia Pignatelli.

218 Piazza San Giovanni – Porta San Sebastiano – along via Appia Antica to Domine Quo Vadis? – along via Ardeatina to Fosse Ardeatine and, with a bit of a hike, the Catacombe di Domitilla.

660 Colli Albani metro station – along via Appia Antica, from Circo di Massenzio to Tomba di Cecilia Metella.

664 Colli Albani metro station – along via Appia Nuova to Villa dei Quintili.

Along the Appian Way

Although it once started at the south-eastern end of the Circo Massimo, the beginning of the Appia Antica is now considered to be the **Porta San Sebastiano**, the best-preserved of the gates that were built by Aurelian when he walled the city in AD 270. Inside the gate is the little **Museo delle Mura** (*see p174*), which once allowed access to the Aurelian Walls to the west; sadly, this has long been closed to the public for structural reasons, although if you ask the custodian he'll let you up on to the tower, from which there's a marvellous view. On the right, ten minutes' walk beyond the gate, is the **Centro Visite Parco Appia Antica** (via Appia Antica 42, 06 512 6314, www.parcoappia antica.org, open 9.30am-5.30pm (4.30pm in winter) Sun & public holidays, telephone for information on weekdays), where you can rent a bicycle (book ahead, €3 an hour, €10 a day) or take a free guided bike tour.

Parco degli acquedotti

Federico Fellini's masterpiece, *La dolce vita*, opens with Marcello Mastroianni flying in a helicopter over a stretch of aqueduct that snakes its way through the concrete post-war suburbs of Rome. Much of the aqueduct is now in the **Parco degli Acquedotti**, which retains a certain Fellini-esque charm. The aqueduct traverses the landscape, with the 1960s church of St Polycarp to one side and the rail line to Naples to the other; nearby, a golf course dotted with olive trees lies cheek by jowl with a more home-made sports club –

four mismatched and rusting exercise bikes propped up with bricks are the meeting point of a number of elderly men. Throw in the occasional flock of sheep and newly-weds in their finery having photographs taken, and Fellini would have been in his element.

The aqueduct in question is in fact two, the double-decker *acque* Claudia and Anio Novo, which both date from AD 38-52 and have their sources in the hills near Tivoli (arches of these are also visible from the bus from Ciampino airport). To save on building costs, the sections of the aqueducts that are above ground were unified, with the line of arches supporting two channels; the Acqua Claudia below and the Anio Novo above. Where the aqueducts are severed, the rectangular *specus* (water channels) are visible above the arches. Together the aqueducts carried over a third of the water supply of Imperial Rome, estimated at one cubic metre (250 gallons) per person per day – more than any city before or since. On the via Tuscolana side of the *acque* Claudia and Anio Novo, the pipe bulging out of the ground is the route of the Renaissance Acqua Felice.

● To get to the Parco, take the metro to Giulio Agricola and walk (10mins) south-west on viale Appio Claudio. Alternatively, take bus 557 from Subaugusta metro station, or the Archeobus (*see p232*), which stops on the viale Appio Claudio side of the park.

Further out on the left is the tiny, austere church of **Domine Quo Vadis?** (open Apr-Oct 8am-7.30pm daily, Nov-Mar 8am-6.30pm daily). Inside the door on a raised tablet are the imprints of two long, flat feet that are said to have been left by Christ when he appeared to St Peter, who was running away from Rome and crucifixion. Christ told Peter he was going to Rome to be crucified again himself, thus shaming Peter into returning too. These prints are a copy; the real ones are at the church of San Sebastiano (*see p174*).

A right fork outside the church along via Ardeatina leads to the **Catacombe di Domitilla** (access from via delle Sette Chiese; *see below*) and the **Fosse Ardeatine** (via Ardeatina 174, 06 513 6742, open 8.15am-3.30pm Mon-Fri, 8.15am-4.45pm Sat & Sun, admission free), this latter a moving memorial to the 335 Italians shot by the occupying Nazis in 1944 in retaliation for a Resistance ambush.

From the centre of the fork, a drive leads up to the **Catacombe di San Sebastiano** (*see p173*). The left fork past Domine Quo Vadis?, on the other hand, opens up two options: straight along via Appia Antica, or left again into via della Caffarella.

The latter choice takes you past sumptuous private villas and clubs before opening up to the vast **Parco della Caffarella**, which offers a choice of bike and walking paths winding across the Roman countryside, past herds of sheep and a few noteworthy objects of antiquity. Follow the main path to the most important one: commonly known as the temple of the god Redicolo, historians say it is in fact a second-century AD tomb, perhaps of a Roman woman named Annia Regilla. It owes its good state of preservation to local farmers who guarded it jealously through the ages… as a useful barn for hay storage. A fortified farmhouse in the middle of the Caffarella valley offers entertainment for children: in spring lambs bleat, roosters crow and mum and dad can buy home-made cheese.

On the Appia Antica, on the other hand, Renaissance walls surround private villas along the road to the **church** (*see p174*) and **catacombs of San Sebastiano** (*see p173*). Beyond here, the Appian Way is as it was… almost. The original volcanic paving stones that lie exposed beneath a canopy of pines and cypresses are those trod by the Roman infantry. All Roman roads were built to handle five soldiers or two carriages abreast, measuring 14 Roman feet (4.2 metres/13.7 feet) across. On either side of the road are bits and pieces of funerary ornaments. On this stretch are the **Mausoleo di Romolo** (behind a very sad-looking palm tree) and the vast **Circo di**

Massenzio (for both, *see p174*). The rise towards the cylindrical **tomb of Cecilia Metella** (*see p174*) marks the end of the lava flow that was exploited for the building of the road. Further south, the villas thin out and the funerary monuments are more prominent. At the fifth Roman mile is the second-century **Villa dei Quintili** (access from via Appia Nuova only; *see p174*). Beyond this point the road is quieter and landscape wilder, with occasional sheep. Any turning to the left will take you to the modern via Appia Nuova. Between via Appia Nuova and via Tuscolana, the **Parco degli Aquedotti** (*see p172*) has striking remains of Roman aqueducts.

Catacombe di Domitilla

Via delle Sette Chiese 282 (06 513 3956). **Open** 9am-noon, 2-5pm Mon, Wed-Sun. Closed Jan. **Admission** €5; €3 6-15 years. **No credit cards**. These catacombs are found on land once belonging to Flavia Domitilla, wife of a first-century consul, banished to the island of Ponza for her faith. The guided visit starts with the fourth-century basilica of Saints Nerius and Achilleus, Roman soldiers martyred for proselytising, probably under Christian-hating Emperor Diocletian. The tomb of the martyrs is in the apse; throughout the church, inscriptions mark the tombs of early Christians who wanted their final resting place to be near these two fearless military men. On a column is a representation of the martyrdom of St Achilleus with his hands tied behind his back. The ensuing galleries of burial places in the soft volcanic rock cover some 12km (7.5 miles), though you won't see all of them. The oldest part is the so-called *hypogeum* of the Flavi, a pagan burial ground taken over by Christians. Frescoes in varying states of preservation are found throughout.

Catacombe di San Callisto

Via Appia Antica 78, 110 & 126 (06 513 0151/ www.catacombe.roma.it). **Open** 9am-noon, 2-5pm Mon, Tue, Thur-Sun. Closed late Jan-late Feb. **Admission** €5; €3 concessions. **Credit** AmEx, DC, MC, V. These are Rome's largest catacombs. Buried in the 29km (18 miles) of tunnels were nine popes (venerated in a chapel known as *il piccolo Vaticano*), dozens of martyrs and thousands of Christians. They are stacked down, with the oldest on the top. Named after the banker, deacon and later pope Callixtus, who was administrator of the catacombs in the early third century, the area became the first official cemetery of the Church of Rome. The crypt of St Cecilia is the spot where this patron saint of music is believed to have been buried before she was moved to her eponymous church in Trastevere (*see p138*); the statue is a copy of the one in the church.

Catacombe di San Sebastiano

Via Appia Antica 136 (06 785 0350). **Open** 9am-noon, 2-5pm Mon, Tue, Thur-Sat. Closed late Jan-late Feb. **Admission** €5; €3 concessions. **Credit** AmEx, MC, V.

The name 'catacomb' originated in this spot, where a complex of underground burial sites situated near a tufa quarry was described as being *kata kymbas* – 'near the quarry'. The guided tour will take you into the crypt of St Sebastian, the martyr always depicted nastily pierced by a hail of arrows (though these were just one of several unpleasant tortures), who was buried here, probably during Diocletian's reign in the late third century; the base of the original monument to him can be seen. The Christian burials that followed his eventually formed three layers of tombs, the second of which is what's on show; this includes the *piazzolo*, where pagan mausoleums re-used by Christians were found.

Circo di Massenzio & Mausoleo di Romolo

Via Appia Antica 153. Closed as this guide went to press but due to reopen in late 2007.

This large area of lovely green countryside contains one of the best preserved Roman circuses. It was built by Emperor Maxentius for his private use, before his defeat and death at the hands of co-ruler Constantine in AD 312. Remains of the Imperial palace are perched above the track, at its northern end. Earthenware jugs (amphorae) were inserted into the upper sections of the long walls: their empty volume helped lighten the load above the vaults. Also at the north end is the mausoleum Maxentius built for his beloved son Romulus. To the left, forming a wall of a farmhouse, is a mausoleum thought to have belonged to the Servilius family. Underneath other ancient ruins next to the road lie more catacombs, largely unexcavated.

Mausoleo di Cecilia Metella

Via Appia Antica 161 (06 780 0093). **Open** (last entry 1hr before closing) *Apr-Oct* 9am-6.30pm daily. *Nov-Mar* 9am-3.30pm daily. **Admission** €6; €3 concessions. *See also p73* **Appia Card**. **No credit cards**.

This colossal cylinder of travertine is the final resting place of, and unusual tribute to, a woman who linked two major families in late first century BC Rome. A large plaque beneath the frieze honours Cecilia as the daughter of Quintus Creticus (probably so-called for his triumph in Crete in 64BC) and the wife of Crassus (a relation of the Crassus who ruled in the triumvirate with Julius Caesar). During the 14th century the powerful Caetani family, relatives of Pope Boniface VIII, incorporated the tomb into a fortress, adding the crenellations to the top; the frieze decorated with skulls gives this area its nickname *Capo di bove* (ox head). Inside is a roofless gallery with a row of headless, toga-clad Romans and other marble objects, including lapidary inscriptions, crematory urns and tomb decorations – all funerary statues that used to line the Appia Antica. The spot where Cecilia was buried is a fine example of brick dome-making. Downstairs, pieces of the volcanic rock used in the construction of the ancient road can be seen. Outside and across the way are what's left of the church of San Nicola, a rare example of Gothic

architecture in Rome, surrounded by further walls of the fortress, which once straddled the road. From this imposing spot the Caetani filled their coffers by exacting tolls from passing travellers.

Museo delle Mura

Via di Porta San Sebastiano 18 (06 7047 5284). **Open** 9am-2pm Tue-Sun. **Admission** €3; €1.50 concessions. **No credit cards**.

Housed in the ancient Porta San Sebastiano, the little Museum of the Walls has a smallish collection of artefacts associated with Roman walls and roads. The museum's greatest attraction used to be the access it gave visitors to a walkway on top of a substantial stretch of the Aurelian Wall itself, but this *passeggiata* was closed in 2001 as the wall started to crumble, with no date set for reopening.

San Sebastiano (church)

Via Appia Antica 136 (06 785 0350). **Open** 8am-7pm daily.

Visitors usually ignore the fourth-century basilica built over the catacombs of the same name (*see p174*), though pilgrims on a tour of Rome's great basilicas understand its importance. The remains of apostles Peter and Paul were hidden in the underlying catacombs in the third century, during the persecutions by Emperor Valerian, hence the church's original name: Basilica Apostolorum. In the ninth century it was rededicated to St Sebastian. A soldier from Gaul, Sebastian was the target of a rain of arrows when he converted, but, tradition says, his wounds were healed by the intercession of another saint. Emperor Diocletian then had him stoned or bludgeoned to finish off the job. Two relics of the saint – an arrow, plus the column to which he was tied while the arrows were flying – are in the first chapel on the right. Also on display is the marble slab in which Christ left his footprints during his miraculous apparition at Domine Quo Vadis? (*see p173*).

Villa dei Quintili

Via Appia Nuova 1092 (06 718 2485). **Open** (last entry 1hr before closing) *Apr-Oct* 9am-7.30pm daily. *Nov-Mar* 9am-4.30pm daily. **Admission** €6; €3 concessions. *See also p73* **Appia Card. No credit cards**.

The wealthy, cultured and militarily gifted Quintili brothers – consuls under Emperor Marcus Aurelius – built this splendid villa with a large bath complex and nymphaeum before Emperor Commodus became jealous and had them killed. He then took over the villa for himself, and essentially ruled from here. Digs in the 18th and 19th centuries unearthed statuary and objects now in the Vatican Museums and others around the world. Recent excavations have brought more rooms to light; the nymphaeum, which has been under restoration, was due to reopen as this guide went to press. The rest of the vast structure is set in splendid isolation amid fields strewn with fragments of the many-coloured marble that once faced its mighty halls. A small antiquarium displays statuary and objects found in the vicinity. Check for evening events in the summer.

The Suburbs

Rome's outer spaces.

In 1871, when Rome became the capital of united Italy, its 212,000 residents rattled around inside the Aurelian Walls, where vast swathes were still given over to vegetable gardens. Only the occasional farmhouse punctuated the rolling *campagna romana* beyond the walls. By 1901 the population had almost doubled to 422,000; in 1931 it was 930,000; by 1971 it was well over two million. These new *romani* were only too happy, in the interests of having a roof over their heads, to endorse the destruction of the countryside, which was swiftly gobbled up, at first by pompous turn-of-the-century *palazzi* and, later, by unauthorised – and often unplumbed – tower blocks.

Today the result mostly looks grim, with a few notable exceptions, especially in the inner suburbs. There are Liberty (art nouveau) *palazzi* along *vie* Salaria and Nomentana, for example, and some memorable Fascist urban planning in EUR. Elsewhere, even some of the most architecturally uninspired districts hide wonderful surprises worth travelling for.

North

Flaminio

For centuries the route along which most travellers entered the Eternal City, the dead-straight via Flaminia nowadays passes through affluent residential *Roma nord* as it shoots north from piazza del Popolo. Along the way are myriad sports facilities: the Stadio Flaminio and Acqua Acetosa running tracks in the east, and the **Foro Italico** and **Stadio Olimpico** football stadium to the west.

It also crosses a mushrooming cultural zone, containing the hyper-active **Auditorium-Parco della Musica** (*see p275*) and **MAXXI** art gallery. Via Flaminia crosses the Tiber at the ancient **Ponte Milvio**; now open to pedestrians only, the second-century BC bridge offers a good view of the neighbouring Ponte Flaminio designed by Armando Brasini, a glorious example of Fascist rhetorical architecture. Federico Moccia's cult novel *Tre metri sopra il cielo* has put Ponte Milvio at the centre of a strange phenomenon: like characters in the book, young Romans attach padlocks painted with sweethearts' names to the bridge and throw the key into the Tiber below.

Foro Italico & Stadio Olimpico

Piazza de Bosis/via del Foro Italico. Bus 32, 69, 271, 280, 910/tram 2. **Map** p353.
A marble obelisk, 36m (120ft) high, with the words 'Mussolini Dux' carved on it, greets visitors to the Foro Italico, a sports complex conceived in the late 1920s by architect Enrico Del Debbio. The avenue leading west of the obelisk is paved with black-and-white mosaics of good Fascists doing Fascist things – flying warplanes, saluting *il Duce* and engaging in physical jerks. It's a wonderfully camp sight today, and amazingly well preserved considering the thousands of feet that trample the tiles every weekend on their way to the Stadio Olimpico beyond (built in the 1950s but modified for the 1990 World Cup), where AS Roma and SS Lazio both play (*see p289* **Football**). Surrounding the Stadio dei Marmi track to the north – also by Del Debbio – are 60 marble statues of naked athletes, each with some kind of sports apparatus, from crossbows to *bocce* (bowling) balls. Other facilities at the Foro Italico include tennis courts, where the Italian Open is held each May, and two swimming pools.

MAXXI

Via Guido Reni 10 (06 321 0181/www.maxximuseo.org). Bus 53, 280, 910/tram 2. **Open** (during exhibitions only) 11am-7pm Tue-Sun. **Admission** free. **No credit cards.**
Works to transform this former army barracks into the Museo delle arti del XXI secolo (MAXXI) have been stop-go since building began in 2001, to a design by Anglo-Iraqi architect Zaha Hadid. But the political wheel turns and at the time of writing, the person who championed the creation of a centre for 21st century arts and architecture in Rome when she was culture minister in the late 1990s is now back in government, and pressing noisily for more funds, faster. When it is finished – no one is willing to guess when that will be – it will certainly be striking but pessimists (aka realists) doubt that it will rival the Tate Modern phenomenon. For the time being, it hosts occasional interesting temporary shows.

Parioli

Expensive, residential Parioli is located north of the Villa Borghese (see p95). Built over some of Baroque Rome's finest private suburban villas, its atmosphere is rather dull, and the late 19th- and early 20th-century architecture not consistently impressive. For Romans, however, a Parioli address is the ultimate status symbol; the consummate pariolino is a rich kid who drives a

Sightseeing

super-shiny SUV, spends summer at the family home in Sardinia, and wears clothes – purchased at Davide Cenci – pressed by a *filipina* maid.

Salario

Via Salaria – the salt road – existed before Rome, when ancient tribes brought vital salt supplies along it from saltpans on the east coast. Today the road begins its north-easterly itinerary from piazza Fiume. The modern district on either side of the Salaria is called Trieste, home to upmarket post-Unification apartment blocks and a bevy of embassies. But the real treasures of the area are the delightful art nouveau **Coppedè quarter** – centred on piazza Mincio – and the leafy shade of the **Villa Ada** public gardens and the **Catacombe di Priscilla**. In via della Moschea, between *vie* Salaria and Flaminia, lies Paolo Portoghesi's mosque (*see p334*), built between 1984 and '92.

Catacombe di Priscilla
Via Salaria 430 (06 8620 6272). Bus 63, 92, 310, 630. **Open** 8.30am-noon, 2.30-5pm Tue-Sun. Closed Jan. **Admission** €5; €3 concessions. **No credit cards.**
This two-storey second-century AD burial place contains bas-reliefs and frescoes, including what is believed to be the first-ever depiction of Mary.

Nomentano

Via Nomentana leads out of Rome to the north-east, flanked on either side by another middle-class residential area, with some charming art nouveau buildings. It has its green lung in the **Villa Torlonia** (again with a touch of art nouveau in the **Casina delle Civette**), its art fest in the **MACRO** contemporary art gallery and perhaps the earliest Christian mosaics in **Santa Costanza**, by the catacombs and church of **Sant'Agnese fuori le Mura**. The area around via Tiburtina is more low-rent.

MACRO
Via Reggio Emilia 54 (06 6710 70400/www.macro. roma.museum). Bus 36, 60Exp, 62, 80Exp, 84, 90Exp. **Open** 9am-6.30pm Tue-Sun. **Admission** €1. **No credit cards. Map** p356 E3.
Rome's sluggish contemporary art scene was given a shot in the arm in the 1990s with the opening of a municipal modern art gallery in a stunningly converted brewery. Rechristened MACRO (Museo d'Arte Contemporaneo di Roma), this space will eventually cover 10,000 sq m (107,500 sq ft), thanks to an extension designed by superstar architect Odile Decq, scheduled for completion in summer 2008. MACRO brings big international names to Rome, gives space to young artists and showcases local artists making place-specific art. Shows and

Slow progress at the new **Palazzo dei Congressi**. *See p178.*

events spill over into some of the dramatic space inside the Mattatoio (*see p143*; open 4pm-midnight Tue-Sun during shows) in Testaccio.

Sant'Agnese fuori le Mura & mausoleum of Santa Costanza
Via Nomentana 349 (06 861 0840/www.santagnese. net). Bus 36, 60Exp, 90Exp. **Open** *Church* 7.30am-noon, 4-7.45pm daily. *Catacombs & Santa Costanza* 9am-noon, 4-6pm Mon-Sat; 4-6pm Sun. **Admission** *Church & Santa Costanza* free. *Catacombs* €5; €3 concessions. **No credit cards.**
The circular fourth-century mausoleum of Santa Costanza, 2km (1.25 miles) along via Nomentana, was built for Constantine's daughters, Constance (a saint only by popular tradition) and Helen. The sarcophagus here, containing the remains of Constance, is a plaster cast of the porphyry original, now in the Vatican Museums. The barrel-vaulted ambulatory, whose arcades rest on exquisite 'pillows' of marble, is decorated with perhaps the world's earliest surviving Christian mosaics. These fourth-century works look more pagan than Christian, with simple pastoral scenes with a spiralling vine encircling figures collecting and treading grapes; but Christian historians insist the wine-making motifs represent Christ's blood, not the pastimes of Bacchus. The vast remains of a fourth-century basilica stand in wasteland nearby. In the adjoining church of Sant'Agnese, dating from the seventh century, is an original apse mosaic showing a diminutive figure of St Agnes standing on the flames of her martyrdom, flanked by two popes. St Agnes was almost certainly buried in the catacombs below this church, though her skull was later moved to the church of

Sant'Agnese in Agone (*see p116*). The catacombs are among Rome's least visited and most atmospheric, but beware: they usually close in January.

Villa Torlonia

Villa Torlonia, via Nomentana 70 (06 8205 9127/ www.museivillatorlonia.it). Bus 36, 60Exp, 62, 84, 90Exp, 140. **Open** *Park* dawn-sunset daily. *Museums & sights* Mar, Oct 9am-5.30pm Tue-Sun; Apr-Sept 9am-7pm Tue-Sun; Nov-Feb 9am-4.30pm Tue-Sun. **Admission** *Casina nobile* €4.50; €2.50 concessions. *Casina delle civette* €3; €1.50 concessions. *All museums* €6.50; €3 concessions. **No credit cards.**

The Villa Torlonia, with its verdant palm-filled park, was the elegant home of the aristocratic Torlonia family from 1797, glorified as Mussolini's suburban HQ in the 1930s and trashed by Anglo-American forces when they made it their high command base (1944-7). When Rome city council bought it in 1978, it was in a disastrous state; the house and its outbuildings disappeared for years behind scaffolding. Enough has now emerged to make this a truly worthwhile hike. The main house – the pretty *Casina nobile* – was revamped in 1832 by architect Giovan Battista Caretti, who commissioned the interior's frescoes and mouldings, which have now been restored to their former glory. Mussolini's bunker beneath the house can be visited by appointment. A number of structures are dotted around the park. Exhibitions are held in the *Casino dei principi*, which also houses the archives of the inter-war *Scuola romana* artistic movement. The *Casina delle civette*, a wacky Swiss chalet-folly, was endowed with all kinds of stupendous stained glass and *boiseries* in 1916-20; the art nouveau fittings have been beautifully restored and supplemented with much more stained glass from the same period. The *Limonaia* – where lemon trees were kept through the winter – is now a pleasant café-restaurant, and the faux-medieval villa by its side is home to Technotown (*see p260*). Beneath the park, and accessible only by appointment, is one of Rome's few Jewish catacombs.

East

Pigneto

Bordered by via Prenestina to the north and via Casilina to the south, the Pigneto district sprang up in haphazard fashion between the 1890s and 1930s as railwaymen and artisans used micro-credits from workers' cooperatives to build dwellings amid the warehouses and railway sheds. The humble industriousness of the area attracted the directors of Italian neo-realism: Rossellini's *Roma città aperta* (1945), Visconti's *Bellissima* (1951) and Pasolini's *Accattone* (1960) were largely shot here. Though fast becoming one of the city's hippest residential zones – with property prices going through the roof – it retains much of its unique

appeal, thanks in large part to the thronging morning food market (Mon-Sat) along pedestrianised via del Pigneto, and a massive flea market held in the same spot on the last Sunday of every month.

Tor Tre Teste

Further along via Casilina, just inside the GRA ring road, is the anonymously ugly suburb of Tor Tre Teste, above which emerges the startling **Dio Padre Misericordioso** church (via F Tovaglieri, 06 231 5833, www.diopadre misericordioso.it, open 7.30am-12.30pm, 3.30-7.30pm daily), designed by American architect Richard Meier. Its three white sails make it look like a mini version of the Sydney Opera House. It stands in splendid isolation, in a sea of asphalt, looking as out of place in this run-down periphery as Meier's Ara Pacis museum (*see p111*) does in the *centro storico*.

South

Garbatella & San Paolo

Lying south of Testaccio and Ostiense (*see p142*), San Paolo is a district of mainly uninspiring 1950s-70s high-rises, while Garbatella is a fascinating area of late 19th- and early 20th-century workers' housing: many of the apartment blocks and adorable single- or two-family villas in private grounds are architecturally outstanding. A strong community feel remains. While Garbatella has no monuments (but some exciting cultural life based around the Teatro Palladium; *see p288*), San Paolo is home to one of Rome's major basilicas, **San Paolo fuori le Mura**.

San Paolo fuori le Mura

Via Ostiense 184 (06 541 0341). Metro San Paolo/ bus 23, 271, 769, 770. **Open** *Basilica* 7am-7pm daily. *Cloister* 9am-1pm, 3-6pm daily. **Map** p353.
Constantine founded San Paolo to commemorate the martyrdom of St Paul at nearby Tre Fontane (*see p179*). The church has been destroyed, rebuilt and restored several times; most of the present basilica – the largest in Rome after St Peter's – is only 150 years old. The greatest damage to the building occurred in a fire in 1823, but restorers also contributed to the destruction of the older church. Features that have survived include 11th-century doors decorated with biblical scenes; a strange 12th-century Easter candlestick, featuring human-, lion- and goat-headed beasts spewing the vine of life from their mouths; and the elegant 13th-century ciborium above the altar, by Arnolfo di Cambio. In the *confessio* beneath the altar is the tomb of St Paul, topped by a stone slab pierced with two holes through which devotees stuff bits of cloth to imbue them with the apostle's holiness.

Sightseeing

Eight more popes and the world ends: **San Paolo fuori le Mura**. See p177.

BENEDICTVS·XVI·

IO·PAVLVS·II·

SED·A·XXVI·M·V·DIES·

The cloister is a good example of cosmatesque work, its twisted columns inlaid with mosaic and supporting an arcade of sculpted reliefs. In the sacristy are the remnants of a series of papal portraits that once lined the nave. The modern church has carried on this tradition, replacing the originals with mosaic portraits of all the popes from Peter to the present incumbent. There are only eight spaces left; once they are filled, the world, apparently, will end.

EUR

Italian Fascism managed to be simultaneously monstrous and absurd, but its delusions of grandeur helped produce some of the most interesting European architecture and town planning of the 20th century. In the early 1930s Giuseppe Bottai, governor of Rome and the leading arbiter of Fascist taste, had the idea of expanding landbound Rome along via Ostiense towards the sea. Imperial Rome had its monuments, papal Rome had its churches. Fascist Rome (*la terza Roma*), Bottai thought, should have its architectural spaces as well. He combined this with the notion of a universal exhibition, pencilled in for 1942 and intended to combine cultural exhibition spaces with a monument to the regime.

Architect Marcello Piacentini was charged with co-ordinating the ambitious project but few of the original designs were ever built. The planning committee became so embroiled in argument that little had been achieved by the outbreak of World War II. After the war, work resumed with a different spirit. Still known as **EUR** (*Esposizione universale romana*), the project united some of Italy's best architects – Giovanni Muzio, Mario de Renzi, Ludovico Quaroni and partners Luigi Figini and Gino Pollini. With its unrelieved planes of

icy travertine and reinterpretations of classical monuments, the bombastic modernism of EUR lets you know you're not in Kansas any more.

Today, EUR continues to grow, though construction work on a new Palazzo dei Congressi is progressing slowly.

On either side of axial via Cristoforo Colombo, Fascist-inspired buildings such as Guerrini's **Palazzo della Civiltà del Lavoro**, popularly known as *il colosseo quadrato* (the square Colosseum), and Arnaldo Foschini's church of **Santi Pietro e Paolo** (piazzale Santi Pietro e Paolo) can be seen alongside post-war *palazzi* like Adalberto Libera's **Palazzo dei Congressi** (piazza JF Kennedy) and Studio BBPR's superbly functional post office (viale Beethoven).

A slew of museums – the **Museo dell'Alto Medioevo**, **Museo della Civiltà Romana** (containing an astronomy museum), **Museo delle Arti e Tradizioni Popolari**, the **Museo Preistorico ed Etnografico** (for all, *see p179*) – allows a glimpse inside these striking monuments to Fascist grandeur.

The 1960 Olympics offered another stimulus for filling out the area. The masterpiece is Nervi and Piacentini's flying-saucer-like **Palazzo dello Sport** (piazza dello Sport), hovering over EUR's artificial lake and now often used for big rock concerts and political conventions. The area contains other attractions, such as the **LUNEUR Park** funfair and the **Piscina delle Rose** swimming pool (*see p293*).

Most Romans never visit EUR except on business or for concerts. At night, however, and especially in summer, there's a definite whiff of rich-kid good times in the air when it becomes the playground of fun-loving, suntanned, wealthy brats. For relief from EUR's relentless modernity, head for the leafy charm of the **Abbazia delle Tre Fontane** (*see p179*).

GETTING THERE

The quickest way from the city centre to EUR is by underground (Metro line B; get off at EUR Fermi or EUR Palasport), but approaching the district from the surface, along via Cristoforo Colombo (bus 30Exp, 170, 714), is the best way to experience the isolated, emerging-from-greenery feel of EUR, which was a significant part of the original architects' design.

Abbazia delle Tre Fontane

Via Acque Salvie 1 (06 540 1655). Bus 716, 761. **Open** *Santi Vincenzo e Anastasio* 6am-12.30pm, 3-8pm daily. *Other churches* 8am-1pm, 3-6pm daily. *Shop* 9am-1pm, 3.30-7pm daily.

To the east of the Tre Fontane sports facilities lies a haven of ancient, eucalyptus-scented green, with three churches commemorating the points where St Paul's head supposedly bounced after it was severed from his body in AD 67. (Being a Roman citizen, Paul was eligible for the relatively quick and painless head-chop, as opposed to the long, drawn-out crucifixion.) These are the grounds of the Trappist monastery of Tre Fontane, where water has gurgled and birds have sung since the fifth century. The church of San Paolo delle Tre Fontane is said to be built on the spot where the apostle was executed; apart from a column to which Paul is supposed to have been tied, all traces of the fifth-century church were done away with in 1599 by architect Giacomo della Porta, who was also responsible for the two other churches. Monks planted the eucalyptus trees in the 1860s, believing they would drive away the malarial mosquitoes; a liqueur is now brewed from the trees and sold in a little shop (no credit cards) along with chocolate and remedies for all ills.

Museo dell'Alto Medioevo

Viale Lincoln 3 (06 5422 8199). Metro EUR Fermi/bus 30Exp, 170, 714. **Open** 9am-7.30pm Tue-Sun. **Admission** €2; €1 concessions. **No credit cards.**

Focusing on the decorative arts between the fall of the Roman Empire and the Renaissance, this museum has intricate gold- and silver-decorated swords, buckles and horse tackle, as well as more mundane objects: ceramic bead jewellery and the metal frames of what may be Europe's earliest folding chairs.

Museo della Civiltà Romana

Piazza G Agnelli 10 (06 592 6135/06 592 6041). Metro EUR Fermi/bus 30Exp, 170, 714. **Open** *Museum* 9am-2pm Tue-Sun. **Admission** €6.50; €3.50 concessions. **No credit cards.**

This museum dates from 1937, when Mussolini mounted a massive celebration to mark the second millennium of Augustus becoming the first emperor. The fact that the celebration came about 35 years too early was overlooked by *il Duce*, who was eager to draw parallels between Augustus' glory and his own. With its blank white walls and lofty, echoing corridors, the building is Fascist-classical at its most grandiloquent. There's a fascinating cutaway model of the Colosseum's maze of tunnels and lifts, as well

as casts of the intricate reliefs on Trajan's column (*see p81*). The centrepiece is a giant model of Rome in the fourth century AD, which puts Rome's scattered fragments and artefacts into context very helpfully. The palazzo also contains the new Museo Astronomico and a planetarium (*see p260*).

Museo delle Arti e Tradizioni Popolari

Piazza G Marconi 8 (06 592 6148/06 591 2669). Metro EUR Fermi/bus 30Exp, 170, 714. **Open** 9am-4pm Tue-Fri; 9am-8pm Sat, Sun. **Admission** €4; €2 concessions. **No credit cards.** **Note:** staff shortages mean opening times can be changed without notice. It pays to call ahead.

This enormous collection is dedicated to Italian folk art and rural tradition. Exhibits include elaborately decorated carts and horse tackle, as well as craft-related implements and a bizarre collection of votive offerings left to local saints. Malevolent-looking puppets fill one room; another has *carnevale* artefacts.

Museo Preistorico ed Etnografico L Pigorini

Piazza G Marconi 14 (06 549 521). Metro EUR Fermi/bus 30Exp, 170, 714. **Open** 9am-2pm Tue-Sun. **Admission** €4; €2 concessions. **No credit cards.**

This museum displays prehistoric Italian artefacts together with material from a range of world cultures. The lobby contains a reconstruction of the prehistoric Guattari cave near Monte Circeo (*see chapter* **Trips Out of Town**), with a genuine Neanderthal skull. On the first floor is the ethnological collection, with a range of hut-urns, arrow-heads, jewellery, masks and a couple of shrunken heads. The second floor has archaeological finds from digs all over Italy, including mammoth tusks and teeth, and some human bones.

West

Monteverde

Climbing the steep hill behind Trastevere and the Gianicolo (*see pp132-138*) is Monteverde Vecchio, a leafy, well-heeled suburb that is home to the vast, green, tree-filled expanse of the **Villa Pamphili** park (map p353). Here, children will enjoy feeding the turtles – if you can find the pond – and riding the ponies (if they're not at their other haunt, the Gianicolo). Nearby, to the south-east, is the smaller but equally lovely **Villa Sciarra** garden (map p359 A4), with its rose arbours, children's play area and miniature big dipper.

From here, spare yourself any further wandering to the south: all you'll find is Monteverde Nuovo, a charmless, more downmarket, predominantly post-war addition of high-rise flats and heavily trafficked streets.

YOU KNOW WHO YOU ARE.
ROME • VIA VITTORIO VENETO 62 A/B
+39-06-4203051 • HARDROCK.COM

©2007 Hard Rock Cafe International, Inc. All rights reserved.

Eat, Drink, Shop

Eating Out

A fresh culinary breeze is blowing through Rome as the traditional trattoria gets a revamp.

Eat, Drink, Shop

Chef Fabio Baldassarre at **L'Altro Mastai**. *See p192*.

Rome is a city that has always taken its food seriously, and a city that has always valued substance over style – at least where vital matters like eating are concerned. So although a swathe of designer restaurants opened here around the turn of the millennium, many have since closed: the survivors being those that were able to offer something more than a few dried twigs in a tall vase and the chance of seeing a once-famous TV starlet at the next table.

Trattorias and osterias, on the other hand, are going great guns, spurred on by the increasing demand for value for money in euro-poor Italy. Some of these restaurants are unreconstructed family-run operations that have been serving up the same dishes for generations – but still do them so well that they pack in the punters day after day. Others, however, are newcomers. The big novelty of the

❶ Purple numbers given in this chapter correspond to the location of each restaurant as marked on the street maps. *See pp354-361*.

last five years or so has been the rise of the *nuova trattoria* – places that take the trattoria formula (informal service, unfussy cooking based on market-fresh ingredients) but give it a twist by upping the creativity quotient in the kitchen, and by offering a range of fine wines. **Uno e Bino** (*see p205*), **L'Arcangelo** (*see p209*), **Tutti Frutti** (*see p203*), **Ditirambo** (*see p196*), **Osteria dell'Arco** (*see p188*), **Al Ristoro degli Angeli** (*see p211*) – these are all, in their ways, successful examples of this.

But it is the focus on the raw materials that is the real innovation. Once upon a time it was only Michelin-starred establishments that would specify provenance in menu descriptions: but now even €25-a-head places point out that the onions are red Tropea onions, the tomatoes are the rare *piennolo* variety grown on Vesuvius, while the beef comes from grass-fed Maremman cattle. Though it's sometimes taken to extremes, this new foodie enthusiasm has upped quality no end, the trickle-down effect meaning that even the most basic trat now generally offers a decent bottle of extra-virgin olive oil with which to dress your salad.

The other positive note is the increasing variety of the Roman dining scene. Twenty years ago the choice was basically between the posh restaurant, the humble trattoria, or the ultra-cheap, no-frills pizzeria. Today the range of options extends to wine bars, mozzarella bars, salad bars, gastropubs, designer restaurants and deli-diners. Even the unchanging pizzeria has been shaken up by the arrival of gourmet pizza emporia like **Dar Poeta** (*see p200*) and **La Gatta Mangiona** (*see p213*). Only the ethnic and international scene still leaves a lot to be desired – though Rome now has more decent Japanese and Indian restaurants than ever before.

In the end, though, Romans are conservative eaters, and will return to their local trattoria as a guitarist returns to a home chord. The great majority of these fine establishments are still family-run, with *mamma* in the kitchen, aided and abetted by the rest of the household. You can be fairly sure that she will be cooking up the same traditional Roman dishes, such as *spaghetti all'amatriciana* or *saltimbocca* (for food terms, *see p342* **The Menu**), that were on the menu last time you visited.

If there is one purely Roman contribution to the Italian culinary tradition, it's creativity with **offal**. Traditional Roman restaurants rely heavily on the *quinto quarto*, or 'fifth quarter' – those parts of the beast left over after the prime cuts of meat, plus the liver and kidneys, were sold off. That means brain (*cervello*), spinal marrow (*schienale*), nerves (*nervetti*), stomach and intestines (*trippa* or *pajata*), hooves (*zampi*), and the thymus and pancreas glands (*animelle*). Even tails are highly thought of by Roman gourmets, as in the classic slaughterhouse worker's dish, *coda alla vaccinara*. The once working-class areas of Testaccio and Trastevere are peppered with trattorias that serve these delicacies. They seem to have weathered the BSE scare – though one of the most Roman dishes of them all, *pajata* (baby calf's intestines with the mother's milk still inside), is now usually made with sheep's intestines rather than veal.

Despite the euro price hike, there are still bargains to be found – particularly if you are prepared to forsake the *centro storico* for the suburbs, where running costs are lower and the clientele less tolerant of *fregature* (rip-offs). The

Eat, Drink, Shop

The best Restaurants

For a top-level gourmet meal
L'Altro Mastai, *p192*; Baby, *p187*; La Pergola dell'Hotel Hilton, *p212*.

For a good-value gourmet meal
Giuda Ballerino!, *p211*; Il Pagliaccio, *p196*.

For eating well on a budget
Il Margutta (lunch), *p191*; Le Mani in Pasta, *p200*; Osteria del Rione, *p188*; Sora Margherita, *p197*; Zampagna, *p212*.

For creative trattoria cuisine
Al Ristoro degli Angeli, *p211*; L'Arcangelo, *p209*; Osteria dell'Arco, *p188*; Trattoria Monti, *p207*; Tuttifrutti, *p203*.

For traditional Roman cuisine
Da Felice, *p203*: Marcello, *p205* Matricianella, *p191*; Osteria dell'Angelo, *p209*; Osteria del Velodromo Vecchio, *p212*; Zampagna, *p212*.

For Roman Jewish cuisine
Da Giggetto, *p196*; Paris, *p200*; Sora Margherita, *p197*.

For alfresco dining
See *p195* **Tables with views**.

For Italian regional cuisine
Capricci Siciliani (Sicily), *p193*; L'Ortica (Naples), *p211*; Trattoria Monti (Marches), *p207*; Velando (Val Camonica), *p209*.

For a snack on the run
Da Michele, *p187*; Le Piramidi, *p199*; Lo Zozzone, *p195*.

For salads
L'Insalata Ricca, *p199*; Il Margutta, *p191*; Vic's, *p192*.

For fish and seafood
Alberto Ciarla, *p199*; San Teodoro, *p185*.

For pizza
Dar Poeta, *p200*; La Gatta Mangiona, *p213*; Pizzarium (takeaway), *p211*; Remo, *p203*.

For vegetarians
Arancia Blu, *p204*; Armando al Pantheon, *p193*; Il Margutta, *p191*.

For wine
Antico Arco, *p199*; Cavour 313, *p209*; Cul de Sac, *p195*; Del Frate, *p210*; Palatium, *p191*; Tramonti & Muffati, *p213*; Uno e Bino, *p205*.

Reading the listings

Times listed under **Meals served** are those of the kitchen, not the restaurant itself – in other words, you can generally sit and finish your meal after the cooks wrap up, as long as you get your order in first (if you turn up near kitchen closing time, it's polite to ask if it's not too late to grab something: *sono/siamo ancora in tempo a mangiare qualcosa?*).

Average restaurant prices are what you are likely to spend per person for three courses (antipasto, primo and secondo or primo, secondo and dessert) with water and half a bottle of house wine. For wine bars, averages are for two dishes and a glass of wine or beer; for pizzerias, they cover a starter (like bruschetta), a pizza and a medium beer.

other advantage of seeking out hostelries like **Osteria del Velodromo Vecchio** (*see p212*), **Zampagna** (*see p212*) or **Marcello** (*see p205*) is a warmer welcome than you'd get in the tourist-weary centre, and the frisson of being the only *straniero* (foreigner) in the house.

GOING THE COURSE

The standard Roman (and Italian) running order is: *antipasto* (hors-d'oeuvre), *primo* (usually pasta, occasionally soup), *secondo* (the meat or fish course) with optional *contorno* (vegetables or salad, served separately), and *dolce* (dessert). You're under no obligation to order four courses – few locals do. It's perfectly normal, for example, to order a pasta course followed by a simple *contorno* (often the only option for vegetarians). Fixed-price meals are not as big here as they are in France, though two- or three-course lunch menus aimed at businessmen and office workers are becoming more common. Top-flight establishments occasionally offer at least one *menu degustazione* (taster menu) in the evening as well, but any establishment offering a *menu turistico* should usually be avoided, especially if it is written in several languages.

DRINKS

One of the biggest changes over the last decade has been the way even humble trattorias and osterias have started to get themselves decent wine lists, in response to a growing demand for fine wines from both locals and tourists. There are still a few spit-and-sawdust places that pride themselves on their paint-stripper house wines, but they are increasingly in the minority. More and more establishments are also now offering a decent selection of wine by the glass (*al bicchiere* or *alla mescita*). In pizzerias, the drink of choice is *birra* (beer) or a variety of soft drinks. Mineral water – *acqua minerale* – comes as either *gasata* (sparkling – if you want it less bubbly they may have a *leggermente frizzante* version) or *naturale* (still) and is usually served by the litre. If you have a full meal, and the

owner takes a shine to you, you may be offered free amaro or grappa at the end. *See also p219* **What the locals drink**.

PRICES, TIPPING AND TIMES

Service is a grey area. It's usually safe to assume it isn't included. Romans themselves tend not to tip much, especially in family-run places. A good rule of thumb is to leave around five per cent. Sure, this is more than most locals would ever leave – but waiters have learned to expect more from tourists. If service has been slack or rude, don't feel ashamed to leave nothing (they won't chase after you as they do in New York) – or to check the bill in detail, as there is still the occasional restaurateur who becomes strangely innumerate when dealing with foreigners.

Italy is less of a cash-only society these days; but there are still a few humble trattorias that do not accept credit cards – plus one or two bona fide restaurants that think the ban gives them authentic salt-of-the-earth kudos. If there is no sticker on the door, always ask. By law, when you pay the bill (*il conto*) you must be given a receipt (*una ricevuta fiscale*) with the name, address and tax number of the restaurant. A few very basic neighbourhood places still prefer to scrawl the total amount on the paper tablecloth.

Opening times can change according to time of year and the owners' whim. In the evening, few proper restaurants open before 7.30pm. Pizzerias begin serving earlier, generally by 6.30pm or 7pm. (*See also above* **Reading the listings**.) Booking is becoming more of a habit, even in places that might appear to be modest trattorias. It's always a good idea to book at least a day ahead for Friday or Saturday evening or Sunday lunch.

KIDS, WOMEN AND ETIQUETTE

Taking children into restaurants – even the smartest – is never a problem in Rome. Waiters will usually produce a high chair (*un seggiolone*) on request and are generally happy to bring *una mezza porzione* – a half-portion.

Also, just about any kitchen in the city will do those off-menu standbys, *pasta al pomodoro* (with tomato sauce) or *pasta in bianco* (plain, to be dressed with oil or butter and parmesan).

Women dining alone will rarely encounter problems, though you have to get used to the local habit of staring frankly (but usually unaggressively) rather than avoiding eye-contact, Anglo-Saxon style. Single diners of either sex can have trouble getting a table in cheaper places at busy times: eating out is a communal experience here, and few proprietors want to waste a table that could hold four diners.

Very few places impose a dress code, though shorts and T-shirts go down badly in formal, upmarket restaurants. Some restaurants will insist that you turn your mobile phone off; and smoking is now illegal in all restaurants except where there is a designated smoking area that meets stringent regulations.

PIZZA

The city's *pizzaioli* have always been proud of their thinner, flatter *pizza romana*, but recently the fickle public has started to defect to the puffier Neapolitan variety. Either way, make sure your pizza comes from a wood-fired brick oven (*forno a legna*); pizzas from electric or gas-fired ovens just don't have the same flavour.

So orthodox is the range of toppings in Roman pizzerias, so eyebrow-raising is any departure from the norm, that it's worth learning the main varieties by heart. For these, and for the various gap-fillers that it is customary to order while you're waiting for your pizza to come out of the oven, *see p342* **The Menu**. Note that pizza is an evening thing – very few places will serve it at lunchtime.

WINE BARS

Neighbourhood *enoteche* (wine shops) and *vini e olii* (wine and oil) outlets have been around in Rome since time immemorial, complete with their huddle of old men knocking back wine by the glass. For a selection of places in which drinking is the main point of the exercise, see the **Cafés, Bars & *Gelaterie*** chapter. Recently, a number of upmarket, international-style wine bars have also sprung up, offering snacks and even full meals to go with their wines. Those included in this chapter range from places that lay out tables among the bottle-lined shelves at lunch to full-blown wine-oriented restaurants like **Ferrara** (*see p201*).

SNACKS

The Roman tradition of sitting down to two full meals each day is fast disappearing; as a result, places designed for eating on the run are on the increase. Roman snack culture, though, lurks in unlikely places. Few new arrivals, for example,

consider stepping into a humble *alimentari* (grocer's) to have their picnic lunch prepared on the spot – and yet for fresh bread and high-quality fillings this is one of the best options. Favourite casing is the ubiquitous white Roman roll, *la rosetta*, or a slice of *pizza bianca* (plain oiled and salted pizza base, eaten as is or filled); fillings are generally ham, salami or cheese, as *alimentari* do not sell fruit and veg.

VEGETARIANS

The city has few bona fide vegetarian restaurants; but even in traditional trattorias, waiters will no longer look blank when you say *non mangio la carne* ('I don't eat meat') – though they do have a charming tendency to offer chicken or *prosciutto* (ham) as an alternative. Despair not: the message will eventually sink in, and there's plenty left to try – from *penne all'arrabbiata* (pasta in a tomato and chilli sauce) through *tonnarelli cacio e pepe* (thick spaghetti with crumbly sheep's cheese and plenty of black pepper) to *carciofi alla giudia* (deep-fried artichokes, a Roman Jewish speciality). If you are at all unsure about the ingredients of any dish, ask.

Capitoline & Palatine

Restaurants

San Teodoro

Via dei Fienili 49-51 (06 678 0933). Bus 30Exp, 44, 81, 95, 160, 170, 628. **Meals served** 1-3.15pm, 8pm-11.30am Mon-Sat. Closed 2wks Jan, 1wk Easter & 1wk Dec. **Average** €60. **Credit** AmEx, MC, V. **Map** p358 E3 & p360 A3 ❶

Of a summer's evening there are few better places for an alfresco meal than this seafood-oriented restaurant around the back of the Forum, in the prettiest of residential squares. Come prepared to splash out, though: it's decidedly upmarket, and attracts a fair amount of expense-account business trade. Some dishes, like the *minestra di broccoli in brodo di arzilla* (broccoli ravioli in skate broth) are pure *cucina romana*; others, like the *tonnarelli* San Teodoro (with shrimps, courgettes and cherry tomatoes) are lighter and more creative; still others are a fusion of tradition and modernity, like the baked sea bass served in a coat of Jewish-style fried artichokes. Don't miss the *gelato di cassata*: an ice-cream take on the classic Sicilian ricotta and candied-fruit cake.

Trevi & Quirinale

Restaurants

Al Presidente

Via in Arcione 94-95 (06 679 7342/www.al presidente.it). Bus 52, 53, 61, 62, 63, 71, 80Exp, 95, 116, 119, 175, 490, 630. **Meals served** 1-3.30pm,

IL BACARO ROMA

sfizi ai fornell

Via degli Spagnoli, 2
Roma
tel. 06.6872554
06.6864110
www.ilbacaro.com
OPEN
TO LATE NIGHT
(closed Sunday)
Reservations advisable

8-11.30pm Tue-Sun. Closed 3wks Jan & 3wks Aug. **Average** €60. **Credit** DC, MC, V. **Map** p357 A/B5 ❷
This born-again family restaurant under the towering walls of the Quirinal palace is one of the few really reliable addresses in the *menu turistico* dominated Trevi Fountain area. When weather permits, you can dine outside, plant-screened from the tourist crocodiles and their umbrella-waving guides; inside, the decor is cool (though a tad bare) and restful antique-modern. The creative Italian menu is strong on fish, but there are plenty of meat dishes as well, including an excellent, ultra-Roman *coda alla vaccinara*. *Primi* take in soups, pasta and rice dishes, including a fine risotto of *verza* (cabbage) and red prawns; one of the highlights of the *secondi* is the *coda di rospo* (anglerfish) on a bed of lentils. Desserts are delicious, and the wine list one of the best in Rome in this price range. There is also a good selection of wines by the glass and, in the evening, an intelligent range of taster menus, from €50 up.

Wine bars & gastropubs

Antica Birreria Peroni
Via di San Marcello 19 (06 679 5310). Bus 62, 63, 81, 85, 95, 117, 119, 160, 175, 492, 628, 630, 850. **Meals served** noon-midnight Mon-Sat. Closed 2wks Aug. **Average** €18. **Credit** AmEx, DC, MC, V. **Map** p357 A6 ❸
This long-standing *centro storico* birreria – which was here decades before all those lookalike Irish pubs – is the perfect place for a quick lunch or dinner. Service is rough-and-Roman but friendly, and the food – five or six hot pasta dishes or risottos, salmon, various salads and cold cuts – is good and relatively cheap. Sausage, though, is the main act: three different types of German-style *wurstel* are on offer. The birreria still retains its original art nouveau decor, with a chiaroscuro frieze featuring such slogans as 'drink beer and you'll live to be 100'. At lunch, if you're in a real hurry, you can join the row of office-worker regulars eating their pasta standing up at the bar. There are four Peroni beers on draught, including the excellent lager (*birra chiara* in Italian). Unusually for Rome, service is included.

Vineria il Chianti
Via del Lavatore 81-82 (06 678 7550/www.vineria ilchianti.com). Bus 52, 53, 61, 62, 63, 71, 80Exp, 95, 116, 119, 175, 490, 630. **Open** 12.30pm-1am Mon-Sat. **Meals served** 12.30-3.30pm, 7-11.30pm Mon-Sat. Closed Aug. **Average** €25. **Credit** AmEx, DC, MC, V. **Map** p357 A5 ❹
In the middle of the Trevi Fountain souvenir belt, this rustic, wood-lined wine bar offers welcome relief from all of the surrounding tack. As the name suggests, wine, food and decor all have a Tuscan slant – though there is now also a small range of traditonal *cucina romana* dishes. Service, too, can occasionally be of the offhand Roman variety. The typical lunch menu might feature a couple of filling grain and bean soups, a pasta dish such as

pappardelle alla lepre (wide pasta strips in hare sauce), and meaty *secondi* such as *abbacchio scottadito* (grilled lamb chops). Pizzas make an appearance in the evening, and there are also some decent *insalatoni* (mega-salads). From 3.30 to 7pm there's a free *aperitivo* buffet. Seating is cosy, not to say cramped. In summer, tables fill the *piazzetta* outside.

Snacks & quick meals
See also above **Antica Birreria Peroni**.

Caffetteria Borromini
Via XX Settembre 124 (06 488 0866). Metro Barberini/bus 40Exp, 52, 53, 60Exp, 61, 62, 63, 64, 70, 71, 80Exp, 95, 116, 119, 170, 175, 490, 630. **Open** 6am-8pm Mon-Fri; 6am-2pm Sat. **Meals served** noon-3pm Mon-Fri. Closed 2wks Aug. **Credit** AmEx, DC, MC, V. **Map** p357 C5 ❺
In three huge bare rooms, this lunch-only joint serves cheap Italian fast food at its best, with two pasta choices, plenty of *secondi* – from salads to *scamorza al salmone* (grilled cheese with smoked salmon) – and real wood-fired pizza, a rarity at lunchtime. The clientele consists mostly of hungry office workers and staff from the British Council around the corner. Allow about €12-€14 for two courses and a glass of wine.

Da Michele
Via dell'Umiltà 31 (349 252 5347). Bus 52, 53, 61, 62, 63, 71, 80Exp, 95, 116, 119, 175, 490, 630. **Open** *Apr-Sept* 8am-10pm Mon-Fri, Sun. *Oct-Mar* 8am-6pm Mon-Fri, Sun. Closed Jewish holidays; 10 days Pesach (usually April). **No credit cards.** **Map** p357 A6 ❻
Recently relocated from the Ghetto to new premises near the Trevi Fountain, Da Michele (formerly Zi' Fenizia) does over 40 flavours of takeaway pizza, all of them kosher, all dairy-free. So don't ask for margherita – instead, try one of their Roman Jewish speciality toppings like *aliciotti e indivia* (anchovies and endives) or smoked salmon and potato.

Veneto & Borghese

Restaurants

Baby
Via Ulisse Aldrovandi 15 (06 322 3993). Tram 3, 19. **Meals served** 12.30-2.30pm, 7.30-10.30pm Tue-Sun. Closed 2wks Jan. **Average** €80. **Credit** AmEx, DC, MC, V. **Map** p356 A1 ❼
Don Alfonso (in Sant'Agata dei due Golfi, on the Amalfi Coast), with its two Michelin stars, is one of Italy's great gourmet stopovers, and this is its Roman, er, baby – born in spring 2004 (but already with one star of its own). The location – in the plush five-star Aldrovandi Palace Hotel, on the north side of the Borghese gardens – is a little remote, but the restaurant has cast off the rather fusty feel of the hotel in favour of a contemporary Zen/ethnic design scheme. It helps, too, that Baby looks on to the

Eat, Drink, Shop

Eat, Drink, Shop

verdant garden and swimming pool – a lovely, priv-ileged spot for summer bathing (in 2006, day passes cost a cool €40, €60 at weekends). The menu com-bines Don Alfonso classics such as *sartù di riso* (Neapolitan baked rice) served on a light tomato *ragù* with less weighty versions of Roman stan-dards: particularly *amusant* is the classic chicken with red peppers – except that the red peppers have morphed into *peperone* ice-cream. Desserts are as spectacular as one would expect of Don Alfonso (we especially liked the *pastiera* soufflé with tangy *granita di limone*). Sure, of an evening, there is the added cost of a taxi ride there and back – but Baby is still an awful lot closer than the Amalfi Coast. And you can always do it the slow way – on the tram.

Cantina Cantarini

Piazza Sallustio 12 (06 485 528/06 474 3341).
Bus 36, 60Exp, 62, 63, 80Exp, 86, 360, 630.
Meals served noon-3pm, 7.30-11pm Mon-Sat.
Closed 3wks Aug & 2wks Dec-Jan. **Average** €35.
Credit AmEx, DC, MC, V. **Map** p357 D4 **8**
This high-quality trattoria is always packed, lunch and dinner, and it's easy to see why: the cooking (from the Marches, on Italy's Adriatic side) is sim-ple but spot-on, and the prices are very reasonable. Meat-based for the first part of the week, it turns fishy from Thursday on. The atmosphere is as *allegro* as seating is tight – though outside tables take off some of the pressure in summer. But the excellent *coniglio al cacciatore* (stewed rabbit), *fritto misto di pesce* (fried mixed fish) and *risotto al nero di seppia* (with squid ink) should easily help to override any concerns about comfort; they also do a surpris-ingly rich and varied take on the humble *insalata mista*.

Osteria dell'Arco

Via G Pagliari 11 (06 854 8438). Bus 36, 38,
60Exp, 61, 62, 84, 80Exp, 88, 90Exp, 490, 491,
495. **Meals served** noon-3pm, 7.30-11pm Mon-Fri;
7.30-11pm Sat. Closed Aug. **Average** €35. **Credit**
AmEx, DC, MC, V. **Map** p356 D3 **9**
The lively residential neighbourhood around piazza Alessandria, just outside Porta Pia, is on the up and up: there's the MACRO art gallery (*see p176*), due for completion sometime in 2008, and a sprinkling of new places to eat and drink. One of the best is this nouveau-rustic wine-oriented osteria, all brick vault-ed ceiling and bottle-lined walls, which offers creative trattoria cooking at competitive prices. Kick off with smoked tuna and swordfish with *misticanza* salad before moving on to *mezzemaniche* (short rigatoni) with cuttlefish and broccoli, or anglerfish fillet with artichokes and *pachino* tomatoes. Desserts are mostly playing-it-safe standards like *crema cata-lana*. Vegetarians will find a better than average selection here, and the worthwhile wine list includes several by-the-glass options.

Osteria del Rione

Via Basento 20 (06 855 1057). Bus 52, 53, 63,
86, 217, 360, 630, 913. **Meals served** 12.30-2.30pm, 7-11pm Mon-Fri; 7-11.30pm Sat. Closed Aug and 1wk Dec. **Set meals** €18. **No credit cards**.
Map p356 D2 **10**
A short walk from Villa Borghese, the Osteria del Rione (a *rione* is one of the districts into which Rome's *centro storico* is divided) is ideal for those sick of nouvelle cuisine and who want to eat like a horse and drink like a fish for a total of €18 per head (the price of the obligatory *menù fisso*). If your

Gourmet spread at **Casa Bleve**.
See p193.

Italian is a little shaky, bearded owner Bruno will recite the menu in his charming English. It always includes an array of *antipasti* such as *bruschette*, grilled vegetables and 'strong ricotta cheese' (a sort of Italian cheddar, from Puglia), plus a taster selection of three pasta dishes, followed by 'meat-a-balls' and other carnivorous treats. The fixed menu includes water, coffee, and all the wine you can drink, and if you are not too hammered by the time the home-made dessert arrives, Bruno will suggest rounding things off with a glass of grappa.

The Tridente

Restaurants

Gino in vicolo Rosini

Vicolo Rosini 4 (06 687 3434). Bus 52, 53, 61, 62, 63, 71, 80Exp, 95, 116, 119, 175, 490, 630. **Meals served** 1-2.45pm, 8-10.45pm Mon-Sat. Closed Aug. **Average** €30. **No credit cards. Map** p355 E4 ⓫
In a hard-to-find lane around the back of the parliament building, off piazza del Parlamento, this rustic neighbourhood osteria with its Arcadian murals is always filled to bursting with MPs, and accompanying political hacks and hangers-on. The cuisine champions the lighter side of the local tradition, in dishes like *tonnarelli alla ciociara* (with mushrooms and tomatoes), pasta and chickpeas in skate sauce, *coniglio al vino bianco* (rabbit in white wine) and *zucchine ripiene* (stuffed courgettes). Desserts include home-made *crostate* (jam tarts) and an excellent tiramisù. Come early, or be prepared to wait for one of the hotly contested tables.

'Gusto

Piazza Augusto Imperatore 9 (06 322 6273/www. gusto.it). Bus 81, 117, 119, 628, 913, 926. **Open** *Wine bar* 11.30am-2am daily. **Meals served** *Pizzeria* 12.30-3.30pm, 7.30pm-1am daily. *Restaurant* 12.30-3.30pm, 7.30-11.30pm daily. **Average** *Pizzeria* €23. *Restaurant* €50. **Credit** AmEx, DC, MC, V. **Map** p354 D3 ⓬
This multipurpose, split-level pizzeria, restaurant and wine bar, with a kitchen shop and bookshop next door, is the granddaddy of the Roman design bunch – the only problem being that, though the interior spaces are great, it's looking rather crumbly these days. The location is ideal: on a warm evening, sitting outside eating a competent pizza and drinking good wine while looking across at the new Ara Pacis museum (*see p111*) is extremely pleasant. And the lunch buffet served in the pizzeria area is abundant and good. But the overpriced fusion food in the upstairs restaurant is mediocre, the Conran c1980-style decor is in need of a makeover and, on a recent visit, the buzzing, stylish winebar out the back – always the part of this establishment we liked best – didn't have the first *five* bottles we asked for.

Maccheroni

Piazza delle Coppelle 44 (06 6830 7895/www. ristorantemaccheroni.com). Bus 52, 53, 61, 62, 63, 71, 80Exp, 95, 116, 119, 175, 490, 630. **Meals served** 1-3pm, 7.30-11pm daily. **Average** €30. **No credit cards. Map** p355 D5 ⓭
With its painted wooden wainscotting and industrial-style iron lights, this feels like a cross between a cricket pavilion and a real downhome workers' trattoria. But the clientele is more rich-kid

Eat, Drink, Shop

GiNa

eat & drink

restaurant

italian bistrò

wine & cocktail bar

tea room

sweets & ice cream

pic nic basket

music lounge

private party

Via San Sebastianello 7/A
(Next to Spanish Steps)
www.ginaroma.com
tel. 0039.06.678.02.51
Open 7/7 no stop 11 a.m 11 p.m

GiNa

eat & drink

than bricklayer, and the table staff are younger and more stylish than the plain cotton tablecloths and humble drinks tumblers suggest. Still, if this is an exercise in peasant chic, it's a successful one, and the filling pasta dishes served from the open-to-view kitchen are perfectly decent takes on *mamma*'s home cooking. Play safe on the *secondi*: the grilled steaks are good, the more elaborate dishes less so. In summer, there's a real *dolce vita* vibe at the outside tables.

Il Margutta

*Via Margutta 118 (06 3265 0577/www.
ilmargutta.it). Metro Spagna or Flaminio/bus 117,
119.* **Meals served** 12.30-3.30pm, 7.30-11.30pm daily. Closed 3wks Aug. **Average** €40. **Credit** AmEx, DC, MC, V. **Map** p354 E3 ⓮
Well-heeled and a tad snobbish, the clientele of this artsy diner is not what one generally associates with veggie restaurants. But Il Margutta occupies a prime piece of real estate on the corner of Rome's historic gallery alley, and the decor pays homage to the area, with plenty of modern art and tasteful greenery. The Green Brunch, available from Monday to Saturday, keeps things busy in the middle of the day: the set price of €15 includes a bowl of soup and one large plate filled with whatever takes your fancy from two well-stocked buffet tables, plus water, fruit juice (disappointingly tinned in flavour), fruit salad, a slice of cake or flan, and coffee. On Sunday the fare is offered on all-you-can-eat basis for €25. You can also choose to dine à la carte in the more formal restaurant, which offers a meatless slant on modern Italian cuisine, with one or two oriental touches; in the evening, this is the only option. There's live jazz on occasional Tuesday evenings; check the website for details.

Matricianella

*Via del Leone 3-4 (06 683 2100/www.
matricianella.it). Bus 70, 81, 117, 119, 629.*
Meals served 12.30-3pm, 7.30-11pm Mon-Sat. Closed 3wks Aug. **Average** €35. **Credit** AmEx, DC, MC, V. **Map** p355 E4 ⓯
A good example of how to upgrade the Roman family trattoria without betraying its roots. Spread over three cosy rooms, this is a friendly, bustling place with great prices. The Roman imprint is most evident in classics such as *bucatini all'amatriciana* or *abbacchio a scottadito*, but there are plenty more creative options, including a tasty *risotto mantecato* (creamy risotto with courgette flowers) and some great *fritti* (fried dishes), including *bucce di patate* (potato skins). The well-chosen wine list is a model of honest pricing; service is friendly but nononsense. Once you've eaten here, you'll understand why it's almost always packed (and why you should be sure to book ahead). When weather permits, they have a few, highly sought-after tables outside.

L'Osteria

*Via della Frezza 16 (06 322 6273/www.gusto.it).
Bus 81, 117, 119, 628, 913, 926.* **Meals served** 12.30-3.30pm, 7pm-1am daily. **Average** €35. **Credit** AmEx, DC, MC, V. **Map** p354 D3 ⓰

The people behind 'Gusto (*see p189*) opened this modernised take on a traditional Italian osteria just down the road from the mothership. The place seats well over a hundred, on two levels, but some warm, bistro-like corners have been carved out of the warehousey space. The idea here is to apply the Spanish *tapas* approach to the trattoria menu: so everything, from the *fritti* (fry-ups of ricotta, innards, polenta, seafood and broccoli) to traditional pasta dishes like *spaghetti alla gricia*, can be ordered either as full portions or as a series of tasters. The full-on hot dishes can be a tad disappointing; our advice is to focus on the excellent cold meat and cheese selection (the place also has a takeaway cheese counter, with around 400 varieties) and explore the ample wine list – which also includes a good by-the-glass selection.

Pizzerias

Pizza Ciro

*Via della Mercede 43 (06 678 6015). Metro
Spagna/bus 52, 53, 61, 62, 63, 71, 80Exp, 95,
116, 119, 175, 490, 630.* **Meals served** 11am-2am daily. **Average** €20. **Credit** AmEx, DC, MC, V. **Map** p357 A5 ⓱
From outside it looks like a small, vaguely touristy pizza parlour. But Ciro is in fact a huge eating factory with 150 places, many of them in a large back room that houses the pizza oven. The pizzas – of the high-crust Neapolitan variety – are not at all bad, and *primi* such as *tubetti alla Ciro* (with rocket and mussels) provide a decent alternative for those who are doughed out. Technicolour Bay of Naples murals set the design tone; the service is brisk but efficient.

Wine bars & gastropubs

See also p220 **Shaki**.

Buccone

*Via Ripetta 19-20 (06 361 2154/www.enoteca
buccone.com). Bus 81, 204, 224, 628, 926.* **Open**
Shop 9am-8.30pm Mon-Thur; 9am-midnight Fri, Sat.
Meals served 12.30-3pm, 7.30-10.30pm Mon-Sat. Closed 3wks Aug. **Average** €22. **Credit** AmEx, DC, MC, V. **Map** p354 D3 ⓲
This historic osteria at the piazza del Popolo end of via di Ripetta began life in the 18th century as a carriage garage for local aristocrats. For years it operated as a takeaway *enoteca* (wine shop) with a few wines available by the glass at the marble counter; but recently tables have been arranged among the high wooden shelves, and in a little room behind, for full meals. There are always three or four pasta dishes or soups, followed by a range of meaty seconds and creative salads. The cooking is more than competent, the prices extremely reasonable, and the service friendly.

Palatium

*Via Frattina 94 (06 6920 2132). Metro Spagna/bus
52, 53, 61, 62, 63, 71, 80Exp, 95, 116, 119, 175,
490, 630.* **Open** noon-midnight Mon-Sat. **Meals**

served 12.30-3pm, 8-10.30pm Mon-Sat. Closed 2wks Aug. **Average** *Restaurant* €30. **Credit** AmEx, DC, MC, V. **Map** p355 E4 ⑲
Though it's backed by the regional government, this new wine bar and restaurant deep in the fashion district is more than just a PR exercise. Dedicated to the wines and produce of Lazio – the region around Rome – it gives punters the chance to go beyond the Frascati clichés to explore lesser-known local wines like Cesanese or Aleatico. There's a bar where you can perch for a glass and a nibble – from 3pm to 7.30pm, charcuterie, cheeses and deep-fried tidbits are provided free of charge with your *aperitivo*. At mealtimes the tables downstairs and in another contemporary-minimalist space upstairs kick into restaurant mode, offering light creative dishes that give centre stage to micro-regional products like Atina cannellini beans or coriander-flavoured sausages from Monte San Biagio.

Snacks & quick meals

See also *p191* **Il Margutta** and *p218* **GiNa**.

Vic's

Vicolo della Torretta 60 (06 687 1445). Bus 52, 53, 61, 62, 63, 71, 80Exp, 95, 116, 119, 175, 490, 630. **Meals served** 7.30-11pm Mon; 12.30-3pm, 7.30-11pm Tue-Sat. Closed 2wks Aug. **No credit cards. Map** p355 D/E4 ⑳
This new-but-old wine and salad bar offers a range of creative salads (€7.50 standard, €9 mega) such as radicchio, pine nuts, sultanas and parmesan. There are also one or two hot pasta or soup dishes, plus

crostini (toasted bread) with mozzarella and various other toppings, and a good selection of crêpes. With its pared-back Roman osteria decor, friendly service and fairly priced wine list, this is a deservedly popular *centro storico* lunch stop.

Pantheon & Navona

Restaurants

L'Altro Mastai

Via Giraud 53 (06 6830 1296/www.laltromastai.it). Bus 40Exp, 46, 62, 64, 916. **Meals served** 7.30-11.30pm Tue-Sat. Closed Aug. **Average** €90. **Credit** AmEx, DC, MC, V. **Map** p355 C5 ㉑
Fabio Baldassarre opened this creative restaurant in 2002. He is now established as one of Rome's top five chefs, and L'Altro Mastai's elegant neo-Pompeiian decor and impeccable service make this one of our favourite places for a splash-out meal. Baldassarre is open to international influences, but his carefully balanced creations are anything but tired fusion. The seasonal menu changes four times a year; in autumn, you might start with sea scallop *carpaccio* with chocolate and walnuts, followed by rabbit and endive tortelli with anchovy butter, before moving on to mallard in black-bean sauce with tarragon. Not a place for a quick snack, in other words – but if you have the time, money and appetite, you're in for a treat. The wine list is satisfyingly vast, the desserts are to die for. For those who haven't eaten in days, there's a seven-course *menu degustazione* at €85. **Photo** *p182*.

Chef Patrizia Mattei creates a strong menu at the **Antico Arco**. *See p199.*

Eat, Drink, Shop

Armando al Pantheon

*Salita de' Crescenzi 31 (06 6880 3034). Bus 30Exp,
40Exp, 46, 62, 63, 64, 70, 81, 87, 116, 492, 628, 780,
H/tram 8.* **Meals served** 12.30-3pm, 7.15-11pm Mon-
Fri; 12.30-3pm Sat. Closed Aug. **Average** €35. **Credit**
AmEx, DC, MC, V. **Map** p355 D5 ②
Armando is a simple, no-frills trattoria of the kind
that is very rare to find just a few yards from an A-
league tourist attraction. But, right by the Pantheon,
it has all the hallmarks of authenticity: cork walls,
indifferent artworks, a pretty, stained-glass entrance
and friendly service from the family that has run it
for the last couple of generations. The menu
is almost unchanging (we can vouch personally for
the last 21 years), with classics like *fettucine
all'Armando* (with mushrooms, peas and tomatoes)
or *ossobuco* – reliable but with few pretensions. The
only concessions to changing times are some filling
vegetarian dishes and a much-expanded wine list,
which now contains seriously interesting bottles.

Capricci Siciliani

*Via di Panico 83 (06 687 3666/www.capricci
siciliani.com). Bus 40Exp, 46, 62, 64, 916.*
Meals served noon-3.30pm, 7-11.30pm Tue-
Sun. Closed Aug. **Average** €40. **Credit** AmEx,
DC, MC, V. **Map** p355 C5 ②
A welcome addition to the capital's roster of Italian
regional eateries, 'Sicilian Caprices' is housed in the
cellars of the imposing Palazzo Taverna – former
stronghold of the Orsini and Borgia families. The
menu reads like a 'Sicily's Greatest Culinary Hits'
compilation: all the classics are there, from *pasta con
le sarde* (*maccheroni* with sardines, pine nuts, sultanas and wild fennel) to *involtini di pesce spada*
(swordfish roulades), all done by the book. Desserts,
too, are in line with island tradition, and include
excellent *cassata* and *cannoli*. Service is professional, the wine list offers some Sicilian vintages that are
well-nigh impossible to find in Rome. Although the
clientele has a rather formal, expense-account edge,
the garden murals adorning the walls and ceiling
vaults keep things light and breezy.

Il Convivio Troiani

*Vicolo dei Soldati 31 (06 686 9432/www.ilconvivio
troiani.com). Bus 30Exp, 70, 81, 87, 116, 492, 628.*
Meals served 8-11pm Mon-Sat. Closed 1wk Jan &
1wk Aug. **Average** €100. **Credit** AmEx, DC, MC, V.
Map p355 D5 ②
The three Troiani brothers run a high-class act in this
temple of foodie excellence just north of piazza
Navona, and seem entirely unfazed by the proximity
of new neighbour Gualtiero Marchesi, whose
Hostaria dell'Orso (not listed in this edition of the
guide) has failed to live up to its promise. Il Convivio,
on the other hand, maintains a steady course of reliable haute cuisine in elegant surroundings – though
only one of the three dining rooms (the one with the
pastel chiaroscuro murals) could be described as
warm and inviting. The brothers are from the
Marches, and although the creations of chef Angelo
are ultra-gourmet, the regional stamp is still

discernible in dishes such as a first-course *risotto
con funghi porcini e quaglia scaloppata* (porcini
mushrooms and quail scallops). *Secondi* – where
fresh vegetables, meat, game and seafood take equal
billing – are also fine (we like the lacquered quail on
a skewer with bitter chestnut honey, ginger, red-
wine sauce and roast mushrooms), and the desserts
are spectacular (don't miss the *zabaione* ice-cream
with praline almonds and balsamic vinegar). The
wine list is extensive and has a few affordable bottles, plus a range of non-Italian labels. For Convivio
beginners, there is a six-dish taster menu (€97).

Trattoria

*Via del Pozzo delle Cornacchie 25 (06 6830 1427).
Bus 30Exp, 40Exp, 46, 70, 81, 87, 116, 492, 628.*
Meals served 12.30-3pm, 7.30-11.30pm Mon-Sat.
Closed 2wks Aug. **Average** €55. **Credit** AmEx,
DC, MC, V. **Map** p355 D5 ②
When it opened in 2003, Trattoria was stronger on
design (cool, Nordic, softened by an abundance of
natural materials – string, copper, leaves) than cuisine. But that all changed in 2004 when ebullient
Sicilian chef Filippo La Mantia was brought in. La
Mantia – who used to be a photojournalist special-
ising in Mafia stories – takes Sicilian standards like
caponata or *pasta alla Norma* and gives them his
own creative twist; the results vary from intriguing
to delicious. You need to be patient, though: service
can be both slow and uncertain. But you see all the
right people in this media and *fashionista* hangout.
For something speedier, try the lunchtime (noon-
3pm Mon-Sat) couscous bar for €15 a head.

Pizzerias

Da Francesco

*Piazza del Fico 29 (06 686 4009). Bus 40Exp, 46, 62,
64, 916.* **Meals served** 11.50am-3pm, 7pm-12.30am
Mon, Wed-Sun; 7pm-12.30am Tue. **Average** €20.
No credit cards. **Map** p355 C5 & p358 C1 ②
Accept no imitations: Da Francesco is the genuine
centro storico pizzeria article. You can try booking
but your reservation is all too likely to be forgotten.
Get there before 8pm, however, and you can generally walk right on in; if you get there much after,
you'll have to join the queue. The reasons for this
popularity are very simple: tasty pizzas; a warm,
traditional ambience; brisk but friendly service; and
a range of competent, classic *primi* and *secondi* for
those who can't face a doughy disc. You often get
the distinct feeling that they are rushing you
through to free up the table – but that's the price you
pay for such a *centro storico* bargain.

Wine bars & gastropubs

Casa Bleve

*Via del Teatro Valle 48-49 (06 686 5970). Bus
30Exp, 40Exp, 46, 62, 63, 64, 70, 81, 87, 116,
492, 571, 628, 630, 780, 916.* **Meals served**
1-3pm, 7.30-10pm Tue, Sat; 1-3pm, 7-10pm

ristorante
pizzeria
wine bar
live music
enoteca
emporio libreria
osteria
formaggeria
pesce e ortaggi

the different tastes of Gusto

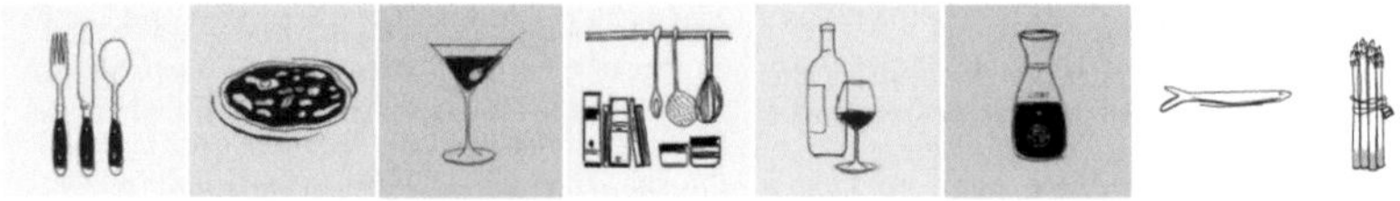

ristorante pizzeria wine bar piazza augusto imperatore 9   roma   tel +39 063226273
osteria formaggeria via della frezza 16   vicolo del corea 2 roma   tel +39 0632111482
ristorante cocktail bar pesce & ortaggi piazza augusto imperatore 28 roma tel +39 0668134221
emporio libreria negozio di vini piazza augusto imperatore 7 roma   tel +39 063236363

www.gusto.it

Wed-Fri. Closed 3wks Aug. **Average** €35. **Credit** AmEx, DC, MC, V. **Map** p355 D6 & p358 D1 ㉗
Wine merchant Anacleto Bleve and his wife Tina pushed the boat out in 2003 when they opened what must be Rome's most elegant wine bar, on the ground floor of Palazzo Medici Lante della Rovere, between piazza Navona and the Pantheon. The main room is a huge colonnaded courtyard roofed over with coloured glass: undeniably impressive, though the tables feel a little lost in all this space. Food is chosen from the entrance buffet, which contains a vast spread of gourmet cold cuts – from cheese to meat to smoked fish – and salads. A mixed plate will set you back about €25; add wine and water and it's by no means a cheap lunch option. Wine remains the star turn here: there is a tremendous selection on offer, both by the bottle and by the glass. We still have a soft spot, though, for the original Bleve *enoteca* in the Ghetto (via Santa Maria del Pianto 9-11, 06 6819 2210, open 8am-8pm Mon-Sat), which runs its own, slightly cheaper, buffet-lunch operation from Monday to Friday (12.30-3pm). **Photo** *p188.*

Cul de Sac
Piazza Pasquino 73 (06 6880 1094). Bus 30Exp, 40, 62, 63, 64, 70, 81, 87, 492, 628, 780/tram 8. **Meals served** noon-4pm, 6pm-midnight daily. **Average** €20. **Credit** MC, V. **Map** p355 C5/D6 & p358 C1 ㉘
Rome's first ever wine bar, the Cul de Sac was founded in 1968. Looking very traditional nowadays, it's cramped inside and out, with long pine benches and tables, and decidedly no-frills. But the location – just off piazza Navona, with a ringside view of the 'talking statue' of Pasquino (*see p113*) – coupled with reasonable prices and an encyclopaedic wine list,

ensures full occupancy all the time. Food is standard wine-bar fare, with mainly cold dishes. The generous Greek salad and the lentil soup stand out.

Enoteca Corsi
Via del Gesù 87-88 (06 679 0821). Bus 30Exp, 40Exp, 46, 62, 63, 64, 70, 81, 87, 492, 628, 780, H. **Meals served** noon-3.30pm Mon-Sat. **Average** €18. **Credit** AmEx, DC, MC, V. **Map** p355 E6 & p358 D1 ㉙
This 1940s wine shop was the first in Rome to begin serving lunch, and is now more trattoria than *enoteca*. The daily-changing menu is written up on the board at the entrance. Dishes follow the traditional Roman culinary calendar – *gnocchi* on Thursdays and stewed *baccalà* (salt cod) on Fridays. A slice of ricotta tart followed by a jolt of espresso makes a fitting end to a hearty meal. No bookings are taken, so get there early or be prepared to queue on workdays, as this *centro storico enoteca* is a deservedly popular venue for a filling, noisy and cheap lunch.

Snacks & quick meals
See also above **Cul de Sac,** *p199* **L'Insalata Ricca** and *p223* **Trinity College.**

Lo Zozzone
Via del Teatro Pace 32 (06 6880 8575). Bus 40Exp, 46, 62, 64, 916. **Open** *Apr-Sept* 9am-9pm Mon-Fri; 9am-11pm Sat, Sun. *Oct-Mar* 9am-9pm Mon-Fri; 9am-11pm Sat. Closed Aug. **No credit cards. Map** p355 C5 & p358 C1 ㉚
Now in new, more spacious premises with (gasp!) outside tables (or at least chairs), the 'dirty old man' (an affectionate Roman nickname that became

Tables with views
There's nothing more pleasant than an alfresco lunch or dinner with a ringside seat on a Roman street or dramatically lit bit of old stonework. Most years the outside dining season runs from March or April right through to October – and with global warming taking a hold, outside tables could soon be a year-round feature (in some places, overhead braziers already ensure winter comfort on all but the coldest days).

The following is a list of our favourite Roman open-air dining experiences:
Ar Galletto, *p196*: admire piazza Farnese ✔ (*see p122*) from one of the tables of this rustic, no-nonsense trattoria.
Cecilia Metella, *p211*: take a break from slogging along the Appia Antica (*see p171*) in this rustic oasis.
Da Francesco, *p193*: enjoy rough-and-ready fare in Fig Tree Square (there *is* a fig tree) not far from piazza Navona (*see p116*).

Da Giggetto, *p196*: in the heart of the Ghetto, get up close and personal with the Portico d'Ottavia (see *p128*).
Da Remo, *p203*: let your kids mix with Testaccio youth on the swings in the park across the road from Remo's rickety tables.
'Gusto, *p189*: the best point from which to view the new Ara Pacis museum (*see p111*).
Maccheroni, *p189*: there's a *dolce vita* vibe in this square a stone's throw from the Pantheon (*see p119*).
Paninoteca da Guido, *p211*: you'll have to fight Swiss guards off for a table at this sandwich bar on a bustling street by St Peter's (*see p164*).
La Pergola dell'Hotel Hilton, *p212*: far from central and very, very pricey, this three-star restaurant has the whole city at its feet.
San Teodoro, p185: dine in a historic piazza in this charming enclave around the back of the Roman Forum (*see p82*).

official with the move) serves up Rome's best *pizza bianca ripiena* – which, as a sign explains, is 'White Pizza With Any Thing You Like Inside'. Fillings range from classics like prosciutto and mozzarella to exotic combinations such as brie, grilled aubergine and rocket. Pay at the till for a standard slab (€3); then join the receipt-waving hordes to get served – and draw inspiration from what regulars are ordering as you wait.

Ghetto & Campo de' Fiori

Restaurants ∕ 3 5 €

Ar Galletto
Piazza Farnese 102 (06 686 1714). Bus 30Exp, 40Exp, 46, 62, 63, 64, 70, 81, 87, 492, 628, 780, H/tram 8. **Meals served** 12.15-3pm, 7.15-11pm Mon-Sat. Closed 10 days Aug. **Average** €35. **Credit** AmEx, MC, V. **Map** p355 C6 & p358 C1 **31**
You don't need to pay the inflated prices charged by other restaurants around here for a ringside view of piazza Farnese. Humbler than the competition, and Roman to its marrow, Ar Galletto has tables on the square in summer. The food is firmly in the local tradition, but dishes like *penne all'arrabbiata, spaghetti alle vongole* or *abbacchio scottadito* (grilled ribs of lamb) are appetising and – for the location – well priced. The only downside is the fact that this lot are Lazio supporters – hence all the sky-blue regalia in the busy main dining room. But nobody's perfect.

Da Giggetto
Via Portico d'Ottavia 21A-22 (06 686 1105/www. giggettoalportico.com). Bus 23, 63, 280, 630, 780, H/tram 8. **Meals served** 12.30-3pm, 7.30-11.30pm Tue-Sun. Closed 2wks July. **Average** €40. **Credit** AmEx, DC, MC, V. **Map** p358 D2 **32**
In this long-running standby in the Ghetto, a troop of old-fashioned waiters serves up plentiful helpings of decent versions of *cucina ebraica* (Jewish cuisine) classics like *carciofi alla giudia* (crunchy fried whole artichokes) and fried *baccalà* (salt cod) to large tables of tourists – both Italian and foreign. The atmosphere is loud, warm and friendly, and an unexpectedly extensive wine list has reasonable markups. When the weather is warmer, sit at the outside tables for a fine view of the first-century Portico d'Ottavia (*see p128*).

Ditirambo
Piazza della Cancelleria 74 (06 687 1626/www. ristoranteditirambo.it). Bus 30Exp, 40Exp, 46, 62, 63, 64, 70, 81, 87, 492, 628, 780, H/tram 8. **Meals served** 7.30-11.30pm Mon; 1-3pm, 7.30-11.30pm Tue-Sun. Closed 3wks Aug. **Average** €35. **Credit** MC, V. **Map** p355 D6 & p358 C1 **33**
This funky trattoria located around the corner from campo de' Fiori serves up good-value food based on fresh, mainly organic ingredients. They specialise in traditional fare with a creative kick, as in the excellent baby squid on a bed of *cicerchie* (a sort of primitive chick-pea), or the decent *girello di vitello*

(veal silverside) braised in coffee. When they try to be out-and-out creative – as in the tuna kebabs coated with almonds and pistacchios in pomegranate and lime sauce – results can be less convincing. There are a few vegetarian main-course options, such as cauliflower *sformato* (bake) with smoked ricotta. Don't come here if you're in a hurry: service can be slow, but it's friendly enough, and there's usually a good buzz, with a mix of young trendsters and older gourmands. Ditirambo's popularity in the evenings means that it's a good idea to book ahead.

Il Pagliaccio
Via dei Banchi Vecchi 129 (06 6880 9595/www. ristoranteilpagliaccio.it). Bus 23, 46, 62, 64, 116, 280. **Meals served** 8-10pm Mon, Tue; 1-2pm, 8-10pm Wed-Sat. Closed 1wk Jan & 2wks Aug. **Average** €70. **Credit** AmEx, DC, MC, V. **Map** p355 C5 & p358 B1 **34**
Though prices have climbed recently – prompted, perhaps, by Pagliaccio's first Michelin star, in the 2007 edition of the guide – Anthony Genovese's *centro storico* restaurant still offers one of the best-value gourmet dinners in Rome. A light makeover in 2006 upped the warmth and intimacy factors and did away with those uncomfortable chairs, allowing diners to focus more clearly on the sheer bravura of Genovese's cuisine. The chef's successful incorporation of oriental influences (unlike some other Italian chefs who have jumped on the fusion bandwagon, Genovese actually studied in Japan) is clearly illustrated in an *antipasto* of grilled scallops with teriyaki-marinated beef and caramel *zabaione*. But his sure touch is equally evident in less pyrotechnic dishes like the *gnocchi* with lamb and two varieties of wild mushroom, or *secondi* such as the John Dory with glacé vegetables, baby octopus tossed in the pan and *scorzonera* (black salsify). The small but interesting wine list is efficiently managed by a Japanese sommelier, and service is affable – though sometimes slow. Leave plenty of space for the excellent desserts, which are prepared by talented Alsatian pastry chef Marion Lichtle. Although there are six-course taster menus at €55 and €80, we recommend ordering à la carte.

Sora Lella
Via Ponte Quattro Capi 16 (06 686 1601/www. soralella.com). Bus 23, 63, 280, 630, 780. **Meals served** 12.45-2.30pm, 7.50-10.45pm Mon-Sat. **Average** €65. **Credit** AmEx, MC, V. **Map** p358 D3 **35**
Sora Lella was a sort of Roman celebrity Queen Mum and TV star. Her son set up this upmarket trattoria on the Tiber Island in her honour after she died in 1993. It avoids folksy kitsch and offers good Roman cooking, with filling classics such as *pasta e patate* (pasta and potatoes) or *gnocchi all'amatriciana* playing off against more creative options like *involtini di manzo con peperoni in umido* (beef rolls with stewed red peppers) or *filetto al Cesanese del Piglio* (beef fillet in a sauce made from a red Lazio wine). Some of the dishes fail to reach the peaks,

Eat, Drink, Shop

and prices are a little high for what you get, but the ambience is warm and welcoming, service efficient and the wine cellar well stocked.

Sora Margherita ✔ ↗

Piazza delle Cinque Scole 30 (06 687 4216). Bus 23, 63, 280, 630, 780, H/tram 8. **Meals served** *Apr-Sept* 12.45-2.45pm, 8-11.30pm Mon-Thur; 8-11.30pm Fri. *Oct-Mar* 12.45-2.45pm, 8-11.30pm Tue-Thur; 8-11.30pm Fri, Sat. Closed Aug. **Average** €20. **No credit cards. Map** p358 D2 ⑯

This spit-and-sawdust, hole-in-the-wall trat offers one of Rome's great local dining experiences. There may or may not be a sign with the restaurant's name stuck inside the glass door; if it's fallen off, you'll just have to go by the street number. Inside, wooden tables are crammed into a couple of narrow rooms, and the volume generated by 20 simultaneous conversations with orders shouted over the top is matched only by the friendliness of the welcome. Sora Margherita is not for health freaks, but no one argues with serious Roman Jewish cooking at these prices. The classic pasta and meat dishes on offer include a superlative *pasta e fagioli*, as well as *tonnarelli cacio e pepe* and *ossobuco* washed down with rough-and-ready house wine. Dessert consists of good, home-made *crostate* (jam or ricotta tarts). In June and July, Sora Margherita closes Sunday and opens on Monday. Licensing laws mean that if you come for dinner on Fridays and Saturdays, you'll need to fill out a (free) membership card.

Wine bars & gastropubs

See also p193 **Casa Bleve**.

L'Angolo Divino

Via dei Balestrari 12 (06 686 4413). Bus 30Exp, 40Exp, 46, 62, 63, 64, 70, 81, 87, 116, 492, 628, 780, H/tram 8. **Open** 6pm-midnight Mon, Sun; 10am-3pm, 6pm-midnight Tue-Sat. Closed 1wk Aug. **Average** €20. **Credit** MC, V. **Map** p355 D6 & p358 C2 ⑰

Over 20 reds, whites and dessert wines are available by the glass, many more by the bottle, at this relaxed wine bar on a quiet street near campo de' Fiori. There's a good range of smoked fish, salami and salads, and a vast selection of cheeses, plus some hot dishes in winter. The furniture is basic, which fits well with the overall laid-back mood – stoked by a jazz soundtrack.

Roscioli

Via dei Giubbonari 21-23 (06 687 5287/www. rosciolifinefood.com). Bus 23, 63, 280, 630, 780, H/tram 8. **Meals served** 12.30-4pm, 8pm-midnight Mon-Sat. **Average** €40. **Credit** AmEx, DC, MC, V. **Map** p355 D6 & p358 C2 ⑱

Although quite a few Roman wine shops are in the habit of laying out tables for lunch and (sometimes) dinner, Roscioli is the first of the city's butchers to do so. In fact, this historic food emporium near campo de' Fiori is more a meat-oriented deli than a standard butcher, and menu entries like Chianina

Community service with a smile at **Trattoria degli Amici**. *See p200.*

Eat, Drink, Shop

L'HI-RES, all'ultimo piano dell'Hotel Valadier,
offre uno scenario incantevole.
Restaurant, Wok corner, Tartar bar, banco Fry-top.

*The HI-RES, on top floor of the Hotel Valadier,
offers an enchanting view of Rome.
Restaurant, Wok corner, Tartar bar, Fry-top corner.*

H I | R E S

H I G H R E S T A U R A N T

HI-RES Via della Fontanella, 15 (PIAZZA DEL POPOLO) - Tel. 06 3212905

Hotels and Restaurant in the heart of Rome 🍸 **groupevaladier.com**

IL VALENTINO Via della Fontanella, 14 (PIAZZA DEL POPOLO) - Tel. 06 3610880

Restaurant Pianobar

Il Ristorante IL VALENTINO offre menù fantasiosi
in un ambiente sobrio e raffinato.
Pianobar, musica dal vivo e American Bar.

*The restaurant IL VALENTINO offers a creative
menu in a refined environment.
Lounge Pianobar, live music and American Bar.*

beef *carpaccio* with carrot julienne and sweet-and-sour leeks reflect this vocation. The ingredients are top-notch, but the meld is not always persuasive, and service can be decidedly offhand. The wine list does have some good bottles at a reasonable markup, but overall we find Roscioli expensive given the no-frills deli ambience. Try it between 6 and 8pm for their *aperitivo* buffet.

Snacks & quick meals

Bruschetteria degli Angeli
Piazza B Cairoli 2A (06 6880 5789). Bus 23, 63, 280, 630, 780, H/tram 8. **Open** 12.30-3.30pm, 7.30pm-1.30am daily. Closed 1wk Aug. **Credit** DC, MC, V. **Map** p358 D2 **39**
This unpretentious, pub-like diner overlooks a little park, set back from via Arenula. As the name suggests, the star turns are the rich house *bruschette* (average €8) – thick toasted bread, here in mega format, with various toppings from red chicory and bacon to grilled courgettes and mozzarella. There are also pasta dishes, grilled steaks and a good range of draught beers.

Il Forno Campo de' Fiori
Vicolo del Gallo 14 (06 6880 6662/www.forno campodefiori.com). Bus 30Exp, 40Exp, 46, 62, 63, 64, 70, 81, 87, 116, 492, 628, 780, H/tram 8. **Open** 7.30am-2.30pm, 5-8pm Mon-Sat. **No credit cards. Map** p355 C6 & p358 C1 **40**
This little bakery does the best takeaway sliced pizza in the campo de' Fiori area by far. Their plain *pizza bianca* base, dressed with extra-virgin olive oil, is delicious in itself, but check out the one with *fiori di zucca* (courgette flowers) too. Next door (or almost – it's separated by the entrance to via dei Cappellari), at campo de Fiori 22, is the main shop, which turns out a variety of delicious breads, biscuits and cakes.

L'Insalata Ricca
Largo dei Chiavari 85 (06 6880 3656/www.insalata ricca.it). Bus 30Exp, 40, 46, 62, 63, 64, 70, 81, 87, 116, 492, 628, 780, H/tram 8. **Open** noon-4pm, 6pm-midnight Mon-Fri; noon-midnight Sat, Sun. **Credit** AmEx, DC, MC, V. **Map** p355 D6 & p358 D1 **41**
L'Insalata Ricca is a good answer to that classic Roman dilemma – where to go when you're dying for a decent salad. The Anglo-Italian menu lists over 30 different types, from *baires* (walnuts, apple and melted gorgonzola) to *speck* (with ham, fontina cheese and croutons). The success of L'Insalata Ricca has led to a rash of lookalikes scattered around the city – but the mothership remains the best. **Other locations**: piazza Pasquino 72, Pantheon & Navona (06 6830 7881).

Le Piramidi
Vicolo del Gallo 11 (06 687 9061/www.cucina raba.com). Bus 30Exp, 40Exp, 46, 62, 63, 64, 70, 81, 87, 116, 492, 628, 780, H/tram 8. **Open** 10am-12.30am Tue-Sun. Closed Aug. **No credit cards. Map** p355 C6 & p358 C1 **42**

Around the corner from campo de' Fiori, Le Piramidi makes for a welcome change from takeaway pizza. The range of Middle Eastern takeaway fare is small, but it's all fresh, cheap and tasty, and the falafel is probably the best in Rome.

Trastevere & Gianicolo

Restaurants

Alberto Ciarla
Piazza San Cosimato 40 (06 581 8668/www.alberto ciarla.com). Bus 780, H/tram 8. **Meals served** 8.30pm-midnight Mon-Sat. Closed 1wk Jan & 1wk Aug. **Average** €70. **Credit** AmEx, DC, MC, V. **Map** p358 C3 **43**
The reputation of this restaurant is stuck in the same 1960s time warp as the decor. But Alberto Ciarla is still one of Rome's best fish restaurants – and a meal here is not prohibitively expensive, especially if you opt for one of the taster menus (from €50 up). A trademark dish like *spigola con le erbe* (sea bass with herbs) strikes the right balance between art and nature, while a *primo* of *pasta e fagioli ai frutti di mare* (pasta and beans with seafood) is strong, decisive and very Roman. The menu is a triumph of *dolce vita* typography, the overriding mood one of charmingly courteous camp. As this guide went to press, Alberto Ciarla was in the midst of opening a winebar next door (12.30-2.30pm, 7.30pm-midnight Mon-Sat).

Alle Fratte di Trastevere ✔ 3 0
Via delle Fratte di Trastevere 49-50 (06 583 5775/ www.allefratteditrastevere.com). Bus 23, 280, 780, H/tram 8. **Meals served** 12.30-3pm, 6.30-11.30pm Mon, Tue, Thur-Sat; 12.30-3pm Sun. Closed 2wks Aug. **Average** €30. **Credit** AmEx, DC, MC, V. **Map** p358 C3 **44**
Trastevere has its fair share of traditional, family-run trattorias, but the cheap and cheerful Alle Fratte has got to be one of the best. It does honest Roman trattoria fare with Neapolitan influences, and the service is friendly, attentive and bilingual (the owner's wife is from Long Island). First courses, like *pennette alla sorrentina* (pasta with tomatoes and runny mozzarella), are served up in generous portions. *Secondi* include oven-roasted sea bream, veal escalopes in marsala and a good grilled beef fillet. Desserts are home-made; the post-prandial *digestivi* flow freely. In summer a few outside tables edge the restaurant's ivy-covered street frontage and spill around the corner.

Antico Arco
Piazzale Aurelio 7 (06 581 5274). Bus 44, 75, 710, 870. **Meals served** 7.30-11.30pm Mon-Sat. Closed 2wks Aug. **Average** €50. **Credit** AmEx, DC, MC, V. **Map** p358 A3 **45**
A January 2007 refit has given the Antico Arco a smart new interior, minimalist but warm, and the cuisine has perked up, too, after a period of stasis. On a busy corner behind Porta San Pancrazio, this Gianicolo restaurant – helmed by chef Patrizia

Mattei – was one of the first of the new wave of creative Roman diners in the 1990s, and unlike some of the others, it can still be highly recommended. Tables are spread over two upstairs and two downstairs rooms, and there's now also a wine-bar lobby where you can imbibe while waiting to be seated. The menu is strong on all fronts, from the *antipasti*, which include an outstanding Tropea onion and *taleggio* cheese flan, to the *primi*, where Antico Arco classics like the risotto with castelmagno cheese are flanked by new entries such as *tonnarelli* with *bottarga* (grey mullet roe), artichokes and coriander. The excellent *secondi* cover the board from meat to fish to game, and the choreographic desserts are no let-down. The wine list is extensive, and sensibly priced. It's still hugely popular, so book at least a couple of days in advance. **Photo** *p192*.

Glass Hostaria

Vicolo del Cinque 58 (06 5833 5903/www.glass-hostaria.com). Bus 23, 280, 780, H/tram 8. **Meals served** 8pm-midnight Tue-Sat. **Closed** 2wks Jan-Feb. **Average** €40. **Credit** AmEx, DC, MC, V. **Map** p358 C3 ⓸⓺

Despite being ultra-modern and kicking against the trad Trastevere dining scene, Glass Hostaria offers surprisingly warm service, a very interesting wine list, and pan-Italian food that is a lot less pretentious than you might expect. True, there are a couple of kooky novelty numbers like ice lasagna with coal mousse, but other creative melds like the pumpkin *gnocchi* with *taleggio* fondue, chestnuts and porcini mushrooms are more persuasive. It's also unexpectedly good value, given the setting and location.

Le Mani in Pasta

Via de' Genovesi 37 (06 581 6017). Bus 23, 280, 780, H/tram 8. **Meals served** 12.30-3pm, 7.30-11.30pm Tue-Sat. Closed 3 wks Aug & 1wk late Dec. **Average** €33. **Credit** AmEx, DC, MC, V. **Map** p358 D3 ⓸⓻

It doesn't look like much from the outside, but this relative newcomer has three things going for it: decent, creative home cooking, served up in huge portions; the friendly, informal service of the lads who run the place; and great value for money. On our last visit we started off with some nicely chargrilled vegetables and a *sauté di cozze e vongole* (clams and mussels), followed up by giant mounds of spaghetti with *seppioline* (baby cuttlefish) and *carciofi* (artichokes), and ended up paying €38 for two, wine and water included. The *secondi*, if you get that far, include a good fillet steak with green peppercorns. The upstairs room has a ringside view of the kitchen action. Unusually for Rome, there's a *sala fumatori* (smoking area) though it's confined to the nether regions. Book ahead.

Paris

Piazza San Calisto 7A (06 581 5378). Bus 780, H/tram 8. **Meals served** 12.30-3pm, 7.45-11pm Tue-Sat; 12.30-3pm Sun. Closed 3wks Aug. **Average** €45. **Credit** AmEx, DC, MC, V. **Map** p358 C3 ⓸⓽

Don't be fooled by the name: this upmarket restaurant is militantly Roman. It's one of the few places where you can still sample *minestra di arzilla ai broccoli* (skate soup with broccoli), a classic of old-school *cucina romana*. Paris highlights the Jewish side of the city's culinary traditions, most obviously in the succulent *gran fritto vegetale con baccalà* (a fry-up of artichokes, courgettes and their flowers, and salt cod). Service is a little slow at times, but reassuringly old-fashioned, like the decor. In summer, there are a few tables outside in the square.

Trattoria degli Amici

Piazza Sant'Egidio 5 (06 580 6033). Bus 23, 280, 780, H/tram 8. **Meals served** 7.30-11pm Mon-Sat. Closed Aug. **Average** €30. **Credit** AmEx, MC, V. **Map** p358 B3 ⓸⓽

This Trastevere trattoria with a difference is owned and run by the Comunità di Sant'Egidio charity, and gives work experience to mentally and physically handicapped people both in the kitchens and front-of-house. That said, it's a real restaurant, not just a laudable project, and most regulars come because of the warm ambience, good home cooking and excellent value for money. The menu is Roman with a few creative and international variations: so a classic local dish like *spaghetti all'amatriciana* might be joined by a radicchio and provolo cheese *involtino* (roulade), or a Tunisian-style couscous. It's proved a real hit, so book well ahead, especially for Friday or Saturday evenings. **Photo** *p197*.

International

Jaipur

Via di San Francesco a Ripa 56 (06 580 3992/www.ristorantejaipur.it). Bus 780, H/tram 8. **Meals served** 7pm-midnight Mon; noon-3pm, 7pm-midnight Tue-Sun. **Average** €25. **Credit** AmEx, DC, MC, V. **Map** p359 C4 ⓹⓪

Jaipur does some of Rome's best Indian food (not that there's much competition), and it's good value too – which helps make up for the garish lighting and colour scheme. The menu ranges from basic starters to a large selection of tandoori specials, curries and *murghs* (the *murgh maccan*, charcoal-grilled chicken with a butter-tomato gravy, is particularly tasty). Vegetarian dishes include an outstanding *baighan bharta* (aubergine purée cooked in a clay oven, dressed with spices).

Pizzerias

Dar Poeta

Vicolo del Bologna 45 (06 588 0516). Bus 23, 280, 780, H/tram 8. **Meals served** 7.30pm-midnight daily. **Average** €15. **Credit** AmEx, DC, MC, V. **Map** p358 B/C3 ⓹⓵

Dar Poeta does a better-quality pizza, based on an innovative slow-rise dough. Creative assemblages include the house pizza (with courgettes, sausage and spicy pepper) and the *bodrilla* (with apples and

Remo. *See p203.*

Wine bars & gastropubs

Enoteca Ferrara

Piazza Trilussa 41A (06 5833 3920). Bus 23, 280, 780, H/tram 8. **Open** *Wine bar & shop* 11am-2am daily. **Meals served** 8-11.30pm daily. **Average** *Wine bar* €25. *Restaurant* €55. **Credit** AmEx, DC, MC, V. **Map** p358 C2 ⊛
This wine bar with culinary pretensions is a real warren of a place, with tables on three levels and a lovely back garden for fair-weather dining. The two wine lists (one huge book for whites, one for reds) provide a happy evening's reading, though it's a shame that there is nothing available for under €18. Some punters come to Ferrara to buy a bottle or a little gastronomic treat from the in-house deli, some for a pre- or post-dinner glass of wine, some ignore the slight diffidence of the bar staff and succumb to one of the wholesome tapas-style dishes on the counter (a selection costing €7-€9 is served from 6pm to 2am). Others opt for the full-on restaurant experience. The cuisine is undeniably creative, with a Slow Food approach that exalts the quality of the raw ingredients, but we find the service a little too frosty for comfort and the pricing on the high side for what is a good but by no means great meal.

Snacks & quick meals

See also p225 **Enoteca Trastevere**, **Friends Art Café** and **Ombre Rosse**.

Sisini

Via San Francesco a Ripa 137 (06 589 7110). Bus 780, H/tram 8. **Open** 9am-10pm Mon-Sat. Closed 3wks Aug. **No credit cards. Map** p358 C3 ⊛
Probably Trastevere's best *pizza rustica* (takeaway pizza) outfit. The flavours are fairly conservative, but there's a wide range and they're all delicious. Roast chicken is another forte.

Aventine, Testaccio & Ostiense

Restaurants

Checchino dal 1887

Via di Monte Testaccio 30 (06 574 6318/www. checchino-dal-1887.com). Bus 95, 673, 719. **Meals served** 12.30-3pm, 8pm-midnight Tue-Sat. Closed Aug and 1wk Dec. **Average** €50. **Credit** AmEx, DC, MC, V. **Map** p359 C/D6 ⊛
Nestling among the trendy bars and clubs opposite Testaccio's former slaughterhouse (Il Mattatoio; *see p143*), the Mariani family's historic restaurant is Rome's leading temple of authentic *cucina romana*. Imagine a pie shop rising to become one of London's leading restaurants, and the odd mix of humble decor, elegant service, hearty food and one of the most extensive wine cellars in Rome falls into place. Vegetarians should give this place a wide berth:

Grand Marnier). The varied *bruschette* are first-rate, and healthy salads offer a break from all those carbs. Leave room for dessert, as the sweet *calzone* stuffed with Nutella and ricotta is to die for. You can eat till late and the waiters are genuinely friendly, but be prepared to queue, as they don't take bookings.

Da Vittorio

Via di San Cosimato 14A (06 580 0353). Bus 780, H/tram 8. **Meals served** 7.30pm-midnight Mon-Sat. **Average** €20. **Credit** MC, V. **Map** p358 C3 ⊛
Vittorio was here long before Neapolitan pizzas caught on in Rome and will no doubt still be here when the fad has passed. The man's as expansively *napoletano* as they come and so are his succulent pizzas, which include the self-celebratory Vittorio (mozzarella, parmesan, fresh tomato and basil). Kids will delight in his heart-shaped junior specials. The place is minute, but bursts with exuberance.

SENSUS FARNESE

RISTORANTE

The pleasure of dining goes by
the name Sensus Farnese.
With space for 25 only, the
restaurant maintains an elegant
atmosphere, where you'll enjoy
authentic Roman and regional
cuisine, prepared with the truest
and most ancient flavours. The
expert staff offers the highest level
of service, and a formidable wine
selection is cared for by a knowing sommelier. This is the place
for the refined gourmand, who
considers dining to be one of life's
greatest pleasures. Sensus Farnese
will surely set the trend for a new
and exclusive way to eat out.

Vicolo del Giglio, 22 (piazza Farnese) Roma
Open 7,00 pm 1,00 am
Closed Sundays - tel. 06.6877966
s.farnese@ergonitalia.com - www.ergonfood.com

specialities include *trippa* and *coda alla vaccinara*. Pasta dishes like the traditional *bucatini all'amatriciana* are delicious. Desserts feature a delicious *stracciatella* cake with ricotta, almonds and chocolate chips. Unusually for Rome, there's an impressive cheese board.

Da Felice ✓ 𝈈

Via Mastro Giorgio 29 (06 574 6800). Bus 23, 30Exp, 75, 95, 170, 280, 716, 781/tram 3. **Meals served** 12.30-3pm, 8-11.30pm Mon-Sat; 12.30-3pm Sun. Closed 3wks Aug. **Average** €30. **Credit** MC, V. **Map** p359 D5 ⑤⑥

This formerly basic trattoria in the heart of trendy Testaccio used to be best known for being almost impossible to get into – Felice, the owner, liked to keep reserved signs on all the tables, and only let in regulars and the few others he liked the look of. But Felice has retired (though he still pops in occasionally) and the place has had a makeover, turning it into a stylishly *moderne* neo-osteria. Thankfully, though, the quality of the cooking has not changed. If anything it's got better, with a few lighter and more creative dishes alongside the Roman classics – *tonnarelli cacio e pepe*, *abbacchio al forno con patate* – which first made the name of this long-running Testaccio institution. The desserts are excellent – especially the *tiramisù al bicchiere* (served in a glass), and the wine list has expanded a little since the days when it was cloudy Castelli romani in a flask or nothing.

Tuttifrutti

Via Luca della Robbia 3A (06 575 7902). Bus 23, 30Exp, 75, 95, 170, 280, 716, 781/tram 3. **Meals served** 8-11.30pm Mon-Sat. Closed 3wks Aug. **Average** €30. **Credit** AmEx, MC, V. **Map** p359 D5 ⑤⑦

Behind an anonymous frosted-glass door, this friendly, artsy trattoria is Testaccio's best-value dining experience. In colourful *romanesco* or even more colourful English, host Michele guides you through a daily changing menu of creative pan-Italian fare, very much dtermined by whatever happens to be in season, and which might include an *antipasto* of *pizzelle* (fried pizza balls with tomato and basil) followed by *fusilli* with sun-dried tomatoes, pecorino, bacon and pine nuts and then baked lamb with potatoes and rosemary. There are always a few options for vegetarians, including a tasty bake of potatoes with *porcini* mushrooms. Though limited, the wine list is excellently priced. Finish up your meal with good desserts or great chunks of convent-made chocolate and sweet wine.

International

Bishoku Kobo

Via Ostiense 110B (06 574 4190). Metro Garbatella/bus 23. **Meals served** 7.30pm-midnight Mon, Sat; 12.30-2.30pm, 7.30pm-midnight Tue-Fri, Sun. Closed 1wk Aug. **Average** €25. **No credit cards. Map** p143 B3 ⑤⑧

This Japanese restaurant on via Ostiense is well placed for visitors to the collection of antique statues in the adjacent Centrale Montemartini (*see p142*). Though the food is classic Japanese, the ambience is pure neighbourhood trattoria – except details like a gloriously kitsch sushi clock. The sashimi, sushi and stuffed vegetables are all good, and the tempura is well worth the extra wait. Prices are reasonably low, and it's always packed with locals, so book ahead, especially if you're going out of your way to get here.

Court Delicati

Viale Aventino 39 (06 574 6108). Metro Circo Massimo/bus 60Exp, 75, 673/tram 3. **Meals served** noon-3pm, 7.30-11pm Tue-Sun. Closed Aug. **Average** €22. **Credit** MC, V. **Map** p361 A5 ⑤⑨

Court Delicati is basically just a decent Chinese restaurant, but it has gained some renown because the FAO (the UN's Food and Agriculture Organisation), with its captive international clientele, is just up the road, and because it's one of the few places to add some Thai and Indonesian dishes to the usual repertoire. So as well as better than average steamed dumplings and hot crispy beef, regulars can also enjoy the violently spicy *tom yam* soups and very passable *nasi goreng* (fried rice). Beer and wine are as reasonably priced as everything else on the menu.

Pizzerias

Piccolo Alpino

Via Orazio Antinori 5 (06 574 1386). Bus 23, 75, 95, 170, 280, 716, 781/tram 3. **Meals served** 12.30-2.30pm, 6-11pm Tue-Sun. **Average** €18. **No credit cards. Map** p359 C5 ⑥⓪

This ultra-cheap, no-frills trattoria-pizzeria in a residential Testaccio sidestreet is about as far as you can get from the tourist herd. There's a telly in the corner (with live football on Sunday evenings), beer on tap and some rough Castelli romani wine in the fridge; but the pizzas are good, and the pasta too, as long as you stick to the house specialities: *spaghetti con le vongole* (with clams) and *penne all'arrabbiata* (in tomato and chilli sauce); for restaurant fare, expect to pay a little more – say €25. In summer tables invade the road, kids play tag among the cars, and it all feels like a scene from Fellini's *Roma*.

Remo ✓ 𝈈

Piazza Santa Maria Liberatrice 44 (06 574 6270). Bus 23, 75, 95, 170, 280, 716, 781/tram 3. **Meals served** 7pm-1am Mon-Sat. Closed 3wks Aug. **Average** €18. **No credit cards. Map** p359 D5 ⑥①

The best place in town for authentic *pizza romana*, Remo is a Testaccio institution, with a prime location on the district's main piazza. You can sit at wonky tables balanced on the pavement, or in the cavernous interior, overseen by Lazio team photos. The *bruschette al pomodoro* are the finest in Rome. A park with swings right across the road makes this a great place to eat with kids. **Photo** *p201*.

Wine bars & gastropubs

See p226 **L'Oasi della Birra**.

Snacks & quick meals

Il Seme e la Foglia

Via Galvani 18 (06 574 3008). Bus 95, 170, 673, 781/tram 3. **Open** *7.30am-2am Mon-Sat; 6pm-2am Sun. Closed 3wks Aug.* **No credit cards.** **Map** p359 D6 ⊕

Right-on and alternative, this lively daytime snack bar and evening pre-club stop is always packed with students and teachers from the Scuola Popolare di Musica across the road. At midday there's generally a pasta dish, plus large salads (€5-€7) and creative filled rolls.

Tallusa

Via Beniamino Franklin 11 (333 752 3506). Bus 95, 170, 673, 719, 781. **Open** *11am-1.30am daily.* **Average** €15. **No credit cards.** **Map** p359 C6 ⊕

Always packed, this tiny eat-in or takeaway joint specialises in southern and eastern Mediterranean cuisine – ranging from Sicilian specialities to falafel and a full range of Lebanese-style mezedes, served with pitta bread. Very friendly, and very cheap.

Celio, San Giovanni & San Lorenzo

Restaurants

See also p226 **Café Café**.

Arancia Blu

Via dei Latini 55-65 (06 445 4105). Bus 71, 492/tram 3, 19. **Meals served** *8.30pm-midnight daily.* **Average** €30. **No credit cards.** **Map** p151 C3 ⊕

This vegetarian restaurant in bohemian San Lorenzo has shaken off its rather earnest macrobiotic origins and become a stylish urban bistro with a great wine list; but it still has serious organic credentials. Service has improved since our last visit, and we would recommend the place even to non-vegetarians looking for a good-value meal in a space with a jazzy, alternative ambience (though be warned: some of the tables for two are very small). A starter of *puntarelle* (chicory stems) with a walnut-balsamic vinegar dressing and aged piave cheese shavings is an interesting twist on a Roman classic, and we liked the potato-filled ravioli topped with pecorino cheese and mint. Some dishes can be a little bland, but the large cheese selection and

Doozo. *See p208.*

well-priced wine list are pluses, and the extensive dessert list – including a chocolate tasting menu with rum – is an original touch. The 'Blue Orange' also organises cooking and wine-tasting courses.

Il Bocconcino

Via Ostilia 23 (06 7707 9175). Bus 60Exp, 75, 85, 87, 117, 571, 810, 850/tram 3. **Meals served** 12.30-3.30pm, 7.30-11.30pm Mon, Tue, Thur-Sun. Closed 3wks Aug. **Average** €28. **Credit** AmEx, DC, MC, V. **Map** p360 C3 ⑭

With its red-check tablecloths and brick vaulted ceilings, this trattoria within a slingshot's range of the Colosseum looks like it's been around for generations, but in fact it only opened in 2005. The welcome is ultra-friendly, the menu – assembled by a chef who used to be a pharmacist – mixes Roman classics like *tonnarelli cacio e pepe* or *abbacchio brodettato* (braised lamb) with more adventurous, Slow-Food-style dishes like *fusilli* with fresh tuna, Tropea onions and capers stewed in wine. On Tuesdays and Fridays, 'poor' fish like anchovies and mackerel take a starring role. The wine list is limited but honestly priced, while the desserts (including *ciambella* biscuits for dipping in Olevano dessert wine) are of the comforting home-made variety. The only downside is the fact that the service, though affable, can be excruciatingly slow.

Luzzi

Via Celimontana 1 (06 709 6332). Bus 60Exp, 75, 85, 87, 117, 571, 810, 850/tram 3. **Meals served** noon-3pm, 7pm-midnight Mon, Tue, Thur-Sun. Closed 2wks Aug. **Average** €22. **Credit** AmEx, DC, MC, V. **Map** p360 C3 ⑯

On busy nights (and most nights are busy here), this heaving neighbourhood trat is the loudest and most crowded 40 square metres in Rome. Not the place for a romantic tête-à-tête – come instead for the human zoo and, of course, for the perfectly decent pizzas, pasta dishes and *secondi*, which stretch from Roman meaty staples to a few piscine options like baked *orata* (bream) with potatoes. The outside tables operate all year round.

Marcello

Via dei Campani 12 (06 446 3311). Bus 71, 492/ tram 3, 19. **Meals served** 7.30-11.30pm Mon-Fri. Closed 3wks Aug. **Average** €18. **No credit cards**. **Map** p151 C3 ⑰

From the outside, this San Lorenzo eaterie looks like one of those spit-and-sawdust places that Romans refer to as *un buco* – a hole in the wall. There's no name outside, just a sign saying 'Cucina'. Inside, hordes of hungry students from the nearby university occupy the old wooden tables. Alongside Roman offal specialities like tripe and *pajata* are lighter and more creative dishes such as *straccetti ai carciofi* (strips of veal with artichokes). The same goes for pasta: as well as reliable traditional recipes (*spaghetti alla carbonara, all'amatriciana* or *alla gricia*), you can also order home-made *ravioloni* filled with fresh cheese, ricotta and walnuts. A surprisingly extensive wine list, strong on big reds, confirms that Marcello – now run by Marcello's son, Isidoro – is a lot more than a *buco*.

Tram Tram

Via dei Reti 44-46 (06 490 416). Bus 71, 492/tram 3, 19. **Meals served** 12.30-3.30pm, 7.30-11.30pm Tue-Sun. Closed 1wk Aug. **Average** €35. **Credit** AmEx, DC, MC, V. **Map** p151 D2 ⑱

Taking its name from its proximity to the tram tracks, this good-value *nuova* trattoria in San Lorenzo attracts a young crowd, who are not fazed by the waiters' rather hassled manner or the lack of elbow room. The menu mixes Roman classics with dishes inspired by the cuisine of Puglia (the heel of Italy) and Sicily. It's particularly strong on fish and vegetables, as in the *tagliolini calamaretti e pesto* (pasta strips with baby squid and pesto). There are a few vegetarian main courses. The wine list is small but well chosen, with very reasonable markups.

Uno e Bino

Via degli Equi 58 (06 446 0702). Bus 71, 492/ tram 3, 19. **Meals served** 8.30-11.30pm Tue-Sun. Closed 2wks Aug. **Average** €45. **Credit** DC, MC, V. **Map** p151 C3 ⑲

Behind an unassuming façade in the rough-edged quarter of San Lorenzo lies an elegantly minimalist, creative Italian restaurant with one of the best

Eat, Drink, Shop

Tuttifrutti

Testaccio, a stone's throw from the market. No sign, just some lettering on the front, but who needs a sign, when people already know the place. Why? Because behind the sign-less door is a simple, homespun kind of restaurant, rather like going round to a friend's for dinner...

Once inside, Michele is always happy to explain what delights Anna, Raffaele and their helpers have prepared for you in the kitchen...

Our dishes all start their life in the market, and with a little care and imagination, turn into part of our unique contribution to Italian cuisine.

TUTTIFRUTTI
Via Luca della Robbia, 3A - 5 - 5A 00153 Roma Tel.: +39 06 575 7902
open for dinner: 7.30 - 11.30 pm closed: Sundays and August
Booking advisable

quality/price ratios in Rome. With such pared-back decor, the place needs to be full to really work – but it usually is. The back wall is all bottles: the result of the oenological peregrinations of host Gloria Gravina's wine-critic brother Giampaolo. New chef Giovanni Passerini has maintained the restaurant's reputation for audacious combinations of vegetables and herbs with fish, meat and game, but has done it his way, sweeping out most of the old classics and introducing his own creations. These vary according to season and what's good in the market, but on a recent visit we were impressed by the *linguine* pasta served with a topping of raw, marinated *dentice* (dentex, a Mediterranean fish), and blown away by the mackerel cracker brulé with Tropea onions and *burrata* (a buttery mozzarella). The desserts are good too, and there's a well-stocked cheese board. Two taster menus are currently pegged at €45 and €55. Book well in advance to guarantee a table.

Monti & Esquilino

Restaurants

Agata e Romeo
Via Carlo Alberto 45 (06 446 6115/www.agatae romeo.it). Metro Vittorio/bus 16, 70, 71, 75, 84, 360/tram 5, 14. **Meals served** 12.30-3pm, 7.30-10.30pm Mon-Fri. Closed 2wks Jan & 2wks Aug. **Average** €90. **Credit** AmEx, DC, MC, V. **Map** p360 D1 ⑦⓪

If we had a couple of hundred euros to blow on a knockout meal for two with a decent bottle of wine, we'd be very tempted to blow it here. 'Agata' is Agata Parisella – a talented chef who was one of the first to demonstrate that Roman cuisine could be refined without sacrificing its flavoursome roots in *mamma*'s home cooking. Among the *primi*, the cannelloni filled with a white duck *ragù* are memorable, their thin home-made pasta gratinéed to a delectable crispness, while the terrine of *coda di vaccinara* in celeriac sauce is an affectionately ironic – and, more importantly, delicious – tribute to a legendary Roman dish. The place is a family affair: Agata's husband, Romeo Caraccio, presides over the dining room and extensive wine list, while their daughter Mariantonietta is fast becoming one of Rome's most original and exciting pastry chefs (don't miss her triple-whammy choc-fest of semi-sweet chocolate cake with chocolate sorbet and chocolate *semifreddo*). The service is very professional, and the decor elegant but welcoming, with well-spaced tables.

Trattoria Monti ✓ ⌗𝔖
Via di San Vito 13A (06 446 6573). Metro Vittorio/bus 16, 70, 71, 75, 84, 360/tram 5, 14. **Meals served** 12.45-2.45pm, 7.45-11pm Tue-Sat. Closed 1wk Easter, 3wks Aug & 1wk Sept. **Average** €35. **Credit** DC, MC, V. **Map** p360 D1 ⑦①

This tiny, upmarket trattoria just south of Santa Maria Maggiore is more difficult to get into than many top restaurants – so book well in advance, especially for a Friday or Saturday evening. The

Eat, Drink, Shop

Eat by the day, eat by the month

Visitors from the land of the global supermarket may find the concept a little strange, but Romans still like to eat by the seasons. There's a real sense of anticipation for the day the first artichokes appear in winter or asparagus in early spring, the week at the beginning of June when cherries suddenly fill market stalls, or the September weekend when wicker baskets of *funghi porcini* are set out as baits for passing gourmets. Today many restaurants offer speciality produce – artichokes are a case in point – all year round; but you will eat better (and encourage more responsible catering) if you stick to seasonal availability.

Here's a quick checklist of the main seasonal debuts:

Spring: *spinaci* (spinach), *zucchini* (courgettes), *fave* (broad beans), *asparagi* (asparagus), *rughetta* (rocket).

Summer: *fragole* (strawberries), *piselli* (peas), *albicocche* (apricots), *ciliegi* (cherries), *pomodori* (tomatoes).

Autumn: *peperoni* (red, green and yellow peppers), *funghi porcini* (porcini mushrooms), *pere* (pears), borlotti beans, *broccoletti* (Roman name of *cime di rape*, or broccoli rabe), *tartufi* (truffles), *zucche* (pumpkins), *finocchi* (fennel).

Winter: *broccoli*, *carciofi* (artichokes), *cavolfiore* (cauliflower), *puntarelle* (Catalogna chicory shoots, traditionally served with an anchovy sauce), *radicchio*, *scarola* (chicory), *indivia* (endive).

There's a daily calendar too, partly influenced by Catholic edicts, partly by time-honoured traditions. Tuesdays and especially Fridays are the main days for fish – particularly salt cod (*baccalà*), which you may see soaking under constantly running water in large basins outside some of the city's more traditional *alimentari* (groceries). And for some reason, Thursday is the canonical day for *gnocchi* (mini potato-flour dumplings), though quite a few restaurants offer them the rest of the week as well.

reasons for its popularity are simple: friendly service and ambience, excellent, good-value food, and a surprisingly extensive wine list with very reasonable markups. The cuisine, like the family that runs the place, is from the Marches – so meat, fish and game all feature on the menu. Vegetarians are well served by a range of *tortini* (pastry-less pies) such as Tropea onion in cheese sauce; pasta-hounds will be kept happy by such treats as *tagliolini* with anchovies, pine nuts and pecorino cheese. Lunch is generally the only time you can walk in without a booking and be fairly sure of a table.

International

Africa

Via Gaeta 26-28 (06 494 1077). Metro Castro Pretorio/bus 36, 38, 75, 217, 310, 360, 492, 649. **Meals served** 9.30am-midnight Tue-Sun. **Average** €20. **Credit** MC, V. **Map** p357 E4

Cheerfully casual, Africa serves up filling Eritrean cuisine at rock-bottom prices. After a starter of falafel served with a spicy dip, you can tuck into spongy, whole-wheat *taita* bread: break pieces off and use them to scoop up the meat or vegetables (there are forks for those who prefer them). The mixed vegetarian plate comes with delicious stewed lentils. The *tibsi* – grilled veal with spicy sauce – is also good. Sweet sesame halva, served with a cup of spicy tea, makes a perfect end to the meal.

Doozo

Via Palermo 51 (06 481 5655/www.doozo.it). Metro Repubblica/bus 40Exp, 60Exp, 64, 70, 71, 116, 117, 170, H. **Meals served** 12.30-3pm, 8-11pm Tue-Sat. **Average** €40. **Credit** DC, MC, V. **Map** p357 C6 & p360 B1

Defining itself as an 'art, books & sushi' gallery, this newcomer (the name means 'welcome') – on a quiet street parallel to the shopping and transport artery of via Nazionale – is an oasis of peace and quality in an area dominated by desultory tourist-oriented eateries. The interior is spacious and cultured (tables spill over into the bookshop and gallery space, where regular art and photography exhibitions are organised), but we especially like the small Zen garden out back, which is open all year, weather permitting (overhead braziers keep off the winter chill). The menu is pure Japanese rather than watered-down Italo-Nipponic, with good sushi, sashimi, tempura and *karaage* chicken served in wooden bento boxes. Green tea is on the house. **Photo** *p204*.

Hang Zhou

Via San Martino ai Monti 33C (06 487 2732). Metro Cavour/bus 16, 75, 84, 360, 649, 714. **Meals served** noon-3pm, 7pm-midnight daily. Closed Aug. **Average** €22. **Credit** AmEx, MC, V. **Map** p360 D1

The vast majority of Rome's Chinese restaurants are cheap and mediocre. Hang Zhou is cheap and decidedly original: not so much for the food (though the menu does make an effort to rise above the herd with a series of interesting daily specials) as for the verve of its media-savvy owner, Sonia, who appears in hundreds of photos plastered on the wall of this packed shoebox of a restaurant, beaming next to anyone who is remotely famous… and quite a few who aren't. It's colourful, friendly, theatrical and incredibly good value: the average price given above

Settembrini. *See p209.*

is for a full spread with wine, but you can easily eat here for €15 a head. No bookings are taken – so come early or be prepared to queue.

Hasekura
Via dei Serpenti 27 (06 483 648). Bus 40Exp, 60Exp, 64, 70, 117, 170, H. **Meals served** noon-2.45pm, 7-10.20pm Mon-Sat. Closed Aug. **Average** €40. **Credit** AmEx, DC, MC, V. **Map** p360 B1 ⑦
The decor might not be old Kyoto, but the food at Hasekura is about the most authentically Japanese in Rome. Partners Ito Kimiji (kitchen) and Franca Palma (up front) serve beautifully presented dishes to tourists and curious Italians alike. The fixed-price set menus (from €32 in the evening, €16 at lunch) are good bets. The soba and tempura options are excellent, though for fish lovers the sushi and sashimi are hard to resist.

Wine bars & gastropubs

See also p226 Al Vino al Vino.

Cavour 313
Via Cavour 313 (06 678 5496). Metro Cavour/bus 75, 84, 117. **Meals served** *June, July, Sept* 12.30-2.30pm, 7.30pm-12.30am Mon-Sat. *Oct-May* 12.30-2.45pm, 7.30pm-12.30am Mon-Sat; 7.30pm-12.30am Sun. Closed Aug. **Average** €25. **Credit** AmEx, MC, V. **Map** p360 B2 ⑦
A friendly atmosphere (despite the gloomy dark-wood decor), a serious cellar and good snacks explain the eternal popularity of this wine bar near the Forum. Prices are reasonable, and there's a selection of hot and cold snacks; in winter, soups are a strong point. With over 500 bottles on the wine list, choosing one is the only problem.

Snacks & quick meals

Indian Fast Food
Via Mamiani 11 (06 446 0792). Metro Vittorio/bus 70, 71, 360, tram 5, 14. **Open** 11am-4pm, 5-10.30pm Mon-Sat; noon-4pm, 5-10.30pm Sun. **No credit cards. Map** p360 E1 ⑦
Rome's only Indian takeaway is just off piazza Vittorio. You can eat in too – at least as well as in the capital's more upmarket Indian restaurants – accompanied by gloriously kitsch Indian music videos. While munching on those vegetable samosas, you can even send a moneygram to Mumbai. Does life get any better?

Vatican & Prati

Restaurants

L'Arcangelo
Via GG Belli 59-61 (06 321 0992). Metro Lepanto/bus 23, 70, 87, 492. **Meals served** 1-2.30pm, 8-11.30pm Mon-Fri; 8-11pm Sat. Closed Aug. **Average** €50. **Credit** AmEx, DC, MC, V. **Map** p354 C3 ⑦

The mood is that of an elegant trattoria: wood panelling below tobacco-coloured walls, linen tablecloths, proper wine glasses and a soft jazz soundtrack. But it's what's on the plate and in the glass that really impresses at this laid-back gourmet magnet just north of piazza Cavour. A pastry-less tartlet of octopus and potato with olive oil is simple but delicious, and the fresh pasta *chitarrini* with marinated anchovies and fried artichokes a worthy follow-up. *Secondi*, like steamed *baccalà* with puréed broccoli and warm ricotta with cocoa beans, are clever variations on the Roman tradition, and taste a lot less pretentious than they read. Service is cordial, though Arcangelo and his wife Stefania can have the occasional vague-out when things get busy. There's a foie gras selection, and a six-course taster menu (€45). The wine list includes some real discoveries from small-scale Italian producers; ask for guidance.

Osteria dell'Angelo
Via G Bettolo 32 (06 372 9470). Metro Ottaviano/bus 23, 32, 70, 490, 913/tram 19. **Meals served** 8-11pm Mon, Sat; 12.30-2.30pm, 8-11pm Tue-Fri. Closed 2wks Aug. **Average** *Lunch* €20. **Set dinner** €25-€30. **No credit cards. Map** p354 A2 ⑦
Five minutes' walk north of the Vatican, Angelo Croce's neighbourhood trattoria is a real one-off, just like the man himself. The decor consists of photos, artworks and memorabilia that celebrate boxing and rugby – the two sporting passions of Angelo and his culinary helpmates, who have cauliflower ears but hearts of gold. The menu – which, in the evening, comes at a fixed price of €25 (or €30 for the luxe grilled-meat option), rough-and-ready house wine included – celebrates the Roman tradition in dishes like *tonnarelli cacio e pepe* (among the best in town) and meatballs flavoured with nutmeg, pine nuts and sultanas. Dessert consists of a glass of sweet wine and *ciambelline* (aniseed biscuits). Following recent building work, the Osteria dell' Angelo now has more table space and a brand-new open grill.

Settembrini
Via Luigi Settembrini 25 (06 323 2617). Metro Lepanto/bus 30Exp, 70, 280, 913. **Meals served** 12.30-4pm, 8-11.30pm Mon-Sat. Closed 2wks Aug. **Average** €35. **Credit** AmEx, MC, V. **Map** p354 C2 ⑧
One of the most interesting new kids on the Roman block, Settembrini mixes design and tradition, both in its warmly minimalist decor and in its menu. In chef Marco Poddi's approach to Italo-fusion, the flavours of his native Sardinia are prominent – as in the spaghetti with Cabras sea urchins – and all ingredients are sourced with an obsessive regard for quality. It's open all day from 11am on, segue-ing from *panini* to buffet lunch to afternoon tea to *aperitivi* (6-8pm) to the full-on dinner experience.

Velando
Borgo Vittorio 26 (06 6880 9955/www.ristorante velando.com). Bus 23, 34, 40Exp, 62, 64, 280. **Meals served** noon-3.30pm, 7-11pm Mon-Sat. Closed 1wk Aug. **Average** €45. **Credit** AmEx, DC, MC, V. **Map** p355 A4 ⑧

Al Ristoro degli Angeli – for clubbers and theatre-goers. *See p211.*

If you've never tried frog-and-vegetable strudel, or *pizzocheri* (buckwheat pasta strips), make up for those startling omissions at this pleasingly *moderne* cherrywood-and-cream restaurant located within strolling distance of the Vatican. The owners, and the cuisine, are from the Val Camonica area of northern Italy – famous for its rock-hewn inscriptions, which find their way into the design scheme. Like the Borgo quarter itself, Velando has more of a lunchtime buzz, and things can get pretty quiet on weekday evenings. But dishes like salmon and prawn terrine, or duck marinated in Moscato wine with prunes and chestnuts, are always adequate – and sometimes very good indeed. Be certain to leave room for one of the rich and creamy desserts, or an excellent fresh fruit platter with caramel sauce. The pricey wine list focuses on northern Italy, with several varieties available by the glass.

International

Zen
Via degli Scipioni 243 (06 321 3420/www.zen world.it). Metro Lepanto/bus 30Exp, 70, 280, 913. **Meals served** 1-3pm, 8-11.45pm Tue-Fri, Sun; 8-11.30pm Sat. Closed 3wks Aug. **Credit** AmEx, DC, MC, V. **Map** p354 B2/3 ㉜
This stylish Roman offshoot of a successful Milanese sushi bar was the first in the capital to have a *kalten* (conveyor belt) for sushi and sashimi. No need to book if you want to perch at the belt – just put your name down on the list at the door and wait for a seat – but you should reserve for the tables around the side and in the large back room, which is open in the evenings only. The more substantial (and expensive) meals served here might consist of seared tuna, or a wooden 'boat' of sashimi or sushi, or an excellent, light tempura. Depending on where you sit and how you consume, a meal here could set you back anything between €20 and €100.

Wine bars & gastropubs

Del Frate
Via degli Scipioni 118 (06 323 6437). Metro Ottaviano/bus 32, 70, 913/tram 19. **Meals served** 1-3pm, 6.30pm-12.30am Mon-Fri; 6.30pm-1.30am Sat, Sun. Closed 2wks Aug. **Average** €35. **Credit** AmEx, DC, MC, V. **Map** p354 A3 ㉝
This historic Prati bottle shop expanded into a wine-bar annexe a few years back, and has since built up a loyal local following. Of an evening, tables spill over into the *enoteca* itself, amid tall wooden shelves crammed with bottles. The menu offers a series of hot and cold dishes that can be combined in various ways. The oven-baked ravioli with salmon and courgette sauce is a good demonstration of the modern approach; *secondi* might include a

scallop of sea bass with pan-fried *cicoria*. The dessert selection features a knockout chocolate fondue. The only off-note is the steep markup on wines: often almost triple what the same bottle would cost to take away (especially painful if you happen to be staring at it on the shelf).

Snacks & quick meals

Paninoteca da Guido
Borgo Pio 13 (06 687 5491). Bus 23, 34, 40Exp, 62, 64, 280. **Open** 8am-6pm Mon-Sat. **No credit cards. Map** p355 B4 🄬
This hole-in-the-wall in pedestrianised Borgo Pio is one of the best places to grab a quick daytime snack in the Vatican area. Guido does filled rolls, made up while you wait from the selection of gourmet ingredients behind the counter: ham, mozzarella, olive paste, rocket. They also do a few pasta dishes at lunchtime. If large groups of crop-haired, unprepossessing young men have staked their claim to the few outside tables, they're probably Swiss Guards. (They don't look half as impressive out of uniform.)

Pizzarium
Via della Meloria 43 (06 3974 5416). Metro Cipro–Musei Vaticani/bus 51, 490, 492. **Open** 9am-10.30pm Mon-Sat. **No credit cards. Map** p165 A1 🄭
Feel a dough craving coming on after staring at all those muscular Sybils on the Sistine ceiling? Then head for this gourmet carry-out pizza joint, which stands in a rather downmarket residential street not far from the Vatican Museums. It's the fiefdom of Gabriele Bonci, a next-generation pizza baker who combines slow-rise dough made from special flours with fresh, seasonal toppings like wild asparagus, or pesto and aubergine.

The Appian Way

Restaurants

Cecilia Metella
Via Appia Antica 125-129 (06 513 6743). Bus 118, 660. **Meals served** 12.30-3.30pm, 7.30-10.30pm Tue-Sun. **Average** €35. **Credit** AmEx, MC, V.
Just across the street from the catacombs of San Sebastiano (*see p172*), this long-established Appia Antica restaurant is one of the few to combine an obvious tourist orientation with an equally obvious concern for quality. Perched on top of a low hill, with a vine-covered terrace for outdoor dining, Cecilia Metella is ideal for a lazy lunch after a visit to the catacombs or nearby Circus of Maxentius. Service is swift and professional, and the cuisine, though a little dated, is still reliable. Specialities include *scrigno alla Cecilia* (baked green pasta strips in cheese sauce) and *pollo al Nerone* (flambéed chicken). The *polenta ai porcini* (polenta with porcini mushrooms) is also extremely tasty.

The Suburbs

Restaurants

Al Ristoro degli Angeli
Via Luigi Orlando 2, South (06 5143 6020/www. ristorodegliangeli.it). Metro Garbatella/bus 673, 715, 716. **Meals served** 8-11.30pm Mon-Sat. Closed Aug and 1wk Sept. **Average** €35. **Credit** AmEx, DC, MC, V. **Map** p143 C3 🄰
The charming 1920s workers' suburb of Garbatella has started to take some of the spillover from the new nightlife axis along via Ostiense, and clubs and eateries are springing up like daisies. Situated right opposite the revamped Palladium theatre (*see p288*), this was one of the first of Garbatella's new restaurants, and it's still one of the best. The vibe and decor are old-style French bistro, but the food is resolutely Italian. The chef's creativity is based on combinations of ingredients and flavours that go back centuries: *passatina di ceci* (chickpea purée) with lightly fried calamari, or *straccetti di maiale* (sautéed pork strips) aromatised with thyme and lemon and coated with toasted almonds, plus a number of vegetarian dishes. Desserts (with an appropriate glass of sweet wine) are delicious, the wine list small but good. In summer you can eat outside under the arcade and watch the world go by. **Photo** *p210*.

Giuda Ballerino!
Via Marco Valerio Corvo 135, East (06 7158 4807/www.giudaballerino.it). Metro Giulio Agricola. **Meals served** 8-10pm Mon, Tue, Thur; 1-2pm, 8-10pm Fri-Sun. Closed Aug. **Average** €50. **Credit** AmEx, DC, MC, V.
The high-rise working-class Tuscolana area is not the kind of place you would expect to find a gourmet restaurant. Inside, it feels like a shed that has had a glamorous makeover: the walls are covered with drawings by Italian graphic artists, some of them signed. (The restaurant's name is the favourite exclamation of Italian comic-book hero Dylan Dog.) But you don't come for the cartoons; you come for dishes like an *antipasto* of seared tuna, served with hazel-nut and potato *quenelle* and a ginger *zabaione*; or rabbit parcels with *taggiasche* olives in a cinammon-flavoured leek sauce. All pretty extreme, but mostly successful, and great value compared with its *centro storico* counterparts. An excellent wine list, sublime desserts and delicious home-made bread (which, for once, comes free of charge) are three more reasons to make the trek out here – which is actually not that much of a trek, given the proximity of the metro.

L'Ortica
Via Flaminia Vecchia 573L, North (06 333 8709). Bus 32, 224. **Meals served** 8pm-midnight Mon-Sat; 12.30-2.30pm Sun. **Average** €50. **Credit** AmEx, DC, MC, V.
If there were a prize for the oddest Roman gourmet restaurant location, L'Ortica would win it. To get there, head north across the unrepentantly Fascist

Eat, Drink, Shop

Ponte Flaminio into busy corso Francia, and locate the Standa supermarket on your right. On the terrace above it – next door to a billiard parlour – stands Vittorio Virno's oasis of culinary excellence. The accent is Neapolitan – militantly so, with all the ingredients brought in fresh from trusted southern suppliers and put to excellent use in dishes such as the *sfizi di Napoli* starter – a platter of gourmet nibbles, from anchovy and mozzarella parcels to a melt-in-the-mouth ricotta. Continue with *linguine scamarro*, with olives, capers and sun-dried tomatoes, or the squid stuffed with endive, sultanas and pine nuts; and don't miss the *misticanza* salad of wild herbs, which the host gathers himself. Virno is a discerning kleptomaniac, and his collection of copper pans, irons, wicker baskets and other domestic antiques adorns a series of elegant, spacious rooms. Outside, the verdant terrace is screened from the surrounding suburban chaos for alfresco dining when the weather warms up.

Osteria del Velodromo Vecchio

Via Genzano 139, East (06 788 6793). Metro Colli Albani/bus 85, 87, 671. **Meals served** 12.30-3pm Mon-Wed; 12.30-3pm, 8-11pm Thur-Sat. Closed Aug. **Average** €30. **Credit** DC, MC, V.
A friendly, good-value osteria in the southern suburbs near a former cycling stadium – hence the name. Inside is one small room with eight tables; in summer a few more are arranged outside on a sheltered patio. The cooking is solidly Roman, but alongside old favourites like *pasta e fagioli* or *rigatoni con la pajata*, there are a few more creative dishes, like *fettucine tonno e zucchine* (with tuna and courgettes). One or two dishes – like the *tortino di aliciotti e indivia* (anchovy and endive pie) – reflect the Jewish contribution to the local tradition. Desserts consist of home-made *crostate* (pastry tarts), or aniseed biscuits with a glass of sweet wine. The wine list is small but surprisingly adventurous.

La Pergola

Via Cadlolo 101, North (06 3509 2154/www. cavalieri-hilton.it). Bus 907, 913, 991, 999. **Meals served** 7.30-11pm Tue-Sat. Closed 3wks Jan & 2wks Aug. **Average** €140. **Credit** AmEx, DC, MC, V.
Heinz Beck is, without a doubt, the most talented chef in Rome right now. But it's not just his technical dexterity and unerring instinct for taste and texture combinations that impress. It's also the fact that, in over ten years, the German chef has not missed a single sitting at the rooftop restaurant of the Cavalieri Hilton hotel, which was finally awarded its third Michelin star in 2006. Once known as 'the chef who doesn't do pasta', Beck is letting Italy get to him: half of the *primi* are now pasta dishes – including, if you dine here in late spring, some melt-in-the-mouth *tortellini di ricotta e pecorino con fave* (pasta parcels filled with ricotta and pecorino cheese, served with shelled broad beans). On our last visit, we were also wowed by a heavenly dish of courgette flowers, fried in a light batter, served with assorted saffron-flavoured crustaceans. Alongside the main

menu and the dessert menu, there is also a water list, a tea list, and a wine list in two volumes – one Italian, the other international. Markups on wine are very steep. But €300 for two with a good bottle of wine still compares favourably with restaurants at the top of the gourmet ladder in London or Paris – and they don't have an almost aerial view of Rome.

Zampagna

Via Ostiense 179, South (06 574 2306). Metro San Paolo/bus 23. **Meals served** 12.30-2.30pm Mon-Sat. Closed Aug. **Average** €20. **No credit cards. Map** p143 B3/4 ➐
There are two reasons for making a pilgrimage to the nether reaches of via Ostiense: one is to see St Paul's Basilica (*see p177*) and the other is to lunch at the Trattoria Zampagna. Maria Zampagna and family offer basic Roman cooking as it once was, with filling dishes for the confirmed carnivore. *Primi* include *spaghetti alla carbonara* or *tagliatelle alla gricia* (with bacon and pecorino cheese), while most of the second courses – whether *bollito alla picchiapò* (boiled beef with onions), *involtini* (rolls of meat stuffed with carrot and celery) or the inevitable, ultra-classic *trippa* (tripe) – are served swimming in the thick house *sugo* (tomato sauce). The *broccoli ubriachi* (literally 'drunken broccoli'), tossed in wine with a sprinkle of chilli, makes for an excellent side dish. Service is brisk but cheery.

L'Ortica. *See p211.*

Eat, Drink, Shop

Pizzerias

La Gatta Mangiona

Via Ozanam 30, West (06 534 6702). Bus 44, H/ tram 8. **Meals served** 7.45-11.30pm daily. Closed 2wks Aug. **Average** €20. **Credit** MC, V.

Rome's best pizzeria? We certainly think so. The 'greedy she-cat' steers a middle course between puffy-rimmed Neapolitan and flat and crunchy Roman, using a special semi-wholemeal dough that spends 48 hours in the fridge, ensuring a slow and healthy rise. Small but filling, the pizzas are a tad more gourmet than the Roman average – courgette, anchovy, *pachino* tomato and *mozzarella di bufala* is a typical example. They also do reasonable pasta dishes and salads, and some simple but effective home-made desserts (including a moreish coffee mousse); but these are very much satellites of the pizza planet. The ambience is bright, chatty and neo-rustic, with plenty of cat-themed mementos and artwork. On Wednesdays and Thursdays there are wine and pizza tastings for groups of at least four. In the backwoods of Monteverde, this pizza mecca is a little out of the way – but worth the journey; it is easily reached by taking the No.8 tram from largo Argentina (get off at piazza San Giovanni di Dio). But book ahead: it's hugely popular.

Wine bars & gastropubs

Tramonti & Muffati

Via Santa Maria Ausiliatrice 105, South (06 780 1342). Metro Colli Albani/bus 16, 85. **Open** *Wine bar & deli* 4.30-8pm Mon-Sat. Closed Aug. **Meals served** 8-11pm Mon-Sat. Closed Aug. **Average** €25. **Credit** DC, MC, V.

This tiny wine bar and delicatessen just off via Appia Nuova has built up a solid reputation. Behind the small shopfront are a grand total of five rustic tables (they can't seat more than five on any one table) for evening dining: needless to say, you should book well ahead. The secret of Marco Berardi's success is an obsessive hunt for the very best Italian wines, bakery goodies and farm products. These delicacies (most of which can also be bought here to take away) are supplemented by a few hot dishes such as *testaroli della Lunigiana* (spongy pasta squares) with pesto sauce and *pinoli* (pine nuts), or a cheese fondue flavoured with truffle shavings. But wine is the real point of the exercise – to the extent that the items on the menu are organised not by courses, but on the basis of what type of wine they best suit. The well-priced list features a number of small but interesting regional producers; if in doubt, ask signor Berardi for his oenological advice.

THE NEW SHAKI STORE AND SHAKI WINE BAR

SHAKI STORE, a friendly and intriguing two-floor boutique can be found at 65, Piazza di Spagna, and is a veritable Aladdin's cave for anyone looking to give a tasteful personal touch to their home furnishings: from porcelain ware of every type and artistic ceramics, to scented candles and glasses decorated with the most exclusive materials.

But that's not all? Discover the world of our all-Italian organic delicatessen: offering a thousand types of pasta, oils, relishes, jams, honeys, in a range of exciting flavours.

And since 2001, the SHAKI brand is also a WINE BAR, located in 29, via Mario de Fiori, near Piazza di Spagna.

Here until the early hours you can enjoy the best wines the regions of Italy have to offer, along with a carefully selected list of foreign labels, accompanied by traditional sliced meats and cheeses, or imaginative salads dressed with excellent oil and balsamic vinegar, named after the most famous streets and piazzas of the historic city centre: Condotti, Margutta, Spagna.

All this, in a modern, original setting.

SHAKI WINE BAR
VIA MARIO DE FIORI 29 - 00187 ROMA
TEL 066791694 - FAX 066797167
VIA DEL GOVERNO VECCHIO, 123 - 00186 ROMA
TEL. 0668308796

SHAKI Shop
PIAZZA DI SPAGNA 65 - 00187 ROMA
TEL/FAX 06.066786605

www.shakiroma.com

Cafés, Bars & *Gelaterie*

From morning till late at night, sit back and enjoy the *dolce vita*.

If you want to really make a Roman mad, walk straight off the plane and demand 'a latte, *por favor*.' And a panini.' *Latte* means milk, and it means cold milk in a Roman bar; *panini* are plural, so how many do you want? The subtext to his indignation is that if you're a habitual orderer and consumer of filthy industrial lattes and iced blended coffees at home, then it's hardly worth serving you on holiday with what is undoubtedly the finest hot beverage in the world. In Italy, you'll find, coffee is an extremely serious matter.

Everyone's day starts with a coffee in their local café or bar (in Italy these amount to the same thing since alcohol and coffee are served all day long in both); there's every chance that it will end there too. There'll invariably be a newspaper you can read on the counter, a public phone, snacks, maybe cigarettes and bus tickets, a clean loo, the hottest gossip and fabulous coffee: it is the heart of the *quartiere* and a backdrop to your social life. (If you do

Enjoying an ice-cream *al fresco*.

become addicted to the café lifestyle, you can try taking it home with you: *see p235* **All that java jazz**.)

Once you are on the tourist track in the *centro storico*, things change slightly. For example, you should think twice before sitting down. Standing at the counter like the locals to knock back your tiny cup of miraculously cheap black nectar, is one thing. But take the weight off your feet at a table or, worse, at a pavement table, and watch the bill double or even treble. Of course, there are moments when nothing in the whole world is more beguiling than sitting in a piazza with your *aperitivo*, or a *digestivo*, drinking in the afternoon sunshine and incomparable vista, and you are quite prepared to pay extra for the pleasure; just be aware that you're paying for the luxury.

Besides coffee, which comes in many different forms (*see p220* **Caffè culture**), most bars have *cornetti* (croissants), which vary widely in quality, *tramezzini* (sandwiches; good when fresh, but usually to be avoided by the afternoon), *pizza romana* (a slab of pizza base brushed with olive oil, sliced through the middle and filled) and *panini* (filled rolls, plural; one is a *panino*). All can be toasted (ask, *me lo può scaldare, per favore*?).

To accompany your snack, bars generally offer *spremute* (freshly squeezed juices) and some have *frullati* (fruit shakes) and *centrifughe* (juiced fruit) too. All offer a range of sodas, juices and mineral waters. Tap water (*acqua semplice, acqua dal rubinetto*) is free; a small bottle of still or sparkling mineral water (*acqua minerale naturale* or *gassata*) costs around one euro. Wine, beer and some liqueurs are also generally on offer. *Digestivi* like *amari* (bitters, infused aromatic liqueurs) and *limoncello* (lemon liqueur) will help you digest your meal; they should be sipped, rather than downed like shots. (*See also p219* **What the locals drink**.)

By law, all bars must have a *bagno* (lavatory), which can be used by anyone, whether or not they buy anything in the bar.

---

❶ Pink numbers given in this chapter correspond to the location of each café and bar as marked on the street maps. See pp354-361.

The *bagno* may be locked; ask the cashier for the key (*la chiave per il bagno*). Bars must also provide dehydrated passers-by with a glass of tap water, again with no obligation to buy. Smoking in all bars, cafés and restaurants is strictly forbidden.

PUBS AND ENOTECHE

Rome's *enoteche* and *vini e olii* (bottle shops) have historically been meeting places for residents of the neighbourhood. Many of these places have recently become, at the very least, charming places to grab a drink and a slice of the *vita romana*. At best, they are chic wine bars or bars with a *dopo cena* (after-dinner) scene, offering a wide variety of drinks – from a glass of Falanghina or Chianti to Caipirinhas, Caipiroskas and Mojitos – and a beautiful crowd for people-watching. Some *enoteche* have developed into fully fledged eateries: for these, *see pp182-213* **Eating Out**. The ones we list below have remained predominantly watering holes. Rome's pubs are divided between a handful of long-standing UK-style institutions and a host of newer casual joints. The best pubs of both categories have been listed in this chapter.

PASTICCERIE AND GELATERIE

Every *zona* of Rome has its *pasticcerie* (cake shops); most of these are bars where freshly baked goodies can be consumed *in situ* with a coffee or some other drink. The range of items on offer rarely varies: choux pastry *bignè* with creamy fillings, *semifreddi* ice-cream cakes, fruit tarts and a large assortment of biscuits. There can be huge variations, however, in the quality and freshness of the goods: the *pasticcerie* listed below are always reliable.

For a change from the usual offerings, try feast-day seasonal delicacies. *Panettoni* – sponge cakes with raisins and candied fruit – are ubiquitous around Christmas. The Easter variation is vaguely bird-shaped and called a *colomba* (dove). Around the feast of San Giuseppe (19 March), *pasticcerie* make fried batter-balls filled with custard. During *carnevale* (the run-up to Lent) you'll find compact balls of fried dough called *castagnole* and crispy fried pastry strips dusted with icing sugar called *frappe*.

Many *gelaterie* (ice-cream bars) in Rome boast a well-stocked freezer cabinet with a sign promising *produzione artigianale* (home-made).

Eat, Drink, Shop

The best Places…

For breakfast
Bernasconi, *p224*; I Dolci di Checco er Carrettiere, *p225*; Pan di Zucchero, *p217*.

For a serious caffeine fix
La Caffettiera, *p223*; Sant' Eustachio, *p221*; Tazza d'Oro, *p221*.

For working on your tan
Canova (afternoon), *p218*; Gran Caffè Esperia (morning), *p228*; Rosati (morning), *p218*.

For a yummy lunch
Café Café, *p226*; Café Notegen, *p218*; Cinecaffè–Casina delle Rose, *p217*.

For a spot of culture
Antico Caffè Greco, *p218*; Caffè Canova-Tadolini, *p218*.

For the view
Ciampini al Café du Jardin, *p218*; La Vineria, *p214*; I Tre Scalini, *p221*.

For calorific afternoon teas
Dagnino, *p227*; Dolci e Doni, *p218*; Palombini, *p228*.

For political discussions
Da Vezio, *p221*.

For an *aperitivo*
Friends Art Café, *p225*; Enoteca Nuvolari, *p228*.

For the *aperitivo* buffet
Freni e Frizioni, *p225*; Gloss, *p223*; Lot 87, *p223*; Société Lutèce, *p221*.

For rubbing shoulders with VIPs
Bar della Pace, *p220*; Stravinskij Bar, *p220*.

For serious wine buffs
Al Vino al Vino, *p226*; Antica Enoteca di Via della Croce, *p220*; Enoteca Trastevere, *p225*; Il Goccetto, *p223*.

For after-dark eats & drinks
Crudo, *p223*.

For a beer
Artù, *p225*; The Druid's Den, *p226*; The Fiddler's Elbow, *p226*; L'Oasi della Birra, *p226*; The Proud Lion, *p228*; Trinity College, *p223*.

For insomniacs
Bar del Mattatoio, *p226*.

This is often a con: it may mean industrial ice-cream mix whipped up on the premises. While this doesn't necessarily mean the ice-cream will be bad – indeed, in some cases this not-so-genuine article can be very good – you'll need to be selective when seeking a truly unique *gelato* experience. Look at the fruit *gelati*: if the colours seem too bright to be real, they probably aren't. Banana should be cream-coloured with a tinge of grey, not electric yellow… you get the picture.

Ice-cream is served in a *cono* (cone) or *coppetta* (tub) of varying sizes, usually costing from €2 to €4. As well as the two main categories, *frutta* or *crema* (fruit- or cream-based ice-cream), there's also *sorbetto* or the rougher *granita* (water ices).

When you've exhausted the *gelato,* you should sample a *grattachecca*. It's the Roman version of water ice, and consists of grated ice with flavoured syrup poured over it. The city was once full of kiosks selling this treat, but now only a handful remains. They are almost always on street corners, and close in winter; in summer opening hours are erratic.

Trevi & Quirinale

Cafés & bars

News Café
Via della Stamperia 72 (06 6992 3473). Metro Barberini/bus 52, 53, 61, 62, 63, 71, 80Exp, 95, 116, 119, 175, 492, 630. **Open** *Apr-Sept* 8am-2am daily. *Oct-Mar* 8am-1am daily. Closed 1wk Aug. **Credit** AmEx, DC, MC, V. **Map** p357 A5 **1**
This is an attempt at a New York-style bar, with steel and wood decor. It pays lip service to the 'news' theme with racks of papers and a non-stop satellite news screen. But behind the façade it's a regular Roman bar with better than average lunch options (salads, soups, pastas, filled rolls) and cakes, including muffins and brownies. The seating is cramped – unless you are lucky enough to secure one of the few outside tables – and the service can sometimes be a little offhand. Be sure to check out the loo… amazing.

Pan di Zucchero
Via del Lavatore 29 (06 679 3214). Bus 52, 53, 61, 62, 63, 71, 80Exp, 95, 116, 119, 175, 492, 630. **Open** *Apr-July, Sept* 7am-8.30pm daily. *Oct-Mar* 7am-9pm Mon-Sat. Closed Aug. **No credit cards**. **Map** p357 A5 **2**
This tiny bar/*pasticceria* is a genuine, old-school bar that caters to real Italians in a heavily touristed area by the Trevi Fountain. It offers a basic selection of Italian favourites to workers from shops, offices and ministry outposts nearby. The *bombe calde* (warm doughnut-like pastries) are legendary.

Pasticcerie & gelaterie

Il Gelato di San Crispino
Via della Panetteria 42 (06 679 3924/www.ilgelato disancrispino.com). Bus 52, 53, 61, 62, 63, 71, 80Exp, 95, 116, 119, 175, 490, 630. **Open** 11am-12.30am Mon, Wed-Sun. Closed mid Jan-mid Feb. **No credit cards**. **Map** p357 A5 **3**
Il Gelato di San Crispino serves what many consider to be the best ice-cream in Rome – some say in the world. The secret is the makers' obsessive control over the whole process. The flavours on offer change according to what's in season – in summer the *lampone* (raspberry) and *susine* (yellow plum) are fabulous. Cones would interfere with the purity of the product: only tubs are allowed. The original branch is out in the sticks; the central branch has the advantage – over and above its location – of offering exquisite Jamaican coffee. On Fridays and Saturdays in summer San Crispino remains open until 1.30am.
Other locations: via Acaia 56, Suburbs: south (06 7045 0412); via Bevagna 90, Suburbs: north (06 3322 1075).

Veneto & Borghese

Cafés & bars
See also p52 **Eden**.

Café de Paris
Via Veneto 90 (06 4201 2257). Bus 52, 53, 63, 80Exp, 95, 116, 119, 630. **Open** 8am-1am Mon-Thur, Sun; 8am-2am Fri, Sat. **Credit** AmEx, DC, MC, V. **Map** p357 B4 **4**
When via Veneto was in the midst of its famed *dolce vita* heyday, Café de Paris was the epicentre of laid-back cool. Here you could be served in your jeans – which was quite something in those days – and eavesdrop on the *paparazzi* as they badmouthed their prey. But times, unfortunately, have changed: the via Veneto is strictly for tourists and this is just another rather bland café. Nonetheless, there's an English tea hour for the homesick, and in the evenings you can sup at the wine bar in the refurbished interior.

Cinecaffè–Casina delle Rose
Largo Marcello Mastroianni 1 (06 4201 6224/ www.cinecaffe.it). Bus 88, 95, 116, 490, 491, 495, C3, M. **Open** 10am-7pm Mon, Sun; 10am-midnight Tue-Sat. **Credit** AmEx, DC, MC, V. **Map** p356 B3 **5**
Via Veneto is a desert if you're looking for a coffee or maybe a light lunch that won't break the bank. Strike off instead through the arches of the Roman Porta Pinciana, into the Borghese gardens, to the ultra-civilised new Casa del Cinema (*see p264*) in the Casina delle Rose. Here, delicious alfresco lunches and weekend brunches, as well as coffee, snacks and drinks, are served to cineastes, enthusiasts and tourists.

The Tridente

Cafés & bars

Antico Caffè Greco
*Via Condotti 86 (06 679 1700). Metro Spagna/bus
52, 53, 61, 71, 80Exp, 85, 95, 116, 119, 160, 850.*
Open 10.30am-7pm Mon, Sun; 9am-7.30pm Tue-Sat.
Closed 2wks Aug. **Credit** AmEx, DC, MC, V.
Map p355 E4 & p357 A4 ⑥
Founded in 1760, this venerable café was once the
hangout of Casanova, Goethe, Wagner, Stendhal,
Baudelaire, Shelley and Byron. Opposition to the
French Occupation of 1849-70 was planned here.
Today it has its sofas packed with tourists, while
locals cram the foyer. Literary and musical evenings
with a light dinner hark back to its artistic past.

Café Notegen
*Via del Babuino 159 (06 320 0855/www.notegen
cafe.it). Metro Spagna/bus 117, 119.* **Open** 7.30am-
midnight Mon-Sat; 10.30am-7pm Sun. Closed 1wk
Aug. **Credit** DC, MC, V. **Map** p354 E3 ⑦
This century-old gathering spot for theatre people,
artists and intellectuals is under charming new
management. It has received a lick of paint and
general sprucing up without, thankfully, falling prey
to the mega-makeover (with accompanying price
hikes) fever sweeping the Tridente. On the ground
floor, hot and cold dishes and great cakes are served
to sophisticated customers seated in elegant booths.
Downstairs, former manager Signora Teresa is still
organising irregular performances of live cabaret
and music, and the odd play.

Caffè Canova-Tadolini
*Via del Babuino 150A (06 3211 0702). Metro
Spagna/bus 117, 119.* **Credit** AmEx, DC, MC, V. **Map** p354 E3 ⑧
Sculptor Antonio Canova signed a contract in 1818
to ensure that this property, in the heart of the old
artists' quarter, would remain an atelier for sculpture. The master's wishes were respected until 1967:
the workshop passed through many generations of
the Tadolini family, descendants of Canova's
favourite pupil and heir, Adamo Tadolini. Now refurbished as a museum-atelier, Canova's workshop has
café tables among its sculpture models and a refined
and elegant old-world feel: dark hardwood floors,
wood-beamed ceilings, chandeliers and mustard-
yellow leather banquettes. Lunch is served, and
the small bar offers cocktails and assorted drinks,
as well as tasty titbits, from canapés to cookies and
pastries. *See also p111* **Extra time**.

Canova
*Piazza del Popolo 16 (06 361 2231). Metro Flaminio/
bus 95, 117, 119, 491.* **Open** 7.30am-midnight Mon-
Fri; 8am-midnight Sat, Sun. **Credit** AmEx, DC, MC,
V. **Map** p354 D/E3 ⑨
Traditionally, Canova's clientele was right-wing and
at daggers drawn with the left-wing rabble at Rosati
(*see below*) across the square, though there has been

little evidence of this recently. The place was undergoing a massive refit as this guide went to press, so
it remains to be seen whether it can redeem itself
after its most recent, characterless manifestation.
That said, outside tables catch the late afternoon
sun, and light lunches served in the garden out back
are good and not too expensive – unlike the *menu
turistico* fare served on the square.

Ciampini al Café du Jardin
*Viale Trinità dei Monti (06 678 5678). Metro
Spagna/bus 52, 53, 61, 71, 80Exp, 85, 95, 116,
119, 160, 850.* **Open** *Apr-mid May, mid Sept-mid
Oct* 8am-8pm daily. *Mid May-mid Sept* 8am-1am
Mon, Tue, Thur-Sun. Closed mid Oct-Mar. **Credit**
AmEx, DC, MC, V. **Map** p357 A4 ⑩
This open-air café near the top of the Spanish
Steps is an oasis surrounded by creeper-curtained
trellises, with a pond in the centre. There's a selec-
tion of sandwiches, salads, pastas, cocktails and ices,
and it also serves a good breakfast. The view is
stunning, especially at sunset, so whet your appetite
by sipping an *aperitivo* in style.

Dolci e Doni
*Via delle Carrozze 85B (06 6992 5001). Metro
Spagna/bus 52, 53, 61, 71, 80Exp, 85, 95, 116,
119, 160, 850.* **Open** *May-Sept* 11am-11pm daily.
Oct-Apr 11am-9pm daily. **Credit** AmEx, DC, MC, V.
Map p355 E4 ⑪
This bijou tearoom, renowned for its cakes and
chocolates, also specialises in breakfasts, brunches
and quick quiche-and-salad lunches. There are cakes
to take away, and catering can be arranged.

GiNa
*Via San Sebastianello 7A (06 678 0251/www.gina
roma.com). Metro Spagna/bus 52, 53, 61, 71, 80Exp,
85, 95, 116, 119, 160, 850.* **Open** 11am-5pm Mon;
11am-11pm Tue-Sat; 11am-8pm Sun. Closed 2wks Aug.
Credit AmEx, MC, V. **Map** p354 E3 & p357 A4 ⑫
This modern *locale* is a relief from the area's posh
tearooms and over-decorated cafés. The decor is
clean and ultra-white, with delicate touches like
votive candles and single pink roses in miniature
jars. It's an all-day kind of place – from late breakfast to light lunch, from evening *aperitivi* to snacky
dinner. The menu is divided into sections ('Be
Warm' – soups, melted brie; 'Be Light' – salads; 'Be
Classic' – Italian staples): then there's a selection of
great ice-cream and peculiarities such as chocolate
fondue. Prices are on the high side – count on around
€20 a head for a very light lunch – but you're
paying for the prime location. They also do a
special summer picnic-hamper service for those who
like the idea of a *déjeuner sur l'herbe* in nearby Villa
Borghese (you drop the basket back later).

Rosati
*Piazza del Popolo 5 (06 322 5859). Metro Flaminio/
bus 95, 117, 119, 491.* **Open** 7am-11pm daily.
Credit AmEx, DC, MC, V. **Map** p354 D3 ⑬
Rosati is the traditional haunt of Rome's intellectual
left: Calvino, Moravia and Pasolini were regulars.

What the locals drink

We call it Frascati, locals call it *Castelli*, but nearly all of the house white served up in traditional Roman *trattorie*, *enoteche* and bars comes from the same place: the Alban hills, aka i Castelli romani. They're the fertile, villa-sprinkled volcanic hills that you see from the plane window as you land just south of Rome at Ciampino airport.

In classical times the area was dotted with the estates of the super rich: Emperor Caligula kept vast barges for orgiastic moonlit parties on tiny, mirror-like Lake Nemi, which nestles in an extinct crater; Augustus grew up at Velletri; Domitian had a holiday villa at Albano. In the Middle Ages feudal types imposed their will from a string of hill-top castles, while the popes spent their summers (and still do) at the airy papal residence at Castelgandolfo. Now, however, the Castelli romani are within commuting distance of the city, and Rome sprawls out to meet them.

These rolling hills have long provided the straw-coloured plonk that is the default option of any wine-fuelled meal in Rome's *centro storico*. Until World War II the plonk was transported to Rome on horse-drawn wagons, precursors of the elderly barrel-loaded trucks double-parked outside the city's pizzerias today. Visitors and ex-pats, who tend to consume vast quantities of *Castelli*, console themselves by arguing that it's not very strong – and, at around 11.5% alcohol content, it isn't (compared with an Amarone or many French *blancs*). And of course, on a

hot day, it's delicious, the nectar of the gods – an opinion that owes nothing, naturally, to the fact that a jug of the stuff costs less than fancy mineral water in some *trattorie*.

But much of it has long been mediocre (or worse). However, for some years now a number of local growers (Paola di Mauro at Colle Picchioni, Piero Costantino at Villa Simone, Fabrizio Santarelli at Castel de Paolis) have been battling to raise standards, producing some startlingly superior DOC or 'super table' wines like Castel de Paolis' Vigna Adriana, a malvasia-viognier-sauvignon blend. A small quantity of red wine from cabernet/merlot blends is also gaining favour with connoisseurs.

At the centre of the Castelli romani area is the town of Frascati (*see p315*), which, in 1450, had more bottle shops than inhabitants. Romans still like to head for the hills in September when the new *vendemmia* is ready: at the annual fair in nearby Marino the town fountains literally flow with wine, balconies are decked with vine leaves, and drunken competitive games involving barrels are played up and down hillier streets.

But you don't really have to leave the city to savour the new breed of *Castelli* wines. Rome's growing number of *enoteche* are the place to start researching the best of Lazio's labels. Palatium (*see p191*) should be your first port of call: sponsored by the regional government, this place is dedicated to the wines and produce of Lazio. If you can't find it here, chances are it doesn't exist.

Caffè culture

Whether neighbourhood bar or smart café, the etiquette is the same: non-regulars are expected to pay at the *cassa* (cash desk) before consuming. Identify what you want, then pay. When you order at the bar, placing a 10¢ or 20¢ coin on your *scontrino* (receipt) will grab the bartender's attention. If you sit down, you will be served by a waiter and charged at least double for the privilege.

To get a short, thick espresso, ask for *un caffè*. A cappuccino is an espresso with steamed, frothy milk added. It is rarely consumed after 11am; Romans wouldn't be caught dead drinking it after a meal.

Variations on the espresso

caffè americano very diluted in a large cup.

caffè corretto with a dash of either liqueur or spirits (indicate which).

caffè freddo iced espresso; comes sugared unless you ask for *caffè freddo amaro*, which, however, is not always available.

caffè Hag espresso decaf.

caffè lungo a bit more water than usual.

caffè macchiato with a dash of milk.

caffè monichella with whipped cream.

caffè ristretto coffee essence lining the bottom of the cup – a tooth-enamel remover.

caffè al vetro in a glass.

Variations on the cappuccino

caffè latte more hot milk and less coffee.

cappuccino freddo iced coffee with cold milk; will come sugared unless you specifically ask for *cappuccino freddo amaro*.

cappuccino senza schiuma without froth.

latte macchiato hot milk with just a dash of coffee for flavour.

The art nouveau interior has remained unchanged since its opening in 1922, though the packed furniture and sea of lunch menus outside rather spoils the overall effect. Try the *Sogni romani* cocktail: orange juice with four kinds of liqueur in red and yellow – the colours of the city (and the Roma football team).

Shaki

Via Mario de' Fiori 29A (06 679 1694). Metro Spagna/bus 52, 53, 61, 71, 80Exp, 85, 95, 116, 119, 160, 850. **Open** 10.30am-1am daily. **Credit** AmEx, DC, MC, V. **Map** p354 E3 & p357 A4 ⑭

Deep in designer territory, this wine bar shook up the local scene when it opened, with its cool, modern, Japanese-influenced design. A few years on it's all looking rather tired and in need of a makeover, but its outside tables – with heaters through the winter – are still a lovely place to sit and watch the expensively dressed world go by… though the price tag of €9 for even the most ordinary glass of red is high. There's a selection of *panini* and salads made with fresh ingredients.

Stravinskij Bar

Via del Babuino 9 (06 328 881/www.hotelderussie.it). Metro Spagna or Flaminia/bus 117, 119. **Open** 9am-1am daily. **Credit** AmEx, DC, MC, V. **Map** p354 E3 ⑮

Located in Sir Rocco Forte's swanky Hotel de Russie (*see p55*), the bar is divided into three sections: the small bar, a larger lounge area with sofas, and the outdoor patio. The first two are filled in cooler months with international business people, the hotel's celebrity guests and a gaggle of deep-pocketed regulars. But the real draw here is the fabulous patio, a sunken area of shady tables surrounded by orange trees. The drinks menu is interesting, the cocktails well executed – although on the patio beneath the Roman sun, the beverage the courteous staff serves most of is simply the finest spumante.

Pubs & *enoteche*

See also *p191* Buccone.

Antica Enoteca di Via della Croce

Via della Croce 76B (06 679 0896). Metro Spagna/bus 52, 53, 61, 71, 80Exp, 85, 95, 116, 119, 160, 628, 850. **Open** 11am-midnight daily. **Credit** AmEx, DC, MC, V. **Map** p354 E3 ⑯

When this place opened in 1842 it was the favourite haunt of the Scandinavian painters who lived on nearby via Margutta. A tasteful revamp has retained most of the original fittings, including the marble wine vats and a venerable wooden cash desk, making it a great place to sip one of many wines offered by the glass. There's a cold *antipasto* buffet at the bar, and a restaurant with tables in the long back room offering a full range of hot dishes at meal-times. It also operates as an off-licence.

Pantheon & Navona

Cafés & bars

Bar della Pace

Via della Pace 3-7 (06 686 1216). Bus 30Exp, 40Exp, 46, 62, 64, 70, 81, 87, 116, 492, 628. **Open** 4pm-3am Mon; 8.30am-3am Tue-Sun. **Credit** AmEx, MC, V. **Map** p355 C5 ⑰

Rome's Antico Caffè della Pace (which is known to all and sundry as Bar della Pace) is eternally *à la mode*. In cooler months the antiques and flower-filled rooms emit a sense of warmth, and the proximity of the tables allows for cosying up to your neighbours. Outdoors, it continues to be a great, albeit pricey, place from which to survey passers-by. Of a summer evening pick a pavement table beneath this establishment's trademark façade clad in swaying ivy and watch the action on the street.

Da Vezio

Via Tor di Nona 37 (06 683 2951). Bus 30Exp, 40Exp, 46, 62, 63, 64, 70, 81, 87, 492, 628. **Open** 7am-8pm Mon-Sat. Closed 3wks Aug. **No credit cards. Map** p355 C5 ⑱

For decades Vezio Bagazzini was a legendary figure in the Ghetto area, on account of his bar behind the former Communist Party HQ. Every square centimetre was filled with Communist icons and trophies – not just Italian, but Soviet and Cuban too. Every Italian leftist leader worth his or her salt visited at some point for a photo with Vezio. Vezio has now moved into new premises in picturesque, arty via Tor di Nona with all his Marxist-Leninist souvenirs and photos. A time warp with great coffee, but probably best not to ask for a Coke…

Salotto 42

Piazza di Pietra 42 (06 678 5804/www.salotto42.it). Bus 62, 63, 81, 95, 117, 119, 160, 492, 628, 630. **Open** 10am-2am Tue-Sat; 10am-midnight Sun. **Credit** AmEx, DC, MC, V. **Map** p355 E5 ⑲

This newish spot on lovely piazza di Pietra is open morning till late. The bar's Roman/Swedish/New York pedigree is seen in little touches throughout. Incredibly comfortable chairs and sofas provide a cosy feel during the day, when a smörgåsbord of ibbles is available. By night, the sleek room becomes a gorgeous cocktail bar with a great (if sometimes over-loud) soundtrack, excellent mixed drinks and local sophisticates. All this plus a vast and cosmopolitan selection of books on fashion, art and design. The loo's worth checking out too.

Sant'Eustachio

Piazza Sant'Eustachio 82 (06 6880 2048/www. santeustachioilcaffe.it). Bus 30Exp, 40Exp, 46, 62, 63, 64, 70, 81, 87, 492, 628, 630, 780, H. **Open** 8.30am-1am Mon-Thur, Sun; 8.30am-1.20am Fri, Sat. **No credit cards. Map** p355 D5 & p358 D1 ⑳

This is one of the city's most famous coffee bars, and its walls are plastered with celebrity testimonials. The coffee is quite extraordinary, if pricier than elsewhere; the barmen turn their backs while whipping up a cup so as not to let their secret out (though a pinch of bi-carb soda is rumoured to give it its froth). Try the *gran caffè*: the *schiuma* (froth) can be slurped off afterwards with spoon or fingers. Unless you specify (*amaro* means 'no sugar'; *poco zucchero* means 'a little sugar'), it comes very sweet.

Tazza d'Oro

Via degli Orfani 84 (06 678 9792/www.tazzadoro coffeeshop.com). Bus 30Exp, 40Exp, 46, 62, 63, 64, 70, 81, 87, 492, 628, 630. **Open** 7am-8pm Mon-Sat. Closed 1wk Aug. **Credit** AmEx, DC, MC, V. **Map** p355 E5 ㉑

The powerful aroma wafting from this ancient *torrefazione* (coffee-roaster's) overlooking the Pantheon is a siren call to coffee lovers. It's packed with coffee sacks, tourists and regulars, who flock for *granita di caffè* (coffee sorbet) in summer, and *cioccolata calda con panna* (hot chocolate with whipped cream) in winter. The chocolate-covered coffee beans are a great take-home present.

I Tre Scalini

Piazza Navona 28-32 (06 6880 1996). Bus 30Exp, 40Exp, 46, 62, 64, 70, 81, 87, 116, 492, 628. **Open** 9am-midnight daily. Closed Jan. **Credit** MC, V. **Map** p355 D5 ㉒

This bar is famous for its *tartufo* – a calorie-bomb chocolate ice-cream concoction with huge lumps of chocolate inside. There are tables outside at which to enjoy food from a wide-ranging menu and a tearoom on the first floor. Beware: sit down inside or out, and the price mark-up is massive. Instead, take your ice-cream away and enjoy it next to Bernini's fountain (*see p116*).

Pubs & *enoteche*

Société Lutèce

Piazza di Montevecchio 17 (06 6830 1472). Bus 30Exp, 40Exp, 46, 70, 81, 87, 116, 492, 628. **Open** 6.30pm-2am Tue-Sun. Closed 2wks Aug. **Credit** AmEx, MC, V. **Map** p355 C5 ㉓

Despite being fiendishly difficult to find, this outpost of a popular bar/café in Turin has caught on quickly with the eclectic Roman hipsters who formerly frequented places like the Vineria (*see p224*) in campo de' Fiori. The cramped quarters cause a spillover into the small piazza, which has not pleased the neighbours (known to dump water and mouldy produce on noisy revellers down below). Still, the *aperitivo* buffet (6.30-10.30pm – unless the food runs out earlier) is plentiful, the employees are as playful as the customers and the vibe is decidedly laid back.

Stardust

Via dell'Anima 52 (06 686 8986). Bus 30Exp, 40Exp, 46, 62, 64, 70, 81, 87, 116, 492, 628. **Open** noon-2am daily. **No credit cards. Map** p355 D5 & p358 C1 ㉔

This stalwart of the Trastevere nightlife scene – which drew a colourful mix of locals, out-of-work actors and expats – was moving house as this guide went to press, to new premises just round the corner from piazza Navona. Proprietors swore the formula would remain unchanged: a tearoom from 4 to 7pm; a bistro from 7 to 10pm, perfect for an *aperitivo* and snack; and then after 11pm a raucous bar/pub where bartenders blast anything from Lenny Kravitz to Cuban jazz, Euro-rap to Czech polkas, and owner Anna's favourite: Italian opera. Brunch is served every Sunday from noon to 5pm: salads and light Mediterranean-themed fare, along with plenty of cocktails for a bit of the 'hair of the dog' from the night before.

Recafé
pizzeria restorant - neapolitan caffetteria

piazza Augusto Imperatore, 36
ph: 06.681.347.30
WWW.RECAFE.IT

Simply wonderful

Trinity College

Via del Collegio Romano 6 (06 678 6472/www. trinity-rome.com). Bus 62, 63, 81, 85, 95, 117, 119, 160, 175, 492, 628, 630, 850. **Open** 11am-3am daily. **Credit** AmEx, DC, MC, V. **Map** p355 E5, p357 A6 & p358 E1 ㉕

This is a city-centre pub much frequented by thirsty employees of the Cultural Heritage Ministry opposite. It has a more authentic feel than many of the capital's 'Irish' pubs, although the thirsty packs of American college students prove 'tis all an illusion.

Pasticcerie & gelaterie

La Caffettiera

Piazza di Pietra 65 (06 679 8147). Bus 62, 63, 81, 85, 95, 117, 119, 160, 175, 492, 628, 630, 850. **Open** 7am-9pm Mon-Sat; 8am-9pm Sun. **Credit** AmEx, DC, MC, V. **Map** p355 E5 ㉘

Politicians and mandarins from the parliament buildings nearby lounge in the sumptuous tearoom of this temple to Neapolitan goodies, while lesser mortals bolt coffees at the counter. The *rum babà* reigns supreme, but ricotta lovers rave over the crunchy *sfogliatella*, flavoured with cinnamon and orange peel, and the *pastiera*, a rich tart filled with ricotta, orange-flower water, citrus peel and whole grains of wheat.

Cremeria Monteforte

Via della Rotonda 22 (06 686 7720). Bus 30Exp, 40Exp, 46, 62, 63, 64, 70, 81, 87, 492, 628, 630, 780, H. **Open** 10am-11pm Tue-Sun. Closed mid Dec-Jan. **No credit cards. Map** p355 D5 & p358 D1 ㉗

This *gelateria*, handily situated round the side of the Pantheon, is a cut above the many others in the area. The flavours (offering the standard selection) are crisp and the texture is creamy and light. Try a cup of rich chocolate *granita* with fresh *panna* (whipped cream) for a delicious alternative to the *gelato*.

Ghetto & Campo de' Fiori

Cafés & bars

See p224 **Bernasconi**.

Pubs & enoteche

Bartaruga

Piazza Mattei 7 (06 689 2299/www.bartaruga.it). Bus 30Exp, 40Exp, 46, 62, 64, 70, 81, 87, 492, 628, 630, 780, H/tram 8. **Open** 6pm-midnight Mon-Thur; 6pm-2am Fri, Sat; 6pm-1am Sun. **No credit cards. Map** p358 D2 ㉓

This exotic baroque *locale* – in peach and midnight blue, with divans, candelabra and a grand piano – overlooks one of the most exquisite fountains in Rome, not to mention a square that has just been restored and provided with that most unusual of Roman accessories: benches. A crowd of beautiful, eccentric people make the most of the backdrop (while trying hard to ignore the rather surly bar staff).

Crudo

Via degli Specchi 6 (06 683 8989/www.crudo roma.it). Bus 40Exp, 46, 62, 64, 116, 916. **Open** 7.30pm-2am daily. **Credit** AmEx, DC, MC, V. **Map** p358 D2 ㉙

It's easy to forget you're in Rome in this ultra-modern venue. The name (*crudo* means raw) conveys perfectly the sheer freshness of the place's style and ingredients. The dazzling designer interior – art installations, plasma screens, leather sofas, DJs – has some of the best *aperitivi* in town, and glamourous dining after you've downed them.

Gloss

Via del Monte della Farina 43 (06 6813 5345/www. glossroma.it). Bus 40Exp, 46, 62, 64, 116, 916. **Open** 6.30-10.30pm Mon; 6.30pm-2am Tue-Sat. **No credit cards. Map** p355 D6 & p358 D2 ㉚

Less intimidating than some of the latest cocktail/culture temples, this inviting bar offers an *aperitivo*-hour buffet (from 7pm) and a wide range of cultural offerings, including ever changing art on its walls. Alternatively, you can just sink into a sofa, knock back a Negroni and listen to the music, live or DJed.

Il Goccetto

Via dei Banchi Vecchi 14 (06 686 4268). Bus 40Exp, 46, 62, 64, 916. **Open** 11.30am-2pm, 6.30pm-midnight Mon-Sat. Closed 1wk Jan & 3wks Aug. **Credit** AmEx, MC, V. **Map** p355 C6 & p358 B1 ㉛

One of the more serious *centro storico* wine bars, occupying part of a medieval bishop's house, Il Goccetto has original painted ceilings, dark wood-clad walls and a cosy, private-club feel. Wine is the main point here, with a satisfying range by the glass from €2.50, but if you're peckish, there's a choice of cheeses, salamis and salads too). It also closes early afternoon on Saturdays in July.

Lot 87

Via del Pellegrino 87 (06 9761 8344/www.lot87. com). Bus 40Exp, 46, 62, 64, 916. **Open** 7am-midnight Mon-Sat. Closed 1wk Aug. **Credit** AmEx, MC, V. **Map** p355 C6 & p358 C1 ㉜

This bar, opened in 2003, is the usual mod Rome offering – steel and blond wood, minimalist design and flat-screen TVs – but service is more down-home friendly and the clientele far from jet-set. There's a long list of expertly made cocktails for only €5. From 6 to 9pm there's an *aperitivo* hour, during which there are free snacks all along the bar.

Sloppy Sam's

Campo de' Fiori 10 (06 6880 2637). Bus 40Exp, 46, 62, 64, 116, 916. **Open** 4pm-2am daily. **Credit** MC, V. **Map** p355 C/D6 & p358 C1 ㉝

From *aperitivo* hour on, this American-owned bar packs in some regulars and swarms of expats. The scene in the campo gets livelier/rowdier from 10pm, when the 'program'-attending denizens of US university-owned accommodation around the campo descend on the bar and its outdoor tables. Sam's is unfortunately popular with the obnoxiously drunk participants of organised bar-crawls.

Eat, Drink, Shop

La Vineria

Campo de' Fiori 15 (06 6880 3268). Bus 40Exp, 46, 62, 64, 116, 916. **Open** *8.30am-2am Mon-Sat. Closed 2wks Aug.* **Credit** *AmEx, DC, MC, V.* **Map** p355 C/D6 & p358 C1 ❸

The longest-running wine bar on the campo, La Vineria is the real thing, where Romans flock to chat and plan the evening ahead over good wines by the glass starting at a remarkably cheap €1.50 (albeit in tiny glasses). By *aperitivo* time, it's a dog-eat-dog battle to grab a table.

Pasticcerie & gelaterie

See also p241 **Dolceroma** and **Forno del Ghetto**.

Alberto Pica

Via della Seggiola 12 (06 686 8405). Bus 23, 63, 280, 630, 780, H/tram 8. **Open** *Jan-Mar, Oct, Nov 8.30am-2am Mon-Sat. Apr-Sept, Dec 8.30am-2am Mon-Sat; 4.30pm-2am Sun. Closed 10 days Aug.* **No credit cards. Map** p358 D2 ❸

Horrendous neon lighting, surly staff… and some of Rome's most delicious ice-cream. These are the hallmarks of this long-running bar by the justice ministry. The rice specialities stand out: imagine eating frozen, partially cooked rice pudding and you'll get the picture. *Riso alla cannella* (cinnamon rice) is particularly wonderful.

Bernasconi

Piazza Cairoli 16 (06 6880 6264). Bus 63, 630, 780, H/tram 8. **Open** *7am-8.30pm Tue-Sun. Closed Aug.* **No credit cards. Map** p358 D2 ❸

Cramped and inconspicuous – like so many of Rome's best cake shops – it's well worth fighting your way inside for *lieviti* (breakfast yeast buns). Bernasconi's chewy, yeasty *cornetti* are unbeatable: the real vintage variety, difficult to find elsewhere.

Close to the synagogue, this spot straddles Rome's Jewish and Catholic worlds, with kosher sweets and Lenten *quaresimale* cookies

Trastevere & Gianicolo

Cafés & bars

Bar Gianicolo

Piazzale Aurelio 5 (06 580 6275). Bus 870. **Open** *6am-1am Tue-Sat; 6am-9pm Sun. Closed 1wk Aug.* **No credit cards. Map** p358 A3 ❸

If you've slogged up here to visit Villa Pamphili (*see p179*) or the site of Garibaldi's doomed battle with the French on the Gianicolo (*see p138*), rest your weary bones on the wooden benches of this tiny bar with an intimate, chatty feel. Carrots and apples are juiced on the spot and a good range of interesting sandwiches and light meals – along with outside tables (slightly too close to passing traffic for comfort) overlooking the Porta di San Pancrazio – make it a good spot for a drink or a snack.

Bar San Calisto

Piazza San Calisto (no phone). Bus 780, H/tram 8. **Open** *5.30am-2am Mon-Sat.* **No credit cards. Map** p358 C3 ❸

Green tourists get their coffee or beer on piazza Santa Maria in Trastevere; locals who know better go to this bar. Its harsh lighting would make Sophia Loren look wan, and the dingy space – inside and out – is no picture postcard. But it's dirt-cheap and as such it has always been the haunt of arty and fringe types (plus many questionable characters after sundown). They're here downing beers or an *affogato* (ice-cream swamped with liqueur), or savouring some of the best chocolate in Rome: hot and thick with fresh whipped cream in winter, and in the form of creamy *gelato* in warmer months.

Freni e Frizioni. *See p225.*

Eat, Drink, Shop

Friends Art Café

Piazza Trilussa 34 (06 581 6111). Bus 23, 280, 780, H/tram 8. **Open** *7.30am-2am Mon-Sat; 6.30pm-2am Sun. Closed 1wk Aug.* **Credit** *AmEx, DC, MC, V.* **Map** p358 C2 ❸

This lively, modern bar is a popular place where habitués meet for everything from a morning *cornetto* and cappuccino to after-dinner cocktails. The chrome detailing, brightly coloured plastic chairs and constant din of fashion TV in the background, lend the place a retro-'80s funhouse feel. Lunch and dinner menus offer *bruschette*, salads and pastas at reasonable prices. There's a free wireless connection too.

Ombre Rosse

Piazza Sant'Egidio 12 (06 588 4155). Bus 780, H/tram 8. **Open** *7.30am-2am Mon-Sat; 5pm-2am Sun.* **Credit** *AmEx, MC, V.* **Map** p358 C3 ❹

In the heart of Trastevere, this café is perfect for morning coffee, a late lunch or a light dinner (try the chicken salad or fresh soups). It fills to bursting point before and after dinner, when bagging one of the outside tables is a coup. Service is slow but friendly: as the bartender hand-crushes the ice for your next Caipiroska, you have plenty of time to watch the Trastevere menagerie go by.

Pubs & *enoteche*

Artù

Largo MD Fumasoni Biondi 5 (06 588 0398). Bus 23, 280, 870. **Open** *6pm-2am Tue-Sun. Closed 3wks Aug.* **Credit** *AmEx, MC, V.* **Map** p358 C2 ❹

This friendly place – in a little square off piazza Sant'Egidio – hovers somewhere between Italian bar and English pub. The selection of high-quality brews, stained-glass and English-speaking regulars lean towards the UK; the wine list, fashion TV and *aperitivo* buffet (6.30-9pm) are reminders that you're still in *bella Italia*. There's also a full menu of 'pub' fare, with sandwiches, pasta and meat courses.

Cioccolata e Vino

Vicolo del Cinque 11 (06 5830 1868). Bus 23, 280, 780, H/tram 8. **Open** *8am-2am Mon; 2pm-2am Tue-Sun.* **Credit** *AmEx, MC, V.* **Map** p358 C2/3 ❹
See p227 **Book bars.**

Enoteca Trastevere

Via della Lungaretta 86 (06 588 5659). Bus 780, H/tram 8. **Open** *6pm-2am Mon, Tue, Thur-Sat; 5pm-1am Sun. Closed 3wks Jan.* **Credit** *AmEx, MC, V.* **Map** p358 C3 ❹

The usual *enoteca* offerings prevail at this neighbourhood favourite: wooden tables and chairs, and a snack menu offering an assortment of cheese, cured meats, *bruschette* and *crostini*, salads and desserts (the rather pretentious full menu is as overpriced as it is badly translated). But this *enoteca* has a couple of less obvious selling points too: a large selection of grappas, distilled liqueurs and *amari* by the glass at reasonable prices, plus a good selection of organic wines.

Freni e Frizioni

Via del Politeama 4-6 (06 5833 4210/www.frenie frizioni.com). Bus 23, 280. **Open** *10am-2am daily.* **Credit** *DC, MC, V.* **Map** p358 C2 ❹

Unlikely ex-garage surroundings – the name means 'brakes and clutches' – for Rome's hippest early evening spot, frequented by arty types and a creative, studenty crowd. A grand buffet is laid out on a snowy white tablecloth decorated with armfuls of long-stemmed roses and candles. There are baskets of focaccia, ceramic bowls of couscous and pasta, guacamole and raw vegetables: help yourself while you sip a cocktail, a beer, or a glass of well-priced wine. The riverside square outside becomes an extension of the place, filling up with the overspill of chatting drinkers. **Photos** *p224.*

La Libreria del Cinema

Via dei Fienaroli 31 (06 581 7724/www.libreria delcinema.roma.it). Bus 780, H/tram 8. **Open** *4-9pm Mon; 10am-2pm, 3-9pm Tue-Fri; 11am-11pm Sat; 11am-9pm Sun. Closed 1wk Aug.* **Credit** *MC, V.* **Map** p358 C3 ❹
See p227 **Book bars.**

Pasticcerie & gelaterie

See also p224 **Bar San Calisto.**

I Dolci di Checco er Carrettiere

Via Benedetta 7 (06 581 1413). Bus 23, 280, 780, H/tram 8. **Open** *6.30am-1am daily.* **No credit cards.** **Map** p358 C2 ❹

Located behind piazza Trilussa, this small bar, annexed to one of Trastevere's oldest restaurants, has outstanding cakes and pastries, plus fresh quiches, crisp *crocchette* and, usually, tasty baked pasta. There's a savvy selection of malt whiskies too, and some of the best *gelato* this side of the Tiber.

Doppia Coppia

Via della Scala 51 (06 581 3174). Bus 23, 280, 780, H/tram 8. **Open** *Feb, Mar, Nov 1-8pm Mon-Fri; 1-10pm Sat, Sun. Apr-Oct 1pm-midnight Mon-Fri; 1pm-1am Sat, Sun. Closed Dec-Jan.* **No credit cards.** **Map** p358 B2 ❹

This tiny *gelateria* on a corner in Trastevere dishes out a fantastic *stracciatella* (chocolate chip), along with about 20 other delicious flavours of ice creams. In summer months it also offers *granita* (water ice) in refreshingly tart lemon, tangerine, coffee or mint.

Sora Mirella

Lungotevere degli Anguillara, corner of Ponte Cestio (no phone). Bus 23, 280, 780, H/tram 8. **Open** *10am-3am daily. Closed Oct-Feb.* **No credit cards.** **Map** p358 D3 ❹

Mirella styles herself *la regina della grattachecca* (the Queen of Water Ices), and there seems no reason to disagree. Sit on the Tiber embankment wall as you tuck into *speciale superfrutta* – fresh melon, kiwi fruit and strawberry (or whatever is in season) with syrups served in a special glass.

Aventine, Testaccio & Ostiense

Cafés & bars

Bar del Mattatoio

Piazza O Giustiniani 3 (06 574 6017). Bus 95, 170, 673, 719, 781/tram 3. **Open** 6am-8.30pm Mon-Sat. Closed 2wks Aug. **No credit cards.** **Map** p359 C6 (49)

This is a brick doll's house of a bar, with unusual Gothic recesses in the front. It's also one of the earliest-opening bars in Rome, which once upon a time catered for the early-bird workers from the slaughterhouse opposite. Nowadays, the early risers have been predominantly replaced by dawn revellers limping home from Testaccio's high-density clubs and stopping off en route to recover over coffee and *cornetti*.

Caffè Letterario

Via Ostiense 83 (392 069 3460/www.caffeletterarioroma.it). Bus 23, 769. **Open** 10am-2am Mon-Fri; 3pm-2am Sat, Sun. Closed 1wk Aug. **No credit cards.** **Map** p143 B2 (50)

See p227 **Book bars**.

Pubs & *enoteche*

L'Oasi della Birra

Piazza Testaccio 41 (06 574 6122). Bus 23, 30Exp, 75, 95, 170, 280, 716, 781/tram 3. **Open** 7pm-12.30am daily. Closed 2wks Aug. **Credit** AmEx, MC, V. **Map** p359 D5 (51)

In the basement of an *enoteca* on Testaccio's market square, this 'Oasis of Beer' has over 500 brews on offer. It's one of the few places in Rome where you can track down the products of Italian microbreweries such as the award-winning Menabrea; the selection of wines by the bottle is almost as impressive. The food ranges from full-scale meals with a Germanic/Eastern European slant (goulash, *wurstel, krauti*) to snacks (*crostini, bruschette*). The outside tables operate year round, weather permitting. Booking is a good idea.

Pasticcerie & gelaterie

Chiosco Testaccio

Via G Branca, corner of via Beniamino Franklin (no phone). Bus 95, 170, 781/tram 3. **Open** noon-1.30am daily. Closed mid Sept-Apr. **No credit cards.** **Map** p359 C5 (52)

Still going strong after over 80 years in this working-class neighbourhood, the Chiosco Testaccio has the unusual selling point of being painted a different colour each year. Push past the lounging local youth for hand-grated ice; the unusual flavours are as varied as the outside paint job is colourful; tamarind and *limoncocco* (lemon-coconut) are specialities.

Celio, San Giovanni & San Lorenzo

Cafés & bars

Bar à Book

Via dei Piceni 23 (06 4544 5438/www.barabook.it). Bus 71, 492/tram 3, 19. **Open** 4pm-midnight Tue-Thur; 4pm-2am Fri, Sat; 11am-8pm Sun. Closed Aug. **Credit** AmEx, DC, MC, V. **Map** p151 D2 (53)

See p227 **Book bars**.

Café Café

Via dei Santi Quattro 44 (06 700 8743). Metro Colosseo/bus 85, 87, 117, 810, 850/tram 3. **Open** *Mid Mar-Sept* 11am-1am daily. *Oct-mid Mar* 11am-1am Mon, Tue, Thur-Sun. **Credit** MC, V. **Map** p360 C3 (54)

This attractive place offers teas, wines, salads and sandwiches for travellers weary after a romp around the Colosseum. There's a brunch buffet from 11.30am to 4pm on Sundays.

Monti & Esquilino

Pubs & *enoteche*

Al Vino al Vino

Via dei Serpenti 19 (06 485 803). Bus 40Exp, 64, 70, 117, 170, H. **Open** 10.30am-2.30pm, 5pm-1am daily. Closed 2wks Aug. **Credit** MC, V. **Map** p360 B1 (55)

This hostelry on lively via dei Serpenti has a range of more than 500 wines, with more than 25 available by the glass. But its real speciality is *distillati*: dozens of fine grappas, whiskies and other strong spirits. In the back room are pretty cast-iron tables, topped with volcanic stone and ceramics. The menu here is strong on Sicilian specialities such as *caponata* (Sicilian ratatouille) and eggplant *parmigiana*.

The Druid's Den

Via San Martino ai Monti 28 (06 4890 4781/www.druidspubrome.com). Metro Cavour/bus 16, 75, 84, 360, 649. **Open** 5pm-2am daily. **Credit** MC, V. **Map** p360 D1 (56)

Like its competitor the Fiddler's Elbow (*see below*), this pub was already well established before the 1990s craze for all things Irish developed in Rome. It serves a decent pint of Liffey water, as well as beaming football in from the British Isles. Happy hour lasts from shutters-up to 8pm daily.

The Fiddler's Elbow

Via dell'Olmata 43 (06 487 2110/www.thefiddlerselbow.com). Metro Cavour/bus 16, 75, 84, 360, 649. **Open** 5pm-1.30am daily. **Credit** MC, V. **Map** p360 C/D1 (57)

One of the oldest, best-known pubs in Rome, the Fiddler's Elbow has a basic wooden-benched interior that hasn't changed for years. Though Italy's smoking ban means it's no longer a fume-filled dive, it still succeeds in giving the impression of being one.

Book bars

For climatic and temperamental reasons, Italians on the whole are do-ers rather than readers: not for them a nice quiet night at home with a book. But a night *out* with a book? Now you're talking!

In a new trend that has taken the city by storm, there's no perching with a plastic cup of coffee substitute while you speed-read the first four chapters of a book you're too mean to buy. Book bars are about print being a reason to get together, have fun, discuss ideas and simply while away your evening in a bar. In Rome, books have become fashionable evening stimulants.

Caffè Letterario (*see p226*) led the charge. Perfectly situated in an area swarming with students from the Terza Università campus, and on the crest of the culture surge accompanying the transformation of the Mattatoio (*see p226*) area from run-down periphery to cutting-edge cool, Caffè Letterario is a style temple showcasing not only new books but the arts in general.

Bohemian Trastevere, just across the river, boasts the highest concentration of book bars. The biggest, **Bibli** (*see p233*), has been around for years as a book shop; nowadays it functions as a book-lined cultural centre, with courses, lectures and concerts. It's also a great place for a healthy lunch: try the couscous and the delicious salads. In the evenings glamorous readers mingle with authors and artists over an *aperitivo*, and maybe

a little something to eat – all that reading can really give you *such* an appetite.

Lettere Caffè (*see p283*) is more intimate, and noisier, with evening DJs, live jazz, poetry slams and readings. **La Libreria del Cinema** (*see p225; photo below*) is heaven for movie buffs with its encyclopedic stock of DVDs and cinema-related books, its busy events programme featuring film directors and screenwriters, and its intimate little bar – where you might just persuade someone to cast you in their next blockbuster. **Cioccolata e Vino** (*see p225*) adds another dimension to guilty pleasures: divine coffee and home-made chocolates upstairs, a well-thumbed selection of second-hand books downstairs.

Naturally, San Lorenzo, the university quarter, has its own book bar – **Bar à Book** (*see p226*) – where weighty tomes mingle with quiches, puddings and rather good wines.

For something more central, if less literary, visit **Salotto 42** (*see p221*), where the books are as stylish as the decor.

Pasticcerie & gelaterie

Dagnino
Galleria Esedra, via VE Orlando 75 (06 481 8660/ www.pasticceriadagnino.com). Metro Repubblica/bus 40Exp, 64, 70, 170, H. **Open** 7am-11pm daily. **Credit** AmEx, MC, V. **Map** p357 C5 ⑬
Stunning 1950s decor sets the scene for this corner of Sicily in the heart of Rome. If it's Sicilian and edible, it's here: from ice-cream in buns to lifelike marzipan

fruits. Regulars come for crisp *cannoli siciliani* filled with salty, chocolate-chip ricotta and the shiny green-iced *cassata*, uniting all the flavours of the south: the perfume of citrus, almond paste and fresh ricotta.

Il Palazzo del Freddo di Giovanni Fassi
Via Principe Eugenio 65-67 (06 446 4740/www. palazzodelfreddo.it). Metro Vittorio/bus 70, 71, 105/tram 5, 14. **Open** noon-midnight Tue-Sun. **No credit cards**. **Map** p360 E2 ㊾

Eat, Drink, Shop

With its breathtakingly kitsch interior and splendid ices, Fassi is a Roman institution. Founded in 1880, its walls are adorned with Edwardian adverts and Fascist-era posters that extol the virtues of the shop's wares. Service is unfailingly irascible, and the crowds can be daunting, but the ices are never less than sublime: best of all are *riso* – the English translation, 'rice pudding', hardly does it justice – and the Palazzo's own invention, *la caterinetta*, a mysterious concoction of whipped honey and vanilla.

Vatican & Prati

Cafés & bars

Gran Caffè Esperia
Lungotevere dei Mellini 1 (06 3211 0016). Bus 30Exp, 70, 280, 492, 913. **Open** *May-Sept 7am-midnight daily. Oct-Apr 7am-9.30pm daily.* **Credit** MC, V. **Map** p355 D4 **60**
Locals vie to conquer pavement tables in the morning sun at this newly restored belle époque café. Join them for a late breakfast of wonderful coffee and toasted *cornetti*; alternatively, forget about the cappuccino and go straight for a glass of *prosecco* and a smoked salmon *tramezzino*. The Esperia offers surprisingly reasonable prices for the pleasure of the location, plus an opportunity to top up the tan.

Il Ristoro
Basilica di San Pietro (06 6988 1662). Metro Ottaviano/bus 23, 40Exp, 62, 64. **Open** *Apr-Sept 8.30am-6pm Mon-Sat. Oct-Mar 8.30am-5pm Mon-Sat.* **No credit cards. Map** p165 D3 **61**

Il Ristoro, on the roof of St Peter's.

You're not going to bump into the Pope up here, but it's still worth paying the price of the St Peter's cupola lift to sip your coffee on the roof of the basilica. There's precious little on the menu except coffee, soft drinks and mineral water – certainly no alcohol – but there's a wondrous view over the city, through the row of giant saints crowning the façade.

Pubs & enoteche

Enoteca Nuvolari
Via degli Ombrellari 10 (06 6880 3018). Bus 23, 40Exp, 62, 280. **Open** *6.30pm-2am Mon-Sat.* **No credit cards. Map** p355 A4 **62**
Named after the legendary Italian racing driver Tazio Nuvolari, this *enoteca* is where the younger denizens of staid old Borgo hang out. A lively cocktail hour (6.30-8.30pm) is accompanied by a free buffet, but nourishing home-made soups and pâtés sustain tardier wine enthusiasts in the candlelit supper room next door (meals served 8pm-1am). Music, plus regular art shows on the walls, make this a fun place.

The Proud Lion
Borgo Pio 36 (06 683 2841). Bus 23, 40Exp, 62, 280. **Open** *11am-2am Mon-Sat.* **No credit cards. Map** p355 A/B4 **63**
This cosy neighbourhood drinking den in the historic Borgo has a vintage Scottish theme, with tartan, old postcards and a fine array of draught and bottled beers. Off-duty Swiss Guards (the very short hair is a giveaway) mingle with regulars watching the footy on TV or playing darts.

Pasticcerie & gelaterie

Pellacchia
Via Cola di Rienzo 103 (06 321 0807/06 321 0446/ www.pellacchia.it). Bus 30Exp, 70, 81, 224, 280. **Open** *6am-1am Tue-Sun. Closed 1wk Aug.* **Credit** AmEx, DC, MC, V. **Map** p354 B3 **64**
This bar on Prati's busiest street produces some of the best ice-cream north of the river. It's the perfect place to recover after slogging around the Vatican.

The Suburbs

Cafés & bars

Palombini
Piazzale Adenauer 12, EUR (06 591 1700/www. palombini.it). Metro Magliana/bus 30Exp, 170. **Open** *7am-10pm Mon-Wed; 7am-midnight Thur, Fri; 7am-1am Sat; 8am-10pm Sun. Closed 2wks Aug.* **Credit** AmEx, DC, MC, V.
In the imposing shadow of the Palazzo del Civiltà del Lavoro (*see p178*) stands this airy pavilion, surrounded by sweeping gardens. The patio area, covered by a steel and plastic tent, is a favourite meeting point for bronzed and sun-glassed young Romans. The ice creams and cakes are both first-rate.

Eat, Drink, Shop

Shops & Services

Visit Rome's temples to style.

Fashionable **via Condotti**.

Shopping in Rome can be rather a refreshing, old-fashioned experience for out-of-towners. There are no huge department stores here; no shopping malls; none of the ubiquitous chains (give or take a Benetton or two) that make every British high street, for example, a carbon copy of all the others. Instead, there are corner grocery shops, dark and dusty bottle-lined wine shops, one-off boutiques catering to every imaginable taste… and, of course, the opulent outlets of Italy's fashion aristocracy.

To some extent, this old-worldliness is an illusion: the corner shop is being driven out by big-name mini-markets; shopping malls would be here were it not for the fact that space restrictions and exorbitant rents keep them in the outer suburbs; there *are* clothing retail chains (just that they have different names here); and international brands are creeping slowly but inexorably on to the Roman high street. Traditionalists just have to draw comfort from the fact that the tiny boutique and the family-run store still maintain a strong presence in Rome's retail sector.

As a fashion centre, Rome has long been overshadowed by the *moda* empire that is Milan, but the past few years have seen a blossoming in the Eternal City, which now looks set to give her foggy northern sister a run for her money. The major Italian names in high fashion are huddled around piazza di Spagna and via Condotti (*see p240* **The A-list**). To

avoid the masses, wend your way around the side streets of the area, where smaller boutiques and cafés make for a peaceful and pretty stroll. For great independent designers and the city's best vintage, on the other hand, make for via del Governo Vecchio (map p355 C5).

Via del Corso – stretching from piazza del Popolo to piazza Venezia – is home to mid-range outlets for everything from books and music to clothing and shoes. Many of the same clothing retailers can be found along via Nazionale (map p357 B/C5/6, p360 B1), and while the street itself is no charmer, the nearby Monti district packs unique boutiques and hip originals along its narrow, hilly streets. Across the river in the Prati area, via Cola di Rienzo (map p354 A/B/C3) is a shorter and less crowded version of via del Corso, with major retail chains, and some great food shopping at **Castroni** and divine deli **Franchi** (for both, *see p241*).

PAYING

The city echoes with complaints about the price hikes introduced during the period of slack regulation and public confusion surrounding the introduction of the euro. Whether buying a banana, a bus ticket or a bikini, if you last came to Rome with the lira you'll notice that it ain't cheap any more, although home-grown designer names are still a little easier on the wallet here than abroad. Bargaining belongs firmly at the flea-market: in shops, prices are fixed.

In theory, you should be given a *scontrino* (receipt). If you aren't, then ask for it: by law, shops are required to provide one, and they and you are liable for a fine in the (wildly unlikely) event of your being caught without it. Major credit cards are accepted just about everywhere, although it's worth checking before queuing.

The rules on taking purchases back are infuriatingly vague. Faulty goods, obviously, must be refunded or replaced. Most shops will also accept unwanted goods that are returned unused with a receipt within seven days of purchase, though this is not obligatory.

TAX REBATES

Non-EU residents are entitled to a sales tax (IVA) rebate on purchases of goods over €155, providing they are exported unused and bought from a shop with the 'Europe Tax Free' sticker. The shop will give you a receipt and a 'Tax Free Shopping Cheque', which should be stamped by customs before departing Italy.

OPENING TIMES

Regardless of their aversion to chain store takeover, most central-Rome shop owners have jumped on the capitalist bandwagon, foregoing the sacred siesta in favour of '*no-stop*' opening hours, from 9.30/10am to 7.30/8pm, Monday to Saturday. The occasional independent still clings to the traditional 1-4pm shutdown. In the centre, stores also increasingly open on Sundays.

Times given in this chapter are winter opening hours; in summer (approximately June to September) shops that opt for long lunches tend to reopen later, at 5pm or 5.30pm, staying open until 8-8.30pm. Most food stores close on Thursday afternoons in winter, and on Saturday afternoons in summer. The majority of non-food shops are closed Monday mornings. Many shops shut down for at least two weeks each summer (generally in August) and almost all are shut for two or three days around the 15 August public holiday. If you want to avoid finding a particular shop *chiuso per ferie* (closed for holidays), be sure to ring ahead.

Although service is improving, many shop assistants seem hell-bent on either ignoring or intimidating customers. This is no time for Anglo-Saxon reticence; be sure to perfect the essential lines *mi può aiutare, per favore?* ('Can you help me please?') and *volevo solo dare un' occhiata* ('I'm just looking') and you're ready for any eventuality.

One-stop shopping

In a city where restricted space means malls are an out-of-town phenomenon, the big new development on the Roman shopping scene

Cartoleria Pantheon. *See p231*.

has been the renovation of the 19th-century Galleria Colonna – now known as **Galleria Alberto Sordi** (map p355 E5), in memory of the Roman cinema legend – off via del Corso. There are more than 20 shops, including bookstore Feltrinelli (with a few novels and guide books in English on the ground floor; *see p231*), teen paradise Jam (trendy togs for rich kids), a branch of cheap-and-cheerful fashion retailer Zara and a couple of bars – all under one beautifully coloured glass roof.

For the concept store **TAD**, *see p239*.

COIN

Piazzale Appio 7, San Giovanni (06 708 0020). Metro San Giovanni/bus 16, 81, 85, 87, 186, 218, 810, 850. **Open** 9.30am-8pm Mon-Sat; 10am-8pm Sun. **Credit** AmEx, DC, MC, V. **Map** off p361 E4.

A reliable if limited department store. Romans come here for tights or sheets that last. The make-up counter and lingerie collection are good points. There's also an excellent houseware department and sturdy kids' clothes; the via Cola di Rienzo branch has a supermarket in the basement.

Other locations: via Cola di Rienzo 173, Prati (06 3600 4298); via Mantova 1B, Suburbs: north (06 841 6279).

MAS

Via dello Statuto 11, Esquilino (06 446 8078). Metro Vittorio/bus 105, 360, 649/tram 5, 14. **Open** 9am-1pm, 3.45-8pm Mon-Sat; 10am-1pm, 3.45-7.30pm Sun. **Credit** AmEx, DC, MC, V. **Map** p360 D1.

This Roman institution in the down-at-heel Esquilino neighbourhood has a mind-boggling (and often strikingly ugly) assortment of clothes, shoes, luggage, jewellery and linen. If you've got the patience to rummage through four floors of bargain bins and racks you will probably find something – and it will be very cheap.

La Rinascente

Largo Chigi 20, Tridente (06 679 7691). Bus 52, 53, 61, 62, 63, 71, 80Exp, 85, 116, 117, 119, 160, 850. **Open** 10am-10pm Mon-Sat; 10am-8pm Sun. **Credit** AmEx, DC, MC, V. **Map** p355 E5.

This old favourite has hats, sun cream and make-up, plus limited ranges of designer and mid-range clothing. There's also a good selection of lingerie. This shop's days are numbered though: the historic *palazzo* that houses it has been purchased by Spanish clothing retailer Zara; by 2009 (or thereabouts), La Rinascente will move into larger, more luxurious premises on nearby via del Tritone. The piazza Fiume branch (06 884 1231) in the northern suburbs has a large homewares department.

Antiques

Some of the best areas for antiques are pricey via del Babuino, via Giulia and via de' Coronari; the last stages antiques fairs in May and October. The dealers/restorers thronging via del Pellegrino may be cheaper, but quality dips too. Occasional bargains can be picked up at flea markets (*see p247*). See also *p245* **Marmi Line**.

Artists' supplies & stationery

Cartoleria Pantheon

Via della Rotonda 15, Pantheon & Navona (06 687 5313). Bus 30Exp, 40Exp, 46, 62, 63, 64, 70, 81, 87, 186, 492, 628, 810, 916/tram 8. **Open** 9.30am-1pm, 3.30am-7.30pm Mon-Sat; 1-7.30pm Sun. Closed 1wk Aug. **Credit** AmEx, DC, MC, V. **Map** p355 D5.

Bring out your literary soul with leather-bound notebooks, hand-painted Florentine stationery and rare paper from Amalfi. Nearly everything for sale has been handcrafted. **Photo** *p230*.

Other locations: via della Maddalena 41, Pantheon & Navona (06 679 5633).

Ditta G Poggi

Art Supplies: via del Gesù 74-75; Paper products: via Pie' di Marmo 38, Pantheon & Navona (06 678 4477/www.poggi1825.it). Bus 30Exp, 40Exp, 46, 62, 63, 64, 70, 81, 87, 186, 492, 628, 810, 916/tram 8. **Open** 9am-1pm, 4-7.30pm Mon-Sat. Closed 2wks Aug. **Credit** AmEx, MC, V. **Map** p355 E6.

This wonderfully old-fashioned shop has been selling paints, brushes, canvases and artists' supplies of every description since 1825. The via Pie' di Marmo shop closes on Saturday afternoons. The main shop remains open through the day on Thursday.

Other locations: via Cardinale Merry del Val 18-19, Trastevere (06 581 2531).

Officina della Carta

Via Benedetta 26B, Trastevere (06 589 5557). Bus 23, 280, 780, H/tram 3. **Open** 10am-1pm, 3.30-7.30pm Mon-Sat. Closed 2wks Aug. **Credit** AmEx, DC, MC, V. **Map** p358 C3.

A tiny shop crammed with handmade notebooks, leather-bound albums and paper-covered gift boxes.

Il Papiro

Via del Pantheon 50, Pantheon & Navona (06 679 5597/www.ilpapirofirenze.it). Bus 30Exp, 40Exp, 46, 62, 63, 64, 70, 81, 87, 186, 492, 628, 810, 916/ tram 8. **Open** 10am-8pm Mon-Fri; 11am-8pm Sun. **Credit** AmEx, DC, MC, V. **Map** p355 D4.

Fine Florentine paper is incorporated into albums, notebooks and more. Don't ruin the effect with a biro: the shop also stocks quill pens and ink in jazzy colours. **Other locations**: salita de' Crescenzi 28, Pantheon & Navona (06 686 8463); via dei Crociferi 17, Trevi & Quirinale (06 6992 0537); via Quattro Novembre 147, Trevi & Quirinale (06 6994 1327).

Pineider

Via dei Due Macelli 68, Tridente (06 679 5884/ www.pineider.it). Metro Spagna/bus 52, 53, 61, 62, 63, 71, 80Exp, 85, 116, 117, 119, 160, 850. **Open** 10am-2pm, 3-7pm Mon-Sat. Closed 2wks Aug. **Credit** AmEx, DC, MC, V. **Map** p357 A5.

The first Pineider shop, opened in 1770s Florence, supplied stationery to princes and poets. Pineider continues to cater for an elite clientele, selling the finest paper and leather goods – many in modern, eye-popping colours – designed by master craftsmen.

Other locations: via della Fontanella Borghese 22, Tridente (06 687 8369).

Bookshops

Al Ferro di Cavallo

Via Ripetta 67, Tridente (06 322 7303). Bus 81, 116, 119, 204, 224, 590, 628, 926. **Open** 9.30am-7.30pm Mon-Sat. Closed Aug. **Credit** AmEx, MC, V. **Map** p354 D3.

Located opposite Rome's Art Academy, this is not only the city's best bookshop for art, architecture and graphic design tomes, but it's also a gallery promoting the work of emerging artists.

Amore e Psiche

Via Santa Caterina da Siena 61, Pantheon & Navona (06 678 3908). Bus 30Exp, 40Exp, 46, 62, 63, 64, 70, 81, 87, 186, 492, 628, 810, 916/tram 8. **Open** 3-8pm Mon; 10am-8pm Tue-Sun. Closed 2wks Aug. **Credit** AmEx, DC, MC, V. **Map** p355 E6.

This cosy, wood-beamed bookshop specialises in psychology texts, but also stocks a decent range of art and poetry books. There are readings for kids on Sundays and occasional book launches.

Bibli

Via dei Fienaroli 28, Trastevere (06 581 4534/www. bibli.it). Bus 23, 280, 780, H/tram 8. **Open** 5.30pm-midnight Mon; 11am-midnight Tue-Sun. Closed 1wk Aug. **Credit** AmEx, DC, MC, V. **Map** p358 C3.

A bookshop-cum-cultural-centre, this warren-like space stocks over 30,000 titles (some in English) and hosts concerts, readings and children's events in the conference room. All this, and a café too.

Feltrinelli

Largo Argentina 5A, Ghetto & Campo (06 6866 3001). Bus 30Exp, 40Exp, 46, 62, 63, 64, 70, 81,

Eat, Drink, Shop

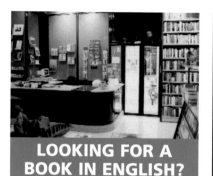

LOOKING FOR A BOOK IN ENGLISH?

We have 40,000 titles in stock to choose from!

ANGLO AMERICAN
BOOKSTORE

Via della Vite 102 (near the Spanish Steps)
Tel. 066795222 - Fax 066783890/0669784312

OUR SHELVES ARE ON INTERNET
BROWSE AND ORDER AT www.aab.it

All major credit cards are accepted

SALON DE COIFFURE
all traditional services
to enhance your personal image,
utilizing creative solutions
at the forefront
of the lastest trends

OPEN EVERYDAY. OPEN AUGUST
00187 Roma, Via Sistina 75
tel. +39 06.6780260
www.femmesistina.com
femmesistina@libero.it

women's clothing

angelo di nepi
MADE IN ITALY

rome
via frattina, 2
via cola di rienzo, 267a
via dei giubbonari, 28
via del babuino, 147-147a
www.angelodinepi.com

To advertise in the next edition of the Rome Guide

Please contact
guidesadvertising@timeout.com

87, 186, 492, 628, 810, 916/tram 8. **Open** 9am-9pm Mon-Fri; 9am-10pm Sat; 10am-9pm Sun. **Credit** AmEx, DC, MC, V. **Map** p358 D1.
This spacious store has a wide range of art, history, literature, philosophy and politics books, as well as videos, DVDs and stationery. There's a selection of titles in English. The shop also contains a branch of the Ricordi music chain (*see p248*) and a café.
Other locations: Galleria Colonna/Galleria Alberto Sordi, Trevi & Quirinale (06 6975 5511); via del Babuino 39-41, Tridente (06 3600 1842); via VE Orlando 78-81, Esquilino (06 487 0171); viale Giulio Cesare 88, Prati (06 3735 1589).

Libreria del Viaggiatore
Via del Pellegrino 78, Ghetto & Campo (06 6880 1048). Bus 30Exp, 40Exp, 46, 62, 63, 64, 70, 81, 87, 492, 628, 810, 916/tram 8. **Open** 4-8pm Mon; 10am-2pm, 4-8pm Tue-Sat. Closed 1wk Aug. **Credit** AmEx, DC, MC, V. **Map** p355 C6.
Dedicated to the traveller, this welcoming shop offers guidebooks for every imaginable location, as well as maps, travel journals and a selection of literature (some in English), history and cookery books organised by country. You'll leave the shop with serious wanderlust.

Mel Giannino Stoppani
Piazza Santissimi Apostoli 59A-62, Trevi & Quirinale (06 6994 1045). Bus 40Exp, 60Exp, 64, 70, 117, 170. **Open** 9.30am-7.30pm Mon-Sat; 10.30am-1.30pm, 4-7.30pm Sun. **Credit** AmEx, DC, MC, V. **Map** p357 A6.
An exclusively children's bookshop, stocking over 20,000 books (including a small selection in English), as well as DVDs, videos and creative toys. An array of kiddie activities is also organised in this colourful shop.

Odradek
Via dei Banchi Vecchi 57, Ghetto & Campo (06 683 3451). Bus 40Exp, 46, 62, 64, 916. **Open** 9am-8pm Mon-Sat. **Credit** AmEx, DC, MC, V. **Map** p355 C5.
A stockist of alternative books by obscure publishing houses, with sections on philosophy, mass media, politics, sci-fi and the artistic avant-garde.

Rinascita
Via delle Botteghe Oscure 1-2, Ghetto & Campo (06 679 7637). Bus 30Exp, 40Exp, 46, 62, 63, 64, 70, 87, 186, 204, 492, 630, 780, 810, 916. **Open** 10am-8pm daily. **Credit** AmEx, DC, MC, V. **Map** p358 E2.
Slightly past its prime, perhaps, but Rinascita still retains its loyal left-wing clientele. It offers literature, comic books, history, art and politics. The record department is next door (*see p248*).

English-language

The Almost Corner Bookshop
Via del Moro 45, Trastevere (06 583 6942). Bus 23, 280, 780, H/tram 8. **Open** 10am-1.30pm, 3.30-8pm Mon-Sat; 11am-1.30pm, 3.30-8pm Sun. **Credit** AmEx, MC, V. **Map** p358 C2.

Not an inch of space is wasted here: a good selection of fiction, as well as history, art, archaeology and more, is displayed on every surface. Check the noticeboard if you're seeking work, lodgings or Italian lessons. Closed Sundays in August.

Anglo-American Book Co
Via della Vite 102, Tridente (06 679 5222/www.aab.it). Bus 52, 53, 61, 62, 63, 71, 80Exp, 85, 116, 117, 119, 160, 850. **Open** 3.30-7.30pm Mon; 10am-7.30pm Tue-Sat. Closed 2wks Aug. **Credit** AmEx, DC, MC, V. **Map** p357 A5.
A good selection of books in English; what isn't in stock, staff will order. There's a vast selection of scientific and technical texts for students at the branch down the road. In summer (June-Sept) the shop is open on Monday mornings and closed on Saturday mornings.
Other locations: via della Vite 27 (06 678 9657).

Feltrinelli International
Via VE Orlando 84, Esquilino (06 482 7878). Metro Repubblica/bus 36, 60Exp, 61, 62, 84, 175, 492, 590, 910. **Open** 9am-8pm Mon-Sat; 10.30am-1.30pm, 4-8pm Sun. **Credit** AmEx, DC, MC, V. **Map** p357 C5.
An excellent range of fiction, non-fiction, magazines and guidebooks in English and other languages.

The Lion Bookshop
Via dei Greci 33, Tridente (06 3265 4007/www.thelionbookshop.com). Metro Spagna/bus 52, 53, 61, 62, 63, 71, 80Exp, 85, 116, 117, 119, 160, 850. **Open** 3.30-7.30pm Mon; 10am-7.30pm Tue-Sun. **Credit** AmEx, DC, MC, V. **Map** p354 E3.
This friendly shop is great for contemporary fiction and children's books. There's also a café, which doubles as a gallery space. Closed on Sundays from mid June to mid September.

Cosmetics & perfumes

Beauty superstores **Sephora** (in Forum Termini, the underground mall at Termini railway station, 06 4782 3445) and **Beauty Point** (piazza di Spagna 12, 06 6920 0947; other branches across the city) are known for stocking big-name ranges plus basic toiletries at non-rip-off prices. The former's own-brand cosmetics line is excellent value. For a more refined experience, follow your nose to one of the city's elegant *profumerie*.

Antica Erboristeria Romana
Via di Torre Argentina 15, Pantheon & Navona (06 687 9493/www.anticaerboristeriaromana.com). Bus 30Exp, 40Exp, 46, 62, 63, 64, 70, 81, 87, 186, 492, 628, 810, 916/tram 8. **Open** 8.30am-7.30pm Mon-Fri; 9am-7.30pm Sat. Closed 1wk Aug. **Credit** AmEx, DC, MC, V. **Map** p358 D1.
Visit this charming 18th-century apothecary-style shop if only to admire the carved wood ceilings and banks of tiny wooden drawers – some etched with skull and crossbones – in which herbal remedies are hidden safely away.

Eat, Drink, Shop

Officina Profumo-Farmaceutica di Santa Maria Novella

Corso Rinascimento 47, Pantheon & Navona (06 687 9608/www.smnovella.it). Bus 70, 81, 87, 116, 186, 492, 629. **Open** 9.30am-7.30pm Mon-Sat. Closed 2wks Aug. **Credit** DC, MC, V. **Map** p355 D5.

From quiet beginnings – it was founded in Florence in 1612 by a group of enterprising Dominican monks – the chic Officina's all-natural products have gained themselves a global following. The handcrafted potions are exquisite; prices, needless to say, don't reflect the products' humble origins.

L'Olfattorio – Bar à Parfums

Via Ripetta 34, Tridente (bookings 06 361 2325/ information 800 631 123/www.olfattorio.it). Metro Flaminio/bus 81, 117, 119, 204, 224, 628, 926. **Open** 11am-7.30pm Tue-Sat. **Credit** MC, V. **Map** p354 D3.

It's strictly personal shopping at this innovative perfumery. 'Bartender' Maria will awaken your olfactory organs and guide you expertly towards your perfect scent. Once determined, exclusive lines of handmade English and French fragrances are available on site. Paradise for perfume lovers.

Profumeria Materozzoli

Piazza San Lorenzo in Lucina 5, Tridente (06 6889 2686). Bus 52, 53, 61, 62, 63, 71, 80Exp, 85, 116, 117, 119, 160, 850. **Open** 3.30-7.30pm Mon; 10am-1.30pm, 3-7.30pm Tue-Sat. Closed 2wks Aug. **Credit** AmEx, DC, MC, V. **Map** p355 E4.

This elegant *profumeria*, founded in 1870, stocks sought-after, cult brands such as Miller Harris, Kiehl's and Diptyque, as well as the rather more prosaic Crest and Listerine.

Pro Fumum Durante

Via della Colonna Antonina 27, Pantheon & Navona (06 679 5982/www.profumum.com). Bus 52, 53, 61, 62, 63, 71, 80Exp, 85, 116, 117, 119, 160, 850. **Open** 2.30-7.30pm Mon; 10am-7.30pm Tue-Fri; 10am-1.30pm, 2.30-7.30pm Sat. Closed 2wks Aug. **Credit** AmEx, DC, MC, V. **Map** p355 E4.

The rare-brand creams, lotions and perfumes you will find in this sophisticated shop are highly tempting… but such high-class pampering doesn't come cheap. **Other locations**: via di Ripetta 10, Tridente (06 320 0306); viale Angelico 87-89, Prati (06 372 5791); piazza Mazzini 4, Suburbs: north (06 321 7920).

Roma – Store

Via della Lungaretta 63, Trastevere (06 581 8789). Bus 23, 280, 780, H/tram 8. **Open** 10am-8pm daily. **Credit** AmEx, DC, MC, V. **Map** p358 C3.

Not to be confused with the rash of shops selling Roma football team merchandise, this blissful sanctuary of lotions and potions stocks an array of gorgeous scents: old-school Floris, Creed and Penhaligon's rub shoulders with modern classics such as home-grown Acqua di Parma and Lorenzo Villoresi. Staff can be very abrupt. From June to September it sometimes stays open until midnight on Friday and Saturday.

Design & household

The area around via delle Botteghe Oscure and via Arenula (map p358 D2) is full of shops that sell linen, fabric, laces, curtain ribbons… many Romans remember being dragged here as kids by their mum and granny on a Saturday. *See also p189* **'Gusto** and *p235* **Moa**.

Celsa

Via delle Botteghe Oscure 44, Ghetto (06 6994 0872). Bus 30Exp, 40Exp, 46, 62, 63, 64, 70, 87, 186, 204, 492, 630, 780, 810, 916. **Open** 9am-1pm, 3.30-7.30pm Mon-Sat. **Credit** AmEx, DC, MC, V. **Map** p358 D2.

This reliable shop stocks an extensive range of fabrics and tailoring odds and ends. Remnants of textiles are sold off cheaply.

C.U.C.I.N.A

Via Mario de' Fiori 65, Tridente (06 679 1275/ www.cucinastore.com). Metro Spagna/bus 52, 53, 61, 62, 63, 71, 80Exp, 85, 116, 117, 119, 160, 850. **Open** 3.30-7.30pm Mon; 10.30am-7.30pm Tue-Sat. **Credit** AmEx, DC, MC, V. **Map** p354 E3.

Even the most adventurous of cooks will find a utensil their kitchen lacks at this temple of culinary gadgetry. It sells a vast range of kitchenware, from bamboo rice steamers to an exhaustive selection of jelly and baking moulds.

L'Olfattorio – Bar à Parfums.

Eat, Drink, Shop

All that java jazz

In the city where the *pausa di caffè* ritual is sacred, the serving of coffee becomes something close to an art form. After a few days of doing it the Italian way, a spoonful of instant and a splash of boiling water in a mug may no longer appeal. So rather than merely brewing up memories, equip yourself to make the real thing back home.

You will be able to find all of the major coffee brands at any supermarket, but for fresh and/or roasted-on-site grinds, check out the city's favourites: **Sant'Eustachio** (*see p221*), **Tazza D'Oro** (*see p221*) and **Castroni** (*see p241*). **Arcioni** (*see p243*) has its own blend too.

A host of other shops around town – including **Leone Limentani** (*see p235*) and **TAD Outlet** (*see p239*) – will cater for your other coffee-making requirements, from appliances to accessories. Otherwise, you could try one of these:

Art'è

Piazza Rondanini 32, Pantheon & Navona (06 683 3907). Bus 30Exp, 40Exp, 46, 62, 64, 70, 81, 87, 116, 186, 204, 491, 628, 916. **Open** 10am-7.30pm Mon-Sat. **Credit** AmEx, DC, MC, V. **Map** p355 D5.
Peruse big names in ultra-modern Italian design, especially the beloved Alessi. This is where you'll find that swank, shiny espresso-maker and cheerful teacups in all imaginable colours.

Leone Limentani

Via del Portico d'Ottavia 47, Ghetto (06 6880 6686). Bus 30Exp, 40Exp, 46, 62, 63, 64, 70, 81, 87, 186, 492, 628, 810, 916/tram 8. **Open** 4-8pm Mon; 9am-1pm, 3.30-7.30pm Tue-Fri; 10am-7.30pm Sat. Closed 2wks Aug. **Credit** AmEx, DC, MC, V. **Map** p358 D2.
A cavernous treasure-trove of high-piled crockery and kitchenware is on display here – at bargain-basement prices. Many big brand names are reduced by up to 20%.

Too Much

Via Santa Maria dell'Anima 29, Pantheon & Navona (06 6830 1187/www.toomuch.it). Bus 30Exp, 70, 81, 87, 116, 186, 204, 628, 491. **Open** noon-midnight Mon-Wed, Sun; noon-1am Thur-Sat. **Credit** AmEx, MC, V. **Map** p355 D5.
Lovers of kitsch need look no further: two storeys crammed floor-to-ceiling with gimmicky design and household objects, from retro T-shirts and badges to fuzzy dice, furry handcuffs and lava lamps.

Euronics Point

Corso Vittorio Emanuele II 101, Pantheon & Navona (06 6880 2998). Bus 30Exp, 40Exp, 46, 62, 64, 70, 81, 87, 116, 186, 204, 491, 628, 916. **Open** 3.30-7.30pm Mon; 9am-1pm, 3.30-7.30pm Tue-Sat. **Credit** AmEx, DC, MC, V. **Map** p355 C6.
A little electronics wonderland, this shop sells all sizes and styles of the Bialetti classic *mokka* stove-top coffee-maker.

Moa

Via Leone IV 1-3, Vatican & Prati (06 3972 3405). Metro Ottaviano/bus 23, 32, 49, 70, 490, 492/tram 19. **Open** 3-7.30pm Mon; 9am-1pm, 3.30-7.30pm Tue-Sat. **Credit** AmEx, MC, V. **Map** p354 A2.
This fancy homewares shop carries the finest porcelain and ceramics (including the exclusive Ginori and Modigliani labels), as well as Alessi, Bialetti and Illy Caffè espresso sets and whimsical teacups.

Tè e Teiere

Via del Pellegrino 85, Ghetto & Campo (06 686 8824). Bus 30Exp, 40, 46, 62, 64, 70, 81, 87, 116, 186, 204, 491, 628, 916. **Open** 3-7pm Mon; 9am-1pm, 3.30-7.30pm Tue-Sat. **Credit** AmEx, DC, MC, V. **Map** p355 C6.
This shop is dedicated to teatime in all its elegance, but the selection of Asian-inspired miniature teacups and trays will add some ethno-glam to your Italian roast.

Fashion

Accessories & leatherwear

See also p239 **Le Tartarughe**, *p238* **DIY dreams** and *p247* **Testaccio Market**.

AVC by Adriana V Campanile

Piazza di Spagna 88, Tridente (06 6992 2355/www.avcbyadrianacampanile.com). Metro Spagna/bus 52, 53, 61, 62, 63, 71, 80Exp, 85, 116, 117, 119, 160, 850. **Open** 10.30am-2.30pm, 3.30-7.30pm Mon-Fri; 10.30am-7.30pm Sat; 11am-2.30pm, 3.30-7.30pm Sun. **Credit** AmEx, MC, V. **Map** p357 A4.
A vast selection of women's shoes from Roman designer Adriana Campanile at the best prices you'll find this close to the Spanish Steps. Upstairs in the piazza di Spagna store there are lovely kids' shoes. **Other locations**: via Frattina 141, Tridente (06 679 0891). *Outlets* largo del Pallaro 1, Ghetto & Campo (06 682 10670); via Mastro Giorgio 66-68, Testacccio (06 5725 0493).

Eat, Drink, Shop

www.urushi.it

CA-DO

E S S E N T I A L   L I V I N G

LINEAR, MINIMAL, ESSENTIAL.
The beds manufactured by URUSHI
mingle together your wish to sleep
naturally with the need to decorate
your private spaces with first-class furniture.
URUSHI's style talks to your soul,
whispering to it. URUSHI's style.

FU-CI

SHIMA

FUTON E ALTRO PER LA TUA VITA

MILANO - corso garibaldi, 65 - 02.86915587   **ROMA** - via margutta, 21/22 - 06.32110358

Borini

Via dei Pettinari 86, Ghetto & Campo (06 687 5670).
Bus 23, 40Exp, 46, 62, 64, 280, 916. **Open** 3.30-
7.30pm Mon; 9am-1pm, 3.30-7.30pm Tue-Sat. Closed
3wks Aug. **Credit** AmEx, MC, V. **Map** p358 C2.
Franco Borini's shop is busily chaotic, packed with
clued-in shoe lovers. His elegant but durable shoes
follow fashion trends religiously and prices are fair.

Borsalino

Via di Campo Marzio 72A, Tridente (06 679 6120).
Bus 52, 53, 61, 71, 80Exp, 85, 160, 116, 850.
Open 3-7.30pm Mon; 9.30am-1.30pm, 3-7.30pm Tue-
Sat. Closed 3wks Aug. **Credit** AmEx, DC, MC, V.
Map p355 E5.
Italian hat-maker Borsalino has been producing the
world's most famous felt hat for over a century, plus
panamas and women's hats and accessories.
Other locations: piazza Trevi 83 (06 678 6816);
piazza del Popolo 20 (06 3265 0838).

Furla

Piazza di Spagna 22, Tridente (06 6920 0363/
www.furla.com). Metro Spagna/bus 52, 53, 61,
62, 63, 71, 80Exp, 85, 116, 117, 119, 160, 850.
Open 10am-8pm Mon-Sat; 10.30am-8pm Sun.
Credit AmEx, MC, V. **Map** p357 A4.
In eye-popping colours or as elegantly subdued classics, Furla's bags are spreading like wildfire all over
the city. Prices won't reduce you to tears, and the line
extends to shoes, sunglasses, wallets and watches.
Other locations: via Condotti 55-56 (06 679 1973);
via Tomacelli 136 (06 687 8230); via Nazionale 54-55
(06 487 0127); via Cola di Rienzo 226 (06 687 4505).

Gallo

Via Vittoria 63, Tridente (06 3600 2174). Metro
Spagna/bus 52, 53, 61, 62, 63, 71, 80Exp, 85, 116,
117, 119, 160, 850. **Open** 3.30-7.30pm Mon; 10am-
2pm, 3.30-7.30pm Tue-Sat. Closed 2wks Aug. **Credit**
AmEx, MC, V. **Map** p354 E3.
Pretty via Vittoria is home to Gallo's splendid socks
and tights in cotton, wool or cashmere. The trademark stripes also feature on scarves in the winter
and lovely bikinis in the summer.

Ibiz

Via dei Chiavari 39, Ghetto & Campo (06 6830
7297). Bus 30Exp, 40Exp, 46, 62, 64, 70, 81,
87, 116, 186, 204, 491, 628, 916. **Open** 9.30am-
7.30pm Mon-Sat. Closed 2wks Aug. **Credit** AmEx,
DC, MC, V. **Map** p358 D2.
Ibiz bags are made by hand in the on-site workshop:
look on as you mull over which of the handbags,
briefcases, and leather accessories you must have.

Loco

Via dei Baullari 22, Ghetto & Campo (06 6880
8216). Bus 30Exp, 40Exp, 46, 62, 64, 70, 81, 87,
116, 186, 204, 491, 628, 916. **Open** 3.30-8.30pm
Mon; 10.30am-8.30pm Tue-Sat. Closed 2wks Aug.
Credit AmEx, DC, MC, V. **Map** p358 C1.
If you like your shoes avant-garde, this is the place.
From classy to wild and eccentric, its pieces are
always one step ahead of the flock.

Scarpe Diem

Via di Parione 40A, Pantheon & Navona (06 6813
6861). Bus 30Exp, 40Exp, 46, 62, 64, 70, 81, 87,
116, 186, 204, 491, 628, 916. **Open** 3-7.30pm
Mon; 10.30am-7.30pm Tue-Sat. **Credit** MC, V.
Map p355 C5.
Owner Franco is a blossoming shoe designer
himself, and several of his hand-painted pairs are on
sale along with comfy Kickers, funky Pura Lopez,
and other whimsical brands.

Silvano Lattanzi

Via Bocca di Leone 59, Tridente (06 678 6119/www.
zintala.it). Metro Spagna/bus 52, 53, 61, 62, 63, 71,
80Exp, 85, 116, 117, 119, 160, 850. **Open** 3-7pm
Mon; 10am-1pm, 3-7pm Tue-Sat. Closed 3wks Aug.
Credit AmEx, DC, MC, V. **Map** p354 E3.
The man the Japanese *cognoscenti* call the 'poet of
shoes' flies to Washington to measure George
Bush's feet. Even Bill Clinton was spotted in this
pretty shop on a recent trip to Rome. The only
drawback? Made-to-measure starts at €3,000.
Ready-to-wear shoes for men and women are
slightly more affordable.

Boutiques

See also p240 **The A-list**.

Angelo di Nepi

Via dei Giubbonari 28, Ghetto & Campo (06 689
3006). Bus 30Exp, 40Exp, 46, 62, 64, 70, 81, 87,
116, 186, 204, 491, 628, 916. **Open** noon-7.30pm
Mon; 9.30am-7.30pm Tue-Sat. **Credit** AmEx, DC,
MC, V. **Map** p358 C2.
This Roman designer's clothes for women are
inspired by the exotic; colours and fabrics are rich,
with occasional beaded details.
Other locations: via Frattina 2 (06 678 6568).

Arsenale

Via del Governo Vecchio 64, Pantheon & Navona
(06 686 1380). Bus 30Exp, 40Exp, 46, 62, 64, 70,
81, 87, 116, 186, 204, 491, 628, 916. **Open** 3.30-
7.30pm Mon; 10am-7.30pm Tue-Sat. Closed 2wks
Aug. **Credit** AmEx, DC, MC, V. **Map** p355 C5.
Patrizia Pieroni's wonderful designs make for
great window displays – not to mention successful party conversation pieces – and have been
going down well with the Roman boho-chic luvvy
crowd for a fair few years.

Battistoni

Via Condotti 60-61A, Tridente (06 697 6111/www.
battistoni.com). Metro Spagna/bus 52, 53, 61, 62,
63, 71, 80Exp, 85, 116, 117, 119, 160, 850. **Open**
3-7pm Mon; 10am-7pm Tue-Sat. **Credit** AmEx, MC,
V. **Map** p357 A4.
A bastion of the Roman establishment, reached
through a pretty courtyard. Made-to-measure suits
for both men and women are glorious but ruinously
expensive. There is also a vast selection of off-the-
peg suits – and an expert alteration service – plus
shoes, ties, shirts, and accessories.

Eat, Drink, Shop

DIY dreams

Any shopper with an eye for the original will have plenty of luck at the boutiques around town. But for those seeking something utterly unique, nothing beats your own design. Beware, though: what starts as a souvenir-quest for friends and family may likely end up in your own closet.

Can't seem to find that perfect handbag? At **Artigianato del Cuoio** you'll find an amazing spread of leathers and synthetics to bring the bag you've always wanted to life. Take your own sketch, or describe your ideal and have the staff draw it for you, before selecting fabrics, belt and buckles… then wait (up to a week) for the finished article to turn up.

Officine overflows with jars, trays and bowls of beads. For a necklace that no one in the world but you will ever have, choose from a variety of cords to assemble them on at home, or have the nimble-fingered staff string you a personalised strand.

I Cervone looks like any shoe shop along via del Corso, but in summer you can pick a colour and style and have the flat-soled lace-up sandal you desire stitched together for you.

There's a Sicilian flavour to **La Coppola Storta**, where the typical southern cap the shop takes its name from can be had in every colour and fabric under the rainbow.

Artigianato del Cuoio
Via Belsiana 90, Tridente (06 678 4435).
Bus 52, 53, 61, 62, 63, 71, 80Exp, 85, 116, 117, 119, 160, 850. **Open** 10am-8pm Mon-Sat. **Credit** DC, MC, V. **Map** p355 E4.

I Cervone
Via del Corso 99, Tridente (06 678 3522).
Bus 52, 53, 61, 62, 63, 71, 80Exp, 85, 116, 117, 119, 160, 850. **Open** 10am-7.45pm Mon-Sat; 10am-1pm, 4-7.30pm Sun. **Credit** AmEx, MC, V. **Map** p354 E3.

La Coppola Storta
Via del Piè di Marmo 4, Pantheon & Navona (06 679 5801). Bus 30Exp, 40Exp, 46, 62, 63, 64, 70, 81, 87, 186, 492, 628, 810, 916/tram 8. **Open** 1-7pm Mon, Sun; 10am-7pm Tue-Sat. **Credit** AmEx, DC, MC, V. **Map** p355 E6.

Officine
Vicolo del Governo Vecchio 60, Pantheon & Navona (06 687 5804). Bus 30Exp, 40Exp, 46, 62, 64, 70, 81, 87, 116, 186, 204, 491, 628, 916. **Open** 3.30-7.30pm Mon; 10.30am-7.30pm Tue-Sat. **Credit** AmEx, MC, V. **Map** p355 C5.
Other locations: via della Stelletta 21, Tridente (06 686 8431).

Corner
Via Belsiana 97, Tridente (06 679 5020). Metro Spagna/bus 52, 53, 61, 62, 63, 71, 80, 85, 116, 117, 119, 160, 850. **Open** noon-7.30pm Mon; 10am-7.30pm Tue-Sat. **Credit** AmEx, DC, MC, V. **Map** p355 E4.
Casual elegance for the ladies by Milanese designer Alberto Aspesi. Bold and classic solids and sophisticated cuts make this line as pretty as it is comfy.

Le Gallinelle
Via del Boschetto 76, Monti (06 488 1017). Metro Cavour/bus 40Exp, 60, 64, 70, 117, 170. **Open** 3.30-7.30pm Mon; 10am-7.30pm Tue-Sat. Closed 2wks Aug. **Credit** AmEx, MC, V. **Map** p360 B1.
Vintage and ethnic garments are reworked by Wilma Silvestri and her daughter Giorgia in their funky shop. For those who shun the outlandish, there are classic linen suits for men and women.

Maga Morgana
Via del Governo Vecchio 27, Pantheon & Navona (06 687 9995). Bus 30Exp, 40Exp, 46, 62, 64, 70, 81, 87, 116, 186, 204, 491, 628, 916. **Open** 10am-8pm Mon-Sat. **Credit** AmEx, DC, MC, V. **Map** p355 C5.
Designer Luciana Iannace's quirky one-of-a-kind creations – including dresses, skirts and stunning hand-knitted sweaters – will provide a talking point at any party. The shop down the road at No.98 (06 687 8095, open 3-8pm Mon, 10am-8pm Tue-Sat) has more knitted and woollen items.

Momento
Piazza Cairoli 9/via dei Giubbonari, Ghetto & Campo (06 6880 8157). Bus 30Exp, 40Exp, 46, 62, 64, 70, 81, 87, 116, 186, 204, 491, 628, 916. **Open** 10am-7.30pm daily. **Credit** AmEx, DC, MC, V. **Map** p358 D2.
The poshest of princesses and her boho cousin will be equally awed over the collection of clothes and accessories at this treasure trove. Definitely for the fearless and colourful, all pieces from jumpers to evening gowns are flirty, feminine and fun. Also a fabulous spot for knock-'em-dead shoes and hand-bags in colour combos you've got to see to believe.
Other locations: via Nazionale 88F, Esquilino (06 474 4723).

NuYorica
Piazza Pollarola 36-37, Ghetto & Campo (06 6889 1243/www.nuyorica.it). Bus 30Exp, 40Exp, 46, 62, 64, 70, 81, 87, 116, 186, 204, 491, 628, 916. **Open** 10am-7.30pm Mon-Sat. Closed 2wks Aug. **Credit** AmEx, DC, MC, V. **Map** p358 C1.

Eat, Drink, Shop

This is the place for extravagant but stylish shoes and clothes by the hippest designers. Owners Cristiano Giovangnoli and Emanuele Frumenti keep the collection seriously fresh... Cameron Diaz approves. Of course, none of this comes cheap. There's a branch (shoes only) inside TAD (see below).

TAD
Via del Babuino 155A, Tridente (06 3269 5122/ www.taditaly.com). Metro Spagna or Flaminio/ bus 117, 119, 590. **Open** noon-7.30pm Mon, Sun; 10.30am-7.30pm Tue-Fri; 10.30am-8pm Sat. Closed 2wks Aug and Sun from June to Sept. **Credit** AmEx, DC, MC, V. **Map** p354 E3.

The concept behind this 'concept store' is that you can shop for clothes, shoes, flowers, household accessories, CDs, mags and perfumes, get your hair done, eat fusion Thai-Italian and drink – all in one super-cool place. Labels include McQueen and Chloé, with some occasional home-grown talent.

Other locations: TAD Outlet, via San Giacomo 5, Tridente (06 3600 1679).

Le Tartarughe
Via Pie' di Marmo 17, Pantheon & Navona (06 679 2240). Bus 30Exp, 40Exp, 46, 62, 63, 64, 70, 81, 87, 492, 628. **Open** 3.30-7.30pm Mon; 10am-7.30pm Tue-Sat. **Credit** AmEx, DC, MC, V. **Map** pE6.

Susanna Liso's sumptuous designs fill this chic boutique near the church of Santa Maria sopra Minerva. The lines of these eminently wearable garments – ranging from cocktail dresses to elegant workwear – are classic with a twist; the colours are eye-catching but never garish. For her gorgeous accessories, head across the road to No.33.

Lingerie

The last couple of years have seen a spate of new lingerie chains; both **Intimissimi** (at via del Corso 167 and many other places, www.intimissimi.com) and **Yamamay** (at via Frattina 86 and all over town, www. yamamay.it) cater for men and women looking for cheap-and-cheerful outfits in surprisingly soft fabrics. Upmarket lingerie shops cluster around the Tridente; **La Rinascente** (see p231) is a good bet for middle-range items.

Demoiselle
Via Frattina 93, Tridente (06 679 3752). Metro Spagna/bus 52, 53, 61, 62, 63, 71, 80, 85, 116, 117, 119, 160, 850. **Open** 10am-8pm Mon-Sat. Closed 1wk Aug. **Credit** AmEx, DC, MC, V. **Map** p357 A5.

Luscious, sexy and classy lingerie is the temptation here, as well as fab swimwear from Missoni, Pucci and hip Roman label Delfina.

La Perla
Via dei Condotti 78, Tridente (06 6994 1934/www. laperla.com). Metro Spagna/bus 52, 53, 61, 62, 63, 71, 80Exp, 85, 116, 117, 119, 160, 850. **Open** 3-7pm Mon; 10am-7pm Tue-Sat. **Credit** AmEx, DC, MC, V. **Map** p357 A4.

From the lace and silk that have made La Perla a favourite for 50 years, to some slightly more affordable lines, this is knicker heaven.

Treppiedi
Via del Teatro Valle 54, Pantheon & Navona (06 6880 6268). Bus 30Exp, 40Exp, 46, 62, 63, 64, 70, 81, 87, 492, 628, 630, 780, 916/tram 8. **Open** 4-7.30pm Mon; 9.30am-1pm, 3.30-7.30pm Tue-Sat. **Credit** AmEx, DC, MC, V. **Map** p355 D5.

For those with awkward lingerie needs, this is the place: an austere *signora* with pins in her mouth will take you under her wing. The on-site workshop can usually carry out alterations in a couple of days, and the sexy lacy bra you always dreamed of is yours.

Mid-range

(Ethic)
Piazza Cairoli 11-12, Ghetto & Campo (06 6830 1063/www.ethic.com). Bus 30Exp, 40Exp, 46, 62, 63, 64, 70, 81, 87, 186, 492, 628, 810, 916/tram 8. **Open** noon-8pm Mon, Sun; 10am-8pm Tue-Sat. Closed 1wk Aug. **Credit** AmEx, DC, MC, V. **Map** p358 D2.

Come here for creative clothes in bright and/or natural colours; evening dresses are complemented by lovely shoes and bags. Very affordable.

Other locations: via del Corso 85, Tridente (06 3600 2191); via del Babuino 152, Tridente (06 3600 2676); via del Pantheon 46-47 (06 6880 3167).

Iron G
Via Cola di Rienzo 50, Prati (06 321 6798). Bus 30Exp, 81, 87, 186, 224, 280, 590, 913. **Open** 10.30am-7.30pm Mon-Sat. Closed 1wk Aug. **Credit** AmEx, DC, MC, V. **Map** p357 B3.

This warehousey boutique with trashy chandeliers supplies clubwear to the fashion victims of this well-heeled neighbourhood. The hippest labels mix with ethnic and local handmade accessories.

Max & Co
Via dei Condotti 46-46A, Tridente (06 678 7946). Metro Spagna/bus 52, 53, 61, 62, 63, 71, 80Exp, 85, 116, 117, 119, 160, 850. **Open** 10am-7.30pm Mon-Sat; 11am-7.30pm Sun. **Credit** AmEx, DC, MC, V. **Map** p357 A4.

The younger and more affordable line of Max Mara (see p240 **The A-list**), accentuated by sweet T-shirts and floaty dresses.

Food & drink

If you hanker after mouth-watering Italian specialities, head for *alimentari* (grocers) like **Volpetti** or **Castroni** (for both, see p241). For fresh (as opposed to long-life) milk or cream, look for any bar labelled *latteria*; otherwise try chiller cabinets in *alimentari* or supermarkets. Food is sold by the *etto* (100g): ask for *un etto*, *due etti* and so on. *Enoteche* (off-licences; see p216) often have counter bars for downing a glass or two. See also p243 **Pack a picnic**.

Eat, Drink, Shop

Confectionery & cakes

Pasticcerie (cake shops) attached to cafés are listed by neighbourhood in the Cafés, Bars & *Gelaterie* chapter.

Moriondo & Gariglio

Via del Piè di Marmo 21, Pantheon & Navona (06 699 0856). Bus 30Exp, 40Exp, 44, 46, 60Exp, 62, 63, 64, 70, 81, 84, 85, 87, 95, 117, 119, 160, 170, 175, 492, 628, 630, 715, 716, 780, 781, 810, 850, 916, H. **Open** 9am-1pm, 3.30-7.30pm Mon-Sat. Closed Aug. **Credit** AmEx, MC, V. **Map** p355 E6.

This fairytale chocolate shop with beautiful gift-boxes is especially lovely at Christmas, when you'll have to fight to get your hands on the excellent *marron glacé*. It usually closes on Saturday afternoons in summer.

Dolceroma

Via Portico d'Ottavia 20B, Ghetto (06 689 2196). Bus 63, 630, 780, H/tram 8. **Open** 8am-8pm Tue-Sat; 10am-1.30pm Sun. Closed July & Aug. **No credit cards. Map** p358 D2.

Though it specialises in Viennese cakes, Dolceroma is also the place for American-style carrot cake and chocolate-chip cookies. It's not cheap.

The A-list

Jostling for space in window-shopping heaven in the grid of streets at the bottom of the Spanish Steps in Tridente, the emporia of the big guns of Italian fashion can be reached from the Spagna metro station or by any bus going to piazza San Silvestro. (Only Davide Cenci is out of the area.) They all take major credit cards.

Roberto Cavalli

Via Borgognona 7A (06 6992 5469). **Open** 1-7.30pm Mon; 10am-7.30pm Tue-Sat; 11am-7.30pm Sun. **Map** p355 E4.
Other locations: Just Cavalli, Piazza di Spagna 82-83 (06 679 2294).

Costume National

Via del Babuino 106 (06 6920 0686). **Open** 3-7pm Mon; 10am-2pm, 3-7pm Tue-Fri; 10am-7pm Sat. **Map** p354 E3.

Davide Cenci

Via Campo Marzio 1-7, Pantheon & Navona (06 699 0681). Bus 62, 63, 81, 85, 95, 117, 119, 160, 175, 492, 628, 630, 850. **Open** 4-8pm Mon; 9.30am-1.30pm, 3.30-7.30pm Tue-Fri; 10am-7.30pm Sat. Closed 1wk Aug. **Map** p355 D5.

Dolce e Gabbana

Via Condotti 51-52 (06 6992 4999). **Open** 10am-7.30pm Mon-Sat; 11am-7pm Sun. **Map** p355 E4.
Other locations: D&G, piazza di Spagna 93 (06 6938 0870).

Fendi

Men: via Borgognona 36-37A & 39-40 (06 696 661). **Open** 10am-2pm, 3-7pm Mon-Sat. **Map** p355 E4.

Women: largo Goldoni 419 (06 696 661). **Open** 10am-7.30pm Mon-Sat; 11am-2pm, 3-7pm Sun. **Map** p355 E4.

Gianfranco Ferrè

Piazza di Spagna 70 (06 679 1451). **Open** 10am-7.30pm Mon-Sat; 11am-2pm, 3-7pm Sun. Closed Sun in Aug. **Map** p357 A4.

Gianni Versace

Via Bocca di Leone 26 (06 678 0521). **Open** 10am-7pm Mon-Sat; 2-7pm Sun. **Map** p357 A4.

Giorgio Armani

Via Condotti 77 (06 699 1460). **Open** 10am-7pm Mon-Sat. **Map** p355 E4.
Other locations: Emporio Armani, via del Babuino 140 (06 322 1581); Armani Jeans, via del Babuino 70A (06 3600 1848); Armani Jeans, via Tomacelli 137 (06 6819 3040).

Gucci

Via Condotti 8 (06 679 0405). **Open** 10am-7pm Mon-Sat; 2-7pm Sun. **Map** p357 A4.
Other locations: via Borgognona 7D (06 6919 0661); Gucci Jewellery Boutique, via Condotti 68A (06 6978 8266).

Max Mara

Via Condotti 17-19A (06 6992 2104). **Open** 10am-7.30pm Mon-Sat; 11am-2pm, 3-7pm Sun. Closed Sun in Aug. **Map** p355 E4.
Other locations: via Frattina 28 (06 679 3638); via Nazionale 28-31 (06 488 5870).

Prada

Via Condotti 90 (06 679 0897). **Open** 10am-7pm daily. **Map** p357 A4.
Other locations: Prada Sport, via del Babuino 91 (06 3600 4884).

Valentino

Via Condotti 13 (06 679 5862). **Open** 3-7pm Mon; 10am-7pm Tue-Sat. **Map** p355 E4.
Other locations: via del Babuino 61 (06 3600 1906); via Bocca di Leone 15 (06 678 3656).

Eat, Drink, Shop

Forno del Ghetto

Via Portico d'Ottavia 1, Ghetto (06 687 8637).
Bus 63, 630, 780, H/tram 8. **Open** 7am-2pm, 3.30-
7.30pm Mon-Thur; 7am-2pm Fri; 7.30am-5pm Sun.
Closed 3wks Aug & Jewish holidays. **No credit
cards. Map** p358 D2.
Run by three dour ladies, this tiny shop has no sign
but is immediately recognisable by the line of slaver-
ing regulars outside. Among other goodies, they
come for the unforgettable damson and ricotta (and
chocolate and ricotta) pies. The lunchtime closing is
suspended during the summer.

Josephine's Bakery

*Piazza del Paradiso 56-57, Ghetto & Campo (06 687
1065). Bus 30Exp, 40Exp, 46, 62, 63, 64, 70, 81,
87, 186, 492, 628, 810, 916/tram 8.* **Open** 3.30-8pm
Mon; 10am-2pm, 3.30-8pm Tue-Sat; 11am-5pm Sun.
Closed Aug. **Credit** AmEx, DC, MC, V. **Map** p358 C1.
This former London model-turned-pastry-goddess,
bakes up sumptuous cheesecake, chocolate fudge
cake, carrot cake, cupcakes and cookies.
Dangerously rich and almost too beautiful to eat.

Valzani

*Via del Moro 37B, Trastevere (06 580 3792). Bus
23, 280, 780, H/tram 8.* **Open** 2-8pm Mon, Tue;
9.30am-8pm Wed-Sun. Closed Aug. **Credit** AmEx,
DC, MC, V. **Map** p358 C3.
A Trastevere institution, surviving eviction orders
and the vicissitudes of sweet-eating fashion.
Sachertorte and spicy, nutty *pangiallo* are specialities, but form the tip of an iceberg of chocolatey
delights, including the must-try chocolate with chilli.

Delis

Ai Monasteri

*Corso Rinascimento 72, Pantheon & Navona
(06 6880 2783/www.monasteri.it). Bus 30Exp,
70, 81, 87, 116, 186, 204, 491, 628.* **Open** 10am-
1pm, 3-7.30pm Mon-Wed, Fri, Sat; 9am-1pm Thur.
Closed 2wks Aug. **Credit** MC, V. **Map** p355 D5.
This shop sells honey, preserves, liqueurs and other
interesting foodie oddities – including an elixir for
long life – made in monasteries across Italy.

Castroni

*Via Cola di Rienzo 196, Prati (06 687 4383/www.
castroni.com). Metro Ottaviano/bus 23, 32, 49, 81,
492, 590, 982/tram 19.* **Open** 8am-8pm Mon-Sat.
Credit AmEx, MC, V. **Map** p354 D3.
This wonderful shop roasts its own espresso beans
and has lots of Italian regional specialities and
imported foodstuffs: it's the place for expats han-
kering after anything from Chinese noodles to HP
Sauce. Online shopping available.
Other locations: via Ottaviano 55, Prati
(06 3972 3279).

Franchi

*Via Cola di Rienzo, Prati (06 687 4651). Bus 23, 32,
49, 81, 492, 590, 982/tram 19.* **Open** 8am-9pm
Mon-Sat. **Credit** AmEx, DC, MC, V. **Map** p354 D3.

Head to **Franchi** for deli delights.

A dream of a deli, for just about anything you
could ever want to eat: cheeses from everywhere,
cured meats and ready-to-eat meat and seafood
dishes prepared fresh.

Innocenzi

*Via Natale del Grande 31, Trastevere (06 581 2725).
Bus 780, H/tram 8.* **Open** 8am-1.30pm, 4.30-8pm
Mon-Wed, Fri, Sat; 8am-1.30pm Thur. Closed 2wks
Aug. **No credit cards. Map** p358 C3.
Pulses spill from great sacks stacked around this
treasure trove of foodie specialities from all over the
world. Currants for your Christmas pud? Crunchy
peanut butter? Look no further.

Panella

*Via Merulana 54, Esquilino (06 487 2344).
Metro Vittorio Emanuele/bus 16, 714.* **Open**
8am-2pm, 5-8pm Mon-Sat. **Credit** AmEx, MC, V.
Map p360 D2.
A boutique of a baker's, where bread, biscuits and
sweet and savoury treats vie for attention with a
selection of speciality cheeses and preserves. The
pizza bianca filled with mortadella is legendary – try
it while leaning at the tiny bar, which is also the spot
to down one of their excellent coffees. Opens 8am-
2pm on Sunday in December.

Volpetti

*Via Marmorata 47, Testaccio (06 574 2352/www.
volpetti.com/www.fooditaly.com). Bus 23, 30Exp,
75, 280, 716/tram 3.* **Open** 8am-2pm, 5-8.15pm
Mon-Sat. **Credit** AmEx, DC, MC, V. **Map** p359 D5.
One of the best delis in Rome, with exceptional
cheese, hams and salamis. It's hard to get away without one of the jolly assistants loading you up with
samples of their wares – pleasant, but painful on the
wallet. If you can't get to Testaccio, at least check
the website: they ship all over the world.

Eat, Drink, Shop

LA COPPOLA STORTA

LA COPPOLA STORTA
deals in "coppole",
the famous Sicilian flat cap.
Our "coppole" are entirely hand-made
using traditional methods, and are available
in a range of over 3,000 different
fabrics and patterns.
Every "coppola" is unique.

We also have a store
in SoHo, in the heart of
New York City.

Spike Lee (at the last Venice Film Festival) wearing one of our highly
original pink and white see-through "Coppola".

LA COPPOLA STORTA - Made in Sicily
via del Piè di Marmo, 4 (Pantheon) - Rome - Tel: +39 06 679 5801
via della Croce 81/A Rome - Tel: +39 06 6785824
246, Mott Street - New Jork Tel: 212-2264104
e-mail: info@lacoppola.com - www.lacoppola.com

Pack a picnic

When spring fever strikes and sunny Roman days seem wasted by lingering lunches indoors, why not round up a basket of goodies and head to one of the city's glorious green spaces? For gourmet-to-go, peruse the counter at **Franchi** (see p241) for everything you'll need, including fine Italian and international cheeses, copious cured meats, traditional pasta, and meat and seafood dishes made fresh throughout the day. Or stock up at deli extraordinaire **Volpetti** (see p241).

Alternatively, do as the Romans used to (pre-supermarket days) and hit the forno for bread, the alimentari (grocers) for cold cuts and cheese, and the frutteria for your apple a day. All these staples can be found with more Roman brio under one roof (so to speak) at open-air markets (see p247 **Markets**).

Otherwise, take advantage of the recent crop of corner supermarcati in the centro storico, including those listed below. Deli counters have all the sandwich essentials from pane to prosciutto at prices slightly lower than those of traditional shops. And though these supermarkets are rather less charming than the neighbourhood alimentari, your taste buds will hardly notice much of a difference.

Despar

Vicolo della Moretta 10-11, Ghetto & Campo (06 6880 1506). Bus 30Exp, 40Exp, 46, 62, 63, 64, 70, 81, 116, 492, 628, 630, 780, 916. **Open** 8am-9pm Mon-Sat; 9am-9pm Sun. **Credit** AmEx, DC, MC, V. **Map** p358 B1.

GS Dì per Dì

Via Poli 47, Trevi & Quirinale (06 6920 2101). Bus 52, 53, 61, 62, 71, 80Exp, 95, 116, 119, 175, 492, 630, 850. **Open** 8am-8pm Mon-Sat. **Credit** AmEx, DC, MC, V. **Map** p357 A5.

Via Monterone 5, Pantheon & Navona (06 689 3608). Bus 30Exp, 40Exp, 46, 62, 63, 64, 70, 81, 87, 116, 492, 571, 628, 630, 780, 916. **Open** 8.30am-8pm Mon-Sat. **Credit** MC, V. **Map** p358 D1.

Via Vittoria 22, Tridente (06 3211 1416). Metro Spagna/bus 52, 53, 61, 63, 71, 80Exp, 85, 116, 119, 160, 850. **Open** 8am-8.30pm Mon-Sat; 9am-7.30pm Sun. **Credit** AmEx, DC, MC, V. **Map** p354 E3.

Standa

Viale Trastevere 60, Trastevere (06 589 5342). Bus 44, 75, 780, H/tram 3, 8. **Open** 8.30am-8pm Mon-Sat; 9.30am-1pm, 4-8pm Sun. **Credit** AmEx, MC, V. **Map** p359 C4.

Drink

For wine bars, where the focus is more on sitting down to drink, see the Eating Out and Cafés, Bars & Gelaterie chapters. See also p191 **Buccone**.

Arcioni

Via della Giuliana 11-13, Prati (06 3973 3205/ www.pierocostantini.it). Bus 23, 30Exp, 31, 49, 87, 280, 492, 926, 990/tram 19. **Open** 9am-2pm, 4-9pm Mon-Sat. **Credit** AmEx, DC, MC, V. **Map** off p354 A2.

The experts at this well-stocked enoteca, which has been in the business since 1932, will suggest sophisticated Italian and international labels – as well as tasty bottles that are easier on your wallet – and possibly proffer you a sample. Or take home a full-bodied, aromatic bag of their own roasted Arabica coffee beans.

Costantini

Piazza Cavour 16, Prati (06 321 3210/www.piero costantini.it). Bus 30Exp, 34, 49, 87, 280, 492, 926, 990. **Open** Shop 4.30-8pm Mon; 9am-1pm, 4.30-8pm Tue-Sat. Wine bar 11am-3pm, 6.30pm-midnight Mon-Fri; 6.30pm-midnight Sat. Closed Aug. **Credit** AmEx, DC, MC, V. **Map** p355 C4.

This cavernous cellar has a seriously comprehensive collection of wines as well as some gourmet extras such as chocolate, olive oil and pasta.

Enoteca al Parlamento

Via dei Prefetti 15, Tridente (06 687 3446/www. enotecaalparlamento.it). Bus 81, 116, 117, 204, 590, 628, 913, 926. **Open** 9.30am-2pm, 4-8.30pm Mon-Sat. Closed 2wks Aug. **Credit** AmEx, MC, V. **Map** p355 D4.

Hundreds of bottles of spirits and the best Italian wines fill the wooden shelves of this warm shop. There's also delectable honey, balsamic vinegar and regional specialities.

Trimani

Via Goito 20, Esquilino (06 446 9661). Metro Termini/bus 75, 86, 92, 217, 360. **Open** 9am-1.30pm, 3.30-8.30pm Mon-Sat. Closed 1wk Aug. **Credit** AmEx, DC, MC, V. **Map** p357 E4.

In the family since 1821, Trimani is Rome's oldest and best wine shop. Purchases can be shipped anywhere.

Ethnic foods

The best place for Indian, Korean, Chinese and African foodstuffs is the area around piazza Vittorio Emanuele, now home to a large slice

Eat, Drink, Shop

of Rome's recent-immigrant population. The market there (*see p247*) has stalls selling halal and kosher meat, along with many other products, spices and vegetables that don't make an appearance anywhere else in the city. There are also kosher shops in the Ghetto (*see p126*).

Pacific Trading Co
Viale Principe Eugenio 17-21, Esquilino (06 446 8406). Metro Vittorio/bus 105, 360, 649/tram 5, 14. **Open** 9am-8.30pm Mon-Sat; 3.30-6pm Sun. **Credit** MC, V. **Map** p360 E2.
Sells an enormous variety of Asian foodstuffs.

Health foods

Il Canestro
Via Luca della Robbia 12, Testaccio (06 574 6287). Bus 23, 30Exp, 75, 280, 716/tram 3. **Open** 9am-7.30pm Mon-Sat. **No credit cards. Map** p359 D5.
Il Canestro offers a huge range of natural health foods, cosmetics and medicines, including some organic versions of Italian regional specialities. Prices tend to be steep. The branch on via San Francesco a Ripa offers nutrition-related courses and alternative medicine.
Other locations: via San Francesco a Ripa 106, Trastevere (06 581 2621); viale Gorizia 51, Suburbs: north (06 854 1991).

Life's essentials

Your two points of reference for all life's essentials – including bus tickets, phone cards and the like – are *edicole* (newsstands) and *tabacchi* (tobacconists).

Scattered across the city, *edicole* are a testament to a generally warm and relatively dry climate. These cute kiosks have just about every journal, magazine and newspaper available in Italy, from national dailies to sports publications (which usually run out first). Stands in major tourist hubs also carry international papers and glossies in English, for those who can't go without their *Vogue*, *Glamour* and *Cosmo*. They also dispense bus tickets, phone cards and maps. They're your best bet for directions, and will generally dispense sound city advice.

Identifiable by a large **T**, *tabacchi* deal not only in tobacco products, but are also the place to top up your Italian mobile phone SIM card (if you've got one), and purchase phone cards, bus tickets and stamps for all those postcards you've been writing. Many *tabacchi* also have a postbox out front. Some double up as stationery shops; others specialise in smoking equipment or playing cards and games. Strangely, all sell salt.

Most *edicole* open early in the morning and close around 9pm. *Tabacchi* generally follow shop hours, so it's not unusual to find them closed between 1pm and 4pm. Those located in central areas usually open around 8am, and stay open late. The *edicole* below feature the widest selection of international publications and tend to stay open a bit later.

Piazza San Pantaleo, Pantheon & Navona (no phone). Bus 30Exp, 40Exp, 46, 62, 63, 64, 70, 81, 87, 492. **Map** p358 C1.

Corner of via Nazionale & piazza della Repubblica, Esquilino (no phone). Metro Repubblica/bus 40Exp, 60Exp, 61, 62, 64, 84, 86, 90Exp, 170, 175, 492, 910, H. **Map** p357 D5.

Piazza Sonnino, Trastevere (no phone). Bus H/tram 8. **Map** p358 2B.

Piazza Santa Maria in Trastevere, Trastevere (no phone). Bus H/tram 8. **Map** p358 2B.

Largo Argentina (no phone). Bus 30Exp, 40Exp, 46, 62, 63, 64, 70, 81, 271, 492, 571, 628, 630, 780, 916/tram 8. **Map** p358 D3.

Corner of via Ottaviano & viale Giulio Cesare, Vatican & Prati (no phone). Metro Ottaviano/ bus 32, 70, 81, 271, 490/tram 19. **Map** p354 A3.

Eat, Drink, Shop

Gifts

Jewellery & watches

While the big names in glitter production, like **Bulgari** (via Condotti 10, 06 679 3876, www.bulgari.com) and **Federico Buccellati** (via Condotti 31, 06 679 0329, www.federico buccellati.com), cluster around piazza di Spagna, it's well worth straying from diamond lane for a look at enviable and original baubles.

Giokeb

Via della Lungaretta 79, Trastevere (06 589 6891). Bus 23, 280, 780, H/tram 8. **Open** 10am-8pm Mon-Sat. Closed 1wk Aug. **Credit** AmEx, MC, V. **Map** p358 D3.
A sparkling array of silver settings adorned with natural stones. The chunky amber collection alone is worth checking out. Pieces here are surprisingly original and won't clean out your wallet.

Damiani

Via Condotti 84, Tridente (06 6920 0477/www. damiani.it). Metro Spagna/bus 52, 53, 61, 62, 63, 71, 80Exp, 85, 116, 117, 119, 160, 850. **Open** 11.30am-7pm Mon-Sat. Closed 1wk Aug. **Credit** AmEx, DC, MC, V. **Map** p357 A4.
Exquisite gems with that celebrity seal of approval: the (former) Aniston-Pitts have designed a range, and Gwyneth Paltrow is in the ads.

Laboratorio Marco Aurelio

Via del Pellegrino 48, Ghetto & Campo (06 686 5570/ www.marcoaurelio.it). Bus 30Exp, 40Exp, 46, 62, 64, 70, 81, 87, 116, 491, 628, 916. **Open** 11am-2pm, 5-9pm Tue-Sat. **Credit** AmEx, DC, MC, V. **Map** p355 C6.
Designer Marco Aurelio creates stunning and often unconventional pieces in hammered and wrought silver, on site. Sizable stones and intricate patterns vaguely recall ancient Roman styles.

Madò

Via del Governo Vecchio 89A, Pantheon & Navona (no phone). Bus 30Exp, 40Exp, 46, 62, 64, 70, 81, 87, 116, 186, 204, 491, 628, 916. **Open** 11am-7.30pm Mon-Sat. **Credit** AmEx, MC, V. **Map** p355 C5.
Housing a glittering collection of oriental-inspired clothing and accessories, this shop feels like an exotic (and wealthy) aunt's closet. There's a fabulous range of ethnic jewellery and pieces from the 1920s.

Tempi Moderni

Via del Governo Vecchio 108, Pantheon & Navona (06 687 7007). Bus 30Exp, 70, 81, 87, 116, 186, 204, 491, 628. **Open** 10am-1pm, 4-7.30pm daily. Closed 2wks July & 2wks Aug. **Credit** AmEx, DC, MC, V. **Map** 333 C5.
There's an eclectic assortment of 20th-century pieces in this boudoir-like shop: elegant art deco necklaces are displayed alongside 1950s Bakelite brooches and chunky retro bangles. A selection of jewel-bright kimonos adds to the effect.

Marble

Bottega del Marmoraro

Via Margutta 53B, Tridente (06 320 7660). Metro Spagna/bus 81, 116, 117, 204, 590, 628, 913, 926. **Open** 8am-7.30pm Mon-Sat. **No credit cards**. **Map** p354 E3.
Stepping into this hole-in-the-wall shop, you'd be forgiven for thinking you'd been teleported back to the workroom of an ancient Roman craftsman: the tiny space is crammed with pseudo-classical inscriptions, headless statues and busts. The jolly *marmoraro* Enrico Fiorentini can make to order.

Galleria Agostini

Via di Monte Brianzo 80, Pantheon & Navona (06 361 1141/www.galleriaitaliana.com). Bus 70, 81, 87, 116, 186, 492, 628. **Open** 9am-1pm, 3-7pm Mon-Sat. Closed Aug. **Credit** AmEx, DC, MC, V. **Map** p355 C5.
Suppliers of classical and neo-classical marble vases, inlaid slabs and huge tabletop tableaux. Purchases, however cumbersome, can be shipped anywhere in the world.
Other locations: Piazza Borghese 1, Tridente (06 687 3632); via Pietro Cavallini 8, Prati (06 361 1141).

Marmi Line

Via dei Coronari 113 & 141-5, Pantheon & Navona (06 689 3795). Bus 40Exp, 46, 62, 64, 280, 916. **Open** 10am-7.30pm Mon-Sat. Closed 2wks Aug. **Credit** AmEx, DC, MC, V. **Map** p355 C5.
Ancient columns, busts, vases and tables are on offer, as well as modern pieces made from Numidian and *rosso antico* marble. Goods can be shipped worldwide.
Other locations: piazza San Pantaleo 11-12, Pantheon & Navona (06 680 2466); via del Lavatore 24, Trevi & Quirinale (06 678 6347); via della Lungaretta 90-90A, Trastevere (06 581 4860).

Studio Massoni

Via della Meloria 90, Vatican & Prati (06 322 7207). Bus 23, 32, 49, 81, 492, 590, 982/tram 19. **Open** 9am-1pm, 3-7pm Mon-Fri. Closed Aug. **No credit cards**. **Map** off p354 A2.
A selection of classical busts in *gesso* (plaster) are for sale, while copies of just about any statue or object can be made to order. They're certainly a lot lighter to carry home than the real thing.

Miscellaneous

Eclectica

Via in Aquiro 70, Pantheon & Navona (06 678 4228). Bus 52, 53, 61, 62, 63, 80Exp, 85, 116, 117, 119, 850. **Open** 4.30-7.30pm Mon; 10.30am-1pm, 4.30-7.30pm Tue-Sat. Closed Aug. **Credit** AmEx, DC, MC, V. **Map** p355 E5.
An assortment of talking-point collectibles and antique toys jostles for space with a vast selection of militaria and, bizarrely, an array of tricks and hats for the professional magician. Pricey.

timeout.com

The hippest online guide to over 50
of the world's greatest cities

Linearia-Museum Store

Corso Vittorio Emanuele 5, Pantheon & Navona
(06 6920 0722). Bus 30Exp, 40Exp, 46, 62, 63, 64,
70, 81, 87, 186, 492, 628, 810, 916/tram 8. **Open**
10.30am-7.30pm Mon-Sat; 11am-2pm, 4-7.30pm Sun.
Credit AmEx, MC, V. **Map** p355 D6.
Two floors of postcards, posters, books and arty
souvenirs from Rome's major museums and others
in Milan, Venice, Florence and around the world.

Markets

Flea markets

Though prices at Rome's many flea markets
have crept up, bargain-hunters needn't despair:
since the trend for all things vintage has yet to
take the city by storm, there's many a find to be
unearthed by those with the patience for some
serious rummaging. At the larger markets, such
as the legendary Porta Portese and via Sannio,
haggling is expected; ignore the dealer's well-
practised air of offended disbelief when you
reject his initial price. No credit cards.

Borghetto Flaminio

Piazza della Marina 32, Suburbs: north (info 06 588
0517/www.creativitalia.com). Bus 88, 204, 231, 490,
495, 628/tram 2, 19. **Open** *Market* mid Sept-mid
July 10am-7pm Sun. *Office* 10am-1.30pm, 2.30-5.30pm
Mon-Fri. **Admission** €1.60. **Map** p354 D1.
A huge garage sale in a former bus depot, with stalls
selling bric-a-brac, costume jewellery and clothes.

La Soffitta Sotto i Portici

Piazza Augusto Imperatore, Tridente (06 3600
5345). Bus 81, 116, 117, 204, 590, 628, 913, 926.
Open 9am-sunset 1st & 3rd Sun of mth. Closed Aug.
Map p355 E4.
Peruse collectibles of all kinds, from magazines to
ceramics, at non-bargain prices.

Porta Portese

Via Portuense, from Porta Portese to via Ettore Rolli,
Trastevere (no phone). Bus 23, 44, 170, 280, 781,
H/tram 3, 8/train to Trastevere. **Open** 5am-2pm
Sun. **Map** p359 C1/2.
Rome's biggest and most famous flea market grew
out of the city's thriving black market after the end
of World War II. A lingering air of illegality still persists, so watch out for pickpockets. Dealers peddle
bootleg CDs, furniture, clothes and fake designer
gear (as well as car stereos of dubious origin).

Via Sannio

Via Sannio, Suburbs: south (no phone). Metro San
Giovanni/bus 16, 81, 85, 87, 186, 218, 650, 850.
Open 8.30am-1.30pm Mon-Fri; 8.30am-6pm Sat.
Map p361 E4.
Three long corridors of stalls piled high with new,
low-priced clothes, and a large second-hand section
behind. Those prepared to sort through the slagheap
of cut-price day- and eveningwear, bags and shoes,
will be rewarded with rare gems.

Produce markets

If you're looking for a bit of local colour, a stroll
through a produce market is the answer. Every
neighbourhood in Rome has at least one (those
in the *centro storico* tend to be pricier), opening
Monday to Saturday from around 6am until
2pm. Some stay open Tuesday and Thursday
afternoons, but much depends on the whims of
individual stallholders. None accept credit cards.
    Apart from the bigger ones listed below,
there are a few tiny central(ish) street markets.
They can be found in **via dei Santi Quattro**
(map p360 D3), a stone's throw from the
Colosseum; **via Milazzo** (map p357E5), near
Termini station; and **piazza Bernini**, on the
San Saba side of the Aventine hill (map p361 A5).

Campo de' Fiori

Campo de' Fiori (no phone). Bus 30Exp, 40Exp, 46,
62, 64, 70, 81, 87, 116, 186, 204, 491, 628, 916.
Map p358 C1.
Despite exorbitant prices and swarms of tourists,
this historic market – the biggest in the *centro
storico* – retains oodles of charm. *See also p122.*

Ex-Piazza Vittorio

Via Lamarmora, Esquilino (no phone). Metro
Vittorio/bus 105, 360, 590, 649/tram 5, 14.
Map p360 E2.
This market used to fill piazza Vittorio Emanuele
and be absolute chaos. In 2003 it moved to rather
more salubrious – though somewhat less colourful
– quarters in a revamped former barracks. An abundance of stalls stock the usual Italian fresh produce,
cheese and meats, supplemented by pulses, halal
meat, spices, African fruits and Asian food, as well
as some exotic fabrics and household goods in the
building across the central piazza.

Mercato Trionfale

Via Andrea Doria, Suburbs: north (no phone). Metro
Cipro–Musei Vaticani/bus 490, 492, 907, 913, 990,
999. **Map** off p354 A1.
Situated five minutes' walk north of the Vatican
Museums, this market is the largest in town. Lining
both sides of the boulevard, while its original
address (an entire city block) undergoes a revamp,
it isn't enormously picturesque, but it is authentic.

San Cosimato

Piazza San Cosimato, Trastevere (no phone). Bus
780, H/tram 3, 8. **Map** p358 C3.
This market in heavily touristed Trastevere retains
its local feel, particularly first thing in the morning.

Testaccio

Piazza Testaccio, Testaccio (no phone). Bus 23, 30Exp,
75, 95, 170, 280, 716, 781/tram 3. **Map** p359 D5.
A glimpse into the true heart of Rome; prices are
considerably lower than at more central markets too.
The whole northern aisle is dedicated to cut-price
shoes, with some real bargains to be had.

Eat, Drink, Shop

Get the look at **Femme Sistina**. See p249.

Music: CDs & records

For larger outlets, head to **Messaggerie Musicali** (via del Corso 472, 06 684 401) or **Ricordi** (branches at via del Corso 506, 06 361 2370; and inside Feltrinelli bookshop, see p231). The via del Corso branch of Ricordi also sells musical instruments, scores and concert tickets, and offers sound equipment for sale or hire.

L'Allegretto

Via Oslavia 44, Suburbs: west (06 320 8224). Bus 186, 224, 280, 628. **Open** 4-7.30pm Mon; 9.30am-1.30pm, 4-7.30pm Tue-Sat. Closed 2wks Aug. **Credit** AmEx, DC, MC, V. **Map** p354 B1.

Though this shop stocks a bit of everything, the emphasis is firmly on opera and classical: you'll find an excellent choice of both here. Closed on Saturday afternoons in the summer.

Disfunzioni Musicali

Via degli Etruschi 4-14, San Lorenzo (06 4543 6094/www.disfu.com). Bus 71, 204, 492/tram 3, 19. **Open** 3-8pm Mon; 10.30am-8pm Tue-Sat. Closed 1wk Aug. **Credit** DC, MC, V. **Map** p151 C2.

Still one of the best sources in Rome for underground records, both new and second-hand. Music and film DVDs are also in stock.

Pink Moon

Via Antonio Pacinotti 3D, Suburbs: south (06 557 3868/www.pinkmoonrecords.com). Bus 170, 766, 780, 781. **Open** 10am-1pm, 4-8pm Mon-Sat. Closed 1wk Aug. **Credit** AmEx, MC, V. **Map** off p143 A1.

This three-storey shop (vinyl is on the top level) is a temple for the heavy metal fraternity.

Radiation

Circonvallazione Casilina 44, Suburbs: east (06 4544 9836/800 901 168/www.goodfellas.it). Bus 81, 412, 810/tram 5, 14, 19. **Open** 4.30-7.30pm Mon; 10am-7.30pm Tue-Sat. Closed 1wk Aug. **Credit** MC, V.

This is the freshest and most original of Rome's alternative and indie music shops. The reggae and punk sections are excellent, as is the choice of rare-label and used vinyl.

Rinascita

Via delle Botteghe Oscure 5-6, Ghetto & Campo (06 6992 2436). Bus 30Exp, 40Exp, 46, 62, 63, 64, 70, 87, 186, 204, 492, 630, 780, 810, 916. **Open** 10am-8pm Mon-Sat; 10am-2pm, 4-8pm Sun. **Credit** AmEx, DC, MC, V. **Map** p358 E2.

A Roman institution, this shop has all the basics, plus friendly and knowledgeable staff. (For the next-door bookshop, see p233.)

Soul Food

Via San Giovanni in Laterano 192-4, San Giovanni (06 7045 2025). Metro Colosseo/bus 85, 117, 650, 850. **Open** 10.30am-1.30pm, 3.30-8pm Tue-Sat. Closed 2wks Aug. **Credit** AmEx, MC, V. **Map** p360 D3.

A cool vintage record shop, stocking indie, punk, beat, exotica, lounge, rockabilly and more. It's record collectors' heaven.

Services

For newsstands and tobacconists, see p244 **Life's essentials**; for shoe repairs, see p249 **Save your soles**.

Dry-cleaning & laundries

The city is bristling with *tintorie monoprezzo* (one-price dry-cleaners) that, despite the name, don't charge the same for all items: tariffs generally start at €3, rising stiffly if there's a pleat to iron in. Most laundries do the washing for you (charging by the kilo).

Wash & Dry

Via della Pelliccia 35, Trastevere (800 231 172). Bus 780, H/tram 8. **Open** 8am-10pm (last wash 9pm) daily. **No credit cards**. **Map** p358 C3.

This self-service launderette is just behind piazza Santa Maria in Trastevere. It costs €3.50 to wash eight kilos (17lbs) and the same to tumble-dry. For 18kg (40lbs), you'll pay €6.50.

Other locations: via della Chiesa Nuova 15, Pantheon & Navona (800 231 172).

Hairdressers & beauticians

Rome's hairdressers shut up shop on Mondays. Appointments are not usually necessary, but be prepared to wait if you haven't booked.

Biancaneve e i Sette Nani

Via Metastasio 17, Tridente (06 686 5409). Bus 81, 116, 117, 204, 590, 628, 913, 926. **Open** 9.30am-1pm, 3-7pm Tue-Sat. Closed 2wks Aug. **No credit cards.** **Map** p355 D5.

This unique, old-fashioned hairdresser for kids is equipped with toys, and chairs shaped like rocking horses. They'll wash and cut your child's hair for about €20. It'll open on Sunday if you book.

Centro Estetico Malò

Piazza Tavani Arquati 120, Trastevere (06 589 8950). Bus 23, 271, 280, H/tram 8. **Open** 3-8pm Mon; 10am-8pm Tue-Sat. Closed 2wks Aug. **Credit** MC, V. **Map** p358 C3.

This friendly Trastevere beautician offers great deals on waxing, manicures and pedicures. They also feature a whole range of face and body treatments for relaxation and glowing skin.

Concept Hair & Make-Up

Via Cimarra 60, Monti (320 926 7635). Metro Cavour/bus 60Exp, 64, 70, 116T, 170, H. **Open** 10am-7.30pm Tue-Sat. **Credit** AmEx, DC, MC, V. **Map** p360 B1.

Forget hectic Rome in this little light-wood heaven with a charming back garden. Bianca and Neil (both speak English) will take care of you with trendy haircuts, make-up and a refreshing cup of herbal tea.

Femme Sistina

Via Sistina 75A, Tridente (06 678 0260/www. femmesistina-rome.com). Metro Spagna/bus 52, 53, 61, 62, 63, 71, 80Exp, 85, 116, 117, 119, 160, 850. **Open** 10am-7pm Mon-Sat; 11am-7pm Sun. **Credit** AmEx, DC, MC, V. **Map** p357 B5.

Going strong since 1959, Femme Sistina was the beauty parlour of the glam and famous during the *dolce vita* era and continues to look like a glorious time warp. But its services – facials, leg-waxing, eyelash tinting, hairdressing – are as up-to-the-minute as you could wish... Nicole Kidman certainly values them, and the old-style care taken of customers by proprietor Lisette Lenzi. **Photo** *p248.*

Opticians

Replacement lenses can usually be fitted overnight, and most opticians will replace a missing screw on the spot (perhaps gracelessly, but nearly always for free). If you're having prescription lenses fitted, it's normal to get a discount on frame prices; if it isn't offered, ask for one. See also *Ottica* in the Yellow Pages.

Mondello Ottica

Via del Pellegrino 97-98, Ghetto & Campo (06 686 1955). Bus 40Exp, 46, 62, 64, 916. **Open** 9.30am-

1pm, 4-7.30pm Tue-Sat. Closed 3wks Aug. **Credit** AmEx, DC, MC, V. **Map** p358 C1.

Giancarlo and Rosaria will frame your face with the most prestigious international designer eyewear. It's worth visiting this gallery-like store just to goggle at the clever window installations by local artists. Lenses can often be replaced on the spot; and adjustments and repairs are done for free – and executed with a smile.

Optissimo

Forum Termini, Stazione Termini, Esquilino (06 4890 5630). Metro Termini/buses to Termini/tram 5, 14. **Open** 8am-10pm daily. **Credit** AmEx, DC, MC, V. **Map** p357 E5.

Save your soles

In a city obsessed with fancy feet and sky-high heels, *calzolai* (cobblers) do a roaring trade. Cobbled streets ensure they make a fortune on lost heel taps alone. It's a wise investment to reinforce the soles of new shoes, as even costly models leave much to be desired on the underside. *Anti-scivolo* (anti-slip) are the Ferrari of sole replacements, and will keep your Prada pumps pumping even in the worst of weather conditions. The *calzolaio* can also stretch that half-size-too-small-but-had-to-have pair, or paste in a heel grip for the blister prone. Rome's cobblers charge reasonable prices for their handiwork and (depending on the job) will have you out and about again within minutes.

Calzolaio

Via della Lungaretta 26, Trastevere (340 762 5463). Bus 23, 280, H/tram 8. **Open** 5.30am-6pm Mon-Fri. **Map** p358 C3.

Cucchiaroni Maurizio

Vicolo della Volpe 14, Pantheon & Navona (06 687 5962). Bus 30Exp, 40Exp, 46, 62, 64, 70, 81, 87, 116, 186, 204, 491, 628, 916. **Open** 10.30am-6.30pm Mon-Fri. **Map** p355 C5.

Fulvimar Bruno Laboratorio

Via Angelo Poliziano 54, Esquilino (06 487 2378). Metro Vittorio/bus 105, 360, 649/tram 5, 14. **Open** 8am-1pm, 4-8pm Mon-Sat. **Map** p360 D2.

Giancimino Giuseppe

Via Vespasiano 79-81, Vatican & Prati (06 3903 0057). Bus 23, 81, 492, 590, 982/tram 19. **Open** 9am-7pm Mon-Sat. **Map** p354 A3.

Eat, Drink, Shop

This bright and shiny chain store in the shopping centre beneath Termini station is open unusually long hours; they do contact lenses too.

Photocopying

In addition to specialised shops, some *tabacchi* (tobacconists) and *cartolerie* (stationers) do photocopies: as a rule, give them a miss if you need crisp, clear copies. Around the university, many copy centres offer discounts to students.

B&M

Piazza Costaguti 13, Ghetto (06 687 5494). Bus 30Exp, 40Exp, 46, 62, 63, 64, 70, 81, 87, 186, 492, 628, 810, 916/tram 8. **Open** 9am-6.30pm Mon-Fri. **Credit** AmEx, MC, V. **Map** p358 D2.
Excellent photocopying, plus plotter and CAD services for architects. You can also send faxes.
Other locations: via Marmorata 79-81 (06 5728 7289).

Xeromania

Viale Trastevere 119, Trastevere (06 581 4433). Bus 780, H/tram 8. **Open** 9am-2pm, 3-7.30pm Mon-Fri; 9am-1pm Sat. **No credit cards. Map** p359 C4.
A general photocopy shop, which also has a reliable fax-sending and -receiving service.

Photo developers

Film can be bought in specialist camera shops, opticians and most tobacconists. Lots of one-hour developing services are scattered around town, but they are not always reliable.

CocaColor

Via del Mascherino 4-10, Vatican & Prati (06 687 9498). Metro Ottaviano/bus 23, 32, 49, 81, 492, 907, 982, 990/tram 19. **Open** 8am-8pm Mon-Fri; 9am-7pm Sat, Sun. **Credit** DC, MC, V. **Map** p355 A4.
This reliable photo shop just outside piazza San Pietro offers one-hour developing.

Foto-Cine di Pennetta

Via Dandolo 2, Trastevere (06 589 6648). Bus 780, H/tram 8. **Open** 8.30am-8pm Mon-Fri; 9am-1pm, 4-7.30pm Sat. Closed 2wks Aug. **Credit** DC, MC, V. **Map** p359 C4.
High-quality photo shop with one-day developing and digital processing; camera repairs too.

Repairs

F Pratesi (Clinica della Borsa)

Piazza Firenze 22, Tridente (06 6880 3720). Bus 52, 53, 61, 62, 63, 71, 80Exp, 85, 116, 117, 119, 160, 850. **Open** 9.30am-1pm, 3.30-7.30pm Mon-Fri; 9.30am-1pm Sat. Closed Aug. **No credit cards. Map** p355 D4.
Specialises in bag repairs… which generally means the patching up of bags slit by thieves – be warned! Repairs take up to three days.

Sartoria Paola e Fabio

Via dei Banchi Vecchi 19, Ghetto & Campo (06 6830 7180). Bus 40Exp, 46, 62, 64, 916. **Open** 8.30am-1pm, 2-7pm Mon-Fri; 8.30am-1pm Sat. Closed 2wks Aug. **No credit cards. Map** p355 C6.
Run by a skilled traditional tailor and a seamstress. Clothing repairs are performed quickly – and at reasonable prices.

Ticket agencies

Expect to pay *diritti di prevendita* (booking fees) on tickets bought anywhere except at the venue on the night. **Ricordi** (*see p248*) sells tickets for classical concerts and for many rock, jazz and other events.

Hello Ticket

Ala Termini, Termini station (by platform 25), via Giolitti, Esquilino (800 907 080/06 4782 5710/www.helloticket.it). Metro Termini/buses to Termini/tram 5, 14. **Open** 10am-5pm Mon-Fri. **Credit** (phone & online bookings) AmEx, DC, MC, V. **Map** p357 E6.
Tickets for most concerts, plays and sporting events.

Travel agencies

Centro Turistico Studentesco (CTS Student Travel Centre)

Via Genova 16, Monti (06 462 0431). Bus 40Exp, 60Exp, 64, 70, 71, 116T, 170, H. **Open** 9.30am-1.30pm, 2-6.30pm Mon-Fri; 10am-1pm Sat. **Credit** MC, V. **Map** p357 C6.
This agency offers discounts on air, rail and coach tickets for all those in full-time education. CTS services can also be used by non-students.
Other locations: corso Vittorio Emanuele 297, Pantheon & Navona (06 687 2672/3/4); via degli Ausoni 5, San Lorenzo (06 445 0141).

Turicam Viaggi

Via di Torre Argentina 80, Ghetto & Campo (06 6819 3343). Bus 30Exp, 40Exp, 46, 62, 64, 70, 81, 87, 810/tram 8. **Open** 9.30am-7pm Mon-Sat. **Credit** AmEx, DC, MC, V. **Map** p355 D6.
Planes, trains, boats and the like are all bookable through this friendly centrally located agency.

Video/DVD rental

You can rent movies in English from outlets all over the city, though it's always worth checking the box – not all DVDs are multilingual.

Hollywood

Via Monserrato 107, Ghetto & Campo (06 686 9197/www.hollywood-video.it). Bus 40Exp, 46, 62, 64, 916/tram 8. **Open** 10am-7.30pm Mon-Sat. Closed Aug. **Credit** MC, V. **Map** p358 C1.
A wide selection of auteur cinema and about 400 original-language films. Lots of film stills and original posters are for sale. Lifetime membership costs €25 and a two-day rental is €3.50.

Eat, Drink, Shop

Arts & Entertainment

Natale (Christmas). *See p254.*

Festivals & Events

Why settle for just one Roman holiday?

The Romans, perennial fun-seekers, have never needed much of an excuse for a knees-up; in ancient times a whopping 150 days were set aside every year for R&R. Though modern-day Romans must make do with a paltry ten annual public holidays, the final total is usually quite a bit more: any holiday that falls midweek is invariably taken as an invitation to *fare il ponte* ('do a bridge') – take an extra day or two off between the official holiday and the weekend.

Important religious holidays tend to shut down the entire city. Different districts of Rome hold smaller-scale celebrations of their own patron saints in their own way, from calorific blowouts to costume parades, to extravagant fireworks displays. Rome's savvy mayor Walter Veltroni has lavished an embarrassment of cultural riches on the city in recent years, striking a good balance between small-scale, independent festivals and bigger-budget citywide events, which make ample use of Rome's endless supply of photogenic venues.

Spring

Festa di Santa Francesca Romana

Monastero Oblate di Santa Francesca Romana, via Teatro di Marcello 32 & 40 (06 679 3565). Bus 30Exp, 63, 95, 628. **Date** 9 Mar. **Map** p358 E2.
In 1433 Santa Francesca Romana founded the Oblate di Maria, an order of nuns who never took final vows. She was believed to possess the gift of dislocation – being in several different places at once – a quality that so endeared her to Italy's pioneer motorists that they made her their patron saint. Devout Roman drivers get their motors blessed at her church in the Foro Romano (*see p82*) on 9 March.

Palazzo Massimo alle Colonne

For listing, see p115. **Date** 16 Mar (8am-1pm).
San Filippo Neri performed one of his most celebrated miracles in the palazzo of the noble Massimo family. Called to administer the last rites to young Paolo Massimo, the saint found the boy already dead; undaunted, he revived Paolo, chatted for a while, then – when the boy was ready to meet his maker – commended him to God. On the anniversary,

> ▶ For more **musical events**, *see p276* and *p282* **Sounds of summer**; for **film festivals** *see pp263-264*; for **dance seasons**, *see p295* **Dancing days**.

after a private mass, a procession of family, servants and altar boys escorts the presiding cardinal or archbishop to a private room for a slap-up buffet. Turn up around 11.30am to witness the spectacle in all its Felliniesque glory.

Festa di San Giuseppe

Around via Trionfale. Metro Ottaviano/bus 23, 32, 81, 492/tram 19. **Date** 19 Mar. **Map** p354 A2.
Though no longer an official public holiday, the feast of St Joseph remains popular, especially in the Trionfale district of northern Rome. In the run-up to the feast, the city's *pasticcerie* are piled high with deep-fried batter-balls called *bignè di San Giuseppe*.

Settimana della Cultura

Information (toll-free) 800 991 199/ www.beniculturali.it. **Date** one week in Spring.
During Cultural Heritage Week, the state-owned museums and monuments throw their doors open to the public without charge.

Maratona della Città di Roma

Information 06 406 5064/www.maratonadiroma.it. **Date** 3rd or 4th Sun in Mar.
Rome's annual marathon now attracts big-name runners. The serious race begins and ends in via dei Fori Imperiali; sign up online (the sooner you register, the lower the fee). The Stracittadina fun-run is a 5km (3-mile) jog through the *centro storico* for those not up to the 42km (26-mile) slog over cobblestones; sign up at the Marathon Village (usually in the Palazzo dei Congressi in EUR, *see p178*, but check online) up to a day before the event.

Festa di Primavera – Mostra delle Azalee

Piazza di Spagna (for listing, see p105). **Date** end Mar, early Apr. **Map** p357 A4.
Spring arrives early in Rome, bringing masses of blooms. When the azaleas come out, some 3,000 vases of them are arranged on the Spanish Steps.

Settimana Santa & Pasqua (Holy Week & Easter)

Vatican (for listing, see p162). **Map** p355 A45.
Colosseum (for listing, see p85). **Date** Mar/Apr.
Map p360 B/C3.
Tourists and pilgrims flood into the city on the Saturday before Palm Sunday, cramming inside St Peter's square for the open-air mass. The non-stop services of Holy Week peak in the pope's Stations of the Cross (*Via Crucis*) and mass at the Colosseum late on the evening of Good Friday. On *Pasquetta* (Easter Monday), tradition coaxes Romans *fuori porta* (outside the city gates) to feast upon lavish

picnics of such specialities as *torta pasqualina* (cheesy bread, with salami and hard-boiled eggs) and *fave e pecorino* (broad beans and cheese).

Natale di Roma
Campidoglio (for listing, see p74). **Date** 21 Apr. **Map** p358 E2.
Not all cities celebrate their birthday… but Rome, 'born' in 753 BC, is no ordinary city. The bulk of the festivities take place at the Campidoglio. The city hall and the other *palazzi* on the hill are illuminated, and enormous quantities of fireworks are set off.

Festa della Liberazione
Date 25 Apr.
This public holiday commemorates the liberation of Italy by Allied forces at the end of World War II.

Giornate FAI
Various locations (information 06 689 6752/ www.fondoambiente.it). **Date** varies (see website).
For one weekend each spring, the Fondo per l'Ambiente Italiano (FAI) persuades institutional and private owners of historic properties to reveal their spectacular interiors, usually off-limits to the public; see the website for information.

FotoGrafia
Various locations (information 06 7047 3500/ www.fotografiafestival.it). **Date** Apr-May.
Rome's annual photography festival puts on a wide range of exhibitions in venues across the city, from historic museums to avant-garde backstreet galleries.

Natale (Christmas) at St Peter's. *See p254.*

Concorso Ippico Internazionale di Piazza di Siena
Piazza di Siena, Villa Borghese (06 638 3818/ www.piazzadisiena.com). Metro Spagna/bus 88, 95, 116. **Date** 2nd half of May. **Map** p356 B2.
Rome's jet-set flock to this international show-jumping event in leafy Villa Borghese.

Primo Maggio
Piazza San Giovanni. Metro San Giovanni/ bus 16, 81, 87, 117, 850/tram 3. **Date** 1 May. **Map** p361 E4.
On May Day, trade unions organise a huge, free rock concert, which is traditionally held in front of the basilica of San Giovanni in Laterano (*see p150*). Performers – mainly Italian, with a smattering of international has-beens – belt out crowd-pleasers from mid afternoon into the small hours.

Campionato Internazionale di Tennis (Italian Open)
Foro Italico, viale dei Gladiatori 31 (06 3283 7240/ www.internazionalibnlditalia.it). Bus 32, 280/tram 2. **Date** 2wks early May.
Every May, Rome hosts the Italian Open tennis tournament, one of the most important European clay-court challenges outside the Grand Slam, and a warm-up event for the French Open.

Summer

Estate Romana
Various locations (www.estateromana.it). **Date** June-Sept.
During the event-packed Estate Romana (Roman Summer) festival, *piazze*, *palazzi*, parks and court-yards come alive with music from local bands, films are shown on outdoor screens late into the night, and cultural events such as readings and gastronomic events take place in venues around town. Many events are free; check local press for details. The website may change its address; it can, however, be accessed through the town council website at www.comune.roma.it. *See also p282* **Sounds of summer**.

Festival delle Letterature
Basilica of Maxentius, via dei Fori Imperiali (06 3996 7850/www.festivaldelleletterature.it). **Date** June.
The floodlit basilica of Maxentius in the Roman Forum provides a theatrical backdrop to readings by some of the most important names in contemporary literature; past guests have included Paul Auster, Hanif Kureishi and Zadie Smith.

Festa di San Giovanni
Piazza di San Giovanni in Laterano. Metro San Giovanni/bus 16, 85, 87, 117, 850/tram 3. **Date** 23 June. **Map** p360 E4.
In the San Giovanni district, locals observe this saint's day by guzzling *lumache in umido* (stewed snails) and *porchetta* (roast suckling pig). The main

Arts & Entertainment

religious highlight is a candlelit procession, usually led by the pope, to San Giovanni in Laterano.

Santi Pietro e Paolo
San Paolo fuori le Mura (for listing, see p177).
Date 29 June.
The two founders of Catholicism are also the twin patron saints of Rome, and each is honoured in his own basilica. At St Peter's a solemn mass is the highlight; celebrations at San Paolo fuori le Mura are focused outside the church, with an all-night street fair on via Ostiense.

AltaRomAltaModa
Venues vary (information 06 678 1313/www. altaroma.it). **Date** 5 days late Jan; 5 days mid July.
Though often in the shade of glitzier, trendier Milan, Rome's fashion community is treated twice a year to a sneak preview of the coming season's collections by Roman designers, and an appearance by a handful of international talent.

Festa de' Noantri
Piazza Santa Maria in Trastevere/piazza Mastai. Bus 23, 280, 780, H/tram 8. **Date** mid-end July.
Map p358 C3.
Though few traces of Trastevere's working-class roots remain today, the area's residents celebrate its humble origins with gusto during the Festa de' Noantri. Festivities kick off with a procession held in honour of the Madonna del Carmine, to whom the whole shebang is theoretically dedicated. Two weeks of arts events and street performances follow, and fireworks round off the closing night.

Festa delle Catene
San Pietro in Vincoli (for listing, see p157).
Date 1 Aug. **Map** p360 C2.
The chains that allegedly bound St Peter in prison in Jerusalem, and those with which he was shackled in Rome, are displayed in a special mass at the church of San Pietro in Vincoli.

Festa della Madonna della Neve
Santa Maria Maggiore (for listing, see p160).
Date 5 Aug. **Map** p357 D6.
August 5 352 saw an unseasonal snowfall on the Esquiline Hill, an event which is still remembered at the basilica of Santa Maria Maggiore. The day is marked with a special mass, culminating in a blizzard of rose petals which flutter down from the roof on to the congregation.

Notte di San Lorenzo
San Lorenzo in Panisperna, via Panisperna 90 (06 483 667). Metro Cavour/bus 71, 117. **Date** 10 Aug. **Map** p360 B1.
On the night of 10 August, Roman eyes turn towards the heavens, hoping to catch a glimpse of one of the night's shooting stars. Some explain the phenomenon as the fall-out of a meteor entering orbit, while the more poetic attribute the falling stars to the tears shed by St Lawrence, martyred in Rome on this day in 258.

Ferragosto (Feast of the Assumption)
Date 15 Aug.
Those who haven't scarpered to the coast for the whole of August take a long weekend for the Feast of the Assumption, and most of the city closes down.

Autumn

RomaEuropa Festival
Various locations (06 422 961/ www.romaeuropa.net). **Date** Sept-Nov.
Rome's cutting-edge performing arts festival offers music, dance and theatre, with an eclectic mix of international acts and emerging young talent. Buy tickets at the venues themselves or by phone or online (www.helloticket.it); book well in advance for big-name acts. *See also p295* **Dancing days**.

La Notte Bianca
Various locations (www.lanottebianca.it).
Date Sat in mid Sept.
The *Notte Bianca* (White Night) sees the city's streets throng with the bleary-eyed and the caffeine-fuelled, making the most of a packed programme of theatre, dance and music events in venues open all night long across the city. Many museums and galleries participate too, offering free entrance into the small hours. Avoid the endless queues by instead visiting the major exhibitions on the warm-up night before the main event: 'Waiting for… *La Notte Bianca*'.

Ognissanti/Giornata dei Defunti
Cimitero del Verano, piazzale del Verano. Bus 71, 163, 492/tram 3, 19. **Date** 1, 2 Nov. **Map** p151 D1.
Otherwise known as *Tutti santi*, All Saints' Day (*Ognissanti*) is followed by *La commemorazioni dei defunti* (or *Tutti i morti*), when the pope celebrates mass at Verano Cemetery. Romans travel en masse to visit family graves.

Winter

See also above **AltaRomAltaModa**.

Immacolata Concezione
Piazza di Spagna (for listing, see p105). **Date** 8 Dec.
Map p357 A4.
The statue of the Madonna in piazza di Spagna is the focus of the Feast of the Immaculate Conception. With the pope looking on, the fire brigade runs a ladder up Mary's column and a lucky fireman gets to place a wreath over her outstretched arm. At the base of the column locals deposit elaborate floral tributes.

Natale & Santo Stefano (Christmas & Boxing Day)
Date 25, 26 Dec.
Tickets for the papal midnight mass at St Peter's can be obtained from the Prefettura (*see p163*); put your request in months ahead. Cribs can be found in most churches, but the most impressive are halfway up the Spanish Steps and in piazza San Pietro. The

Country knees-ups

Festivals are observed with gusto in villages around Rome. Whether events are in honour of an obscure saint or the year's crop of *porcini* mushrooms, merrymaking is guaranteed.

Infiorata

Genzano, 5km beyond Castelgandolfo on via Appia (see also p316). www.infiorata.it. **Date** mid June.

For over two centuries locals have decorated Genzano's town centre with some 5,000kg (11,000lbs) of petals, in a carpet of pictorial representations from the church of Santa Maria della Cima to the main square. Once artists have sketched their designs on the paving stones, petals are placed on top to create stunning tableaux... until the town's children run rampant the following day, obliterating the delicate pictures in seconds.

Festa dell'Inchinata

Tivoli (see also p311). **Date** 14, 15 Aug.

Dating back to 1524, this festival marks the assumption of the Virgin Mary's soul into heaven. On 14 August two processions of the faithful – one from the church of Santa Maria Maggiore bearing the image of the Madonna, the other from the cathedral with the image of Christ – meet in piazza Trento, where the effigies bow to each other three times under

arches of greenery before being carried into the church. The following day, after a final bow, they part company for another year.

Palio del Lago

Trevignano Romano (see also p306). www.trevignanoromano.it. **Date** 15 Aug.

The volcanic lake at Trevignano Romano is the picturesque setting for a boat procession to mark the Feast of the Assumption, but what really draws the crowds is the *Palio* – a dragon-boat regatta during which the three lakeside towns of Trevignano, Anguillara and Bracciano battle it out for victory.

I Facchini di Santa Rosa

Viterbo (see also p308). www.facchinidisantarosa.it. **Date** 3 Sept.

When the parents of a Viterbo girl, Rosa, born in 1233, thwarted her dreams of becoming a nun, she took to the streets, lugging a crucifix and preaching to anyone who would listen. Proclaimed a saint after her death at 18, Rosa was credited with saving the citizens of Viterbo from the plague in 1657, and every 3 September she is remembered with much ceremony; an ornately decorated 28m (92ft) column is borne through the streets on the shoulders of solemn-faced, white-robed men with knotted handkerchiefs on their heads.

Roman Christmas Day is a gluttonous affair: locals feast upon *fritti* (calorific fried offerings), followed by *panettone* (currant sponge) and *torrone* (slabs of nutty chocolate or nougat). The pope says a special mass and gives his '*Urbi et orbis*' blessing in St Peter's. **Photo** *p253*.

San Silvestro & Capodanno (New Year's Eve & New Year's Day)

Date 31 Dec, 1 Jan.

Hordes of Romans flock to piazza del Popolo to see in the new year with a free concert and fireworks display; check the city council website (www.comune.roma.it) for a full list of events. Some people add to the fun with home-grown pyrotechnics and flying *spumante* corks, turning the *centro storico* into something resembling a war zone. Beware: some older residents still honour the tradition of chucking unwanted consumer durables off their balconies.

Epifania – La Befana (Epiphany)

Piazza Navona (for listing, see p116). **Date** 6 Jan.

From mid December up to 6 January, piazza Navona hosts a Christmas fair, with market stalls peddling sweets and cheap tat. The fair is dedicated to *La Befana* – the old witch. As the pagan legend goes,

on the day of Epiphany this 'Mother Christmas' brought presents to good children only; naughty ones found their shoes filled with coal. The climax of the fair comes late on 5 January, when *La Befana* herself touches down in the piazza.

Festa di Sant'Antonio Abate

Sant'Eusebio, piazza Vittorio Emanuele II 12A. Metro Vittorio/bus 70, 71, 105, 360/tram 5, 14. **Date** 17 Jan. **Map** p360 E1.

In a rare example of Italian devotion to animal welfare, Romans commemorate the protector of animals, Sant'Antonio Abate, in the church of Sant'Eusebio on 17 January; those keen to ensure their pets get a place in heaven bring them along to have them blessed.

Carnevale

Date week before Ash Wednesday (Feb/early Mar).

In the Middle Ages this riotous last fling before the rigours of Lent was celebrated with wild abandon on Monte Testaccio (see p140). Renaissance popes, anxious to keep an eye on their debauched subjects, brought the ceremony to via del Corso (see p106). Nowadays young Roman tykes dressed up in their finery are paraded about by their proud parents.

Children

Interactive museums, ruins to explore and the world's best ice-cream…
Who says Rome isn't for kids?

If you've been surfing the web for ideas on what to do with your children in Rome, don't be put off by those dreary bloggers who say that the city has little to offer younger visitors, and suggest you leave your offspring at home. It's true there are no theme parks, Imax cinemas or giant amusement arcades. But approached in the right way, Rome itself is one fascinating, city-wide theme park. And even though the country's birth rate is now one of the world's lowest, Italian culture is traditionally family-oriented: there's nothing that the average local enjoys more than making your brood feel welcome and admiring your courage in producing more than one child. In fact, you're *much* more likely to be sold the juiciest fruit and veg at the market, offered a seat on a crowded bus or given priority treatment in the pizzeria if you have several small ones in tow.

Most British junior schools include some ancient history on their curriculum, but to guarantee a successful Roman family holiday it's best to brush up on your emperors and popes, so you can bring some colourful characters to life. A trip to your local library or, better still, a bookshop to invest in a good children's guide will help to get kids' imaginations going and introduce them to some of the architectural and artistic treasures waiting to be discovered: triumphal arches and pagan temples, towering statues and Imperial tombs.

If you're flying into Ciampino, the excitement may start even before you land: the Colosseum can sometimes be spotted from the air. As you point it out, whet their appetites with some gory tales about Christians being fed to the lions, or gladiators fighting to the death, and hopefully you'll have them hooked.

PRACTICALITIES

Since there's not much in the way of baby-changing or feeding facilities, don't be afraid to corner the friendliest looking face in a café, bookshop or children's clothes store: more often than not they'll find you a quiet corner where you can do both.

If you're visiting in the heat and humidity of the summer months, you'll have to slog far from the centre to find leisure centres or public pools (*see p293* **Swimming**). But you can take advantage of the drinking fountains located on street corners and in *piazze* all over the city: unless they say *non potabile* they all have excellent quality drinking water. Though climbing into fountains is officially forbidden, there are few better ways to revive your flagging youngsters than letting them cool off, splash around and fill up their water bottles from a spout while you plan the next stage of your tour.

Food, of course, is part and parcel of the Rome experience: here, after all, they can sample some of the world's best *gelato*. Rather than heading for the ubiquitous fast-food chains, with their mass produced nuggets, burgers and chips, let yours pick out their favourite pizza topping on a takeaway slice to revive their spirits or choose several different flavoured scoops on an ice-cream cone to delight even the fussiest child. Though you won't find any special children's menus, most restaurants are more than happy to provide you with a plate of plain cheese or tomato pasta even if it's not listed. And you needn't fret if your little terror runs riot around the restaurant while you try to figure out the menu: chances are the Italians will find your bored and noisy offspring utterly charming.

The parks and gardens (*see p260*) dotted around the city centre – many of them incorporating spectacular views – have in recent years had some decent swings and slides added to their fountains and ponds, statues and other archeological remains, which themselves make for a great game of hide-and-seek.

Many children's workshops, shows and other activities are listed in weekly events magazines such as *Roma C'è* and *Trovaroma* (*see p332*); and special kiddie events supported by the city council abound during the long, hot summer holidays (mid June to mid September).

GETTING AROUND

Children under ten travel free on Rome's city transport; older children pay the full price for single-journey and one- or three-day bus passes. If you're here longer term, invest in a travel pass (€18 per calendar month) for school-age children.

An increasingly broad selection of bus tours (*see p323*) with English commentary is a good way to whisk your family past the major sights. When this palls, electric mini-buses (116, 117, 119) connect some of the most central sights (though they're often packed).

Though much of Rome suffers from chronic traffic congestion, many of the city's central squares and streets are now officially designated pedestrian zones with plenty of pigeons for toddlers to chase while older kids continue their treasure hunts inside the atmospheric churches and exhibit-packed museums. Negotiating cars parked on pavements and avoiding mad moped drivers can be a problem, so a sling or backpack is often better than a buggy for babies.

Sightseeing

If you're travelling with offspring, don't expect too much from most of the city's museums and galleries: they're not renowned for being user-friendly and exhibits can often be unlabelled, badly lit and definitely hands-off. Much better to take the family on a bus tour (or get them walking) and challenge them to spot a pyramid, an elephant with an obelisk on its back, an angel on top of a castle – the possibilities are endless. And with a few facts at your fingertips, you can keep the kids entertained and informed with tales of popes fleeing invading armies, great artists competing for their patron's favours and emperors worshipping the stars and the sun.

If you've neglected to visit the history section of your local library before departure, you could begin your sightseeing with a whirlwind trip through the past three millennia of Roman history at the **Time Elevator** (*see p260*). After taking part in a game-show-type quiz to reveal the depth of your ignorance about Rome's art and architecture, time travellers are invited to take their flight-simulator seats and don the appropriate language headphones for their jolting journey back in time. Starting with brothers Remus and Romulus, who founded Rome some time around 753 BC, this half-hour video touches briefly on some of the key people (Julius Caesar, Nero, Michelangelo) and events (the advent of Christianity, the birth of the Baroque) that marked the city. It's pricey, and not recommended for under-fives (or anyone who's had a large meal recently), but it's a slick performance that will grab your children's attention.

After the virtual tour, it's time to tackle ancient Rome for real, starting a stroll away at the **Foro romano** (*see p82*). As there's a high risk of the kids refusing point-blank to waste time looking at heaps of old stones, you could do worse than invest in one of the 'then and now' guidebooks on sale from the many souvenir stalls around the area: they may seem tacky to you, but they could help bring the place to life for your children. Better still, if you're visiting during the summer months you may be able to catch a performance of the

Romans have a soft spot for *bambini* – and there are plenty of places for kids to let loose.

Miracle Players, an English-language theatre troupe that stages short comedy shows based on the works of classical writers in the Forum. Productions such as *Rome in a Nutshell*, *The Seven Kings of Rome* and *Caesar – More than Just a Salad!* pack in plenty of fascinating facts in an original and entertaining way. For details of performances call 06 7039 3427 or check out their website (www.miracleplayers.org). The **Colosseum** (*see p85*) is a little further down the via dei Fori Imperiali. (Beat the lengthy queues by buying your ticket en route at the entrance to the Palatine.) Make sure you immortalise your Roman holiday by posing with some of the ersatz gladiators and centurions in full regalia.

Remember *Ben-Hur*? The **Circo Massimo** (*see p84*) – once a grandiose track for chariot races – is now an elongated expanse of patchy grass that's less than salubrious after dark. But during the day it's a perfect (if unshaded) place to let your kids work off excess energy while re-enacting the Hollywood epic. A short walk away at the Tiber end of the track, you'll find queues of tourists waiting in the front porch of the church of **Santa Maria in Cosmedin** (*see p131*), home to the *bocca della verità* ('mouth of truth'), an ancient drain cover that is supposed to chomp off the hand of anyone unwise enough to tell a fib.

St Peter's (*see p164*) may seem like 'just another church' to your kids but, again, you can tickle their imagination with a few stories of murder and intrigue that have accompanied the long history of papal Rome. Younger kids may be more impressed by the Swiss Guards' brightly coloured costumes or the flocks of pigeons in St Peter's square. While you admire Bernini's magnificent piazza, keep the children busy by telling them to find and stand on the small round plaques embedded in the pavement in front of each 'arm' of the colonnade: they'll be amazed to see the three tiers of columns perfectly aligned to form a single row. Once inside the

Strictly educational

With its ruins and catacombs, churches and ubiquitous art, Rome is an education in itself. But if you're seeking something less cultural for your kids (or the generally glorious Roman weather has let you down), then you are in luck: the Eternal City has recently sprouted some entertaining youngster-specific venues of an educational bent.

Explora – Museo dei Bambini di Roma (Rome Children's Museum; *see p260*) is housed inside a old bus depot a stroll away from Villa Borghese. With energy-generating solar panels on the roof, this hands-on play-town is designed for the under-12s, with activities ranging from car maintenance and plumbing to commerce and communications. The museum has also teamed up with the UN's World Food Programme to provide simple interactive information and games about the problems of world hunger and humanitarian relief work. In other sections, younger kids will be fascinated to watch what happens when you flush a toilet, while older visitors can try their hands with real television cameras. There's also a good gift- and bookshop, a restaurant, and a terrace bar from which you can keep an eye on the adventure playground while waiting for your session to begin.

Technotown (*see p260*), inaugurated in 2006, is a science and technology activity centre for 11- to 17-year-olds located on two floors of a recently restored faux-medieval structure inside the Villa Torlonia (*see p177*) public park. Visitors can take 3D photos, create cinematic special effects and explore sound through graphic representation – though some knowledge of Italian comes in handy.

Not far from Termini railway station, the unlikely sounding **Museo dell'Istituto Centrale della Patologia del Libro** (yes, the Book Pathology Museum; via Milano 76, Esquilino, 06 4829 1229, icplform@tin.it) offers free workshops in which kids (and their parents) can learn all about the production of parchment, paper, pens and inks in different cultures down the centuries, and put together their own manuscript or book. Guided tours and workshops must be booked well in advance.

For books with no pathological problems, take your kids to the **Biblioteca Centrale per i Ragazzi** (via San Paolo alla Regola 16, Ghetto & Campo, 06 6880 1040, www.biblioteche diroma.it), Rome's main children's library. Downstairs is well designed to encourage toddlers and first readers, while the first floor has a selection of English, French, German and Spanish books for older kids, as well as a computer room, a video library and an events notice board. Non-residents can use the library, but not borrow books. The library usually moves to a tent in a park for most of the summer; check the website for details.

Arts & Entertainment

church, challenge them to find the foot on the statue of St Peter that has been worn away by the lips of devout pilgrims or the boastful brass markers set into the floor that show how much bigger this basilica is than any other church. A trip up to the dome is always a favourite (don't try this with babes in arms or with a bulky pushchair), with wonderful views both down into the church and out across Rome. There's now a café (Il Ristoro; *see p228*) halfway up.

The **Vatican Museums** (*see p166*) offer nothing in the way of children's itineraries, so it's up to you to decide what might catch their attention: perhaps the well-preserved mummies in the Egyptian section, or the grisly, tormented faces of Michelangelo's figures descending into hell on the altar wall of the Sistine Chapel? If you're looking for a bribe or some extra energy as you trudge the 15-minute walk along the Vatican walls from St Peter's to the museum entrance, stop in at the Old Bridge ice-cream shop, just past piazza Risorgimento. Nearby **Castel Sant'Angelo** (*see p170*) has handy swings and slides in the gardens outside (not to mention some spectacular frescoes and trompe l'oeil effects inside).

If it's art you're after, then take heart: both the imposing **Palazzo Barberini** (*see p92*) and the elegant **Galleria Borghese** (*see p99*) are well situated for a picnic in **Villa Borghese** (*see p95*), where you can recover from cultural overload by hiring individual or family-size bikes or taking a rowing boat out on the artificial lake. On the northern side of Villa Borghese is the recently revamped **Bioparco** – formerly the plain old Zoo – and the nearby **Museo di Zoologia** (*see p260*). The zoo's facelift has sent ticket prices up, but a train ride around the grounds, a snazzy, well-stocked reptile house and a decent-size picnic and play area make it a safe bet for the younger ones.

Not far from Villa Borghese is **Explora – Museo dei Bambini di Roma** (Rome Children's Museum), while **Technotown** is within the precincts of the verdant Villa Torlonia in the suburbs to the north (for both, *see p258* **Strictly educational**).

Other museums that may entertain your kids include **Crypta Balbi** (*see p122*), which supplements its fascinating displays on Rome in the Dark Ages with computer games to show how the ancient city was gradually incorporated into the modern; and **Palazzo Massimo alle Terme** (*see p159*), where the cellar is home to computer activities based around ancient trade routes.

The **Museo della Civiltà Romana** (*see p179*), which is a hike out into the southern

The **Colosseum** will enthral almost any youngster. *See p258.*

suburb of EUR, but rewarding for its huge plaster models of how ancient Rome looked before the rot set in. Within this enormous building there is now a new **Planetario** with a varied programme of star-gazing shows for both adults and children. As well as watching planets moving slowly across the huge domed roof, it's a remarkably relaxing way to spend an hour reclining in the auditorium's comfy armchairs. The museum is also conveniently close to the rather run-down **LUNEUR Park** funfair (www.luneur.it) and the **Piscina delle Rose** swimming pool (*see p293*).

Last but not least, don't forget to join the crowds around the sides of the **Trevi Fountain** (*see p88*) and dig out your small change so that the kids can chuck coins over their shoulders, thus ensuring a return visit to the city some day.

Bioparco-Zoo

Piazzale del Giardino Zoologico 1, Veneto & Borghese (06 360 8211/www.bioparco.it). Bus 217, 910/tram 3, 19. **Open** 9.30am-5pm (last entry 4pm) daily. **Admission** €8.50; €6.50 3-12s & OAPs. *Reptile house* €1.50 extra. **Credit** MC, V. **Map** p356 B1/2. For guided tours (in English) call 06 361 4015 from 9.30am to 1pm. From April to September the Zoo remains open until 7pm on Saturdays and Sundays.

Explora – Museo dei Bambini di Roma

Via Flaminia 82, Veneto & Borghese (06 361 3776/ www.mdbr.it). Metro Flaminia/bus 88, 95, 204, 490, 491, 495/tram 2, 19. **Open** (1hr 45min sessions) 10am, noon, 3pm, 5pm Tue-Fri; 10am, noon, 3pm, 5pm Sat, Sun. **Admission** €6; €7 3-12 year olds; €5 for all on Thur afternoon; free under-3s. **Credit** MC, V. **Map** p354 D2.
Booking is essential at weekends and strongly advised on other days.

Planetario & Museo Astronomico

Piazza G Agnelli 10, Suburbs: EUR (06 8207 7304/www2.comune.roma.it/planetario). Metro EUR Fermi/bus 30Exp, 170. **Open** 9am-2pm Tue-Fri; 9am-7pm Sat, Sun. **Admission** €6.50; €4.50 6-18s; free under-6s. **No credit cards.** **Map** p353.
Booking is essential for Planetarium shows.

Technotown

Villa Torlonia, via Spallanzani 1A, Suburbs: north (06 8205 9127/www.technotown.it). Bus 36, 60Exp, 62, 84, 90Exp, 140. **Open** 4-7pm Tue-Fri; 2-7pm Sat; 9am-7pm Sun. **Admission** €5. **No credit cards.** **Map** p353.
See p258 **Strictly educational**.

Time Elevator

Via dei Santissimi Apostoli 20, Trevi & Quirinale (06 9774 6243/www.time-elevator.it). Bus 62, 63, 81, 85, 95, 117, 119, 160, 175, 492, 628, 630. **Open** 10.30am-7.30pm daily. **Admission** *History of Rome* €11; €8 concessions. *Big bang, House of horrors* (each) €8; €6 concessions. **Credit** MC, V. **Map** p358 E1.

Parks & gardens

Besides the large, central expanse of **Villa Borghese** (*see p95*), with its bikes, skates and rowing boats for hire, other parks with children's attractions include:
● **Villa Celimontana** (*see p149*) has swings, a cycle/skating track for tinies and a fishpond that can double (against all rules) as a paddling pool – in lush green shade dotted with classical marble fragments.
● **Villa Pamphili** (*see p179*), sprawling out to the west, is Rome's biggest park. It comes replete with swings, lakes, woods, pony rides: you name it, they've got it. The only problem is whether you can find the

particular attraction you're looking for – not always an easy task in 1.5 square kilometres (one square mile) of parkland.
● **Villa Sciarra** (*see p179*), a little gem of a park, offers lots of swings and climbing frames, a mini-big dipper, rides, fountains, manicured lawns and a pigeon-filled aviary.
● **Villa Ada** (*see p175*), on the north side of the city, was recently restored and has swings, rides, ponies and basic exercise equipment.

Puppets, theatre & music

Italy's puppet tradition centres on Sicily and Naples, but Rome also offers some good productions. One of the best-known *burattinai* (puppeteers) operates on the Gianicolo (*see p138*) and is identifiable by the sign *Non Tirate Sassi!* (Don't throw stones!). Another is in Largo K Ataturk, EUR (*see p178*), conveniently near a Giolitti ice-cream emporium. Both serve up Pulcinella, just as violent and misogynistic as his English descendant Mr Punch, delivered in a Neapolitan accent so thick that most local kids understand it no better than foreigners do: it's the whacks on the head that count, anyway.

Puppet Theatre (piazza dei Satiri, 06 589 6201) stages performances of popular fairy tales at 5pm each Sunday. If you make an advance group booking, they'll do it in English.

Rome's best-known children's theatre, **Teatro Verde** (circonvallazione Gianicolense 10, 06 588 2034, www.teatroverde.it, closed Aug & Sept), offers puppet shows and plays, mostly in Italian. Visit the costume and prop workshop half an hour before the curtain goes up.

For classical concerts and events aimed at youngsters, *see p277* **Musical mums**.

Babysitters & crèches

If you're staying any length of time with little ones, check out the **Ladybirds** mums-and-toddlers group that meets in All Saints' English church (06 3600 1881, www.allsaintsrome.org; *see p333*) every Wednesday morning. The church also runs a Sunday School and crèche during the 10.30am service and has a good selection of children's books, cards and videos on sale at the end of the service.

Higher-range hotels have their own baby-sitting services, and all but the most basic hotels will arrange a babysitter for you.

Angels

Via dei Fienili 98, Capitoline & Palatine (06 678 2877/338 667 9718/http://web.tiscali.it/angelsstaff). Tried and tested English-speaking babysitters are provided by Brit Rebecca Harden, who also handles domestic staff, teachers, secretaries and waitresses for longer-term visitors to Rome and all over Italy.

Film

The action's hotting up on Rome's cinema scene.

Seventy years after the Cinecittà studios were inaugurated, and almost 50 since Anita Ekberg took her famous dip in the Trevi Fountain in Federico Fellini's *La dolce vita*, Rome has finally got itself a film festival (*see p263* **How to launch a film festival**) to match its iconic cinematic status. It was about time. For many years the reality of Rome as a city of cinema has failed to live up to the legend, and the media buzz that surrounded the first edition of the clunkily named **Cinema – Festa Internazionale di Roma** (aka RomeFilmFest) in October 2006 was a much-needed shot in the arm for the city's once glorious film industry.

That glory centred around Cinecittà, unveiled with Fascist pomp in 1937, on 99 acres of what had been virgin farmland south-east of the city (today, Rome marches right out to meet the studios along the busy, traffic-clogged via Tuscolana). It was only after the war that Cinecittà began to make a name for itself, when US producers discovered just how cheap it was to film here and the great era of 'Hollywood-on-the-Tiber' began. The Christians-to-the-lions

Roman Holiday brought Hepburn and Peck.

romp *Quo Vadis?* (1951) opened the floodgates to *gli americani*, much to the delight of the post-war public and nascent paparazzi. *Roman Holiday* (1953) brought Gregory Peck and Audrey Hepburn; *The Barefoot Contessa* (1954) drew Ava Gardner and Humphrey Bogart; and Charles Vidor's *Farewell to Arms* (1957) brought Rock Hudson and Jennifer Jones. Meanwhile, Fellini was consecrating his elaborate visions in Teatro 5, the largest of Cinecittà's studio sheds, sandwiching *La dolce vita* between two US sword-and-sandal blockbusters, *Ben-Hur* (1959) and *Cleopatra* (1963). Spaghetti Westerns and Viscontian epics kept the place riding high through to the mid '60s, but thereafter its decline was rapid. Soon Fellini's second home was churning out the director's bugbear: low-grade TV variety shows.

The 1990s saw something of a revival, with the return of big Hollywood productions, from Sylvester Stallone vehicles *Cliffhanger* and *Daylight* to Anthony Minghella's *The Talented Mr Ripley*. There was even a reprise of the over-budget glory days when Martin Scorsese's *Gangs of New York* roadshow rolled into town with Leonardo DiCaprio and Cameron Diaz. Since then the *Exorcist* prequel *Exorcist: The Beginning*, Mel Gibson's *The Passion* and Wes Anderson's *The Life Aquatic* have kept the studios' costume-makers, carpenters, post-production technicians and stuntmen busy, while all-star crime caper *Ocean's Twelve* used the studios' production and office facilities. But the biggest production of recent years has been an HBO-BBC TV series, *Rome* – television yes, but on a truly cinematic scale.

It's not just foreign directors whose cameras are rolling in Rome. Italians are still making around a hundred films a year. True, Italian cinema ain't what it used to be. Masterpieces of the calibre of *La dolce vita, L'Avventura* and *Rocco e i suoi fratelli* have been thin on the ground in the last couple of decades or so; but there are stirrings of talent among the younger generations of Italian directors.

Matteo Garrone's *L'imbalsamatore* (The Embalmer, 2002), Paolo Sorrentino's *Le conseguenze dell'amore* (The Consequences of Love, 2004) and Saverio Costanzo's *Private* (2006) are three small but fascinating films that all prove there's life in the old dog yet. Working on a larger canvas, Emanuele Crialese's symbolic US immigration saga *Nuovomondo* (The Golden Door, 2006) demonstrates a breadth of vision that has not been seen in Italy for some time. Meanwhile, some directors from an older generation are still going strong, including intense maverick Marco Bellocchio and politicised clown Nanni Moretti.

MOVIE-GOING IN ROME
Italians are enthusiastic movie-goers. Rome, especially, has seen a picture-palace renaissance in recent years: since the beginning of the 1990s the number of screens in the city has more than doubled, and audiences have kept pace. This has been due partly to the conversion of older cinemas into two- or three-screen miniplexes, but also to the creation of purpose-built mega-cinemas, especially in the outer suburbs.

Art-house fans are well served by the Circuito Cinema chain, which controls nine first-run outlets (including **Quattro Fontane**), and the first-run independent **Nuovo Sacher**, owned by cult director Nanni Moretti. The most recent additions to the art-house scene are the **Filmstudio** – a two-screen reincarnation of the club that launched a thousand earnest film buffs in the 1960s and '70s – and the **Sala Trevi**, a *centro storico* single-screen space dedicated to retrospectives.

Another new arrival, **Casa del Cinema**, has a more institutional role: housed in a former pleasure pavilion in the Villa Borghese gardens, and sponsored by Rome city council, the 'house of cinema' hosts film-related exhibitions, press conferences and presentations. But it also has an eclectic screening programme.

The downside is the dubbing. Italian dubbers are recognised as the world's best, but that's no consolation if you like to hear films in the original language (*lingua originale* or *versione originale* – VO in newspaper listings); subtitles are rare. That said, you're better served in Rome than in any other Italian city for original-language films – which generally means English. The historic Pasquino in Trastevere closed abruptly in 2005 and shows no signs of reopening, but the two-screen **Nuovo Olimpia**, just off via del Corso, seems to have taken over its role as Rome's VO picturehouse. The **Metropolitan** also has regular VO programming, while the **Warner Village Moderno** sometimes shows a Warner blockbuster in English on one of its screens. The **Alcazar** and **Nuovo Sacher** often show their current attraction in *lingua originale* on Monday and/or Tuesday.

For a standard 90-minute film, the four daily screenings are usually at 4.30pm, 6.30pm, 8.30pm and 10.30pm, and the box office opens half an hour before the first showing (some now accept credit cards, but this is still a rarity). Nowadays most larger cinemas stay open all year, but many cinemas and most cineclubs still close down completely in July and August. Compensation is found in the open-air cinemas and festivals around the city (*see p264*).

The best source of information for what's on, including summer venues, is the local section of daily newspaper *La Repubblica*, while the www.trovacinema.it site provides programme details for almost all first-run cinemas in Italy.

First-run cinemas

Most first-run cinemas offer lower prices for the first two screenings (generally 4.30pm and 6.30pm) from Monday to Friday. Programmes change on Fridays. *See also p264* **Filmstudio**.

Alcazar
Via Cardinale Merry del Val 14, Trastevere (06 588 0099). Bus 780, H/tram 8. **Tickets** €7; €5 reductions. **No credit cards**. **Map** p358 C3.
All red and plush, this was one of the first major Rome cinemas to screen VO films on Mondays. For the last two showings it's wise to book ahead (tickets must be picked up 30mins beforehand).

Metropolitan
Via del Corso 7, Tridente (06 3260 0500). Metro Flaminio/bus 88, 95, 117, 119, 495, 628, 926/ tram 2. **Tickets** €7; €5 reductions. **No credit cards**. **Map** p354 D2.
This modern miniplex at the piazza del Popolo end of via del Corso has all today's cinema-goer could want, from popcorn to automatic ticketing and Dolby sound – plus an above-average bar with pavement tables. Anything from blockbusters to films from the artier edge of Hollywood often run in the *lingua originale* on one of the four screens.

Nuovo Olimpia
Via in Lucina 16G, Tridente (06 686 1068). Bus 52, 53, 61, 62, 63, 71, 80, 85, 116, 117, 119, 160, 850. **Tickets** €7; €5 reductions. **No credit cards**. **Map** p355 E4.
Hidden away just off via del Corso, this two-screener belongs to the art-house-oriented Circuito Cinema group; its main interest is that one or both screens now usually show films in the *lingua originale*.

Nuovo Sacher
Largo Ascianghi 1, Trastevere (06 581 8116). Bus 44, 75, 780, H/tram 3, 8. **Tickets** €7; €5 reductions. **No credit cards**. **Map** p359 C4.
The Nuovo Sacher is owned and run by veteran director Nanni Moretti, who set it up out of irritation at the poor state of film distribution in Rome. A meeting place for local cinematic talent, it supports small independent Italian filmmakers and presents foreign art-house titles on long runs. VO films are usually shown on Mondays. There's a small bar and bookshop.

Arts & Entertainment

How to launch a film festival

1) **Do** make sure your mayor is a film buff. (Rome's head honcho, Walter Veltroni, even loaned his voice to one of the turkeys in *Chicken Little* when the film was dubbed into Italian.)

2) **Do** curry favour with the locals by stressing that this is a people's event, with a jury of 50 ordinary Roman film-goers, rather than a snooty critics' summit.

3) **Do** get a raftload of money (€7 million) from a mix of public and private sponsors, but without going through parliament, so you're less open to governmental pressure.

4) **Do** spend a large part of the dosh on an eight-month city-wide publicity campaign (at one point, every single Rome bus seemed to be sporting the festival's she-wolf logo). Spend an even larger amount on roping in a raft of A-list talent, from Nicole Kidman (*pictured, with Mayor Walter Veltroni*) to Leonardo DiCaprio (and be shameless: ensure Sean Connery turns up by dedicating a retrospective to him). Also, be generous to the world's press, offering complimentary four- or five-star hotel rooms for the duration (unheard of at Cannes, or Berlin, or Venice).

5) **Do** needle your long-established rival (Venice) by not only matching its budget but also by choosing a similar autumn slot – but let your rival go first to avoid outright war. (In 2006, Venice opened on 30 August and closed on 9 September, while Rome's first edition ran from 14 to 23 October.) And exploit Venice's failure to develop a serious film market even after 63 editions by launching your own fledgling marketplace for film buyers, sellers, movers and shakers – and locate it in via Veneto, original home of *La dolce vita*.

6) **Do** link up with another feisty little newcomer, New York's Tribeca Film Festival, to ensure arthouse kudos *and* the presence at your sister do of Tribeca founding father Robert De Niro.

7) **Do** collar four or five major world or European premières (in 2006 these included Steven Shainberg's *Fur* with Nicole Kidman, Lasse Hallstrom's *The Hoax* with Richard Gere, and Christopher Nolan's *The Prestige* with Hugh Jackman and Christian Bale)

... and what *not* to do:

8) **Don't** undermine the authority of the event by putting 16 small, marginal films in your official competition – most of which have already screened at other festivals.

9) **Don't** alienate the press you've been so eager to court by scheduling major preview screenings in cinemas that only hold a third of those who want to get in.

10) **Don't** start gala screenings over an hour late.

Well, seven out of ten isn't bad for a festival that's still in its infancy. The second edition of this event is scheduled for 18-27 October 2007. Check the festival website for further details.

● *www.romacinemafest.org*

Arts & Entertainment

Quattro Fontane
Via Quattro Fontane 23, Trevi & Quirinale (06 474 1515). Bus 40Exp, 60Exp, 64, 70, 170. **Tickets** €7; €5 reductions. **No credit cards**. **Map** p357 C5.
This is the designer showcase miniplex of indie distribution cartel Circuito Cinema (*see p262*). It has state-of-the-art sound system and a small bar for post-screening analysis. Small domestic indies often get their only Italian outing in Sala 4.

Warner Village Moderno
Piazza della Repubblica 45-46, Esquilino (06 4777 9202). Metro Repubblica/bus 40, 60, 61, 62, 64, 90, 170, 175, 492, 910. **Tickets** €7.50; €5.50 reductions. **Credit** AmEx, DC, MC, V. **Map** p357 D5.
The full-on American Movie-going Experience. Warner Village has two outposts in Rome: this more restrained five-screen central branch (in a venerable former porn palace, now sanitised) is remarkable only for the fact that it often dedicates one screen to

original-language Hollywood blockbusters. The other branch is an 18-screen multiplex at Parco de' Medici, just off the Fiumicino airport road.

Cinema d'essai & cineclubs

Generally small and cheap, *cinema d'essai* mainly feature classics or contemporary arthouse cinema, occasionally in *versione originale*. In these, and even smaller cineclubs, the best of Italy's cinema heritage can be seen. Some *centri sociali* (*see p279*) offer screenings of alternative or difficult-to-see films. A *tessera* (membership card) is required by many clubs, but these are free or carry a minimal charge.

Azzurro Scipioni
Via degli Scipioni 82, Prati (06 3973 7161/www. azzurroscipioni.com). Metro Lepanto/bus 30, 70, 81, 280, 913. **Tickets** (with annual €6 membership) €5; €4 reductions. **No credit cards. Map** p354 B3.
Azzurro Scipioni is run by director Silvio Agosti. It has two screens: the Sala Chaplin shows more recent art-house successes, while Sala Lumière, with a video projector, is devoted to world cinema classics and themed seasons.

Casa del Cinema
Largo Marcello Mastroianni 1, Veneto & Borghese (06 423 6019/www.casadelcinema.it). Bus 88, 95, 116, 490, 495. **No credit cards. Map** p356 B3.
This new film space in a restored pavilion in the Villa Borghese park is used for cinema-related presentations, but also has its own screening schedule, organised around themed days of the week. There's also a bookshop and a café (*see p217*). Admission to screenings is free.

Detour
Via Urbana 47A, Monti (06 4859 0845/www. cinedetour.it). Metro Cavour/bus 75, 84, 117. **Tickets** (with annual €5 membership) €3. **No credit cards. Map** p360 C1.
A small but committed cineclub with an eclectic programme – cinema classics, world cinema, shorts – but poor projection quality. Workshops, debates and art exhibitions are also organised.

Filmstudio
Via degli Orti di Alibert 1C, Trastevere (06 6819 2987). Bus 23, 280. **Tickets** (€6); €4.50 reductions. **No credit cards. Map** p358 A1.
This historic Rome film club returned from oblivion to its old home at the end of 2000, with new, comfortable seats and state-of-the-art screening facilities. It alternates first-run art-house films with more *recherché* treats and themed seasons, which include the occasional film in the *lingua originale*.

Sala Trevi 'Alberto Sordi'
Vicolo del Puttarello 25, Trevi & Quirinale (06 678 1206). Bus 52, 53, 61, 63, 71, 80, 85, 95, 116, 119, 160, 850. **Tickets** €5; €4 reductions. **No credit cards. Map** p357 A6.

This brand new 100-seater art cinema belongs to the Cineteca Nazionale, Italy's national film archive. Named after late, great actor Alberto Sordi, the cinema is dedicated to restored Italian classics by Fellini, Pasolini, Sergio Leone and others, plus the occasional foreign interloper. It shares its basement location with a 400sq m (4,300sq ft) archaeological site based around two ancient Roman *insulae* (apartment blocks), which can be seen through the glass panels at the side of the main screening room. Closed on Mondays. You can get a ten-ticket deal for €30.

Festivals & summer programmes

Around the beginning of July, as cinemas are closing and box-office figures take a nosedive, Rome becomes a great place to take in a movie. A raft of second-run or art-house open-air cinema feasts is launched as part of the **Estate Romana** festivities (*see p253*), many of them in breathtaking settings. In addition, several *arene* (open-air screens) provide a chance to catch that blockbuster you missed or to take in an underground classic.

Two regular mini-festivals – **Cannes a Roma** and **Venezia a Roma** – show a selection of original-language films from the Cannes and Venice film festivals a few days after the festivals themselves close (in May and September respectively). They were joined in 2006 by a rather more ambitious venture, the **Cinema – Festa Internazionale di Roma** (*see p263* **How to launch a film festival**).

Festivals and *arene* come and go, so always check local press for details of what's on. The following are regular summer fixtures.

Cineporto
Parco della Farnesina, Suburbs: north (06 3600 5556/www.cineporto.com). Bus 32, 224, 280. **Date** usually July & Aug. **No credit cards.**
One of the most successful and popular summer festivals is in the park by the Stadio Olimpico (*see p290*). There are two separate screens, each of them showing two dubbed films a night, often recent releases. Live concerts of mainly Italian bands are presented between shows on many nights.

Massenzio
www.massenzio.net. **Date** July & Aug. **No credit cards.**
The biggest and most politically correct of all Rome's open-air film festivals, featuring about 200 films every year. The venue changes annually (in 2006 it was in the Parco del Celio, overlooking the Colosseum), so check for details. The imaginative programmes are organised around directors, actors, countries, genres or themes; there's usually a large viewing area for the more commercial films and a smaller art-house space.

Arts & Entertainment

Galleries

The Eternal City is finally getting up off its laurels to embrace the contemporary.

Galleria Sala 1.
See p267.

The famously lacklustre Roman contemporary art scene is positively buzzing these days. Not only is mega dealer Larry Gagosian planning to open his first Continental gallery here within the year, but many galleries are choosing the capital over Milan, formerly the commercial centre for the Italian art world. Established galleries based in other cities – including Lipanje Puntin of Trieste, Romberg of Latina, and Studio Trisorio of Naples – have opened branches in Rome within the last two years. In this way Italy is reflecting the current state of the international art world, with the burgeoning of many small centres of vibrant activity, notably Naples and Turin, sustained by growing numbers of art fairs and biennials.

Although private galleries seem to be thriving, some city projects are moving slowly. The construction of **MAXXI** (Museo del XXI Secolo – Museum of the 21st Century; *see p175*), a spectacular sinuous structure designed by Zaha Hadid, has been delayed due to budget constraints. In the meantime exhibitions linking architecture and art are hosted in a former military barracks on the site. A revamp of the **Palazzo delle Esposizioni** (*see p93*) ground to a halt in 2004 when a construction worker died when part of the building collapsed; it's now slated to open in September 2007.

However, the two **MACRO** (Museo d'Arte Contemporanea di Roma, *see p176*) spaces have become vibrant art centres. Both galleries are successfully converted industrial spaces: the headquarters in via Reggio Emilia is a former brewery (with a stunning glass addition by French architect Odile Decq due in 2008); its cavernous ancillary space in Testaccio occupies part of the former municipal slaughterhouse; a new pavilion is due to open there later in 2007.

Other great spaces dedicated to modern and contemporary art include **Galleria Termini**, inside Termini railway station (*see p158*); **Cinecittàdue Arte Contemporanea** (viale Palmiro Togliatti 2, 06 722 0910), inside the slick Cinecittà Due shopping mall in the eastern suburbs; the harmonious space dedicated to art in Renzo Piano's **Auditorium-Parco della Musica** (*see p273*); and the archaeological area inside the **Mercati di Traiano** (Trajan's markets, *see p81*), where monumental ruins provide a dramatic setting for contemporary installations and photography. The **Centrale Montemartini** (*see p142*), a decommissioned generating station, displays the city's stores of classical statuary as well as temporary exhibitions of fashion and photography.

Major shows of modern and contemporary art and photography are held at the **Museo di Palazzo Venezia** (*see p77*) and inside the **Vittoriano** complex (*see p80*). Other large central venues include the **Scuderie del Quirinale** (*see p94*), **Palazzo Ruspoli** (*see p109*), the **Museo del Corso** (*see p119*) and the **Chiostro del Bramante** in Santa

Arts & Entertainment

Maria della Pace (*see p115*). The **Palazzo di Montecitorio** (*see p109*) is always worth checking out: shows here are free, generally of good quality, and give you a chance to get into the parliament building without booking. (Avoid weekends: queues can be hours long.)

Cultural events at foreign academies can include top-class exhibitions. Check local press (*see p331*) for programmes at the Académie de France (www.villamedici.it), Accademia di Spagna (www.academiaroma.com), Accademia d'Ungheria (www.magyarintezet.hu), British School (www.bsr.ac.org), Goethe Institut (www.goethe.de/roma), Instituto Cervantes (http://roma.cervantes.es) and the American Academy (www.aarome.org), in particular.

In the spring the ever-growing **FotoGrafia Festival Internazionale di Roma** (06 492 7141, www.fotografiafestival.it) encompasses photographic exhibitions in museums and galleries as well as less mainstream venues.

To find out what's going on at any given time, pick up the *Art Guide* (www.artguide.it), a free handout available in most galleries. It provides listings of exhibitions and information about openings. The 'Trovaroma' supplement of Thursday's *La Repubblica* has a comprehensive arts section with reliable reviews; you'll find an English-language summary at the back. *Wanted in Rome* (*see p332*), an English-language fortnightly magazine, has an exhaustive section with venue details and exhibition reviews.

Only the most renowned or reliable galleries are listed below. Note that opening times and summer closures can vary from year to year.

The Tridente

Il Gabbiano
Via della Frezza 51 (06 322 7049/www.galleria ilgabbiano.com). Metro Flaminio/bus 117, 119, 628. **Open** 10am-1pm, 4.30-7.30pm Tue-Sat. Closed Aug. **No credit cards. Map** p354 D3.

Situated behind the trendy restaurant 'Gusto (*see p189*), this classic gallery has been showing the work of well-known artists since 1967.

Magazzino d'Arte Moderna
Via dei Prefetti 17 (06 687 5951/www.magazzino artemoderna.com). Bus 62, 63, 81, 85, 95, 116, 117, 119, 160, 175, 492, 628, 630, 850. **Open** 11am-3pm, 4-8pm Tue-Fri; 11am-1pm, 4-8pm Sat. Closed Aug. **No credit cards. Map** p355 D4.
Strong on installations, videos and photography, this gallery works closely with the artists it promotes.

La Nuova Pesa
Via del Corso 530 (06 361 0892). Metro Flaminio/ bus 117, 119. **Open** 10.30am-1pm, 3-7pm Mon-Fri. Closed Aug. **No credit cards. Map** p355 E4.
In the 1950s, La Nuova Pesa organised the first post-war Italian shows of Picasso, Gris and Léger. The gallery now works with upcoming Roman artists and big international names alike.

Valentina Moncada Arte Contemporanea
Via Margutta 54 (06 320 7956/www.valentina moncada.com). Metro Spagna/bus 117, 119. **Open** noon-6pm Mon-Fri. Closed mid July-early Sept. **No credit cards. Map** p354 E3.
Federico Fellini lived on this street, fashionable in the 1950s and now filled with small galleries and antique dealers. Hidden away in a picturesque garden among a series of purpose-built 19th-century artists' studios, this gallery focuses on photography, alternating between 20th-century masters and emerging artists.

Pantheon & Navona

Studio Trisorio Roma
Vicolo delle Vacche 12 (06 6813 6189/www.studio trisorio.com). Bus 30Exp, 40Exp, 46, 62, 64, 87, 628, 916. **Open** 4-8pm Tue-Sat. Closed Aug. **No credit cards. Map** p355 C5.
Run by mother-and-daughter team Lucia and Laura Trisorio, this recently opened branch of a Naples gallery shows the work of important artists such as Rebecca Horn, Tom Wesselman and Enzo Cucchi.

Sacred and profane

Right beneath one of Catholic Rome's holiest relics – the Scala Santa (Holy Stairs; *see p151*) – lies a truly unique Roman institution, the non-profit gallery **Sala 1** (*see p267*). The stunning ex-basilica was restored and opened as an art centre in 1970 by priest-sculptor Tito Amodei. For almost 40 years it has been a pioneer in Rome's art world, hosting premières of young artists and groundbreaking international exhibitions, such as *Moscow: Third Rome*, Italy's first look at Russian artists of the perestroika era; *Affinities*, the first show of South African art, including the debut of William Kentridge; and the first retrospective for French performance artist Orlan, whose medium is her own body. Directed with energy and enthusiasm by American curator Mary Angela Schroth, the progressive programme is supported by private companies and individuals as well as public funding, allowing unlimited independence and freedom in its activities.

VM21 Arte Contemporanea
Via della Vetrina 21 (06 6889 1365/www.vm21 contemporanea.com). Bus 30Exp, 40Exp, 46, 62, 64, 87, 628, 916. **Open** 11am-7.30pm Mon-Fri; 4.30-7.30pm Sat. Closed mid July-Aug. **No credit cards. Map** p355 C5.
This spacious, attractive gallery, which opened in 2004, collaborates with notable Italian and foreign artists working in a representative selection of media. The small gallery across the street, 9 via della Vetrina Contemporanea, is also worth checking out.

Ghetto & Campo de' Fiori

Galleria Alessandra Bonomo
Via del Gesù 62 (06 6992 5858/www.bonomo gallery.com). Bus 30Exp, 40Exp, 46, 62, 63, 64, 70, 81/tram 8. **Open** 3-7pm Mon-Sat. Closed Aug. **No credit cards. Map** p358 D1.
Tucked away in a peaceful palazzo courtyard, this gallery – run by yet another member of the Bonomo dynasty – shows a mix of established Italian and emerging foreign artists.

Lipanje Puntin Arte Contemporanea
Via di Montoro 10 (06 6830 7780/www.lipanjepuntin. com). Bus 40Exp, 46, 62, 64, 116, 916. **Open** 2-8pm Tue-Sat. Closed Aug. **No credit cards. Map** p355 C6.
This branch of a 12-year-old Trieste gallery shows a roster of successful artists, whose bold work is often focused on the pop genre or photography.

NextDoor
Via di Montoro 3 (06 4542 5048/www.galleria nextdoor.com). Bus 40Exp, 46, 62, 64, 116, 916. **Open** 1-7pm Tue-Sat. Closed Aug. **No credit cards. Map** p355 C6.
Previously focusing on photography, this tiny space is now venturing into site-specific installations.

Il Ponte Contemporanea
Via di Monserrato 23 (06 6880 1351/www.ilponte contemporanea.com). Bus 23, 40Exp, 46, 62, 64, 116, 280, 916. **Open** noon-8pm Mon-Sat. Closed Aug. **No credit cards. Map** p355 C6.
This stylish gallery focuses mostly on photography and installation art. Pierre & Gilles and Tracey Moffat had their first Italian shows here.

Romberg Arte Contemporanea
Piazza de' Ricci 127 (06 6880 6377). Bus 23, 40Exp, 46, 62, 64, 116, 280, 916. **Open** 2-8pm Tue-Sat. Closed Aug. **Map** p355 C6.
This recently opened branch of the long-standing gallery in Latina (south of Rome) exhibits some interesting mid-career Italian painters.

Valentina Bonomo Arte Contemporanea
Via del Portico d'Ottavia 13 (06 683 2766/www. galleriabonomo.com). Bus 23, 30Exp, 63, 280, 780, H/tram 8. **Open** 11am-1pm, 3.30-7.30pm Mon-Wed, Fri, Sat; 3.30-7.30pm Thur. Closed Aug-mid Sept. **No credit cards. Map** p358 D2.

Directed by a daughter of Marilena Bonomo, owner of an influential Bari gallery since 1971, this space exhibits work by both established international artists and young photographers.

Trastevere & Gianicolo

Galleria Lorcan O'Neill
Via Orti d'Alibert 1E (06 6889 2980/www.lorcan oneill.com). Bus 23, 280. **Open** noon-8pm Mon-Fri; 2-8pm Sat. Closed 3wks Aug. **No credit cards. Map** p358 A1.
Headed by the former director of a major London gallery, Lorcan O'Neill is perhaps Rome's most fashionable private gallery. Inaugurations of blue-chip exhibitions invariably turn into social events in which the jet set mixes with artists.

Stefania Miscetti
Via delle Mantellate 14 (06 6880 5880). Bus 23, 280. **Open** 4-8pm Tue-Sat. Closed July-Sept. **No credit cards. Map** p358 B1.
One of the more established of Trastevere's commercial art galleries, Miscetti holds unusual shows of sculpture and installations.

Volume!
Via di San Francesco di Sales 86 (06 7030 1433/ www.volumefnucci.it). Bus 23, 280. **Open** 6-8pm Tue-Sat. Closed mid July-mid Sept. **Map** p355 B2.
A meeting place for those who are passionate about experimental art, the Volume! space shows almost exclusively site-specific installations.

Celio & San Giovanni

Galleria Sala 1
Piazza di Porta San Giovanni 10 (06 700 8691/www. sala uno.com). Metro San Giovanni/bus 81, 85, 87, 186, 571, 850/tram 3. **Open** 4.30-7.30pm Tue-Sat. Closed mid July-late Aug. **No credit cards. Map** p360 E3.
See *p266* **Sacred and profane**. Photo *p265*.

Galleria SALES
Via dei Querceti 4-5 (06 7759 1122/www.galleria sales.it). Metro Colosseo/bus 60Exp, 85, 87, 117, 850/tram 3. **Open** 3.30-7.30pm Tue-Sat. Closed Aug. **No credit cards. Map** p360 D3.
What used to be one of Trastevere's hippest art galleries has now moved to the relatively quiet Celio district, where it continues to show rising young international artists.

Vatican & Prati

Monitor
Viale delle Mura Aurelie 19 (06 3937 8024/www. monitoronline.org). Metro Ottaviano/bus 23, 32, 34, 49, 81, 492/tram 19. **Open** 3.30-8pm Tue-Sat. Closed Aug. **No credit cards. Map** p355 A5.
This gallery is dedicated to young, up-and-coming artists working mainly in video.

Arts & Entertainment

Gay & Lesbian

The Rome scene is slowly stepping out of the closet.

These are heady times in the *Bel paese*. With a centre-left government putting the recognition of *coppie di fatto* (common-law couples) – whatever their sexual orientation – back on the political agenda, Italy's gay men and lesbians are enjoying a higher profile than ever. While it remains to be seen whether same-sex couples will one day celebrate their nuptials in piazza del Campidoglio, gay and lesbian life in the Italian capital has undoubtedly become more mainstream. This increased visibility is matched by new organisations, venues and facilities, and the historic **Mario Mieli** group – flanked by the newer, hyperactive **Di'Gay Project** (for both, *see p271*) – is doing an excellent job of adding more social goodies to the shopping trolley.

Likewise, the gay market continues to diversify and cater for distinct clienteles, with restaurants, pubs, clubs and bars attracting punters of all ages. A proliferation of mixed one-nighters also mirrors the ever increasing number of places where men and women have fun under the same roof. Or, for that matter, in the open air: one of the successes in the Roman calendar is the summer **Gay Village** (*see p269*). With its concerts, various dancefloors and bars, it's now worth staying in the city for the traditionally becalmed months of July and August.

THE GREAT OUTDOORS

Once upon a time, the gay scene in Rome was synonymous with outdoor cruising, and there are still hedonistic delights to be had on the Monte Caprino side of the Capitoline hill (*see p75*), though the usual caution is advised. Rome's nudist beach at Capocotta also survives as one of the gay community's alfresco glories. *Il Buco* ('the hole') is a short stretch of sandy dunes located between the family-fun resorts of Ostia and Torvaianica (*see p304* **Buckets & spades**). Gay men and women of all ages flock to *il Buco* from June to September, looking to enjoy sun, sand and (less than crystal-clear) sea. Nudism was once the order of the day, but swimming costumes are now tolerated. To get there by public transport, take the train from the Roma–Ostia Lido station (Metro Piramide) to Lido di Ostia–Cristoforo Colombo, then the 07 bus (summer months only) from outside the station and get off at the 10km stop.

Bars, clubs & restaurants

Admission prices to Rome's bars and clubs can be confusing. Some places may charge no entrance fee but will oblige you to buy a drink, while others include a first drink in the admission price. A growing number of venues also ask for an **Arcigay card**, which costs €15 for annual membership, though an €8 monthly version is available for out-of-towners. The card can be bought at any venue that requires it and is valid throughout Italy. In most bars you're given a printed slip on which the bar staff tick off what you consume; you pay the total amount on leaving. Where we have not specified an admission price, entry is free.

Rome now has a few rainbow-flagged restaurants. At the **Asinocotto** (via dei Vascellari 48, 06 589 8985, www.asinocotto. com, closed Mon, average €45), cook Giuliano Brenna impresses as much with his right-on

Coming Out. *See p269.*

Arts & Entertainment

political stance as with his culinary skills, while **Edoardo II** (vicolo Margana 14, 06 6994 2419, www.edoardosecondo.com, closed Tue, average €35) serves up double-entendre specialities like their chocolate *orgasmo* dessert.

Gay Village

Venue changes from year to year (no phone/ www.gayvillage.it). **Open** *Late June-early Sept* 7pm-3am daily. **Admission** approx €15/wk. **No credit cards**.
A ten-week open-air bonanza that makes summer the pinkest season of the year: bars, restaurants, live acts, discos, cinema – a great place for boys and girls alike. Venue and contact details change from year to year, but the website reveals all as the date approaches.

Aventine & Testaccio

L'Alibi

Via di Monte Testaccio 40-44 (06 574 3448). Metro Piramide/bus 23, 95, 716, 92N/tram 3. **Open** 11.30pm-5am Thur-Sun. **Admission** €15 (incl 1 drink). **Credit** MC, V. **Map** p359 D6.
The Alibi paved the way for Testaccio's boom as a nightlife quarter with an alternative feel, although its increasingly straight-friendly approach (with a special Friday 'hetero' night) has diluted its success with punters of all persuasions. Potentially, it's still a great place to bop the night away, with a well-oiled sound system covering two floors in winter and three in summer, when the roof garden comes into its own. If you can get yourself on to the guest list, admission costs €10. **Photo** *p272.*

Celio & San Giovanni

Coming Out

Via San Giovanni in Laterano 8 (06 700 9871/www. comingout.it). Metro Colosseo/bus 85, 850, 55N. **Open** 10am-2am daily. **Credit** MC, V. **Map** p360 C3.
This unassuming but popular pub offers quick lunches, evening snacks, beers and cocktails to a predominantly youthful crowd of men and women. A useful address if you need a place to meet before heading off in search of something a bit more frantic, though the CO team occasionally provides its own midweek entertainment with karaoke (Wed) and live music (Thur). **Photo** *p268.*

Skyline

Via Petremoli 36 (06 700 9431/www.skylineclub.it). Metro San Giovanni/bus 360, 55N/tram 3. **Open** 10.30pm-4am Mon-Sat; 5pm-4am Sun. **Admission** (with Arcigay card) free with compulsory drink. **No credit cards**. **Map** off p361 E4.
Skyline keeps getting better, even more so now that it has new, two-floor premises. The relaxed mixed crowd ensures there's constant movement between the bar areas, the video parlour and the cruisy cubicle and dark areas. Hosts naked parties on Mondays.

Monti & Esquilino

Hangar

Via in Selci 69A (06 488 1397/www.hangar online.it). Metro Cavour/bus 75, 84, 40N. **Open** 10.30pm-2.30am Mon, Wed-Sun. Closed 3wks Aug. **Admission** (with Arcigay card) free. **No credit cards**. **Map** p360 C2.
American John Moss has been at the helm of Rome's oldest gay bar since it opened over two decades ago. Hangar maintains its friendly but sexy atmosphere whether half full (occasionally midweek) or packed (at weekends and for porn-video Monday and striptease Thursday). Two bar zones are linked by a long, dark passage, designed for cruising before consuming. Much to the delight of visiting tourists, and the twenty- and thirtysomething clientele, the venue also has a small dark area.

Max's Bar

Via A Grandi 7A (06 7030 1599/www.maxsbar.net). Metro Manzoni/bus 29N/tram 3, 5, 14, 19. **Open** 10.30pm-3.30am Mon, Thur-Sun. **Admission** free Mon; €6 Thur, Sun; €10 (incl 1 drink) Fri, Sat. **No credit cards**. **Map** off p151 C4.
Max's is a fairly relaxed, mainstream venue near Porta Maggiore. Its dancefloor (disco-commercial) and bars are popular with all ages and walks of life, which may explain its chummy charm – and why it attracts its fair share of Roman silver foxes.

Sphinx

Piazza M Fanti 40 (06 444 1312/www.sphinx40.it). Metro Termini/bus 70, 45N, 91N/tram 5, 14. **Open** 11pm-2am Tue-Sun. **Admission** (with Arcigay card) free Tue-Thur, Sun; €10 (incl 1 drink) Fri, Sat. **No credit cards**. **Map** p360 D1.
A venue originally aimed at the leather and bear community, though gay men of any age should feel more than welcome. The small bar area has cubicles to the right and a dark room to the left, all of which fill up as the night progresses. Dress code is not strictly enforced except for the special Leather Club Roma nights (*see p271*).

One-nighters

Muccassassina

at Qube, via di Portonaccio 212, Suburbs: east (06 541 3985/www.muccassassina.com). Metro Tiburtina/ bus 409. **Open** 11pm-4am Fri. **Admission** (incl 1 drink) €15. **No credit cards**.
The Mario Mieli crew (*see p271*) were trail-blazers of the gay one-nighter – and their Friday night fest at the Qube still packs them in. Three floors of pop and house create a great atmosphere throughout. Circolo Mario Mieli members get in for €10.

> ▶ Many gay venues, even if free, require an **Arcigay card** for entry. For details, see **p268 Bars, clubs & restaurants**.

Arts & Entertainment

Cruising the Casilina

All roads may lead to Rome, but many also lead straight out again to a plethora of cruising clubs that have sprung up on the eastern outskirts of the city. Sex in the suburbs is flourishing. The working-class via Casilina, much loved by Pasolini, was the first to set the trend with **K Men's Club**, the first venue in the capital wholly devoted to the joy of the dark encounter. The latest to appear is nearby **Cock's**, where ersatz Roman ruins make for that profane catacomb experience. In both clubs, bar space is reduced to a minimum, favouring labyrinthine consumption of a more basic kind.

Moving to the via Prenestina area, **Il Diavolo Dentro** is a stark, candle-lit basement that opens its doors to weekend thirtysomething hedonists, whose inner devils are tempted at the club's theme nights. Anyone for an orgy or a black mass (hoods free of charge)?

Further south, along via Appia Nuova, is **Frequency**, an unassuming sex club with a large bar area, which indulges its young regulars with an 'extreme naked Thursday', a 'black' candle-lit Friday and a fine choice of underwear or the all-together for its Sunday evening meets. Finally, Saturday night punters still on the prowl should head back to the Casilina district for the after-hours cruisy chill-out at **Frutta e Verdura**.

Words of warning. It is a truth universally acknowledged that the harder-core and further-flung the club, the greater chance there is for sudden closure – so ring ahead. As well as the 105 bus, the Casilina area is served by the Termini–Pantano tram service. Night buses back to the centre can be irregular so take your chances or ask the doorman to call you a taxi.

Cock's

Via Galeazzo Alessi 163, Suburbs: east (06 241 3687/www.thecocks.it). Bus 105, 50N/tram Termini–Pantano (Filarete stop). **Open** 3pm-3am Mon-Thur, Sun; 3pm-4am Fri, Sat. **Admission** (with Arcigay card; incl 1 drink) €5. **No credit cards**.

Il Diavolo Dentro

Largo Itri 23, Suburbs: east (347 728 5891/ www.ildiavolodentro.com). Bus 20, 12N/ tram 5, 14. **Open** 3-7pm Tue; 11pm-5am Fri, Sat; 6pm-3am Sun. **Admission** (with Arcigay card; incl 1 drink) €10 Fri; €8 Sat; €6 (undressed), €10 (dressed) Sun; free Tue. **No credit cards**.

Frequency

Via Enea 34, Suburbs: east (06 785 1504/ 340 693 9719/www.thefrequency.it). Metro Furio Camillo/bus 628, 55N. **Open** 10pm-3am Mon, Wed, Thur, Sun; 10pm-4am Fri, Sat. **Admission** (with Arcigay card) free Mon, Wed; €5 Thur-Sun. **No credit cards**.

Frutta e Verdura

Via P Zurla 68/70, Suburbs: east (347 879 7063/347 244 6721/www.fruttaeverdura. roma.it). Bus 105, 50N/tram Termini–Pantano (Alessi stop). **Open** 4.30-10.30am Sun & 1 Sat each month (check website for details). **Admission** (with Arcigay card; incl 1 drink) €13. **No credit cards**.

K Men's Club

Via A Amati 6-8, Suburbs: east (06 2170 1268). Bus 105, 50N/tram Termini–Pantano (Filarete stop). **Open** 10pm-4am Tue-Thur, Sun; 10pm-5am Fri, Sat. **Admission** (with Arcigay card) €5. **No credit cards**.

Omogenic

at Circolo degli Artisti (for listing, see p288). **Open** 11pm-late Fri. **Admission** €6. **No credit cards**. The Di'Gay Project's (see p271) Friday rival to the Muccassassina always attracts an eclectic crowd of young boppers. Di'Gay Project members get in for €5.

Saunas

Europa Multiclub

Via Aureliana 40, Veneto & Borghese (06 482 3650). Metro Repubblica/bus 36, 60Exp, 60N. **Open** 1pm-midnight Mon-Thur; 1pm Fri until midnight Sun. **Admission** (with Arcigay card) €14; €12 after 11pm Fri, Sat. **Credit** MC, V. **Map** p357 D4.

Europa has 1,300 sq m (4,300 sq ft) of gym facilities and pools, complete with waterfalls. Leave your togs in multicoloured lockers and cruise down to the steam and sweat rooms and romantically star-lit booths. It's a mixed crowd, with young, muscled tendencies. Open 24hrs over the weekend.

Mediterraneo

Via Villari 3, Esquilino (06 7720 5934/www.sauna mediterraneo.it). Metro Manzoni/bus 85, 87/tram 3. **Open** 1pm-midnight daily. **Admission** (with Arcigay card) €14. **No credit cards**. **Map** p360 D3. Tasteful decor and an emphasis on hygiene set this sauna apart from its rivals. The steam room and jacuzzi provide repose prior to exertion in the 'relax rooms'. All body types, ages and nationalities.

Rio's

Via dei Colli Albani 10, Suburbs: south (06 7814 7828/www.riossauna.it). Metro Colli Albani/bus 85, 87, 55N. **Open** 1pm-midnight Mon-Fri, Sun; 1pm-2am Sat. **Admission** (with Arcigay card) €11 Mon; €12 Tue-Sat; €13 Sun. **No credit cards.**
As the new kid on the Roman sauna block, Rio's is determined to make a mark with its extensive cabin and cruise area, plus bar and internet points. It attracts a heterogeneous clientele, but isn't quite as popular as its more central rivals.

Information & organisations

There are over 70 gay activist organisations in Italy, mostly in the north. Foremost among these are the organisations belonging to the Bologna-based Arcigay network.

Arcigay Nazionale

Via Don Minzoni 18, 40121 Bologna (051 649 3055/www.arcigay.it).

Arcigay Roma

Via Goito 35B, Esquilino (06 6450 1102/www.arcigayroma.it). Metro Termini/buses to Termini/tram 5, 14. **Map** p357 D4.
The local Arci group gets together on Wednesday (Welcome Group) and Friday evenings (6-9pm both evenings).

Circolo Mario Mieli di Cultura Omosessuale

Via Efeso 2A, Suburbs: south (06 541 3985/www.mariomieli.org). Metro San Paolo/bus 23. **Open** 10am-6pm Mon-Fri.
This is the most important gay, lesbian and trans-gender group in Rome, named after pioneer author and thinker Mario Mieli. It provides a base for debates and events, and offers counselling and care facilities. Its Muccassassina one-nighters (*see p269*) are highly popular and it also organises summer Pride events (www.romapride.it).

Di'Gay Project

Via Costantino 82, Suburbs: south (06 513 4741/www.digayproject.org). Metro San Paolo/bus 23. **Open** *Sept-June* 3.30-8pm daily. Meetings 7-9pm Thur.
Hosts the summer Gay Village (*see p269*) as well as a series of other worthy events. A welcome group meets at 3.30pm on Sundays.

Epicentro Ursino Romano

Information 392 579 6357/www.epicentroursino.com.
Rome's burgeoning bear community is well served by the enterprising EUR. Check the website for details of their Subwoofer parties, held the last weekend of the month.

Leather Club Roma

www.lcroma.com.
The LCR, a group devoted to leather and fetish lifestyles, holds strictly dress-code-only parties on the second Saturday of the month at the Sphinx club (*see p269*). In early December it organises the international Catacombs weekend.

Publications & outlets

Edicole (newsstands) are often good for gay books and videos; the *edicole* in *piazze* dei Cinquecento (map p357 D5) and Colonna (map p355 E5) are treasure troves of porn: discreet amounts are displayed by day, but piles of it come out at night.

Aut

A monthly magazine published by the Circolo Mario Mieli (*see above*), containing interesting articles and fairly up-to-date listings. It's available free at many gay venues.

Babilonia

A lively monthly magazine (€3.90 at selected newsstands) that contains a detailed listings guide for the whole of Italy.

Libreria Babele

Via dei Banchi Vecchi 116, Ghetto & Campo (06 687 6628/www.libreriababeleroma.it). Bus 40Exp, 46, 62, 64, 916. **Open** 3-7pm Mon; 11am-7pm Tue-Sat. Closed 2wks Aug. **Credit** AmEx, DC, MC, V. **Map** p355 C5.
This friendly outlet is the largest exclusively gay and lesbian bookshop in Rome. A good selection of books, videos, guides and magazines – and a small toys cabinet for the young at heart.

Studio Know How

Via San Gallicano 13, Trastevere (06 5833 5692). Bus 23, 280/tram 8. **Open** 10.30am-2pm, 3-8pm Tue-Sat. Closed 3wks Aug. **Credit** AmEx, DC, MC, V. **Map** p358 C3.
This Roman branch of a Milanese sex-shop chain focuses exclusively on gay and lesbian accoutrements.

Lesbian Rome

There are two identifiable factions in *Roma lesbica*: older lesbian groups, which meet at the **Buon Pastore** centre (*see p272*), have their roots in 1970s feminism and continue to claim separate identity from men, gay or straight; younger lesbians, on the other hand, tend to favour the less separatist **Arci-Lesbica** association or join the lads at **Circolo Mario Mieli** or the **Di'Gay Project** (for both, *see above*). Rome has yet to host a permanent lesbian club, but joint ventures like **Gay Village**, **Muccassassina** and other one-nighters (*see p269*) get a good turnout from lesbians as well as gay men, and bars like **Coming Out** (*see p269*) are also popular with women. Check noticeboards at gay and women's bookshops or stop by the Buon Pastore. Try www.listalesbica.it and www.arcilesbica.it too.

Arts & Entertainment

One-nighters

Venus Rising
at Goa (for listing, see p285). **Open** 11pm-late
last Sun of month. **Admission** (incl 1 drink) €10.
No credit cards.
While Muccassassina (*see p269*) and Omogenic (*see
p270*) attract their fair share of women, Venus Rising
is the only women-only one-nighter in the capital.

Organisations

See also p271 **Circolo Mario Mieli di
Cultura Omosessuale**.

Arci-Lesbica Roma
*Viale G Stefanini 15, Suburbs: north (06 418 0211/
www.arcilesbica.it/roma). Metro Santa Maria del
Soccorso.* **Open** 8.30-10.30pm Mon.
Arci-Lesbica organises weekly meetings and the
occasional get-together. Phone them or consult the
website for information.

Casa Internazionale delle Donne
(Centro Buon Pastore)
*Via della Lungara 19, Trastevere (06 6840 1720/
www.casainternazionaledelledonne.org). Bus 23, 280.*
Map p358 B2.

L'Alibi embraces all types. *See p269.*

Once an abandoned 17th-century convent, this vast
riverside complex is still better known as the Centro
Buon Pastore (Good Shepherd Centre). Following a
splendid multi-million-euro makeover, over 40
women's associations now use the building. There
are also various facilities for visitors, including
accommodation (*see below*).

Collegamento lesbiche
italiane (CLI)
*Casa Internazionale delle Donne, via San Francesco
di Sales 1B, Trastevere (06 686 4201/www.clrbp.it).
Bus 23, 280.* **Map** p358 B2.
This separatist group has midweek meetings in the
Buon Pastore women's centre; you don't need to be
a member to take part. It also organises conferences,
literary evenings, concerts and dances. The
Coordinamento lesbiche italiane, little sister of the
CLI, meets here Thursdays at 9pm. Both associa-
tions groups are part of the Centro Femminista
Separatista (Separatist Feminist Centre).

Accommodation, outlets
& restaurants

See also p271 for both **Libreria Babele** and
Studio Know How.

La Foresteria Orsa Maggiore
*Via San Francesco di Sales 1A, Trastevere (06 6840
1724/www.casainternazionaledelledonne.org). Bus
23, 280.* **Credit** MC, V. **Map** p358 B2.
The Orsa Maggiore (Great Bear) hostel provides
out-of-towners with 13 bright, second-floor rooms,
some with en-suite bathrooms. Prices range from
€26 to €75 per person per night.

Luna e L'altra
*Via San Francesco di Sales 1A, Trastevere (06 6840
1727/www.casainternazionaledelledonne.org). Bus
23, 280.* **Open** 1-2.30pm, 8.30-11pm Mon-Fri; 8.30-
11pm Sat. **Credit** AmEx, DC, MC, V. **Map** p358 B2.
A restaurant within the walls of the historic Buon
Pastore women's centre. Self-service lunch gives
way to an *à la carte* evening service with an emphasis on imaginative vegetarian dishes. Male diners
are only allowed at lunchtimes.

Zipper Travel
*Via Castelfidardo 18 (second floor), Esquilino
(06 488 2730/www.zippertravel.it). Metro Castro
Pretorio/bus 75.* **Open** 9.30am-6.30pm Mon-Fri.
Credit DC, MC, V. **Map** p357 E4.
One of only a few travel agencies in Italy to offer
customised travel for gay women.

Zora Neale Hurston Association
*Via San Francesco di Sales 1A, Trastevere (06 6819
3001). Bus 23, 280.* **Map** p358 B2.
This Buon Pastore association offers a range of book
presentations, readings, creative writing workshops
and other events for the literary-inclined. There is
also wall space for art exhibitions.

Music: Classical & Opera

Symphonic and chamber music are rising to a crescendo but opera still falls flat.

Slowly but surely, the face of the city started to change back in 2000, the much celebrated Jubilee Year during which some 26 million pilgrims flocked to the Eternal City. In preparation for that occasion, Rome received a radical facelift – and the city's centre-left administration began to channel much-needed funds into the moribund cultural scene. The results are now showing, and the music panorama is the one in which, arguably, horizons have changed the most: Rome is back on the music-lovers' map of Europe after more than a century of neglect.

This is thanks, mainly, to the activity of the **Auditorium-Parco della Musica** (*see p275*), inaugurated in 2002 and now working at full steam. The complex of concert and exhibition spaces, designed by internationally acclaimed architect Renzo Piano, has gone from strength to strength, enticing Romans of all tastes with a programme of such extraordinary breadth it is second only to the New York Lincoln Center for the variety of its offerings. In fact, it has become much more than a simple centre for the arts. Its democratically eclectic programme – which ranges from symphonies to soul, from jazz to jugglers – has cast its spell over citizens who have never set foot in a classical-music venue in their lives, driving them to rethink their relationship with the performing arts. The year 2006 saw a record number of over a million attendances. Even more miraculous, in a country where the arts are traditionally a financial black hole, the Auditorium is self-funding and making money.

But the Auditorium is not the only venue in Rome for music. Many of the more traditional concert halls and locations have also benefited from the surge of energy and extra funding, and many boast high-quality programmes with resident and visiting artists. The large number of music festivals that are organised throughout the year by a variety of institutions are another feather in Rome's cap, especially since these often take place in remarkably beautiful church settings, aristocratic *palazzi*, or in the magnificent residences of many of the city's foreign academies.

So Rome is more or less sorted for 'serious' music – opera being the one glaring exception: notwithstanding two glorious locations, the programmes are constipated and productions are generally mediocre (*see p275*).

The classical scene

The **Accademia Nazionale di Santa Cecilia** (06 8024 2501, www.santacecilia.it) is Italy's national music academy, with its prestigious *conservatorio*, and choir and orchestra directed by world-class conductor Antonio Pappano. It resides in Rome and plays out its season at the Auditorium-Parco della Musica. Pappano promotes the Accademia's trend of thematic cycles, with a series of mini-festivals dedicated to single composers, artists or themes in bursts throughout the season. Meanwhile, Santa Cecilia also continues to attract some of the world's greatest conductors for its symphonic season, and renowned soloists for its chamber music programme.

Also based at the Auditorium-Parco della Musica is the city-council-funded **Orchestra di Roma e del Lazio** (06 8024 1278, www. orchestradellazio.it), which holds a high-quality symphonic season under the stern direction of Chinese conductor Lu Jia. You can catch up with this ensemble every Sunday in the Auditorium's Sala Sinopoli.

Many other institutions of all sizes make their voices heard. The **Accademia Filarmonica Romana** (06 320 1752, www.filarmonica romana.org) was founded in 1821 and boasts an illustrious history, with composers such as Rossini, Donizetti, Paganini and Verdi among its founders. It offers a varied programme of chamber music, ancient music, ballet and chamber opera. It's also particularly active in co-producing multimedia events in conjunction with festivals and foreign academies.

Another major concert provider is the **Istituzione Universitaria dei Concerti** (IUC, 06 361 0051, www.concertiiuc.it), founded after World War II to inject some life into Rome's university campus. The IUC offers a varied calendar that includes often outstanding

Arts & Entertainment

The **Auditorium-Parco della Musica** has energised Rome's music scene. *See p273*.

– and frequently experimental – international and Italian recitals and chamber music at La Sapienza's main auditorium, the rather stark **Aula Magna** (*see p275*).

The 16th-century **Oratorio del Gonfalone** (*see p275*) hosts a chamber music season that reflects the joyous personality of director Angelo Persichilli. Every concert and recital on the programme, which runs from December to May, seems to have been lovingly chosen to fit the beautiful surroundings, and to show off the Oratorio's magnificent 18th-century organ. In recent years, however, it has been giving more and more space to concerts and recitals with an ethnic, folk and contemporary flavour.

The **Orchestra Sinfonica di Roma** (06 4425 2303, www.artsacademy.it) directed by conductor Francesco La Vecchia, offers a somewhat traditional symphonic season at the newly renovated **Auditorium Conciliazione** (*see below*), where famous conductors or soloists often feature as guest artists.

At the genteelly decaying **Teatro Ghione** (*see p276*), director Christopher Axworthy is behind the surprising **Euromusica Master Series**, which runs from January to June with a brief prelude in September dedicated to the guitar. This series consists of mostly piano recitals, studded with some brilliant jewels, such as Peter Katin, Fou Ts'ong, Mikhail Pletnev and Alicia De Laroccha. Notwithstanding the stellar programme, the theatre and staff remain approachable and ticket prices extremely reasonable. Many of the artists are elderly personal friends of Axworthy, some of whom rarely perform because of their advanced age.

The **La Stravaganza** music association (06 7707 2842, www.lastravaganzamusica.it) is a tiny, privately run endeavour that organises delightful chamber music concerts or recitals inside the historic **Palazzo Doria Pamphili** (*see p119*). During the interval or after the concert, the public is invited to wander into some of the adjacent rooms to enjoy the Doria Pamphili art collection hanging on the walls.

The **Quirinale** (*see p94*; for programme information visit www.quirinale.it) also opens its doors to the public, on Sunday mornings, for a cycle of chamber music concerts and recitals in the *cappella Paolina*.

And of course, many churches and basilicas scattered throughout the city host chamber ensembles, choirs and soloists of differing artistic worth, so keep an eye on street posters and the daily press for events and details, and remember, as the Catholic Church does not allow paying concerts on consecrated ground, many of these events are free of charge.

The opera

An evening at the opera makes for an interesting experience. The drab exterior of the **Opera di Roma**'s 19th-century **Teatro Costanzi** gives way to a beautiful and harmonious interior with a good-sized stage and perfect acoustics. And in summer the breathtaking majesty of the **Terme di Caracalla** (*see p141*) is a unique backdrop and setting for lyrical productions. Popular conductor Gianluigi Gelmetti has been at the helm of the Opera di Roma since 2001. He has worked his musicians hard, moulding the 100-strong orchestra and its chorus of 80 into

a harmonious ensemble. The result of his efforts has been a huge increase in audience numbers, even for operas considered 'difficult'. The dreary **Teatro Nazionale**, just down the road from the Teatro Costanzi – and often not worth the trip – provides the stage for most of the smaller productions, including chamber opera, contemporary works and ballets. Top-name singers rarely stay around after the opening night, so keep an eye on cast lists to avoid second-rate substitutes.

Auditoria

See also p296 **Teatro Il Sistina**.

Auditorium Conciliazione

Via della Conciliazione 4, Vatican (899 5000 55/ www.auditoriumconciliazione.it). Metro Ottaviano/ bus 62, 23, 34, 40Exp, 982, 271. **Box office** 11am-6pm Mon-Fri. **No credit cards. Map** p355 B5.
This was Rome's prime serious music venue until the national academy shifted its season to the Auditorium-Parco della Musica. It has since been renovated to reveal a good-sized stage that is suitable for dance. And dance – with some star-studded events – makes up part of its varied programme, which also includes music and conferences.

Auditorium–Parco della Musica

Via P de Coubertin 15, Suburbs: north (06 80 242/ box office 06 808 2058/fax 06 8024 1211/www. auditorium.com). Bus 53, 910, M/tram 2. **Box office** July-Sept 11am-6pm Mon-Fri. Oct-June 11am-6pm daily; until interval on concert days. **Credit** MC, V.
Tickets can be booked online. Guided tours cost €10 (€5 concessions; no credit cards) and take place at intervals throughout the day: times change frequently so call ahead or check the website. Alternatively, wander in (open 10am-6pm daily, admission free) and have a look around the place for yourself. **Photo** *p274*.

Aula Magna dell'Università la Sapienza

Piazzale Aldo Moro, Esquilino (06 361 0051/fax 06 3600 1511/www.concertiiuc.it). Metro Policlinico/bus 61, 490, 495/tram 3, 19. **Season** Oct-Apr. **Box office** 10am-1pm, 2-5pm daily; up to 1hr before concerts. **Credit** MC, V. **Map** p151 B1.
With kitsch Fascist decor but reasonable acoustics, this is the main auditorium for the Istituzione Universitaria dei Concerti (IUC; *see p273*) season.

Oratorio del Gonfalone

Via del Gonfalone 32, Ghetto & Campo (06 687 5952). Bus 40Exp, 46, 62, 64, 116, 916. **Box office** 10am-4pm Mon-Fri. **No credit cards. Map** p355 B6.
This beautiful frescoed little auditorium is located in a 16th-century oratorio adjacent to the Baroque church of the Gonfalone. It provides a suitable home for one of the city's most precious organs.

Arts & Entertainment

Teatro dell'Opera di Roma – Teatro Costanzi

Piazza B Gigli 1, Esquilino (06 4816 0255/www. opera.roma.it). Metro Repubblica/bus 40Exp, 60Exp, 64, 70, 117, 170. **Box office** 9am-5pm Tue-Sat; 9am-1.30pm Sun; until 15mins after performances begin. **Credit** AmEx, DC, MC, V. **Map** p357 D5.

The lavish late 19th-century *teatro all'italiana* interior comes as quite a surprise after the grey, angular, Mussolini-era façade and its esplanade with tacky potted palms. There are towering rows of boxes, and loads of stucco, frescoes and gilding everywhere. The acoustics vary greatly: the higher (cheaper) seats are unsatisfactory, so splash out on a box… it's all part of the experience.

Teatro Ghione

Via delle Fornaci 37, Vatican & Prati (06 637 2294/www.ghione.it). Bus 34, 46, 64, 916. **Box office** 10.30am-1pm, 4-7pm Tue-Sat; 4-7pm Sun. **Credit** DC, MC, V.

This plush little red and gold theatre regales its faithful public with extraordinary recitals by some legendary – and mostly ancient – performers.

Antony Hegarty at the **RomaEuropa** fest.

Teatro Olimpico

Piazza Gentile da Fabriano, Suburbs: north (06 326 5991/www.teatroolimpico.it). Bus 53, 280, 910/tram 2, 19. **Season** Oct-May. **Box office** 11am-7pm daily; from 8pm on concert days. **Credit** MC, V. **Map** off p354 C/D1.

Great for all types of performances, the Olimpico has good acoustics, even for cheaper seats. Go for the central front and second row seats in the gallery. It's owned by the Accademia Filarmonica (*see p273*) and used for their Thursday concerts.

Festivals

Most of Rome's summer festivals take place under the **Estate Romana** umbrella (*see also p253* and *p282* **Sounds of summer**). This overwhelming event-fest runs from June to September and provides such quantities of entertainment of all descriptions that it's difficult to know where to start. But one thing is for sure: it all comes to an end during the increasingly successful **Notte Bianca** (*see p254*), when the city doesn't close down but instead offers an all-night choice of some 500 different happenings, many of which are musical, and many of which are free of charge.

The **Accademia Nazionale di Santa Cecilia** offers a full summer programme of quality crowd-pleasers, including international orchestras and classical/popular crossovers, in the outside *cavea* of the Auditorium-Parco della Musica performing arts complex.

For the **RomaEuropa** festival, *see p254*.

Concerti all'Orto Botanico

Largo Cristina di Svezia 24, Trastevere (06 686 8441/06 3936 6322/fax 06 3936 6229/www. assmusrom.it). Bus 23, 280, 630, 780, H/tram 8. **Season** July. **Box office** at venue before concerts. **No credit cards. Map** p358 B2.

Organised by the Associazione Musicale Romana, these concerts – which include Gershwin and Piazzola as well as mainstream chamber music – take place in the botanical gardens, where a natural amphitheatre makes for a lovely venue for a limited number of spectators. Booking essential.

Concerti del Tempietto

Various venues (06 8713 1590/fax 06 2332 26360/ www.tempietto.it). **Box office** at venues from 1hr before concerts. **No credit cards.**

The Associazione Il Tempietto organises year-round concerts under the Festival Musicale delle Nazioni banner in various venues, mainly the Sala Baldini (piazza Campitelli 9), the church of San Nicola in Carcere (*see p130*), in the archaeological site around the Teatro di Marcello (*see p131*) in summer, and the art nouveau Casina delle Civette in Villa Torlonia (*see p177*). It's mostly low-level musically, but there's a concert almost every evening and the venues are enchanting. You can book online.

Musical mums

Maybe the idea arose because Rome doesn't really cater much for children or mums... or families for that matter, and the need is keen; or maybe it just sounded like fun and the new Auditorium-Parco della Musica (*see p273*) provided the perfect setting. Whatever the reason behind the Accademia Nazionale di Santa Cecilia's initiative for expecting mums, breastfeeding mums and babies, it has proved so popular there are hardly enough tickets to go around, so if it takes your fancy, make sure that you book well in advance (by phone on 06 808 2058, or online at www.santacecilia.it).

Musica in-Attesa (this clever play on words means both 'Expecting Music' and 'Unexpected Music'), is a series of concerts developed for pregnant women and their partners: the concert programmes are conceived to soothe, lull and positively stimulate the foetus (and parents) according to studies that show that the unborn child develops hearing in the fifth month.

The **Micronote** series is the next step, with interactive concerts for children from birth to two years of age. During these performances, toddlers are encouraged to move, sway and clap to the music, interacting with a handful of musicians and their instruments. Parents with babes in arms can be seen rocking to the rhythm with the tinies. More sporadic are the concerts presented under the **Allattamento al... suono** banner, during which nursing mums are invited to take a seat with their babies for a good relaxing feed to the sound of music.

All these initiatives take place within a broader project geared towards families, **Tutti a Santa Cecilia**, which caters for children of all ages. It also includes a popular series of family concerts, with shorter-than-usual daytime performances that are preceeded by an explanation of what the audience is about to hear. Also noteworthy is the musical baby-sitting service provided alongside many events, at the end of which the children perform a mini-concert for their mums and dads.

International Chamber Ensemble

Sant'Ivo alla Sapienza, corso Rinascimento 40, Pantheon & Navona (06 8680 0125/www.inter ensemble.org). Bus 30Exp, 70, 81, 87, 116, 204, 280, 492, 628. **Season** mid June-mid Aug. **Box office** 10am-7pm Mon-Fri; 10am-1pm Sat. **No credit cards. Map** p355 D5.
Chamber and symphonic music, as well as opera, takes place in a splendid example of Renaissance architecture: the courtyard of Sant'Ivo alla Sapienza, the hallowed 15th-century seat of Rome university.

Mille e Una Nota

Arco della Pace 5, Pantheon & Navona (06 780 7695). Bus 30Exp, 40Exp, 46, 62, 63, 64, 70, 81, 116, 492, 628, 630, 780, 916. **Season** Aug. **Box office** 1hr before concerts. **No credit cards. Map** p355 C5.
This charming little chamber music festival has been going for over ten years in the magnificent cloister of Santa Maria della Pace (*see p115*).

New Operafestival di Roma

Piazza San Clemente 1, Celio (347 852 4241/www. newoperafestivaldiroma.com). Metro Colosseo/bus 60Exp, 85, 87, 117, 810, 850/tram 3. **Season** mid July-mid Aug. **Box office** 2hrs before concerts. **Credit** AmEx, MC, V. **Map** p360 D3.
This festival offers talented young musicians and singers from Italy and the US the chance to perform in the courtyard of the basilica of San Clemente (*see p145*). There's always at least one fully fledged opera, plus chamber music and a series of recitals.

Stagione Estiva del Teatro dell'Opera

Terme di Caracalla, viale delle Terme di Caracalla, Aventine, Testaccio & Ostiense (06 4816 0255/ www.opera.roma.it). Metro Circo Massimo/bus 60Exp, 75, 81, 118, 175, 628, 714. **Season** July-Aug. **Box office** (at Teatro dell'Opera; *see p276*) 9am-5pm Tue-Sat; 9am-1.30pm Sun. **Credit** AmEx, DC, MC, V. **Map** p361 C5.
The spectacular venue for the Opera di Roma's summer season is a breathtaking archaeological site. Set designers usually exploit the unique backdrop of majestic Roman ruins with few props and dramatic lighting. Back-row seats are very far away from the stage – so don't forget binoculars. Bookings can be made online at www.chartanet.it.

Out of town

Festival Pontino

Castello Caetani, Sermoneta/Abbazia di Fossanova, Priverno (information 0773 605 551/bookings 0773 480 672/fax 0773 628 498/www.festivalpontino.it). **Season** late June-late July. **Box office** at venues before performances. **No credit cards.**
This little festival has a family feel to it and draws excellent musicians from all over Europe. Classical and contemporary music are part of the programme and are performed in a scattering of outstandingly atmospheric venues, including the medieval Castello Caetani in the hill town of Sermoneta, south of Rome, and the Gothic abbey of Fossanova.

Arts & Entertainment

Nightlife & Live Music

Rome has a lively year-round scene but things really heat up in summer.

Micca Club. See p287.

Since he won his first mandate in 2001, Rome's jazz- and cinema-loving mayor, Walter Veltroni, hasn't let national government cuts to city funding stop him from promoting arts and culture enthusiastically. The trickle-down effect on the nightlife and music scene is tangible: growing cultural, artistic and musical vibrancy feeds an ongoing renaissance that is slowly turning the once sleepy Eternal City into a lively European capital.

Surprisingly enough in this hide-bound country, established artists are not the only ones benefitting from the changes: young, cutting-edge artistic communities are being given more space to bring their innovative entertainment projects into the open. This flurry of activity seeps into Rome's nightlife, where dancing to the best international DJs and hearing the latest bands has become almost as easy as in London or Berlin. You will, however, need some inside information to avoid the Eurotrash dished out by the plethora of commercial venues playing disco on weekends.

For details of upcoming events, consult listings magazines *Trovaroma*, *Roma C'è* (for both, *see p332*) or the trendy *Zero6* (a monthly, free in shops and pubs). For an alternative look at Rome's nightlife, check out www.romastyle. info, which is especially good for techno and drum 'n' bass nights, and www.musicaroma.it and www.indierock.it for gigs. Fans of indie and punk rock music can have a look at www.pogopop.it and www.myspace.com/ romecityrockers, while reggae addicts can browse at www.reggae.it.

Rome gives its best over the long summer, when the *ponentino* breeze makes nights fresh and almost magical. For information on the plethora of summer happenings, *see p282* **Sounds of summer**.

NIGHTLIFE

New compulsory closing times forcing most *centro storico* bars to shut at 2am have cancelled the unwritten 'open until the last punter stumbles out the door' rule, which long gave Roman nights their uniquely relaxed feel.

Discos and live venues continue to stay open until the small hours, though, allowing Romans to keep up their habit of starting the evenings late and ending them even later: concerts rarely kick off before 10.30pm and most clubs close after 4am, even on weekdays. When picking your club for the night, bear in mind that many mainstream clubs serve up commercial house or retro '80s tunes on Fridays and Saturdays. Established venues like **Goa** (*see p285*), **La Saponeria** (*see p286*) and **Micca Club** (*see p287*) can always be relied upon to offer quality DJ sets. For something alternative, try the Brit-pop/punk rock served up by the Beatles-lookalike DJs of **Fish & Chips** (on Fridays at Radio Café, via Principe Umberto 57, Esquilino, www.radiocaferoma.org) or dance the night away at **Screamadelica** (at Circolo degli Artisti; *see p288*), where international live acts are joined by DJs playing rock, pop and indie. Otherwise, check out what's on at places like **Locanda Atlantide** (*see p287*) or the tiny **Metaverso** (*see p286*). On Tuesdays DJ Andrea Esu and guests spin their electro-house and tech sounds at **L-Ektrica** (at Akab; *see p285*). If reggae's your thing, then the **One Love Hi Pawa** (on Thursdays at Brancaleone; *see p288*) is your best bet. Vintage enthusiasts will find gold at **Twiggy**, Rome's best '60s night, where Italy's top live bands precede expert DJs Luzy L and Corry X (one Saturday a month at Metaverso; see p286 or check out www.myspace.com/twiggy60sparty).

LIVE MUSIC

To a large extent, the recent rise in the popularity of concert-going in Rome is due to the **Auditorium-Parco della Musica** (see p273), a multifunctional complex – opened in 2002 and snowballing ever since – hosting not only theatre and classical music, but also pop, jazz and rock events. Rome's vocation for live music is also being prodded along by a string of smallish live clubs, and by the daring programme of goodies on offer at the cool **Teatro Palladium** (see p288). Moreover, city hall continues to fund the exciting **RomaEuropa Festival** (see p254), the cutting-edge **Enzimi** festival (see p282 **Sounds of summer**) and the occasional free mega-concert. Strangely, Rome still lacks a major outdoor venue for musical events.

CENTRI SOCIALI

Until very recently, the *centri sociali* – disused buildings occupied by dissatisfied youth and transformed into spaces for art, music and politics – were a motor of Rome's musical and artistic renaissance, playing a key role in its transition from historic showcase to vibrant capital by hosting avant-garde artists and musicians. With more opportunities elsewhere, *centri sociali*'s importance has waned, but they still have plenty to offer at bargain prices (admission is usually €5). With occasional evictions taking place, this is an ever-changing scene: besides long-established *centri sociali*, there are many that only last a few years. Listings magazines and the Rome listings pages of *La Repubblica* give details of their activities.

LATIN AMERICAN

Rome has hosted an energetic Latin American community since the 1970s, and Romans swarm to dance courses to get into tangoing trim. The Brazilian dance *capoeira* is one of the latest

Tune in

There's more to Italian music than the melodic pop successes of Eros Ramazzotti and Laura Pausini, who sell millions of records worldwide.

On the electronic front, the highly popular **Subsonica** and their Motel Connection disco project continue to dish out top-quality sounds with poetic lyrics.

Now that their super-charismatic vocalist Dan Black is busy with his UK pop band The Servant, Naples' **Planet Funk** are not enjoying the kind of success they had a few years ago when hits like *Who Said* played on every radio in Europe. And yet, their eclectic sounds, sung in English, make it difficult not to get up and dance.

For rock-pop, seek out **Tiromancino**, sweet, melancholic **Riccardo Senigallia**, smart, politically engaged **Daniele Silvestri**, popular **Neffa** or new-wave pop group **Baustelle**. Indie rock is played by internationally known band **Marlene Kuntz** (very much inspired by Sonic Youth) and **Afterhours**.

The Italian hip hop and rap scene, which had been flourishing in the early 1990s, is now left with only a few icons (notably **Assalti Frontali** and **Mondo Marcio**); the once-commercial singer Lorenzo Cherubini, formerly known as **Jovanotti**, now offers a mix of world music and hip hop that has gone beyond thoughtful to soapy.

Instrumental surf is in the capable hands of **Bradipo's IV**. The ska and hardcore scene is best represented by **Meganoidi**, **Statuto** and **Punkreas**. **Giuliano Palma and the Bluebeaters** serve up happy ska. The niche scene of jazzcore-experimental music has in Rome one of its best-known bands, the **Zu**.

Grab any chance to see the multi-ethnic **Orchestra di Piazza Vittorio**. Composed of musicians from five continents, this energetic ensemble, which inspired a documentary, often plays in Rome's theatres and cinemas.

In the easy listening and lounge scene – which originates from the film soundtracks of Piero Umiliani and Piero Piccioni – look for the sophisticated-funny sounds of the duo-twins **Montefiori Cocktail**, who draw from northern Italy's orchestral folk tradition. Another easy-listening and lounge star is the DJ-producer **Nicola Conte**, who also produces the Rome-resident, Brazilian singer **Rosalia De Souza**.

One of the most interesting phenomena of the past decade has been the revisiting of Italian folk traditions, such as *pizzica*, trance-like dance music from the southern region of Apulia. **AllaBua**, **Nidi d'Arac**, **Officina Zoè** and the legendary **Uccio Aloisi** are some of the better known groups in this genre.

And if you're lucky enough to be in Rome when he plays, be sure not to miss Italy's best songwriting export, **Paolo Conte**.

Arts & Entertainment

supperclubroma

supper**club** presents a new dining experience...

supper**club** presents a multi-sensory experience, rediscovering and renewing the origins of the roman banquet.

as a platform dedicated to creativity, we serve our guests a dynamic experience through a combination of cuisine, music, visuals and performances.

supper**club** provides an exceptional venue for social, cultural, and fashionable events and we thereby offer a stage to the innovators of every level of artistic expression; chefs, sommeliers, dj's, vj's, lj's, performers, artists, designers and creative people in general.

as a result, supper**club** rome was selected by the skilled commission of the prestigious magazine "**Conde Nast-Traveller**" as the best restaurant of 2003 of both italy and abroad due to its "*innovative and unusual combination of food, unique atmosphere, multi sensorial and eclectic offer*".

supper**club** Roma via De'Nari 14 00186 Roma

for information, please contact
Ivana Carmen Mottola (sales & event manager)
tel: 06 68301011.

fads, and schools run by resident Brazilians have popped up all over town. As well as clubs, discobars and a few tango cafés, lovers of Latin American tunes head en masse, especially on Thursdays, to **Palacavicchi** (via RB Bandinelli 130, Suburbs: south, 06 7932 1797, 349 290 7356) or, on Saturdays, to **Alpheus** (see p285). **Caruso** (see p285) offers live bands almost every night while **Fiesta** (see p282 **Sounds of summer**) livens up Rome's summer nights.

WHERE TO GO

With a few exceptions, Rome's nightlife is concentrated in a few easily accessible areas.

Testaccio is one of Rome's liveliest quarters, with nightlife action concentrated around **Monte Testaccio** (map p359): you'll be spoilt for choice – just walk around until you find the vibe you're after. The area around **via Libetta**, off via Ostiense (map p143), teems with trendy clubs and is poised to become even more crowded: the city council has slowly begun to develop the whole district as an arts hub based around the old fruit and vegetable market.

Fashionistas head for the *centro storico*: join them in the **triangolo della Pace** (map p355) to be part of trendy Roman life. The **campo de' Fiori** area (map p358), once a fashionista meeting spot, has become increasingly chaotic and, as the evening progresses, squalid.

The **San Lorenzo** quarter (map p151) is less pretentious: drinks are cheaper, and there's always something new going on.

Trastevere has lovely alleys packed with friendly, crowded bars. If you're longing for company but your Italian's weak, this is the place for you: English is the lingua franca. Note though that around piazza Trilussa, the scene gets seriously seedy in the small hours.

GETTING THROUGH THE DOOR

Getting into *centri sociali* or alternative, down-to-earth venues is easy enough – just join the chaotic queues at the door and use your elbows. But making it inside fashionable mainstream clubs can be stressful, no matter how elegantly you're dressed. Intimidating bouncers will bar your way, asking 'can I help you?' while supposed VIPs are whisked through the door.

Clubs and discobars generally charge an entrance fee at weekends but not on weekdays; you often have to pay for a *tessera* (membership card) on top of, or sometimes instead of, the entrance fee. *Tessere* may be valid for a season or for a month, and in some cases they're free. Admission tickets often include a 'free' drink, but you can expect the other drinks you buy to be pricey. Another popular formula is to grant 'free' admission while forcing you to buy a drink (generally expensive). To get out again

you have to hand a stamped drink card to the bouncer, so hold on to whatever piece of paper they give you or you'll be forced to pay twice.

Where we haven't specified a price for entrance in the listings, admission is free.

Tridente

Gregory's

Via Gregoriana 54 (06 679 6386/www.gregorys jazzclub.com). Metro Spagna or Barberini/bus 116, 117, 119, 590. **Open** 6pm-3.30am Tue-Sun. Closed Aug. **Credit** AmEx, DC, MC, V. **Map** p357 A5.
This cosy venue oozes jazz culture from every pore. On the ground floor, sip a glass of whisky from one of Rome's widest selections while admiring old portraits of jazz musicians. In the small upstairs room, you can jazz up your ears to top live acts while sitting comfortably among soft lights and lacquered tables.

Pantheon & Navona

Anima

Via Santa Maria dell'Anima 57 (347 850 9256). Bus 30Exp, 40Exp, 62, 64, 70, 81, 492, 628, 916. **Open** 6pm-4am daily. **Credit** DC, MC, V. **Map** p355 D5.
The improbable baroque gilded stucco that decorates this small venue could put some off, but there's a buzzing atmosphere and good drinks, and a mixed crowd of all ages and nationalities. The musical focus is on hip hop, R&B, funk, soul and reggae. There's an *aperitivo* evening on Sundays.

Bloom

Via del Teatro Pace 30 (06 6880 2029). Bus 30Exp, 40Exp, 62, 64, 70, 81, 492, 628, 916. **Open** 7pm-3am Mon, Tue, Thur-Sat. Closed July & Aug. **Credit** AmEx, DC, MC, V. **Map** p355 C5.
A restaurant, cocktail bar and disco (generally, but not always, on Fridays and Saturdays), Bloom is cooler than ice. A fashionable crowd hangs out in its designer interiors. At Bloom you can eat in the sushi bar, sip an *aperitivo*, dance or simply relax at the bar while you check out other people's outfits. The door policy can be strict, and booking is essential for dinner as there are only 25 seats.

La Cabala

Via dei Soldati 25C (06 6830 1192/www.hosteria dellorso.it). Bus 30Exp, 70, 87, 116, 117, 492, 916. **Open** *Piano bar* 11.30pm-3.30am Tue-Thur; 11.30pm-4.30am Fri, Sat. *Disco* 12.30am-5am Fri, Sat. Both closed June-Aug. **Admission** free with compulsory drink (€15). **Credit** AmEx, DC, MC, V. **Map** p355 D5.
One of the favourite haunts of Rome's well-heeled, La Cabala nestles on the third floor of a 15th-century palazzo that's also home to the Osteria dell'Orso restaurant of super-chef Gualtiero Marchese and a quaint ground-floor piano bar. To get to La Cabala, walk past the sing-along punters in the piano bar and head for the stairs: the music may be nothing special – a mix of house and chart hits – but the place rocks and the view over the Tiber is romantic.

Arts & Entertainment

La Maison

Vicolo dei Granari 4 (06 683 3312). Bus 40Exp, 46, 62, 64, 70, 81, 97, 189, 304, 492, 628, 916. **Open** 11pm-4am Wed-Sat. Closed June-Sept. **Admission** free. **Credit** AmEx, DC, MC, V. **Map** p355 D5.

The ice-cool barmen and a VIP room almost as big as the club itself speak volumes: this is one of the clubs of choice of Rome's fashion-victims. Huge chandeliers, dark red walls and curvy sofas give La Maison an opulent, courtly feeling. And yet, surprisingly, the place is not snobbish, the music on offer is not banal and the atmosphere is buzzing. Be warned: the doormen can be very picky.

Supperclub

Via de' Nari 14 (06 6830 1011/www.supperclub.com). Bus 30Exp, 40Exp, 62, 64, 70, 186, 492, 628, 916. **Open** 8.30pm-3.30am Mon, Tue, Thur-Sun. Closed Aug. **Credit** AmEx, DC, MC, V. **Map** p355 D6.

Although it may be better known for its popular, sofa-lounging restaurant (booking strongly advised) and artistic performances than it is for its club-bar nights, the upmarket Supperclub offers a good array of cocktails (served by super-stylish waiters). Themed club events take place on slow-moving evenings; check the website for details. There's a downstairs room for dancing. Be warned: the crowd selection at the door can be strict.

Late bars

See also p221 **Société Lutèce**.

Bar del Fico

Piazza del Fico 26-28 (06 686 5205). Bus 30Exp, 40Exp, 46, 62, 64, 70, 81, 87, 116, 304, 492, 628, 916. **Open** *Sept-July* 8.30am-2.30am Mon-Sat; noon-2.30am Sun. *Aug* 4pm-2am daily. **No credit cards.** Map p355 C5.

Although it was undergoing extensive renovation work as this guide went to press, this long-established *centro storico* fixture – named after the ancient fig tree (*fico*) outside – will reopen bigger and more chic in mid 2007. From breakfast until the small hours it's perfect for exchanging glances with sultry strangers at the next table.

Sounds of summer

On long summer nights Rome really comes into its own, bursting with an astounding number of festivals, often held in such breathtaking locations as Roman ruins, Renaissance villas or ancient amphitheatres. Besides providing top performances, they allow access to some of the city's artistic and architectural treasures that are normally beyond the reach of tourists.

The warm season starts with the free **Labour Day concert** organised by Italy's trade unions on 1 May (Primo Maggio; *see also p253*). It's traditionally held in piazza San Giovanni in Laterano and hosts Italian – and a handful of international – stars, drawing half a million people from all over Italy.

In mid June, the **Estate Romana** kicks off. An umbrella for most of Rome's outdoor summer festivals sponsored by city hall, it runs to the end of September. Every year, a couple of major concerts (Madonna and Depeche Mode in 2006) are held in the Stadio Olimpico (via del Foro Italico), while one or two free big-names concerts are held in July or August. In 2006 Bryan Adams and Billy Joel each played before huge crowds of enthusiastic Romans in front of the Colosseum; the venue for 2007 is the nearby Circus Maximus. There are more headliners at the **Cornetto Free Music Festival**, which consists of a major one-day festival or a series of concerts held at various

venues; the Black Eyed Peas were on the bill in 2006. A full programme of summer events can be accessed from late spring through the city council website (www.comune.roma.it).

For an incursion into an all-Italian phenomenon, look out for festivals organised by Italy's political parties (**Festa dell'Unità** by the Democratici di sinistra, and **Festa di Liberazione** by Rifondazione comunista). At these festivals – which are popular with supporters and non-affiliates alike – there are arty crafty stalls for browsing, food, live music, theatre and, of course, political debates. Check in the local press for details.

The summer season is rounded off in style by two of the city's best events: the cutting-edge **Enzimi** festival (*see below*) and the **Notte Bianca** (*see p254*) – one night in early September when bars, clubs, museums, libraries and shops are open all night long, bringing the whole city out on to the streets.

Other summer events to look out for are:

Cosmophonies – Festival Internazionale di Ostia Antica

Teatro Romano-Scavi Archeologici di Ostia Antica, viale dei Romagnoli 717 (333 200 4329/www.comsophonies.com). **Date** June-mid Sept. **Tickets** €15-€65. **No credit cards.** Held in the breathtaking scenario of the ancient Roman theatre of Ostia Antica (*see p300*), Cosmophonies is an international

Fluid
*Via del Governo Vecchio 46-47 (06 683 2361/www.
fluideventi.com). Bus 30Exp, 40Exp, 62, 64, 70,
492, 628, 916.* **Open** 6pm-2am daily. Closed 3wks
Aug. **Credit** AmEx, DC, MC, V. **Map** p355 C5.
Ultra-sleek, with black floors, stunning chandeliers
and plasma screens, this designer bar tries hard to
be trendy but ends up being somewhat characterless.
The crowd isn't always as cool as the interiors.

Ghetto & Campo de' Fiori

Rialtosantambrogio
*Via Sant'Ambrogio 4 (06 6813 3640/www.rialto
santambrogio.org). Bus 23, 30Exp, 40Exp, 62, 64,
70, 95, 492, H/tram 8.* **Open** days & times vary.
Closed Aug. **Admission** free or €5. **No credit
cards. Map** p358 D2.
A winding staircase leads you into this lively *centro
sociale* housed in a picturesque building hidden
away in the Ghetto. The Rialtosantambrogio, which
also has a charming courtyard garden that's perfect

for the summer months, hosts performances, art
exhibitions, live music and disco nights headlined
by cutting-edge DJs and VJs. The funk and bossa
Condominio club night (one Friday a month) gets
especially crowded, as does the electronica-meets-
arthouse-cinema Blueroom (Saturdays). A meeting
point for the radical crowd. The 'smoke as much as
you like' policy – flying in the face of Italy's no-
smoking legislation – turns the place into a smoke
chamber in the small hours.

Late bars
See p223 **Gloss.**

Trastevere & Gianicolo

Lettere Caffè
*Via San Francesco a Ripa 100-101 (06 6456 1916/
www.letterecaffe.org). Bus 44, 75, 780, H/tram 3, 8.*
Open 5pm-2am daily (concerts begin 10.30pm).
Closed Aug. **Credit** AmEx, MC, V. **Map** p359 C4.

festival of theatre, dance and music dishing
out acts like Sonic Youth, Morrissey, Caetano
Veloso and Jackson Browne. No matter
what's happening on stage, these unique
surroundings make for a memorable night.

Enzimi
*Various venues (www.enzimi.festival
roma.org).* **Date** generally 2wks mid-Sept.
Admission free.
This free music, theatre and arts festival –
a showcase for the best up-and-coming
artists – is council-funded and aimed at
thirtysomethings and younger. Held in an
array of unlikely locations, it hosts cutting-
edge local bands and some international
stars, skilfully mixing mainstream acts with
offbeat sounds – the perfect opportunity to
see what's new in the city's artistic circles.

Fiesta
*Via Appia Nuova 1245, Suburbs: east
(06 7129 9858/toll-free credit card
bookings 199 109 910/www.fiesta.it).
Metro Colli Albani/bus 590, 650, 671.*
Date mid June-mid Aug.
This hectic Latin American-themed festival
regularly attracts almost a million people
over the summer months with performances
by Latin American bands, plus appearances
by some international rock, pop and hip hop
stars. There are four dancefloors, scores

of restaurants and stalls... and lots of salsa
and merengue. Come early: transport and
parking can be a nightmare.

Jazz & Image Festival
*Villa Celimontana, Celio (06 5833 57817/
www.villacelimontanajazz.com). Metro
Colosseo/bus 81, 673/tram 3.* **Date** early
June-Aug. **Admission** €5-€30 per event.
Credit (online bookings only) DC, MC, V.
Map p361 C4.
This festival takes place in the leafy Villa
Celimontana park (*see p149*) and features
acclaimed artists (from Incognito to Italian
jazz star Stefano Bollani) in an astonishingly
beautiful setting. Lots of candles and torches
give the place a magical aura. Wine and food
stands complete the idyll.

Roma Incontra il Mondo
*Villa Ada, via di Ponte Salario, Suburbs: north
(06 4173 4712/06 4173 4648/www.villa
ada.org). Bus 63, 92, 231, 235, 310.* **Date**
mid June-early Aug. **Admission** €4-€12 per
event. **No credit cards. Map** p353.
Musicians from around the world play on a
lakeside stage beneath the venerable trees
of the Villa Ada park. Lights reflected in the
water and cool breezes make this one of the
most atmospheric and relaxing of the summer
festivals. If the music palls there are bars and
stalls purveying ethnic food, music and books.

Arts & Entertainment

THE SHORTLIST
WHAT'S NEW | WHAT'S ON | WHAT'S BEST

Barcelona
WHAT'S NEW | WHAT'S ON | WHAT'S NEXT

Berlin
WHAT'S NEW | WHAT'S ON | WHAT'S NEXT

London
WHAT'S NEW | WHAT'S ON | WHAT'S NEXT

Manchester
WHAT'S NEW | WHAT'S ON | WHAT'S BEST

New York
WHAT'S NEW | WHAT'S ON | WHAT'S NEXT

Paris
WHAT'S NEW | WHAT'S ON | WHAT'S NEXT

Prague
WHAT'S NEW | WHAT'S ON | WHAT'S NEXT

Rome
WHAT'S NEW | WHAT'S ON | WHAT'S NEXT

Coming soon…

Amsterdam
2008
WHAT'S NEW | WHAT'S ON | WHAT'S NEXT

Dubrovnik
WHAT'S NEW | WHAT'S ON | WHAT'S NEXT

Las Vegas
WHAT'S NEW | WHAT'S ON | WHAT'S NEXT

Tokyo
WHAT'S NEW | WHAT'S ON | WHAT'S NEXT

Venice
WHAT'S NEW | WHAT'S ON | WHAT'S NEXT

- **POCKET–SIZE GUIDES**
- **WRITTEN BY LOCAL EXPERTS**
- **KEY VENUES PINPOINTED ON MAPS**

ble at all major bookshops at only
and from timeout.com/shop

Time
SHOR

While retaining its vocation for poetry and literature (see p227 **Book bars**), the Lettere Caffè has bounced back cooler and stronger with new management and a choice of live concerts and DJ sets. From rockabilly to jazz, passing through '60s beat, the Lettere is both a showcase of new talent and a place to listen to well-known DJs and bands from Rome and beyond. An excellent selection of wines and spirits that won't empty your wallet and yummy home-made cakes complete the picture.

Big Mama

Vicolo San Francesco a Ripa 18 (06 581 2551/ www.bigmama.it). Bus 75, 170/tram 3, 8. **Open** 9pm-1.30am Tue-Sat. Closed mid June-mid Sept. **Admission** free with membership (annual €13, monthly €8); extra charge (€8-€22) for big acts. **Credit** DC, MC, V. **Map** p359 C4.

Rome's blues heart throbs in this pared-back but welcoming venue, which hosts an array of respected Italian and international artists every evening. The blues menu is punctuated with jazz, rock and ethnic music. There are drinks and hot meals to consume while listening to the top-quality music on offer. Book if you want to get a table.

Aventine, Testaccio & Ostiense

Akab

Via di Monte Testaccio 68-69 (06 5725 0585/www. akabcave.com). Metro Piramide/bus 23, 30Exp, 75, 95, 719, 29N, 30N, 91N/tram 3. **Open** midnight-5am Tue-Sat. Closed Aug. **Admission** (incl 1 drink) €10-€25. **Credit** AmEx, DC, MC, V. **Map** p359 D6.

Formerly a carpenter's workshop, this busy, long long-term fixture of the Testaccio scene hosts well-known international DJs, especially on Tuesdays at L-Ektrica. Come here for retro on Wednesdays, R&B on Thursdays and house on Fridays and Saturdays. It has two levels: an underground cellar and a street-level room, plus an outside garden.

Alpheus

Via del Commercio 36 (06 574 7826/www. alpheus.it). Metro Piramide/bus 23, 769, 770, 40N, 80N. **Open** 10.30pm-4am Fri-Sun; other evenings vary. Closed July & Aug. **Admission** €5-€20. **Credit** AmEx. **Map** p143 A2.

An eclectic club with a miscellaneous crowd, the Alpheus has four big halls for live gigs, music festivals, theatre and cabaret, all followed by a disco. The music changes every night and varies depending on the room you're in: rock, chart R&B, Latin, world music, retro and happy trash. Alpheus also hosts Tocodance (www.tocodance.it), an irregular word-of-mouth dance-event frequented by a creative, international crowd of thirty- and forty-somethings.

Caruso-Caffè de Oriente

Via di Monte Testaccio 36 (06 574 5019/www. carusocafedeoriente.com). Metro Piramide/bus 23, 30Exp, 75, 95, 280, 716, 719, 91N/tram 3. **Open**

10.30pm-3.30am Tue-Thur, Sun; 11pm-4.30am Fri & Sat. Closed July-mid Sept. **Admission** (incl 1 drink) €8 Tue-Thur; €10 Fri; €10 women, €15 men Sat; free Sun. **No credit cards. Map** p359 D6.

A must for lovers of salsa and the like, this club offers Latin American tunes every night (apart from Saturdays, when it veers towards hip hop and R&B) and live acts almost daily. Shimmy your way in between scores of dancing couples to enjoy the warm atmosphere in these three, ethnic-themed, orange-hued rooms – or head up to the roof terrace.

Caffè Latino

Via di Monte Testaccio 96 (06 5728 8556). Metro Piramide/bus 23, 30Exp, 75, 95, 280, 716, 719, 29N, 30N, 91N/tram 3. **Open** 10.30pm-3am Wed-Sat. Closed June-Sept. **Admission** free; €8-€15 for special events. **No credit cards. Map** p359 D6.

This is one of the oldest clubs in the Testaccio area, offering a choice of live music and DJs, ranging from jazz to ethnic, Latin American to funky. If you don't feel like dancing, you can relax on comfy chairs.

Classico Village

Via Libetta 3 (06 574 3364/www.classico.it). Metro Garbatella/bus 29, 769, 770, 40N, 80N. **Open** 9pm-1.30am Mon-Thur; 11pm-4am Fri, Sat. **Admission** €5-€15. **Credit** DC, MC, V. **Map** p143 B3.

This former factory space in super-hip Ostiense comprises three rooms, often offering three different acts simultaneously. The whole thing faces on to a courtyard, which is heaven in the warmer months. The live bands and DJ sets veer towards the rock end of the musical spectrum.

Fake

Via di Monte Testaccio 64 (347 794 8859). Metro Piramide/bus 23, 30Exp, 75, 95, 280, 716, 719, 29N, 30N, 91N/tram 3. **Open** 11pm-4am Fri, Sat. **Admission** €10-€20. **No credit cards. Map** p359 D6.

When it opened in 2005, this club proclaimed itself to be at the cutting edge of hipness. And Fake certainly looks the part, starting from the decor – a stunning mix of white, '60s space-age design, pop-art motifs and ancient red bricks. But we're still waiting for it to happen. The music on offer is centred around electronica but includes hip hop, R&B and '60s beat.

Goa

Via Libetta 13 (06 574 8277). Metro Garbatella/ bus 29, 769, 770, 40N, 80N. **Open** midnight-4am Wed-Sat. Closed mid May-mid Sept. **Admission** (incl 1 drink) €10-€25. **Credit** AmEx, DC, MC, V. **Map** p143 B3.

In trendy Ostiense, this is one of the best of Rome's fashionable clubs. Goa marries iron and steel with curvy, 1960s-style whites. The quality of its Italian and international DJs is generally above the competition. Ultrabeat on Thursdays, organised by top Italian DJ Claudio Coccoluto, brings the cream of Europe's electronic music DJs to Rome. There are occasional Sunday openings (5pm-4am), including a women-only event on the last Sunday of the month. Note that the doormen can be picky.

Arts & Entertainment

Linux

Via Libetta 15C (06 5725 0551/www.linuxclub.it).
Metro Garbatella/bus 29, 769, 770, 40N, 80N.
Open 5pm-3.30am daily. Closed Aug. **Credit**
AmEx, DC, MC, V. **Map** p143 B3.
Linux is a club, a bar, a cultural association and an
internet point, committed to the promotion of Linux,
other open-source software and the not-for-profit
sector in general. The decor is minimal except for some
flat screens. On Saturdays, drum 'n' bass devotee DJ
AndyPop organises the Romastyle club night.

Metaverso

Via di Monte Testaccio 38A (06 574 4712/www.
metaverso.com). Metro Piramide/bus 23, 30Exp, 75,
95, 280, 716, 719, 29N, 30N, 91N/tram 3. **Open**
10.30pm-5am Fri, Sat. Closed July & Aug. **Admission**
€5-€7. **No credit cards. Map** p359 D6.
This inexpensive, friendly little club plays host to
international DJs from well-known labels, along
with several of Rome's home-grown best, pulling
in an alternative crowd. Weekends are mostly dedicated to electronica and hip hop apart from one
Saturday a month, when it's '60s galore in a cool
party called 'Twiggy'. It also hosts exhibitions of
works by local artists.

Rashomon

Via degli Argonauti 16 (347 340 5710/www.
myspace.com/rashomonclub). Metro Garbatella/bus
29, 769, 770, 40N, 80N. **Open** 11pm-4am Thur-Sat.
Closed July & Aug. **Admission** free-€10. **No credit
cards. Map** p143 B3.
This dark-walled club in Ostiense has an authentic
underground feel – which is confirmed by the choice
of DJs and live bands on the roster. Run by a group
of young people with a passion for the alternative
clubs of London and Berlin, Rashomon lets loose
with electro-rock, electronica, indie and new wave,
plus showcases of emerging bands.

La Saponeria

Via degli Argonauti 20 (393 966 1321/www.
lasaponeria.com). Metro Garbatella/bus 29, 769,
770, 40N, 80N. **Open** 11.30pm-5am Thur-Sat.
Closed mid May-mid Sept. **Admission** €10-€15.
Credit DC, MC, V. **Map** p143 B3.
One of the liveliest clubs in Ostiense's via Libetta
area, La Saponeria is a curvy space with a large bar
in the middle. It gets hopelessly packed on weekends. Fridays revolve around hip hop and R&B,
Saturdays are house with the Minima crowd. Expect
queues on popular nights.

Jazz up your ears

Rome's appetite for jazz has been growing
steadily over the past decade, culminating
in the 2005 opening of the charming **Casa
del Jazz** (viale di Porta Ardeatina 55, 06 704
731, bookings 199 109 783, www.casajazz.it;
photo below) in a 1930s villa confiscated from
a *mafioso*, close to the Baths of Caracalla
(*see p141*). A project sponsored by Rome's
jazz-loving mayor, Walter Veltroni, this 'Home
of Jazz' focuses on the Italian scene, but also
hosts international stars. It features a 150-
seat auditorium, as well as a large garden, a
bookshop (open from 7pm on concert nights),

a library (open 6-9pm on concert nights),
a café and a restaurant (06 700 8370,
both open 7.30pm-midnight Tue-Sat, noon-
midnight Sun). In addition to concerts, it
hosts lectures and readings.

For something more central, check out
Gregory's (*see p281*), located just around
the corner from the Spanish steps, or **Big
Mama** (*see p285*) in Trastevere. In Testaccio,
jazz is on the menu at **BeBop Jazz & Blues
Live Club** (via Giulietti 14, 06 5728 8959,
www.bebopmusicclub.it) and the nearby
Classico Village (*see p285*). In Prati, near

the Vatican, you can catch a
jam session at the legendary
Alexanderplatz (*see p287*) or
The Place (*see p287*).

In summer, you can enjoy
concerts at the **Jazz & Image
Festival** (*see p283*) or at the
summer festival in the **La
Palma** courtyard (*see p288*).

Italian jazz has several
excellent names to watch out
for, including Antonello Salis,
Roberto Gatto, Paolo Fresu,
Enrico Pieranunzi, Rosario
Giuliani, Stefano di Battista
and singer Ada Montellanico.

Arts & Entertainment

Celio, San Giovanni & San Lorenzo

Beba do Samba

Via dei Messapi 8 (339 878 5214/www.bebado samba.it). Bus 71, 163, 204, 443, 448, 490, 491, 492, 495, 649/tram 3, 19. **Open** 10pm-2am daily. Closed July & Aug. **Admission** free with annual membership (€5). **No credit cards**. **Map** p151 C3.

This popular, buzzing little venue in San Lorenzo attracts a studenty crowd for live music – mostly ethnic, world music and jazz – almost every night, often followed by a DJ.

Locanda Atlantide

Via dei Lucani 22B (06 4470 4540/www. locandatlantide.it). Bus 71, 163, 204, 443, 448, 490, 491, 492, 495, 649/tram 3, 19. **Open** 9.30pm-3am Tue-Sun. Closed mid June-Sept. **Admission** €3-€10. **No credit cards**. **Map** p151 C3.

This friendly, unpretentious venue in the buzzing San Lorenzo neighbourhood hosts an array of events ranging from concerts and DJ acts to theatrical performances. It may open earlier in the evening for book launches; there are occasional events on Mondays too. It pulls an alternative crowd and can be relied upon to offer a good night out.

Micca Club

Via Pietro Micca 7A (06 8744 0079/www.micca club.com). Metro Vittorio or Manzoni/bus 71, 105, 12N, 50N/tram 3, 5, 14. **Open** 10pm-2am Wed; 10pm-4am Thur-Sat; 6pm-2am Sun. Closed June-Aug. **Credit** MC, V. **Admission** free Wed, Thur, Sun; €5 Fri, Sat; €10 for special events. **Credit** MC, V. **Map** p151 B4.

Some might be put off by the makeover that has turned this interesting space (a cellar with red-brick vaults) into an impractical venue with a small dance floor and a stage inexplicably stuck at the very end of the space. Yet Micca's top-notch DJ sets and live acts, plus smooth advertising, ensure that it's full every night. From '60s beat to soul, from funk to jazz and rock'n'roll, the music on offer is varied and interesting. The programme also includes, once a month, the rising London star of burlesque striptease, Lady Luck. On Sunday evenings there's a crowded flea market held here. **Photo** *p278*.

Monti & Esquilino

Living Room

Via Solferino 9A (348 280 2891/www.livingroom roma.com). Metro Castro Pretorio or Termini/buses to Termini/tram 5, 14. **Open** 7am-4am Mon, Wed-Sat; 7am-7pm Tue; 7pm-4am Sun. **Admission** free with compulsory drink (€10). **Credit** DC, MC, V. **Map** p357 E5.

With its sleek design and mix of red brick and steel, the Living Room gives itself airs but does not quite live up to its aspirations. Still, it's very lively, and has DJs and a space for dancing.

The lovely **Teatro Palladium**. *See p288.*

Vatican & Prati

Alexanderplatz

Via Ostia 9 (06 3974 2171/www.alexanderplatz.it). Metro Ottaviano/bus 32, 34, 49, 81, 492, 590, 982/ tram 19. **Open** 8.30pm-1.30am daily. Closed June-Sept. **Admission** free with monthly (€10) or annual (€30) membership. **Credit** DC, MC, V. **Map** p354 A3.

Jazz is increasingly popular in Rome, and new venues pop up every year. But the pioneer of them all, *the* jazz club in Rome, is still the Alexanderplatz. It offers nightly concerts with famous names from the Italian and foreign scene. In summer it runs the popular Jazz & Image open-air festival (*see p283*) in Villa Celimontana. Dinner is served from 8.30pm; live music starts at 10.30pm. Booking advised.

aBlueNote

Via Fabio Massimo 113 (06 323 1005). Metro Ottaviano. Bus 70, 590, 913/tram 19. **Open** 5pm-2am Tue-Sun. **Credit** AmEx, DC, MC, V. **Map** p354 B3.

This small jazz venue with a cramped stage and a slightly Arabic feel offers concerts, jam sessions and singer-songwriter evenings in a homely atmosphere.

The Place

Via Alberico II 27 (06 6830 7137/www.theplace.it). Bus 23, 34, 49, 80Exp, 280, 492, 982, 990. **Open** 8.30pm-2.30am daily. Closed mid June-Sept. **Admission** €8-€15. **Credit** AmEx, DC, MC, V. **Map** p355 B4.

A swish, vibrant club with a stage for live acts, The Place caters for a thirty- and forty-something crowd by serving up Italian – and a sprinkling of foreign – singer-songwriters and jazz bands. Dinner is served on a platform overlooking the stage. DJs spin commercial and house after the weekend acts.

Arts & Entertainment

Late bars

BarBar
Via Ovidio 17 (06 6880 5682). Bus 32, 34, 49, 81, 492/tram 19. **Open** 10pm-4am Tue-Sat; 8pm-2am Sun. Closed June-Aug. **Credit** AmEx, DC, MC, V. **Map** p354 b3.
Stylish interiors – including a bar 50m (165ft) long that wends its way through the whole club – make BarBar a design jewel, one popular with a young label-clad crowd. On Sundays, *aperitivo* evenings turn into dancing nights. There's a wide, though pricey, choice of cocktails.

Suburbs

See also p273 **Auditorium-Parco della Musica**.

Brancaleone
Via Levanna 11, Suburbs: north (06 8200 4382/ www.brancaleone.it). Bus 36, 60Exp, 90Exp. **Open** 10pm-4.30am Thur-Sat. Closed June-mid Sept. **Admission** €5-€10. **No credit cards.**
What used to be the best-run of the city's *centri sociali* – and the Roman beacon for hosting the best electronic musicians and DJs in Europe – is now on a decline, and it's not clear whether it's reversible. The live and DJ acts on offer continue to be top-notch but the crowd has become rowdy. Weekends get packed but weekdays can be lively too, especially the reggae Thursdays; there are occasional events on Wednesdays. The venue also houses a cinema, a rehearsal studio and an organic products bar.

Circolo degli Artisti
Via Casilina Vecchia 42, Suburbs: south-east (06 7030 5684/www.circoloartisti.it). Bus 81, 105, 412, 810/tram 5, 14, 19. **Open** 9.30pm-3.30am Tue-Thur; 9pm-4.30am Fri-Sun. Closed Aug. **Admission** €6 and up. **No credit cards.**
This is Rome's most popular venue for small- and medium-scale bands from international alternative music circuits. (Inexplicably, the owners still haven't sorted out the patchy acoustics.) On Fridays it hosts a popular gay night (*see p270*). On Saturdays (admission free after midnight) the established Screamadelica night has concerts by some of Europe's best alternative artists and emerging Italian bands, followed by a DJ spinning indie, electric pop and new wave. The large, cool garden is a great place for chatting with friends or making new ones.

La Palma
Via G Mirri 35, Suburbs: south (06 4359 9029/ www.lapalmaclub.it). Metro Tiburtina/bus 163, 211, 309, 409, 443, 448. **Open** 8.30pm-1.30am Tue-Thur; 8.30pm-5am Fri, Sat. Closed Aug. **Admission** (with annual €2 membership) varies considerably, from free to €15. **Credit** AmEx, DC, MC, V.
An oasis in a post-industrial landscape, this club housed in a former farm has good concerts and DJ sets. The schedule is eclectic, though jazz-focused;

you might also catch avant-garde rock, ethnic, soul or lounge, sometimes followed by a DJ. In the summer it hosts a jazz festival in a charming, spacious outside courtyard complete with restaurant.

PalaLottomatica
Piazzale dello Sport, Suburbs: EUR (199 128 800/ www.forumnet.it). Metro EUR Palasport/bus 30Exp, 671, 714, 780, 791. **Open** days & times vary. **Admission** varies.
After a lengthy period of refurbishment, the flying-saucer-shaped PalaLottomatica, designed by architect and engineer Pierluigi Nervi for the 1960 Rome Olympics, reopened in 2003 to become the space for large indoor concerts that Rome never had. So far, it has not lived up to expectations, though a system of movable panels has improved the once appalling acoustics. Tickets are available from the usual large-event outlets (*see p250*).

Teatro Palladium
Piazza Bartolomeo Romano 8, Suburbs: south (06 5706 7761/06 5706 7768/www.teatro-palladium.it). Metro Garbatella/bus 716. **Box office** 4-8pm Tue-Sun; until 9pm on performance days. **Open** days & times vary. **Admission** varies. **Credit** AmEx, DC, MC, V. **Map** p143 C3.
This beautiful 1920s theatre – furnished with brightly coloured chairs – offers a fascinating mix of electronic-music acts, cutting-edge theatre and art performances. It is one of the venues of choice for the exciting, eclectic RomaEuropa Festival (*see p254*) in the autumn. **Photo** *p287*.

Traffic Drink 'n' Roll Live Club
Via Vacuna 98, Suburbs: north (328 054 7412/ www.trafficlive.org). Metro Tiburtina/bus 111, 211, 440, 163. **Open** 10pm-3am Tue-Sun. Closed July & Aug. **Admission** (with annual €2 membership) €3-€5. **No credit cards.**
With the motto of 'we rock, they don't', Traffic has become Rome's hottest live stage for underground and soon-to-be-famous bands. Every night it pumps out alternative tunes ranging from punk, rock'n'roll and hard core to power pop, '60s beat and surf. Hidden in a side street close to Tiburtina station, this basic club is on two levels: concerts take place downstairs and there's a pub upstairs.

Zoobar
Via Benvenga 1, Suburbs: north (339 272 7995/ www.zoobar.roma.it). Bus 36, 60Exp, 84, 211, 60N. **Open** 11pm-4.30am Fri, Sat. Closed Aug. **Admission** (with annual €2 membership) €10 Fri; €4 Sat. **No credit cards.**
This down-to-earth club used to host live acts of up-and-coming international bands, drawing crowds to its venue in club-packed Testaccio. At the time of writing, it had just moved to the northern suburbs. There's no room in the new place for live bands, making it unclear exactly what Zoobar's future holds. But the club continues to offer a steady DJ diet of pop, indie, Brit pop and '80s retro to a studenty crowd. Fridays are open-bar nights.

Arts & Entertainment

Sport & Fitness

Nothing exercises Romans like watching a football match.

Ever since the days when the ancient masses headed to the Colosseum in droves for their dose of gladiator-slaying, the Romans have been fanatical about sport… so long as they can enjoy it sitting down. Like their slothful forebears, today's Romans prefer to save their energy for gesticulating from the sidelines, though in recent years a general obsession with looking good has sent them scurrying to work off the pasta pounds at the city's gyms, no longer the province of the perma-tanned and super-honed. Though more alternative fitness centres are opening up, yoga and Pilates are still regarded as exotic ways to get fit.

For the seriously sporty, facilities in the city remain rather limited. The Foro Italico complex in the northern suburbs – the result of a campaign by Mussolini in the 1920s and '30s to prod his layabout countrymen into action – has impressive facilites… for professionals only.

The hallowed *calcio* (football), with its all-star cast of modern-day gladiators, has long been the Romans' spectator sport of choice. Rome boasts two first-class football teams, one of which plays at home almost every weekend from September to June. To do sport as the Romans do, make the weekend pilgrimage to the Stadio Olimpico, and cheer from the stands.

Cycling

Occasional Sunday closures to cars of the *centro storico* (see local press) provide an opportunity for exploring the city on two wheels in relative safety. It's a weekly occurrence further out: the

ancient Appian Way offers especially serene (if somewhat bumpy) pedalling on traffic-free Sundays; the via Appia Antica visitors' centre (*see p172*) has bikes for hire that day only. For other **bike hire** outlets, *see p325*.

Two **cycle paths** – one beginning at Ponte Milvio and heading north, the other at Ponte Sublicio and heading south – follow the banks of the Tiber as far as the city's GRA ringroad; it's a pleasant ride, mostly on good surfaces, with an alternation of inner suburb and urban green along the route. Plans to join the two tracks are moving slowly, but it is just about possible to get from one to the other along the bumpy riverside promenade on the Tiber's right bank. There's a ramp to wheel your bike down at Ponte Sublicio, and elsewhere steps have tracks for easy pushing. You may find the odd questionable character lurking under bridges but on the whole it's safe – and a peaceful way to get around the city well below the level of the thundering traffic.

Football

Romans' passionate loyalty as supporters has always distinguished them, though their commitment wavered slightly in the wake of a dramatic match-fixing scandal in 2006, when it was alleged that a football ring led by 'Lucky' Luciano Moggi, manager of super-squad Juventus, had been fiddling the results for years. Moggi was banned from football for five years. Blasé Italians would generally struggle to raise an eyebrow at the news of a

Arts & Entertainment

AS Roma's modern-day gladiators. *See p290.*

scandal, but Moggi-gate so shamed Italian sport that many formerly die-hard fans professed themselves ambivalent about the outcome of the World Cup... until they started winning. Italy's victory over France was an excuse for weeks of city-wide celebration, kicking off with a victory procession to the Circo Massimo (*see p84*), where half-a-million ecstatic fans bellowed as Italian team captain Fabio Cannavaro hoisted the trophy aloft.

At weekends during the season the 20 teams of Italy's **Serie A** (Premier League) meet, under the gaze of 50 million Italians. Rome boasts two first-class football clubs: **AS Roma** (www.as romacalcio.it) and **SS Lazio** (www.sslazio.it). The two teams share the **Stadio Olimpico** (*see below*), and tension is thick across the city whenever they play each other. Derbies are an excuse for *romanisti* and rival *laziali* to attempt to out-do each other with the wittiest banners, the rudest chants and the most impressive displays of team-colour pyrotechnics.

Lazio was founded in 1900. After winning the championship (*lo scudetto*) in 2000, they have languished mid-division ever since, and in 2006 the club was publicly shamed for its involvement (though to a lesser extent than Juventus) in the match-fixing scandal; they were docked valuable points as punishment. The younger Roma (founded in 1927; **photo** *p289*) won its third *scudetto* in 2001. Though some of its stars have jumped ship since, the team is still a solid presence in Serie A, largely thanks to playmaker Francesco Totti, who has been all but deified in his native Rome.

A recent spate of stadium violence – culminating in the death of a police officer in the Sicilian city of Catania in 2007 – prompted tough new legislation. As a result, **tickets** can no longer be purchased directly from the Stadio Olimpico box office. You'll need to get them online from **www.listicket.it** or from the merchandising outlets listed below. Tickets are personal and non-transferable. You can purchase up to ten tickets at a time; to do so, you'll need to present your photo ID and provide the names and dates of birth of all the other people for whom you are buying tickets. Each must present photo ID (corresponding, obviously, with the name on the ticket) at the turnstiles when they get to the stadium.

Once inside the stadium, die-hard Roma fans flock to the *curva sud* (south end), marking their territory with red and yellow, while the sky blue and white of the Lazio faithful occupies the *curva nord* (north end). Team mascots (Roma's wolf, Lazio's eagle), are much in evidence. The *curve* have the best pyrotechnics and cheapest seats, but for a better view, opt for the more expensive Tribuna Tevere or Tribuna Monte Mario.

Stadio Olimpico

Viale dello Stadio Olimpico, Suburbs: north (06 323 7333). Bus 32, 224, 280/tram 2. **Tickets** €10-€100. **No credit cards.** **Map** p353.
Important matches sell out quickly. Even the cheaper seats have a decent view.

Essential accessories

An array of unofficial team scarves, jerseys and flags can be bought outside the stadium on match days. For better quality items go to the club shops listed here. They also sell match tickets up to seven days in advance.

AS Roma Store

Piazza Colonna 360, Tridente (06 678 6514/www. asromastore.it). Bus 52, 62, 95, 116, 175, 492. **Open** 11am-7.30pm Mon-Sat; 11am-7.30pm Sun. **Credit** AmEx, DC, MC, V. **Map** p355 E5.
AS Roma stores have an endless array of club merchandise, from scarves to baby booties – all of it emblazoned with the highly recognisable red-and-yellow AS Roma logo.
Other locations: piazza Indipendenza 8, Esquilino (06 4470 2689).

Original Fans Lazio

Via Farini 34, Esquilino (06 482 6688). Metro Termini/bus 40Exp, 64, 70, 170, 175, 492. **Open** 9am-7pm Mon-Sat. Closed 1wk Aug. **Credit** AmEx, DC, MC, V. **Map** p357 D6.

Golf

Golf is still an exclusive game in Italy. Most clubs will ask to see a membership card from your home club and proof of handicap, although it's not normally necessary to be introduced by a member. Green fees, including those quoted below, are normally per day rather than per round.

Circolo del Golf Roma Acquasanta

Via Appia Nuova 716, Suburbs: east (06 780 3407/ www.golfroma.it). Metro Colli Albani then bus 663 or 664. **Open** 8am-sunset Tue-Sun. **Rates** (green fees incl use of range) €80 Tue-Fri; €100 Sat, Sun. *Driving range* €15 Tue-Fri; €20 Sat, Sun. *Club hire* €18. *Golf cart hire* €45. **Credit** DC, MC, V.
The capital's most prestigious club, situated in the green belt east of the city.

Country Club Castelgandolfo

Via Santo Spirito 13, Castelgandolfo (06 931 2301/www.countryclubcastelgandolfo.com). Metro Anagnina then taxi. **Open** 8.30am-7pm daily. **Rates** (green fees incl use of range) €60 Mon-Fri; €70 Sat, Sun. *Driving range* €10. *Club hire* €15. *Electric cart hire* €35 Mon-Fri; €40 Sat, Sun. *Trolley hire* €5. **Credit** AmEx, DC, MC, V.
Near the Pope's summer residence in this lakeside town, this course, designed by American golf architect Robert Trent Jones, is overlooked by a 16th-

Arts & Entertainment

century clubhouse. The course is impossible to reach by public transport and beyond most taxis' circuits, so consider hiring a car from Rome and visiting the nearby Castelli romani (*see chapter* **Trips Out of Town**) before or after your round. Reserve tee times in advance by phone or online.

Gyms

Dabliu Parioli
Viale Romania 22, Suburbs: north (06 807 5577/ fax 06 855 2433/www.dabliu.com). Bus 910. **Open** 7am-10.30pm Mon-Fri; 9am-7pm Sat; 10am-5pm Sun. Closed 1wk Aug. **Rates** €40/day. **Credit** DC, MC, V. **Map** off p356 D1.
This new shiny gym has state-of-the art Technogym machines, classes in everything from spinning to salsa, and a spa area with sauna, Turkish bath and hydromassage.

Farnese Fitness
Vicolo delle Grotte 35, Ghetto & Campo (06 687 6931/www.farnesefitness.com). Bus 40Exp, 46, 64, 116, 492/tram 8. **Open** 9am-10pm Mon, Wed; 8am-10pm Tue, Thur; 9am-9pm Fri; 11am-7pm Sat; 10.30am-1.30pm Sun. Closed Aug. **Rates** €12/day. **Credit** AmEx, DC, MC, V. **Map** p358 C2.
This friendly *centro storico* gym is handily located for a post-sightseeing workout. Classes in the downstairs aerobics studio – a 16th-century cellar – are included in the daily membership fee. The Sunday opening is suspended from June to September.

Roman Sport Center
Viale del Galoppatoio 33, Veneto & Borghese (06 320 1667/www.romansportcenter.com). Metro Spagna/bus 52, 53, 63, 116, 495, 630. **Open** 8am-10pm Mon-Sat; 9am-3pm Sun. Closed Sun from June to Aug. **Rates** €26/day; €220/mth. **Credit** AmEx, DC, MC, V. **Map** p356 A3.
'La Roman' offers aerobics studios, saunas, hydromassage pools, squash courts and two Olympic-size swimming pools.

Jogging & running

Traffic-choked streets and crowds of sight-seers make a casual jog through central Rome nigh-on impossible – except during the city's marathon and fun-run (*see p252*). The pavements along the *lungotevere* (riverside drive) are an option, if you're prepared to hurdle tree roots, but the best jogging and strolling is to be had in parks, most of which are just outside the *centro storico*.

Circo Massimo
A taste of ancient Rome while you're working up a sweat. **Map** pp360-361.

Parco della Caffarella
Just off via Appia Antica, this park has shady trails and open fields dotted with ruins. **Map** p173.

Terme di Caracalla
Serious runners congregate opposite Caracalla's ancient baths. **Map** p361.

Villa Ada
This large park has running paths around its ponds and lakes. **Map** p353.

Villa Borghese
Great for joggers, but can get crowded at weekends. **Map** p354 & p356.

Villa Pamphili
The city's largest park contains picturesque walkways with workout stations. **Map** p353.

Riding

Cavalieri dell'Appia Antica
Via dei Cerceni 15, Appian Way (06 780 1214/328 208 5787). Bus 118, 660. **Open** (call in advance to book excursions) 10am-6pm Tue-Sun. Closed Aug. **Rates** €25/hr. **No credit cards.**

Arts & Entertainment

Running commentary

Why has no one ever thought of it before? See Rome... with a lycra-clad tour guide by your side. The appropriately named Carolina Gasparetto launched SightJogging in 2005, combining a whistle-stop tour of the sites with a workout, for those who can't bear to take a holiday from their ab crunches. The super-fit guides are knowledgeable enough to pant out brief explanations of the major sites as you hurtle past them at breakneck speed, but there's no pausing to take in the finer architectural details, and no leisurely cappuccino breaks. The trainers/guides can pick you up from your hotel, and you can choose between 11 routes emphasising art, culture or nature, tailored to your fitness level and sightseeing requirements. Even if you don't learn much, you'll see the sites at an impressive rate, and all those endorphins ought to make one of the world's most beautiful cities seem even more so.
● *Book online (www.sightjogging.it) or by phone (347 335 3185), at least 24hrs in advance. Prices start at €84/hour for one person; €120 for two; €124 for three; €168 for four.*

Spa-gazing

The ancient Roman masses got their pampering fix at the city's vast bath complexes, languishing poolside and dousing themselves in perfumed unguents. Today image-conscious Romans flock to modern-day spas for the latest in sculpting, smoothing and cellulite-zapping treatments. It's now *de rigueur* for luxury hotels to have their own beauty centre; prices can be steep, and some charge a hefty extra fee for non-hotel residents. The city's independent day spas, equally luxurious, more than hold their own in the fluffy towelling bathrobe stakes.

Acanto Benessere Spa

Piazza Rondinini 30, Pantheon & Navona (06 6813 6602). Bus 40Exp, 46, 64, 70/ tram 8. **Open** 10am-10pm Tue-Sat; 2-10pm Sun. **Credit** AmEx, DC, MC, V. **Map** p355 D5.
This unisex day spa is a tranquil haven with futuristic glass treatment rooms, a great range of massages and treatments, and a Turkish bath.

Centro Benessere de Russie

Hotel de Russie, via del Babuino 9, Tridente (06 328 881). Metro Flaminio/bus 117, 119. **Open** 7am-9pm daily. **Credit** AmEx, DC, MC, V. **Map** p354 E3.
The €40 entrance fee covers sauna, Turkish bath and gym; treatments cost extra and are as high-tech as you'd expect from Rome's swankiest hotel (*see also p55*). Those in the know come here for hot stone therapy.

El Spa

Via Plinio 15C/D, Vatican & Prati (06 6819 2869/www.elspa.it). Bus 30Exp, 492, 926. **Open** 10am-9pm Mon-Thur; 10am-10pm Fri, Sat; noon-9pm Sun. **Credit** AmEx, DC, MC, V. **Map** p354 B3.
Decorated in warm, Middle-Eastern style, this spa (*pictured below, left*) specialises in holistic treatments. Try the *mandi lulur*, an ancient Indonesian treatment that leaves you with blissfully silky-soft skin.

Paradise Spa

Hotel Aleph, via di San Basilio 15, Veneto & Borghese (06 4229 0075). Metro Barberini/bus 61, 62, 116, 175, 492, 590. **Open** 9am-9pm Mon-Sat; 10am-6pm Sun. **Credit** AmEx, DC, MC, V. **Map** p357 C4.
In the basement of trendy Hotel Aleph (*see p52*), this spa has a relaxation room in what was once a bank vault – presumably chosen for its cocooning effect. Entrance fee for non-residents is €35.

Salus Per Aquam

Via Giulia 4, Ghetto & Campo (06 687 7449). Bus 30Exp, 40Exp, 64, 116. **Open** 9.30am-7pm Mon-Sat. Closed 3wks Aug. **Credit** AmEx, DC, MC, V. **Map** p355 C6.
This swanky spa (*pictured below, right*) – catering to many of Rome's beautiful people – offers an enticing range of treatments for men and women, plus a hammam and hairdressing. By appointment only.

El Spa.

Salus Per Aquam.

Arts & Entertainment

This rustic facility offers excursions along the ruin-strewn via Appia Antica for small groups. Friendly owners Sandro and Armanda speak almost no English, but their easy-tempered horses are suitable for beginners. Ask about moonlight rides, and reserve well in advance for excursions at weekends.

Rugby

Though football reigns supreme, the city also has a strong rugby subculture. Since 2000 the national side has been in the Six Nations' Championship, with home games played at the Stadio Flaminio. Rome also boasts a first-class rugby side in **RDS Roma**, who play their league matches at the Stadio Tre Fontane.

Stadio Flaminio
Viale Tiziano, Suburbs: north (06 3685 7309/ www.federugby.it). Bus 53, 910/tram 2. **Tickets** *Regular games €22-€143. Six Nations games €50-€233.* **No credit cards.**

Stadio Tre Fontane
Via delle Tre Fontane, Suburbs: EUR (06 591 7633). Metro Magliana/bus 30Exp, 671, 780. **Tickets** €5. **No credit cards.**

Swimming

Romans flock to the coast at the first hint of warm weather. If you don't mind the crowds, the cruising and the murky water, **Ostia** is a straightforward hop from Rome (Roma–Lido train from next to the Piramide metro station, get off at the Cristoforo Colombo stop). Sea-front *stabilimenti* (beach clubs) charge a daily fee (around €20, including sun lounger and parasol). **Fregene** (the strip to the north), with its chic beach clubs and thriving nightlife, is deluged by beautiful people in the summer months. If you're happy to fight for towel space on the packed free beaches, head south from Ostia to the sand dunes of **Capocotta** (catch one of the buses that stop along the coast road). Next to the presidential hunting reserve and within the protected Parco del Litorale Romano, this stretch of coast was once an infamous nudist beach (there are still nudist and gay stretches; *see also p268*); it's now council-run, and relatively clean and well-kept. (*See also p304* **Buckets & spades**)

Swimming pools are scarce in the city and, with a few far-flung exceptions, those that do exist are privately run. The **Roman Sport Center** (*see p291*) has Olympic-sized pools.

Piscina delle Rose
Viale America 20, Suburbs: EUR (06 592 6717/ www.piscinadellerose.it). Metro EUR-Palasport/bus 30Exp, 714, 780. **Open** *May-June, Sept 9am-7pm daily. July-Aug 9am-10pm daily.* **Admission** €16

full day; €13 half day (9am-2pm or 2-7pm); €9 1-4pm Mon-Fri; free under-4s & 5-12s accompanied by an adult with day ticket; €130 Mon-Fri monthly ticket. **No credit cards.**

This Olympic-size public pool in the heart of the suburban EUR district is often crowded with Roman *bambini* on warmer days.

Hotel pools

Space is tight in central Rome, and only the swankiest of hotels have their own pool. The following pools can be used by non-residents – at a price.

Cavalieri Hilton
Via Cadlolo 101, Suburbs: west (06 35 091/www. cavalieri-hilton.it). Bus 907, 913. **Open** *May-mid Oct 9am-7pm daily.* **Admission** €45 Mon-Fri; €65 Sat, Sun. **Credit** AmEx, DC, MC, V.

This almost-Olympic-sized pool is a draw for serious swimmers and style-conscious sun-seekers alike: it's one of the chicest poolsides in Rome, as evidenced by the array of designer swimwear modelled by lounger-bound lovelies.

Parco dei Principi
Via Frescobaldi 5, Suburbs: north (06 854 421/www. parcodeiprincipi.com). Bus 52, 53, 217, 910/tram 3, 19. **Open** *May-Sept 10am-6.30pm daily.* **Admission** €45 Mon-Fri; €60 Sat, Sun. **Credit** AmEx, DC, MC, V.

On the edge of the Villa Borghese gardens, this pool is a favourite with locals (it can be busy at weekends). Weather permitting, it remains open into October.

Tennis

Circolo della Stampa
Piazza Mancini 19, Suburbs: north (06 323 2452). Bus 53, 280, 910/tram 2. **Open** *8am-10pm Mon-Fri; 8am-8pm Sat, Sun.* **Rates** *Court (50mins) €10 singles; €12 doubles. Floodlights (50mins) €12 singles; €14 doubles.* **No credit cards.**

Owned by the Italian journalists' association, but friendly and open to non-members, the Circolo offers both clay and synthetic grass courts. There's no dress code, but studded trainers are not allowed. Booking is advised.

Yoga

Several of the gyms we list (*see p291*) also offer yoga classes; phone to check.

L'Albero e la Mano
Via della Pelliccia 3, Trastevere (06 581 2871/www. lalberoelamano.it). Bus 23, 280, 630, 780, H/tram 8. **Open** *depends on course schedule. Closed Sat & Sun and mid July-mid Sept.* **Rates** €12-€13/class. **No credit cards. Map** p358 C3.

This incense-scented studio offers classes in Ashtanga and Hatha yoga, as well as t'ai chi, belly-dancing and Shiatsu, Ayurvedic and Thai massage.

Theatre & Dance

Drama in Rome may be staid rather than edgy, but there's an increasingly vibrant scene of dance festivals and seasons.

It isn't easy for an Anglo-Saxon audience to find satisfaction in the Italian theatre scene. The Italian school of drama, with its strong traditions and roots in the *Commedia dell'Arte*, and the stiff style imposed by its stuffy dramatic arts academy, is worlds apart from what British, Irish or North American theatre-goers are used to. If you're thinking of an evening at the theatre, don't expect the daring performances of Edinburgh's Fringe or the delightful plays of London's West End. Instead, you're on safer ground if you go for big names and classic titles, plus all the glitz of a fashionable theatre.

That said, the effects of globalisation are encroaching, and the Roman theatre-going public is becoming ever more sophisticated, its standards raised mainly thanks to some excellent seasonal festivals (in particular the **RomaEuropa** festival; *see p254* and *p295* **Dancing days**) that bring the best national and international fare to the city's excitement-starved stages. What's more, a few emerging names do stand out and are beginning to change the face of a rather unexciting panorama, namely those of rising star Emma Dante, a young Sicilian playwright who has raked in a host of prestigious prizes in the past few years; the multidisciplinary theatre of Giorgio Barberio Corsetti and his Fattore K company; the socially committed Marco Baliani, who brings groups of African Aids orphans to star in adapted musicals; and the new trend of readings and one-man shows by accomplished actors with live musical accompaniment at the **Auditorium-Parco della Musica** (*see p273*).

One interesting project is the relatively new **Casa dei Teatri** (*see p295*). The aim of this centre is to give a multifaceted perspective to drama, integrating performances with training, workshops and research. The complex – located inside the Villa Pamphili park in the suburb of Monteverde – hosts a library, as well as a photographic archive, a space for screenings, conferences, lectures and workshops, and a permanent art collection.

Rome has no lack of performing arts venues: there are at least 80 theatres in the city. The Italian drama board ETI is responsible for the 18th-century **Teatro Argentina**, the modern **Teatro India**, the delightful **Teatro Valle** and the bleaker **Teatro Quirino**.

Alongside these, valiant private foundations and organisations offer fare of very uneven quality. The modern **Teatro Vascello** often hosts international companies and experimental productions; the brand new **Teatro Tor Bella Monaca**, directed by actor Michele Placido, has mainly contemporary theatre and a handful of old favourites; the rather stuffy **Teatro Il Sistina** hosts mostly musicals and comic monologues, as does the **Teatro Olimpico** (*see p276*); the **Teatro Ambra Jovinelli** delivers variety shows and jazz concerts; the freshly refurbished **Teatro Palladium** (*see p288*) runs a wide-ranging programme; and Rome's own version of Shakespeare's Globe Theatre, the **Silvano Toti Globe Theatre** in Villa Borghese, offers a summer programme of mostly Shakespearean fare and Sunday matinée shows for children.

RomaEuropa gives the arts scene a lift.

Arts & Entertainment

DANCE

Dance has always been considered the Cinderella of the arts in Italy, notwithstanding its glorious beginnings in the court of Caterina de' Medici in Florence and the subsequent string of influential Italian dancers and choreographers such as Maria Taglioni and Enrico Cecchetti, who set standards and created a ballet method that is still taught worldwide. The problem is a financial one, as dance institutions have to make do with crumbs left over from the ever-inadequate arts funding package. It comes as no surprise, therefore, to discover that many excellent young Italian dancers find fame and fortune abroad, then drop in here occasionally to star as guest artists in Italian corps de ballet. However, the spurt of artistic vitality produced by the city's Auditorium-Parco della Musica, and the concern for the arts shown by the current city council, means that Cinderella is allowed out of the kitchen much more often nowadays, and features regularly – in various forms – in a host of festivals and seasonal programmes (*see right* **Dancing days**).

Dance fans keep an eye on the programme at the Teatro Olimpico, which quite regularly hosts visiting international companies. There are some festival dance events at the Teatro Argentina, Teatro Valle and Teatro Palladium. The **Teatro Greco**, Teatro Vascello, the Auditorium-Parco della Musica and the newly refurbished **Auditorium Conciliazione** (*see p275*) are all possible venues for touring Italian and international dance companies.

The **Teatro dell'Opera** (*see p276*) and its offspring, the **Teatro Nazionale**, are where the Opera's corps de ballet stretches its limbs (*see also p275*). Its seasonal programme invariably includes two or three classics and a handful of contemporary works. The standard leaves much to be desired; in fact, good soloists and sometimes brilliant stars are overshadowed by kitsch productions, mouldy old sets and costumes, and second-rate choreographers.

Theatre and dance listings can be found in local newspapers and magazines (*see p331*). For ticket agencies, *see p250*.

Main public theatres

See also p275 **Auditorium Conciliazione**, *p273* **Auditorium-Parco della Musica** and *p275* **Teatro Palladium**.

Casa dei Teatri

Villino Corsini, Villa Doria Pamphili, Suburbs: west (06 4544 0707/www.casadeiteatri.culturaroma.it). Bus 44, 75, 710, 870. **Box office** *May-Sept* 10am-7pm Tue-Sun. *Oct-Apr* 10am-5pm Tue-Sun. **No credit cards**. **Map** p358 A3.

Dancing days

Although dance has benefited from the arts boost brought upon the city by the Auditorium-Parco della Musica (*see p273*), balletomanes must rely on festivals rather than regular dance seasons to satisfy their appetites. The Auditorium itself inaugurates its seasonal activities in September with **Festival Metamorphosi** (06 662 4626, www.festivalmetamorfosi.it), purportedly a border festival between theatre and circus, but with much appeal for dance lovers. In mid-September comes a world-class tango festival, **Buenos Aires Tango** (06 8024 1281, www.auditorium.com), featuring fantastic tango dancers and performances as well as open classes and a *milonga*.

Malnourished dance fans especially await the delicacies that the **RomaEuropa** festival (06 422 961, www.romaeuropa.net, late Sept-late Nov) can be relied upon to serve up. This arts festival features a programme of multimedia events, concerts and happenings in classic and alternative venues all over the city. Big names of the dance world such as Alain Platel, Sylvie Guillem and Akram Khan grace the programme of this sophisticated event, but so do many emerging artists with dance/video performances and other genre-busting events; an interesting sideline of the programme always includes dancers and companies from far-away places like China, Thailand or Mongolia.

Next in line is the **Equilibrio Oltre** (06 80 241 281, www.auditorium.com), with an interesting programme – from October to May, though events are concentrated in February – that includes Italian and international contemporary dance as well as dance theatre, plus film and video projections on dance and other multimedia events. The **Teatro Vascello** (*see p296*) also kicks off its autumn and winter season with a mini-festival dedicated to dance, be it experimental, tango or folk.

In mid July the place to look is Villa Pamphili (*see p179*), which hosts the annual dance feast **Invito alla Danza** (06 5831 0086, 06 3973 8323, www.invito alladanza.it) in its beautiful gardens. The programme, with both classical and modern offerings, presents a performance every evening for about two weeks, and often includes international companies and stars.

Since September 2004, the elegant 18th-century Villa Corsini inside the Villa Pamphili park (*see p179*) has been a centre for drama and drama-making, with a stage, spaces for workshops and study, and two prestigious libraries, as well as the important collection of theatrical documents donated by actor Carmelo Bene. For information on performances, call the Teatro Argot on 06 589 8111 or 06 581 4023.

Teatro di Roma – Argentina

Largo Argentina 52, Ghetto & Campo (06 6840 00345/www.teatrodiroma.net). Bus 30Exp, 40Exp, 46, 62, 63, 64, 70, 81, 87, 492, 628, 810, 916/ tram 8. **Box office** 10am-2pm, 3-7pm Tue-Sun. **Shows** *Oct-June* 9pm Tue, Wed, Fri, Sat; 5pm Thur, Sun. **Credit** AmEx, DC, MC, V. **Map** p358 D1.
Rome's plush flagship theatre has a wide-ranging programme, including some dance and poetry.

Teatro di Roma – India

Lungotevere Papareschi/via L Pierantoni 6, Suburbs: south (06 5530 0894). Bus 170, 780, 781. **Box office** 30mins before shows, or at Teatro Argentina (*see above*). **No credit cards.** **Map** p143 A2.
This converted industrial space, with three stages, is used for more experimental offerings.

Teatro Tor Bella Monaca

Via Bruno Cirino/viale Duilio Cambellotti, Suburbs: east (06 201 0579/www.teatrotorbellamonaca.it). Metro Anagnina then bus 20. **Box office** 3.30-7.30pm Tue-Sat; from 7.30pm on day of performance. **No credit cards.**
The city's latest theatrical initiative has found space in the eastern suburbs, as part of the mayor's thrust to bring culture to peripheral areas. It's a multifunctional edifice with two theatres, rehearsal space, an open-air arena and rooms for workshops, conferences and lectures. At the helm is actor Michele Placido, whose varied programme includes many free events and concerts. Leonardo DiCaprio presented his environmental documentary initiative here in 2006.

Teatro Valle

Via del Teatro Valle 23A, Pantheon & Navona (06 6880 3794/www.enteteatrale.it/www.teatrovalle.it). Bus 30Exp, 40Exp, 46, 62, 63, 64, 70, 81, 87, 492, 628, 810, 916/tram 8. **Box office** 10am-7pm Tue, Thur-Sat; 10am-5pm Wed, Sun. **Shows** *Oct-May* 8.45pm Tue, Thur-Sat; 4.45pm Wed, Sun. **Credit** AmEx, DC, MC, V. **Map** p355 D6.
This beautiful little chocolate-box of a theatre hosts an interesting range of performances plus the occasional concert or ballet. A gem.

Private & smaller venues

See also p276 for both **Teatro Ghione** and **Teatro Olimpico**.

Teatro Ambra Jovinelli

Via G Pepe 41-45, Esquilino (06 4434 0262/www. ambrajovinelli.com). Metro Vittorio/bus 70, 71, 105, 360, 649/tram 5, 14. **Box office** 10am-7pm Tue-Sat; 3-7pm Sun. **Credit** AmEx, DC, MC, V. **Map** p360 E1.

Restored and reopened in 2000, this shrine to Italy's comic heritage – with a school for comic writing and acting, and a video and research library – also puts on top-quality jazz and other concerts.

Teatro Greco

Via R Leoncavallo 16, Suburbs: north (06 860 7513/ www.teatrogreco.it). Bus 63, 135, 342, 630. **Box office** 10am-1pm, 4-7pm Tue-Sun. **Shows** 9pm daily. **No credit cards.**
A well-designed venue that programmes some Italian dance and has a penchant for little-tried writers, both foreign and domestic.

Teatro Il Sistina

Via Sistina 9, Veneto & Borghese (06 420 0711/ www.ilsistina.com). Metro Barberini or Spagna/bus 52, 53, 61, 62, 63, 71, 80Exp, 95, 116, 119, 175. **Box office** 10am-7pm daily. **Shows** 9pm Tue-Sat; 5pm Sun. **Credit** AmEx, DC, MC, V. **Map** p357 B5.
A tacky, over-heated theatre with decent acoustics and a lot of red velvet.

Teatro Vascello

Via G Carini 72, Suburbs: west (06 588 1021/06 589 8031/www.teatrovascello.it). Bus 44, 75, 710, 870, 871. **Box office** 10am-5pm Mon; 10am-9pm Tue-Fri; 3-8pm Sat; 10.30am-8pm Sun. **Shows** 9pm Tue-Sat; 5pm Sun. **No credit cards.** **Map** p359 A4.
Presents decent experimental theatre and dance productions, plus conferences and workshops.

Summer venues

Anfiteatro della Quercia del Tasso

Passeggiata del Gianicolo, Gianicolo (06 575 0827). Bus 870. **Box office** from 7pm before shows. **Shows** *July-mid Sept* 9.15pm daily; occasional afternoon matinées. **No credit cards.** **Map** p358 A6.
This open-air amphitheatre was built in the 17th century. It specialises in Greek and Latin theatre and 18th-century Venetian comedy.

Silvano Toti Globe Theatre

Largo Aqua Felix, Villa Borghese (06 8205 9127/ www.globetheatreroma.com). **Box office** *June-Sept* 1-9.15pm Tue-Sun. **No credit cards.** **Map** p356 B2.
Rome's Elizabethan theatre, a wooden O, can hold 1,250 people, including 420 standing in the stalls. Under the direction of popular actor Gigi Proietti, it offers a mostly Shakespearean menu with a few incursions into Goldoni and Molière and special performances for children.

Teatro Romano di Ostia Antica

Scavi di Ostia Antica, viale dei Romagnoli 117, Ostia Antica (06 6840 00345). Train from Ostiense to Ostia Antica. **Box office** from 6pm before shows; also at Teatro Argentina (*see above*). **Shows** *Mid July-mid Aug* 8.30pm daily. **No credit cards.**
This superbly preserved Roman theatre fills the summer with prestigious productions of Roman and Greek classics, plus concerts and ballets. The seats are stone so bring a cushion – and mosquito repellent.

Arts & Entertainment

Trips Out of Town

Features

Maps

Villa Lante. *See p307.*

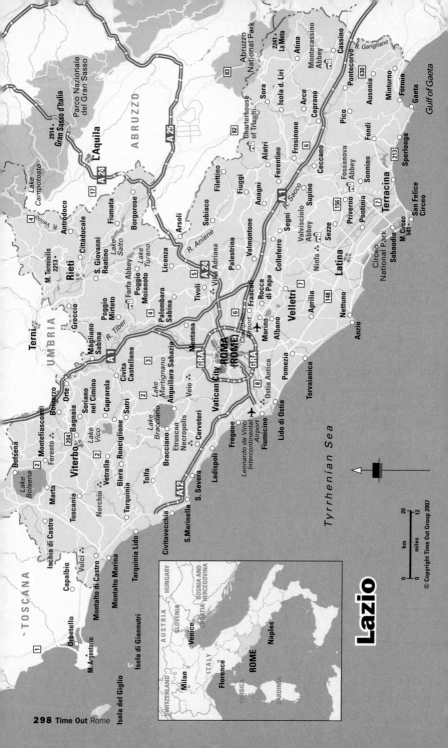

Lazio

© Copyright Time Out Group 2007

Trips Out of Town

Head for the hills... or make a break for the coast.

Proof that Etruscans rivalled Greeks at the **Museo Nazionale** in **Tarquinia**. *See p303.*

Getting started

Maps p298 & p368.

The economic miracle of the 1970s may have brought prosperity to Italy but it wreaked havoc on its landscape, particularly around major cities. The great magnet, Rome, suffered worst of all, with high-rise blocks striding out across what had once been glorious *campagna romana* – hailed in song and verse from antiquity – in unregulated ranks. But beyond – and even between – the eyesores, there's much to draw the city-weary visitor out of Rome.

If you do head into the Lazio countryside, chances are you'll be travelling along a route that has been trodden for millennia. The *consolari* (the consular roads) of the Romans were well paved and well maintained: perfect conduits, in fact, for the military muscle that allowed this people to conquer and rule their neighbours. But most of these *consolari* weren't, strictly speaking, Roman in origin: they merely consolidated much older routes. Today the *consolari* are still key traffic corridors; but along them you'll find Roman (and earlier) remains, grand *palazzi*, quaint villages, lovely countryside and some perfectly acceptable beaches.

Getting around

By car

For more on car hire and driving, *see p324*.

The *Grande Raccordo Anulare* (GRA) ring road links with the network of *autostrade* (motorways) and *strade statali* (SS – most of which follow ancient *consolari*). Traffic on the GRA and city approach roads can be intense in rush hour, and on Friday and Sunday evenings, with long queues at motorway tollbooths. You can save time (but not money) at tollbooths by using a **Viacard** debit card, costing €25, €50 or €75 and available from *tabacchi* (*see p336*) and most motorway service stations. Tollbooths also accept credit cards (AmEx, DC, MC, V).

Isoradio (103.3FM; occasional English-language bulletins in summer) gives regular traffic updates for major roads; **www. autostrade.it** also details current conditions.

By train

For rail transport map, *see p368*; for mainline services, *see p320*.

The network of local railways, the Ferrovie Regionali (FR) and Ferrovie Urbane, is handy for destinations outside Rome. You can get information toll-free on 800 431 784 or from www.atac.roma.it. Trains can be picked up at **Flaminio** (Roma–Viterbo); **Ostiense** (FR1 to Fiumicino airport; FR3 to Bracciano and Viterbo; FR5 to Fregene and Civitavecchia); **Roma–Lido** (services to Ostia Antica and Ostia); **Tiburtina** (FR1; FR2 to Tivoli); **Termini** (FR4 to Frascati; FR6 to Frosinone; FR7 to Latina; FR8 to Nettuno: Roma–Pantano to the eastern suburbs); and **Trastevere** (FR1, FR3, FR5) stations.

By bus

The Lazio transport authority **COTRAL** (information toll-free 800 150 008, www.cotral spa.it) covers the region efficiently; most services ply the consular roads. Buses leave from several city termini, each serving a different direction (as indicated in the 'Getting there' listings for each section of this chapter).
Anagnina Metro Anagnina.
Cornelia Metro Cornelia.
Laurentina Metro Laurentina/bus 30Exp, 761.
Magliana Metro Magliana/bus 780.
Ponte Mammolo Metro Ponte Mammolo.
Saxa Rubra Train from Roma Nord–Flaminio (map p354 D2) to Saxa Rubra.
Termini Metro Termini/buses to Termini (map p357 E5).
Tiburtina Metro Tiburtina/bus 492, 495.

Via Ostiense: Rome's sea port

Naples has Pompeii, made famous by a cataclysmic natural disaster. Rome has **Ostia Antica** – arguably a far better site for getting a feel for everyday life in a working Roman town – which disappeared quietly under river silt over the centuries only to be dug up equally quietly, beginning in the early 20th century. Ostia Antica receives a fraction of the attention lavished on its southern counterpart, which is far less than it deserves.

If you're thinking of making the punishing trip to Pompeii during your holidays, forget it and do a comfortable day-trip here instead. You could begin with a stopover at the **Museo della Via Ostiense** (*see p143*), which has a large-scale model of Ostia Antica in its heyday.

If you're driving, you'll get to Ostia Antica along **via Ostiense**, the shortest of the *consolari*, connecting Rome with the mouth (*ostia*) of the Tiber, which in antiquity lay 30 kilometres (18 miles) from the road's origin at Porta San Paolo. Via Ostiense still follows its 2,300-year-old path; the parallel **via del Mare** was laid out by Mussolini to relieve congestion on the Ostiense, and is a notorious accident blackspot. The Roma–Lido railway (from the station of the same name, adjoining the Piramide metro station) has regular services to Ostia Antica (30mins) along roughly the same route. After the residential quarters of Garbatella and San Paolo, via Ostiense becomes grim, with miles of junkyards and tower blocks. Only as you approach Ostia Antica does this give way to open spaces and umbrella pines.

Legend says that Ostia was founded by Ancus Martius, the fourth king of Rome, in the second half of the seventh century BC, although the oldest remains date 'only' from c330 BC. Ostia was Rome's main port for over 600 years, until its decline in the fourth century AD. Abandoned after sackings by barbarians in the

Flight plan

Being stuck for hours in airports waiting for delayed flights seems an ever more probable hazard for the traveller. And Rome's airports offer little in the way of dead-time entertainment. If you're delayed at **Ciampino airport**... good luck to you and we can only hope that you have a great book to read.

An enforced stopover at **Fiumicino airport** used to provide the perfect opportunity to explore ancient trade routes at the Museo delle Navi (*see p301*) but this delightful museum is currently undergoing an inexplicable – and inexcusable – ten-year restoration. Thankfully, however, there are regular (three per hour) buses between the airport, the nearby fishing port of **Fiumicino** and the seaside resort of **Ostia**. You may not feel moved to dip into Ostia's less-than-salubrious water, but the seafront promenade can be pleasant and some of the 1960s and '70s bathing establishments are charming. The little port of Fiumicino offers some fine gastronomic opportunities (*see p302*) plus a chance to walk along the river and sea walls, and let that sea breeze blow the sense of frustration out of your head.

Trips Out of Town

fifth century, the town was gradually buried. Over the centuries the Tiber changed its course and the coastline receded, leaving Ostia landlocked and obsolete. Visit the **Scavi di Ostia Antica** site on a sunny weekday and bring a picnic (not actually allowed but keep a low profile and you probably won't be ejected). With fascinating remains around every corner, Ostia Antica deserves to be taken at a leisurely pace; purchasing a site plan is a good idea.

The *decumanus maximus* (high street) runs from the Porta Romana for almost a kilometre (half a mile), past the theatre and forum, before forking left to what used to be the seashore (now three kilometres/two miles away at Ostia). The right fork, via della Foce, leads to the Tiber. On either side of these main arteries is a network of intersecting lanes where the best discoveries can be made.

Behind the theatre is one of Ostia's most interesting features: the Forum of the Corporations. Here the various trade guilds had their offices, and mosaics on the floor of small shops that ring the open square refer to the products each guild dealt in – shipowners had ships on the floor, ivory dealers had elephants. Further along on the right is the old mill, where both the grindstones and the circular furrows ploughed by the blindfolded donkeys that turned them are still visible. In the tangle of streets between the decumanus and the museum, don't miss the *thermopolium* – an ancient Roman bar, complete with marble counter, a fresco advertising the house fare and a garden with a fountain. Located off the forum to the south-east are the forum baths – the preserved terracotta pipes that heated the walls are still visible. Nearby is the *forica*, or ancient public latrine. In mostly residential districts off via della Foce, the House of Cupid and Psyche is an elegant fourth-century construction; the House of the Dioscuri has beautiful mosaics; the Insula of the Charioteers still has many of its frescoes. The wealthy lived in the garden apartments at the western end of the site, set back from the busy streets. The **museum** has a good collection of artefacts from the site, including statues, fresco fragments and bas-reliefs of scenes of ordinary life; there's a café and well-stocked bookshop next door.

Five minutes' walk from the entrance to the excavations, the medieval village of Ostia Antica has a **castle** (*see below*) – built in 1483-6 for the bishop of Ostia, the future Pope Julius II – and picturesque cottages, once inhabited by the people who worked in the nearby salt pans.

If you have your own transport (and it's the right day, and you've booked…), you might consider prefacing your Ostia jaunt with a look at the port that eclipsed Ostia in the second

century. As Rome's population grew to around a million at the height of the Empire, its port activities overflowed five kilometres (three miles) north from Ostia to a more sheltered section of the coast. The earliest port here, built by Emperor Claudius in the 40s AD, had a unique jetty: a ship built to transport the Egyptian obelisk now in St Peter's square was sunk in front of the harbour and a lighthouse mounted on it. Claudius' port was later absorbed by the larger and more efficient **Porto di Traiano** (AD 110), where the hexagonal harbour could cater for up to 200 ships at once. Canals were cut to link the harbours to the Tiber, along which river barges were hauled the 35 kilometres (20 miles) to Rome. Almost nothing is left of Claudius' port – what there is lies between airport runways – but in Fiumicino (ancient Portus), the ruins of the Porto di Traiano can be visited on guided tours (*see below*). Tours depart from the charming **Museo delle Navi**, whose ancient ships and displays on ancient trade have, disgracefully, been shut for years, and where 'restoration' work is now scheduled to last until 2010. Or you can visit the **Oasi di Porto** (*see below*), where horse-drawn carriages take you around the perimeter of Trajan's harbour.

With private transport, it's a short hop from here to Rome's closest beach resort, at Ostia (the modern one; *see p304* **Buckets & spades**), and to its fishing port – and seafood restaurants – at **Fiumicino** (not to be confused with the airport of the same name).

Castello di Giulio II (Castle of Julius II)

Piazza della Rocca, Ostia Antica (06 5635 8024). **Open** (guided tours only) 10am, noon Tue; 10am, noon, 3pm Thur. **Admission** free.
Tours can be booked at other times at the number given above.

Oasi di Porto

Via Portuense 2264, Fiumicino (06 588 0880/ www.oasidiporto.it). **Open** 10am-4pm Thur, Sun. Closed June-Sept. **Admission** €8; €4 concessions. **No credit cards.**
Booking essential for carriage rides around the port.

Porto di Traiano

06 652 9192. **Open** (guided tours only; own transport essential) 9.30am 1st Sat, last Sun of mth. **Admission** free.
Tours leave from the Museo delle Navi (via A Guidoni 35, Fiumicino Aeroporto); visits at other times can be arranged for groups.

Scavi di Ostia Antica

Viale dei Romagnoli 717, Ostia Antica (06 5635 8099/www.itnw.roma.it/ostia/scavi). **Open** (Tue-Sun) *Mar* 8.30am-5pm. *Apr-Oct* 8.30am-6pm. *Nov-Feb*

8.30am-4pm. **Admission** €4; €2 concessions.
No credit cards.
Note: the museum officially has the same opening
hours as the site, but this is often not the case.

Where to eat

Before or after a visit to the Ostia Antica ruins,
follow the aroma of fish to **Allo Sbarco di
Enea** (via dei Romagnoli 675, 06 565 0034,
www.paginegialle.it/sbarcoenea, closed Mon
and 2wks Jan, average €40). In the fishing port
of Fiumicino you're spoiled for choice: try the
catch of the day at **Marina del Rey**
(lungomare della Salute 46, 06 658 4641, closed
Mon, average €30) or splash out on some of the
best seafood around at **Bastianelli al Molo**
(via Torre Clementina 312, 06 650 5358, 06 650
5118, closed Mon, average €80).

Getting there

By car
Ostia Antica: via del Mare or via Ostiense.
Ostia: via Cristoforo Colombo or via del Mare.
**Fiumicino, Museo delle Navi, Porto di
Traiano**: autostrada Roma–Fiumicino.

By train
Ostia Antica, Ostia: train from Roma–Lido
station, next to Piramide metro: for downtown Ostia,
get off at Lido Centro; for full-on beach umbrellas,
use the Stella Polare or Cristoforo Colombo stops; for
Capocotta and Torvaianica, go to Cristoforo Colombo
and take bus 061 (all year), 06 or 07 (Mar-Oct).
Museo delle Navi, Porto di Traiano: FR1 to
Fiumicino Aeroporto.
Fiumicino: FR1 to Fiumicino Aeroporto, then
frequent bus services to Fiumicino town.

By bus
COTRAL services run to Fiumicino (Aeroporto, and
in town at piazza Marinai d'Italia) from EUR
Magliana metro station and Cornelia; Cornelia also
has buses to Fregene. There is no direct bus to Ostia
but there are connections from Fiumicino; the half-
hourly service stops in front of Lido Centro station.

Via Aurelia: Etruscan places

Built in the third century BC, **via Aurelia**
not only connected Rome with upper
Tyrrhenian seaports, it also had the advantage
of cutting the mysterious, sophisticated (and
declining) Etruscans off from their port at
Pyrgi, thus effectively crippling this once-
powerful trading people. Along and just off
the Aurelia are a host of Etruscan places,
most notably Cerveteri and Tarquinia. And if
you need a break from all that antiquity, there's
plenty of opportunity for swimming along
the way (*see p304* **Buckets & spades**).

From piazza Irnerio in Rome's western
suburbs, the road travels due west, curving
north at Ladispoli to follow the coast,
eventually reaching Genoa. (It can also
be picked up by heading out of Rome to the
south-west on the fast link road to Fiumicino
airport, and then turning north on the A12
Rome–Civitavecchia motorway.) Despite the
occasional unfortunate outbreak of modern
eyesores – including the entire town of
Ladispoli – the Aurelia today remains a pretty
drive. Widened and repaved for modern traffic,
it travels through rolling hills and by the sea,
with the occasional Roman tomb or medieval
watchtower along the way. Unless you're
looking for a beach (*see p304* **Buckets &
spades**), ignore signposts to the seaside towns
of Maccarese, Fregene and unforgivably ugly
Ladispoli, and head straight for the town of
Cerveteri and, nearby, one of the most
important sites in Etruscan Lazio.

With three ports, Etruscan Kysry – known to
the Romans as Caere, now **Cerveteri** – was one
of the great Mediterranean trading centres from
the seventh to fifth centuries BC. It was situated
on the same volcanic spur as modern Cerveteri
but covered an area 20 times greater. The 16th-
century Orsini castle here houses the small
Museo Cerite, stocked with local finds.

Much more interesting than the town itself
is the **Necropoli di Banditaccia**, a pleasant
30-minute walk into the countryside from the
central piazza. This town of the dead – with
streets, *piazze* and tidy little houses – is one of

The Banditaccia necropolis in **Cerveteri**.

the most touching archaeological sites in Italy. There's plenty of ancient atmosphere here, with a wilderness of vines, cypresses and oaks growing on and around tufa-cut tumuli (mound-shaped tombs). You can only visit a small part of the total site today, but even here there are some 2,000 tombs. The most important are clearly labelled in both English and Italian; the earliest date from the seventh century BC and the latest from the third, by which time there had been a progressive impoverishment of tomb size and decoration. Don't miss the well-preserved sixth-century BC Tomba dei Capitelli (with finely-carved stone), the fourth-century BC Tomba dei Rilievi (with bas-reliefs of weapons and utensils), and the three parallel streets of fifth- and sixth-century BC cube-shaped tombs between via degli Inferi and via delle Serpi. Outside the main gate, the Tomba degli Scudi e delle Sedie has chairs carved out of rock and bas-reliefs of shields.

The Etruscan port of **Pyrgi** was the main sea outlet for Cerveteri. Its remains lie offshore from the squat Orsini **Castle of Santa Severa**. On a calm day you can just about make out the channel that was built to allow vessels to approach the port; when the sea is rough, retreating waves partially reveal its structure. Pygri was the site of an important sanctuary to the Etruscan goddess Uni (whom Romans called Juno), the remains of which lie near the shore a short walk from the small **Antiquarium di Pyrgi**, which contains finds from the excavations.

Northwards, past the family resort of **Santa Marinella**, the power stations and industrial waste of **Civitavecchia** scupper the theory that the further from Rome, the cleaner the sea gets. Located a kilometre (half a mile) north of Civitavecchia are the **Terme Taurine**, Roman baths that were built here to exploit the hot sulphurous springs.

Further north again, **Tarquinia** lies three kilometres (two miles) inland from the Aurelia, bristling with medieval defensive towers. Once a major Etruscan stronghold, Tarquinia has a **necropolis** with the art that Cerveteri's lacks: some 100 tombs, hidden beneath a grassy hill about two kilometres (1.25 miles) out of town, are vividly painted with scenes of work and social life, athletic contests, mysterious rituals and erotic encounters. The Tomba della Caccia e della Pesca has delightful fishing and hunting scenes; in the Tomba dei Leopardi, couples recline at a banquet (note the man passing his partner an egg – a recurrent symbol, though experts disagree about what it represents). There's a similar scene with dancers in the elegant Tomba delle Leonesse. The Tomba dei Tori, one of the oldest, depicts Achilles waiting to ambush Troilus and contains '*un po' di pornografico*', as Etruscan fan DH Lawrence gleefully (if ungrammatically) described it. (Note that only a handful of the tombs are open at any one time.) Housed in the impressive, 15th-century Palazzo Vitelleschi, the **Museo Nazionale** in Tarquinia (**photo** p299) has one of the best Etruscan collections

Trips Out of Town

Buckets & spades

Taking a dip in the Tyrrhenian Sea is quick and easy from Rome; but how pleasant the experience is depends partly on your expectations, and partly on how far you're prepared to travel.

The closest seaside resort to the capital is **Ostia** (*moderna*, as opposed to *antica*; *see also p300*) take the Roma–Lido train from the station next to Piramide metro and get off at either Lido Centro or Lido Cristoforo Colombo). This is the hub of Rome's 'riviera', a lively if not beautiful coastal town laid out in the 1930s. Its *centro* is at the end of via Ostiense; the town's southern end, where beaches are less crowded, is served by via Cristoforo Colombo, which leaves Rome near the Baths of Caracalla. Ostia's water isn't the cleanest, but the dark volcanic sand is believed to have special tan-accelerating properties. Most of the shore consists of brash, pay-on-entry beach clubs full to bursting every summer.

If you aren't convinced by the murky sea here, head towards **Torvaianica**, which lies 11 kilometres (seven miles) to the south. The water is a bit cleaner and laudable efforts are made to keep the sand rubbish-free, both at Torvaianica itself and along the Castelporziano/Capocotta beach between here and Ostia. This stretch has been a nature reserve since 1996; there is a backdrop of sand-dunes, rather than hideous construction. There are good beach-bars and restaurants as well as a gay section (*see p268*) and a nudist stretch (signposted '*Oasi Naturista di Capocotta*', nine kilometres/5.5 miles south of Ostia). The nudist beach has far and away the best of the restaurants (costume obligatory). This beach can be reached on buses 07, 061 and 070 (summer months only) from Lido Cristoforo Colombo station. (For resorts further south, *see p317* **Via Pontina**.)

The northern part of Rome's 'riviera' comprises the area around **Fregene**

(accessible on the FR5 train from Ostiense or Trastevere, then local buses), where Roman families have coveted convenient summer getaways for decades. Again, the water here is so-so, and the beach not always pristine. But you can make up for this with some great seafood: **Il Mastino**, in Fregene's Villaggio dei Pescatori (via Silvi Marina 19, 06 6656 0966, closed dinner Nov-Feb, average €40), is a cheerful barn of a place with a huge terrace set right on the sand where you can feast on spaghetti with scampi, sea bass or mullet roe, fish soup and catch of the day *all'acqua pazza* (cooked and served in its own stock).

Just inland from Fregene is **Maccarese**, with its 32 square-kilometre (12 square-mile) agricultural estate and 14th-century castle, now in the hands of the Benetton family. The WWF runs a portion of the Benetton estate's Mediterranean scrubland as the **Macchiagrande** reserve for marine birds (to book a visit, call 06 668 5487). Lying in the shadow of the castle, the **Ristorante San Giorgio** (piazza della Pace 6, 06 667 8060, closed Wed, average €40) serves up fish and seafood plus the odd meat dish (the beef is sourced from a local organic farm). Try fried artichoke hearts with monkfish, sun-dried tomatoes and thyme or the linguine with shrimp, olives and cherry tomatoes. *Secondi* depend on the day's catch.

The FR5 train continues north to **Santa Severa** – with its outsize sandcastle-like Castello Orsini and the Etruscan port of Pyrgi (for both, *see p305*) – and **Santa Marinella**, two perfectly acceptable family beach resorts. Anything nearer to the industrial port at Civitavecchia, or the beach-side power station at Montalto di Castro, is decidedly less salubrious. Cross the Tuscan border (mainline trains), on the other hand, and you'll come to clean sea and sand at **Chiarone**, chic **Capalbio** and the upmarket holiday destination of **Ansedonia**.

outside Rome. Among some marvellous examples of carved sarcophagi and exquisite Attic vases, its chief exhibit is a pair of fourth-century BC terracotta winged horses – proof that the artists of Etruria could rival even Greek finesse. On the top floor, there are reconstruction of several tombs, with original paintings moved here from the necropolis for their own protection.

At this point, you can leave the Aurelia and cut 25 kilometres (16 miles) north-east through the hills to reach **Tuscania** (*see p307*), another important Etruscan centre (although access is easier from via Cassia; *see p306*).

Some 16 kilometres (10 miles) north of Tarquinia, just past the huge bulk of the decommissioned power station overlooking the sea at Monalto di Castro, a right turn off the Aurelia will bring you to **Vulci**, once a large and important Etruscan town. Built on a volcanic plateau on the Tuscany/Lazio border, it reached its heyday in the sixth century BC. Lying a short distance from the sea, it was a maritime power. It was also famous for its production of ceramics and objects in bronze, but after being conquered by Rome in 280 BC, it rapidly declined. DH Lawrence found 'something disquieting, something very beautiful' in Vulci. Although the Etruscan and Roman remains are relatively scant at the **Parco Naturalistico Archaeologico Vulci**, the extensive open site (situated in a lonely, uninhabited area) is rather lovely. Tracts of the early city walls (including two of the original city gates) can be seen, while within the walls are the remains of a fourth-century BC temple and a long stretch of Roman road. Four necropoli containing over 15,000 tombs have been found around the city, mostly dating from the eighth century BC. The Vulci tombs had statues of imaginary beasts guarding the entrances; the most famous is the François tomb with paintings (now removed) depicting scenes from Etruscan and Greek mythology.

Antiquarium di Pyrgi

Castello di Santa Severa (0766 570 194/www.museo santasevera.org). **Open** *Antiquarium* 9am-7pm Tue-Sun. *Tours of the site* 9am-one hour before sunset Tue-Sun. **Admission** *Antiquarium* free. *Tours of the site* €4.50. **No credit cards**.
Guided tours of the castle and the archaeological site at Pyrgi leave the ticket desk at the museum hourly.

Museo Cerite & Necropoli di Banditaccia

Museum: piazza Santa Maria, Cerveteri. Necropolis: via della Necropoli (06 994 1354/www.caere.it). **Open** *Museum* 8.30am-7pm Tue-Sun. *Necropolis* (last entry 1hr before closing) Apr-Sept 8.30am-7pm Tue-Sun; Oct-Mar 8.30am-5pm Tue-Sun. **Admission** *Museum or necropolis* €4; €2 concessions. *Both* €6.50; €3.25 concessions. **No credit cards**.

Museo Nazionale & Necropolis

Museum: Palazzo Vitelleschi, piazza Cavour, Tarquinia (0766 856 036/www.tarquinia.net). Necropolis: via Ripagretta (0766 856 308). **Open** *Museum* 8.30am-7.30pm Tue-Sun. *Necropolis* Apr-Oct 8.30am-7.30pm Tue-Sun. Nov-Mar 8.30am-2pm (last entry 1hr 30mins before closing) Tue-Sun. **Admission** *Museum or necropolis* €4; €2 concessions. *Both* €6.50; €3.25 concessions. **No credit cards**.

Parco Naturalistico Archaeologico Vulci

Via della Volta Buia, Montalto di Castro (0766 879 729/www.vulci.it). **Open** *Jan, Dec* 9am-5pm Sat, Sun. *Feb, Mar* 9.30am-5.30pm Mon, Wed-Sun; 2.30-5.30pm Tue. *Apr-Aug* 10am-6pm Mon, Wed-Sun; 2.30-5.30pm Tue. *Sept-Nov* 9am-5.30pm Mon, Wed-Sun; 2.30-5.30pm Tue. **Admission** €5; €3.50 concessions; €13 family ticket (3-5 people). **No credit cards**.

Terme Taurine

Parco Archeologico e Botanico delle Terme Taurine, via delle Terme di Traiano, Civitavecchia (0766 20 299/www.termetaurine.com). **Open** 10am-sunset Tue-Sun. **Admission** €8; €5 concessions. **No credit cards**.
The tourist office (number given above), which is located by the Porta Michelangelo entrance to Civitavecchia's port, can organise a free minibus ride from the office to the springs.

Where to eat

A plate of home-made pasta or fresh fish on the piazza-side tables of Cerveteri's **Antica Locanda Le Ginestre** (piazza Santa Maria 5, 06 994 0672, closed Mon and 2wks Jan, average €35) is the perfect end to a day's tomb-hopping. The menu turns up surprises such as spaghetti with artichokes and shrimps, truffle-honeyed fillet of *cinta senese* pork, and a wicked hot chocolate soufflé.

Civitavecchia may be ugly, but it's home to some good fish restaurants. At **La Bomboniera** (corso Marconi 50, 0766 25744, closed Mon, average €38), an excellent wine list compliments a generous *antipasto di mare* (marinated tuna, oysters, sautéed clams and mussels), risotto with scampi and courgette flowers, spaghetti with *bottarga* (smoked mullet roe), and oven baked turbot with porcini mushrooms and potatoes.

If your stomach is rumbling in the area of Tarquinia, you could do a whole lot worse than turn into the no-frills roadside **Ristorante Brizi** (SS Aurelia km83, 0766 841 017, closed dinner Sat & Sun, average €25, fixed-price menu €15), situated on the Aurelia just at the point where it joins the A12 motorway. The car park is likely to be full of lorries at lunchtime (always a good sign in Italy), so join the truckers and the blaring TV for wholesome local pasta and fresh fish dishes such as *zuppa di pesce* (fish soup) or *fritto misto* (mixed fried seafood).

You'll find more sea-side restaurants, on *p304* **Buckets & spades**.

Getting there

If you're visiting the Aurelia by public transport, you'll be hard pressed to cover more than one site in a day, though combining the Pyrgi Antiquarium, or the Necropolis at Cerveteri, with a swim is perfectly feasible. Vulci, on the other hand, cannot be reached by public transport.

By car

The A12 motorway runs parallel to via Aurelia as far as Civitavecchia; beware the huge Sunday evening queues at city-bound tollbooths.

By train

Ladispoli-Cerveteri, Santa Marinella, Civitavecchia: FR5 from Ostiense or Trastevere. A local bus connects Marina di Cerveteri station (the stop after Ladispoli) to Cerveteri.
Tarquinia: mainline services from Termini, Ostiense or Trastevere.

By bus

COTRAL services along the Aurelia from Cornelia.

Via Cassia: lakes & gardens

Leading north-west out of Rome and passing through the heart of ancient Etruria to Siena and Florence, **via Cassia** winds through Lazio's lakeland, slaloming around water-filled volcanic craters and through gentle hilly countryside dotted with picturesque towns built on Etruscan or Roman foundations. It also passes by a number of glorious gardens.

Little is known of the origins of this ancient road: nobody seems sure exactly who built it or when. From the ring road, the ancient road's modern alter ego, via Cassia Veientana (or Cassia *bis*), parallels it to the east. Built to share the load of suburban cars during rush hour, the Cassia *bis* joins the old road after about 15 kilometres (nine miles). Between the old and new roads (but best reached from the former), the **Parco Regionale di Veio** – just before you reach the medieval village of Isola Farnese and across a bridge over an impressive waterfall – surrounds **Veio**, an Etruscan city founded in the eighth century BC and which until the fourth century BC was Rome's chief rival for control of the Tiber's right bank. The site contains rare examples of Etruscan houses and temples, plus a striking sixth-century BC sanctuary of Apollo, with a canopy-covered altar area and a pool.

In the crater of an extinct volcano, pretty **Lago di Bracciano** – about 40 kilometres (24 miles) north of Rome – is a water-sports haven, ringed by sailing, windsurfing and canoeing clubs. The lake is Rome's emergency water supply, so it's kept reasonably clean; the best swimming spots are just north of Bracciano town on the western shore, and on the eastern side near Trevignano. Boats run around the lake from Bracciano in summer.

A handful of pretty villages overlook this body of water. Medieval **Anguillara** is perched on a rocky crag and is especially beautiful at sunset. **Bracciano**, the main town on the lake, is dominated by the rather grim-looking

Castello Orsini-Odescalchi, built in 1470, with fine apartments decorated by Antoniazzo Romano and the Zuccari brothers. (It enjoyed a brief moment of glory in November 2006 when Tom Cruise and Katie Holmes chose it to stage their OTT wedding bash.)

Overshadowed by a ruined Roman *rocca* (fortress), lively **Trevignano** has a pretty medieval centre with a hotchpotch of stone houses and cobbled lanes, and is perfect for scenic strolls along its plane-tree-lined lakeside promenade, where cafés and restaurants share peaceful waterfront views. On the western shore of Lago di Bracciano lies **San Liberato**, a garden designed by Russell Page (1905-85); the English landscape architect tinkered for ten years with a series of graceful terraces. A garden of simples and sweet-smelling roses surrounds the house and fourth-century chapel; the sweeping lawns are dotted with exotic trees, which provide shade in summer and colour through the autumn.

Just to the south-east is tranquil **Lago di Martignano**, with a beach where you can rent sailing boats, pedalos and canoes. You'll need your own transport to reach it.

Further north on the Cassia is the town of **Sutri**, which sits on a tufa rock outcrop above its ancient amphitheatre; the original settlement was built on the lower level. Argument still rages over when this amphitheatre was carved out of the rock: some attribute it to the Etruscans; others say it dates from the first century BC. The amphitheatre is located in the lovely **Parco Urbano dell'Antica Città di Sutri**, where an itinerary with good descriptions (also in English) leads you past ancient Sutri's remains, including a necropolis and a mithraeum.

Just past the town, a winding local road heads north off the Cassia towards medieval **Ronciglione** and on to **Lago di Vico**, which sits in the crater of the extinct Monte Cimino volcano; most of the area (known for its hazelnuts) is a natural park. Skirt around the eastern rim of the volcano for about four kilometres (2.5 miles) and turn right for **Caprarola**, a little town dwarfed by the imposing **Palazzo Farnese**, a huge pentagonal villa designed by Sangallo the Younger and Baldassare Peruzzi. It started out as a castle, but was transformed into something less fortified by Vignola in the 1560s. You can visit the lavishly decorated rooms accessed by a spiral staircase, which Cardinal Alessandro Farnese – grandson of Pope Paul III and responsible for commissioning Vignola – used to climb on horseback. Behind the villa are two formal gardens and a steep, wooded park (*barchino*) that leads up to the fountains of the *Giardino grande* and the *Palazzina del piacere* summer house.

Trips Out of Town

About 15 kilometres (9.5 miles) to the north east (via country roads that pass through the small towns of Carbognano and Fabrica) lies the **Castello Ruspoli** at Vignanello, originally built in the ninth century by Benedictine monks but subsequently enlarged and much altered. Its superb formal garden was laid out by Ottavia Orsini (daughter of Duke Vicino Orsini, creator of the Sacro Bosco park at Bomarzo; *see p310*) in 1610. A large rectangle divided into 12 compact parterres of box grown into elaborate geometrical patterns, it was recently restored to its original glory by current *castellana* Claudia Ruspoli.

Six kilometres (3.5 miles) east of Viterbo (*see also p308* **Viterbo**), the hill town of **Bagnaia** is dominated by **Villa Lante**. The villa's two identical palaces (closed to the public except for two frescoed loggias), built by Vignola in rather forbidding dark grey stone in the 1570s for Cardinal Gambara, are surrounded by a stunning formal Italian garden, punctuated by fountains, statues and pools. Water originally cascaded down five terraces, with spectacular effects. Some of it still works: the ropework cascade, the stone dining table with central wine-cooling rivulet and the grand fountain are impressive. The carved prawn motif you see all over the garden is the Gambara family crest (*gambero* is Italian for prawn).

Some 24 kilometres (15 miles) west of Viterbo is **Tuscania**, an Etruscan town in an eerie landscape of low hills; the area is full of Etruscan remains. Tuscania was an important city around the fourth century BC and enjoyed a few glory years in the Middle Ages. Its lovely medieval centre has some exceptionally fine buildings around piazza Basile, where a fountain has been flowing since Etruscan times. Tuscania's most important buildings are the two unique Romanesque-Lombard churches of **San Pietro** and **Santa Maria Maggiore**, situated on the Colle San Pietro, a hill just outside the centre. The *colle* was the site of an Etruscan and then a Roman settlement; fragments of the pre-Christian acropolis are incorporated into the apse of San Pietro. Founded in the eighth century, the church was reworked from the 11th to the 13th centuries, when the adjacent bishop's palace and towers were added. The façade is startling: three-faced trifrons, snakes and dancers owe more to pagan culture than to Christian iconography. The interior has a cosmatesque pavement and 12th-century frescoes. Built at the same time, Santa Maria Maggiore (strada Santa Maria) has tamer beasts on its façade and a more harmonious interior. The main Etruscan sight here is in the small **Museo Archaeologico**, in the cloisters of the convent of Santa Maria del Riposo. Inside, four generations of the same Etrusco-Roman family gaze from the lids of their sarcophagi.

Castello Orsini-Odescalchi

Piazza Mazzini 14, Bracciano (06 9980 4348/ www.odescalchi.com). **Open** (last entry 1hr before

Formal parterres and water features at the **Villa Lante**.

Viterbo

Viterbo was an important Etruscan town and an insignificant Roman one. In the eighth century it was fortified by the Lombard King Desiderius as a launching pad for sacking Rome. Caught up in the medieval quarrels between the Holy Roman Empire and the Church, Viterbo played host to popes and anti-popes, several of whom relocated here when things got too hot in Rome.

Today, Viterbo's *centro storico* is a jumble of narrow streets concealing a mix of rather grand *palazzi*, medieval laundries, ancient porticoes, imposing towers and crenellated buildings, as well as the ubiquitous lion (the symbol of Viterbo) and many fountains. The medieval quarter of San Pellegrino lies at the city's southern edge, flanked by piazza della Morte. Across the bridge is the elegant 12th-century cathedral of **San Lorenzo**, which has been much altered and restored through the centuries. Next door is the **Palazzo Papale**, built for the popes in the 13th century and restored in the 19th. The pretty 12th-century church of **Santa Maria Nuova** (open 8am-noon, 4-7pm) has an ancient head of Jupiter (on the façade), and a pulpit from which St Thomas Aquinas preached. Behind it are the remains of a small Lombard cloister (always open).

Piazza del Plebiscito is dominated by the early 16th-century **Palazzo Comunale**, or town hall (open to the public 10am-1pm, 3-8pm daily), whose lavishly frescoed senate rooms are still used by the town council.

Outside the walls, opposite Porta della Verità, is the 12th-century **Santa Maria della Verità** (open 8am-noon, 4-7pm). In 1469 local boy Lorenzo da Viterbo painted some of the most Tuscan frescoes outside of Tuscany in its Gothic Cappella Mazzatosta. In the old convent next door is the renovated **Museo Civico**, with Etruscan finds, works of art from local churches, and two canvases by Sebastiano del Piombo.

There are several bubbling pools of sulphurous water, where local residents wallow, smeared in greeny-white clay, within a short radius of the town. At the **Bagnaccio**, four basins of varying degrees of heat allow you to admire the surrounding countryside through the steam rising off the water in which you're submerged. To get there, leave Viterbo on the Montefiascone road, and after five kilometres (three miles) turn left on to the road to Marta. After a kilometre (half a mile) you'll see a ruin on your left. Just before this, an unpaved road branches off to the Bagnaccio. If you prefer to wallow in luxury, head for the **Hotel Terme dei Papi** (just off the Tuscania road to the west), which offers anything from a dip in a sulphurous pool to a full range of spa treatments involving mud and sulphur-rich thermal waters.

Viterbo also offers some fine eating options, including the friendly, informal **Porta Romana** (via della Bontà 12, 0761 307 118, closed Sun and 2wks Aug, average €22), where the menu is based on local produce and features *tortelli* stuffed with pumpkin or broccoli and walnuts, salt cod with sultanas, and *involtini* in a tomato sauce. The offerings at **Enoteca La Torre** (via della Torre 5, 0761 226 467, closed lunch Mon, all Sun and 4wks July-Aug, average €33) are a little more sophisticated. Choose between *rigatoni* with broccoli and spicy sausage, rabbit casserole with black olives and anchovies, and calf liver with wild fennel.

Museo Civico

Piazza Crispi 2, Viterbo (0761 348 275). **Open** Apr-Oct 9am-7pm Tue-Sun. Nov-Mar 9am-6pm Tue-Sun. **Admission** €3.10. **No credit cards**.

Terme dei Papi

Strada Bagni 12, Viterbo (07 613 501/ www.termedeipapi.it). **Open** 9am-7pm daily. **Credit** AmEx, DC, MC, V.
A shuttle bus service (€4 one-way) departs from piazza Mancini in Rome at 8.30am Mon-Sat and returns from Terme dei Papi at 1.15pm. Reservations are requested.

closing) *Apr-Aug* 10am-noon, 3-6pm Tue-Sun. *Sept-Mar* 10am-noon, 3-5pm Tue-Sun. **Admission** €7; €5 concessions. **No credit cards**.

Castello Ruspoli

Piazza della Repubblica 9, Vignanello (0761 755 338/ 0761 754 707). **Open** Easter-Sept 10.30am-1.30pm, 3.30-6.30pm Sun. **Admission** €7. **No credit cards**. Groups of 20 or more can book year-round.

Museo Archaeologico

Largo Professore Moretti, Tuscania (0761 436 209). **Open** 8.30am-7.30pm Tue-Sun. **Admission** free.

Parco Regionale di Veio

Isola Farnese (06 3089 0116). **Open** 8.30am-2.30pm Tue, Wed, Fri, Sun; 8.30am-4pm Thur, Sat. **Admission** €2; €1 concessions. **No credit cards**.

Parco Urbano dell'Antica Città di Sutri

Via Cassia km49.5 (0761 609 380). **Open** *Park*
24hrs. *Amphitheatre* May-Sept 8am-6pm Tue-Sat,
8am-1.30pm Sun; Oct-Apr 8am-1.30pm Tue, Wed,
Fri, Sun; 8.30am-5pm Thur, Sat. **Admission** free.
To visit the mithraeum, ask at the ticket
office: if there are any takers, tours will depart
from there on the hour from 9am to 4pm (extended
to 6pm in summer).

Tenuta di San Liberato

*Via Settevene Palo 33, Bracciano (06 998 8384/06
9980 5460/fax 06 9980 2506/www.sanliberato.it).*
Open (guided tours only, by appointment) May-mid
June & mid Sept-mid Nov. **Admission** €9; €6
concessions; €4 under-12s. **No credit cards**.

Villa Farnese

Caprarola (0761 646 052). **Open** *Villa* 8.30am-
6.45pm Tue-Sun. *Gardens* Apr-Oct tours depart
10am, 11am, noon, 3pm, 4pm Tue-Sat; Nov-Mar
tours depart 10am, 11am, noon, 3pm Tue-Sat.
Admission €2. **No credit cards**.

Villa Lante

Bagnaia (0761 288 008). **Open** (last entry 1hr
before closing) *Mar* 8.30am-5.30pm Tue-Sun. *1 Apr-
mid Apr, mid Sept-Oct* 8.30am-6.30pm Tue-Sun. *Mid
Apr-mid Sept* 8.30am-7.30pm Tue-Sun. *Nov-Feb*
8.30am-4.30pm Tue-Sun. **Admission** €2; €1
concessions. **No credit cards**.

Where to eat

In Bracciano, on warm days, tables are laid on
a terrace in the shadow of the Castello Orsini-
Odescalchi at **Vino e Camino** (piazza Mazzini
11, 06 9980 3433, closed Mon and 2wks Aug,
average €30). This excellent wine bar-
restaurant serves traditional local fare with
an occasional creative slant, such as spelt
salad with mackerel and mint, or fusilli with
a lemon-spiked lamb sauce. Fish dishes may
include *orecchiette* pasta with local perch and
ricotta salata (salty, hard ricotta). There's a
wonderful selection of local cheeses and a fine,
honestly priced wine list.

The terrace of the **Locanda del Gusto** (via
Garibaldi 79, 06 999 9822, closed Mon, Wed &
Thur lunch and all Tue in winter, average €28),
overlooks the lake at Trevignano. The menu
at this modern osteria is based mainly on fish
dishes such as sea bass with Sicilian pesto, and
fresh tuna in a sesame crust. There's a choice
of interesting wines too.

Trattoria del Cimino (via F Nicolai 44,
0761 646 173, closed Sun lunch, all Mon and
2wks July, average €25) is a hospitable and
family-friendly establishment in Caprarola
offering hearty local specialities such as game
and polenta during the winter months. There
are some good fishy choices too.

Tuscania has one of northern Lazio's better
restaurants: **Al Gallo** (via del Gallo 22, 0761
443 388, www.algallo.it, closed Mon and Jan-
mid Feb, average €45) offers taster menus at
€30 and €40, while the carte lists dishes such as
stoccafisso (dried cod) and sweet pepper bake,
truffle risotto, and sea bass in a courgette crust.

Getting there

By car

**Veio, Caprarola, Viterbo, Bagnaia, Sutri,
Ronciglione, Tuscania**: take the Cassia (SS2).
Lago di Bracciano & around: exit the Cassia at
La Storta and take via Claudia-Braccianense (SS493).
Trevignano: take the Cassia bis.

By train

Veio: FR3 to La Storta, then bus to Isola Farnese.
Lago di Bracciano & around: FR3 to Anguillara
or Bracciano.
Sutri: hourly services from Ostiense or Trastevere.
Viterbo: the Roma–Viterbo train from Flaminio
station; or FR3 from Ostiense and Trastevere.

By bus

COTRAL services from Saxa Rubra.

Via Flaminia & via Tiberina: Romans & monsters

Ancient **via Flaminia** leads north-east along
the Tiber river valley to the Adriatic coast.
Once it was a wide country road with the
occasional hamlet or farm; now it takes a while
to get to the idyllic parts. Sandwiched between
the A1 motorway and railway lines, the first 25
kilometres (16 miles) beyond the GRA ring road
are heavily trafficked and lined with tasteless
modern developments. But concealed within
the nightmarish shells of towns like Sacrofano,
Riano, Morlupo and Rignano Flaminio are
medieval churches and churches: keep your eyes
peeled for yellow signs pointing to '*borgo
medioevale*' or '*chiesa medioevale*'.

Running parallel to, and east of, the Flaminia,
via Tiberina is less congested and looks much
more like an ancient road should. About five
kilometres (three miles) south of Fiano Romano
is **Lucus Feroniae**, an ancient religious and
trading hub of the Sabine people. By the third
century BC, when it was colonised by the
Romans, the city was famous for ceremonies
held at its sanctuary of Feronia (goddess of
agriculture). Hannibal took a break from his
march on Rome in 211 BC to help himself to
the treasure but, despite the sacking, Lucus
Feroniae continued to grow; heavily rebuilt
during Augustus' reign, it flourished
throughout the Imperial age and into the early
Middle Ages. What remains is a fascinating

Lucus Feroniae.

microcosm of a Roman urban centre, complete with a basilica, bath complex with black and white mosaics, forum and, further to the north-west, a charming little circular amphitheatre. There's a museum too, with finds from the dig – but there are also chronic staff shortages, so it pays to ring before you head out here.

Further north on via Tiberina, turn off for Nazzano and the **Riserva Naturale Tevere-Farfa** wetlands. This small protected stretch of the Tiber river offers great bird-watching. Rising sharply from the low-lying undulating hills of the Tiber valley is the silhouette of **Monte Soratte**, shaped distinctly like the scaly back of a sleeping dinosaur (though many Italians see Mussolini's profile in it).

Just off the Flaminia, **Città Castellana** is a pretty medieval town atop a massive tufa outcrop. Originally known as Falerii Veteres, it was razed by the Romans in the third century BC. The Falisci people were forced to pack up and move west to conspicuously indefensible flatlands in the valley, creating a settlement called Falerii Novi. It was not until the 11th century, when Normans invaded, that the locals once again took advantage of their natural stronghold and hiked back up the hill. Città Castellana has a lovely medieval centre and a solemn 15th-century castle, the **Rocca** (aka Forte Sangallo); commissioned by the Borgia Pope Alexander VI, it was completed under

Julius II by Antonio da Sangallo the Elder. Inside is the **Museo Nazionale dell'Agro Falisco** (0761 513 735, open 1.30-6.30pm Tue-Sun). The **Duomo** (open 8.30am-noon, 4-6pm daily) is a gorgeous Romanesque church from the 12th century, with a perfectly preserved portico that was decorated in delicate gold, porphyry and green geometric mosaic motifs in the early 13th century; some of the decorative elements on the façade are from the abandoned town of Falerii Novi. Inside, the bright white, sugar-frosted extravaganza is the result of an unfortunate 18th-century makeover – thankfully, the cosmatesque floors were left unmolested.

To reach **Falerii Novi**, go six kilometres (3.5 miles) west of Città Castellana towards Fabrica di Roma. Take the road (left), opposite a white building; after 20 metres (70 feet), turn left on to a dirt path and go through the arch. Not much remains of the city except its impressive outer walls. You'll find yourself trudging around the back of a Romanesque church and through fields to a small pit containing uninspiring blocks of tufa – all that remains of a monumental building in a once-bustling Roman colony. A sign points to an amphitheatre; there are wagon ruts in paving stones. And that's it – a veritable Twilight Zone.

Equally surreal is the *parco dei mostri* (monster park) at **Bomarzo**, ten kilometres (six miles) west of Orte. Duke Vicino Orsini (1523-84) had the park built in his **Sacro Bosco** gardens after his wife died; but it's more Renaissance theme park than dignified retreat. Using the volcanic *peperino* stone that dotted his estate, Orsini spent years filling the park with surreal, sometimes grotesque, sculptures that were completely at odds with the tastes of his day. Lurking in the undergrowth are a skewed house and enormous, absurd beasts.

Lucus Feroniae

Via Tiberina, km18.5 (06 908 5173). **Open** 8.30am-7.30pm Tue-Sun. **Admission** free.
Note: Times given above are the official opening hours; in fact, severe staff shortages mean the site generally closes at 2pm. Even in the morning, it's best to call ahead to make sure it's open.

Sacro Bosco

Località Giardino, Bomarzo (0761 924 029). **Open** 8.30am-sunset daily. **Admission** €9; €7 4-8s. **No credit cards.**

Getting there

By car

Lucus Feroniae: A1 to Fiano Romano, then follow signs for Capena.
Bomarzo: Flaminia, then SS315; or A1 to Attigliano exit, then minor road to Bomarzo.

By train

Città Castellana: frequent services from Tiburtina, Ostiense or Flaminio.
Bomarzo: FR1 to Orte, then mainline train to Attigliano-Bomarzo (5km/3 miles from the park).

By bus

COTRAL services from Saxa Rubra (for Bomarzo, change at Riello).

Via Tiburtina: *ville* & monasteries

Via Tiburtina more or less follows the Aniene river, which wends its way from the Monti Simbruini east of Rome to join the Tiber north of the city centre. Far from the most attractive way to exit the city, the early section of this consular road contains such sights as the Rebibbia high-security prison. Beyond the GRA (ring road) the congested traffic bumps and lurches through a landscape scarred by decades of unregulated construction; to avoid the chemical plants and ugly high-rise apartment blocks, take the faster Roma–L'Aquila *autostrada* (A24) and head straight for via Tiburtina's original, ancient destination, Tibur (modern Tivoli).

Just 20km (12.5 miles) from Rome (and a world away from the Tiburtina's unpromising beginnings) are two UNESCO World Heritage Sites – Villa d'Este (*see p313*), in Tivoli itself, and Hadrian's Villa (*see p312*), five kilometres (three miles) down the hill – which make it ideal for a day-trip.

As you approach Tivoli, the foul stink of the *acque albule* sulphur springs fills the air; the curative properties of the water beloved by the ancients can still be experienced at the spas in **Bagni di Tivoli**. The Tiburtina passes massive quarries of travertine (*see also p33* **Lapis tiburtinus**), where gaping chasms of limestone are still exploited; today it's mostly used for flash kitchens in Malibu rather than blood-sport arenas and Baroque fountains.

Just south of the Tiburtina is the town of **Villa Adriana**, site of the spectacular second-century AD retreat designed and built by Emperor Hadrian (*see p312*).

High on a hill five kilometres (three miles) from Villa Adriana, the town of **Tivoli** was founded by an Italic tribe, and conquered by the Romans in 338 BC. The town was littered with temples, and the surrounding territory became a popular location for country villas – Horace, Nero and Trajan had built in the area before Hadrian came along. Dominating Tivoli itself is the **Villa d'Este**, a lavish pleasure palace built over a Benedictine monastery in 1550 for Cardinal Ippolito D'Este, son of Lucrezia Borgia.

Across town are a Republican, circular **Temple of Vesta**, and a second-century AD, rectangular **Temple of the Sibyl** (both on via della Sibilla). From here you can catch a glimpse of the **Villa Gregoriana** across the rocky gorge: it's a wild park next to two waterfalls much favoured by 18th- and 19th-century artists seeking the picturesque.

The cathedral of **San Lorenzo** (via Duomo), reconstructed in the Baroque style in 1635, contains a carved 13th-century *Descent from the Cross*. At the town's highest point (piazza delle Nazioni Unite) is **Rocca Pia**, a 15th-century castle built by Pope Pius II.

In 300 BC work began to extend via Tiburtina from Tivoli eastwards across the Apennines, to the Adriatic at Pescara. The new road made conquering hostile tribes easier, and the territory gained was doled out to noble Roman families. It also brought the abundant mountain springs feeding the Aniene river under the control of the Romans; in 272 BC work began on four aqueducts, which routed large quantities of fresh water to the metropolis for centuries.

The area's limpid waterways and verdant countryside attracted the ancient jet set; in 33 BC 'Maecenas' (Mecenate) invited Rome's hottest poet, Horace, to move into his country villa outside Licenza. When Nero ordered the construction of a pleasure villa in around AD 60, Subiaco was the chosen spot. In the late fifth century, Western monasticism was born here when St Benedict holed up in a cave in Subiaco. Between the tenth and 11th centuries, the Church and nobility constructed fortresses on the hills along the strategic Aniene valley. The feudal castles still dominate the landscape as you roll along via Tiburtina.

Past Roviano, the SS411 forks off to the south towards **Subiaco** (Sublaqueum, 'under the lakes'). Its narrow gorges and wooded mountains attracted Emperor Nero, who dammed the Aniene to create a massive lake next to his grandiose villa – estimated by archaeologists to have covered 75 hectares (185 acres). The lake has since disappeared and only traces of the villa survive: the emperor abandoned it soon after its completion when lightning struck the table in front of him as he dined – a very bad omen. Much of the land where the villa stood is private property and little has been excavated, but a small thermal complex and part of **San Clemente** – the first monastery built by St Benedict, which is made from villa masonry – can be seen; call ahead to the Monastero di Santa Scolastica (*see p312*) to visit. This isolated area became popular with assorted ascetics, and when young nobleman Benedict of Norcia turned his back on the licentious hedonism of his late fifth-century contemporaries, it was at a cave on Monte Taleo that he did his praying. The **Monastero di San Benedetto** (*see below*) grew up around the *Sacro speco* – the 'Holy Cavern' where Benedict spent those three long years.

After three years of solitude Benedict had attracted such a flock of disciples that he founded the first of 13 monasteries inside the ruins of Nero's villa. Only one is still going: the **Monastero di Santa Scolastica** (*see below*), named after Benedict's twin sister, whose dedication to her sacred sibling earned her a place among the saints too.

Not only is Subiaco the birthplace of Western monasticism, but it was also a cradle of Italian printing. In 1464 two Germans set up a Gutenberg press at the St Scholastica monastery. They printed three titles, using the unique *sublacensi* characters. Only one work printed here remains at the monastery, a copy of Lactantius' *De divinis institutionibus.* Behind the monastery lies the **Biblioteca Nazionale Santa Scolastica** (*see below*).

Biblioteca Nazionale Santa Scolastica

Via dei Monasteri (0774 85 424/www.scolastica. librari.beniculturali.it). **Open** *Mid July-Aug* 8.30am-1pm Mon-Sat. *Sept-mid July* 8.30am-6.30pm Mon-Fri; 8.30am-1.30pm Sat. Closed Easter weekend, 2wks Aug & religious holidays. **Admission** free.

The National Library of St Scholastica houses over 100,000 volumes, including ninth- and tenth-century manuscripts. Only a fraction is on display in the library's two lower rooms; for the well being of the books, there's no artificial lighting (bad on a cloudy day); and there's little by way of explanation.

Monastero di San Benedetto & Sacro Speco

Via dei Monasteri (0774 85 039/www.benedettini-subiaco.it). **Open** 9am-noon, 3-5.30pm daily. **Admission** free.

Note: during Sunday mass (9.30am & 11am) the upper part of the monastery is closed to visits.

The Monstery of St Benedict is a mountain-hugging complex of twisting corridors and stairways. The Upper Church (*Chiesa superiore*) is covered in early 15th-century frescoes of the Sienese school, while the Lower Church (*Chiesa inferiore*) dates from the second half of the 13th century. On the right of the stair-case is the *Sacro speco* – the cave where Benedict spent three years pondering his vocation – with a 17th-century marble statue of the young hermit by Bernini's pupil, Antonio Raggi, and one of the life-saving food hampers that were lowered regularly into the cave by a friendly local. The *Scala santa* (Holy Staircase) leads further down, its undulating walls decorated with frescoes; on your left there is a simplistic identification of the processes of

decomposition, on your right a horse-riding Death wields his scythe. Part-way down the staircase, the Cappella della Madonna was decorated by the same Sienese artists as the Upper Church. At the bottom of the *Scala santa*, the *Grotta dei pastori* (Shepherds' Grotto) is where Benedict first taught in the sixth century; on the right, fragments of an eighth-century Byzantine Madonna and child remain.

Up the spiral staircase beside the *Grotta dei pastori* is the Chapel of St Gregory. Decoration dates from the first half of the 13th century and includes a fresco of St Francis of Assisi (behind glass). The portrait of St Francis – shown pre-halo and stigmata – was probably done soon after he visited the monastery in 1218.

Monastero di Santa Scolastica

Via dei Monasteri (0774 82 421/www.benedettini-subiaco.it). **Open** 9am-12.30pm, 3.30-6.30pm Mon-Sat; 11.30am-6.30pm Sun. **Admission** free.

The sixth-century chapel of St Silvester is the oldest remaining bit of the monastery; the church dedicated to Scholastica was erected in 981. Most of the rest is the result of a late 18th-century makeover – with the exception of the beautiful campanile, built in 1053. A shop near the main entrance sells monk-made 'curative' spirits, thick liqueurs, chocolate, chunky fruit jams and herbal products.

Villa Adriana (Hadrian's Villa)

Via di Villa Adriana, Villa Adriana (0774 382 733). **Open** (daily; last entry 90mins before closing) *Feb* 9am-6pm. *Mar, Oct* 9am-6.30pm. *Apr, Sept* 9am-7pm. *May-Aug* 9am-7.30pm. *Nov-Jan* 9am-5pm. **Admission** €6.50; €3.25 concessions. *Special exhibitions* €2.50 extra. **No credit cards.**

Strewn across a gentle slope, the Villa Adriana (Hadrian's Villa) was built from 118 to 134 and has some fascinating architectural spaces and water features. Hadrian was an amateur architect and is believed to have designed many of the unique elements in his villa himself. He drew on inspiration from his travels in Greece and Egypt, making the villa an echo of the Empire itself. After the emperor's death in 138, the villa was used by his successors. In the centuries following the fall of the Empire it became a luxury quarry for treasure-hunters. At least 500 pieces of statuary in collections around the world have been identified as coming from this site, and marble and mosaic finds from the villa now make up a significant portion of the collections of Roman art at the Capitoline (*see p75*) and Vatican (*see p166*) museums. The restored remains lie amid olive groves and cypresses and are still impressive; the model in the pavilion just up the hill from the entrance gives an idea of the villa's original size. The layout of the complex is seemingly haphazard: it's easy to get lost and just as easy to stumble upon charming surprises.

Where the original entrance to the villa lay is uncertain; today the first space you'll encounter after climbing the road from the ticket office is the *pecile* (or *poikile*), a large pool that was once surrounded by a portico with high walls, of which only one remains. As it was constructed on land that originally sloped dramatically (the eastern end was 15 metres/47 feet higher than the western), a massive complex of sub-structures (the 'hundred chambers') was built to level things off. The *poikile* was probably used for post-prandial strolling: seven laps around the perimeter of the space constitute two Roman miles, the distance that ancient doctors recommended walking after meals.

Directly east of the *poikile*, the *Teatro marittimo* (Maritime Theatre) is one of the most delightful inventions in the whole villa, and one of the parts generally attributed to Hadrian himself. A circular brick wall (45 metres/150 feet in diameter) encloses a moat, at the centre of which is an island of columns and brickwork; it was a self-sufficient *domus* (mini-villa) – complete with its own baths, bedrooms and gardens. Today a cement bridge crosses the moat, but originally there were wooden bridges, which could be removed to give the impression of absolute isolation. South of the Maritime Theatre is a three-storey building known simply as the 'building with a fish pond' (*peschiera*), or the Winter Palace (*Quartiere invernale*). The highest of the structure's levels, where traces of a heating system are preserved, may have been the emperor's private residence, with a large banquet hall overlooking the Nymphaeum-Stadium and the plains towards Rome. The 'fish pond' is a now-empty rectangular basin in the east side of the structure, beneath which visitors can walk along the perfectly preserved *cryptoporticus*. Continuing south, locate the *Piccole terme* (Small Baths), where intricate plaster mouldings are amazingly intact on some of the vaulted ceilings, giving an idea of the grandeur of the entire villa's decoration.

In the valley below is the lovely *Canopus*. Built to recall the canal that connected Alexandria to the city of Canopus – famous for its temple of Serapis – on the Nile data, this is a long, narrow pool, framed on three sides by columns and statues, including a marble crocodile. At the far (southern) end of the pool is a structure called the *Serapeum*, used for lavish entertaining, where sculpture once embellished the apse; despite its Egyptian inspiration, the architectural style couldn't be more Roman. Summer guests enjoyed an innovative form of air-conditioning – a sheet of water poured from the roof over the open face of the building, enclosing diners. The villa also included extensive guest and staff apartments, dining rooms, assembly halls and libraries, a stadium and theatres. The whole complex was connected by underground passages, so that servants were invisible whenever possible.

Villa d'Este

Piazza Trento 1, Tivoli (0774 332 920/www.villa destetivoli.info). **Open** (Tue-Sun) *Feb* 9am-4.30pm. *Mar* 9am-5.15pm. *Apr* 9am-6.30pm. *May-Aug* 8.30am-6.45pm. *Sept* 9am-6.15pm. *Oct* 9am-5.30pm. *Nov-Jan* 9am-4pm. **Admission** €6.50; €3.25 concessions. **Credit** (online bookings) AmEx, DC, MC, V.

Mannerist architect Pirro Ligorio made detailed studies of Hadrian's Villa (*see p312* **Villa Adriana**), and he drew on these in his plans for the Villa d'Este and its gardens. Inside the villa there are frescoes and paintings by artists such as Correggio, Da Volterra and Perin Del Vaga (including, in the Hall of the Fountain, views of the villa shortly after its construction). The gardens are the main attraction, drawing busloads of day-trippers to admire their ingenious fountains.

Ligorio developed a complex 'hydraulic machine' that channelled water from the Aniene river (still the source today) through a series of canals under the garden. Using know-how borrowed from the Romans, he created a homage to the natural springs on the hillsides of Tivoli in the 51 fountains spread around the terraced gardens. The sibyls (pagan high priestesses) are a recurring theme – it was at Tivoli that the Tiburtine sibyl foretold the birth of Christ – and the grottoes of the sibyls behind the vast fountain of Neptune echo with thundering artificial waterfalls.

Technological gimmickry was another big feature; the Owl Fountain imitated an owl's song using a (sadly long-lost) hydraulic mechanism, while the *Fontana dell'organo idraulico* (restored in June 2004 and now fully functioning) used water pressure to compress air and play tunes. There is a bar (all year round) and a restaurant (Apr-Oct), both with splendid views, and a programme of summer evening openings and events at the villa. Electric carts are provided for disabled visitors to tour the gardens; booking essential.

Where to eat

Across the car park from Villa Adriana is the smart **Adriano** (largo M Yourcenar 2, 0774 535 028, www.hoteladriano.it, average €35). The pasta is home-made and the menu surprisingly sophisticated given the provincial setting; the large shady garden is great for alfresco eating. There's also a €25 Sunday brunch.

In Subiaco, the *foresteria* (guesthouse) of the **Santa Scolastica** monastery (0774 85 569; *see p312*) serves huge meals at reasonable prices (fixed-price menus €15 & €21). **Agriturismo La Parata** (via dei Monasteri 40, 0774 822 748, average €25) specialises in freshwater fish.

Getting there

By car
A24 (exit Tivoli) or via Tiburtina (SS5).

By bus
Tivoli: COTRAL services from Ponte Mammolo. Note that the bus marked *autostrada* is a quicker (although less frequent) service; the regular service is marked 'via Tiburtina' and takes about 45mins. Get off at the main square (piazza Garibaldi) for Villa d'Este.

Villa Adriana: Most Rome–Tivoli services also stop at Villa Adriana. As well, frequent local buses connect Tivoli town to Villa Adriana (10mins). The site is not very well signposted: ask where to get off.
Subiaco: Some buses continue on from Tivoli. There are infrequent local services from Subiaco town centre to the monasteries.

Via Prenestina: a goddess, an oracle & one big temple

For a totally unexpected (and very rewarding) taste of the ancient world, head to the unassuming town of **Palestrina**, the chief 'modern' claim to fame of which is as birthplace of the 16th-century motet and madrigal composer Giovanni Palestrina (c1525-94)

Nowadays it's an uninspiring little town. In antiquity, however, Praeneste was an important Etruscan settlement, which battled long and hard against Rome until capitulating around 338 BC. The town was known for its huge temple and the shrine of an oracle who foretold the future using *sortes* – pieces of wood with letters carved on them. Parts of the temple, dedicated to the goddess Fortuna Primigenia, date from the sixth century BC. Under Roman control the temple complex was rebuilt on a grander scale on a series of mountainside terraces, and Praeneste became a fashionable holiday resort (Pliny the Younger had a villa here). The oracle shut up shop in the fourth century AD, the temple fell into disuse, and a medieval town – Palestrina – was built on top. It wasn't until World War II that air raids devastated the town but unearthed the lower part of the temple. The sprawling complex was a semicircular affair crowned by a statue of the goddess Fortuna where the 17th-century **Palazzo Colonna-Barberini** now stands.

The view from the town's approach road gives a good idea of the vast size of the temple. In the main piazza Margherita, to the right of the cathedral, are scant remains of a shrine to Juno (who, until she became the great goddess of Rome, was protector of women and their sexual life). But what makes Palestrina really worth a stopover is the **Museo Archeologico** (*see below*), housed in the palazzo.

Museo Archeologico di Palestrina

Piazza della Cortina (06 953 8100). **Open** (last entry 1hr before closing) *Museum* 9am-8pm daily. *Archaeological site* 9am-1hr before sunset daily. **Admission** *Museum & site* €3; €1.50 concessions. **No credit cards**.

This fascinating museum is located inside the Palazzo Colonna-Barberini, which was built on the highest terrace of the temple to Fortuna. Today the palazzo-museum incorporates some remains of the ancient construction (plexiglas floor tiles show

where the columns once stood), while a model on the top floor shows how the temple complex might have been. There's a selection of Republican and Imperial Roman artefacts: art, instruments and objects either found in the area or associated with the worship of Fortuna. But the star exhibit is the second-century BC Nile mosaic, a work admired by Pliny, which came from the most sacred part of the temple (where the cathedral now stands). It is an intricately detailed, bird's-eye representation of the flora and fauna of the flooded banks of the Nile from Ethiopia to Alexandria. Gallant warriors hunt exotic animals, and diners recline while pipers pipe and goddesses preach. If your Greek is good, you'll be able to identify the labelled beasts.

In a niche off the ground-floor entrance hall, look out for the *Capitoline Triad*, a second-century AD sculpture of Minerva, Jupiter and Juno sitting together on one throne – the only known portrayal of Rome's three tutelary gods together. This sculpture was stolen in 1992, but subsequently salvaged from the murky underworld of stolen artefacts. Your museum ticket is also good for seeing the archeological excavations. **Photo** *p315*.

Getting there

By car
Via Prenestina (SS155) or via Casilina. Also reached from the A1 (exit San Cesareo or Valmontone) or the A24 (exit Tivoli) motorways, then local roads.

By bus
COTRAL services run from Anagnina or Ponte Mammolo.

Via Tuscolana: Castelli & *palazzi*

Via Tuscolana forks off via Latina (an ancient alternative route to via Appia, *see p316*), passes the centre of Italian filmmaking at Cinecittà (*see p261*), heads out through the rolling Alban hills and the Castelli romani and ends at the ruined city of Tusculum. En route, in Rome's outer, most run-down eastern suburbs, it passes close to the undervisited **Parco degli Acquedotti** (*see p172*).

Frascati is the closest to Rome of the Castelli romani – a group of towns so-called for the grand abodes erected here by Rome's papal and patrician glitterati. Twentieth-century additions have tarnished the gloss, but the towns still have a certain charm.

The name 'Frascati' may be synonymous with uninspiring Italian wine, but you'd do well to give it another try here (*see also p219* **What the locals drink**); local tipplers claim that it has to be drunk *sul posto* – on site. There are Renaissance villas sprinkled over the hillside

A mighty temple and a magnificent mosaic at the **Museo Archeologico di Palestrina.**

behind the town, but only the garden of the 17th-century **Villa Aldobrandini**, built in 1598-1603 by Giacomo della Porta for Cardinal Pietro Aldobrandini, is open to the public. In nearby **Villa Torlonia** – a public park – Carlo Maderno's 16th-century *Teatro delle acque* fountain has been gloriously restored; there's an elegant smaller fountain here too, by Gianlorenzo Bernini.

Four kilometres (2.5 miles) down the road, but a world away from Frascati's summer crowds, ancient **Tusculum** (always open) is part pastoral green and part archaeological treasure trove. The remnants of a volcano that last blew its top 70,000 years ago are now grassy slopes covered by oaks and umbrella pines, fanned by cool breezes. From the picnic ground, the ancient via dei Sepolcri winds up to a Roman cistern and tomb. Or start from the main parking lot at the top of the hill and head west to find the spectacular remains of the **Villa di Tibero** – presumed to have been one of the many villas of Emperor Tiberius. To the east is a second-century BC theatre and forum. Ignore the hideous cross made out of what look like recycled water pipes and enjoy more great views from the summit; if you search among the twisted oaks and blackberry bushes here, you'll come across more ruins of the acropolis.

South of Frascati, on via Latina (SS511), **Grottaferrata** is a lively town whose main street leads to the tenth-century **Abbazia di San Nilo**, the only Greek Orthodox abbey in the province of Rome. The abbey was founded by Bartholomew and Nilus, two Basilian monks from Calabria. The mainly Romanesque monastery was fortified in the 15th century, and the abbey church has a fine 12th-century campanile and an even finer carved marble portal. Inside, the *cappella di San Nilo* (chapel of St Nilus) contains beautiful frescoes by Domenichino.

Abbazia di San Nilo
Corso del Popolo 128, Grottaferrata (06 945 9309). **Open** *May-Sept* 9am-noon, 4.30-6.30pm daily. *Oct-Apr* 9am-noon, 4.30-6pm daily. **Admission** free.

Villa Aldobrandini
Via CG Massaia, Frascati (06 942 0331). **Open** (gardens only) *May-Sept* 9am-1pm, 3-6.30pm Mon-Fri. *Oct-Apr* 9am-1pm, 3-5pm Mon-Fri. **Admission** free, but call first to arrange a visit.

Where to eat & drink

In Frascati you're spoilt for choice when it comes to eating and drinking. **Cacciani** (via A Diaz 13-15, 06 942 0378, www.cacciano.it, closed dinner Sun, all Mon and 10 days Jan & 10 days

Aug, average €45) is an upmarket hotel restaurant, with creative dishes based on fresh seasonal produce – much of it grown by the owners. For something simpler, try **Zarazà** (viale Regina Margherita 45, 06 942 2053, closed dinner Sun from Oct to Apr, all Mon and 3wks Aug, average €33).

Many make the pilgrimage to Frascati not to eat, but to pay their respects to Bacchus. For the hard core, there's the **Osteria dell'Olmo** (piazza dell'Olmo 3, no phone, closed Mon): half wine-making museum and half anthropological study, this *osteria* serves only its own wines and you're expected to provide your own food (stop at the nearby piazza del Mercato to get a *porchetta* – roast suckling pig – sandwich to go). It's not a place for the meek or solitary.

La Briciola (via G D'Annunzio 12, 06 945 9338, closed dinner Sun, all Mon and 1wk Jan & 3wks Aug, average €35) in Grottaferrata uses the freshest of local ingredients.

Getting there

By car
Grottaferrata, Frascati: best reached using via Appia (*see below*) and minor roads.
Tusculum: take via Tuscolo from Frascati.

By train
Frequent trains (FR4) leave from Termini for the 20min ride to Frascati (and Castelgandolfo, *see below*). Check destinations carefully: the FR4 route divides and not all stops are covered.

By bus
COTRAL services run from Anagnina every 30mins.

Via Appia: further along the Way

(For the stretch of via Appia nearer Rome, *see chapter* **The Appian Way**.)

While a trip down the ancient *regina viarum* – or Queen of Roads, as **via Appia Antica** was known – is today an enchanting experience thick with antiquity, you're unlikely to be captivated by modern **via Appia Nuova** (SS7), which is thick only with traffic fumes. Persevere, though, and the SS7 leads past Rome's second airport at Ciampino and out to the lake-dotted countryside south of Rome, along via dei Laghi (SS217) and to the southern side of the Castelli romani and the Alban hills.

Perched on the lip of the **Lago Albano** crater, **Castelgandolfo** is best known as the town where the pontiff spends his summer hols. (Pope Clement VII began the tradition in the 1500s.) The papal palace and pretty, cobbled piazza della Libertà – with its enchanting view

of the lake – were completed by Bernini. In August you can catch the pope delivering his Sunday Angelus here at noon. Enjoy the same breezes the pope does by taking a stroll around the lakeshore; indulge in pleasures that are off-limits to the pontiff by renting a pedalo or lakeside deckchair.

A few kilometres to the south, **Albano Laziale** was the site of a huge army base built by Septimus Severus for the Second Legion, and its remains – such as the main gate and a third-century cistern – can be seen all over the town. The church of **Santa Maria della Rotonda** (which looks a bit like the Pantheon in miniature) was once the nymphaeum of a huge Roman baths complex; you can still see mosaic fragments depicting sea monsters.

Overlooking **Lago di Nemi**, the town of **Genzano** is renowned for its Infiorata festival (*see p255* **Country knees-ups**), which is held on the first Sunday after Corpus Domini (late May or early June). Tons of brilliantly hued flowers are used to create elaborate pictures on the streets.

The road leading from Genzano towards the lake passes the **Museo delle Navi** (Roman Ship Museum). When the lake was partially drained in 1929, two massive (formerly) floating temples emerged. Followers of Isis worshipped the Egyptian goddess on sacred vessels on lakes at the full moon. Emperor Caligula – an Isis devotee – had two fabulously decorated vessels built on Lake Nemi; after his demise, the disapproving Roman Senate had them sunk. The museum built for the 70-metre (230-foot) ships was destroyed during World War II, but today there are scale models and reproductions of artefacts found on board.

Of all the Castelli romani villages, **Nemi** is the most picturesque, perched on the edge of a tree-covered crater overlooking the lake. The name comes from the Latin word *nemus* (forest); the surrounding woods were once the haunt of worshippers of Diana, goddess of the hunt. For centuries Nemi has been famous for its fruit: the medieval village is synonymous with strawberries, now grown by the lake under glass and plastic. Avoid visiting on Sundays, when Nemi fills up with Roman strollers.

Situated on the plain south-east of the Castelli romani, **Ninfa** was named – local legend says – after a nymph who was so devastated by the loss of her lover that she cried herself a river. Today a stream flows though some of Italy's most beautiful gardens, which ramble around the ruins of a medieval town. The origins of Ninfa are obscure, but in the 12th century it made the mistake of supporting a rival to the pope and was sacked. It rallied, and by the early

1380s had 150 large *palazzi*. Afterwards, however, the town came to grief in clan warfare, followed by outbreaks of malaria. The Caetani family acquired Ninfa in the 14th century, but showed little interest in their ghost estate until the 1920s, when Don Gelasio Caetani decided to plant his vast collection of exotic species here. The result of his botanical dabbling – the **Oasi di Ninfa** – is pure magic, though visiting times are very limited so you'll have to plan your visit carefully if you want it to coincide (note that tickets can be bought in Rome).

To learn more about the history of the area, and particularly the reclaiming of the malarial marshland that once dominated this plain, turn right off the Appia at Borgo Faiti and head for the excellent **Piana delle Orme**, where huge barns contain old military vehicles (used in *The English Patient* and *Life Is Beautiful*) and agricultural equipment, models of the Anzio landing and Battle of Cassino, plus antique toys and interactive scenes of life between the wars and marsh-draining. Home-grown produce is on offer at a shop and restaurant, and there's a well-equipped playground and plenty of space for picnics.

Museo delle Navi
Via Diana 15, Genzano (06 939 8040/06 3996 7900). **Open** (last entry 1hr earlier) 9am-1.30pm, 2.30-5pm Mon-Sat. **Admission** €2. **No credit cards**.

Oasi di Ninfa
Doganella di Ninfa (0773 633 935/www.fondazione caetani.org). **Open** *Apr-June, Oct, Nov* 1st Sat, 1st Sun & 3rd Sun of mth 9am-noon, 2.30-6pm. *July-Sept* 1st Sat & 1st Sun of mth 9am-noon, 3-6.30pm. **Admission** €8; €7 concessions; free under-11s. **No credit cards**.
Tickets can also be purchased from the Fondazione Caetani in Rome (via delle Botteghe Oscure 32, 06 687 3056, open 9am-7pm Mon-Fri). Groups can arrange private visits at other times.

Piana delle Orme
Via Migliara km43, Borgo Faiti (0773 258 708/ www.pianadelleorme.it). **Open** *May-Sept* 9am-6pm daily. *Oct-Apr* 9am-5pm daily. **Admission** €10; €8 6-12s, over-65s. **No credit cards**.

Where to eat

In Albano Laziale, the **Antica Abbazia** (via San Filippo Neri 19, 06 932 3187, closed Mon, average €30) serves excellent local seasonal food with the odd creative touch, and has a good wine list.

Though there's not much to see in Genzano, your stomach won't regret stopping by. **Pietrino e Renata** (Via Cervi 8, 06 939 1497, closed Mon and 2wks July-Aug & 2wks

Dec-Jan, average €32) is an old-style family restaurant where *mamma* Renata's seasonally changing menu is built around everything that's freshest. **La Scuderia** (piazza Sforza Cesarini 1, 06 939 0521, closed Mon, average €30) uses fresh ingredients from local producers to re-create traditional dishes, while excellent wines can be sampled in the front rooms of the **Ristorante Enoteca La Grotta** (via I Belardi 31, 06 936 4224, closed dinner in winter, all Wed and 1wk Aug, average €35) or fresh fish in the restaurant out back.

In Nemi, the **Sirena del Lago** (via del Plebiscito 26, 06 936 8020, closed Mon from Oct to Mar, average €20) is family-run, serves excellent grilled trout and game, and has perhaps the best view in town.

At Borgo Faiti, **La Locanda del Bere** (via Foro Appio 64, 0773 258 620, closed Sun and 2wks Aug, average €30) is one of the best places to eat – and drink – in the area.

Getting there

By car
For all destinations, take the Appia (SS7). **Nemi**: exit after Ciampino and take via dei Laghi. **Ninfa**: exit at Tor Tre Ponti, then follow signs to Latina Scalo and Ninfa.

By train
Ninfa: take mainline services from Termini to Latina Scalo, then haggle with waiting taxi drivers for the 9km (5-mile) ride to the gardens. **Castelgandolfo**: the FR4 runs hourly from Termini.

By bus
COTRAL services run from Anagnina to Genzano and Castelgandolfo. For Nemi, change at Genzano. There are also services from Frascati (*see p314*) and Grottaferrata (*see p315*) to Genzano and Nemi.

Via Pontina: Romans & beaches

Slicing south from the city, **via Pontina** (SS148) can make no claim to antiquity. It was built in the 1930s to connect Mussolini's capital to the Pontine marshes – which had been recently reclaimed from brackish water and squadrons of malarial mosquitoes – and 'ideal' Fascist settlements like Littorio (now Latina, a dingy centre of provincial life) and the smart beach resort of Sabaudia.

It now has a reputation as one of the region's deadliest roads, though at weekends you'll wonder how anyone gets up enough speed to wreak death and destruction in the bumper-to-bumper traffic. Pick it up just outside EUR (*see p178*) and head through the soulless, high-rise dormitory suburbs. Before the industrial town of Pomezia (with its factory-door outlets for cheap designer clothes), signs point off to the right (west) for beaches around **Torvaianica** (*see p304* **Buckets & spades**), a miasma of roasting human flesh in high season. About five kilometres (three miles) south of Pomezia, a minor road heads coastwards towards Tor San Lorenzo. Here, at a property called **La Landriana**, British landscape architect Russell Page worked with owner Lavinia Taverna to create a glorious garden in which colours and atmosphere change through successive 'rooms', beyond which a rose-filled valley opens up towards a lake.

At Aprilia the SS207 forks right to **Anzio**, where the Allies landed in 1944 to launch their victorious march on Rome, and **Nettuno**, with its serried rows of heart-rending white crosses in the British and American military cemeteries.

The first cleanish sea south of Rome is at **Sabaudia**. With its striking 1930s architecture, the town (set one kilometre/half a mile back from the coast) is a favourite with Italy's holidaying intelligentsia. It owes its miles of unspoilt sandy beaches to the fact that it is inside the **Parco Nazionale del Circeo**. Forget the dusty exhibits in the park's museum and visitors' centre; hire bikes or set out on foot for walks and picnics instead (note that mosquito repellent is as important as water and sandwiches in this former swamp).

Looming to the south is **Monte Circeo**, where Odysseus was waylaid by the enchantress Circe, who turned his ship's crew into pigs. A hike to the top through cork- and holm-oak forests on the western, seaward side is spectacular – though best attempted in the cooler months. Or drive most of the way up from the landward side to explore the ancient ruins along the ridge. East of the outcrop, a road winds up to **San Felice Circeo**, a pretty little town and a poseurs' paradise in summer.

The Pontina merges with the Appia (becoming the SS213) at **Terracina**, which is a port town with two centres. The pleasant modern part is down by the sea, while the medieval town above lies on top of the forum of the Roman port of Anxur. Its cathedral was built in a Roman temple to Augustus; above the portico is a 12th-century mosaic frieze, and below it is a big basin that was reputedly used for boiling Christians. The paving slabs in the piazza are from the forum. World War II bombing uncovered the ancient remains and made space for the modern town hall and **Museo Civico di Terracina**. Standing above the town is the first-century BC Tempio di Giove (Temple of Jupiter).

Sperlonga is a pretty seaside resort. The whitewashed medieval town on the spur above the two beaches – its narrow lanes lined with potted geraniums, boutiques and restaurants – fills with well-heeled Romans in the summer. The **Museo Archeologico di Sperlonga**, at the end of the southerly beach, contains important second-century BC sculptures of scenes from the *Odyssey*; the ticket includes a tour of **Tiberius' Villa and Grotto**.

La Landriana

Via Campo di Carne 51, località Tor San Lorenzo, Ardea (039 608 1532/when garden is open 06 9101 4140/www.giardinidellalandriana.it). **Open** *Apr, May* 10am-noon, 3-6pm Sat, Sun. *June* 4-7pm Sun. *July* 4-7pm 1st & 3rd Sun of mth. *Sept, Oct* 10am-1pm Sun. **Admission** €8; €4 concessions; free under-8s. **No credit cards.**

Museo Archeologico di Sperlonga & Villa di Tiberio

Via Flacca km1.6, Sperlonga (0771 548 028). **Open** 8.30am-7.30pm daily. **Admission** €2; €1 concessions. **No credit cards.**

Museo Civico di Terracina

Piazza Municipio, Terracina (0773 707 313). **Open** *July, Aug* 9am-2pm Mon; 8am-8pm Tue-Sat; 9am-1pm, 3-9pm Sun. *Sept-June* 9.30am-2pm Mon; 8am-8pm Tue-Sat; 9am-1pm, 3-6pm Sun. **Admission** €1.55. **No credit cards.**

Where to eat

In Sabaudia, try **Sirene** (via Lungomare km20.9, località Bufalara, 0773 534 108, closed Jan & Dec, average €38); in winter opening times can be erratic. You can watch the buffalo that are used to produce the area's renowned mozzarella as they graze outside. **Bottega Sarra 1932** (via San Francesco 54, 0773 702 045, closed Mon & Tue and lunch in Aug, average €50), in Terracina, serves excellent renditions of simple local fare. The family-run **La Bisaccia** (via Romita 19, 0771 548 576, closed Tue and Nov, average €35), in Sperlonga, has great fish.

Getting there

By car

Head south out of Rome, and pick up the Pontina (SS148) in EUR. For minor destinations, your own transport is essential.

By train

Sabaudia, Terracina, Sperlonga: mainline train to Priverno (for buses to Sabaudia and buses/trains to Terracina) and Fondi (for buses to Sperlonga).

By bus

Sabaudia, Terracina, Sperlonga: COTRAL services run from Laurentina.

Directory

Features

Santa Maria in Aracoeli. *See p79.*

Directory

Getting Around

By air

Rome has two major airports: Fiumicino, about 30km (18 miles) west of the city, handles scheduled flights; Ciampino, 15km (nine miles) south-east of the city, is a military airbase, also used by low-cost airlines and for charter flights.

Aeroporto Leonardo Da Vinci, Fiumicino

Via dell'Aeroporto di Fiumicino 320 (switchboard 06 65 951/information 06 6595 3640/www.adr.it). **Open** 24hrs daily.

There's an **express rail service** between Fiumicino airport and Termini railway station, which takes 31mins and runs every 30mins from 6.37am until 11.37pm daily (5.52am-10.52pm to Fiumicino). Tickets in either direction cost €9.50. The **regular service** from Fiumicino takes 25-40mins, and stops at Trastevere, Ostiense, Tuscolana and Tiburtina stations. Trains leave about every 15mins (less often on Sun) between 5.57am and 11.27pm (5.06am-10.36pm to Fiumicino). Tickets cost €5. You can buy tickets for both these services with cash or by credit card for the express service) from automatic machines in the airport lobby and rail stations, and at the airport rail station ticket office (open 7am-9.30pm daily) and the airport *tabacchi*. Some carriages have wheelchair access (*see also p327*). Stamp your ticket in the machines on the platform before boarding.

Terravision (06 6595 8646, www.terravision.it) runs a **coach service** from Fiumicino to Termini, which also makes stops in the northern suburbs (along via Aurelia) and at Lepanto (journey time to Termini: 70mins). Departures are about every two hours between 8.30am and 8.30pm daily. Coaches from Termini to Fiumicino leave from via Marsala 7 (opposite the multi-storey car park) from 6.30am to 6.30pm. Tickets cost €7 single, €12 return (€3.50/€6 5-12s), and can either be booked in advance online, or paid for in cash at the Terravision desk located in the

arrivals hall, at the Terravision Office (Agenzia 365 in the Termini station forecourt) or on the bus.

During the night, a **bus service** runs between Fiumicino (Terminal C) and Tiburtina railway station. Tickets cost €4 from machines or €5 on the bus. Buses leave Tiburtina at 12.30am, 1.15am, 2.30am and 3.45am, stopping at Termini railway station 10mins later. Departures from Fiumicino are at 1.15am, 2.15am, 3.30am and 5am. Neither Termini nor Tiburtina are attractive places at night, so it's advisable to get a taxi from there to your final destination. Buses are infrequent; metro line B at Termini and Tiburtina closes at 11.30pm (12.30am Sat); for an unspecified period, metro line A closes at 9pm daily, with shuttle buses replacing the service at night (*see p322*).

Aeroporto GB Pastine, Ciampino

Via Appia Nuova 1650 (06 794 941/ www.adr.it). **Open** 24hrs daily.

The most hassle-free way to get into town from Ciampino is to take the Terravision **coach service** (06 7949 4572, 06 7949 4621, www.terravision.it) to Termini station (journey time: 40mins). Buses leave from outside the arrivals hall after each arrival. Buses from Termini to Ciampino leave from via Marsala 7, opposite the multi-storey car park. This is a dedicated service for the low-cost airlines, so you will need to show your ticket or boarding pass. Bus tickets (€8 single, €14 return, €4/€7 5-12s) can be booked online, or bought (cash only) in the arrivals hall at Ciampino or at the Terravision office in the Termini forecourt (next to Benetton) or on the bus.

A rival company, Bus Shuttle (06 591 7844, www.sitbusshuttle.it), has recently begun a frequent service from Termini (via Marsala) to Ciampino (€6, 4.30am-11.15pm), and Ciampino to Termini (€5, 8.30am-12.30am). Tickets can be purchased on the bus or online.

Alternatively, Schiaffini **buses** (800 700 805, www.schiaffini.it) runs a service between Ciampino and Anagnina metro station every 30-40mins between 6am and 10.40pm daily and to Ciampino station (where frequent trains depart for Termini) between 5.45am and 11.25pm daily; both cost €1. They also run a direct

service from the airport to Termini station at 12.15am and 12.45am and from Termini to Ciampino at 4.45am, which costs €5. Buy tickets on board the bus, which leaves from in front of the arrivals hall; at Termini, it departs from via Giolitti, by the station's side entrance.

After the last bus has departed, getting into the city is well-nigh impossible, as taxis don't bother to pass by. If you are arriving late, phone ahead and organise a taxi before your arrival (*see p323* and *p321* **Taxi troubles**).

Airlines

Alitalia *Via L Bissolati 11, Veneto & Borghese (06 22 22/06 65 631/ domestic flights 06 65 641/ international flights 06 65 642/ www.alitalia.it). Metro Barberini/bus 61, 62, 175, 492, 590, 45N, 60N.* **Open** 9am-6pm Mon-Fri. **Credit** AmEx, DC, MC, V. **Map** p357 C4. The Fiumicino airport office is open 24hrs daily.
British Airways *(reservations 199 712 266/www.ba.com).* **Open** 9am-6pm Mon-Fri; 9am-5pm Sat. **Credit** AmEx, DC, MC, V.

By bus

There is no central long-distance bus station in Rome. Most coach services terminate outside these metro stations: Lepanto, Ponte Mammolo and Tiburtina (routes north); Anagnina and EUR Fermi (routes south). For further information, *see p300*.

By train

Mainline trains are operated by Ferrovie dello Stato (FS)/ Trenitalia (www.trenitalia.it). Most long-distance trains arrive at Termini station, also the hub of Rome's transport network – and pickpockets, so beware. Night trains arrive at Tiburtina or Ostiense, both some way from the *centro storico*. The metro, bus routes

492 and 649, and night bus 40N run from Tiburtina into the city centre; if you arrive after midnight, it's a good idea to take a taxi.

Some daytime trains bypass Termini, while others stop at more than one station in Rome:

Stazione Ostiense *Piazzale dei Partigiani, Testaccio. Metro Piramide/ bus 60Exp, 95, 175, 280, 719, 91N.* **Map** p143 C1.

Stazione Piazzale Flaminio (Roma Nord) *Piazzale Flaminio, Suburbs: north. Metro Flaminio/bus 88, 95, 204, 490, 491, 25N, 55N/ tram 2.* **Map** p354 D2.

Stazione Termini *Piazza dei Cinquecento, Esquilino (customer services 06 4730 6599). Metro Termini/bus 16, 36, 38, 40Exp, 64, 70, 75, 84, 86, 90Exp, 92, 105, 170, 175, 204, 217, 310, 360, 590, 649, 714, 910, C, H, 6N, 12N, 40N, 45N, 50N, 55N, 78N, 91N/tram 5, 14.* **Map** p357 E5.

Stazione Tiburtina *Circonvallazione Nomentana, Suburbs: south. Metro Tiburtina/bus 71, 111, 163, 168, 204, 211, 309, 409, 443, 448, 490, 491, 492, 495, 545, 649, C, 40N.* **Map** p353.

Stazione Trastevere *Piazzale Biondo. Bus 170, 228, 719, 766, 773, 774, 780, 781, 786, 871, H, 72N, 96N/tram 3, 8.* **Map** p353.

TRAINS AND TICKETS

For bookings and information on Italian rail services, phone the Trenitalia call centre (7am-9pm daily) on 892 021 – 199 166 177 from mobile

phones – or consult the useful official website (www.trenitalia.it).

Tickets can be bought at stations (over the counter or from machines; both accept credit cards), from travel agents with an FS sign, or online; ticketless travel is also available (*see below*). Under-12s pay half fare; under-4s travel free. For information on wheelchair access, *see p327*.

Train timetables can be purchased at any *edicola* (newsstand) or can be checked online. Slower trains (*diretti, espressi, regionali* and *interregionali*) are cheap; faster services – InterCity (IC), EuroCity (EC), Eurostar Italia (ES) – are closer to European norms. Advance reservation is obligatory and free on ES trains. Booking a seat on IC and internal EC routes costs €3, and is worth it to avoid standing in packed corridors at peak times. If your plans change, partial refunds are given (contact the Trenitalia call centre). If your IC or ES train is more than 25mins late and you have booked a seat, a voucher for up to 30% of the ticket price can be claimed back at booths marked *rimborsi*.

Queues at ticket desks at Termini can be soul-destroying; however, if you've already planned your journey, you can speed things up by using one of the many automatic ticket machines; most accept credit cards.

Trenitalia's **Ticketless** service allows you to book tickets with a credit card online (www.trenitalia.it) or by phone up to ten minutes before the train's departure time. Either way, you'll be provided with a carriage and seat number, and a booking code, which will be checked by the ticket inspectors on board. The service is

available on all ES and some IC trains. Seat reservation is obligatory for all passengers using this service.

Note: with paper tickets, you *must* stamp your ticket and supplements in the yellow machines at the head of the platform, before boarding. You risk being fined if you don't.

Public transport

For train and bus transport maps, *see pp366-368*.

Rome's transport system, run by public and private companies, is co-ordinated by **ATAC**. City-centre and inner-suburb destinations are served by the buses and trams of the Trambus transport authority. The system is relatively easy to use and as efficient as the traffic-choked streets allow. Pickpocketing is a problem on buses and metros, particularly major tourist routes, notably the 64 and 40 Express between Termini and the Vatican.

ATAC & MetRo

Via Ostiense 131L (06 46 951/toll-free 800 431 784). Metro Piramide/ bus 23, 271, 769. **Open** *Office* 9am-5pm Mon-Fri. **Map** p143 B3. ATAC's customer services office sells public transport maps. The phone line is Italian-speaking only; the toll-free information number operates 8am-8pm Mon-Sat.

Taxi troubles

Most of Rome's taxi drivers are friendly types, only too happy to squeeze out what English they know in order to share their city's secrets, and perfectly honest when it comes to charging. Unfortunately, most of the drivers who don't fit this description congregate at the airports: taxi-ing into Rome is often (though not always) an unpleasant, not to mention expensive, experience.

In 2006 city hall attempted to curb the greed of these rogues by imposing fixed tariffs between the city, and Fiumicino (€40) and Ciampino (€30) airports. Whatever your driver tells you, this is the all-inclusive fee: not the per-person fee or any variation that they might invent. Moreover, the common practice of piling two couples, say, or a single passenger and a group of three into

one car and then charging each party the whole official fare is totally against the rules.

That said, you might find it very difficult to get a *tassista* to accept you if you protest before getting into his vehicle. You may find it's better to be vague as you climb aboard, then make it clear you intend to pay only the official fee as you get close to your destination. If your driver protests, take down the number written on the metal plaque inside the back door, and the phone number of his cooperative, written on the outside of the taxi and report him to that cooperative. Asking for a receipt (*una ricevuta*) can have a positive effect, as can enlisting the help of a doorman or porter if you're staying at a medium- to high-class hotel.

See also p323 **Taxis**.

Directory

Buses to Termini

For convenience, we have indicated '**buses to Termini**' in the listings in this guide, as all of the following bus routes pass by (or terminate at) Termini rail station: 16, 36, 38, 40Exp, 64, 70, 75, 84, 86, 90Exp, 92, 105, 170, 175, 204, 217, 310, 360, 590, 649, 714, 910, C, H; and night buses 6N, 12N, 40N, 45N, 50N, 55N, 78N, 91N. (Trams 5 and 14 terminate at Termini as well).

Tickets

The same tickets are valid on all city bus, tram and metro lines, whether operated by Trambus, MetRo (for both, *see below*) or regional transport authority COTRAL (*see p300*). They are not valid on express services to Fiumicino airport (*see p320*). Tickets must be bought before boarding, and are available from ATAC ticket machines, information centres, some newsstands and bars and all *tabacchi* (*see p336*). Newer buses have ticket dispensers on board.

BIT (*biglietto integrato a tempo*) is valid for **75mins**, during which you can take an unlimited number of city buses, plus one metro trip; €1.
BIG (*biglietto integrato giornaliero*) is valid for **one day**, until midnight, and covers the urban network; €4.
BTI (*biglietto turistico integrato*) is a **three-day** pass, covering all bus and metro routes, and local mainline trains (second class) to Ostia; €11. (Before purchasing a BTI, consider whether the three-day **Roma Pass** might not be better value; *see p73*.)
BIRG (*biglietto integrato regionale giornaliero*) is valid for **one day** on rail journeys within the Lazio region. The price varies from €2.50 to €10.50, depending on the zones covered. It is valid on metro, buses and local mainline trains (second class), but not Fiumicino airport lines.
CIS (*carta integrata settimanale*) is valid for **seven days**; it covers all bus routes and the metro system, including the lines to Ostia; €16.
Abbonamento mensile Valid for unlimited travel on the entire metropolitan transport system during the **calendar month** in which the ticket was bought; €30 (€18 for under-20s and over-65s who should, theoretically, be Roman residents but it isn't very likely that inspectors would ask).

Note: when you board, you *must* stamp tickets in the machines on board.

Under-10s travel free; older kids have to pay the adult fare, as must pensioners. Discounts for students, the disabled and pensioners are only available for residents. Fare-dodging is common, but if caught without a validated ticket, you'll be fined €51 on the spot, or €101 if you pay later at a post office.

Metro

MetRo is responsible for Rome's two metro lines, which cross beneath Termini mainline train station. Line A runs from south-east to north-west; line B from EUR to the north-eastern suburbs. Line B is open 5.30am-11.30pm (until 12.30am Sat & Sun). Line A also opens at 5.30am but closes at 9pm daily for work on line C (due to have its first phase open in 2008). As long as work goes on, two Trambus shuttle bus services replace metro line A, operating every 2-7mins (9-11.30pm Mon-Fri, 9pm-12.30am Sat, Sun): **Metro-bus** A1 runs from Battistini at the north-western end of the line to Arco di Travertino in the southern suburbs; the A2 runs from Flaminio to Anagnina, the southern end of metro line A.

Buses

Trambus routes are added or suspended and numbers change with some regularity: pick up a copy of the latest city bus map from ATAC HQ (*see p321*) or buy the regularly updated *Roma Metro-Bus* map (€6 from news kiosks). The ATAC website, www.atac.roma.it, has a useful journey planner and maps to download.

Regular Trambus services run 5.30am-midnight daily, every 10-45mins, depending on the route. The doors for boarding (usually front and rear) and alighting (usually centre) are clearly marked. A sign at each bus stop displays the lines and routes they take.

Note that the 'Express' buses make few stops along their route: check before boarding so you don't get whisked past your destination. A small fleet of electric mini-buses also serves the centre, navigating *centro storico* alleys too narrow to accommodate regular buses. The 116, 116T, 117 and 119 connect places such as piazza di Spagna, campo de' Fiori and piazza Venezia with via Veneto and Termini.

Trams

Tram routes mainly serve suburban areas. An express tram service – No.8 – links largo Argentina to Trastevere and the western suburbs.

Suburban transport

For transport map, *see p368*.

MetRo (*see p322*) operates three suburban railway lines – from Termini, Porta San Paolo and Roma Nord stations – that are integrated with local lines of the **Ferrovie dello Stato** (FS; state railway). Regular bus, tram and metro tickets are valid on trains as far as the stations in red on the map. **COTRAL** coaches cover more distant destinations.

For more information on travel to destinations in the vicinity of Rome, *see p300*. For tickets, stations and general information about rail travel, *see p320*.

Tour buses

Trambus's city-tour bus, the **110** (06 4695 2252, www.trambusopen.com), leaves Termini station every 10mins (8.30am-8.30pm). It makes 11 stops on a two-hour circuit, including the Colosseum, Circus Maximus, piazza Venezia, St Peter's, and the Trevi Fountain. Tours include commentary (in six languages). An all-day stop-and-go ticket costs €13. Buy tickets on board, online or at the booth in front of Termini train station.

The **Roma Cristiana** service departs from Termini and St Peter's every 30mins (8.30am-7.30pm daily), and takes in all the major basilicas and pilgrim sites. Tickets can be purchased on board, and at Termini station, San Giovanni in Laterano or at piazza Pio near St Peter's. A 24hr stop-and-go ticket costs €13.

The **Archeobus** passes by the Baths of Caracalla and along via Appia Antica (the Appian Way; see p171) to the Catacombs, the tomb of Cecilia Metella, the Villa dei Quintili and the Parco degli Acquedotti, leaving Termini station about every 40mins (9am-4pm daily). Stop-and-go tickets cost €8; without stops, the trip takes about two and a half hours.

A ticket that combines the 110 and Archeobus tours costs €20 and is valid for two days. Tickets that combine the tours with museum entrance are also available, including those listed below. Tickets for these can be purchased at the booth in front of Termini station, on board or online (www.trambusopen.com).

110 Open + Polo Museale

Bus ticket valid one day; museum ticket valid five days, giving you free entry to any two of these five museums: Museo Nazionale di Palazzo Venezia, Galleria Spada, Castel Sant'Angelo, Galleria Nazionale di Arte Antica and Palazzo Barberini; €20.

110 Open + Polo Museale + Archeobus

Bus ticket valid two days that combines both routes; museum ticket valid five days, includes free admission to any two of the five museums listed above; €25.

Taxis

See also p321 **Taxi troubles**. Licensed taxis are painted white and have a meter. Touts are rife at Termini and other major tourist magnets; ignore them if you don't want to risk an extortionate fare.

FARES & SURCHARGES

When you pick up a taxi at a rank or hail one in the street, the meter should read zero. As you set off, it will indicate the minimum fare – currently €2.33 (€3.36 on Sundays and public holidays) or €4.91 if you board 10pm-7am. After the first 200m (700ft), the charge goes up according to time, distance and route. There's a €1.04 charge for each item of luggage placed in the boot. Tariffs outside the GRA, Rome's major ring road, are much higher, but the city council and taxi unions have agreed to fixed airport tariffs (€40 to/from Fiumicino; €30 to/from Ciampino); check with the driver first (*see also p321* **Taxi troubles**).

Most of Rome's taxi drivers are honest; if you do suspect you're being fleeced, take down the driver's name and number from the metal plaque inside the car's rear door. The more ostentatiously you do this, the more likely you are to find the fare returning to its proper level. Report complaints to the drivers' co-operative (phone number on the outside of each car) or, in serious cases, the police (*see p333*).

TAXI RANKS

Ranks are indicated by a blue sign with 'Taxi' written on it in white. In the centre, there are ranks at largo Argentina, the Pantheon, piazza Venezia, piazza San Silvestro, piazza Sonnino (Trastevere), piazza di Spagna and Termini station.

River boats

Battelli di Roma operates river-boat tours along the Tiber, with stops en route. A one-hour trip down the river without commentary costs €1 during the week, €3 at weekends (cash only; buy tickets on board). From Wednesday to Sunday boats leave roughly every hour between 10am and 6pm (there's a reduced service on Mondays and Tuesdays; check website for details) from the Calata Anguillara jetty on the Trastevere bank (by the Tiber Island), and stop at Ponte Duca d'Aosta; you can also travel in the opposite direction.

Guided boat tours (€12; 1hr 10mins) depart from Ponte Sant'Angelo at 11am, 12.30pm, 4pm and 5.30pm; tours with dinner included (€53; 2hr 15mins) leave from the same jetty at 9pm. You can pay at the jetty or buy online. Advance booking is advisable for guided tours; passengers should be at the jetty 15mins before departure.

Battelli di Roma

Info & bookings 06 678 9361/www. battellidiroma.it. **Credit** AmEx, DC, MC, V.

Directory

Phone cabs

When you phone for a taxi, you'll be given the taxi code-name (always a location followed by a number) and a time, as in *Bahama 69, in tre minuti* ('Bahamas 69, in three minutes'). Radio taxis start the meter from the moment your phone call is answered.

Cooperativa Samarcanda
06 5551/www.samarcanda.it.
Credit AmEx, DC, MC, V.
Cosmos Radio Taxi *06 88 177/ 06 8822.* **Credit** AmEx, DC, MC, V.
Società Cooperativa Autoradio Taxi Roma *06 3570/www.3570.it.*
Credit AmEx, DC, MC, V.
Società la Capitale Radio Taxi
06 49 94. **Credit** AmEx, DC.

Driving

If you plan to drive a car here, brace yourself for Roman driving. To the uninitiated it may seem like every-man-for-himself chaos, but it's really a high-speed conversation, with its own language of glances, light-flashing and ostentatious acceleration.

Short-term visitors should have no trouble driving with their home licence, although if they are in less common languages an international licence can be useful. All EU citizens are obliged to take out an Italian driving licence after being resident for one year.

Remember:

● You are required by law to wear a seat belt at all times, both in the front seats and back seats, and to carry a warning triangle and reflective jacket in your car.
● Outside urban areas, you must drive with headlights on at all times.
● You must keep your driving licence, vehicle registration and personal ID on you at all times.
● Do not leave anything of value in your car. Take all luggage into your hotel when you park.
● Flashing your lights in Italy means that you will not slow down (contrary to British practice).
● Traffic lights flashing amber mean stop and give way to the right.
● Beware death-defying mopeds and pedestrians. Pedestrians assume they have the right of way in the older, quieter streets without clearly designated pavements.

RESTRICTED AREAS

Large sections of the city centre (marked ZTL – *zona a traffico limitato*) are closed to non-resident traffic during business hours, and sometimes in the evening. Municipal police and video cameras guard these areas; any vehicle without the required pass will be fined €68.25 if it enters at restricted times. A strictly enforced no-car policy applies in the city centre on the first Sunday of most months.

If you need to reach accommodation in a restricted area, make arrangements with your hotel before arrival.

PETROL

Petrol stations sell unleaded petrol (*senza piombo* or *verde*) and diesel (*gasolio*). Liquid propane gas is *GPL*. Most stations offer full service on weekdays; pump attendants don't expect tips. At night and on Sundays many stations have self-service pumps that accept €5, €10, €20 and €50 notes, in good condition. Unofficial 'assistants' may offer to do the job for you for a small tip (€1).

Breakdown services

Before taking a car to Italy it's advisable to join a national motoring organisation, like the AA or RAC in Britain or the AAA in the US. They have reciprocal arrangements with the Automobile Club d'Italia (ACI), offering breakdown assistance and giving general information. Even for non-members, ACI is the best number to call if you have any kind of breakdown.

If you require extensive repairs, pay a bit more and go to a manufacturer's official dealer: the reliability of any garage depends on having built up a good client-mechanic relationship. Dealers are listed in the Yellow Pages under *auto*, along with specialist

repairers such as *gommista* (tyres), *marmitte* (exhausts) and *carrozzerie* (bodywork). The *English Yellow Pages*, available from most English bookshops (*see p233*), has a list of garages where English is spoken.

Automobile Club d'Italia (ACI)

06 49 981/24hr traffic report, information & emergency line (in Italian) 803 116/www.aci.it.
The ACI has English-speaking staff and provides services for all foreign drivers, either free or at low prices. Members of associated organisations are entitled to basic repairs free, and to other services at lower rates. Non-members will be charged, but prices are reasonable.

Touring Club Italiano (TCI)

Via del Babuino 20, Tridente (06 3600 5281/www.touringclub.it).
Metro Spagna/bus 117, 119. **Open** *Office & bookshop* 9.30am-7.30pm Mon-Sat. **Map** p354 E3.
The Rome office has a good bookshop with an English-language section and a travel agency. English is spoken and there's a 20% discount on books for all members, including those from European sister clubs.

Parking

A system in which residents park for free and visitors pay is in place in many areas of the city. It's efficiently policed, so watch out for the telltale blue lines. Buy parking tickets (€1 per hour) at pay-and-display ticket dispensers or from *tabacchi*. In some areas you can park for free after a certain time (usually 11pm) or on Sundays, so check the instructions on the machine.

Your vehicle may be clamped if it's improperly or illegally parked: you will have to pay a fine, plus a charge to have the clamp removed. If your car is in a dangerous position or blocking trams and buses, it will be towed away (*see p325* **Car pounds**).

In zones with no blue lines, anything resembling a parking place is up for grabs, but with some exceptions: watch out for signs saying *Passo carrabile* ('access at all times') or *Sosta vietata* ('no parking'), and disabled parking spaces (marked by yellow stripes on the road). The sign *Zona rimozione* ('tow-away area') means no parking, and is valid for the length of the street or until the sign is repeated with a red line through it. If a street or square has no cars parked in it, assume it's a strictly enforced no-parking zone. In some areas, self-appointed *parcheggiatori* will 'look after' your car for a small fee; it may be illegal and an absurd imposition, but it's probably worth paying up to ensure your tyres remain intact.

Cars are fairly safe in most central areas, but you may prefer the hefty rates charged by underground car parks to keep your vehicle off the street. Centrally located include:

ParkSi Villa Borghese

Viale del Galoppatoio 33, Veneto & Borghese (06 322 5934/7972/ www.sabait.it). Metro Spagna/bus 88, 95, 116, 204, 490, 491, 495. **Open** 24hrs daily. **Rates** *Cars* €1.30/hr for up to 3hrs; €1/hr for 4-15hrs; €16 for 16-24hrs. *Scooters & motorbikes* 80¢/hr; €3 for 24hrs. **Credit** AmEx, DC, MC, V. **Map** p356 A3.
Vehicle entrances are on via del Muro Torto (from both sides of the road). The car park is linked to the Spagna metro station, with 24hr pedestrian access to piazza di Spagna.

Valentino

Via Sistina 75E, Veneto & Borghese (06 678 2597). Metro Spagna/bus 590. **Open** 7am-1am Mon-Sat; 7am-12.30pm, 6pm-1am Sun. **Rates** €3/hr for up to six hours; €30-€33 for 24hrs. **Credit** AmEx, MC, V. **Map** p357 B5.

CAR POUNDS

If your car is not where you left it, it may have been towed. Phone the municipal police (*Vigili urbani*) on 06 67 691 and quote your number plate to find out which pound it's in.

Car hire

To hire a car you must be over 21 – in some cases 23 – and have held a licence for at least

a year. You will be required to leave a credit card number or substantial cash deposit. It's advisable to take out collision damage waiver (CDW) and personal accident insurance (PAI) on top of basic third-party cover. Companies not offering CDW are best avoided.

Avis

Via Sardegna 38A, Veneto & Borghese (06 4282 4728/www. avisautonoleggio.it). Metro Spagna/ bus 52, 53, 95, 116, 116T, 119, 204. **Open** 8am-8pm Mon-Fri; 8am-5pm Sat; 8am-1pm Sun. **Credit** AmEx, DC, MC, V. **Map** p356 C3.
Fiumicino airport (06 6595 4146/ 06 6501 1531). **Open** 7am-midnight daily.
Ciampino airport (06 7934 0195). **Open** 8am-1.30pm, 2-10pm Mon-Fri; 8.15am-2.45pm, 4.30-10pm Sat, Sun.
Termini station, Esquilino (06 481 4373). Metro Termini/buses to Termini/tram 5, 14. **Open** 7am-8pm Mon-Sat; 8am-6pm Sat; 8am-1pm Sun. **Map** p357 E5.

Maggiore

Fiumicino airport (06 6501 0678/ toll-free 848 867 067/www. maggiore.it). **Open** 7am-midnight daily. **Credit** AmEx, DC, MC, V.
Ciampino airport (06 7934 0368). **Open** 8am-10pm Mon-Fri; 8am-noon, 5.30-9pm Sat, Sun.
Termini station, Esquilino (06 488 0049). Metro Termini/buses to Termini/tram 5, 14. **Open** 7am-8pm Mon-Fri; 8am-6pm Sat; 8am-1pm Sun.

Cycles, scooters & mopeds for hire

To hire a **scooter or moped** (*motorino*) you need a driving licence, photo ID, credit card and/or a cash deposit. Helmets are required on all motorbikes, scooters or mopeds (the police are very strict about this). You must be at least 14 to drive a 50cc bike, though recent changes to Italian law mean that 14-18 year olds need to have passed a test and obtained a pre-driving licence to use a *motorino*. A full driver's licence is required for anything over 50cc. For hiring bicycles, you can usually leave ID rather than pay a deposit.

Apart from the companies listed below, there are useful pay-and-ride bike-hire stands outside Spagna metro, in piazza del Popolo, by the car park under Villa Borghese, at a tiny bar in piazza di Ponte Milvio (it's at the start of a cycle path that takes you out of central Rome along the banks of the Tiber), in piazza San Lorenzo in Lucina and in via San Leo.

Bici & Baci

Via del Viminale 5, Monti (06 482 8443/www.bicibaci.com). Metro Repubblica/bus 40Exp, 60Exp, 64, 70, 84, 86, 90Exp, 170, 175, 492, 910, H. **Open** 8am-7pm daily. **Rates** (per day) €9 bicycles; €32 mopeds (50cc); from €50 scooters (125cc). **Credit** MC, V. **Map** p357 C6.
This friendly outlet also offers hourly and weekly rates.

Romarent

Vicolo dei Bovari 7A, Ghetto & Campo (phone/fax 06 689 6555). Bus 46, 62, 64, 116, 116T, 916. **Open** 9.30am-7pm daily. **Rates** (per day) €12 bicycles; €40 mopeds (50cc); €50-€70 scooters (125cc); €80 scooters (250cc). **Credit** AmEx, MC, V. **Map** p358 C1.

Scoot a Long

Via Cavour 302, Monti (06 678 0206). Metro Cavour/bus 75, 84, 117. **Open** 9.30am-7.30pm daily. **Rates** (24hrs) from €35 mopeds; €45 scooters (125cc); €80 motorbikes. **Credit** AmEx, MC, V. **Map** p360 B2.
A credit card or deposit of €350 (125cc)/€200 (50cc) required. This company offers student discounts.

Scooters for Rent

Via della Purificazione 84, Veneto & Borghese (06 488 5485/www.travel.it/ roma/scooters). Metro Barberini/bus 52, 53, 61, 62, 63, 80Exp, 95, 116, 119, 175, 492, 590, 630. **Open** May-Sept 9am-7pm daily. *Oct-Apr* 9am-6pm daily. **Rates** (per day) €30 mopeds; €50-€60 scooters (125cc); €80-€100 scooters (250cc) **Credit** AmEx, DC, MC, V. **Map** p357 B5.
Weekly rates are available. A deposit of €155 or credit card is required.

Treno e Scooter Rent

Piazza dei Cinquecento, Esquilino (06 4890 5823/www.trenoescooter. 191.it). Metro Termini/buses to Termini/tram 5, 14. **Open** 9am-2pm, 4-7pm daily. **Rates** €5/hr bikes; scooters (50cc) €8/hr, €35/day (9.30am-7.30pm), €37/24hrs. **Credit** AmEx, DC, MC, V. **Map** p357 E5.
Piaggio sponsors this outlet, located on the Termini station forecourt. Prices drop for weekly rentals.

Directory

Resources A-Z

Age restrictions

Cigarettes and alcohol cannot be sold to under-16s (for hard liquor or alcopops you must be 18). Over-14s can ride a moped or scooter of 50cc, but 14-18s are required to pass a practical test and obtain a pre-licence first (*see also p324* **Driving**). The age of heterosexual and homosexual consent is 14, rising to 16 if one partner is in a position of responsibility.

Business

If you are doing business in Rome, visit your embassy's (*see p328*) commercial section. You'll find trade publications and databases of fairs, buyers, sellers and distributors. Use any personal recommendations you have shamelessly: in Italy these will always smooth your way immensely.

Business centres

Finding temporary office space can be difficult. Try these for basic facilities, and conference and secretarial services:
Centro Uffici Parioli *Via Lima 41, Suburbs: north (06 844 981/fax 06 8449 8332/www.centrouficiparioli.it). Bus 53, 168, 360/tram 3, 19.*
Pick Center *Via Attilio Regolo 19, Prati (06 328 031/fax 06 3280 3227/www.pickcenter.com). Metro Lepanto/bus 81.* **Map** p354 B3.

Conferences

Rome offers superb facilities for conferences in magnificent *palazzi* and castles. Most major hotels cater for events of all sizes. A number of agencies can help handle the details.
Studio Ega *Viale Tiziano 19, Suburbs: north (06 328 121/ fax 06 322 2006/www.ega.it). Bus 52, 204, 910/tram 2.*
Tecnoconference Europe *Via A Luzio 66, Suburbs: east (06 7835 9617/fax 06 7835 9385/ www.tecnoconference-europe.com). Bus 87.*

Triumph Congressi *Via Lucilio 60, Suburbs: north (06 355 301/fax 06 3534 0213/www.gruppotriumph.it). Bus 990.*

Couriers

International couriers include:
DHL *06 790 821/199 199 345/ www.dhl.it*
Federal Express *toll-free 800 123 800/www.fedex.com*
TNT *toll-free 803 868/from mobile phones 199 803 868/fax 049 769 855/www.tntitaly.it*
UPS – United Parcel Service *toll-free 800 877 877/www.ups.com*

For local deliveries, try:
Easy Rider *06 5823 7506/ www.easyrider2.it*
Speedy Boys *06 39 888/ www.speedyboys.it*

Interpreters & translators

CRIC
Viale Aventino 102, Aventine (06 574 5323/fax 06 5728 9426/ www.cric-interpreti.com). Metro Circo Massimo/bus 3, 60Exp, 75, 118, 271, 673/tram 3. **Map** p361 A5.

Rome At Your Service
Via VE Orlando 75, Esquilino (06 484 583/06 482 5589/fax 06 484 429/www.romeatyourservice.it). Metro Repubblica/bus 36, 60Exp, 61, 62, 84, 175, 492, 590, 910. **Map** p357 C5.

Customs

Travellers arriving from EU countries are not required to declare goods imported into or exported from Italy if they are for personal use, up to the following limits:
● 800 cigarettes or 400 cigarillos or 200 cigars or 1kg of tobacco;
● Ten litres of spirits (over 22% alcohol) or 20 litres of fortified wine (under 22% alcohol).

For people arriving from non-EU countries, the following limits apply:
● 200 cigarettes or 100 cigarillos or 50 cigars or 250 grams of tobacco;
● One litre of spirits or two litres of wine;
● One bottle of perfume (50 grams), 250 millilitres of eau de toilette;

● Merchandise not exceeding €175. Anything above that will be subject to taxation at the port of entry.

There are no restrictions on the importation of cameras, watches or electrical goods. For further information call Italian customs (*dogana*) on 041 269 9311 or visit www.agenziadogane.it.

Disabled travellers

Rome isn't the easiest city for disabled people, especially wheelchair-users. You'll almost certainly have to depend on other people more than you would at home. Narrow streets make life awkward for those who can't flatten themselves against a wall to let vehicles by. Cobblestones turn wheelchairs with excellent suspension into bone-rattlers and getting on to pavements is well-nigh impossible due to bumper-to-bumper parked cars. Off the streets, old buildings tend to have narrow corridors and the lifts (if any), are usually much too small.

Blind and partially sighted people often find there's no kerb between the road proper and the bit of street pedestrians are entitled to walk on (the one exception is a smooth brick walkway laid into the cobbles leading from the Trevi Fountain to piazza Navona, with Braille notes about landmarks on bronze plaques along the way).

Wheelchair-accessible public toilets are found in many central areas... which is no guarantee they'll be in working order or open.

Information

Information for disabled people is available from Enjoy Rome, the APT tourist office (for both, *see p337*) and the following organisations:

CO.IN
*Via E Giglioli 54A, Suburbs: east
(06 5717 7001/www.coinsociale.it).*
Open 9am-6pm Mon-Fri.
Contact CO.IN for information
on disabled facilities at museums,
restaurants, shops, theatres, stations
and hotels. The group also organises
transport for disabled people (up to
eight places), which must be booked
several days in advance but can
cover airport journeys as well as
travel within Rome. Its phone service,
in Italian and English, offers up-to-
date information (toll-free 800 271
027; operates 9am-5pm Mon-Fri,
9am-1pm Sat, only from within Italy).

Roma per Tutti
06 5717 7094/www.romapertutti.it.
Open 9am-5pm Mon-Fri.
An information line run by CO.IN
(*see above*) and the city council.
English-speaking staff answer
questions on accessibility in hotels,
buildings and monuments.

Sol.Co.Roma
*Piazza Vittorio Emanuele 31,
Esquilino (06 490 821/fax 06 491
623/www.solcoroma.net). Metro
Vittorio/bus 71, 105, 360, 590,
649/tram 5, 14.* **Open** 9am-6pm
Mon-Fri. **Map** p360 A1.
Sol.Co's free *Cammina Cammina*
guide was published in December
2002. With info and itineraries in
Italian and English, plus simple
symbols, it's easy to follow.

Sightseeing
Well-designed ramps, lifts
and toilets have been installed
in many attractions; CO.IN's
Roma per Tutti (*see above*)
has up-to-date information.

Museum
06 513 9855/www.assmuseum.it
This volunteer group offers tours
of some galleries and catacombs for
individuals or groups with mobility
or, especially, sight problems. Their
museum guides – some speak
English; if not, an interpreter can be
arranged – have Braille notes, copies
of paintings in relief, and permission
to touch artefacts. Guides also make
works of art comprehensible to the
non-sighted with music cassettes and
recorded text. A voluntary donation
to cover costs is requested.

Transport
Rome's buses and trams are
being made more accessible:
about half of the current fleet
can accommodate wheelchairs.

On the metro, most of the
central stations on line A are
no-go areas. All stations on
line B have lifts, disabled WCs
and special parking spaces,
except for Circo Massimo,
Colosseo and (southbound)
Cavour. Check MetRo's website
(www.metroroma.it) for
wheelchair-accessible stations.

Most taxi drivers will carry
(folded) wheelchairs; when you
can, phone for a cab rather
than hailing one (*see p323*).

To ascertain which trains
have wheelchair facilities, call
(or visit) the *ufficio disabili*
(office for the disabled) at your
departure station (Termini's is
in the main concourse, 06 488
1726, open 7.30am-8.30pm
Mon-Fri) or consult the official
timetable: there's a wheelchair
symbol next to accessible
trains. You must phone or fax
the relevant *ufficio disabili*
24hrs prior to departure and,
before boarding the train, fill in
a form requesting assistance.
Reserve a seat when buying
your ticket, and make sure you
arrive at least 45mins early.

This also applies to trains
to and from Fiumicino airport;
in theory, you must call or
fax your airline to arrange
assistance the day before
arrival; in practice, you'll be
helped on the train anyway.

Both Rome's airports have
adapted toilets and waiting

rooms. Inform your airline
of your needs so that it can
contact the office at Fiumicino
or Ciampino airport.

Wheelchair hire

Ortopedia Colosseo
*Via Capo d'Africa 24B, Celio &
San Giovanni (06 700 5709). Bus
85, 117, 850.* **Open** 8.30am-1pm,
3.30-7pm Mon-Fri; 8.30am-1pm Sat.
No credit cards. Map p360 C3.
Rents all kinds of wheelchairs (from
€3 per day). These can be delivered
by taxi: you pay the fare unless you
are in one of the larger hotels with
which the shop has an agreement.
Other locations: via Carlo Felice
91-3 (06 7720 9393). **Credit** MC, V.

Where to stay & eat
There may be a greater
number of accessible hotels –
CO.IN (*see above*) has details –
but cheaper hotels and *pensioni*,
often housed on upper floors
of *palazzi*, can be a problem. If
you have special needs, make
them known when you book.

Local by-laws require
restaurants to have disabled
access and toilets; in practice,
few have made the necessary
alterations. If you phone ahead
and ask for an appropriate
table, most will try to help. In
summer the range of outdoor
restaurants makes things
easier, but getting to toilets can
be almost impossible.

Travel advice

For current information on travel to a specific country –
including the latest news on health issues, safety and
security, local laws and customs – contact your home
country's government department of foreign affairs. Most
have websites with useful advice for would-be travellers.

Australia
www.smartraveller.gov.au

Canada
www.voyage.gc.ca

New Zealand
www.safetravel.govt.nz

Republic of Ireland
http://foreignaffairs.gov.ie

UK
www.fco.gov.uk/travel

USA
http://travel.state.gov

Directory

Most bars open on to the street at ground level, and/or have tables outside. Again, most bar toilets are tiny dark holes down long staircases.

Drugs

As this guide went to press, Italy's drug laws were once again under review. The law currently states that it is an offence to buy, sell or even give away drugs. Anyone caught in possession of narcotics of any kind must be taken before a magistrate. The severity of the punishment depends upon the quantity of drugs, and whether they are deemed *leggera* (light) or *pesante* (heavy). For a small amount, you will probably be let off with a fine or ordered to leave the country. Habitual offenders will be offered rehab. Holders of Italian driving licences may have them temporarily suspended.

Sniffer dogs are a fixture at most ports of entry into Italy; customs police are likely to allow visitors entering with even negligible quantities of narcotics to stay no longer than it takes a magistrate to expel them from the country.

Electricity

Most wiring systems work on 220V – compatible with UK-bought appliances (with a plug adaptor); US 110V equipment requires a current transformer. Adaptors can be bought at any electrical or hardware shop (*elettricità* or *ferramenta*).

Embassies & consulates

For a full list of embassies, see *Ambasciate* in the phone book.

Except where indicated, consular offices (which provide the majority of services of use to tourists) share the same address as these embassies.

Australia *Via Antonio Bosio 5, Suburbs: north (06 852 721/www.italy.embassy.gov.au). Bus 36, 60Exp, 62, 84, 90Exp.*
Britain *Via XX Settembre 80A, Esquilino (06 4220 0001/fax 06 4220 2334/www.britain.it). Bus 36, 60Exp, 61, 62, 84, 90Exp, 490, 491.* **Map** p357 E4.
Canada Embassy: *via Salaria 243, Suburbs: north (06 854 441/06 8544 43937/www.canada.it). Bus 53, 63, 86, 92, 168, 630/tram 3, 19.* Consulate: *via Zara 30, Suburbs: north. Bus 36, 60Exp, 62, 84, 90Exp.*
Ireland *Piazza Campitelli 3, Ghetto (06 697 9121/www.ambasciata-irlanda.it). Bus 30Exp, 44, 63, 81, 95, 160, 170, 628, 630, 715, 716, 780, 781, H.* **Map** p358 E2.
New Zealand *Via Zara 28, Suburbs: north (06 441 7171/www.nzembassy.com). Bus 36, 60Exp, 62, 84, 90Exp.*
South Africa *Via Tanaro 14, Suburbs: north (06 852 541/www.sudafrica.it). Tram 3, 19.* **Map** p356 E1.
US *Via Vittorio Veneto 119, Veneto & Borghese (06 46 741/www.usembassy.it). Metro Barberini/bus 52, 53, 61, 62, 63, 80Exp, 95, 116, 116T, 119, 175, 204, 590, 630.* **Map** p357 C4.

Emergencies

See also below **Health & hospitals**; *p335* **Safety & security**; *p333* **Police**; *p332* **Money**.

Thefts or losses should be reported immediately at the nearest police station. Report the loss of travellers' cheques and/or credit cards immediately to your credit card company (*see p332*), and of passports to your consulate/embassy (*see above*).

National emergency numbers
Police *Carabinieri* (English-speaking helpline) 112; *Polizia di Stato* 113
Fire service *Vigili del fuoco* 115
Ambulance *Ambulanza* 118
Car breakdown *See p324.*

Domestic emergencies
Report a malfunction in any of the main services to these 24hr emergency lines.
Electricity *ACEA 06 57 991/ toll-free 800 130 330 (8am-7pm)/ toll-free 800 130 332*
Gas *Italgas 06 57 391/toll-free 800 900 999/toll-free 800 900 700*
Telephone *Telecom Italia 187*
Water *ACEA toll-free 800 130 335*

Health & hospitals

Emergency health care is available through the Italian national health system; hospital accident and emergency departments (*see below*) treat all emergency cases for free. If you are an EU citizen, the EHIC (European Health Insurance Card; *see p330*) entitles you to free consultation with any doctor. Non-EU citizens are advised to obtain private health insurance (*see p330*).

Accident & emergency

If you need urgent medical care, go to the *pronto soccorso* (casualty department). All the hospitals listed here offer 24hr casualty services. If your child needs emergency treatment, head straight for the excellent Ospedale Bambino Gesù.
Ospedale Fatebenefratelli *Isola Tiberina, Ghetto (06 68 371). Bus 23, 63, 271, 280, 630, 780, H/ tram 8.* **Map** p358 D2.
Ospedale Pediatrico Bambino Gesù *Piazza Sant'Onofrio 4, Gianicolo (06 68 591/www.opbg.net). Bus 23, 115, 116, 280, 870.* **Map** p355 A6.
Ospedale San Camillo-Forlanini *Via Portuense 332, Suburbs: west (06 55 551/06 58 701/www.scamilloforlanini.rm.it). Bus 228, 710, 719, 773, 774, 786, 791, H/tram 8.*
Ospedale San Giacomo *Via Canova 29, Tridente (06 36 261/ www.aslromaa.it/ospedali/osg.htm). Metro Spagna/bus 117, 119, 590.* **Map** p354 D/E3.
Ospedale San Giovanni *Via Amba Aradam 8, San Giovanni (06 7705 3444/www.hsangiovanni. roma.it). Metro San Giovanni/bus 81, 117, 650, 673, 714.* **Map** p360 E3.
Policlinico Umberto I *Viale Policlinico 155, Suburbs: north (06 49 971/www.policlinicoumberto1.it). Metro Policlinico/bus 61, 310, 490, 491, 495, 649/tram 3, 19.*

Contraception & abortion

Condoms (*preservativi*) are relatively inexpensive and on sale near checkouts in supermarkets or over the

Directory

counter in pharmacies; the pill is available on prescription. Abortion, available on financial hardship or health grounds, is legal only when performed in public hospitals.

Despite funding cuts and pressure from the former right-wing Lazio regional government, most districts maintain a local health authority *consultorio familiare* (family planning clinic). EU citizens with an EHIC (*see p330*) form pay the same low charges as locals. Phone first to make an appointment. The most centrally located is:

Piazza Castellani 23, Trastevere (06 7730 6006). Bus 23, 280. **Open** 9am-noon, 3-5pm Mon, Wed; 9am-noon Tue, Thur, Fri. **Map** p358 D3.

These private gynaecological clinics are also recommended:

AIED
Via Toscana 30, Veneto & Borghese (06 4282 5314). Metro Barberini/ bus 52, 53, 63, 80Exp, 95, 630. **Open** 9am-7pm Mon-Fri; 9am-1pm Sat. **Credit** MC, V. **Map** p356 C3.
Offers check-ups, contraceptive advice, menopause counselling and smear tests. You buy a membership card (*tessera*) for €5, then check-ups cost €39.50. Smear tests are €15.50.

Artemide
Via Sannio 61, San Giovanni (06 7047 6220). Metro San Giovanni/ bus 87, 360. **Open** 10am-7pm Mon-Fri; 10am-1pm Sat. **No credit cards**. **Map** p361 E4.
Gynaecological check-ups here are €70, smear tests are €25, and there's a wide range of other services. Appointments should be made a few days in advance, but emergencies are invariably dealt with immediately.

Dentists

For serious dental emergencies, head to a hospital casualty department (*see p328*).

Most dentists (see *Dentisti* in the Yellow Pages) in Italy work privately; treatment is not cheap and may not be covered by your health insurance, but you can wait months for a dental appointment in a national health service hospital (children are somewhat better

served at the out-patients department of the Ospedale Bambino Gesù; *see p328*).

Doctors

See also p335 **Relocation: Doctors**.
EU nationals with an EHIC (*see p330*) can consult a national health service doctor free of charge, and buy drugs at prices set by the Health Ministry. Tests and out-patient treatment are charged at fixed rates too. Non-EU nationals who consult a health service doctor will be charged a small fee at the doctor's discretion.

Helplines & agencies

Alcoholics Anonymous
06 474 2913/www.aarome.info
An English-speaking support group holds meetings at the church of St Paul's Within the Walls at via Napoli 56. Phone for meeting times.

Associazione Differenza Donna
Viale Villa Pamphili 100, Suburbs: west (06 581 0926). Bus 44, 710, 871.
A helpline for victims of sexual violence. The women-only volunteers (some English-speaking) can offer support and legal assistance.

Samaritans
Toll-free 800 860 022. **Open** 24hrs daily.
Staffed by native English speakers.

Telefono Azzurro
19 696. **Open** 24hrs daily.
A toll-free helpline for children and young people suffering abuse (normally Italian-speaking only).

Telefono Rosa
06 3751 8261. **Open** 10am-1pm, 4-7pm Mon-Fri.
Offers counselling and legal advice for women who have been victims of sexual abuse or sexual harassment.

Hospitals

Rome's public hospitals (*see p328*) offer good-to-excellent treatment, though the quality of nursing may appear slack to anyone used to the standards at Anglo-Saxon hospitals.

Opticians

See p249.

Pharmacies

Farmacie (identified by a green cross) give informal medical advice, as well as making up prescriptions. Most also sell homeopathic and veterinary medicines, and all will check your height/weight/blood pressure on request. Make sure you know the generic as well as the brand name of your regular medicines: they may be sold under a different name here. The best-stocked pharmacy in the city is in the Vatican: it has a whole range of medicines not found elsewhere in Italy.

Normal pharmacy opening hours are 8.30am-1pm, 4-8pm Mon-Sat. Outside these hours, a duty rota system operates. A list by the door of any pharmacy (and in local papers) indicates the nearest ones open at any time. A surcharge of €3.87 per client (not per item) applies when only the special duty counter is open.

Farmacia della Stazione *Piazza dei Cinquecento 49-51, Esquilino (06 488 0019). Metro Termini/buses to Termini/tram 5, 14.* **Open** 24hrs daily. **Credit** AmEx, DC, MC, V. **Map** p357 E5.

Farmacia del Vaticano *Porta Sant'Anna entrance, Vatican (06 6988 3422). Metro Ottaviano/bus 23, 32, 49, 62, 81, 492, 590, 982, 990/tram 19.* **Open** 8.30am-6pm Mon-Fri; 8.30am-1pm Sat. **Credit** MC, V. **Map** p355 A4.

Piram *Via Nazionale 228, Esquilino (06 488 0754). Metro Repubblica/ bus 40Exp, 60Exp, 64, 70, 71, 170, H, 78N, 91N.* **Open** 24hrs daily. **Credit** DC, MC, V. **Map** p357 C5.

ID

You are required by law to carry photo ID with you at all times. You must produce it if stopped by traffic police (along with your driving licence, which you must carry when you're in charge of a motor vehicle) and when you check

Directory

into a hotel. Smaller hotels may try to hold on to your passport/ID card for the length of your stay; you are within your rights to ask for it back.

Insurance

See also p328 **Health & hospitals**; and *p333* **Police**. EU citizens are entitled to reciprocal medical care in Italy provided they leave their own country with an **EHIC** (European Health Insurance Card), which has replaced the old form E111. In the UK, you can apply for an EHIC online (www.ehic.org.uk) or by post using forms available at any post office. If used for anything but emergencies (which are treated free anyway in casualty departments; *see p328*), you'll need to deal with the intricacies of the Italian state health system. For short-term visits, it is advisable to take out private travel/health insurance. Non-EU citizens should take out private medical insurance before setting off.

Visitors should also take out adequate insurance against loss or theft. If you rent a car, motorcycle or moped, make sure you pay the extra for full insurance cover and, for a car, sign the collision damage waiver (CDW).

Internet & email

Most budget hotels will allow you to plug a modem into their phone system; more upmarket places should have built-in dataports. There are also ever more places offering internet access around Rome.

Much of central Rome, plus the major parks – *ville* Ada, Borghese, Pamphili, Torlonia – and the Auditorium-Parco della Musica zone, is covered by wireless hotspots sponsored by the city council. As soon as you open your browser, you'll be asked to log on; initially you'll need to register, giving

a mobile phone number when you do so. As this guide went to press, access was free. For further information, including a map of the hotspots, see www.romawireless.com.

A number of Italian ISPs offer free access, including Caltanet (www.caltanet.it), Libero (www.libero.it), Tiscali (www.tiscalinet.it), Kataweb (www.kataweb.com) and Telecom Italia (www.tin.it).

EasyEverything

Via Barberini 2, Trevi & Quirinale (www.easyeverything.com). Metro Barberini/bus 52, 53, 61, 62, 63, 80Exp, 95, 116, 119, 175, 204, 492, 590, 630. **Open** 8am-2am daily. **Rates** €1-€3/hr (depending on the number of computers in use; peak time is 4-7pm). **No credit cards. Map** p357 C5.
Three floors, 250 computer terminals (with webcam and scanner), digital photo, and printer services… as well as a coffee bar.

Left luggage

The left-luggage office by platform 24 in Termini station (06 4782 5543) is open 6am-midnight daily. A suitcase costs €3.80/hr (for up to 5hrs); 60¢/hr from the sixth to the 12th hour; thereafter, 20¢/hr. At Fiumicino airport, left luggage in Terminal C is open 6.30am-11.30pm daily. Each item costs €2 for 7hrs; thereafter €3.50 per day. Hotels will generally look after your luggage during the day, even after you've checked out.

Legal help

Legal advice should first be sought at your embassy or consulate (*see p328*).

Libraries

Rome's libraries are dogged by red tape, restricted hours and patchy organisation. All libraries listed are open to the public; other specialist libraries can be found under *Biblioteche* in the phone book. Always take some ID along; in

some cases, a letter from your college stating the purpose of your research will be required.

Archivio Centrale dello Stato (State Archives)

Piazzale Archivi 27, Suburbs: EUR (06 545 481/fax 06 541 3620/ www.archivi.beniculturali.it/acs). Metro EUR Fermi/bus 703, 707, 765, 767. **Open** 9am-7pm Mon-Fri; 9am-1pm Sat. Closed 1wk Aug.
The original documents, historical correspondence and many other items at this efficiently run archive have to be consulted *in situ* (but most can be photocopied). Arrive before noon to order the ones you want.

Biblioteca Alessandrina

Piazzale Aldo Moro 5, Esquilino (06 447 4021/www.alessandrina.librari. beniculturali.it). Metro Policlinico/ bus 71, 310, 492, C. **Open** 8.30am-7.30pm Mon-Fri; 8.30am-1pm Sat. Closed 2wks Aug. **Map** p151 C1.
This library is grossly inefficient for the needs of La Sapienza (*see p335*), Europe's largest university. Books must be requested by 6.30pm Mon-Fri and 12.30pm Sat.

Biblioteca Nazionale

Viale Castro Pretorio 105, Esquilino (06 49 891/www.bncrm.librari. beniculturali.it). Metro Castro Pretorio/bus 310, 492, 649, C. **Open** 8.30am-7pm Mon-Fri; 8.30am-1.30pm Sat. Closed 2wks Aug. **Map** off p357 E5.
The national library holds 80% of everything that's in print in Italy, as well as books in other languages. A computerised catalogue system allows access to library archives dating from 1987.

Biblioteca dell'Università Gregoriana

Piazza della Pilotta 4, Trevi & Quirinale (06 6701 5131/www. unigre.it/newbiblio). Bus 40Exp, 60Exp, 62, 63, 64, 70, 81, 85, 95, 160, 170, 175, 204, 492, 628, 630, 850, H. **Open** 8.30am-6.30pm Mon-Fri; 8.30am-12.30pm Sat. Closed Aug. **Map** p357 A6.
Better organised than Biblioteca Alessandrina (*see above*), but books here are not allowed off the premises.

Biblioteca Vaticana

Via di Porta Angelica, Vatican (06 6987 9411/www.vatican.va). Metro Ottaviano/bus 23, 32, 49, 62, 81, 492, 982, 990/tram 19. **Open** (postgrads only) 8.45am-5.15pm Mon-Fri. Closed mid July-mid Sept. **Map** p355 A4.

Directory

To obtain an entrance card, students need a letter on headed paper, signed by a professor, stating their research purpose. This must be presented between 8.45am and noon (or 3-4pm Mon & Thur).

The British School at Rome
Via Gramsci 61, Veneto & Borghese (06 326 4931/www.bsr.ac.uk). Bus 52, 926/tram 19. **Open** *Library* 9am-1pm, 2-6.30pm Mon-Thur; 9am-1pm, 2-5pm Fri. Closed July & Aug. **Map** p354 E1.
The library has English and Italian books on all aspects of Rome, especially art history, archaeology and topography. To get in, students require one photo and a letter from a museum or university, or photocopy of their degree. No lending facilities.

Lost property

Anything mislaid on public transport, or stolen and subsequently discarded, may turn up at one of the lost-property offices below.

Ufficio oggetti smarriti
At the time of writing, the ATAC bus and tram network lost property office was in the process of moving from its old address to new premises: call 06 581 6040 (8.30am-1pm Mon, Wed, Fri; 8.30am-1pm, 3-5pm Tue; 8.30am-5pm Thur; mornings only in Aug) or ask at the terminus of the bus in which the object was lost.

MetRo
Line A (Termini) 06 487 4309. **Open** 9am-12.30pm Mon, Wed, Fri. *Line B (Piramide) 06 5753 2265.* **Open** 8.30am-6.30pm Mon-Sat.

COTRAL
The regional transport authority has no central lost-property office. Instead, enquiries can be made at Anagnina (06 722 2153), Cornelia (06 662 3555), Tiburtina (06 4424 2419), Laurentina (06 591 0531), Ponte Mammolo (06 418 1338) or Saxa Rubra (06 332 8331) stations.

Ferrovie dello Stato/ Stazione Termini
Termini station, platform 24, Esquilino (06 478 25543/www.grandistazioni.it). Metro Termini/ buses to Termini/tram 5, 14. **Open** 6am-midnight daily. **Map** p357 E5.
Items found on FS trains anywhere in Rome are sent to this collection point; the office is part of the left-luggage office. The office charges €3 per day it has held the found object, payable upon collection.

Media

Magazines

For English-language publications, *see p332* **Listings & small ads**.

Panorama and *L'Espresso* each provide a generally high-standard round-up of the week's news, while *Magazine* and *Venerdì* – the colour supplements of *Corriere della Sera* (Thur) and *La Repubblica* (Fri) respectively – have nice photos but are textually weak; *La Repubblica*'s rather glossy Saturday supplement *D* is the best of the lot. For tabloid-style scandal, try the weird mix of sex, glamour and religion in *Gente* and *Oggi*, or even the compulsively awful *Eva 3000* and *Cronaca Vera*. Rather more highbrow, *Internazionale* (www.internazionale.it) provides a readable digest of articles gleaned from the world's press over the previous week. *Diario della Settimana* (www.diario.it) offers informed investigative journalism. But the biggest-seller is *Famiglia Cristiana* – available from newsstands and in most churches – which alternates between Vatican line-toeing and Vatican-baiting, based on the current state of relations between the Holy See and the idiosyncratic Paoline monks who produce it.

National dailies

Long, indigestible political stories with little in the way of background predominate in Italian newspapers. On the plus side, dailies are refreshingly unsnobbish and happily blend news, leaders by internationally known commentators, and well-written, often quite bizarre, human-interest stories. Sports coverage is extensive; and there are always the mass-circulation sports papers *Corriere dello Sport*, *La Gazzetta dello Sport* and *Tuttosport*.

Free papers are distributed on weekdays in metro and bus stations and are widely read: *Leggo*, *Metro*, *City* and *Epolis* all contain brief news articles as well as details of the day's happenings in the city. *Ventiquattrominuti* is an afternoon freesheet produced by the authoritative *Il Sole-24 Ore* financial daily.

Corriere della Sera
www.corriere.it
To the centre of centre-left, this solid, serious but often dull Milan-based paper is good for foreign news.

Il Manifesto
www.ilmanifesto.it
A reminder that there is still some corner of central Rome where hearts beat Red.

La Repubblica
www.repubblica.it
Rome-based, centre-ish, left-ish; good selection of supplementary inserts.

La Stampa
www.lastampa.it
Part of the massive empire of Turin's Agnelli family; it offers good (albeit pro-Agnelli) business reporting.

Local dailies

La Repubblica and *Corriere della Sera* (*see above*) have large daily Rome sections.

Il Messaggero
www.ilmessaggero.it
The Roman daily *per eccellenza*. Particularly useful classified ads – with many flat rents – on Saturdays.

L'Osservatore Romano
www.vatican.va
The Vatican's official newspaper reflects the conservative orthodoxies issuing from the top. Weekly English edition on Wednesdays.

Il Tempo
www.iltempo.it
A high-circulation right-wing paper.

Foreign press

The *Financial Times, Wall Street Journal, USA Today, International Herald Tribune* and most European dailies can be found on the day of issue at central newsstands; US dailies can take 24hrs to appear.

Directory

Listings & small ads

The American Magazine
www.theamericanmag.com
Monthly English-language magazine on Italian cultural and political life, with useful classified ads.

Porta Portese
www.porta-portese.it
Essential reading for flat-hunters in Rome (to rent or buy). Published Tuesday and Friday, it also has sections on household goods and cars. Place ads free on 06 70 199.

Roma C'è
www.romace.it
Comprehensive listings for theatre, music, dance film and nightlife every Wednesday, with a small English-language section.

Solocase
www.solocase.it
Houses for sale and rent. Comes out on Saturdays.

Trovaroma
Free with *La Repubblica* every Thursday; its English-language section covers the week's concerts, exhibitions and guided tours.

Wanted in Rome
www.wantedinrome.com
Essential information and upmarket housing ads for English-speaking expats; out fortnightly.

Radio

These state-owned stations play a programme of classical and light music, interspersed with chat shows and regular, excellent news bulletins:
RAI 1 89.7 FM, 1332 AM
RAI 2 91.7 FM, 846 AM
RAI 3 93.7 FM, 1107 AM
www.rai.it

For UK and US chart hits, mixed with home-grown offerings, try:
Radio Capital 95.8 FM/
www.capital.it
Radio Centro Suono 101.3 FM/
www.radiocentrosuono.it
Radio Città Futura 97.7 FM/
www.radiocittafutura.it
Italy's most PC 24hr station.
Radio Kiss Kiss Network 97.25 FM/*www.kisskissnetwork.it*
Radio 105 96.1 FM/*www.105.net*
Vatican Radio 105 FM, 585 MW/
www.vaticanradio.org
World events, as seen by the Catholic church, broadcast in English.

Television

Italy has six major networks (three are owned by the state broadcaster RAI, three by Silvio Berlusconi's Mediaset group), and two channels that operate across most of the country: La7 and MTV. Local stations provide hours of tacky programming, from tarot-reading to zero-budget soaps.

The standard of TV news varies, but most channels offer a breadth of international coverage. La7 broadcasts CNN in English from about 4am, while RAI 3's 2pm, 7pm and 10.30pm news programmes have regional round-ups.

Money

See also p336 **Tax**.
The Italian currency is the euro, with banknotes of €5, €10, €20, €100, €200 and €500, and coins worth €1 and €2, plus 1¢, 2¢, 5¢, 10¢, 20¢ and 50¢ (*centesimi*). Money from any Eurozone country is valid tender. Vatican euros are a highly collectable rarity.

ATMs

Most banks have 24hr cash-point (*Bancomat*) machines. The vast majority accept cards with the Maestro, Cirrus and Plus logos, and will dispense up to a daily limit of €250.

Banking hours

Opening hours vary, but most banks operate 8.30am-1.30pm, 2.45-4.30pm Mon-Fri. Some central branches now also open until 6pm Thur and 8.30am-12.30pm Sat. All banks close on public holidays, and work reduced hours the day before a holiday (many close by 11am).

Bureaux de change

Banks usually offer better exchange rates than private bureaux de change (*cambio*).

Take a passport or other photo ID, particularly if changing travellers' cheques or making a credit card withdrawal. Commission rates vary (from nothing to €5 per transaction). Beware 'no commission' signs: the rate will likely be terrible.

Many city-centre bank branches have automatic cash-exchange machines, which accept most currencies (notes in good condition only). Main post offices also have exchange bureaux (€2.58 commission; no travellers' cheques); *see p333* **Postal services**.

American Express
Piazza di Spagna 38, Tridente (06 67 641). Metro Spagna/bus 52, 53, 61, 71, 80Exp, 117, 119, 160, 850. **Open** 9am-5.30pm Mon-Fri; 9am-12.30pm Sat. **Map** p357 A4.
Travellers' cheque refund service, card replacement, poste restante, a cash machine that can be used with AmEx cards, and 24hr money-transfer from any other AmEx office.

Travelex
Piazza Barberini 21, Veneto & Borghese (06 4202 0150/fax 06 482 8085/www.travelex.it). Metro Barberini/bus 52, 53, 61, 62, 63, 80Exp, 95, 116, 119, 175, 492, 590, 630. **Open** *June-Sept* 9am-8pm Mon-Sat; 9.30am-5pm Sun. *Oct-May* 9am-7pm Mon-Sat; 9.30am-5pm Sun. **Map** p357 B5.
The Travelex branches in Rome are among the few exchange offices open on Sundays. Commission of 8.5% is charged on all transactions apart from travellers' cheques bought in Travelex outlets (with proof of purchase). Visa and MasterCard holders can also withdraw cash here (€50-€230); €5 commission is charged on these cash withdrawals. **Other locations**: via della Conciliazione 23-25 (06 6830 0435); via del Corso 23 (06 320 0224); Metro B Colosseo (06 4782 5894); Metro A & B Termini (06 4891 3004).

Credit cards

Nearly all hotels of two stars and above now accept at least some of the major credit cards; all but the cheapest local eateries will take them too.

Should you lose a credit card, phone one of the 24hr emergency numbers below.

American Express *06 7290 0347/*
06 7228 0371/US cardholders 800
874 333/travellers' cheques 800 872
000 or 800 914 912
Diner's Club *800 864 064*
MasterCard *800 870 866/*
travellers' cheques 800 872 050
Visa *800 877 232/travellers' cheques*
800 785 0065 or 800 874 155

Police

The principal *Polizia di Stato*
station, the Questura Centrale,
is at via San Vitale 15 (06 46
861, www.poliziadistato.it).
Others, and the Carabinieri's
Commissariati, are listed in the
phone directory under *Polizia*
and *Carabinieri*. Incidents can
be reported to either.

Postal services

For postal information, call
803 160 (8am-8pm Mon-Sat)
or visit www.poste.it.

The once-notorious Italian
postal service is now generally
efficient. If you still have any
doubts, the Vatican Post Office
(*see below*) is run in association
with the Swiss postal service.

Most postboxes are red
and have two slots, *per la città*
(for Rome) and *tutte le altre*
destinazioni (everywhere else).

On the whole, mail arrives
swiftly – up to 48hrs delivery
in Italy, three days for EU
countries and between five
and nine days for other
countries (in zones 2 and 3).
A letter of 20g or less to Italy
costs 60¢; to other countries
in the EU costs 65¢; to zone 2
costs 85¢; to zone 3 costs €1.

The *Posta Celere* service
costs more (€10 for up to 3kg)
and promises (though often
doesn't achieve) 24hr delivery.
You can, however, track the
progress of your letter on
the website or by phoning
(details as above).

Registered mail (ask for
raccomandata) starts at €2.80
for a letter of 20g or less.

Parcels can be sent from any
post office. It is advisable to
send any package worth more
than €50 insured.

There are local post offices
(*ufficio postale*) in each district;
opening hours can vary, but
they are generally 8.30am-6pm
Mon-Fri (8.30am-2pm Aug),
8.30am-1.30pm Sat and any
day preceding a public
holiday. They close two hours
earlier than normal on the last
day of each month. Main post
offices in the centre have
longer opening hours and offer
a range of additional services,
including fax facilities (though
not at the Posta Centrale).
Several postal services are
available online; visit www.
poste.it to avoid the queues.

Posta Centrale

Piazza San Silvestro 19, Tridente
(06 6973 7232/information 803 160).
Bus 52, 53, 61, 71, 80Exp, 85, 116,
116T, 117, 119, 160, 850. **Open**
8am-7pm Mon-Sat. **Map** p357 A5.
The hub of Rome's postal system
has been treated to a facelift: shiny
new internet terminals, numerous
counters, an information desk…
and vastly reduced queues. Letters
sent poste restante/general delivery
(*fermo posta*) to Rome should be
addressed to Roma Centro
Corrispondenza, Posta Centrale,
piazza San Silvestro, 00186 Roma.
You'll need your passport to collect
and have to pay a small charge.

Other main offices

Piazza Bologna 3, Suburbs: east
(06 4411 6211). Metro Bologna/bus
61, 62, 93, 168, 309, 310, 445, 542.
Via Marmorata 4, Testaccio
(06 5701 8264). Metro Piramide/
bus 23, 30Exp, 75, 280, 673, 716,
719/tram 3. **Map** p359 E5.
Viale Mazzini 101, Suburbs: north
(06 377 09268). Bus 30Exp, 88,
495. **Map** p354 B1.
Via Taranto 19, Suburbs: south
(06 7727 91). Metro San Giovanni/
bus 85.

Poste Vaticane

Piazza San Pietro, Vatican (06 6988
3406). Metro Ottaviano/bus 23, 49,
62, 81, 492, 590, 982, 990/tram 19.
Open 8am-7.30pm Mon-Fri; 8.30am-
6.30pm Sat. **Map** p355 A4.

Queuing

Lining up doesn't come easy
to Romans, but despite the
apparent chaos, queue-jumpers
are given short shrift. Hanging
back deferentially, though, is

taken as a sign of stupidity –
if you're not careful the tide
will sweep contemptuously
past you. In busy shops and
bars, be aware of who was
there before you and who
arrived after; when it's your
turn, make your presence felt.
In many shops you have to
take a number as you enter:
this isn't always obvious as the
dispenser is often well hidden.

Religion

For information about papal
audiences, *see p163*.

There are over 400 Catholic
churches in Rome, but few hold
mass in English. The main
English-speaking Catholic
church is San Silvestro
(piazza San Silvestro 17A,
06 697 7121); San Patrizio (via
Boncompagni 31, 06 420 3121,
www.stpatricksrome.com) is
the principal Irish church; the
American Catholic church
is Santa Susanna (via XX
Settembre 15, 06 4201 4554,
www.santasusanna.org).

Anglican

All Saints, via del Babuino 153B,
Tridente (06 3600 1881/www.
allsaints.org). Metro Spagna/bus
117, 119, 590. **Services** 8.30am,
10.30am Sun; 8.30am, 10.30am, 6pm
last Sun of month. **Map** p354 E3.
All Saints hosts a programme of
cultural events, including regular
concerts, and activities for children.

Episcopal

St Paul's Within the Walls, via
Napoli 58, Esquilino (06 488
3339/www.stpaulsrome.it). Metro
Repubblica/bus 40Exp, 60Exp,
64, 70, 116T, 170, H. **Services**
8.30am, 10.30am, 1pm (in Spanish)
Sun. **Map** p357 C5.

Jewish

Comunità Israelitica Ebraica di
Roma, lungotevere Cenci, Ghetto
(06 6840 0661/www.museoebraico.
roma.it). Bus 23, 63, 271, 280, 630,
780, H. **Map** p358 D2.
There are daily services, but times
vary. Guided tours of the synagogue
are offered from the Museo d'Arte
Ebraica (*see p128*).

Methodist

Ponte Sant'Angelo Church, via del
Banco di Santo Spirito, Pantheon

& Navona (06 686 8314). Bus 40Exp, 46, 62, 64, 98, 280, 870, 881, 916. **Services** 10.30am Sun. **Map** p355 B5.

Muslim

Moschea di Roma, viale della Moschea, Suburbs: north (06 808 2167). Train to Campi Sportivi/bus 230.
Paolo Portoghesi's masterpiece is always open to Muslims for prayer. Non-Muslims can visit 9-11.30am Wed and Sat.

Presbyterian

St Andrew's, via XX Settembre 7, Veneto & Borghese (06 482 7627). Bus 36, 60Exp, 61, 62, 84, 175, 492, 590, 910. **Services** 11am Sun. **Map** p357 C4.

Relocation

Foreign nationals residing in Italy are obliged to pick up a series of forms and permits. The basic set is described below. EU citizens should have no difficulty getting their documentation once they are in Italy (see the website www.portaleimmigrazione.it, or contact the toll-free number 800 309 309), but non-EU citizens are advised to enquire at an Italian consulate before travelling. There are agencies that specialise in obtaining documents for you if you can't face the procedures yourself – but at a price (see Pratiche e certificati – agenzie in the Yellow Pages).

Carta d'identità (identity card)

You will need three passport photographs, the original and one photocopy of your permesso di soggiorno (see below), your passport and a form that will be given to you at your circoscrizione – the local branch of the central records office, which eventually issues the ID card. There's a €5.42 charge for the card. Consult the phone book (Comune di Roma: Circoscrizioni) for your area's office.

Codice fiscale & Partita IVA (tax code & VAT number)

A codice fiscale is essential for opening a bank account or setting up utilities contracts. Take your passport and permesso di soggiorno

(see below) to your local tax office (ufficio delle entrate; see below). Fill in a form and return a few days later to pick up the card. It can be posted on request.
The self-employed or anyone doing business in Italy may need a Partita IVA. The certificate is free. Most people pay an accountant to handle the formalities. Take your passport and codice fiscale to your nearest tax office. Be sure to cancel your VAT number when you no longer need it: failure to do so may result in a visit from tax inspectors years later.
Call the Finance Ministry's info line (848 800 444, www.finanze.it) for details of uffici delle entrate (revenue offices); addresses are also in the phone book under Ministero delle Finanze. The office you should visit depends on the city district (circoscrizione) in which you live; offices open 9am-1pm Mon, Wed, Fri; 9am-1pm, 2.50-4.50pm Tue, Thur.

Permesso/carta di soggiorno (permit to stay)

You need a permesso di soggiorno if you're staying in Italy for over three months; you should, in theory, apply for one within eight days of arrival in Italy. Requirements vary depending on whether or not you are an EU citizen. You'll need four passport photographs, your passport (and a photocopy), proof that you have some means of support and reason to be in Italy (preferably a letter from an employer or certificate of registration at a school or university) and a stamp (marca da bollo – EU citizens don't, in theory, need this) costing €14.62, available at tabacchi.
The system has recently been overhauled, and some confusion reigns. Both EU and non-EU citizens can now, in theory, apply for their permesso/carta di soggiorno at main post offices. Complicated cases may find themselves redirected to the ufficio immigrazione in via Teofilo Patini (no street number – the office is on the corner of via Salviati; open 8.30-11.30am Mon, Wed, Fri; 8.30-11.30am, 3-4.30pm Tue, Thur). To get to the office, take Metro B to Rebibbia, then bus 437 or 447. For information call 06 4686 3098 or 06 4686 2375.
The carta (card) di soggiorno is similar to the permesso but allows you to stay in Italy indefinitely – though it has to be renewed every five years. EU citizens who have been resident in Italy for at least five years and who also have a renewable permesso di soggiorno can request a carta. If a foreigner already has a carta, their spouse can also request one.

Permesso di lavoro

Most EU citizens do not require a work permit; only those from new member states, as well as non-EU citizens, are legally obliged to have one, though many don't. A policy introduced in January 2005 places limits on the numbers of people in the latter two categories officially allowed to work in the city. Employers are therefore required to put in a request to the Direzione Provinciale del Lavoro (www.welfare.gov.it) before taking them on. Once authorisation has been granted, a passport and permesso di soggiorno (plus photocopies) are needed for a permesso di lavoro, obtained from the Direzione's office at via dei Vestini 13 (06 4487 1642, open 9am-noon Mon, Wed, Fri; 9am-noon, 2.45-4.30pm Tue, Thur). The whole business is fiendishly complicated, and you may feel that it's worth leaving it in the hands of an agency (see Pratiche e certificati – agenzie in the Yellow Pages) or a lawyer.

Residenza (residency)

This is your registered address in Italy. It's required to buy a car, get customs clearance on goods brought here from abroad and many other transactions. You'll need your permesso di soggiorno (see above; it must be valid for at least another year), your passport and a residency request form (downloadable from the website www.comune.roma.it). Take everything to your local circoscrizione (see above), where staff will check that rubbish-collection tax (nettezza urbana) for your address has been paid (ask your landlord about this) before issuing the certificate.

Accommodation

Try Porta Portese, the American Magazine and/or Wanted in Rome (for all, see p332) and English-language bookshops (see p233). Look out for affittasi ('for rent') notices on buildings, and check the classifieds in Il Messaggero (Thur, Sat). When you move into an apartment, it's normal to pay a month's rent in advance, plus two months' deposit (it should be refunded when you move out, but some landlords create problems over this). You'll probably get a year's renewable contract. Renting through an agency will cost the equivalent of two months' rent in commission.

Bank accounts

To open an account, you'll need a valid *residenza* or *permesso di soggiorno*, proof of regular income (or a fairly substantial deposit), a *codice fiscale* and your passport.

Doctors

See also p328 **Health & hospitals**; and *p330* **Insurance**.

If you are officially resident in Rome and have a valid *permesso* or *carta di soggiorno* and *codice fiscale* (tax code), you are entitled to the same medical care from the national health service (*Servizio sanitario nazionale*, SSN) that Italians receive. Take the above documents and *certificato di residenza* (plus photocopies) to your nearest USL (*Unità sanitaria locale*, also known as ASL, info 06 884 8992, 06 7730 2439). Branches are listed in the telephone directory under *Azienda Unità Sanitaria Locale*. You will be able to choose from a list of local doctors. You are eligible for medical treatment for as long as your *permesso* is valid. Non-residents and holders of student *permessi*, though not entitled to free medical treatment, can still receive SSN medical care by paying monthly health service contributions.

Work

Casual employment can be hard to find, so try to sort out work in advance. English-language schools and translation agencies are mobbed with applicants, so qualifications and experience count. The classified ads paper *Porta Portese* has lots of job ads. Other good places to look are *Wanted in Rome* (for both, *see p332*) and noticeboards in English-language bookshops (*see p233*). You can also place

ads in any of the media above. For serious jobs, check *Il Messaggero* and *La Repubblica*, or these agencies:

Adecco

Via Ostiense 91A, Testaccio (06 574 5701/fax 06 5713 5133/ www.adecco.it). Metro Piramide/ bus 23, 60Exp, 118, 271, 280, 716, 719, 769/tram 3. **Open** 9am-12.30pm Mon-Fri.

Manpower

Via Barberini 58, Trevi & Quirinale (06 4287 1339/fax 06 4287 0833/ www.manpower.it). Metro Barberini/ bus 52, 53, 61, 62, 63, 80Exp, 95, 116, 119, 175, 492, 590, 630. **Open** 9am-6pm Mon-Fri. **Map** p357 C5. **Other locations:** via Molajoni Pio 70 (06 4353 5349/fax 06 4353 5357).

Safety & security

Muggings are fairly rare in Rome, but pickpocketing is rife in the main tourist areas. Below are a few basic precautions:

● Don't carry wallets in back pockets, particularly on buses. If you have a bag or camera with a long strap, wear it across the chest.

● Keep bags closed, with your hand on them. If you stop at a pavement café or restaurant, don't leave bags or coats where you cannot see them.

● When walking down a street, hold cameras and bags on the side of you towards the wall – you're less likely to become the prey of a motorcycle thief.

● Avoid groups of ragged children brandishing pieces of cardboard, or walk by quickly keeping hold of your valuables. The cardboard is to distract you while accomplices pick your pockets or bags.

If you are the victim of crime, call the police helpline (*see p328*) or go to the nearest police station and say you want to report a *furto* (theft). A *denuncia* (written statement) of the incident will be made. It's unlikely your things will be found, but you will need the *denuncia* for insurance claims.

Smoking

A law introduced in January 2005 prohibits smoking in all public places in Italy except for those that provide a distinct, ventilated smokers' room. Possible fines of between €27.50 and €275 (or up to €550 if you smoke in the presence of children or pregnant women) for transgressors are the reason you'll find small groups puffing away *outside* most restaurants, pubs and clubs.

Study

See also p330 **Libraries**.

The state universities – La Sapienza (www.uniroma1.it), Tor Vergata (www.uniroma2.it) and Roma Tre (www.uniroma3.it) – plus the private LUISS (www.luiss.it) offer exchanges with other European universities. All EU citizens have the same right as Italians to study in Rome's universities, paying the same fees. Get your certificates translated and validated by the Italian consulate in your own country before lodging your application at the *ufficio stranieri* (foreigners' department) of the university of your choice.

Several US universities have campuses in Rome, which students attend on exchange programmes. Private Catholic universities run some of Italy's most highly respected medical faculties. Specialist bookshops are near La Sapienza in San Lorenzo, and on viale Ippocrate (north-east of the campus).

Bureaucracy & services

Foreigners studying in Italy must obtain a permit to stay (*see p334*). Student offices in the universities themselves will help, and there are private agencies that take care of enrolment formalities.

Agenzia Athena

*Viale Ippocrate 150, Suburbs: east
(06 445 0236). Metro Policlinico/
bus 310/tram 3, 19.* **Open** 9am-
12.30pm, 3-6pm Mon-Fri. Closed
Aug. **Credit** AmEx, DC, MC, V.
Offers foreigners and locals advice
on university matters and deals with
enrolment, exam registration and
other time-consuming details.

Centro Turistico Studentesco (CTS)

*Via Genova 16, Monti (199 501 150/
06 462 0431/www.cts.it). Bus 40Exp,
60Exp, 64, 70, 170, H.* **Open** 9.30am-
1pm, 2-6.30pm Mon-Fri; 10am-1pm
Sat. **Credit** MC, V. **Map** p357 C5.
CTS issues discount cards (€30,
valid for one calendar year) for
travel, museums and more.

Tabacchi

Tabacchi or *tabaccherie*
(identifiable by signs with a
white 'T' on black or blue) are
the only places you can legally
buy tobacco products. They
also generally sell stamps,
telephone cards, tickets for
public transport, lottery tickets
and the stationery required
for dealing with Italian
bureaucracy. Most *tabacchi*
keep shop hours, but some are
attached to bars and so stay
open into the night. (*See also
p244* **Life's essentials**.)

Tax

For sales tax rebates, *see p230*.
  Sales tax (IVA) is charged at
varying rates on most goods
and services. It's usually
quoted as part of the price,
with occasional exceptions
such as top-end hotels and
some tradespeople. The
implication from the latter is
that, by paying cash and not
demanding a receipt, you won't
have to pay the 19% or so IVA.

Telephones

Dialling & codes

There are three main types of
phone numbers in Rome:
● Land-lines have the area
code 06, which must be used

whether calling from within
or outside the city. Numbers
generally have eight digits. If
you can't get through, it may
be an old number; check the
directory or ring enquiries (*see
below*). When phoning Rome
from abroad, keep the initial 0.
● Numbers beginning 800 are
toll-free. Numbers beginning
840 and 848 are charged at
low set rates, no matter where
you're calling from or how
long the call lasts. These
numbers can be called from
within Italy only; some of
them function only within
a single phone district.
● Mobile numbers begin
with a 3.

Fax

Faxes can be sent from most
large post offices (*see p333*),
charged by the number of
sheets sent. Page rates within
Italy are €3.10 for the first
page, then €1.30/page, or
€5.10/page for Europe. Some
photocopying outlets also send
faxes (with a hefty surcharge).
Do-it-yourself fax/phones can
be found in main stations and
at Fiumicino airport.

International calls

For international calls from
Rome, dial 00, followed by the
country code, area code (omit
the initial zero of area codes
in the UK) and number. Codes
include: Australia 61; Canada
1; Irish Republic 353; New
Zealand 64; United Kingdom
44; United States 1.
  To call Rome from abroad,
dial the international code (00
in the UK, 011 in the US), then
39 for Italy and 06 for Rome
(*don't* drop the zero), followed
by the individual number.

Mobile phones

See also above **Dialling
& codes**.
GSM phones can be used
on both 900 and 1800 bands;

British, Australian and New
Zealand mobiles work fine, but
US mobiles are on a different
frequency that doesn't work
(unless it's a tri-band phone).
The main mobile phone
networks in Italy are Tim
(www.tim.it), Vodafone
(www.vodafone.it) and Wind
(www.wind.it). All three have
numerous branches located
throughout the city.

Operator services

To reverse the charges (make
a collect call), dial 170 for the
international operator. If you
are reversing the charges from
a phone box, insert a 10¢ coin
(refunded after your call).
  The following services
operate 24hrs daily:
Operator & Directory Enquiries
(in Italian) 1254
(in Italian & English) 892 412
International Operator 170
**International Directory
Enquiries** 892 412
Communication problems
(national calls) 187
(international calls) 170
Wake-up calls 4114; an automatic
message asks you to dial in the time
you want your call (on a 24hr clock)
followed by your phone number.

Public phones

Rome has no shortage of
public phone boxes and many
bars have payphones, most of
which are readily available as
locals are addicted to mobiles.
Most only accept phone cards
(*schede telefoniche*); a few also
accept major credit cards.
Phone cards cost €5, €15 and
€30 and are available from
tabacchi (*see above*), some
newsstands and some bars.
Phone cards have expiry dates
(usually 31 Dec or 30 June),
after which they are useless.
  The Vatican City has its
own special phone cards,
available from the Vatican
post office (*see p333*) and
usable only within the city-
state. Public coin phones
accept 10¢, 20¢, 50¢ or €1
coins (minimum call is 10¢).

Rates

Competition has brought Telecom Italia charges down, though they remain among Europe's highest, particularly for international calls. Calls cost more from public pay phones. You can keep costs down by phoning off-peak (6.30pm-8am Mon-Sat, all day Sun). Hotel phones may carry extortionate surcharges.

Time

Italy is one hour ahead of London, six hours ahead of New York, eight hours behind Sydney and 12 hours behind Wellington. In all EU countries clocks are moved forward one hour in early spring and back again in late autumn.

Tipping

Foreigners are generally expected to tip more than Italians, but the ten or more per cent that is customary in many countries is considered generous even for the richest-looking tourist in most eateries, where anything between €1 and €5 is normal; some smarter places, however, now include a 10-15% service charge. For drinks, follow the example of many locals, who leave a 10¢ or 20¢ coin on the counter when ordering at a bar. Taxi drivers will be happy if you round the fare up to the nearest whole euro.

Toilets

If you need a toilet, the easiest thing to do is go to a bar (it won't necessarily be clean or provide toilet paper). There are modern lavatories at or near most major tourist sites, some with attendants to whom you must pay a nominal fee. Fast-food restaurants and department stores may also meet the need. For wheelchair-accessible toilets, *see p326.*

Tourist information

For tours, *see p323* **Tour buses** and *p323* **River boats**; for the Vatican tourist office, *see also p163.*

The offices of Rome's tourist board, APT, and the state tourist board, ENIT, have English-speaking staff, but surprisingly limited amounts of printed tourist information. For visitors looking for more personal service, the private Enjoy Rome agency is highly recommended. Rome's city council operates a number of well-stocked green-painted tourist information kiosks (PIT) that are open 9.30am-7/7.30pm daily (apart from the Fiumicino airport and Termini branches, which open 8am-9pm daily).

APT (Azienda per il Turismo di Roma)

Via Parigi 5, Esquilino (06 4889 9200/infoline 06 8205 9127/www. romaturismo.com). Metro Repubblica/ bus 16, 36, 60Exp, 61, 62, 84, 90Exp, 175, 492, 590, 910. **Open** *Phoneline* 9am-6pm daily. *Office* 9.30am-1pm, 2.30-4.30pm Mon, Thur. **Map** p357 D5.
Other locations: Fiumicino airport, terminal B (06 6595 4471).

Enjoy Rome

Via Marghera 8A, Esquilino (06 445 1843/fax 06 445 0734/www. enjoyrome.com). Metro Termini/ buses to Termini/tram 5, 14. **Open** *Apr-Oct* 8.30am-7pm Mon-Fri; 8.30am-2pm Sat. *Nov-Mar* 9am-6.30pm Mon-Fri; 8.30am-2pm Sat. **No credit cards. Map** p357 E5.
This friendly English-speaking private agency is handy for both information and advice. The office provides a free accommodation booking service and arranges walking tours.

PIT (Punti Informativi Turistici)

Piazza Pia, Vatican & Prati (06 6880 9707). Bus 23, 34, 40Exp, 62, 280, 982. **Open** 9.30am-7pm. **Map** p355 B4.
Piazza delle Cinque Lune, Pantheon & Navona (06 6880 9240). Bus 30Exp, 70, 81, 87, 116, 116T, 186, 492, 628. **Open** 9.15am-7pm. **Map** p355 D5.

Piazza del Tempio della Pace, Capitoline & Palatine (06 6992 4307). Bus 60Exp, 75, 85, 87, 117, 175, 186, 810, 850. **Open** 9.30am-7pm. **Map** p360 B2.
Via Nazionale, Trevi & Quirinale (06 4782 4525). Bus 40Exp, 60Exp, 64, 70, 71, 116, 116T, 170, H. **Open** 9.30am-7.30pm. **Map** p357 C6.
Piazza Sonnino, Trastevere (06 5833 3457). Bus 23, 280, 630, 780, H/tram 8. **Open** 9.30am-7.30pm. **Map** p358 D3.
Via Minghetti, Tridente (06 678 2988). Bus 62, 63, 81, 85, 95, 117, 119, 160, 175, 204, 492, 628, 630, 850. **Open** 9.15am-7pm. **Map** p357 A6.
Termini station, platform 24, Esquilino (06 4890 6300). Metro Termini/buses to Termini/tram 5, 14. **Open** 8am-9pm. **Map** p357 E5.
Fiumicino airport, terminal C (06 6595 5423). **Open** 9am-7pm.
Piazza Santa Maria Maggiore (06 4740 955). Metro Termini/bus 16, 70, 71, 75, 84, 105, 360, 590, 649, 714, H. **Open** 9.30am-7.30pm. **Map** p360 C1.

Ufficio Pellegrini e Turisti

Piazza San Pietro, Vatican (06 6988 1662/www.vaticano.va). Bus 23, 34, 40Exp, 62, 280, 982. **Open** 8.30am-6.30pm Mon-Sat. **Map** p355 A5.
The Vatican's own tourist office.

Visas

EU nationals and citizens of the US, Canada, Australia and New Zealand do not need visas for stays of up to three months. For EU citizens a passport or national ID card valid for travel abroad is sufficient; non-EU citizens must have full passports. In theory, all visitors must declare their presence to the local police (*see p333*) within eight days of arrival. If you're staying in a hotel, this will be done for you.

Water

Most of Rome's water comes from a vast underground lake to the north of the city and is completely safe for drinking. Some areas of the *centro storico* still get water through the ancient aqueducts that

Directory

draw from springs in the countryside: this water is so good that Romans come from the suburbs to fill up plastic containers with it.

When to go

For information on annual events in the city, see *pp252-255* **Festivals & Events**.

Climate

Increasing numbers of visitors to Rome are cottoning on to the fact that spring and autumn are the best times in which to see Rome; the weather's pleasantly balmy and the city is bathed in a glorious, raking yellow light. To visitors arriving from chillier climes, the weather in May, June, September and October may seem like a fairly convincing approximation of summertime, but the actual Roman summer is a different matter altogether: searing, 40°C heat and energy-sapping humidity mark July and August, when the city empties as Romans scurry for the hills and sea. You may be tempted to do the same.

Between November and February the weather is very unpredictable: you may strike

it lucky with a run of crisp, bright, sunny days, maybe punctuated by the odd bone-shakingly icy blast of wind buffetting in from northern Europe… or you may arrive in the midst of a torrential downpour that shows no sign of letting up, putting a dampener on your sightseeing plans. But there is some compensation: a relative scarcity of other tourists.

Public holidays

On public holidays (*giorni festivi*) virtually all shops, banks and businesses close, although (with the exception of May Day, 15 August and Christmas Day) bars and restaurants tend to stay open. There's only limited public transport on 1 May and Christmas afternoon.

New Year's Day (Capodanno) 1 Jan
Epiphany (La Befana) 6 Jan
Easter Monday (Pasquetta)
Liberation Day 25 Apr
May Day 1 May
Patron Saints' Day (Santi Pietro e Paolo) 29 June
Feast of the Assumption (Ferragosto) 15 Aug
All Saints (Tutti i santi) 1 Nov
Immaculate Conception (Festa dell'Immacolata) 8 Dec
Christmas Day (Natale) 25 Dec
Boxing Day (Santo Stefano) 26 Dec

Women

Rome is generally a safe city for women. Stick to central areas and if you do find yourself being hassled, take comfort in the fact that Italian men are generally all mouth and no trousers. Common sense is usually enough to keep potential harassers at bay: if you're not interested, ignore them and they'll probably go away.

Young Roman blades head for major tourist magnets, like piazza Navona, piazza di Spagna and the Trevi Fountain, to pick up foreign talent. If you would rather enjoy Rome's nocturnal charm without the benefit of a self-appointed guide, stick to the areas around campo de' Fiori, Testaccio or Trastevere. The Termini station area gets seriously seedy after the sun has gone down.

Accommodation

The vast majority of Rome's hotels and *pensioni* are perfectly suitable for women.

If you're worried, avoid those near Termini station and via Nazionale (a major shopping artery that's deserted once the shops shut); stick to more populated areas in the *centro storico*. For women-only accommodation, *see p272* **La Casa Internazionale delle Donne**.

Health

See also p328 **Health & hospitals**; and *p329* **Helplines & agencies**.

In case of gynaecological emergencies, head for the nearest *pronto soccorso* (accident & emergency department; *see p328*). Tampons (*assorbenti interni*) and sanitary towels (*assorbenti esterni*) are cheapest in supermarkets, but also sold at pharmacies and *tabacchi*.

Average climate

Month	Avg High (°C/°F)	Avg Low (°C/°F)	Rainfall (mm/in)	Sunshine (hrs/day)
Jan	12/54	4/39	71/2.8	4
Feb	14/57	4/39	62/2.4	4
Mar	15/59	6/43	57/2.2	6
Apr	18/64	8/46	51/2.0	7
May	23/73	13/55	46/1.8	8
June	26/79	16/61	37/1.5	9
July	30/86	19/66	15/0.6	11
Aug	30/86	20/68	21/0.8	10
Sept	26/79	17/63	63/2.5	8
Oct	22/72	13/55	99/3.9	6
Nov	17/63	9/48	129/5.1	4
Dec	13/55	6/43	93/3.7	4

Directory

Glossary

Amphitheatre oval open-air theatre in ancient Rome

Apse large recess at the high-altar end of a church

Atrium courtyard

Baldacchino canopy supported by columns

Baroque artistic period in the 17th-18th centuries, in which the decorative element became increasingly florid, culminating in the rococo (*qv*)

Basilica ancient Roman rectangular public building; rectangular Christian church

Campanile bell tower

Caryatid supporting pillar carved in the shape of a woman

Cavea step-like seating area found in a theatre (*qv*) or amphitheatre (*qv*)

Chiaroscuro from Italian *chiaro* (light) and *scuro* (dark), juxtaposition of light and shade to bring out relief and volume

Ciborio dome-shaped canopy on columns over the high altar

Clivus ancient name for a street on the side of a hill

Cloister exterior courtyard surrounded on all sides by a covered walkway

Column upright architectural element that can be round, square or rectangular; usually structural, but sometimes merely decorative, and usually free-standing; conforms to one of the classical orders (*qv*)

Confessio crypt beneath a raised altar

Cosmati, cosmatesque mosaic technique using coloured marble chips, usually to decorate floors and church furniture

Cryptoporticus underground corridor

Cubicolum bedroom

Decumanus main road, usually running east–west

Domus Roman city house

Entablature section above a column or row of columns that includes the frieze and cornice

Ex-voto an offering given to fulfil a vow; often a small model in silver of the limb, organ or loved one cured as a result of prayer

Fresco painting technique in which pigment is applied to wet plaster

Giallo antico yellowish marble

Gothic architectural and artistic style of the late Middle Ages (from the 12th century), of soaring, pointed arches

Greek cross (of a church) in the shape of a cross with arms of equal length

Grisaille painting in shades of grey to mimic sculpture

Insula a multi-storey city apartment block

Intarsio form of mosaic made from pieces of wood of different colours; also known as intaglio

Latin cross (of a church) in the shape of a cross with one arm longer than the others

Loggia gallery open on one side

Lunette semicircular area, usually above a door or window

Maiolica fine earthenware with coloured decoration on an opaque white glaze

Mannerism High Renaissance style of the late 16th century; characterised in painting by elongated, contorted human figures

Matronium gallery (usually screened) where women sat in early Christian and Byzantine basilicas

Mithraeum temple, usually underground, to the deity Mithras

Narthex enclosed porch in front of a church

Nave main body of a church; the longest section of a Latin-cross (*qv*) church

Necropolis literally, 'city of the dead'; graveyard

Nymphaeum grotto with pool and fountain dedicated to the Nymphs (female water deities)

Ogival (of arches, windows, etc) curving in to a point at the top

Orders rules governing the proportions and decoration of columns, the most common being the very simple Doric, the curlicue Ionic, and the Corinthian, which is decorated with stylised acanthus leaves

Palazzo large and/or important building (not necessarily a palace)

Pendentives four concave triangular sections on top of piers supporting a dome

Peristyle temple or court surrounded by columns

Piazza (or **largo**) square

Pilaster rectangular column projecting slightly from a wall

Pillar upright architectural element, always free-standing, but not conforming to classical orders (*qv*); *see also* **column**

Rococo highly decorative style of the 18th century

Romanesque architectural style of the early Middle Ages (c500-1200), drawing on Roman and Byzantine influences

Rosso antico red-coloured marble brought from Matapan, Greece, by the Romans

Sarcophagus stone or marble coffin

Spandrel the near-triangular space between the top of two adjoining arches and the ceiling (or other architectural feature) resting above them

Tepidarium warm (as opposed to hot), steam-filled room in a Roman baths complex

Theatre in ancient times, a semicircular open-air theatre

Titulus early Christian meeting place

Transept shorter arms of a Latin-cross (*qv*) church

Travertine cream-coloured calcareous limestone

Triclinium dining room

Triumphal arch arch in front of an apse (*qv*), usually over the high altar; monumental victory arch

Trompe l'oeil decorative painting effect to make surface appear three-dimensional

Vocabulary

Romans always appreciate attempts at spoken Italian, no matter how incompetent. In hotels and all but the most spit-and-sawdust restaurants, there's likely to be someone with at least basic English.

There are two forms of address in the second person singular: *lei* (formal, used with strangers and older people) and *tu* (informal). The personal pronoun is usually omitted.

Italian is pronounced as it is spelled.

Pronunciation

a – as in ask.
e – like a in age or e in sell.
i – like ea in east.
o – as in hotel or hot.
u – as in boot.

Romans have a lot of trouble with their consonants. **C** often comes out nearer **g**; **n**, if in close proximity to an **r**, disappears. Remember: **c** and **g** both go soft in front of e and i (becoming like the initial sounds of **ch**eck and **gi**raffe respectively). An **h** after any consonant makes it hard; before a vowel, it is silent.

c before a, o and u: as in **c**at.
g before a, o and u: as in **g**et.
gl like **ll**i in mi**ll**ion.
gn like **ny** in ca**ny**on.
qu as in **qu**ick.
r always rolled.
s has two sounds, as in **s**oap or ro**s**e.
sc like the sh in **sh**ame.
sch like the sc in **sc**out.
z can be sounded ts or dz.

Useful phrases

hello/goodbye (informal) *ciao, salve*
good morning *buon giorno*
good evening *buona sera*
good night *buona notte*
please *per favore, per piacere*
thank you *grazie*
you're welcome *prego*
excuse me, sorry *mi scusi* (formal), *scusa* (informal)
I'm sorry, but... *mi dispiace...*
I don't speak Italian (very well) *non parlo (molto bene) l'italiano*
do you speak English? *parla inglese?*
can I use/where's the toilet? *posso usare/dov'è il bagno/la toilette?*
open *aperto*
closed *chiuso*
entrance *entrata*
exit *uscita*

Female self-defence

no thank you, I can find my own way *no grazie, non ho bisogna di una guida*
can you leave me alone? *mi vuole* (or *vuoi* – informal) to make it clear you feel superior) *lasciare in pace?*

Times & timetables

could you tell me the time? *mi sa* (formal)/*sai* (informal) *dire l'ora?*
it's ... o'clock *sono le* (number)
it's half past... *sono le* (number) *e mezza*
when does it (re)open? *a che ora (ri)apre?*
does it close for lunch? *chiude per pranzo?*

Directions

(turn) left *(giri a) sinistra*
(it's on the) right *(è a/sulla) destra*
straight on *sempre diritto*
where is...? *dov'è...?*
could you show me the way to the Pantheon? *mi potrebbe indicare la strada per il Pantheon?*
is it near/far? *è vicino/lontano?*

Transport

car *macchina*
bus *autobus, auto*
coach *pullman*
taxi *tassì, taxi*
train *treno*
tram *tram*
plane *aereo*
bus stop *fermata (d'autobus)*
station *stazione*
platform *binario*
ticket/s *biglietto/biglietti*
one way *solo andata*
return *andata e ritorno*

(I'd like) a ticket for... *(vorrei) un biglietto per...*
where can I buy tickets? *dove si comprono i biglietti?*
are you getting off at the next stop? (ie get out of my way if you're not) *che, scende alla prossima?*
I'm sorry, I didn't know I had to stamp it *mi dispiace, non sapevo che lo dovevo timbrare*

Communications

phone *telefono*
fax *fax*
stamp *francobollo*
how much is a stamp for England/Australia/the US? *quanto viene un francobollo per l'Inghilterra/l'Australia/gli Stati Uniti?*
can I send a fax? *posso mandare un fax?*
can I make a phone call? *posso telefonare?*
letter *lettera*
postcard *cartolina*
courier *corriere, pony*

Shopping

I'd like to try the blue sandals/black shoes/brown boots *vorrei provare i sandali blu/le scarpe nere/gli stivali marroni*
do you have it/them in other colours? *ce l'ha in altri colori?*

I take (shoe) size... *porto il numero...*
I take (dress) size... *porto la taglia...*
it's too loose/too tight/just right *mi sta largo/stretto/bene*
can you give me a little more/less? *mi dia un po' di più/meno?*
100 grams of... *un etto di...*
300 grams of... *tre etti di...*
one kilo of... *un kilo/chilo di...*
five kilos of... *cinque chili di...*
a litre/two litres of... *un litro/due litri di*

Accommodation

a reservation *una prenotazione*
I'd like to book a single/twin/double room *vorrei prenotare una camera singola/doppia/matrimoniale*
I'd prefer a room with a bath/shower/window over the courtyard *preferirei una camera con vasca da bagno/doccia/finestra sul cortile*
can you bring me breakfast in bed? *mi porti la colazione al letto?*

Eating & drinking

I'd like to book a table for four at eight *vorrei prenotare una tavola per quattro alle otto*
that was poor/good/delicious *era mediocre/buono/ottimo*
the bill *il conto*
is service included? *è incluso il servizio?*
I think there's a mistake in this bill *credo che il conto sia sbagliato*

Days & nights

Monday *lunedì*; **Tuesday** *martedì*; **Wednesday** *mercoledì*; **Thursday** *giovedì*; **Friday** *venerdì*; **Saturday** *sabato*; **Sunday** *domenica*

yesterday *ieri*; **today** *oggi*; **tomorrow** *domani*; **morning** *mattina*; **afternoon** *pomeriggio*; **evening** *sera*; **night** *notte*; **weekend** *fine settimana, weekend*

Numbers & money

0 *zero*; **1** *uno*; **2** *due*; **3** *tre*; **4** *quattro*; **5** *cinque*; **6** *sei*; **7** *sette*; **8** *otto*; **9** *nove*; **10** *dieci*; **11** *undici*; **12** *dodici*; **13** *tredici*; **14** *quattordici*; **15** *quindici*; **16** *sedici*; **17** *diciassette*; **18** *diciotto*; **19** *diciannove*; **20** *venti*; **30** *trenta*; **40** *quaranta*; **50** *cinquanta*; **60** *sessanta*; **70** *settanta*; **80** *ottanta*; **90** *novanta*; **100** *cento*; **200** *duecento*; **1,000** *mille*; **2,000** *duemila*

how much is it/does it cost? *quanto costa/quant'è/quanto viene?*
do you take credit cards? *si accettano le carte di credito?*
can I pay in pounds/dollars/travellers' cheques? *posso pagare in sterline/dollari/con i travellers?*

The Menu

acqua water; olio d'oliva olive oil; pane bread; pepe pepper; sale salt; zucchero sugar; vino wine.

Sughi, condimenti e ripieni – sauces, toppings & fillings

alle vongole with clams; al pesto with a sauce of pine nuts, pecorino and basil; al ragù 'bolognese' (a term not used in Italy), ie with minced meat and tomatoes; al sugo with puréed cooked tomatoes; all'amatriciana with tomato, chilli, onion and sausage; all'arrabbiata with tomato and chilli; alla carbonara with bacon, egg and parmesan; alla puttanesca with olives, capers and garlic in hot oil; cacio e pepe with sheep's cheese and black pepper; (ravioli) ricotta e spinaci (ravioli) stuffed with cottage cheese and spinach; agnolotti, tortellini like ravioli but usually meat-filled.

Carne – meat

abbacchio, agnello lamb; capra, capretto goat, kid; coniglio rabbit; maiale pork; manzo beef; pancetta similar to bacon; pollo chicken; prosciutto cotto ham; prosciutto crudo Parma ham; tacchino turkey; vitello veal.

Roman offal specialities

coda alla vaccinara oxtail braised in a celery broth; pajata veal/lamb intestines with the mother's milk still inside; fagioli con le cotiche beans with pork scratchings; animelle pancreas and thymus glands, generally fried; tripa tripe; cervello brain; lingua tongue; guanciale cured pig's cheek; nervetti strips of cartilage.

Piatti di carne – meat dishes

carpaccio, bresaola thinly sliced cured beef; ossobuco beef shins with marrow jelly inside; polpette meatballs; porchetta roast piglet; salsicce sausages; saltimbocca veal strips and ham; spezzatino casseroled meat; spiedini anything on a spit; straccetti strips of beef or veal, stir-fried.

Formaggi – cheeses

cacio, caciotta cow's milk cheese; gorgonzola strong blue cheese, in creamy (dolce) or crumbly (piccante) varieties; parmigiano parmesan; pecorino romano hard, tangy sheep's cheese; ricotta crumbly white soft cheese; stracchino creamy, soft white cheese.

Pesce – fish

Sarago, dentice, marmora, orata, fragolino bream of various kinds; alici, acciughe anchovies; baccalà salt cod; branzino, spigola sea bass; cernia grouper; merluzzo cod; pesce San Pietro John Dory; pesce spada swordfish; razza, arzilla skate or ray; rombo turbot; salmone salmon; sarde, sardine sardines; sogliola sole; tonno tuna; trota trout.

Frutti di mare – seafood

astice, aragosta lobster; calamari squid; cozze mussels; crostacei shellfish; gamberi, gamberetti shrimps, prawns; granchio crab; mazzancolle king prawns; moscardini baby octopus; ostriche oysters; polipo, polpo octopus; seppie, seppioline cuttlefish; telline small clams; totani baby flying squid; vongole clams.

Verdura/il contorno – vegetables/side dish

asparagi asparagus; basilico basil; broccoli siciliani broccoli; broccolo green cauliflower; broccoletti tiny broccoli sprigs, cooked with the leaves; carciofi artichokes (alla romana steamed; alla giudea deep-fried); carote carrots; cavolfiore cauliflower; cicoria green leaf vegetable resembling dandelion; cipolle onions; fagioli haricot or borlotti beans; fagiolini green beans; fave broad beans; funghi mushrooms; funghi porcini boletus mushrooms; insalata salad; lattuga lettuce; melanzane aubergine; patate potatoes; patatine fritte french fries; peperoncino chilli; peperoni peppers (capsicum); piselli peas; pomodori tomatoes; porri leeks; prezzemolo parsley; puntarelle bitter Roman salad usually dressed with an anchovy sauce; radicchio bitter purple lettuce; rughetta, rucola rocket; scarola type of lettuce; sedano celery; spinaci spinach; verza cabbage; zucchine courgettes.

Frutta – fruit

albicocche apricots; ananas pineapple; arance oranges; cachi persimmons; ciliege cherries; coccomero, anguria watermelon; fichi figs; fragole, fragoline strawberries, wild strawberries; frutti di bosco woodland berries; mele apples; nespole loquats; pere pears; pesche peaches; prugne, susine plums; uva grapes.

Dolci/il dessert – desserts

gelato ice cream; pannacotta 'cooked cream', a very thick, blancmange-like cream; sorbetto sorbet; tiramisù mascarpone and coffee sponge; torta della nonna flan of pâtisserie cream and pine nuts; torta di mele apple flan; millefoglie flaky pastry cake.

Pizza & pizza toppings

calzone a sealed pizza pie, usually filled with cheese, tomato and ham; capricciosa ham, hard-boiled eggs, artichokes and olives; funghi mushrooms; marinara plain tomato, sometimes with anchovies; margherita tomato and mozzarella; napoli, napoletana tomato, anchovies and mozzarella; quattro formaggi four cheeses; quattro stagioni mozzarella, artichoke, egg and mushrooms.

Pizzeria extras

bruschetta toast with garlic rubbed into it and oil on top, and usually diced raw tomatoes; crochette potato croquettes; crostini slices of toast, usually with a grilled cheese and anchovy topping; filetto di baccalà deep-fried salt cod in batter; olive ascolane deep-fried olives stuffed with sausage meat; supplì deep-fried rice balls with mozzarella inside (may contain minced meat).

Good veggie options

orecchiette ai broccoletti/cima di rape ear-shaped pasta with broccoli sprigs/green turnip-tops; pasta e ceci soup with pasta and chickpeas; pasta e fagioli soup with pasta and borlotti beans; pasta alla puttanesca/alla checca based on olives, capers and tomatoes, though anchovies (alici) are sometimes slipped into the former; penne all'arrabbiata pasta with tomato sauce and lots of chilli; ravioli acceptable if filled with ricotta e spinaci and served with burro e salvia (butter and sage); spaghetti aglio, olio e peperoncino with garlic, chilli and olive oil; spaghetti cacio e pepe with crumbled salty sheep's cheese and black pepper; fagioli all'uccelletto haricot beans with tomato, garlic and olive oil; melanzane alla parmigiana aubergine with mozzarella (occasionally has meat in the topping); scamorza grilled cheese – specify without ham (senza prosciutto) or without anchovies (senza alici).

Directory

Further Reference

Books

Classics

Catullus *The Poems*
Sometimes malicious, sometimes pornographic

Juvenal *Satires*
A contemporary view of ancient Rome's seedy underbelly

Ovid *The Erotic Poems*
Ovid's handbook for cynical lovers got him banished from Rome

Suetonius *The Twelve Caesars*
Salacious biographies of rulers from Julius Caesar to Domitian

Virgil *The Aeneid*
Rome's foundation myth is a great yarn

Fiction & literature

Lyndsey Davis The Falco series
Ancient detective romps around the Empire

Michael Dibdin *Vendetta*
Thriller set in contemporary Rome

George Eliot *Middlemarch*
Dorothea's big honeymoon let-down takes place in 19th-century Rome

Nathaniel Hawthorn
The Marble Faun
A quaint, moralising novel about two female artists in Rome

Henry James *The Portrait of a Lady*
Besides *Portrait*, try *Daisy Miller* and a couple of essays in *Italian Hours*

Elsa Morante *History*
A compelling evocation of life for the very poor in wartime Rome

Shakespeare *Julius Caesar, Antony and Cleopatra, Titus Andronicus, Coriolanus*

Non-fiction

Donald Dudley *Roman Society*
Culture, politics and economics from 9th century BC to 4th century AD

Paul Ginsborg *Italy and its Discontents*
Excellent introduction to the ups and downs of post-war Italy

Michael Grant *History of Rome*
Highly readable and full of facts

Peter Hebblethwaite *In the Vatican*
Opinionated insight into the inner workings of the Vatican

Christopher Hibbert
Biography of a City
Engaging account of Rome's history

Tobias Jones *The Dark Heart of Italy*
Exploration of some of the country's dark contemporary secrets

John Kelly *The Oxford Dictionary of Popes*
The life stories of the pontiffs

Georgina Masson *Queen Christina*
Biography of the Catholic Church's illustrious Protestant convert, giving great insights into 17th-century Rome

Alexander Stille *The Sack of Rome, Excellent Cadavers*
Studies of Italy under Berlusconi, and of the Mafia

Rudolf Wittkower *Art and Architecture in Italy 1600-1750*
All about the Baroque

Films

Italian

See also pp261-264 Film.

Accattone
(Pier Paolo Pasolini, 1961)
Sub-proletarian no-hoper Franco Citti careers from bad to worse to ignominious early death in Testaccio in this devastating portrait of the lowest of Rome's low

Bellissima
(Luchino Visconti, 1951)
Screen-struck mamma Anna Magnani pushes her plain and ungifted daughter through the agony of the film-studio casting circuit

Caro Diario (Dear Diary)
(Nanni Moretti, 1994)
As much a wry love letter to Moretti's home town as a diary

La Dolce Vita
(Federico Fellini, 1960)
The late, great Fellini's unforgettable portrait of the fast-lane, paparazzo-fuelled life in 1950s and '60s Rome

Fellini's Roma
(Federico Fellini, 1972)
Patchwork of cameos with visual gems that only the master could pull off

Mamma Roma
(Pier Paolo Pasolini, 1962)
Anna Magnani in a gut-wrenching performance as a mother striving, and failing, to keep her son from a bad end in the mean streets of Rome's outskirts

Roma, Città Aperta
(Roberto Rossellini, 1945)
This semi-documentary on the wartime Resistance is considered the foundation stone of neo-realism

International

The Agony & the Ecstasy
(Carol Reed, 1965)
Charlton Heston – looking much like a muscly Michelangelo statue if not the artist himself – daubs the Sistine ceiling as Pope Rex Harrison looks on

Ben-Hur
(William Wilder, 1959)
Charlton Heston pushes sexual ambivalence to its limits in this epic, with religion and a chariot race chucked in for good measure

Gladiator
(Ridley Scott, 2000)
Russell Crowe's general Maximus flexes his muscles in the Colosseum, watched by Emperor Commodus

Ocean's Twelve
(Steven Soderbergh, 2004)
George, Brad, et al target a Roman art museum for their big heist

Quo Vadis?
(Mervyn Le Roy, 1951)
Blood, sand and love in the lions' den; a huge – and hugely long – epic

Roman Holiday
(William Wyler, 1953)
Endlessly endearing story of bored Princess Audrey Hepburn on the lam in Rome – uniquely for its time, it was filmed on location

The Roman Spring of Mrs Stone
(Jose Quintero, 1961)
Fading, widowed Vivien Leigh tries to spice up her Roman holiday with an affair with gigolo Warren Beatty

Spartacus
(Stanley Kubrick, 1960)
Kirk Douglas does his best to get the slaves revolting in another marathon

The Talented Mr Ripley
(Anthony Minghella, 1999)
Jude and Matt play out part of their tortuous relationship against a Roman background

Three Coins in the Fountain
(Jean Negulesco, 1954)
Rome looks like one big, luscious postcard, and the three American tourist lasses get their Latin lovers

Websites

For information on museums and archaeological sites in the city, try the Cultural Heritage Ministry's exhaustive website:
www.beniculturali.it
Other informative sites include:

www.atac.roma.it
Transport in and around the city, with a useful journey-planner

www.enjoyrome.com
Informative site of the ever-reliable Enjoy Rome agency (*see p337*)

www.pierreci.it
Constantly updated guide to museums and exhibitions

www.romaturismo.com
The city council/APT (*see p337*) site has information on exhibitions, theatres and what to do wth your kids

Index

Note: page numbers in **bold** indicate section(s) giving key information on a topic; *italics* indicate photos.

Index

Advertisers' Index

Please refer to relevant pages for full contact details.

Place of interest and/or entertainment	■
Railway station	■
Parks	■
Area name	TRIDENTE
Metro lines	✕
Hospital	**H**
Church	⛪

Maps

COMMUNICATIONS

englishyellowpages.it

online **directory** of **english-speaking**

professionals and businesses in italy,

culture shock **blog**,

free **classified ads**,

English speakers' **job bank**,

photo gallery of events

and more...

"Helping English speakers in Italy for over 20 years."

Rome
Overview

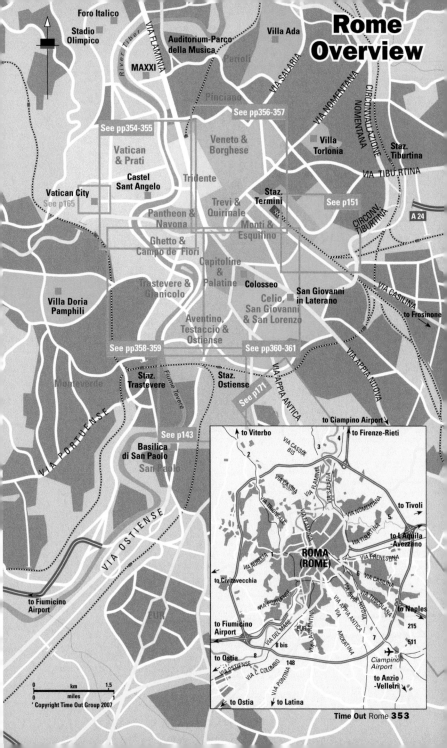

Foro Italico

Stadio Olimpico

VIA FLAMINIA

River Tiber

Auditorium-Parco della Musica

MAXXI

Villa Ada

VIA SALARIA

Parioli

Pinciano

See pp354-355

VIA NOMENTANA

CIRCONVALLAZIONE NOMENTANA

Vatican & Prati

Veneto & Borghese

See pp356-357

Villa Torlonia

Staz. Tiburtina

Castel Sant Angelo

Tridente

VIA TIBURTINA

Vatican City

See p165

Pantheon & Navona

Trevi & Quirinale

Staz. Termini

See p151

CIRCONV. TIBURTINA

A 24

Ghetto & Campo de' Fiori

Monti & Esquilino

Capitoline & Palatine

Trastevere & Gianicolo

Colosseo

San Giovanni in Laterano

VIA CASILINA

Villa Doria Pamphili

Celio, San Giovanni & San Lorenzo

to Frosinone

Aventino, Testaccio & Ostiense

See pp358-359

See pp360-361

VIA APPIA NUOVA

Monteverde

Staz. Trastevere

Fiume Tevere

Staz. Ostiense

VIA APPIA ANTICA

See p171

to Ciampino Airport

VIA PORTUENSE

See p143

to Viterbo

to Firenze-Rieti

VIA CASSIA BIS

3   4

Basilica di San Paolo

San Paolo

2

VIA CASSIA

VIA FLAMINIA

VIA SALARIA

to Tivoli

VIA TRIONFALE

VIA FLAMINIA

VIA NOMENTANA

5

VIA OSTIENSE

VIA TIBURTINA

to L'Aquila -Avezzano

VIA AURELIA

1

ROMA (ROME)

VIA PRENESTINA

to Civitavecchia

6

VIA CASILINA

VIA PORTUENSE

VIA APPIA NUOVA

VIA TUSCOLANA

to Naples

to Fiumicino Airport

VIA DEL MARE

EUR

VIA APPIA ANTICA

VIA ARDEATINA

215

to Fiumicino Airport

8 bis

VIA LAURENTINA

VIA C. COLOMBO

7

511

to Ostia

8

148

VIA PONTINA

Ciampino Airport

VIA OSTIENSE

to Ostia

to Latina

to Anzio -Velletri

to Fiumicino Airport

km   1.5

miles

Copyright Time Out Group 2007

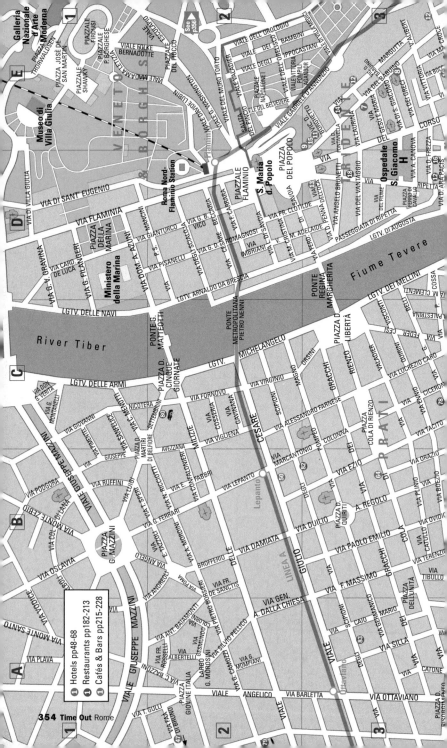

Galleria Nazionale d'Arte Moderna

PIAZZA JOSÉ DE SAN MARTIN

PIAZZA THORWALDSEN

PIAZZALE P. BORGHESE

PIAZZALE SHAWAN

Museo di Villa Giulia

V E N E T O — B O R G H E S E

PIAZZA DI SIENA

VIA MADAMA LETIZIA

VIALE FOLKE BERNADOTTE

PIAZZALE DEL PICCO

PIAZZALE FIRDUSI

See p356

PIAZZALE DEL OROLOGIO

VIALE DEL MURO TORTO

VIALE DELL'OROLOGIO

VIALE DEI BAMBINI

VIALE DEGLI OBELISCHI

VIALE DELL'IPPOCASTANI

VIALE NAPOLEONE I

VIALE VITTORIA PINCIANA

VIALE GABRIELE D'ANNUNZIO

SALITA DEL PINCIO

VIALE DEL BELVEDERE

VIA LUDOVISI

T R I D E N T E

VIA DI S. GIACOMO

VIA DEL BABUINO

VIA GESÙ E MARIA

VIA DEI GRECI

VIA DELLA CROCE

VIA VITTORIA

VIA DELLA VITE

VIA DELLA BOCCA

CORSO

VIA MARGUTTA

V. ALIBERT

VIA BOCC

PIAZZA DEL POPOLO

S. Maria d. Popolo

PIAZZALE FLAMINIO

Roma Nord-Flaminio Station

VIA FERDINANDO DI SAVOIA

VIA PR. CLOTILDE

VIA ANGELO BRUNETTI

VIA DELLA PENNA

VIA DELL'OCA

VIA DEL VANTAGGIO

VIA DEL FIUME

VIA DEL CORSO

Ospedale S. Giacomo H

VIA CANOVA

VIA D. FONTANELLA BORGHESE

VIA RIPETTA

PIAZZA DEL FERRO DI CAVALLO

PIAZZA D. ARA PACIS

PASSEGGIATA DI RIPETTA

LGTV. DI AUGUSTA

VIA FLAMINIA

PIAZZA DELLA MARINA

VIA G. GRAVINA

VIA CARD. DE LUCA

VIA G. FILANGERI

VIA DI VILLA GIULIA

VIA DI SANT'EUGENIO

VIA MANCINI

VIA G. GIANTURCO

VIA DEGLI SCIALOJA

VIA P.S. MANCINI

VIA DOM. A. AZUNI

VIA PISANELLI

VIA G. B. VICO

VIA G. SACCHI

VIA G. B. DE ROSSI

VIA F. CARRARA

VIA CESARE BECCARIA

VIA CROMAGNOSI

VIA L. DI SAVOIA

VIA M. CRISTINA

VIA FERD. DI SAVOIA

VIA FERD. ADELAIDE

VIA IMBRIANI

PIAZZA D. LIBERTÀ

Ministero della Marina

LGTV. DELLE NAVI

LGTV. ARNALDO DA BRESCIA

PONTE REGINA MARGHERITA

Fiume Tevere

LGTV. DEI MELLINI

LGTV. IN AUGUSTA

VIA M. CLEMENTI

COSSA

River Tiber

LGTV. DELLE ARMI

PONTE G. MATTEOTTI

PIAZZA D. CINQUE GIORNATE

PONTE METROPOLITANA PIETRO NENNI

LGTV.

MICHELANGELO

MAGNO ORSINI

VIA VIRGINIO

VIA SCIPIONI

GRACCHI

RIENZO

PIAZZA D. LIBERTÀ

LGTV. LUCREZIO CARO

PALESTRINA

VIA CRESCENZIO

VISCONTI

CESI

VIA FEDER

VIA TACITO

VIA CICERONE

NICOTERA

VIA SETTEMBRINI

VIA FORNOVO

VIA COSSERIA

VIA COLA DI RIENZO

P R A T I

VIA ENNIO

VIA TACITO

VIA DON G. VERITÀ

VIA G. MONTANELLI

VIA SAN FELICE

VIA PIMENTEL

VIA GIOVANNI

VIA GRINVIANA

VIA VIGLIENA

VIA MILIZIE

VIA ALESSANDRO FARNESE

POMPEO

COLONNA

PIAZZA COLA DI RIENZO

VIA ORAZIO

VIA PLINIO

VIA BOEZIO

GIUSEPPE

PIAZZA D. MARTIRI DI BELFIORE

AVEZZANA

VIA N. RICCIOTTI

VIA CONFALONIERI

VIA MARCANTONIO

VIA EZIO

A. REGOLO

VIA POMPEO

VIA OVIDIO

VIA MONTE ZEBIO

VIA COL

VIA LUIGI

VIA T. SPERI

VIA G. FERRARI

VIA LEPANTO

Lepanto

DEGLI

PIAZZA D. QUIRITI

VIA POGORA

VIA RUFFINI

VIA DUILIO

VIA COLA

VIA CATTULLO

VIA OSLAVIA

VIALE GIUSEPPE MAZZINI

VIA ANGELO

BROFFERIO

VIA DELLE

VIA DAMIATA

VIA PAOLO EMILIO

GRACCHI

VIA TERENZIO

VIA TIBULLO

PIAZZA G. MAZZINI

VIA SILVIO PELLICO

VIA GEN. A. DALLA CHIESA

VIA F. MASSIMO

SCIPIONI

CAIO MARIO

PIAZZA DELL'UNITÀ

VIA MONTE ZEBIO

VIA COL DI LANA

VIA A. MORDINI

VIA E. TAZZOLI

VIA FR. BORSIERI

VIA PIETRO BORSIERI

LINEA A

GIULIO CESARE

VIA GERMANICO

VIA SILLA

VIA MONTE SANTO

VIA MONTE NEVOSO

VIA PLAVA

VIA ANT. BAIAMONTI

VIA ANDREOLI

VIA FR. ROSSELLI

VIA G. ALBERTELLI

VIA CARLO MONTI

LARGO G. MORDINI

VIA G. MOMPIANI

VIA GEN.

VIALE ANGELICO

VIA BARLETTA

PIAZZA DELLA GIOVINE ITALIA

VIALE GIUSEPPE MAZZINI

Ottaviano

VIA OTTAVIANO

VIA CATONE

PIAZZA DEL RISORGIMENTO

1 Hotels pp48-68
1 Restaurants pp182-213
1 Cafés & Bars pp215-228

VIA T. GULLI

VIA A. DI BRUNO

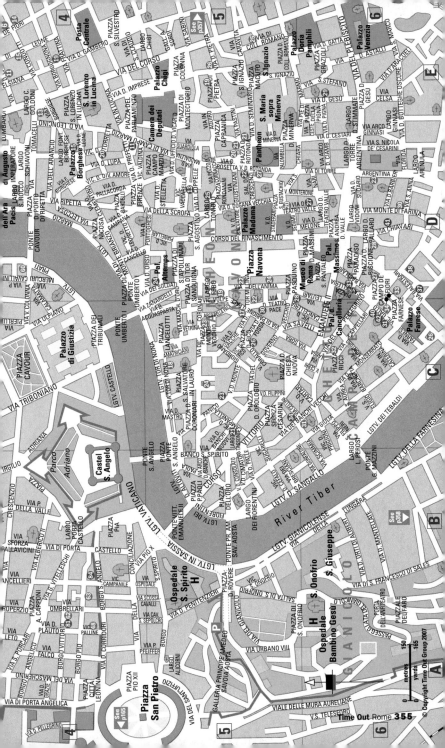

© Copyright Time Out Group 2007

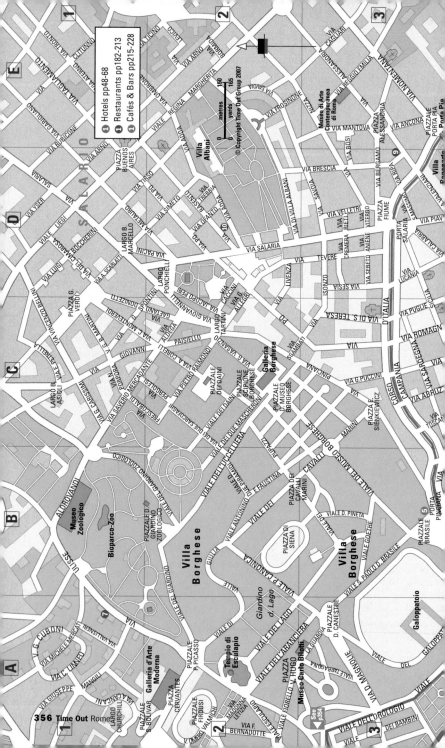

- 1 Hotels pp48-68
- 1 Restaurants pp182-213
- 1 Cafés & Bars pp215-228

metres 150
yards 165
© Copyright Time Out Group 2007

1 E **1** D **1** C **1** B **1** A

2 E **2** D **2** C **2** B **2** A

3 E **3** D **3** C **3** B **3** A

VIA TAGLIAMENTO
VIA DEI TRONTI
VIA METAURO
VIA TICINO
VIA ARNO
VIA ADIGE
VIA MARGHERITA
VIA PO
VIA SAVOIA
VIA NOMENTANA
VIA CAGLIARI
VIA ALESSANDRIA
VIA REGGIO EMILIA

VIA BURRICONE
VIA GABAGLIANO
VIA GARIGLIANO
PIAZZA
BUENOS
AIRES
Villa
Albani
VIA FROSINONE
Museo di Arte
Contemporanea
di Roma
VIA MANTOVA
PIAZZALE
PORTA PIA
Villa

VIA V SER
VIALE LIEGI
VIA DE' CHIAVARESI
VIALE B. BUOZZI
LARGO B.
MARCELLO
VIA SALARIA
VIA BRESCIA
VIA BOSI
VIA BERGAMO
VIA RIPA
VIA ANCONA
PIAZZA
ALESSANDRIA
Villa

VIA SCARLATTI
VIA PACINI
LARGO
PONCHIELLI
VIA DI VILLA ALBANI
VIA VELLETRI
VIA VITERBO
PIAZZA
FIUME
PORTA
SALARIA
VIA PIAV
VIA CALABRIA

PIAZZA G.
VERDI
VIA VINCENZO BELLINI
VIA SPONTINI
VIA GIOVANNI
PAISIELLO
VIA G. CACCINI
VIA G.
ALLEGRI
VIA TEVERE
VIA CREMERA
VIA ANIENE
VIA SESIA
VIA SEBETO
VIA LUCANIA
VIA PUGLIE
VIA SICILIA
VIA ROMAGN
VIA TOSCAN
VIA SARDEGNA
VIA ABRUZZ

LARGO B.
ASIOLI
VIA N.
PORPORA
VIA SALVERO MERCADANTE
VIA PERGOLESI
VIA PIETRO RAIMONDI
VIA PIETRO RAIMONDI
PIAZZALE
DEI DAINI
PIAZZALE
SCIPIONE
BORGHESE
Galleria
Borghese
PIAZZALE
DEL MUSEO
BORGHESE
CORSO
PIAZZA
SIENKIEWICZ
VIA G. PUCCINI
VIA CAMPANIA

VIALE DEL GIARDINO
ZOOLOGICO
PIAZZALE DEL
GIARDINO
ZOOLOGICO
VIALE DEL GIARDINO
VIALE DELL'UCCELLIERA
VIALE DEI DUE MASCHERONI
VIALE DELLE DUE MASCHERONI
VIALE DEL MUSEO BORGHESE
PIAZZA DEI
CAVALLI
MARINI
CAVALLI
MARINI

ALDROVANDI
Museo
Zoologico
Bioparco-Zoo
VIA ULISSE
Villa
Borghese
VIALE P. CANONICA
PIAZZA DI
SIENA
VIALE GOETHE
Villa
Borghese
PIAZZALE
BRASILE
PIAZZALE
BRASILE

VIA G. CUBONI
VIALE DELL'ANNO
VIALE ANTONINO
GIULIA
Giardino
d. Lago
VIALE DEL LAGO
VIALE D. PINETA
VIALE D.

VIA GIUSEPPE
Galleria d'Arte
Moderna
PIAZZA
CERVANTES
PIAZZALE
F. PICASSO
Tempio di
Esculapio
VIALE DELL'ARANCIERA
Museo Carlo Bilotti
PIAZZALE
D. CANESTRE
GALOPPATOIO
Galoppatoio

LARGO
CHURCHILL
PIAZZALE
S. BOLIVAR
PIAZZALE
FIRDUSI
VIA MADONNA
LETIZIA
VIA F.
BERNADOTTE
PIAZZA
FIORELLO - V. HUGO
VIALE DELL'OROLOGIO
VIALE DEI BAMBINI

See
p354

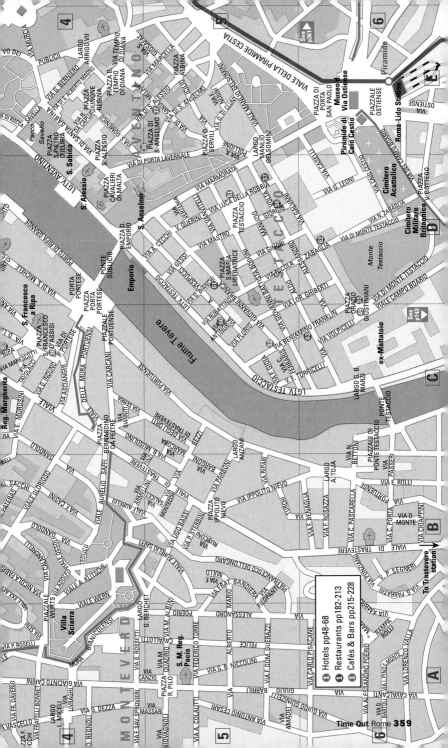

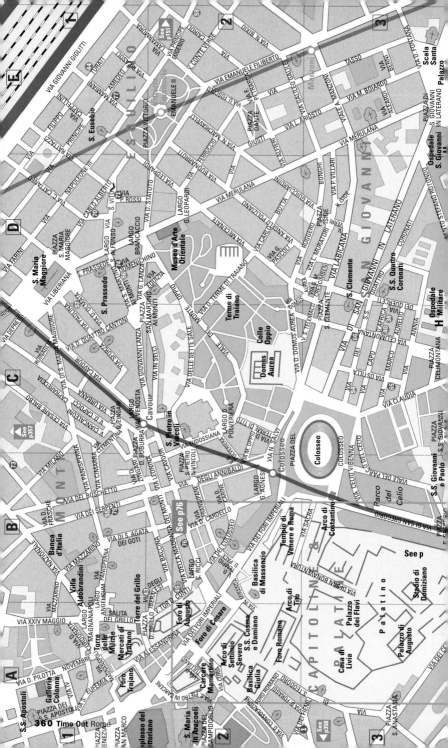

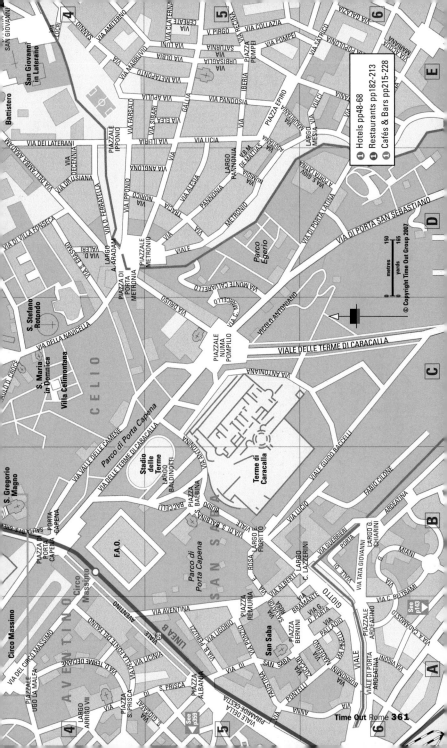

Hotels pp48-68
Restaurants pp182-213
Cafés & Bars pp215-228

© Copyright Time Out Group 2007

Street Index

Marsi via dei - 151 C3
Martini GB. via - 356 C1
Martiri di Belfiore pza - 354 B1
Marzi G. B. Igo - 359 C6
Marzio Igtv - 355 D4
Maschera d'Oro via - 355 C5
Mascherino via del - 165 D2
Mascherone via - 358 C2
Masdea E. pza - 143 C3
Masina via - 358 A3
Massaia vie - 143 D3/D4
Massari via - 359 A5
Massimi pza dei - 355 D6
Massimo F. via - 354 B3
Mastai pza - 354 C2
Mastro Giorgio via - 359 D5
Mastro via - 355 C5
Mattei pza - 358 D2
Matteotti ponte - 354 C2
Matteucci P. via - 143 B1
Mattonato via del - 358 B3
Mauritania via - 361 E5
Mazzarino via - 360 B1
Mazzarino via - 357 B6
Mazzini G. pza, vie - 354 A3
Mazzini ponte - 355 B6
Mecenate via - 360 D2
Medici via - 358 A3
Mellini Igtv dei - 354 D3
Melone via del - 355 D6
Meloria via - 165 A1
Mengoli M. via - 143 A3
Menotti C. via - 354 C1
Mentana via - 357 E4
Mercadante S. via - 356 C1
Mercanti pza - 358 D3
Mercantili via - 358 A3
Mercati M. via - 354 A1
Mercede via - 357 A5
Mercuri via - 355 D4
Merini F. via - 359 E5
Merulana via - 360 D2/E3
Mesia via - 361 E6
Messapi via - 151 C3
Metaponto via - 361 E5
Metauro via - 356 D1
Metronio pde, vle - 361 D5
Miani G. via - 143 C1
Micca P. via - 151 B4
Miceli L. Igo - 359 A4
Michelangelo bastioni di - 165 C1
Michelangelo Igtv - 354 C2
Mignanelli pza - 357 A4
Milano via - 357 C6
Milazzo via - 357 E5
Milizie vle delle - 354 A2/C2
Mille via dei - 357 E5
Millelire D. via - 165 A2
Mincio via - 356 E1
Minerva pza, via della - 355 E5
Minghetti via - 357 A6
Miranda via in - 360 B2
Misericordia via - 358 E3
Modelli via - 357 A6
Modena via - 357 C5, 358 C3
Moletta via - 143 C2
Molise via - 357 B4
Mompiani via - 354 A2
Monserrato via - 355 C6
Montanelli G. via - 354 C1
Monte Aureo rampa di - 358 B3
Monte Brianzo via di - 355 D4
Monte Calvarello via - 361 D5
Monte di Farina via - 355 D6
Monte Oppio vle del - 360 C2/D2
Monte Santo via - 354 A2
Monte Testaccio via di - 143 A1
Monte Zebio via - 354 B1
Montebello via - 357 E4
Montecchi via - 359 B5
Montectorio pza di - 355 E5
Montecorvino G. da via - 143 D3
Montemartini G. Igo - 357 D5
Monterone via - 355 D6
Montevecchio pza - 355 C5
Montoro via - 355 C6
Montuori Comboni via - 143 C4
Mordini via - 354 B2
Moro Aldo pzle - 151 B1
Moro via del - 358 C2/C3
Moroni vic - 358 C2
Morosini E. via - 359 C4
Morosini Igo - 354 A2
Munari via - 143 C3
Mura Aureliane vle delle - 355 A6
Mura Gianicolensi vle delle -
358-359 A3/A4
Mura Portuensi vle delle - 359 C4
Mura Vaticane clivio delle - 165 A2
Muratori via - 360 D3
Muratte via delle - 357 A6
Murcia via - 359 A4
Muro Torto vle del - 354 E2,
356-357 A3/A4
Museo Borghese pzle del - 356 C2
Museo Borghese vle del - 356 B3
Musolino via - 359 C5

Nansen via - 143 B2
Napoleone I pzle - 354 E2
Napoleone III via - 360 D1
Napoli via - 357 C5
Nari via - 355 D6
Natale del Grande via - 358 C3
Navi Igtv delle - 354 D1
Navicella via della - 361 C4
Navona pza - 355 D5
Nazionale via - 357 B6/D5
Nazzareno via di - 357 A5
Negri F. via - 143 C2
Nenni P. ponte - 354 C2
Nerva via - 357 D4
Niccolini via - 359 A5
Nicolò da Pistoia via - 143 C2
Nicolò V via - 165 A4
Nicotera G. via - 354 C1
Nievo I. pza, via - 359 B5
Nizza via - 356 D3/E2
Nomentana via - 356 E3
Norico via - 361 D5
Novembre IV via - 360 A1
Nullo F. via - 359 B5
Numa Pompilio pzle - 361 C5
Numidia via - 361 D5
Obelisco vle del - 354 E2
Oca via dell' - 354 D3
Odero N. via - 143 C4
Ofanto via - 356 D2
Olbia via - 361 E5
Olmata via - 360 C2
Olmetto via - 358 D3
Olona via - 356 E1
Ombrellari via - 355 A4
Ombrone via - 356 E2
Oppio via - 360 C2
Oratorio pza del - 357 A6
Orazio da Pennab. via - 143 D3
Orazio via - 354 B3
Orgoglio vle del - 354 E2
Orlando L. via - 143 C3
Orlando VE. via - 357 D5
Oro pza dell' - 355 B5
Orologio pza del - 355 C5
Orsini V. via - 354 C2/C3
Orso via del - 355 D5
Orsucci via - 358 D3
Orti di Alibert via - 355 B6
Orti di Trastevere via degli - 359 C5
Osci Igo di - 151 C2/C3
Oslavia via - 354 B1
Ospedale via - 355 B4/B5
Ossoli vle - 359 B4
Ostiense circonvallazione - 143 C2
Ostiense pzle - 143 B1
Ostiense via - 143 B1/B4
Ostiense vic - 143 B3
Ostilia via - 360 C3
Ottaviano via - 354 A3
Ovidio via - 354 B3
Pacini via - 356 D2
Pacinotti A. via - 143 A1
Paganiga via - 358 D2
Pagano via - 357 C4
Paglia via delle - 358 B3
Paisiello G. via - 356 C1/C2
Palatino ponte - 358 D3
Palermo via - 357 C6
Palestrari via - 355 D6
Palestro via - 357 E4
Pallacorda via - 355 D4
Palladio via - 361 A5
Pallaro Igo di - 355 D6
Palle via delle - 355 B5
Palline vic delle - 355 A4
Pallotti pza - 358 C2
Palombella via - 355 D5
Pandosia via - 361 E5
Panetteria via della - 357 A5
Panico via - 355 C5
Panieri via del - 358 B3
Panisperna via - 360 B1/C1
Pannonia Igo, via - 361 D5
Pantera pza - 143 C3
Paola via - 355 B5
Paoli P. pza - 355 B5
Paolina via - 360 C2
Papa di Pietra Igtv - 143 A3/A4
Papa P. via di - 143 A2
Papareschi Igtv dei - 143 A2
Paradiso pza - 355 D6, 358 C1
Parboni via - 359 B5
Parco del Celio vle del - 360 B3
Parco S Paolo pzle - 143 B3
Parco Tiburtino pza di - 151 C2
Parco di Villa Corsini via di - 358 A2
Parigi via - 357 B6
Parione O Pace via - 355 C5
Parlamento pza del - 355 E4
Paroli via - 357 B6
Parrasio G. via - 359 B6
Partigiani pzle dei - 143 C1
Pascarella C. via - 359 B6
Pascoli G. via - 360 D2
Pasquino pza - 355 D5
Passalacqua via - 151 C4

Passamonti S. Igo - 151 D2
Passeri via - 359 B6
Passino F. via - 143 C4
Pastini via - 355 E5
Pastrengo via - 357 D4
Pateras via - 359 B4
Pazzoli via - 354 A2
Peano via - 143 A3
Pelasgi via dei- 151 B2
Pelgni via - 151 B2
Pellegrino D. via - 165 D2
Pellegrino via del - 355 C6
Pellicciai via dei - 358 C3
Pellico S. via - 354 A2
Penitenza via della - 358 B2
Penitenzieri via del - 355 A5
Pepe via - 151 A3
Peretti via - 358 D3
Pergolesi via - 356 C2
Peri J. via - 356 C2
Perosi Igo - 355 B6/C6
Perotti via - 359 A6
Persico I. via - 143 C3
Peruzzi via - 361 A5
Pession via - 143 A3
Petrarca F. via - 360 D2
Petrella via - 356 C1
Petroselli via - 358 E3
Pettinari via - 358 C2
Pfeiffr via - 355 A5
Pia pza - 355 B4
Piacenza via - 357 B6/C5
Pianellari vic dei - 355 D5
Piave via - 356-357 D3/D4
Picasso pzle - 356 A2
Piceni via - 151 D2
Piè di Marmo via - 355 E6
Piemonte via - 356-357 C3/C4
Pierleoni Igtv di - 358 E3
Pietra pza, via di - 355 E5
Pietrasanta via - 143 C3
Pigafetta via - 143 C2
Pigna pza, via della - 355 E6
Pilo R. pza - 359 A5
Pilotta pza, via - 357 A6
Pimentel via - 354 C1
Pinciana via - 356 C3
Pincio salita del - 354 E2
Pindemonte via - 359 B6
Pinelli via - 361 A5
Pineta vle della - 356 B3
Pio borgo - 165 D2
Pio X via - 165 C2, 355 B4/B5
Pio XII pza - 165 D3
Piombo via del - 358 E1
Piramide Cestia via della - 359 E5
Pirgo via - 361 E5
Pisacane C. via - 359 A6
Pisanelli via - 354 D2
Piscinula pza in - 358 D3
Plauto via - 355 A4
Plava via - 354 A1
Plebiscito via del - 355 E6
Plinio via - 354 B3
Po via - 356 C3/D1
Podgora via - 354 B1
Poerio A. via - 359 A5/A6
Pola pza - 357 A5
Polacchi via - 358 E2
Policlinico vle del - 357 E4
Poliziano A. via - 360 D2
Pollaiolo pza - 358 C3
Pollione A. via - 359 E5
Polo Marco vle - 143 C1
Polveriera Igo, via della - 360 C2
Polverone via - 358 C2
Poma via - 354 B2
Pompei pza, via - 361 E5
Pompeo Magno via - 354 B3/C2
Ponchielli Igo - 356 D2
Ponte Cavallo salita - 357 B6
Ponte Rotto via - 358 D3
Ponte S Angelo pza - 355 B5
Ponte Savello pza - 358 D3
Ponte Testaccio pzle di - 359 B6
Ponte Umberto I pza - 355 D4
Ponte Venti via - 356 C1
Pontelli via - 361 A5/A6
Ponziani pza di - 358 D3
Ponziano via - 359 B6
Ponzio via - 361 A5
Popolo pza del - 354 D2
Populonia via - 361 E6
Porcari S. via - 355 A4
Porpora via - 356 C1
Porta Angelica via di - 165 D2
Porta Ardeatina vle - 361 A5
Porta Ardeatina via di - 143 D1
Porta C. via - 359 B6
Porta Capena pza - 361 B4
Porta Castello Igo, via di - 355 B4
Porta Cavalleggeri via di - 165 C4
Porta G. via - 361 A5
Porta Labicana via - 151 C3
Porta Latina via di - 361 C5/D6
Porta Lavernale via di - 359 E5

Porta Maggiore pza - 151 C4
Porta Maggiore via di - 151 B4
Porta Metronia pza di - 361 D4
Porta Pia pzle - 356 E3
Porta Pinciana - 356 B3
Porta Pinciana via di - 357 B4
Porta Portese pza, via di - 359 C4
Porta S Giovanni pza di - 361 E4
Porta S Lorenzo pzle - 151 B3
Porta S Lorenzo via - 151 B2
Porta di S Pancrazio Igo - 358 A3
Porta di S Pancrazio via - 358 B3
Porta S Sebastiano via di - 361 D6
Porta Salaria - 356 D3
Porta Tiburtina via - 151 B2
Portico via del - 358 D2
Porto di Ripetta pza di - 355 D4
Porto Fluviale via del - 143 A1
Porto via di - 359 D4
Portoghesi via dei - 355 D5
Portuense pzle, via - 359 C4
Posta via - 165 C2
Pozzo delle Cornacchie via - 355 D5
Prati Igtv - 355 D4
Prefetti via - 355 D4
Pretoriano vle - 151 B1
Pretorio Castro via - 151 A1
Prigioni vic delle - 355 C6
Principe Amedeo via - 357 D5/E6
Principe Amedeo Savoia Aosta
  ponte - 355 B5
Principe Amedeo Savoia Aosta
  galleria - 355 A5
Principe Eugenio via - 151 A3/A4
Principe Umberto via - 151 B3
Propaganda via della - 357 A5
Properzio via - 355 A4
Publicii clivio dei - 359 E4
Publicii pza - 359 D3
Puglie via - 356 C3
Pullino G. via - 143 C3
Pupazzi vle del - 356 B3/C2
Purificazione via della - 357 B4/B5
Quadrio M. via - 359 A5
Quattro Cantoni via dei - 360 C1
Quattro Fontane via delle - 357 C5
Querini via - 359 D5
Quirinale pza, via del - 357 B6
Quirini Visconti E. via - 354 C3
Quiriti pza - 354 B3
Raffaello Sanzio Igtv - 358 C2
Raimodi via - 356 C2
Ramni via dei - 151 B2
Randaccio via - 143 C3
Rasella via - 357 B5
Rattazzi via - 360 E1
Recina via - 361 E5
Reggio Emilia via - 356 E3
Regina Margherita ponte - 354 D3
Regina Margherita vie - 356 E2
Regnoli O. via - 359 A4
Regolo A. D. via - 354 B3
Remuria pza - 361 A5
Renella via - 358 C3
Repubblica pza della - 357 D5
Reti via dei - 151 D2
Revere via - 359 A6
Rialto via - 143 B1
Riari via dei - 358 B2
Ricasoli via - 151 A3
Ricci C. Igo - 360 B2
Ricci via - 143 B1
Riciotti via - 354 B2
Rieti via - 357 D3
Righi Augusto via - 143 A4
Rinascimento corso del - 355 D5
Ripa Grande porto di - 359 D4
Ripa Igtv - 358 D3
Ripa via - 356 D3
Ripari via - 359 B6
Ripetta passeggiata di - 354 D3
Ripetta via - 354-355 D3/D4
Risorgimento pza - 165 D1, 354 A3
Rocca Savella clivio de - 359 E4
Rocco via - 143 B3
Roh G. via - 143 D4
Rolli E. via - 359 B6
Rolli rampa - 359 A6
Roma Libera via - 358-359 C3/C4
Romagna via - 356 C3
Romagnosi GD. via - 354 D2
Romita via - 357 D5
Roncinotto via - 143 D1
Rondanini pza - 355 D5
Rosa E. via - 361 B5
Rosa S. via - 361 A3
Rosazza via - 359 B6
Roselli via - 359 A4
Rosetta via della - 355 D5
Rosmini via - 357 D6
Rossetti G. via - 359 A4
Rossi P. via - 360 D1
Rotonda pza, via della - 355 D5
Rotto ponte - 358 D3
Rovere pza - 355 B5
Rubattino via - 359 C5